June 15–19, 2015
Portland, Oregon, USA

Association for Computing Machinery

Advancing Computing as a Science & Profession

HPDC'15

Proceedings of the 24th International Symposium on
High-Performance Parallel and Distributed Computing

Sponsored by:
ACM SIGARCH and The University of Arizona

Supported by:
**U.S. Department of Energy, NSF, IBM Research,
and Center for Research in Extreme Scale Technologies (CREST)**

**Association for
Computing Machinery**

Advancing Computing as a Science & Profession

The Association for Computing Machinery
2 Penn Plaza, Suite 701
New York, New York 10121-0701

ISBN: 978-1-4503-3550-8 (Digital)

ISBN: 978-1-4503-3874-5 (Print)

Additional copies may be ordered prepaid from:

ACM Order Department
PO Box 30777
New York, NY 10087-0777, USA

Phone: 1-800-342-6626 (USA and Canada)
+1-212-626-0500 (Global)
Fax: +1-212-944-1318
E-mail: acmhelp@acm.org
Hours of Operation: 8:30 am – 4:30 pm ET

Printed in the USA

HPDC15 Chairs' Welcome

Welcome to the *24th ACM Symposium on High-Performance Parallel and Distributed Computing (HPDC'15)*. HPDC'15 follows in the long tradition of providing a high-quality, single-track forum for presenting new research results on all aspects of the design, implementation, evaluation, and application of parallel and distributed systems for high-end computing. The HPDC'15 program features seven sessions on systems, networks, and memory for high-end computing; data analytics and I/O; performance and modeling; resource management and optimizations; graphs and architectures; cloud and resource management; and accelerators and resilience. Each session consists of both full and short papers, giving a mix of novel research directions at various stages of development. Nightly social events include a reception and poster session, and the conference dinner. Awards for best paper, best talk, and best poster will be given in the concluding session on Friday. The program is complemented by an interesting set of workshops on a range of timely and related systems and application topics.

The conference program features two keynote presentations by *Professor Allen D. Malony* of the University of Oregon and *Dr. Ewa Deelman* of the University of Southern California.

Dr. Ewa Deelman is the recipient of the 4th annual HPDC Annual Achievement Award. The purpose of this award is to recognize individuals who have made long lasting, influential contributions to the foundations or practice of the field of high-performance parallel and distributed computing, to raise the awareness of these contributions, especially among the younger generation of researchers, and to improve the image and the public relations of the HPDC community. The process of selecting the winner of the award was formalized this year with an open call for nominations.

HPDC'15 is affiliated with the ACM Federated Computing Research Conference, which brings together fourteen leading computer science conferences and workshops in one place. FCRC is featuring keynotes each day on research topics of broad interest. You are welcome to stop in and visit other conferences, where space permits, and we hope you will have the opportunity to meet new people at the meals and breaks.

The HPDC'15 call for papers attracted *116 paper submissions*. In the review process this year, we followed two established methods that were started in 2012: a two-round review process and an author rebuttal process. In the first round review, all papers received at least three reviews, and based on these reviews, 65 papers went on to the second round in which virtually all of them received another two or three reviews. In total, 474 reviews were generated by the 52-member Program Committee along with a number of external reviewers. For many of the 65 second-round papers, the authors submitted rebuttals. Rebuttals were carefully taken into consideration during the Program Committee deliberations as part of the selection process. On March 12-13, the Program Committee met at IBM Almaden Research Center (San Jose, CA) and made the final selection. Each paper in the second round of reviews was discussed at the meeting. At the end of the 1.5-day meeting, the Program Committee accepted *19 full papers*, resulting in an acceptance rate of 16.3%. In addition, the committee accepted *11 submissions as short papers*. We would like to thank all contributing authors, regardless of the results of their submissions. We are very grateful to the Program Committee members for their hard work and for providing their reviews on time, in what was a very tight review schedule and a very rigorous review process.

This conference could not happen without the hard work of many people listed on the following pages. Thank you for all of your contributions. We would also like to acknowledge the support of the US Department of Energy, the US National Science Foundation, and IBM Research.

Enjoy the conference!

Thilo Kielmann
HPDC'15 General Chair
VU University Amsterdam, The Netherlands

Dean Hildebrand
HPDC'15 Program co-Chair
IBM Almaden Research Center, USA

Michela Taufer
HPDC'15 Program co-Chair
University of Delaware, USA

Table of Contents

Keynote Address 1

Session Chair: Dean Hildebrand *(IBM Research Almaden)*

Session 1: Systems, Networks, and Memory for High-end Computing

Session Chair: John (Jack) Lange *(University of Pittsburgh)*

Session 2: Data Analytics and I/O

Session Chair: Kathryn Mohror *(Lawrence Livermore National Laboratory)*

Session 3: Performance and Modeling

Session Chair: Kenjiro Taura *(University of Tokyo)*

Keynote Address 2
Session Chair: Michela Taufer *(University of Delaware)*

Session 4: Resource Management and Optimizations
Session Chair: Naoya Maruyama *(RIKEN Advanced Institute for Computational Science)*

Session 5: Graphs and Architectures
Session Chair: Matei Ripeanu *(University of British Columbia)*

Session 6: Cloud and Resource Management
Session Chair: Ali R. Butt *(Virginia Tech)*

Session 7: Accelerators and Resilience

Session Chair: Thilo Kielmann *(VU University Amsterdam)*

Author Index

HPDC'15 Organization

General Chair: Thilo Kielmann *(VU University Amsterdam, The Netherlands)*

Program Co-Chairs: Dean Hildebrand *(IBM Research Almaden)*
Michela Taufer *(University of Delaware)*

Workshops Co-Chairs: Abhishek Chandra *(University of Minnesota, Twin Cities, USA)*
Ioan Raicu *(Illinois Institute of Technology and Argonne National Laboratory, USA)*

Posters Chair: Ana-Maria Oprescu *(VU University Amsterdam, The Netherlands)*

Publicity Co-Chairs: Ioan Raicu *(Illinois Institute of Technology and Argonne National Laboratory, USA)*
Torsten Hoefler *(ETH Zurich, Switzerland)*
Naoya Maruyama *(RIKEN Advanced Institute for Computational Science, Japan)*

Publications Chair: Antonino Tumeo *(Pacific Northwest National Laboratory)*

Sponsorship Chair: Martin Swany *(Indiana University, USA)*

Travel Award Chair: Ming Zhao *(Florida International University, USA)*

Webmaster: Kaveh Razavi *(VU University Amsterdam, The Netherlands)*

Steering Committee: Franck Cappello *(Argonne National Lab, USA and INRIA, France)*
Andrew A. Chien *(University of Chicago, USA)*
Peter Dinda *(Northwestern University, USA)*
Dick Epema *(Delft University of Technology, The Netherlands)*
Renato Figueiredo *(University of Florida, USA)*
Salim Hariri *(University of Arizona, USA)*
Thilo Kielmann *(VU University Amsterdam, The Netherlands)*
Arthur "Barney" Maccabe *(Oak Ridge National Laboratory, USA)*
Manish Parashar *(Rutgers University, USA)*
Matei Ripeanu *(University of British Columbia, Canada)*
Karsten Schwan *(Georgia Tech, USA)*
Doug Thain *(University of Notre Dame, USA)*
Jon Weissman *(University of Minnesota, USA)* (Chair)
Dongyan Xu *(Purdue University, USA)*

Program Committee (continued):

Vasily Tarasov *(IBM Research, USA)*
Kenjiro Taura *(University of Tokyo, Japan)*
Douglas Thain *(University of Notre Dame, USA)*
Ana Varbanescu *(University of Amsterdam, The Netherlands)*
Richard Vuduc *(Georgia Institute of Technology, USA)*
Jon Weissman *(University of Minnesota, USA)*
Dongyan Xu *(Purdue University, USA)*
Rui Zhang *(IBM Research, USA)*

Additional reviewers:

Leonardo Bautista-Gomez
Wesley Bland
Prasad Calyam
Xi Chen
Alexandru Costan
Sheng Di
Javier Diaz-Montes
Matthieu Dorier
Aiman Fang
Yuanwei Fang
Hajime Fujita
Mark K. Gardner
Kyle Hale
Shadi Ibrahim
Matt Kappel
Imrul Kayes
Youngjae Kim
Min Li
Francis Liu
Raphael Poss
Thomas Ropars
Lukas Rupprecht
Michael Sevilla
Rryota Shioya
Balaji Subramaniam
Maciej Swiech
Radu Tudoran
Noah Watkins
Mingyuan Xia
Fan Yang
Xiang Zuo

HPDC'15 Sponsors & Supporters

Sponsors: SIGARCH

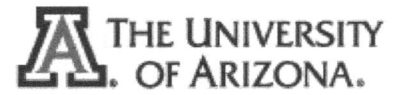

THE UNIVERSITY OF ARIZONA.
Arizona's First University.

Supporters: U.S. DEPARTMENT OF ENERGY

NSF

IBM Research

CREST
Center for Research in Extreme Scale Technologies

Through the Looking-Glass: From Performance Observation to Dynamic Adaptation

Allen D. Malony
Department of Computer and Information Science
University of Oregon
malony@cs.uoregon.edu

Abstract

Since the beginning of ``high-performance" parallel computing, observing and analyzing performance for purposes of finding bottlenecks and identifying opportunities for improvement has been at the heart of delivering the performance potential of next-generation scalable systems. Interestingly, it is the ever-changing parallel computing landscape that is the main driver of requirements for parallel performance technology and the improvements necessary beyond the current state-of-the-art. Indeed, the development and application of our TAU Performance System over many years largely follows an evolutionary path of addressing measurement and analysis problems in new parallel machines and programming environments. However, the outlook to future parallel systems with high degrees of concurrency, heterogeneous components, dynamic runtime environments, asynchronous execution, and power constraints suggests a new perspective will be needed on the role of performance observation and analysis in respect to tool technology integration and performance optimization methods. The reliance on post-mortem analysis of application-level ("1st person") performance measurements is prohibitive for exascale-class machines because of the performance data volume, the primitive basis for performance data attribution, and the fundamental problem of performance variation that will exist. Instead, it will be important to provide introspection support across the exascale software stack to understand how system ("3rd person") resources are used during execution. Furthermore, the opportunity to couple a global performance introspection capability (a "performance backplane") with online performance decision analytics inspires the concept of an autonomic performance system that can feed back policy-based decisions to guide the computation to better states of execution. The talk will explore these issues by giving a brief retrospective on performance tool evolution, setting the stage for current research projects where a new performance perspective is being pursued. It will also speculate on what might be included in next-generation parallel systems hardware, specifically to make the exascale machines more performance-aware and dynamically-adaptive.

Categories and Subject Descriptors:
C.2.0 [**Computer Systems Organization**]: Performance of systems.

Keywords
High-performance computing; runtime environments; optimization methods

Bio
Dr. Allen D. Malony is a Professor in the Department of Computer and Information Science at the University of Oregon (UO) where he directs parallel computing research projects, notably the TAU parallel performance system project. He has extensive experience in performance benchmarking and characterization of high-performance computing systems, and has developed performance evaluation tools for a range of parallel machines during the last 25 years. His research interests also include computational science and neuroinformatics. Malony was awarded the NSF National Young Investigator award, was a Fulbright Research Scholar to The Netherlands and Austria, and received the prestigious Alexander von Humboldt Research Award for Senior U.S. Scientists by the Alexander von Humboldt Foundation. He is funded by the Department of Energy, the National Science Foundation, and the Department of Defense. Malony is the Director of the UO Neuroinformatics Center and the CEO of ParaTools, Inc., which he founded with Dr. Sameer Shende in 2004.

HPDC'15, June 15–20, 2015, Portland, Oregon, USA.
ACM 978-1-4503-3489-1/15/06.
http://dx.doi.org/10.1145/2749246.2749247

Turning Centralized Coherence and Distributed Critical-Section Execution on their Head: A New Approach for Scalable Distributed Shared Memory

Stefanos Kaxiras, David Klaftenegger, Magnus Norgren, Alberto Ros[†], Konstantinos Sagonas
Department of Information Technology, Uppsala University, Sweden
[†]Computer Engineering Department, University of Murcia, Spain

ABSTRACT

A coherent global address space in a distributed system enables shared memory programming in a much larger scale than a single multicore or a single SMP. Without dedicated hardware support at this scale, the solution is a software distributed shared memory (DSM) system. However, traditional approaches to coherence (*centralized via "active" home-node directories*) and critical-section execution (*distributed across nodes and cores*) are inherently unfit for such a scenario. Instead, it is crucial to make decisions locally and avoid the long latencies imposed by both network and software message handlers. Likewise, synchronization is fast if it rarely involves communication with distant nodes (or even other sockets). To minimize the amount of long-latency communication required in both coherence and critical section execution, we propose a DSM system with a novel coherence protocol, and a novel hierarchical queue delegation locking approach. More specifically, we propose an approach, suitable for data-race-free (DRF) programs, based on self-invalidation, self-downgrade, and passive data classification directories that require *no message handlers*, thereby incurring no extra latency. For fast synchronization we extend Queue Delegation Locking to execute critical sections in large batches on a single core before passing execution along to other cores, sockets, or nodes, in that hierarchical order. The result is a software DSM system called *Argo* which *localizes* as many decisions as possible and allows high parallel performance with little overhead on synchronization when compared to prior DSM implementations.

1. INTRODUCTION

Regardless of scale, the prevailing architectural paradigm to build shared memory parallel computers is intrinsically distributed: CPUs are tightly coupled with local memory in which copies of the data in global memory are cached and manipulated. This paradigm spans the spectrum from the ubiquitous multicore (where cores are serviced by their private caches which are further serviced by a proxy of the main memory in the form of a large shared last level cache), to the other end of systems consisting of networked nodes (processors+memory) where shared memory is implemented as a software layer that distributes virtual memory across the nodes (distributed shared virtual-memory or simply DSM). Hardware DSM can be made to scale well, but at a considerable cost [32], and thus it is not the dominating architecture in large installations. In this work, we re-examine the case of the software distributed shared memory.

We believe that the way the prevailing shared memory architectural paradigm is implemented instills it with two fundamental flaws that restrict its scale. The first is that coherence control of *shared* data is *centralized* to a single point in the system, to a directory entry responsible for keeping coherence for these data. The second is that inherently *serial execution*—in particular critical sections using the same lock—is *distributed* across the compute nodes, forcing unnecessary movement of data to where the execution takes place (migratory sharing [41]). Considering that coherence control of the migratory data is centralized (as per our previous point), distributing the serialized execution of critical sections can only worsen performance and, according to Amdahl's law, this effect will be detrimental to scalability.

These two flaws can be safely ignored when the latencies involved are small. Thus, it is feasible to build an efficient (single-chip) multicore using *hardware* directory coherence and distributed critical section execution, which becomes only moderately worse with the increased latencies found in a (single-node) multi-socket board. Industry examples abound. However, the situation changes dramatically in a software DSM system consisting of commodity networked nodes, because of three reasons: i) we are faced with larger network latencies, ii) software message handlers introduce further latency on every coherence action, and iii) because of the increased latencies, critical-section synchronization becomes a serious bottleneck.

Why now? Historically, when the first DSM systems appeared both network latency and network bandwidth were orders of magnitude worse than the corresponding main memory latency and bandwidth. In that setting, the overhead of message handler execution was relatively small (compared to the network latencies) making software coherence possible. On the other hand, coherence protocols were burdened to minimize both latency (e.g., hiding latency with relaxed consistency models [17]) and bandwidth (e.g., by minimizing data transfer using diffs).

Advances in network technology over the last two decades closed the latency and bandwidth gap with exponential im-

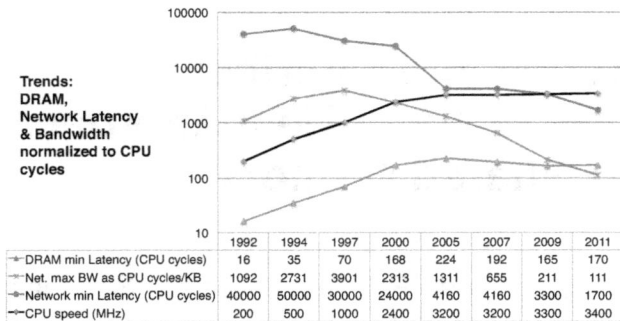

Figure 1: Trends for network bandwidth and latency normalized to CPU speed. (Adapted from Ramesh's thesis [35].)

	1992	1994	1997	2000	2005	2007	2009	2011
DRAM min Latency (CPU cycles)	16	35	70	168	224	192	165	170
Net. max BW as CPU cycles/KB	1092	2731	3901	2313	1311	655	211	111
Network min Latency (CPU cycles)	40000	50000	30000	24000	4160	4160	3300	1700
CPU speed (MHz)	200	500	1000	2400	3200	3200	3300	3400

provements. Figure 1 plots the trends for the top CPU speed (in MHz), DRAM latency, network latency, and the *inverse* of network bandwidth, all normalized to CPU cycles. The last metric is interesting with respect to a DSM implementation because it gives the latency in CPU cycles to transfer a block of data (e.g., 1 Kbyte). In the past, despite the rapid growth in network bandwidth, processor speed increased even faster. Consequently, *increasingly more* CPU cycles were needed to transfer a block of data with each passing year! This trend reversed as network bandwidth continued to improve rapidly but CPU frequency improvement stalled. Whereas the evolvement of network bandwidth with respect to CPU speed was a *deterrent* for DSM development in the past, it now is an incentive. On the other hand, whereas in the early days a DSM was easily realizable with software message handlers, this is not the case today. As Figure 1 shows, in terms of CPU cycles, network latency improved from being tens of thousands of CPU cycles (easily overshadowing any message handler latency) to just a couple of thousand CPU cycles (just an order of magnitude worse than DRAM latency). These technology trends point to the tradeoffs that we should make today to scale shared memory to a distributed system: i) trade using more bandwidth to reduce latency, ii) minimize message handler execution, and iii) minimize movement of data for *dependent* computation (e.g., critical section execution) as network latency is still an order of magnitude worse than memory latency.

Contributions. Motivated by these tradeoffs, we flip the way coherence and critical-section execution is done.

- Inspired by recent efforts to simplify coherence in multi-cores [37, 15], we use self-invalidation (no invalidations and no write-misses) and self-downgrade (no indirection via a home directory) to reduce the latency of servicing each individual miss. Effectively, we are *distributing* coherence control, so that coherence decisions (invalidation and downgrade) are made locally by each node without communication.

- To reduce the *number* of self-invalidation misses and consequently the *average access latency*, we introduce a novel home-node directory protocol *without* message handlers, where all operations are performed by RDMA reads and writes, initiated by the requesting core—no other node is involved in servicing a coherence miss. This approach increases network traffic, but in return we achieve a *message-handler-free* protocol. Further, we systematically trade bandwidth for latency, e.g., by prefetching and by avoiding to create and transmit diffs when we can.

- We consolidate hierarchically the execution of critical sections that use the same lock (to the core or node that happens to get the lock first) in order to minimize wasteful movement of migratory data. This dramatically reduces synchronization latency and critical-section overhead. We achieve this by extending a state-of-the-art queue delegation locking algorithm [18, 20]. To take full advantage of this approach some source code changes are necessary, but the required effort is modest.

The result is a highly scalable DSM system called *Argo*[1] with a novel coherence protocol (*Carina*) based on passive classification directories (*Pyxis*) and a new locking system (*Vela*).

Argo is a page-based, user-space, DSM and its prototype implementation is built on top of MPI. It runs unmodified Pthreads (data-race-free) shared memory programs and with some source code modifications, optimizes the locking performance of such programs with a novel hierarchical extension of queue delegation locking [18, 20].

We evaluate the prototype implementation with a set of seven benchmarks and characterize the effects of our design decisions. We show that Argo is able to scale the set of benchmarks to a large number of nodes, competing with message-passing or Partitioned Global Address Space implementations, as well as to sustain the performance level of critical section execution in a distributed environment.

2. BACKGROUND

2.1 Coherence

Of course, we are not the first to note distributed shared memory problems and aim to address them. A large body of prior work set the same goals. Regarding the problem of centralized coherence the line of attack has been to relax the memory consistency, notably going from Sequential Consistency (SC) [21] to weak memory models that rely on synchronization to enforce ordering. These memory models made it possible to relax the constraints on coherence and ameliorate the centralization problem. We call attention here to Release Consistency (RC) [10], Lazy Release Consistency [17], Entry Consistency [2], and Scope Consistency [13], all of which were invented to optimize the coherence of distributed shared memory architectures: a hardware architecture for RC—the DASH prototype [23] built at Stanford—and software distributed shared virtual memory systems for the rest [24, 2, 16]. However, none of these approaches arrived at a truly distributed coherence solution. Self-invalidation and self-downgrade (write-through) enables fully distributed coherence protocol (that theoretically requires no directory). Practically, however, it is not enough. There is a steep price to pay for excessive self-invalidation. One of the contributions of our work is to address this deficiency by introducing a directory to classify pages according to the number of sharers and the number of writers on each. The novel aspect of our approach is that the directory is *passive*, i.e., it is only accessed by RDMA and does not introduce message handlers in the system.

PGAS/UPC. Using only RDMA to access shared data is comparable to Partitioned Global Address Space (PGAS)

---

[1]In ancient times Argo Navis (or simply Argo) was a large constellation in the southern sky that has since been divided into a number of smaller constellations: Carina (the Hull), Pyxis (the Compass), Vela (the Sail), among others.

4

approaches such as Unified Parallel C [40]. For this reason we will use UPC as a representative base case in our evaluation. In PGAS the address space is logically divided between processes but the main difference with our approach is that there is no remote caching. Shared data can of course be local to a node, but determining this at runtime is costly, and therefore programmers are advised to cast such pointers to local pointers where necessary. Remote accesses are fine grained, and, similarly to our approach, using a relaxed memory model [40] each access can be delayed until the next synchronization point, making it possible to hide the latency of remote accesses with computation on local data. Without caching, it is often necessary for UPC programmers to manually move data from the global address space to thread-local space in bulk transfers, which is then similar to message passing paradigms in the way that the programmer needs to think about communication patterns rather than thinking about how threads are exploiting locality. Critical sections in UPC are programmed with UPC-specific lock/unlock primitives, which ensures that all memory operations have been completed before both the lock and unlock call. Since critical sections by nature make most threads access and write non-local data they incur a high penalty in UPC, as each operation in the critical section is a remote operation without any possibility to run it locally. We address all these issues with our approach.

2.2 Synchronization

Over the years, many locking algorithms have been developed to speed up critical section execution. Traditionally, these algorithms focus on acquiring and releasing a lock as quickly as possible, while also considering the time required for handovers. Queue-based locks, like MCS [28] and CLH [5, 27], reduce cache coherence traffic to achieve higher performance on multicore systems. At the same time they order critical sections without taking the location of data into consideration, which results in performance degradation on NUMA systems, due to the higher latency and lower bandwidth between processors. On NUMA systems these locks are outperformed by algorithms that distribute work in a less fair manner, e.g. the HBO lock [34], the hierarchical CLH lock [26] or more recently the *Cohort lock* [7]. They all aim to hand over the lock to a thread that is "nearby" to exploit the faster transfer of data to some parts of the system.

Delegation locking is a different approach, which takes this idea to the extreme by sending operations to where the lock is held instead of transferring the lock and data to each thread. This allows data to stay in the caches of a helper thread for all cache levels, resulting in higher throughput. Algorithms enabling delegation locking include flat combining [12], remote core locking [25], CC- and H-Synch [8]. Additionally, some algorithms allow threads that delegate critical sections to detach the execution, continue with other work, and only wait for the critical sections' execution if and when needed. Of these, detached execution [31] does not perform as well as other delegation algorithms while Queue Delegation Locking (QDL) [18, 20] combines a fast delegation method with the ability to detach execution. It allows to either collect operations from the entire system concurrently, or (in the case of a NUMA system) restrict the collection to a single NUMA node [20]. This Hierarchical Queue Delegation Locking (HQDL) allows for faster delegation at the cost of less exploitable parallelism in the system.

In a related approach, Suleman *et al.* [39] propose consolidating the execution of critical sections (which is inherently serial) in one fat, fast, and power-hungry core, while distributing parallel execution on thin and power-efficient cores, in a heterogeneous multicore consisting of both types of cores. This addresses Amdahl's law by speeding up the serial part of the programs.

2.3 Other Forward-Looking Approaches

A new DSM system that has focused on latency tolerant programming is Grappa [30]. Similarly to our motivation, the authors recognize that latency is the critical issue to address, at the expense of increasing bandwidth demands. Grappa has, similarly to this paper, tackled the problem of executing critical sections in the global address space. They use another synchronization mechanism called flat-combining. Grappa implements a system where it is possible to send critical sections to the node where the data the critical section wants to access is residing in the global address space. However, Grappa is a new programming paradigm that focuses more narrowly on throughput computing with a vast number of threads. We concentrate on offering efficient shared memory that can run the large library of parallel algorithms that have been developed over the years.

3. THE ARGO SYSTEM

Similarly to other DSM systems [24, 2, 16, 33], Argo implements shared memory using the facilities provided by the virtual memory system. Argo is a user-level DSM, implemented entirely in user space on top of MPI. While a custom network layer tailored to Argo would likely offer greater performance, we opted for the portability and flexibility of MPI for the prototype implementation.

Argo works on page granularity (4KB) and sets up a shared virtual address space spanning all nodes. This address space is first initialized by each node, allocating the same range of virtual addresses using the mmap system call. These addresses are then available for allocation using our own allocator.

Argo is a home-based DSM where each virtual page is assigned a home node. Currently, virtual pages are interleaved across nodes so that for a system containing N nodes, $node_0$ serves the lower addresses of the global memory and $node_{N-1}$ serves the higher addresses. While this is a simplistic approach, we note that more sophisticated data distribution schemes are orthogonal to what we describe here and are left for future work.

Each node caches remote pages in a local page cache. Coherence must be enforced among all the page caches in the system. Typically in prior work, a directory would be responsible to keep a home node's pages coherent. This means keeping track of the readers and the writers of every page and sending invalidation and downgrade messages when necessary. The most important optimization proposed for such DSM systems is to relax the memory model and allow consolidation of coherence traffic on synchronization points [17]. In many cases, this means that downgrading dirty data necessitates the creation and transmission of diffs [17].

Our aim is to eliminate the centralized bottleneck of directories and arrive at a genuinely distributed solution. The reason is twofold: First, any operation that involves a directory is costly because of the latencies involved in a DSM. This is especially true for invalidation and indirection (locating the last writer and obtaining the latest value of the data via the directory) where multiple network hops may be needed. Second, directory operations that involve even simple state transitions or sending new messages, require that a message handler be invoked at the directory side to perform such operations. Potentially a handler is needed also on the receiving side of a directory message to take an action there.

Thus, prior DSM systems rely on directories and page caches that are *active agents* requiring their own computing resources to *process* (receive and respond to) messages. Whether these active agents are implemented as software message handlers that poll the network interface for coherence messages, or are invoked via interrupts, is of little consequence; they consume resources, introduce latency into every access, and can easily become bottlenecks and compromise scalability in the presence of hot spots. Given our analysis in the introduction, the improvement in network latency has increased the relative overhead of software message handlers. Instead, what we would ideally like to do is use remote memory accesses—RDMA—for all coherence actions without the need to execute *code* on the receiving sides. This is perhaps one of the most significant differences between Argo and prior DSM systems.

We achieve this goal by relying on self-invalidation and self-downgrade as the main mechanisms of our coherence. Self-invalidation means that any node is allowed to read any data block as long as it promises to self-invalidate this block before passing a synchronization point. Similarly, self-downgrade means that a node can freely write any data block without obtaining any permission from a directory, as long as it makes the write visible to all other nodes *before* crossing a synchronization point.

The significance of this approach in DSM is twofold. First, self-invalidation eliminates explicit invalidations on writes. This means that no sharers need to be tracked by a home-node directory. Second, self-downgrade eliminates directory indirection on read misses to find the latest version of the data; instead, the correct data are always found in the home node on any read miss. This means neither the writers need to be tracked in the directory, thereby eliminating the need for a directory altogether.

While on first sight this would seem ideal for a DSM, in reality self-invalidation can seriously degrade performance if applied without constraint. This is where our first contribution comes in. We propose a *classification* directory to manage self-invalidation. To the best of our knowledge, this is the first *passive* directory protocol, i.e., without *any* message handlers (active agents) but using exclusively RDMA initiated by requestors to perform all protocol actions. This approach enables a distributed and highly-scalable coherence solution, which we call *Carina*.

As with any protocol that is based on self-invalidation, e.g., [22, 14, 37, 4], our approach imposes a weak memory model in which Sequential Consistency (SC) for DRF programs can be guaranteed when synchronization is fully exposed to the system [1]. We discuss this in the following section.

3.1 Exposing Synchronization to Carina

We expose program synchronization to the coherence layer using "fences" in the application programs. Fences are implicit for synchronization primitives in the Argo synchronization libraries and no source code modification is needed for DRF programs using the Argo Pthreads or HQDL libraries.

There are two fences available in Argo: an SI_fence for self-invalidation and an SD_fence for self-downgrade. On an SI_fence, all pages in a page cache are invalidated before the fence completes. On an SD_fence, all the writes of modified pages are made globally visible before the fence completes.

The memory model of Argo corresponds to a weak memory model if on every synchronization (lock, unlock, signal, wait, barrier, or even synchronization via spin loops and flags), we apply *both* fences. For Release Consistency [10], it is sufficient to use an SI_fence on acquire points and SD_fence on release points. In Section 4 we will show how we use these fences for the memory model of queue delegation locks.

3.2 Carina: Argo's Coherence

Unrestricted self-invalidation (and to a lesser extent unrestricted self-downgrade) can seriously degrade performance considering that: i) on each acquire point, all the data cached in a node are self-invalidated, even if they have not been modified; and ii) on each release point, all the writes must be reflected back to the home node, even if they are not subsequently read by another node, or even if further updates to the data would render exposing these writes to other nodes premature and unproductive. It is therefore important to reduce these costs. We achieve this by classifying pages at home-node classification directories [11, 6, 37].

Any node accessing a page at a home node simply *deposits* its ID (separately for reads and writes) in the directory. This directory information indicates to future accessing nodes whether:

- the page is *Private, P*, (only one node is accessing it) or *Shared, S*, (more than one node are accessing it)
- the page has *No Writers, NW*[2] or the page has a *Single Writer, SW*, (only one node writes it) or *Multiple Writers, MW*, (more than one node write the page).

Note that classification transitions (P→S, NW→SW, and SW→MW) happen at most once per page, i.e., they are rare. Also note that this information concerns the global address space (where potentially everything can be shared) and not the thread-private space which is not shared across nodes. Thus, the term "Private" is somewhat of a misnomer here, as it does not imply perpetual privacy, but temporary privacy for data declared as shared.

In our current implementation these two types of classifications are one-way and non-adaptive: from private to shared and from no-writers to a single-writer to multiple-writers. However, it is straightforward to extend the classification to adaptive (reverting back to private or no-writers/single-writer) using simple "decay" techniques [36], if need arises. For the workloads we examined, such adaptation was not deemed necessary and is left for future work.

Table 1 shows the types of classifications we can do. The first, S, represents the case where no classification is performed in the system and all pages self-invalidate and self-downgrade. The second, P/S, simply distinguishes between private and shared pages, while the third, P/S3, further distinguishes shared pages to NW, SW, and MW, depending on the number of writers. We use this data classification to filter self-invalidation, e.g., exclude private pages, or shared pages without any writer from self-invalidation. While we could also optimize self-downgrade, we actually chose to do the

---

[2] Equivalently: *Read-Only, RO*

Classification	State	SI	SD	Comment
S: No classification	S	✓	✓	All pages shared
P/S: Simple P/S classification	P	—	✓	SD to avoid P→S forced downgrade
	S	✓	✓	
P/S3: Full P/S and Writer classification	P	—	✓	SD to avoid P→S forced downgrade
	S, NW	—	✓	
	S, SW	— (✓)	✓	SW does not SI but other nodes do
	S, MW	✓	✓	

Table 1: Three classifications: S, P/S, P/S3. Argo uses the full P/S3 classification.

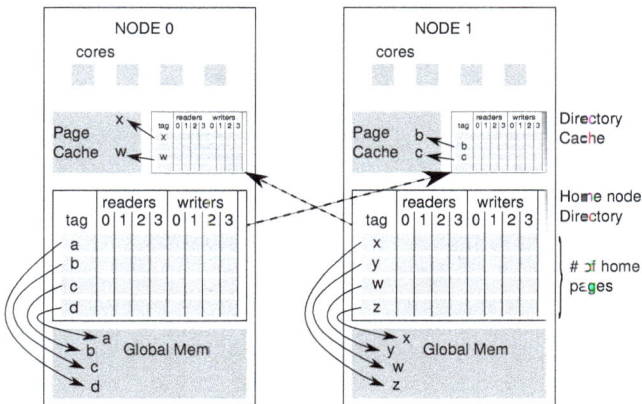

Figure 2: Directory organization (two nodes). Each node holds a "home" directory and a directory cache caching the remote directory entries.

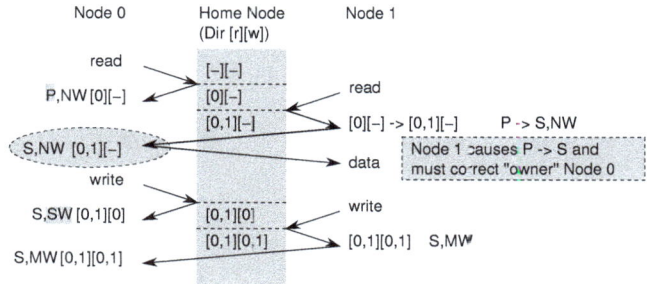

Figure 3: Overview of P→S and NW→SW→MW. The example shows "instant" transitions of state in node 0 (shaded) which would require a local active agent.

updated reader and writer full maps which are stored locally.

To facilitate notifying a node on a classification change without a message handler, we keep copies of all remote directory entries for all the pages in its page cache (Figure 2).[3]

A node is notified of a directory change by simply updating its local copy of the directory entry. The update is observed by the node on its next synchronization or its next request. I.e., a node's perception of the home node classification may be stale until its next synchronization point. This is allowed simply because of the DRF semantics.

3.4 P/S Classification

Let us see now how this classification can reduce the number of self-invalidations. Initially all pages start as uninitialized and without any readers or writers. Initialization writes to the pages do not count and this is a rudimentary form of adaptation that we implement: at the end of initialization and the start of the parallel section of the programs the reader and writer full maps are reset to null.

The first node accessing a page leaves its ID in the directory (as a reader). A single ID signifies that the page is Private as shown in Figure 3 for Node 0 when it first reads a page. The page does not need to be self-invalidated or self-downgraded as there is no sharing. When a new node (Node 1 in Figure 3) misses in its page cache and accesses the same page it observes that there is already a node (Node 0) that considers the page as private, the "private owner." The private owner needs to be notified that the classification has changed and the page is now shared, which means that:

1. the page should be self-invalidated at any subsequent synchronization point
2. any updates to this page previously performed by the private owner (Node 0) need to be made globally visible and certainly visible to the newcomer node (Node 1) before the latter continues.

Recall that the directory is passive, i.e., there is no directory agent to detect the classification change and appropriately notify the private owner. Recall also that the private owner is also "passive:" it can initiate requests but cannot respond to such. The burden for this falls on the node that causes the classification change (e.g., Node 1). Since this node updates the directory with its ID and in the process

---

[3] For simplicity we keep a *full* copy of any accessed remote directory. This is not a significant overhead in the systems we examined, and one can always "compress" the directory copies to a few bits per entry, if need be. Essentially, we want to know if a page has a single reader or single writer; if there is more than one reader or more than one writer, we do not care to know their identity.

---

opposite. For example, we chose to self-downgrade private pages. We do this to eliminate the need for message handlers to service classification transitions.

Our classification is in line with the philosophy we set forth in the introduction of trading bandwidth (increase traffic from self-downgrades) for latency (reducing self-invalidation and eliminating message handlers). Further, the distinction between SW and MW allows us to suppress the creation of diffs (latency) in the case of a single writer, since there can be no false sharing to corrupt data on downgrade, at the expense of transmitting more data (bandwidth). However, this optimization increases the complexity of the protocol and is left for future work.

3.3 Pyxis: Passive Classification Directory

But how do we implement a coherence protocol so that *no active agents—software message handlers—are needed* to respond to messages or generate new requests? In our approach the home node directories are simply metadata structures that are remotely read and written (RDMA) by the requesting nodes. Information is simply deposited in the directories for the *passive* classification of data and all protocol actions are performed by the requesting node.

Figure 2 shows the directory organization. The directory is simply a structure holding, for each page, its reader(s) and its writer(s). There is no explicit state for the page—this is inferred by the accessing nodes. We use a *full map* to keep track of the readers and writers.

When a node (read or write) misses in its page cache it accesses the directory for the page using a Fetch&Add atomic operation. This operation sets the node ID in the reader or writer full map (depending on the miss) and *returns the*

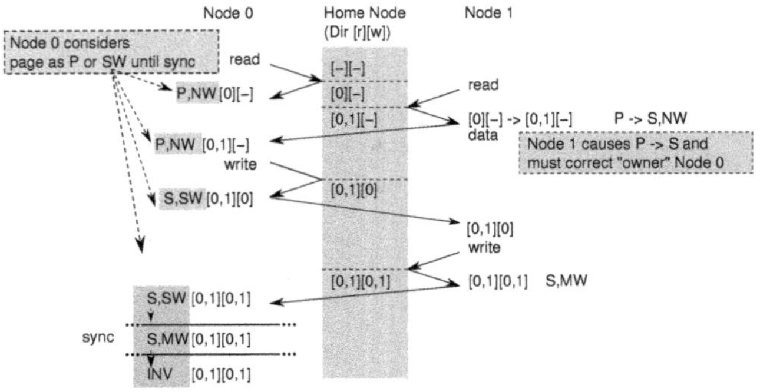

Figure 4: Deferred invalidation: Node 0 ignores P→S (and SW→MW) until its next synchronization.

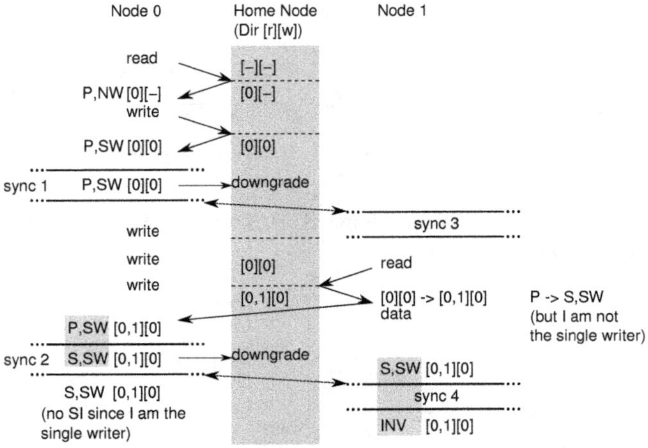

Figure 5: Self-downgrade of private pages.

receives the reader and writer full maps, it detects that the private owner needs to be notified. There is always just a single node that needs to be notified in the P→S transition. Since the private owner is known (from the reader full map), updating it is simply a remote update of its *cached copy* of the directory entry. *In essence, we use the cached directory entries in each node to reflect the updates in the home directory without the need to have active agents in the node.*

3.4.1 Deferred Invalidation

The private owner does not need to immediately notice the P→S transition as shown in Figure 3. There is no action taken at the time of the transition and this means that *no active agent is needed in Node 0.* The transition will be detected and action taken by Node 0 at its *next synchronization point* where it will include the shared page in the self-invalidation. We call this *deferred (self-)invalidation* and show it in Figure 4. In general, a node can consider a page "private" from the initial read to the next synchronization (Figure 4), and—as we already noted—this is valid simply because of the DRF semantics.

3.4.2 Self-Downgrading Private Pages

While deferred invalidation eliminates the need to have an agent to respond to a directory-cache update, the same unfortunately is not true for the second requirement of a P→S transition: obtaining (possible) private-owner modifications before continuing with the Node 1 access that causes the P→S transition in the first place. The problematic point is shown in Figure 3 marked with a grey oval. Normally, this would require an active agent in Node 0 to stall all local threads from accessing (potentially modifying) this page, until the home node and Node 1 are updated with the latest version of the data. Note that as per the DRF semantics Node 1 can only expect to see the writes of Node 0 at most up to the point of Node 0's last synchronization point. In addition, from the moment Node 0's data are made shared, any further writes must be self-downgraded at Node 0's *next* synchronization point as a *diff*. The last two points are critical in making the P→S transition work correctly.

Naïve Solution. A naïve solution would then be to checkpoint all modified private pages prior to any synchronization point and service P→S transitions from these checkpoints. As we will see in Section 5.1 creating these checkpoints is an expensive proposition as it significantly delays synchronization. The overhead largely invalidates the potential benefit of PS classification.

Carina's Solution. To solve this conundrum, we trade-off bandwidth for latency. In this case, we *self-downgrade all Private pages at synchronization points as if they were Shared!* The latency benefit is twofold: 1) private pages are still excluded from self-invalidation (and do not need to be re-fetched as long as they remain private) and 2) we update private owners without active agents. In addition, checkpointing for diffs happens only on a write miss and its latency affects only the thread that incurs the write miss.

An example is shown in Figure 5. Node 0 is the private owner that starts to downgrade once it writes the page. At synchronization points all its modifications are put back to the home node. When Node 1 reads, it obtains the latest data directly from the home node. It does not matter that Node 0 keeps writing in parallel. As per the DRF semantics Node 1 is only guaranteed to "see" Node 0's modifications *prior* to sync 1.

3.5 P/S3 Classification

P/S3 classification adds writer classification (NW, SW, MW) on top of P/S classification. The distinction is meaningful for the shared, S, classification, since as we have explained the private, P, classification always self-downgrades and does not self-invalidate. The reason why it matters for the S classification is that it adds two more opportunities to eliminate self-invalidation: shared pages with no writers, and shared pages with a single writer. A comparison of P/S and P/S3 classification with respect to self-invalidation and self-downgrade is depicted schematically in Figure 6.

If there are no writers (yet) for a page, it can be considered as a read-only page and is classified as "No-Writer" (NW). Any node caching a page may go ahead and write it at any point without needing to obtain any kind of permission to do so. This is because of the DRF semantics: nodes will have no conflicting accesses (i.e., accesses not separated by synchronization). Therefore, any node can write its cached page copy at will, considering itself the single writer. If it is the first time a node writes a page, it deposits its ID at the directory and obtains the full map of writers to check whether there are others. We discern the following cases depending on the home-node state of the page:

- Private, and written by the private owner: In this case, the page becomes P,SW and starts to self-downgrade as described earlier (e.g., Figure 5 sync 1).

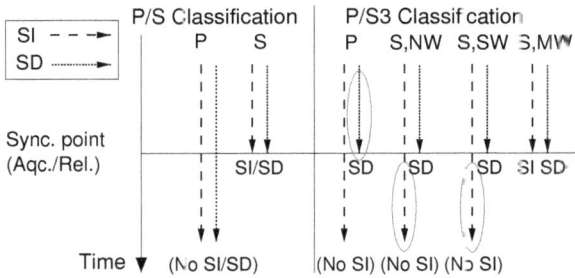

Figure 6: Trading bandwidth for latency. Self-invalidation (extra latency) is represented by dashed lines stopping at the synchronization point. Self-downgrade (extra bandwidth) is represented by dotted lines stopping at the synchronization point. Lines that cross the synchronization point do not require any action.

- Private, but written by a new node: The page transitions both to Shared and SW and the (single) private owner is notified accordingly.
- Shared, NW: The page is already shared by more than one node, and this is the first write (that reaches the home-node directory). In this case *all* nodes caching the page must be notified that there is a writer.
- Shared, SW: The page is already shared with a single writer, written now by a new node. *Only the single writer* is notified.
- Shared, MW: The page is shared with multiple writers. A new writer does not need to take any action.

A single writer node self-downgrades on synchronization. At downgrade, it checks its local directory cache to see if more writers have appeared (Figure 5 **sync 2**). If it is still the only writer then it does not need to self-invalidate—there are no other updates to this page! An example is shown in Figure 5 **sync 2**, where the single writer of a shared page can keep it after the synchronization. This is an optimization that works well in a producer-consumers scenario: the producer creates new data without invalidating its cached page on synchronization, and the consumers read the data directly from the home node—no indirection—as they invalidate their copies on their respective synchronization points (e.g., Figure 5 **sync 4**, the page is S,SW but Node 1 is *not* the single writer and must invalidate).

However, if more writers appear then the page transitions to Multiple Writers (MW) and *all* nodes must both self-invalidate and self-downgrade (if they write) this page. The transition SW→MW is exactly analogous to the P→S transition. As with the private owner there is initially only one "single writer" in the home-node directory and *only* this single writer needs to be notified (by the second writer) about the transition. No other node needs to be notified as it makes no difference: for all other nodes except the single-writer, the SW and MW states are equivalent and mean both self-invalidation and self-downgrade (if written). The transition of the single writer to MW is also *deferred*: it is discovered at the single writer's next synchronization point.

3.6 Additional Techniques

3.6.1 Write Buffers

Downgrading only on synchronization may cause considerable traffic (all the "dirty" pages need to be put downgraded

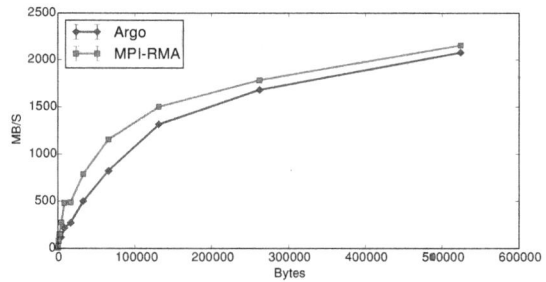

Figure 7: Bandwidth comparison: Argo cache-line read vs passive one-sided communication in OpenMPI 1.6.4. x-axis is cache line or MPI message size.

to their corresponding home nodes) and thus is a serious performance bottleneck. To address this problem we use the equivalent of a write buffer that drains slowly (and downgrades pages) as it is filled with new dirty pages. When a page is marked as dirty we put in a FIFO write buffer of configurable size. Each time the buffer is full we simply write back the copy that was first entered in the buffer to its home node, then setting the memory protection for the virtual addresses mapping to the cache to read-only, meaning that any subsequent write to that memory will trigger a new write miss. Using a write buffer we ensure that all writes are propagated at a good pace to their home nodes, and guarantee an upper bound when flushing the write buffer on synchronization. Again this is an example of trading bandwidth for latency: a write buffer increases write-through traffic but limits the latency of SD_fence synchronization.

3.6.2 Prefetching

For underlying communications, our current implementation (prototype), uses passive one-sided communications of MPI. A limitation imposed by this choice is that only one thread can use the interconnect at any point in time to fetch a page. To mitigate this bottleneck and make better use of the available bandwidth, upon a cache miss Argo fetches not only the requested page but a "line" of consecutive pages. The cache line size and the number of cache lines provided are user configurable. The cache is direct mapped and maps each page to a fixed position in the cache using a simple mapping function. Subsequent threads causing a miss on a page that is being prefetched as part of a cache line (spatial locality) have to wait for that request to complete. Figure 7 shows the achievable bandwidth in Argo while reading a cache line of pages. Clearly, Argo tracks well the MPI data transfer rate with increased cache line size (x-axis).

4. EFFICIENT SYNCHRONIZATION

Efficient synchronization is of paramount importance in making Argo perform well, for two reasons: First, while Argo's coherence handles DRF accesses with ease, thread synchronization essentially constitutes a data race. Data races are problematic in a software DSM, especially in one that is based on self-invalidation and abolishes software message handlers to process (receive and respond to) messages. To implement data races one has to self-invalidate and self-downgrade every access involved in a race. Second, synchronization plays a vital role in Argo's Carina coherence since it determines the points where Carina self-invalidates or self-downgrades. Once synchronization is achieved via a data race, Carina must self-invalidate and/or self-downgrade (depending on the acquire/release semantics of the achieved synchronization) all cached data. While Carina aims to minimize self-invalidation with the P/S3 classification, it is obvious that programs with intensive synchronization will suffer considerably more misses than a comparable DSM using an explicit invalidation protocol.

These two reasons require a complete re-think of synchronization for the Argo system. We discern two types of synchronization: barrier and lock-based synchronization. They are treated separately in Argo's Vela synchronization system that provides the necessary API for both (among other primitives such as signal/wait that are not discussed further due to the limited space in this paper). We will start with the barrier which is the easiest, and proceed with lock-synchronization which will be the main focus of this section.

4.1 Barrier Synchronization

One of the most prevalent synchronization mechanisms in distributed programming is the barrier. This is due to barriers being usually among the easiest methods to implement efficiently. In Argo all that is required is a hierarchical barrier protocol that first ensures each node has written back its data, and then that each node can only read the updated data. To this effect, a node-local barrier is used before a self-downgrade to ensure that all threads on a node have reached the barrier. An MPI barrier call is then used to make sure all the nodes have successfully completed the self-downgrade, after which they all self-invalidate. Finally, the threads on each node can be notified to continue their work, which for simplicity is implemented using another node-local barrier.

4.2 Lock-based Synchronization Using HQDL

Lock-based synchronization is expensive in any DSM, since it involves frequent long-latency transactions among nodes. Worse, lock-based synchronization is typically used in critical sections that access a common dataset. Not only the lock acquire operations are expensive but also the execution of the ensuing critical section is penalized if it switches nodes. The reason is that accessing the same data inside a critical section necessitates their transfer between nodes; in other words data accessed in critical sections are *migratory*. Coalescing the execution of critical sections on the same node as much as possible reduces the inter-node transfers of the lock-protected data and is a beneficial policy on any DSM.

In Argo, there is a further incentive to execute as many critical sections in one node before being forced to switch. The reason is the destructive effect of self-invalidation on the rest of the cached data on nodes (those that are not-protected by the lock). Argo's Carina coherence enforces self-invalidation on synchronization with acquire semantics and self-downgrade on release. This holds for *all data*. The situation is worsened by the fact that Carina implements a common page cache for all threads running on the same node. While a common page cache (as opposed to a per-thread or per-core cache) brings spatial and temporal locality benefits in the epochs of synchronization-free execution, a synchronization on *any* thread, self-invalidates or self-downgrades *all other threads'* data.

While this is a interesting problem for further research, in this paper we approach it by lock-based synchronization that does not cause global synchronization between each and every

critical section. Similar to how barriers use local barrier calls before global ones, locking algorithms like *cohort locks* [7] (developed for NUMA systems) prioritize synchronization on a single node. Such a hierarchical approach brings the overall performance of a chain of critical sections to (at most) the performance achievable using a single node. It is thus essential to use the fastest algorithm available to execute critical sections on a single node. As delegation locking [18, 20, 19] currently outperforms any traditional locking algorithm, the Argo system introduces primitives for *hierarchical queue delegation locking* (*HQDL*).

Let us describe how HQDL is constructed starting from simple (flat) queue delegation. Similarly to delegation locking, HQDL uses a different interface than traditional locks: Each critical section is issued with a single "delegate" call per critical section, and optionally waits (wait) for the section's execution immediately or at a later point. Often, small source code modifications are needed to "package" critical sections into callable functions in order to be able to delegate them to another thread. Note that threads are allowed to execute non-dependent code between the delegate and the wait but we do not take advantage of this feature in this paper, as it requires—sometimes non-trivial—modifications of application source code. HQDL streamlines the execution of many sections into a single thread, thus reusing local hardware caches more efficiently than if many threads each access the same data. As there is no method of synchronization beyond the ones implemented in Vela, no additional work is required from the programmer.

To build a global QD lock in a distributed system one needs a self-invalidate (SI_fence) when opening the delegation queue and a self-downgrade (SD_fence) when flushing (closing) the queue. The trouble is that allowing transmission of operations to a *remote node* necessitates a self-downgrade by the delegating thread. Additionally, when a thread wants to know if its critical section has been executed successfully (e.g., by executing a wait), we also need to perform self-invalidation in order to be able to see the updates performed by the critical section on possibly *other* nodes. Evidently queue delegation to other nodes does not save us any self-invalidations and self-downgrades. Furthermore, the helper thread which executes critical sections may have to slow down to wait for remote nodes delegating sections.

To address these issues, in the Argo system HQDL only allows delegation of critical sections from the same node as the lock holder is on. Permission to open a delegation queue is determined hierarchically by acquiring a global lock. The node that holds the global lock is the currently active node. On the active node, a self-invalidation is performed in order to "see" data possibly written in earlier executions of critical sections in other nodes. However, after this initial self invalidation, there is no need for more self-invalidations or self-downgrades as long as critical sections are delegated and executed locally. Once the execution of the critical sections finishes (either because there are no more, or a limit is reached) a self-downgrade is performed to make the writes of the executed critical sections globally visible and the global lock is released. This type of locking structure uses significantly fewer SI_fence/SD_fence which would otherwise be very costly: First we eliminate the need for self-invalidating data upon waiting for a specific critical section. This is instead done for the whole node when accessing the global lock. Second, when delegating a critical section, we do not need

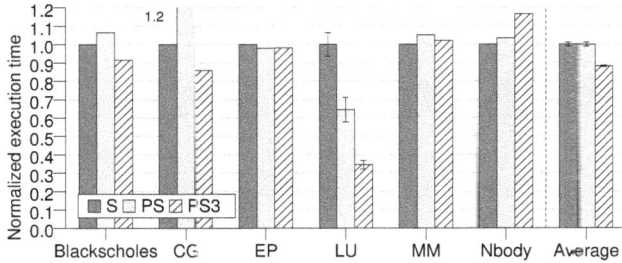

Figure 8: Classification impact on execution time.

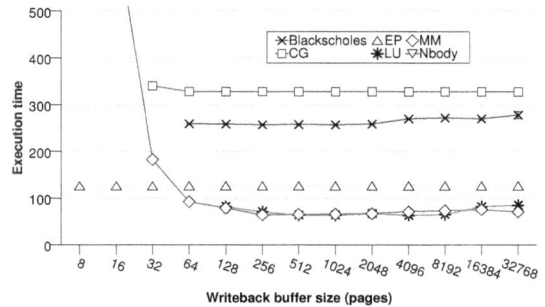

Figure 9: Runtime for different write-buffer sizes.

to flush any buffers, as local node coherence is sufficient.

While this approach reduces the number of threads that can simultaneously delegate to the same lock, it still improves performance: If the program depends on lock performance, it has enough work even on a single node, otherwise there are only negligible stalls on other nodes.

5. EVALUATION

We implement and evaluate Argo on a large distributed cluster in our installation primarily used for HPC workloads. We use at least up to 32 and when possible up to 128 nodes to run our experiments. Each node is equipped with two AMD Opteron 6220 processors featuring two quad-core CPUs per chip, connected using the same interconnect as for communicating with separate processors. Therefore, for NUMA purposes, each machine has four memory nodes, each with only four cores that share a local memory hierarchy (16 cores total). The nodes have at least 64 GB of memory, and are set up with Scientific Linux 6.4, running Linux kernel version 2.6.32-431.20.3.el6.x86_64. All nodes are interconnected with a 2:1 oversubscribed QDR Infiniband fabric. Argo is in its prototype stage and as such it does not have its own custom fine-tuned network layer. Instead, it is built on top of MPI. We use OpenMPI 1.8.4 supporting the MPI3 RMA standard [29]. MPI handles all the bookkeeping needed to start a parallel program on multiple nodes. Each node contributes an equal share of memory to the globally shared memory of the system, and uses an equal amount of memory as a local cache for the global memory. On each run, the amount of memory (user specified) is sized to be large enough to fit the desired workload. Argo uses only 15 out of the 16 available cores of a node, leaving one to take the OS overhead (MPI and UPC use all 16 cores of a node). All results are normalized to a single thread (Pthreads or OpenMP).

5.1 Protocol Choices: S, P/S, P/S3

We first examine the impact of the design choices made for Argo's Carina coherence. As discussed in Section 3.2, Carina implements data classification via the Pyxis passive directory structure. The classification is intended to curb self-invalidation. A fundamental design decision is to avoid message handlers by using more bandwidth, which leads to choices such as the downgrade of private pages (Section 3.4.2). Here, we examine the impact of the three data classification choices: S (no classification—all shared), P/S (the naïve version of P/S classification where private pages are *not* downgraded), and P/S3 the full Carina classification (with private page self-downgrade and writer classification).

Execution time normalized to the S classification for six

benchmarks (on four nodes—64 cores) is shown in Figure 8. While the P/S classification aims to reduce latency by not self-invalidating private pages, it incurs a significant checkpointing overhead during synchronization points, in order to service P→S transitions. The end result is that the naïve P/S classification is no better than the S classification. The P/S3 classification overcomes this problem by self-downgrading private pages. The private/shared classification provides the major part of the benefit in terms of reducing the self-invalidation miss rate. For the six benchmarks we examined, additional writer classification further reduced miss rates but by small amounts. The NW (no writer or read-only) and the SW (single writer) classifications exclude shared read-only pages and pages written by a (single) producer from self-invalidation but these behaviors are not prevalent in our benchmark set: i) while there may be abundant read-only data, a single write disqualifies a whole page from being read-only; ii) there is not enough *stable* single-producer/consumer sharing at page granularity.

Lessons learned. P/S classification provides the most benefit in reducing self-invalidation misses but must be performed at a minimal cost: i.e., by self-downgrading private pages. Writer classification offers further small improvements which perhaps are significant at a different granularity, or in benchmarks with different sharing patterns (e.g., dominated by producer/consumer sharing at a coarser granularity) than those we examined.

5.2 Write-Buffer Sensitivity Analysis

While writes are not as critical to performance as reads, excessive write traffic can still be detrimental to performance. The parameter that controls write traffic in Argo is the size of the write buffer that coalesces writes between synchronizations. However, a very large write buffer (that must empty on synchronization) can adversely affect synchronization latency, with serious performance implications. Figure 9 shows execution time as a function of write-buffer size. With small write-buffer sizes, some of our benchmarks exceed their preallocated run time on the HPC cluster and do not even complete (the corresponding points are missing from Figure 9). For all intents and purposes, the performance of these benchmarks is devastated if the write-buffer size falls below a critical point. Execution time correlates well with the number of writebacks, as shown in Figure 10.

On the other hand, for very large buffer sizes there is a slight slowdown, caused by the overhead on synchronization and other overheads directly related to write buffer size. The set of benchmarks shown here has very little synchronization (in the form of a handful of barriers). Through experimenta-

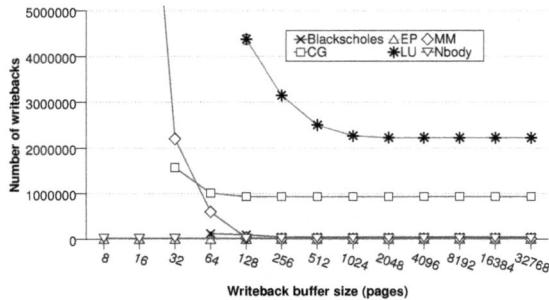

Figure 10: Writebacks for different write-buffer sizes.

tion, the write buffer was chosen to contain 8192 pages for Blackscholes, Nbody and LU, 256 pages for GC, 128 pages for MM, and 32 pages for EP in the remaining experiments.

Lessons learned. A minimum write buffer size is often required to run a program, but increasing the size further neither yields greater benefits, nor hurts performance when synchronization is light.

5.3   Lock Algorithms: Cohort vs HQDL

Since the benchmarks examined so far do not have significant synchronization (no lock synchronization), Argo's behavior in the face of intensive lock synchronization is analyzed using an appropriate micro-benchmark constructing a concurrent priority queue from a fast sequential implementation and a lock to access it. This kind of benchmark is regularly used to evaluate locking algorithms [12, 8, 20]. In particular, the benchmark uses a *pairing heap* [9], which has been shown to outperform non-blocking priority queue implementations when used together with flat combining [12].

The benchmark measures throughput: the number of operations that N threads, starting at the same time and executing a loop, can perform during a period of t seconds. The loop body consists of some amount of thread-local work and a global operation (either `insert` or `extract_min`) which is selected randomly with equal probability. While `extract_min` operations wait for their result, `insert` operations do not expect a result back and therefore can continue immediately after successful delegation. The seed for the random number generator is thread-local to avoid false sharing between threads. The thread-local work can be specified in work units, where each work unit performs updates to two randomly selected elements of a thread-local array of 64 integers. Figure 11 shows the scaling behavior of different locking algorithms on a single machine. As can be seen, Pthreads has performance issues even on a single NUMA machine, and QDL outperforms the alternative Cohort locks.

The benchmark results shown in Figure 12 use 48 local work units and 15 threads per node. Clearly, the benchmark does not scale, but this is to be expected of an application

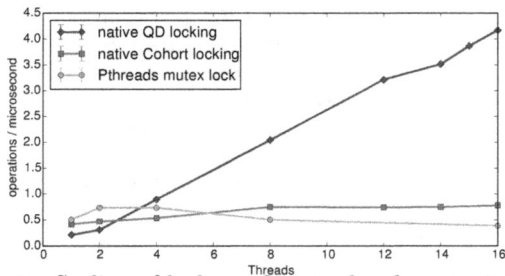

Figure 11: Scaling of lock-synchronized code on a single node.

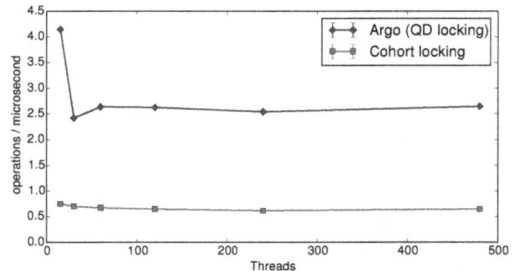

Figure 12: Scaling of lock-synchronized code using DSM.

which is dominated by its critical sections. When going from a single node to two, Argo's Vela HQDL performance drops by 42% compared to the performance of QDL within a node, but stays stable across a large number of nodes and significantly outperforms a state-of-the-art Cohort lock implementation under the same conditions (Figure 12).

Lessons Learned. Delegating critical sections to remote nodes does not save self-invalidations and/or self-downgrades. Instead hierarchical queue delegation should be performed that delegates only locally.

5.4   Scalability and Comparison to MPI

The benchmarks here are written for regular multicore systems using Pthreads, with the necessary adaptions made to run on our system. For comparison, all graphs also show the behavior of the unmodified code on a single machine.

For our first benchmark, we only show scalability compared to its Pthreads implementation. We use the well-known matrix triangulation benchmark from SPLASH-2, commonly known as LU [38]. The results are shown in Figure 13a. As this benchmark involves a lot of data migration within the system, there is significant overhead when running it on Argo. Still, using multiple nodes outperforms the Pthreads version on a single machine, and continues to gain performance up to eight nodes.

Figure 13b shows the scaling of a custom implementation of the n-body problem. It uses a simple iterative approach, separating iteration steps with barriers. The additional cost of synchronization over a network is barely noticeable for large problem sizes and does not prevent scaling of this benchmark up to 32 nodes (512 cores), exceeding that of the MPI port. The blackscholes benchmark from Parsec [3] uses only a single barrier synchronization at the end of each benchmark iteration, resulting in the very good scaling shown in Figure 13c for up to 128 nodes (2048 cores), in contrast to the MPI version that stops scaling at 16 nodes (256 cores). Variations in Argo's speedup (at 32, 48 and 64 nodes) are mainly due to the overly simplistic data distribution and its negative interaction with Argo's prefetching. We implemented a naïve Matrix Multiplication benchmark and show its scaling with two input sets: 2000×2000 and 5000×5000. Speedup is shown in Figure 13d. The MPI version has an algorithmic advantage as it is already faster in a single node. However, whereas the MPI version with the small input cannot maintain its advantage beyond one node, Argo scales well up to eight nodes (128 cores) before flattening out. For the large input, Argo scales in a similar way to the MPI version but the initial difference in the single-node speed is carried all the way up to 32 nodes (512 cores).

---

[3]Thanks to Tobias Skoglund for providing this benchmark.

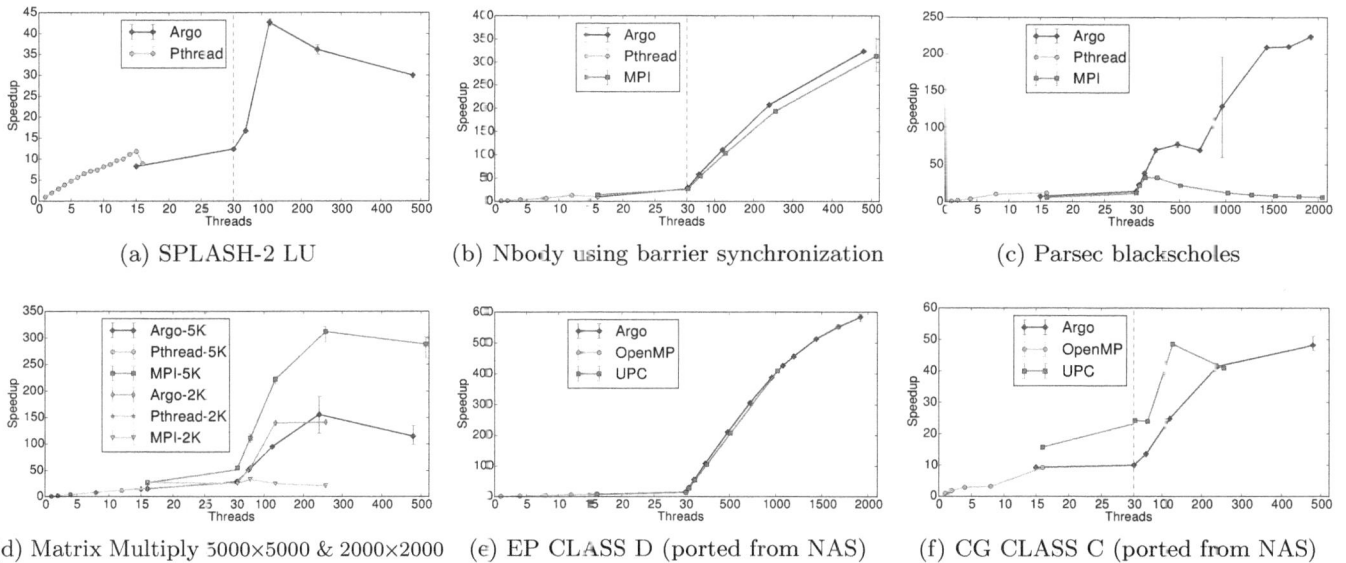

(a) SPLASH-2 LU   (b) Nbody using barrier synchronization   (c) Parsec blackscholes

(d) Matrix Multiply 5000×5000 & 2000×2000   (e) EP CLASS D (ported from NAS)   (f) CG CLASS C (ported from NAS)

Figure 13: Benchmark scaling to 32(128) nodes, 512(2048) cores.

5.5 Comparison to UPC

Our final comparison is against UPC benchmarks. The scaling of the highly-parallel EP benchmark, from the NAS Parallel Benchmark suite, is shown in Figure 13e. In this case the scaling behaviour continues similarly to that on a single machine for both UPC and Argo up to 128 nodes (2048 cores; UPC is limited to 1024 cores). This shows that Argo can compete directly with PGAS systems that require significant effort to program in. The CG benchmark from the NAS suite (Figure 13f) is another case of the non-Pthreads benchmark starting with a significant advantage over the Argo implementation in one node. This advantage, however, withers as the UPC version stops scaling earlier than Argo (at eight nodes, 128 cores) whereas Argo continues up to 32 nodes (512 cores). Whereas UPC performance is initially higher, due to an optimized implementation, Argo still achieves good scaling without changing the algorithm.

6. CONCLUSIONS

In this paper we are re-thinking software distributed shared memory in relation to the technology trends as they developed over the last decade. We have identified the latency of a centralized coherence protocol that indirects via a home node directory, the overhead of software message handlers, the latency of remote synchronization, and the accompanied overhead of data migration incurred by the distributed execution of critical sections, as major impediments to the end performance and hence scalability of a DSM. To this end, we propose a new approach to coherence and a new approach to synchronization that overturn standard practices. The result is exemplified in a prototype implementation of a page-based, user-space DSM system called Argo, which currently is built on top of MPI.

Argo's coherence (Carina) takes distributed decisions using self-invalidation and self-downgrade and does not use message handlers. Instead all actions are performed via RMA by requesting nodes. To reduce the number of misses caused by self-invalidation we introduce passive directories (Pyxis) that perform data classification to help nodes filter what to self-invalidate. The novelty of the Pyxis directory structure is that it is implemented without any message handlers. To handle synchronization and critical section execution we turn to the current performance-leading paradigm of queue delegation locking but we observe that it is not appropriate for a distributed environment where one may have to delegate remotely. Thus, we propose a hierarchical extension of queue delegation locking (implemented as the Vela synchronization system), that prioritizes local delegation before switching to other nodes.

Argo is in its prototype phase and uses MPI as its networking layer. We have ported an initial set of benchmarks—expanding rapidly—to assess our design decisions. Despite the limitations of a prototype implementation, results are highly encouraging. Several benchmarks show significant performance improvements due to Argo's distributed coherence and easily match or exceed their message-passing or PGAS implementations. However, the full potential of Argo is not tapped yet. As more benchmarks come online, future work will rework them for *detached delegation* of critical sections where one can overlap their execution with useful work. Further, we plan to examine the relation of granularity, data placement, and classification to enhance the opportunities offered by the P/S3 classification scheme to reduce miss rates.

Acknowledgements

This work was carried out within the Linnaeus centre of excellence UPMARC (Uppsala Programming for Multicore Architectures Research Center).

7. REFERENCES

[1] S. V. Adve and M. D. Hill. Weak ordering – a new definition. In *17th ISCA*, pages 2–14, June 1990.

[2] B. N. Bershad, M. J. Zekauskas, and W. A. Sawdon. The midway distributed shared memory system. Tech. rep. 865207, Carnegie Mellon University, Jan. 1993.

[3] C. Bienia, S. Kumar, J. P. Singh, and K. Li. The PARSEC benchmark suite: Characterization and architectural implications. In *17th PACT*, Oct. 2008.

[4] B. Choi, R. Komuravelli, H. Sung, R. Smolinski, N. Honarmand, S. V. Adve, V. S. Adve, N. P. Carter, and C.-T. Chou. DeNovo: Rethinking the memory hierarchy for disciplined parallelism. In *20th PACT*, pages 155–166, Oct. 2011.

[5] T. S. Craig. Building FIFO and priority-queuing spin locks from atomic swap. Tech. rep., Dept. of CSE, University of Washington, Seattle, 1993.

[6] B. Cuesta, A. Ros, M. E. Gómez, A. Robles, and J. Duato. Increasing the effectiveness of directory caches by deactivating coherence for private memory blocks. In *38th ISCA*, pages 93–103, June 2011.

[7] D. Dice, V. J. Marathe, and N. Shavit. Lock cohorting: a general technique for designing NUMA locks. In *17th PPoPP*, pages 247–256, 2012. ACM.

[8] P. Fatourou and N. D. Kallimanis. Revisiting the combining synchronization technique. In *17th PPoPP*, pages 257–266, 2012. ACM.

[9] M. L. Fredman, R. Sedgewick, D. D. Sleator, and R. E. Tarjan. The pairing heap: A new form of self-adjusting heap. *Algorithmica*, 1(1):111–129, 1986.

[10] K. Gharachorloo, D. Lenoski, J. Laudon, P. Gibbons, A. Gupta, and J. L. Hennessy. Memory consistency and event ordering in scalable shared-memory multiprocessors. In *17th ISCA*, pages 15–26, 1990.

[11] N. Hardavellas, M. Ferdman, B. Falsafi, and A. Ailamaki. Reactive NUCA: Near-optimal block placement and replication in distributed caches. In *36th ISCA*, pages 184–195, June 2009.

[12] D. Hendler, I. Incze, N. Shavit, and M. Tzafrir. Flat combining and the synchronization-parallelism tradeoff. In *22nd SPAA*, pages 355–364, 2010. ACM.

[13] L. Iftode, J. P. Singh, and K. Li. Scope consistency: A bridge between release consistency and entry consistency. In *8th SPAA*, pages 277–287, June 1996.

[14] S. Kaxiras and G. Keramidas. SARC coherence: Scaling directory cache coherence in performance and power. *IEEE Micro*, 30(5):54–65, Sept. 2011.

[15] S. Kaxiras and A. Ros. A new perspective for efficient virtual-cache coherence. In *ISCA*, pages 535–547, 2013.

[16] P. J. Keleher, A. L. Cox, S. Dwarkadas, and W. Zwaenepoel. TreadMarks: Distributed shared memory on standard workstations and operating systems. In *USENIX*, pages 115–132, Jan. 1994.

[17] P. J. Keleher, A. L. Cox, and W. Zwaenepoel. Lazy release consistency for software distributed shared memory. In *19th ISCA*, pages 13–21, May 1992.

[18] D. Klaftenegger, K. Sagonas, and K. Winblad. Brief announcement: Queue delegation locking. In *26th SPAA*, pages 70–72, 2014. ACM.

[19] D. Klaftenegger, K. Sagonas, and K. Winblad. Delegation locking libraries for improved performance of multithreaded programs. In *Euro-Par*, LNCS, 2014.

[20] D. Klaftenegger, K. Sagonas, and K. Winblad. Queue delegation locking, 2014. http://www.it.uu.se/research/group/languages/software/qd_lock_lib.

[21] L. Lamport. How to make a multiprocessor computer that correctly executes multiprocess programs. *IEEE Transactions on Computers*, 28(9):690–691, 1979.

[22] A. R. Lebeck and D. A. Wood. Dynamic self-invalidation: Reducing coherence overhead in shared-memory multiprocessors. In *22nd ISCA*, pages 48–59, June 1995.

[23] D. Lenoski, J. Laudon, K. Gharachorloo, W.-D. Weber, A. Gupta, J. L. Hennessy, M. A. Horowitz, and M. S. Lam. The Stanford DASH multiprocessor. *IEEE Computer*, 25(3):63–79, Mar. 1992.

[24] K. Li. IVY: A shared virtual memory system for parallel computing. In *ICPP*, pages 94–101, Aug. 1988.

[25] J.-P. Lozi, F. David, G. Thomas, J. Lawall, and G. Muller. Remote core locking: Migrating critical-section execution to improve the performance of multithreaded applications. In *USENIX*, pages 65–76, USA, 2012. USENIX Association.

[26] V. Luchangco, D. Nussbaum, and N. Shavit. A hierarchical CLH queue lock. In *12th ICPP*, pages 801–810, 2006. Springer-Verlag.

[27] P. S. Magnusson, A. Landin, and E. Hagersten. Queue locks on cache coherent multiprocessors. In *8th ISPP*, pages 165–171, 1994. IEEE Computer Society.

[28] J. M. Mellor-Crummey and M. L. Scott. Algorithms for scalable synchronization on shared-memory multiprocessors. *ACM TOCS*, 9(1):21–65, Feb. 1991.

[29] MPI Forum. MPI: A Message-Passing Interface Standard. Version 3.0, September 2012. available at: http://www.mpi-forum.org/docs (January, 2015).

[30] J. Nelson, B. Holt, B. Myers, P. Briggs, L. Ceze, S. Kahan, and M. Oskin. Grappa: A latency-tolerant runtime for large-scale irregular applications. Tech. Rep, Dept. of CSE, Univ. of Washington, Feb 2014.

[31] Y. Oyama, K. Taura, and A. Yonezawa. Executing parallel programs with synchronization bottlenecks efficiently. In *IWPDC*, pages 182–204. 1999.

[32] S. Phillips. M7: Next generation SPARC. In *26st HotChips Symp.*, Aug. 2014.

[33] Z. Radović and E. Hagersten. DSZOOM – low latency software-based shared memory. Technical report, Parallel and Scientific Computing Institute, 2001.

[34] Z. Radović and E. Hagersten. Hierarchical backoff locks for nonuniform communication architectures. In *9th HPCA*, pages 241–252. IEEE Comp. Society, 2003.

[35] B. Ramesh. *Samhita: Virtual Shared Memory for Non-Cache-Coherent Systems*. PhD thesis, Virginia Polytechnic Institute and State University, July 2013.

[36] A. Ros, B. Cuesta, M. E. Gómez, A. Robles, and J. Duato. Temporal-aware mechanism to detect private data in chip multiprocessors. In *42nd ICPP*, pages 562–571, Oct. 2013.

[37] A. Ros and S. Kaxiras. Complexity-effective multicore coherence. In *21st PACT*, pages 241–252, Sept. 2012.

[38] J. P. Singh, W.-D. Weber, and A. Gupta. SPLASH: Stanford parallel applications for shared-memory. *Computer Architecture News*, 20(1):5–44, Mar. 1992.

[39] M. A. Suleman, O. Mutlu, M. K. Qureshi, and Y. N. Patt. Accelerating critical section execution with asymmetric multi-core architectures. In *14th ASPLOS*, pages 253–264, New York, NY, USA, 2009. ACM.

[40] UPC Consortium. UPC language specifications, v1.2. Tech. Rep, Lawrence Berkeley National Lab, 2005.

[41] W.-D. Weber and A. Gupta. Analysis of cache invalidation patterns in multiprocessors. In *3th ASPLOS*, pages 243–256, Apr. 1989.

Uni-Address Threads: Scalable Thread Management for RDMA-Based Work Stealing

Shigeki Akiyama
The University of Tokyo
7-3-1 Hongo Bunkyo-ku
Tokyo, Japan
akiyama@eidos.ic.i.u-tokyo.ac.jp

Kenjiro Taura
The University of Tokyo
7-3-1 Hongo Bunkyo-ku
Tokyo, Japan
tau@eidos.ic.i.u-tokyo.ac.jp

ABSTRACT

Task-parallel systems have been widely used to parallelize programs. They provide automatic load balancing and programmers can easily parallelize sequential programs, including irregular ones, without considering task placement to physical processors.

Despite the success of shared memory task parallelism, task parallelism on large-scale distributed memory environments is still challenging. The focuses of our work are flexibility of task model and scalability of inter-node load balancing. General task models provide functionalities for suspending and resuming tasks at any program point, and such a model enables us flexible task scheduling to achieve higher processor utilization, locality-aware task placement, etc. To realize such a task model, we have to employ a thread—an execution context containing register values and stack frames—as a representation of a task, and implement thread migration for inter-node load balancing. However, an existing thread migration scheme, *iso-address*, has a scalability limitation: it requires virtual memory proportional to the number of processors in each node. In large-scale distributed memory environments, this results in a huge virtual memory usage beyond the virtual address space limit of current 64bit CPUs. Furthermore, this huge virtual memory consumption makes it impossible to implement one-sided work stealing with Remote Direct Memory Access (RDMA) operations. One-sided work stealing is a popular approach to achieving high efficiency of load balancing; therefore this also limits scalability of distributed memory task parallelism.

In this paper, we propose *uni-address*, a new thread management scheme for distributed memory task parallelism. It significantly reduces virtual memory usage for thread migration and enables us to implement RDMA-based work stealing. We implement a lightweight multithread library supporting RDMA-based work stealing based on the uni-address scheme, and demonstrate its lightweight thread operations and scalable work stealing on Fujitsu FX10 super-computing system with three benchmarks: Binary Task Creation, Unbalanced Tree Search, and NQueens solver. As a result, we confirmed all the benchmarks works with less than 144KB virtual memory for thread migration in each processor and achieved more than 95% parallel efficiency on 3840 processing cores, relative to the results on 480 processing cores.

Categories and Subject Descriptors

D.1.3 [**Programming Techniques**]: Concurrent Programming—*Parallel Programming*

General Terms

Algorithms, Design, Performance

Keywords

Task parallelism; lightweight multithreading; thread migration; distributed work stealing; remote direct memory access

1. INTRODUCTION

Dynamic, hierarchical, and fine-grain parallelism are increasingly believed to play a key role in programming extreme scale systems, to achieve load balancing, to hide latency, to combat against performance variability, and to enhance programmability. Systems supporting such parallelism, which we collectively call *task-parallel* systems, have been widely adopted in shared memory machines [11, 5, 16, 21, 28, 18]. On large-scale distributed memory machines, research efforts are under way but we are yet to see a widely used implementation, as there are many intricate issues associated with the lack of shared memory and the scale of such machines. They include how to implement dynamic task migration without shared memory, what happens on pointers upon migration, how to scale dynamic load balancing to extremely large systems, etc.

Previous research efforts take a variety of forms; some systems support task parallelism on distributed machines, but do not support global load balancing [6, 7]; many implement a restrictive "bag of tasks" or "atomic tasks" model as a target (see Section 2). There are a few systems general enough to express fork-join parallelism, but to the best of our knowledge, all assume tasks are tied to a specific processor, which may lower processor utilization. In addition, most systems supporting fork-join parallelism are built with a significant source or bytecode processing [4, 26], which renders them difficult to reuse across multiple languages. The situation contrasts with shared memory machines, where we have task-parallel *libraries* [16, 28, 21], which can be used from most C/C++ programs compiled with ordinary C/C++ compilers.

The main goal of the present work is to narrow this gap, by implementing a library satisfying the following.

- It supports general lightweight threading primitives (creating a thread and joining a thread) on large-scale distributed memory environments.

- In particular, it supports general migration of native threads across nodes, written in ordinary C/C++ programs.

- It does not require a special source code processing or a new code generator; the user program can be compiled with ordinary C/C++ compilers.

The main issue is how to migrate native threads, whose stack may contain ambiguous pointers. We propose a new implementation scheme, *uni-address*, which overcomes a scalability limitation of a previously proposed *iso-address* [2] scheme. We implemented the library, *uni-address threads*, on Fujitsu FX10 system [12] and tested its scalability up to 3840 cores.

Novel contributions of this paper are as follows:

- We propose a new native thread migration scheme, called *uni-address*, which significantly reduces the usage of virtual address space.

- Based on this technique, we design and implement a work stealing scheduler with *one-sided* task stealing, which can take advantage of Remote Direct Memory Access (RDMA).

- We evaluated virtual memory usage and performance of uni-address threads on 3840 processing cores in three benchmark programs: Binary Task Creation, Unbalanced Tree Search, and NQueens. We confirmed all benchmarks works with less than 144KB virtual memory for thread migration in each processor and achieved more than 95% parallel efficiency on 3840 processing cores, relative to the results on 480 processing cores.

The rest of this paper is organized as follows. Section 2 discusses related work. In Section 3, we describe the task model assumed in this paper. Section 4 presents iso-address thread migration scheme and its scalability limitations. In Section 5, we describe uni-address scheme and presents the implementation of RDMA-based work stealing and inter-task synchronization on top of it. Section 6 shows an experimental evaluation of uni-address scheme, and Section 7 concludes this paper.

2. RELATED WORK

To position the present work in context, this section gives a taxonomy of task-parallel systems on distributed memory environments. By task-parallel systems, we broadly mean systems that support creation of tasks at runtime and their dynamic load balancing. Implementation strategies and complexities are heavily affected by synchronization patterns supported by the system.

Bag of tasks.

Some systems such as Scioto [8, 9] and X10/GLB [30] support only independent "bag of tasks"; tasks neither synchronize nor communicate with other tasks. Note that X10 supports async-finish primitives, but native X10 tasks do not migrate across nodes (places); X10/GLB is a system built on top of X10 for global load-balancing. Bag of tasks are particularly simple to implement; it suffices to represent a task with a data structure (e.g., a function pointer + arguments to the function) and exchange the task structure among nodes to achieve load balancing. Bag of tasks is clearly very restrictive and cannot express many important divide-and-conquer algorithms naturally.

Atomic tasks.

Some other systems support dependencies (synchronizations) among tasks but assume a task is "atomic," in the sense that a task never blocks and always runs until completion once it gets started [4, 29]. We say such systems support "atomic tasks" model in the rest of the discussion.

Atomic tasks admit an implementation strategy similar to that for bag of tasks, with only the difference being that it has to keep track of the status (ready to execute or not) of each task. From the programmability standpoint, this model forces a cumbersome programming style in which a logically sequential flow of computation needs to be "split" at each synchronization point and data used by the continuation of a synchronization must be manually packaged as a data structure. Arguably, atomic tasks are not for human programmers and can only be useful as a compiler target.

Fork-join and more general models.

Then there are systems that support a natural expression of fork-join parallelism or more general synchronization patterns. Examples are abundant on shared memory environments (Cilk [11], OpenMP tasks [5], TBB [16], MassiveThreads [21], Qthreads [28], Java fork-join [18]), but scarce on distributed memory environments; notable exceptions are Satin [26], HotSLAW [19], and Grappa [22]. A task can create any number of child tasks and then call a "wait" function that waits for its outstanding children to finish. The calling task suspends until its children finish and then continues; the programmer does not have to package variables used after the synchronization. Figure 1 contrasts the Fibonacci function in atomic tasks and fork-join.

Implementation of fork-join is more involved than atomic tasks, as it is now the system's responsibility to package the variables used by the continuation of a synchronization. Load balancing entails passing the representation of the migrating task's continuation between workers. In procedural programming languages such as C, a task's continuation is essentially its stack of activation frames.

Implementing fork-join with tied tasks.

To avoid complication that stems from such "continuation passing" between workers, many of the systems mentioned above, including Satin, HotSLAW, and Grappa, avoid migrating tasks already started; when a task is created, a task is put in a task pool; only before it gets started can it be stolen by other workers. In other words, once a task gets started by a worker, it is "tied" to the worker. This scheme allows an implementation strategy similar to atomic tasks, as an yet-to-be-started task can be simply represented by

```
1   thread Fib(cont int k, int n) {
2     if (n < 2) {
3       send_argument(k, n);
4     } else {
5       cont int x, y;
6       spawn_next Sum(k, ?x, ?y);
7       spawn Fib(x, n - 1);
8       spawn Fib(x, n - 2);
9     }
10  }
11  thread Sum(cont int k, int x, int y) {
12    send_argument(k, x + y);
13  }
```

```
1   long fib(long n) {
2     if (n < 2) {
3       return n;
4     } else {
5       long r0, r1;
6       r0 = spawn fib(n - 1);
7       r1 = spawn fib(n - 1);
8       sync;
9       return r0 + r1;
10    }
11  }
```

Figure 1: Fibonacci in atomic tasks model (left [4]); and in fork-join model (right [11])

a function pointer + its arguments, similarly to the atomic tasks. On the other hand, it can lose some opportunities for load migration and thus potentially lower processor utilization.

Despite its potential performance problem this scheme seems popular as it can be readily implemented by ordinary procedure calls and returns [16, 18, 26, 19]; when a worker encounters a synchronization point, it repeats executing a task in its local task pool or stealing one from others, until all tasks it waits for finish. Either way it is just an indirect procedure call. The technique, which seems first described in [27], is particularly attractive when implemented in high-level languages, e.g., Java, that do not support non-local jumps.

"Genuine" task migration.

This paper focuses on an efficient implementation scheme supporting "genuine" task migration, in the sense that a task can migrate even after it is started. Specifically, we implement a work stealing scheduling algorithm (child-first execution order upon task creation + FIFO stealing) first proposed by Mohr et al. in [20] and adopted in Cilk [11] and other systems [21, 28], which are possible only when a task's continuation can migrate at each task creation and each synchronization point. This particular scheduling policy is important both in theory and in practice. In theory, an established time bound of the work stealing scheduler [3] applies only when any task, started or not, can be stolen by any idle worker. A bound on extra cache misses [1] applies only when each worker preserves the serial order of execution except when a task steal happens. In practice, the work stealing scheduler is important because it tends to migrate coarse-grain tasks and its execution order tends to minimally deviate from the sequential execution, making it easy to reason about tasking overhead and data locality.

In shared memory environment, migrating a task in the middle of its execution can be done simply by passing the address of the stack, as both workers share the same address space [11, 21]. In distributed memory environments, it entails copying the stack frames of the task. Since address spaces are not shared by workers, pointers from/to the stack further complicate the issue. A scheme proposed in the literature, iso-address, as well as our proposed scheme, uni-address, are further elaborated in Section 4 and 5. There are two systems using iso-address thread migration—Adaptive MPI [14] and Charm++ [17]. Adaptive MPI uses iso-address to migrate MPI processes for dynamic load balancing on distributed memory systems, and Charm++ uses iso-address to

```
1   template <class T, class F, class... Args>
2   task<T> spawn(F f, Args... args);
3
4   template <class T>
5   void join(task<T> t, T *result);
```

Figure 2: Fork-join task API

support migratable threads as threaded entry methods for concurrent objects.

Other Task-Parallel Systems.

Tascell [13] is a "logical thread"-free task-parallel framework based on backtracking-based approach for shared and distributed memory environments. Tascell supports a fork-join model and genuine task migration by both compiler support and explicit packing of task's continuation, similar to atomic tasks, in language level.

3. TASK-PARALLEL MODEL

In this section, we describe a task-parallel model that we assume in this paper. In our model, a *task* is a unit of parallelism. A program starts with a main task, and there is no parallelism at this program point. In order to utilize parallelism of computational resources, a programmer has to spawn new tasks. Our model provides fork-join primitives for creating a task and waiting for completion of a task, shown in Figure 2.

Each task has its own call stack. This stack memory is managed according to underlying C calling convention so that a task can use C programming language features such as local variable accesses and function calls.

In our task model, tasks are automatically load-balanced. The runtime system automatically detects load imbalance, and then migrate tasks among processors across shared memory nodes. Therefore, programmers can write programs in a processor-oblivious manner; they do not have to be concerned about processor and node boundaries.

In order to support automatic load balancing among computational nodes, tasks should be isolated. A call stack is task-local and unable to be shared among tasks, and a task must not access the call stack of another task by passing C pointers. In order to share data among tasks, programmers can use task arguments and global memory features provided existing global address space frameworks such as partitioned global address space systems and distributed shared memory systems.

Our task model permits the runtime system to migrate a task between processors at *migration points*. A migration point is defined as a program point where a task may switch to another task. They include points where a task creates a new task and points where a task waits for the completion of another task.

4. ISO-ADDRESS

This section reviews *iso-address*, which inspires our work most. As noted in Section 2, migrating a task already started involves copying the currently active stack frames of the task—representation of variables used in the rest of the task. Simply copying the stack frames does not complete the job, however, as there are pointers from/to stack, which might need to be "fixed" when a stack moves across address spaces and changes its address.

One way to solve this problem is to implement a compiler that leaves enough information about stack frame and data layout, so that the runtime system knows which slots of a stack frame or which fields of a structure might contain pointers that need to be fixed. This approach is good for type-safe languages but is very difficult if not impossible to apply to languages with ambiguous pointers such as C and C++.

Iso-address [2] is a scheme that makes fixing pointers unnecessary, by ensuring stacks are copied into exactly the same address in the new address space. Intra-stack pointers (pointers from within the migrating stack to inside it) just continues to be valid after migration. Pointers to heap objects outside the migration stack (heap objects) are also copied to the same address in the new address space; they are allocated by a special memory allocation routine `pm2_iso malloc` so that the system knows where they are. In [2], it is assumed that pointers to such heap objects are not passed between threads and there are no inter-stack pointers.

The main advantage of iso-address scheme is that it just works with languages with ambiguous pointers and their ordinary compilers unaware of migration. Also, as the simple bit-wise copy suffices to copy a stack, migration is efficient.

Bringing this technique to a large-scale environment has several problems, however.

1. Iso-address requires the address of each live stack to be *globally* unique in the entire system, and *each* node to reserve these addresses. This results in consuming a huge *virtual* address space.

   In parallel divide-and-conquer algorithms, typical use cases of task-parallel systems, the number of simultaneously live tasks is roughly the maximum depth of the task tree × the number of hardware concurrency (workers) [3]; thus, with concurrency of largest machines already surpassing three million [25], and expected to only increase, allocating a few hundred kilobytes per stack has a risk of running out a *virtual* address space.

   As a point of reference, assume we have 4 million (2^{22}) hardware concurrency, the depth of the task tree is ten thousand or 2^{13}, a number that happens in an unbalanced tree search benchmark, and the size of a stack for each task is a modest 16KB (2^{14}) [1]; the total vir-

tual address space that needs to be reserved for tasks is $2^{22+13+14} = 2^{49}$, which surpasses the virtual address space size the current x86-64 processors support (2^{48}).

2. While allocating a virtual address does not immediately translate into consuming a physical memory, address usage in iso-address may still result in significant growth in physical memory usage. Operating systems generally allocate a physical page for a logical page when it is touched for the first time. Microscopically, when a node steals a task and hosts the incoming stack to its designated address, it may be the first touch on this page by that node.

   More quantitatively, the growth is determined by how many nodes, on average, will ever touch each logical page in the reserved area. When a particular page is reused by r distinct tasks in the lifetime of the application and each task migrates m times on average, tasks allocated on that page experience mr migrations in total; thus, roughly $(1 + mr)$ physical pages will be committed for that page in the entire system. Note that we expect r to be small ($\ll 1$), yet for long running applications, whose r is proportionally large, the overall growth may be significant.

   Also, note that it will also increase the number of page faults due to on-demand paging. Note that the scheme relies on on-demand paging in an essential way; it is obviously not possible to populate (pre-fault) the pages. In a SPARC64IXfx processor, a page fault takes 21K cycles on average, so this may degrade work stealing performance considerably.

3. Iso-address has another issue that it practically prohibits us taking advantage of now common hardware support of Remote Direct Memory Access (RDMA), or one-sided communication, for copying a stack upon migration. With RDMA, a node can trigger a data transfer without involving the host CPU on the target node. One-sided task stealing is a common practice in shared memory machines [11], and has been proved important in distributed memory environments [9].

   The problem is that, RDMA generally requires the region accessed by a remote node to be pinned to the physical memory, but we obviously do not have the luxury of pinning the entire region reserved for stacks. We might consider a more sophisticated strategy that pins (only) the migrating stack on demand, but it would hinder the original benefit of RDMA—stealing a task without involving the victim.

4. Less imminent but potentially an important issue is that, the luxury use of virtual address space may conflict with other techniques relying on sparsely populating a huge linear address range.

---

[1] This estimation (16KB) practically assumes each task has its dedicated linear stack, so as to be compatible with or-dinary C compilers. Alternatively, the ordinary procedure calls may obtain frames from a general free list shared by many tasks (heap frames, split stack, cactus stack, etc.), in which case the initial stack size per each task can be made minimum (just a single frame, in an extreme case). One might expect task stacks not to grow to their limits at the same time, in which case the maximum virtual address range that must be reserved can be reduced accordingly. Yet, as we want to impose a minimum allocation size (e.g., 4KB) to keep the overhead of frame allocation low, the overall conclusion is similar.

5. UNI-ADDRESS SCHEME

5.1 The Basic Idea

In order to address the problem of iso-address, which is reserving a huge virtual address space for stacks, we propose a uni-address scheme and RDMA-based work stealing on top of it. In order to simplify the exposition, we first describe its basic idea without performance considerations.

Recall that iso-address scheme maintains the validity of intra-stack pointers by copying a stack into the same address upon migration. The key idea behind uni-address scheme is that, in order to maintain validity of intra-stack pointers, all we need to guarantee is to map the stack on the designated address *when the task is actually running*. Stacks of not running tasks can be put at *an arbitrary address*; we put them into a reserved, RDMA-accessible region to make them available for task stealing.

A crucial assumption is that there are no pointers pointing to a stack from outside (i.e., there are neither inter-stack pointers nor heap-to-stack pointers). Were there such pointers, it is unsafe to relocate stacks even when the task is not running. Iso-address also made the assumption.

For stack-to-heap pointers, we are separately working on a global address space library supporting explicit global references and assume objects potentially referenced by multiple threads are always referenced by a global pointer. To dereference a global pointer, a function must be called, which can trigger data transfer if necessary. We currently do not support thread-private heaps that can be referenced by ordinary C pointers, but it is possible to add a mechanism similar to pm2_isomalloc. Further details about memory model of our system are beyond the scope of the paper and will be addressed in a separate paper.

To summarize, in its simplest and crudest form, uni-address scheme works as follows.

1. It creates a separate address space for each worker (a hardware concurrency such as a CPU core and a hardware thread).

2. It reserves a region of virtual addresses accommodating a *single* stack. This region is *the* stack for running a task, always used to run a task. We call this region *the uni-address region*.

3. It reserves a region of virtual addresses accommodating stacks for not running tasks and pins them to physical memory. Their addresses do not matter, as long as they can be reached from other nodes by RDMA. We call the region *RDMA region*.

4. Whenever a task switches, the previously running task is swapped out from the uni-address region to RDMA region and the next task is brought into the uni-address region.

Unlike iso-address, which *never* changes the stack addresses even if the task is not running, we do not have to reserve a sparsely used huge virtual address range; we only have to reserve a region large enough to accommodate the number of tasks *simultaneously live in a single address space*.

Note that we have a separate address space for each worker so that all workers can allocate *the* uni-address region at the same virtual address. In practice, it means we need to

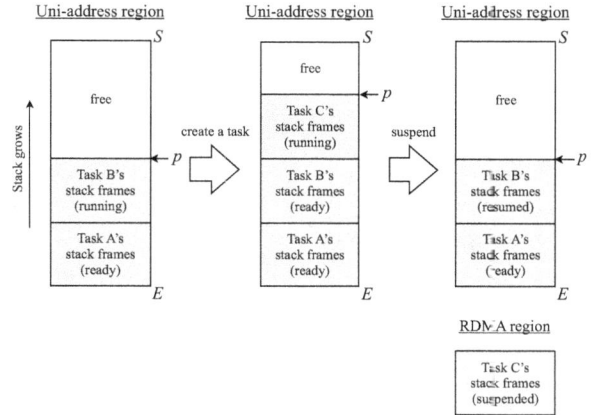

Figure 3: Uni-address region.

create a process per core. This is to guarantee that, at any moment of execution, any ready task can be run by any idle worker. In order to reduce the number of processes, we might alternatively have multiple workers and uni-address regions in each address space. In this case, a task allocated to a particular uni-address region can migrate to uni-address regions of the same address (of a different address space); in unlucky cases, there may be many unfilled regions and many ready yet not running tasks, due to their unmatching addresses. This may lower processor utilization. Further elaborating and quantifying the impact of this approach is our future work. The present paper explores only the basic, process-per-core approach.

5.2 An Optimized Scheme

This crude scheme just mentioned is simple but obviously inefficient, as it incurs two stack copies upon every context switch. Especially in the child-first work stealing scheduler, which immediately switches to the new child upon every task creation, it will be very inefficient.

To address this issue, we developed a better stack management technique.

The key observation is that, we do not have to allocate all stacks on the same address. The real requirement is each task, when executed, always occupies the same address as the address allocated to it upon creation. At least conceptually, a new stack can be allocated at any address in the uni-address region, as long as we ensure that the area the new stack may grow into is empty. More specifically, our memory management works as follows (Figure 3):

1. Assume the address range of the uni-address region is $[S, E)$.

2. Each address space manages a pointer p in the uni-address region (i.e., $S \le p < E$) pointing to the next free address, much like the stack pointer of sequential languages. Assuming a stack grows downwards, we have addresses $\in [p, E)$ are used, and addresses $\in [S, p)$ are free.

3. When a new task is created, its stack is allocated just below p, much like allocating a new frame from a linear stack, and the task immediately starts. We maintain

19

```
1   void do_create_thread(context *ctx, thread_func_t f, void
                *arg) {
2       // push the parent thread
3       taskq_entry entry;
4       entry.frame_base = ctx->rsp;
5       entry.frame_size = ctx->parent_ctx->rsp + sizeof(
                context) - ctx->rsp;
6       entry.ctx = ctx;
7       TASK_QUEUE_PUSH(entry);
8
9       // start a child thread
10      current_worker()->parent = ctx;
11      f(arg);
12
13      // pop the parent thread
14      bool ok = TASK_QUEUE_POP(&entry);
15      if (!ok) go_to_scheduler();
16  }
17  void create_thread(thread_func_t f, void *arg) {
18      context *parent = current_worker()->parent;
19      save_context_and_call(parent, do_create_thread,
20                              f, arg);
21      current_worker()->parent = parent;
22  }
```

Figure 4: Optimized implementation of task creation function.

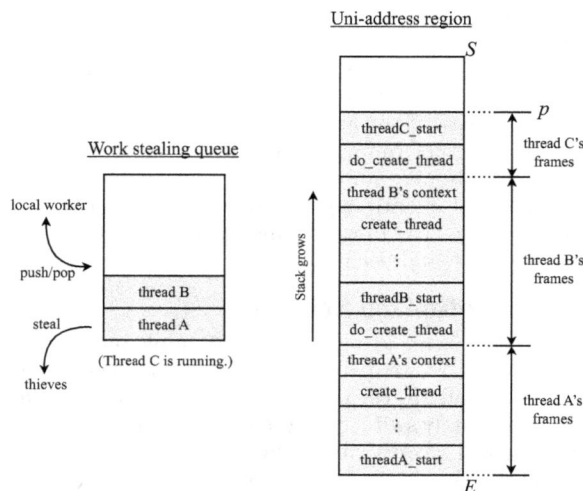

Figure 5: A work stealing queue and the corresponding uni-address region.

an invariant that the running task occupies the lowest addresses of the used region.

4. When a task is suspended, its task is copied out from the uni-address region into any free address in the RDMA region, and resume the task just above it if there is one. This way, we maintain the above invariant.

5. Only when the uni-address region becomes empty, does the process steal work from another node. Thus, the uni-address region of this process can accommodate any task.

In this scheme, a task creation is very efficient, as it is much like an ordinary procedure call, except that we need to save registers before task creation so that the caller can be stolen.

Figure 4 shows the implementation of task creation based on this idea, and Figure 5 illustrates a work stealing queue and the corresponding uni-address region. The thread creation function **create_thread** saves the context of the running thread and call **do_create_thread** function (Line 19-20) by **save_context_and_call** function shown in Appendix A. Then, **do_create_thread** function first pushes an entry to the work stealing queue (Line 3-7). The entry contains information for resuming the parent thread when the thread is stolen. Next, **do_create_thread** function executes a given thread start function (Line 11). After the function call, it pops an entry from the work stealing queue. If it succeeds, the parent thread has not been stolen and resumes the thread after removing the saved context on the stack. Otherwise, the parent thread has been stolen, so the control goes to the scheduler code to execute waiting threads or perform work stealing. Executing a child thread does not evict the parent thread from the uni-address region. The overhead of task creation consists of only save and restoration of the parent thread and manipulations of the work stealing queue.

5.3 RDMA-based Work Stealing

Under random work stealing, a processor selects a victim processor and steals a task from the victim's task queue when the processor becomes idle. To steal a thread with RDMA operations, the following memory regions are pinned to physical memory: the uni-address region, RDMA region, and work stealing queues. Under the requirement, we now explain the implementation of RDMA-based work stealing.

The implementation of a task queue is one of the most important parts in work stealing. A task queue is accessed from a local worker upon a task creation and a local exit from a task, and accessed from remote workers upon a work stealing. Therefore, naive locking scheme for mutual exclusion does not scale well especially on large-scale distributed memory machines [9]. To address this issue, we implement THE protocol [11] with RDMA READ, WRITE, and fetch-and-add. THE protocol is used in several task-parallel systems on shared memory machines, such as Cilk [11] and MassiveThreads [21], and because it eliminates locking from local accesses to a task queue, it reduces tasking overhead and improves scalability of work stealing.

Figure 6 shows the pseudo-code of our work stealing implementation. A thief first selects a victim process and calculates the remote address of the task queue of the victim process. Next, the thief tries to lock the task queue with RDMA fetch-and-add operation, and if it failed, the steal process aborts. If the locking succeeds, the thief tries to steal an entry from the task queue. If the task queue is empty, the steal process aborts. Otherwise, the thief starts migrating the thread in the stolen task queue entry. In thread migration, we first calculate the remote address of the stack region for RDMA operation, and then perform an RDMA READ operation from the remote address to the uni-address region without changing the address of the thread stack. At this point, the context of the thread becomes valid; the saved register values and the contents of the stack become readable. Next, the thief releases the lock of the task queue and resumes the thread loaded to the uni-address stack.

```
1   void resume_remote_context(saved_context_t *sctx,
            taskq_entry e) {
2       WAIT_QUEUE_PUSH(sctx);
3       void *remote_base = get_remote_base(e.stack_base,
            victim);
4       RDMA_GET(e.stack_base, remote_base, e.stack_size,
            victim);
5       taskq_unlock(q, victim);
6       resume_context(e.ctx);
7   }
8   void steal() {
9       int victim = select_victim_randomly();
10      taskq *q = get_remote_taskq(victim);
11      if (!try_lock(q, victim))
12          return;
13
14      taskq_entry e;
15      if (!taskq_steal(q, victim, &e)) {
16          taskq_unlock(q, victim);
17          return;
18      }
19      suspend(resume_remote_context, e);
20  }
```

Figure 6: Implementation for RDMA-based work stealing

```
1   void resume_saved_context_1(saved_context *next_sctx) {
2       // restore stack frames
3       memcpy(next_sctx->stack_top, sctx->stack_buf,
            next_sctx->stack_size);
4       // restore the execution state of the next thread
5       resume_context(next_sctx->ctx);
6   }
7   void resume_saved_context(saved_context *sctx,
            saved_context *next_sctx) {
8       WAIT_QUEUE_PUSH(sctx);
9
10      /* after moving SP to unused area by the suspending
11         thread and resuming thread, call the function.
12         This is implemented in assembly. */
13      CALL_WITH_SAFE_SP(resume_saved_context_1,
14              next_sctx);
15  }
16  void join(task<T> t, T *result) {
17      T value;
18      while (!try_join(t, result)) {
19          // first try to switch to a ready thread
20          bool ok = TASK_QUEUE_POP(&entry);
21          if (ok) {
22              suspend(resume_context, entry->ctx);
23          } else {
24              // start work stealing
25              ok = steal();
26              if (!ok) {
27                  // execute a waiting thread if the steal
            fails
28                  saved_context_t *sctx = WAIT_QUEUE_POP();
29                  suspend(resume_saved_context, sctx);
30              }
31          }
32      }
33  }
```

Figure 7: Implementation of join function

5.4 Inter-Thread Synchronization

In this section, we describe an implementation of inter-thread synchronization in the optimized uni-address scheme, and we take join operation, an operation to wait for the exit of a thread, as an example. Figure 7 shows the implementation. The join function checks whether the target thread has terminated or not with **try_join** function. If it has, the function returns with the result of the thread. Other-

```
1   typedef struct {
2       void *ip, *sp;
3       context_t *ctx;
4       uint8_t *stack_top;
5       size_t stack_size;
6       void *stack_buf;
7   } saved_context_t;
8   typedef void (*suspend_func_t)(saved_context_t *sctx,
            void *arg);
9
10  void do_suspend(context_t *ctx, suspend_func_t f,
11              void *arg) {
12      // calculate the stack range of the thread
13      uint8_t *parent_sp = current_worker()->parent->rsp +
            sizeof(context_t);
14      uint8_t *stack_top = ctx->rsp;
15      size_t stack_size = parent_sp - stack_top;
16
17      // pack the suspending thread
18      saved_context_t *sctx = pinned_malloc(sizeof(
            saved_context_t));
19      sctx->ip = ctx->rip; sctx->sp = ctx->rsp;
20      sctx->ctx = ctx; sctx->stack_top = stack_top;
21      sctx->stack_size = stack_size;
22      sctx->stack_buf = pinned_malloc(stack_size);
23      memcpy(sctx->stack_buf, stack_top, stack_size);
24
25      // execute a thread start function
26      current_worker()->parent = ctx;
27      f(sctx, arg);
28      // not reached
29  }
30  void suspend(suspend_func_t f, void *arg) {
31      context_t *parent = current_worker()->parent;
32      save_context_and_call(prev_ctx, fp, do_suspend, arg);
33      // here, this thread is resumed
34      current_worker()->parent = parent;
35  }
```

Figure 8: Implementation of suspend function

wise, the function suspends the running thread with **suspend** function, pushes the suspended thread to a wait queue, and switches to another thread. We have three kinds of threads as a target of a context switching: a ready thread in the work stealing queue, a suspended thread in the wait queue, and a thread stolen by work stealing. As mentioned in Section 5.2, the uni-address region has to be empty when a worker steals work from another worker. Hence, the join function first tries to resume a ready thread on the work stealing queue (Line 20). Next, it tries to steal a thread from another worker and resume it if the steal succeeds (Line 25). Otherwise, it tries to resume a suspended thread in the wait queue (Line 28-29).

Figure 8 shows the suspend function; it saves the context of the running thread (Line 32), swaps out the stack frames of the thread from the uni-address region to the RDMA region (Line 12-23), and calls a given function resuming a next thread (Line 27).

In such an implementation of join operation, a swap-out of a thread in the uni-address region occurs only when the target thread is executing on another worker due to work stealing. In typical cases where the parent thread is not stolen, the join function only confirms termination of a target thread by **try_join** function.

6. EXPERIMENTAL RESULTS

This section evaluates the efficiency and performance of uni-address threads. We conducted experiments on a Fujitsu PRIMEHPC FX10 supercomputing system and a single

Fujitsu PRIMEHPC FX10 system	
CPU	SPARC64IXfx 1.848GHz, 16 cores
Memory	32GB/node
Interconnect	Custom interconnect (Tofu)
OS	XTCOS (GNU/Linux 2.6.25.8 based)
Compiler	GCC 4.6.1 (option -O3)
MPI	Fujitsu MPI Library 1.2.1
a single node x86-64 server	
CPU	Xeon E5-2660 2.2GHz * 2, total 16 cores
Memory	64GB/node
OS	Debian 6.0.4 (GNU/Linux 2.6.32.5)
Compiler	GCC 4.9.1 (option -O3)

Table 1: Experimental setup.

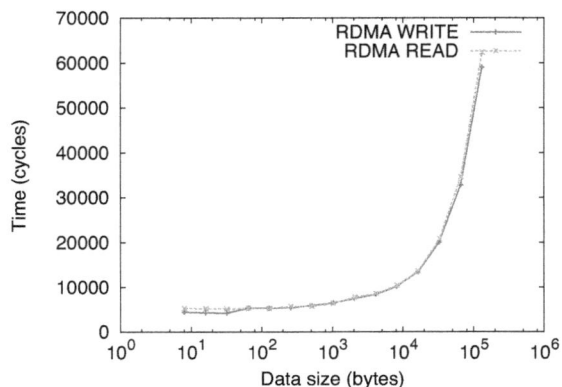

Figure 9: RDMA READ/WRITE latencies of FX10 system.

	SPARC64IXfx	Xeon E5-2660
Uni-address threads	413 cycles	100 cycles
MassiveThreads	658 cycles	110 cycles
Cilk	47 cycles	59 cycles

Table 2: Thread creation overhead.

node Xeon server. Table 1 shows the hardware and software configuration in our experiments. We used up to 256 nodes for the experiments.

Although FX10 system provides RDMA READ and WRITE operations as Fujitsu RDMA interface, RDMA fetch-and-add is not provided. Therefore, we implemented a software implementation of remote fetch-and-add operation. To simulate hardware remote fetch-and-add operation, the fetch-and-add implementation reserves a processing core within a node in advance and use it as a communication server handling fetch-and-add requests from other nodes. The fetch-and-add requests are sent with "RDMA Write with remote notice" operation, which is an RDMA WRITE operation that notifies the target node of the completion of the operation. Because there is a communication server within a node, our experiments use only 15 cores within a node for computation. Figure 9 shows the communication latencies of RDMA READ/WRITE operations in FX10 system. The latency of the software-based remote fetch-and-add operation is 9.8K cycles on average.

For comparison, we used two existing lightweight multithread frameworks—MassiveThreads and MIT Cilk. MassiveThreads is a lightweight multithread library written in C, which can be extended to support inter-node load balancing with iso-address thread migration. Cilk is a lightweight multithread framework implemented with source code processing specialized for a fork-join model. These frameworks support a child-first work stealing scheduler similar to uni-address threads. In our experiments, we used MassiveThreads 0.95 and MIT Cilk 5.4.6.

Confidence intervals in the following figures are calculated with 95% confidence level.

6.1 Benchmark Programs

To evaluate scalability of work stealing in our library, we chose three benchmarks—Binary Task Creation (BTC) benchmark, Unbalanced Tree Search (UTS) benchmark, and NQueens solver:

BTC Binary Task Creation benchmark generates tasks recursively. It has two parameters *depth* and *iter*. *Depth* means the depth of a generated task tree, and each task repeats, *iter* times, spawning two child tasks and waiting for their completions. When $iter \geq 2$, parallelism rapidly grows and shrinks during execution; therefore, it requires high load balancing performance.

UTS Unbalanced Tree Search benchmark [23] is a benchmark to evaluate performance of dynamic load balancing algorithms and implementations. UTS benchmark traverses an unpredictable, tree-based state space generated by a probability distribution. The detailed description of parameters of UTS benchmark are in [23]. In our experiments, We chose a tree whose nodes have 0-4 child nodes based on a geometric distribution and performed experiments with tree cutoff depth = 17 and 18. The command-line arguments is "`-t 1 -r 0 - b 4 -a 3 -d {17,18}`".

NQueens NQueens benchmark is a benchmark to calculate the number of possible ways to place N queens on a $N \times N$ chess board. The program used in our experiments is based on the one in BOTS Benchmark [10].

Because ordinary work stealing schedulers do not work well with parallel loops that appear in UTS and NQueens, we modified them to an efficient divide-and-conquer traversal over loops in which each task generates zero or two subtasks. Such an optimization is common in work stealing schedulers; in fact, Intel Cilk Plus [15] performs such an optimization for its `cilk_for` statement.

6.2 Task Creation Overhead

We measured the overhead of a task creation in uni-address threads on a SPARC64 IXfx processor and a Xeon E5-2660 processor. For comparison, we also measured the overhead of task creation in MassiveThreads and MIT Cilk.

Table 2 shows the results. The task creation overhead of uni-address threads is 413 cycles and 100 cycles on average on the SPARC64IXfx processor and the Xeon E5-2660 processor, respectively. Here, we can see that uni-address threads achieved a comparable performance to an

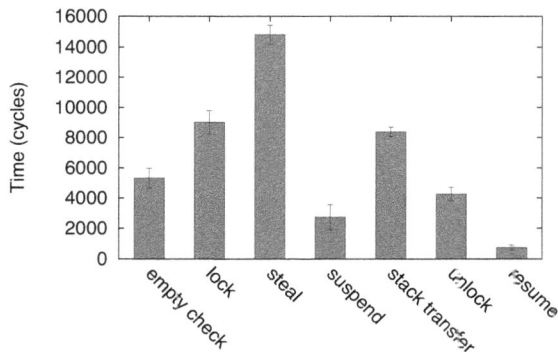

Figure 10: Breakdown of work stealing time

existing lightweight multithread library, MassiveThreads, on both of the processors. For reference, task creation of uni-address threads takes 8.8x and 1.7x more time than Cilk in SPARC64IXfx and Xeon E5-2660.

6.3 Work Stealing Overhead

We measured the overhead of work stealing in uni-address threads on the FX10 system. In this experiment, two workers steal a single thread from each other and measure the execution time and its breakdown of a steal operation. The size of the stolen stack frame is 3055 bytes. To eliminate effects of performance noises, we removed the time of the first steal from the results.

Figure 10 shows the execution time breakdown of inter-node work stealing, and Table 3 shows the operations constituting work stealing. A work stealing takes 42K cycles in total, and suspend and resume operations, which is the main source of overhead of uni-address scheme, take 3.5K cycles, or 7.7% of the total work stealing time. The other overheads are mostly from RDMA operations.

Here, we attempt to compare uni-address and iso-address scheme. As described in Section 4, iso-address scheme frequently causes page faults at thread migration, which takes 21K cycles in FX10 system; therefore, we can estimate that work stealing time of uni-address threads is approximately 71% of iso-address scheme, assuming the stack transfer time are comparable in both schemes [2].

6.4 Load Balancing Scalability

In this section, we evaluate stack memory usage in the uni-address region and the parallel performance of uni-address threads with the three benchmark programs. Table 4 shows the basic information of the benchmarks—total number of generated nodes, execution time, and stack memory usage in the uni-address region on 3840 cores. Note that all benchmarks worked with less than 144KB virtual memory.

Figure 11 shows the parallel performance of uni-address threads with the three benchmark programs. In all benchmarks, the parallel performance is reported as the total throughput of processed tasks or nodes per second.

In summary, all benchmarks scale well in large problems. In Figure 11(a), BTC benchmark ($iter = 1$) scales well to

---

[2] Actually, stack transfer in iso-address scheme requires assistance of a remote node, so it takes longer time than stack transfer in uni-address scheme, which is performed by an RDMA READ operation.

3840 cores. The throughput on 3840 cores is 16.7 and 16.5 billion tasks per second for $depth = 38$ and 39, respectively, and the efficiencies are 97% and 98%, respectively, compared to the performance on 480 cores. In Figure 11(b), the throughput of BTC benchmark ($iter = 2$) on 3840 cores is 11.1 and 16.6 billion tasks per second for $depth = 19$ and 20, respectively, and the efficiencies are 97% and 98%, respectively, compared to the performance on 480 cores.

In Figure 11(c), UTS benchmark scales well to 3840 cores. The throughput on 3840 cores is 1.53 and 1.55 billion nodes per second for $depth = 17$ and 18, respectively, and the efficiencies are 97% and 99%, respectively, compared to the performance on 480 cores. These results are comparable to existing dynamic load balancing frameworks for distributed memory supercomputers [9, 24] when normalizing their clock frequencies and integer performance.

In Figure 11(d), NQueens benchmark scales well to 3840 cores in the case $N = 18$. The throughput on 3840 cores is 168 and 187 million nodes per second, and the performance achieves 78% and 95% efficiency relative to 480 cores in the case $N = 17$ and 18.

7. CONCLUSION

In this paper, we presented uni-address, a scalable thread management technique for RDMA-based work stealing. Uni-address scheme solves scalability problems in applying an existing thread migration scheme, iso-address, to large-scale distributed memory supercomputers. Iso-address consumes a huge amount of virtual address space proportional to the number of processing cores in each node, and therefore thread migration cannot be implemented with RDMA operations, which are important for scalable work stealing. Uni-address significantly reduces virtual memory usage for thread migration and enables RDMA-based work stealing.

We implemented uni-address threads, a lightweight multithread library supporting distributed work stealing with uni-address scheme. The library is implemented in C++ and a few assembly codes, and therefore it can easily be integrated with existing application codes, libraries, and programming languages. We evaluated the performance and efficiency of uni-address threads with microbenchmarks and three benchmarks: Binary Task Creation, Unbalanced Tree Search, and NQueens. Microbenchmark results indicate that the task creation takes 413 cycles on a SPARC64 processor and 100 cycles on an x86-64 processor, and the context switching takes 3.5K cycles, 7% of the total work stealing time on a Fujitsu PRIMEHPC FX10 system. On the three benchmarks, uni-address threads worked with less than 144KB virtual memory for thread migration in each processor and achieved more than 95% parallel efficiency with 3840 processing cores on the FX10 system.

8. ACKNOWLEDGMENTS

This project was partially supported by JST, CREST through its research program: "Highly Productive, High Performance Application Frameworks for Post Petascale Computing." In addition, this research was conducted using the Fujitsu PRIMEHPC FX10 System (Oakleaf-FX, Oakbridge-FX) in the Information Technology Center, The University of Tokyo.

Operation	Description
empty check	A operation to check whether a remote task queue is empty or not. It consists of an RDMA READ operation.
lock	A lock operation for a remote task queue. It consists of a remote fetch-and-add operation.
steal	An operation to steal an entry from a remote task queue. It consists of two RDMA READ and an RDMA WRITE operations.
suspend	An operation to suspend a running thread.
stack transfer	An operation to transfer stack frames. It consists of an RDMA READ operation.
unlock	A unlock operation for a remote task queue. It consists of an RDMA WRITE operation.
resume	An operation to resume a stolen thread.

Table 3: Operations consisting of work stealing.

Benchmark	Parameters	Total tasks or nodes	Time	Stack usage
Binary Task Creation (*iter* = 1)	$depth = 38$	550 billion tasks	65.67 sec	43,568 bytes
	$depth = 39$	1,099 billion tasks	33.37 sec	44,688 bytes
Binary Task Creation (*iter* = 2)	$depth = 19$	367 billion tasks	32.96 sec	22,288 bytes
	$depth = 20$	1,466 billion tasks	88.14 sec	23,408 bytes
Unbalanced Tree Search	$depth = 17$	110 billion nodes	71.62 sec	139,536 bytes
	$depth = 18$	439 billion nodes	282.2 sec	147,392 bytes
NQueens	$N = 17$	8 billion nodes	47.60 sec	74,272 bytes
	$N = 18$	59 billion nodes	317.8 sec	79,120 bytes

Table 4: The number of generated tasks or nodes in three benchmark. *Time* is average execution time on 3840 cores. *Stack usage* is maximum usage of the uni-address region.

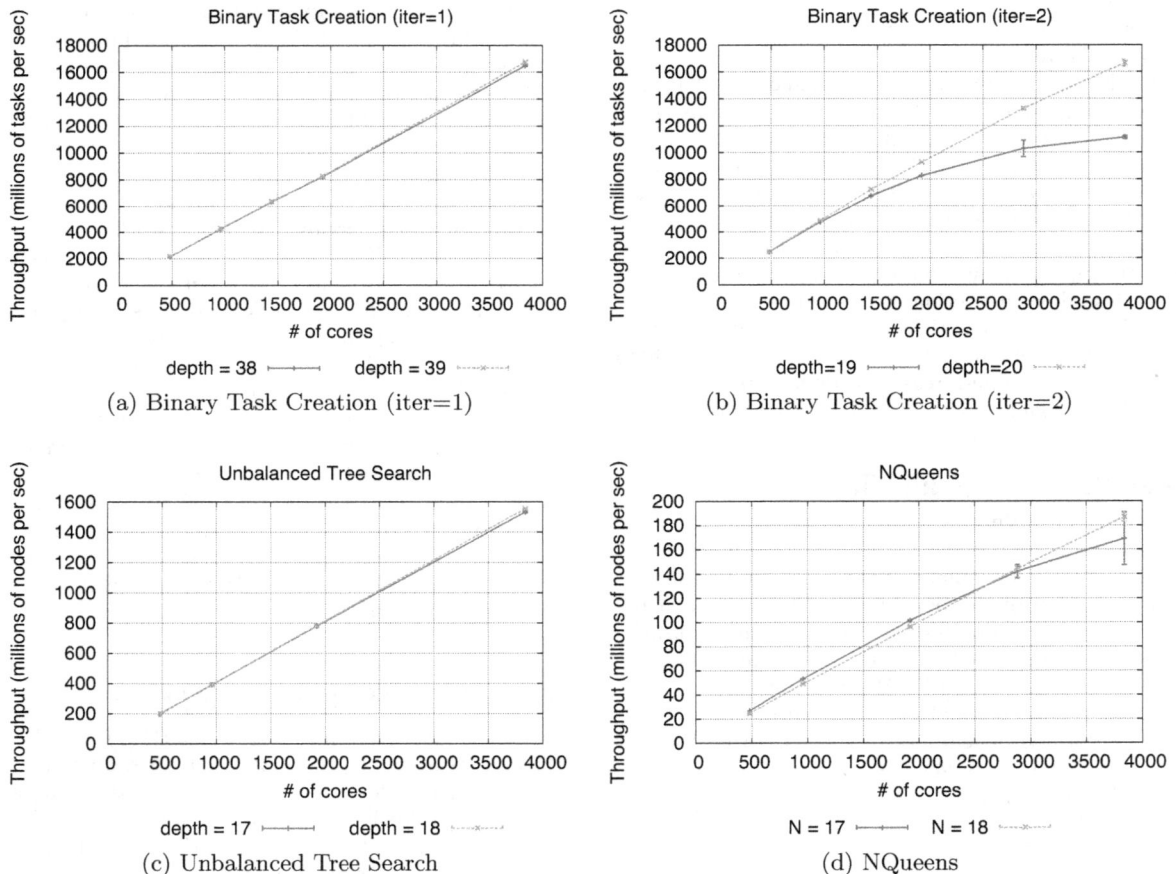

(a) Binary Task Creation (iter=1)

(b) Binary Task Creation (iter=2)

(c) Unbalanced Tree Search

(d) NQueens

Figure 11: Parallel performance in three benchmarks.

9. REFERENCES

[1] U. A. Acar, G. E. Blelloch, and R. D. Blumofe. The data locality of work stealing. In *Proceedings of the twelfth annual ACM symposium on Parallel algorithms and architectures*, SPAA '00, pages 1–12, 2000.

[2] G. Antoniu, L. Bougé, and R. Namyst. An efficient and transparent thread migration scheme in the pm2 runtime system. In *Proceedings of the 11 IPPS/SPDP'99 Workshops Held in Conjunction with the 13th International Parallel Processing Symposium and 10th Symposium on Parallel and Distributed Processing*, pages 496–510, 1999.

[3] R. D. Blumofe and C. E. Leiserson. Scheduling multithreaded computations by work stealing. *J. ACM*, 46(5):720–748, Sept. 1999.

[4] R. D. Blumofe and P. A. Lisiecki. Adaptive and reliable parallel computing on networks of workstations. In *Proceedings of the Annual Conference on USENIX Annual Technical Conference*, ATEC 97, pages 10–10, 1997.

[5] A. R. Board. OpenMP application program interface version 3.0. Technical report, May 2008.

[6] P. Charles, C. Grothoff, V. Saraswat, C. Donawa, A. Kielstra, K. Ebcioglu, C. von Praun, and V. Sarkar. X10: an object-oriented approach to non-uniform cluster computing. In *Proceedings of the 20th annual ACM SIGPLAN conference on Object-oriented programming, systems, languages, and applications*, OOPSLA '05, pages 519–538, 2005.

[7] H. P. Z. David Callahan, Bradford L. Chamberlain. The cascade high productivity language. *International Workshop on High-Level Programming Models and Supportive Environments*, 0:52–60, 2004.

[8] J. Dinan, S. Krishnamoorthy, D. B. Larkins, J. Nieplocha, and P. Sadayappan. Scioto: A framework for global-view task parallelism. In *Proceedings of the 2008 37th International Conference on Parallel Processing*, ICPP '08, pages 536–593, Washington, DC, USA, 2008. IEEE Computer Society.

[9] J. Dinan, D. B. Larkins, P. Sadayappan, S. Krishnamoorthy, and J. Nieplocha. Scalable work stealing. In *Proceedings of the Conference on High Performance Computing Networking, Storage and Analysis*, SC '09, pages 53:1–53:11, 2009.

[10] A. Duran, X. Teruel, R. Ferrer, X. Martorell, and E. Ayguade. Barcelona OpenMP Tasks Suite: A set of benchmarks targeting the exploitation of task parallelism in OpenMP. In *Proceedings of the 2009 38th International Conference on Parallel Processing*, ICPP '09, pages 124–131, Sept 2009.

[11] M. Frigo, C. E. Leiserson, and K. H. Randall. The implementation of the Cilk-5 multithreaded language. In *Proceedings of the ACM SIGPLAN 1998 conference on Programming language design and implementation*, PLDI '98, pages 212–223, 1998.

[12] Fujitsu Co., Ltd. Fujitsu supercomputer PRIMEHPC FX10. http://www.fujitsu.com/global/products/computing/servers/supercomputer/primehpc-fx10/. [Online; accessed 20-January-2015].

[13] T. Hiraishi, M. Yasugi, S. Umatani, and T. Yuasa. Backtracking-based load balancing. In *Proceedings of the 14th ACM SIGPLAN symposium on Principles*

[14] C. Huang, G. Zheng, L. Kalé, and S. Kumar. Performance evaluation of Adaptive MPI. In *Proceedings of the Eleventh ACM SIGPLAN Symposium on Principles and Practice of Parallel Programming*, PPoPP '06, pages 12–21, 2006.

[15] Intel Corporation. Intel® Cilk™ Plus. http://www.cilkplus.org/.

[16] Intel Corporation. *Intel® Threading Building Blocks reference manual*, 2009.

[17] L. Kale and J. Lifflander. Controlling concurrency and expressing synchronization in Charm++ programs. In G. Agha, A. Igarashi, N. Kobayashi, H. Masuhara, S. Matsuoka, E. Shibayama, and K. Taura, editors, *Concurrent Objects and Beyond*, volume 8665 of *Lecture Notes in Computer Science*, pages 196–221. 2014.

[18] D. Lea. A Java fork/join framework. In *Proceedings of the ACM 2000 conference on Java Grande*, JAVA '00, pages 36–43, 2000.

[19] S.-J. Min, C. Iancu, and K. Yelick. Hierarchical work stealing on manycore clusters. In *In Fifth Conference on Partitioned Global Address Space Programming Models*, PGAS '11, 2011.

[20] E. Mohr, D. A. Kranz, and R. H. Halstead, Jr. Lazy task creation: A technique for increasing the granularity of parallel programs. *IEEE Trans. Parallel Distrib. Syst.*, 2:264–280, July 1991.

[21] J. Nakashima and K. Taura. MassiveThreads: A thread library for high productivity languages. In G. Agha, A. Igarashi, N. Kobayashi, H. Masuhara, S. Matsuoka, E. Shibayama, and K. Taura, editors, *Concurrent Objects and Beyond*, volume 8665 of *Lecture Notes in Computer Science*, pages 222–238. 2014.

[22] J. Nelson, B. Holt, B. Myers, P. Briggs, L. Ceze, S. Kahan, and M. Oskin. Grappa: A latency–tolerant runtime for large-scale irregular applications. In *International Workshop on Rack-Scale Computing (WRSC w/EuroSys)*, April 2014.

[23] S. Olivier, J. Huan, J. Liu, J. Prins, J. Dinan, P. Sadayappan, and C.-W. Tseng. UTS: an unbalanced tree search benchmark. In *Proceedings of the 19th international conference on Languages and compilers for parallel computing*, LCPC'06, pages 235–250, 2007.

[24] V. A. Saraswat, P. Kambadur, S. Kodali, D. Grove, and S. Krishnamoorthy. Lifeline-based global load balancing. In *Proceedings of the 16th ACM symposium on Principles and practice of parallel programming*, PPoPP '11, pages 201–212, 2011.

[25] TOP500.org. TOP500 supercomputer site. http://www.top500.org. [Online; accessed 20-January-2015].

[26] R. V. Van Nieuwpoort, G. Wrzesińska, C. J. H. Jacobs, and H. E. Bal. Satin: A high-level and efficient grid programming model. *ACM Trans. Program. Lang. Syst.*, 32:9:1–9:39, March 2010.

[27] D. B. Wagner and B. G. Calder. Leapfrogging: A portable technique for implementing efficient futures. In *Proceedings of the Fourth ACM SIGPLAN*

Symposium on Principles and Practice of Parallel Programming, PPoPP '93, pages 208–217, 1993.

[28] K. Wheeler, R. Murphy, and D. Thain. Qthreads: An API for programming with millions of lightweight threads. In *2008 IEEE International Symposium on Parallel and Distributed Processing*, IPDPS '08, pages 1–8, April 2008.

[29] A. YarKhan. *Dynamic Task Execution on Shared and Distributed Memory Architectures*. PhD thesis, University of Tennessee, 2012.

[30] W. Zhang, O. Tardieu, D. Grove, B. Herta, T. Kamada, V. A. Saraswat, and M. Takeuchi. GLB: lifeline-based global load balancing library in X10. http://arxiv.org/abs/1312.5691, Dec. 2013.

APPENDIX

A.   X86-64 ASSEMBLY TO SAVE CONTEXT

```
1   /*
2   typedef struct {
3       void *rip, *rsp, *rbp, *rbx, *r12, *r13, *r14, *r15;
4       context *parent;
5   } context_t;
6
7   typedef void (*context_func_t)(context_t *ctx,void *arg);
8   void save_context_and_call(context_t *parent,
9                               context_func_t f, void *arg);
10  */
11  save_context_and_call:
12      push    %rdi            /* save parent context */
13      push    %r15,%r14       /* save callee-saved regs */
14      push    %r13,%r12,%rbx,%rbp
15      lea     -16(%rsp), %rax /* save current SP */
16      push    %rax
17      lea     1f(%rip), %rax    /* save IP for resume */
18      push    %rax
19      /* call a thread start function */
20      mov     %rsi, %rax      /* function f */
21      mov     %rsp, %rdi      /* argument ctx */
22      mov     %rdx, %rsi      /* argument arg */
23      call    *%rax
24      add     $8, %rsp        /* pop IP */
25  1:  /* here, jumped from resume_context */
26      add     $8, %rsp        /* pop SP */
27      pop     %rbp,%rbx       /* restore callee-saved regs */
28      pop     %r12,%r13,%r14,%r15
29      add     $8, %rsp        /* pop parent context */
30      ret
31
32  /* void resume_context(context_t *ctx); */
33  resume_context:
34      mov %rdi, %rsp          /* restore SP (== ctx) */
35      ret                     /* pop IP and restore it */
```

A Case for Transforming Parallel Runtimes Into Operating System Kernels

Kyle C. Hale and Peter A. Dinda
Dept. of Electrical Engineering and Computer
Science, Northwestern University
{k-hale,pdinda}@northwestern.edu

ABSTRACT

The needs of parallel runtime systems and the increasingly sophisticated languages and compilers they support do not line up with the services provided by general-purpose OSes. Furthermore, the semantics available to the runtime are lost at the system-call boundary in such OSes. Finally, because a runtime executes at user-level in such an environment, it cannot leverage hardware features that require kernel-mode privileges—a large portion of the functionality of the machine is lost to it. These limitations warp the design, implementation, functionality, and performance of parallel runtimes. We summarize the case for eliminating these compromises by transforming parallel runtimes into OS kernels. We also demonstrate that it is feasible to do so. Our evidence comes from Nautilus, a prototype kernel framework that we built to support such transformations. After describing Nautilus, we report on our experiences using it to transform three very different runtimes into kernels.

Categories and Subject Descriptors

D.4.7 [**Operating Systems**]: Organization and Design; D.1.3 [**Programming Techniques**]: Concurrent Programming—*parallel programming*

Keywords

hybrid runtimes; HRTs; parallel runtimes; Nautilus

1. INTRODUCTION

Modern parallel runtimes are systems that operate in user mode and run above the system call interface of a general-purpose kernel. While this facilitates portability

This project is made possible by support from Sandia National Laboratories through the Hobbes Project, which is funded by the 2013 Exascale Operating and Runtime Systems Program under the Office of Advanced Scientific Computing Research in the United States Department Of Energy's Office of Science.

and simplifies the creation of some functionality, it also has consequences that warp the design and implementation of the runtime and affect its performance, efficiency, and scalability. First, the runtime is deprived of the use of hardware features that are available only in kernel mode. This is a large portion of the machine. The second consequence is that the runtime must use the abstractions provided by the kernel, even if the abstractions are a bad fit. Finally, the kernel has minimal access to the information available to the parallel runtime or to the language implementation it supports.

The complexity of modern hardware is rapidly growing. In high-end computing, it is widely anticipated that exascale machines will have at least 1000-way parallelism at the node level. Even today's high-end homogeneous nodes, such as the one we use for evaluation in this paper, have 64 or more cores or hardware threads arranged on top of a complex intertwined cache hierarchy that terminates in 8 or more memory zones with non-uniform access. Today's heterogeneous nodes include accelerators, such as the Intel Xeon Phi, that introduce additional coherence domains and memory systems. Server platforms for cloud and datacenter computing, and even desktop and mobile platforms are seeing this simultaneous explosion of hardware complexity and the need for parallelism to take advantage of the hardware. How to make such complex hardware programmable, in parallel, by mere humans is an acknowledged open challenge.

Some modern runtimes, such as the Legion runtime [1, 22] we consider in this paper, already address this challenge by creating abstractions that programmers or the compilers of high-level languages can target, abstractions that mirror the machine in portable ways. Very high-level parallel languages can let us further decouple the expression of parallelism from its implementation. Parallel runtimes such as Legion, and the runtimes for specific parallel languages share many properties with operating system (OS) kernels, but suffer by not *being* kernels. With current developments, particularly in virtualization and hardware partitioning, we are in a position to remove this limitation. In this paper, we give an overview of the case for transforming parallel runtime systems into kernels, and report on our initial results with a framework to facilitate just that.

We argue that for the specific case of a parallel runtime, the user/kernel abstraction itself, which dates back to Multics, is not a good one. It is important to understand the kernel/user abstraction and its implications. This abstraction is an incredibly useful technique to enforce isolation and protection for processes, both from attackers and from each other. This not only enables increased security, but also reduces the impact of bugs and errors on the part of the programmer. Instead, programmers place a higher level of trust in the kernel, which, by virtue of its smaller codebase and careful design, ensures that the machine remains uncompromised. However, because the kernel must be all things to all processes, the kernel has grown dramatically bigger over time, as has its responsibilities within the system. This has forced kernel developers to provide a broad range of services to an even broader range of applications. At the same time, the basic model and core services have necessarily ossified in order to maintain compatibility with the widest range of hardware and software. In a general-purpose kernel, the needs of parallelism and a parallel runtime have not been first-order concerns.

Runtime implementors often complain about the limitations imposed by a general-purpose kernel. While there are many examples of significant performance enhancements within general-purpose kernels, and others are certainly possible to support parallel runtimes better, a parallel runtime as a user level component is fundamentally *constrained* by the kernel/user abstraction. In contrast, as a kernel, a parallel runtime would have full access to all hardware features of the machine, and the ability to create any abstractions that it needs using those features. We show in this paper that, in fact, breaking free from the user/kernel abstraction can produce measurable benefits for parallel runtimes.

At first glance, transforming a parallel runtime into a kernel seems to be a particularly daunting task because language runtimes often have many dependencies on libraries and system calls. It is important to be clear that we are focused on the performance or energy-critical core of the runtime where the bulk of execution time is spent, not on the whole functional base of the runtime. The core of the runtime has considerably fewer dependencies and thus is much more feasible to transform into a kernel. As we describe in Section 2, virtualization and hardware partitioning in various forms have the potential to allow us to partition the runtime so the non-core elements run at user-level on top of the full software stack they expect, while the core of the runtime runs as a kernel. We refer to such a kernel as a hybrid runtime (HRT) as it is a hybrid between a kernel and a runtime. Our focus in this paper is on the HRT.

We make the following contributions:

- We describe the limitations of building parallel runtime systems on top of general-purpose operating systems and how these limitations are avoided if the runtime *is* a kernel. That is, we motivate HRTs.

- We introduce Nautilus, a prototype kernel framework designed to facilitate the porting of existing parallel runtimes to run as kernels, as well as the implementation of new parallel runtimes directly as kernels. That is, we create an essential tool for easily making HRTs.

- We summarize our experiences in using Nautilus to transform three runtimes into kernels, specifically Legion, NESL, and a new language implementation named NDPC that is being co-developed with Nautilus. That is, we make HRTs, demonstrating their feasibility.

Readers should refer to our technical report [16]. for a more detailed discussion than is possible in this summary.

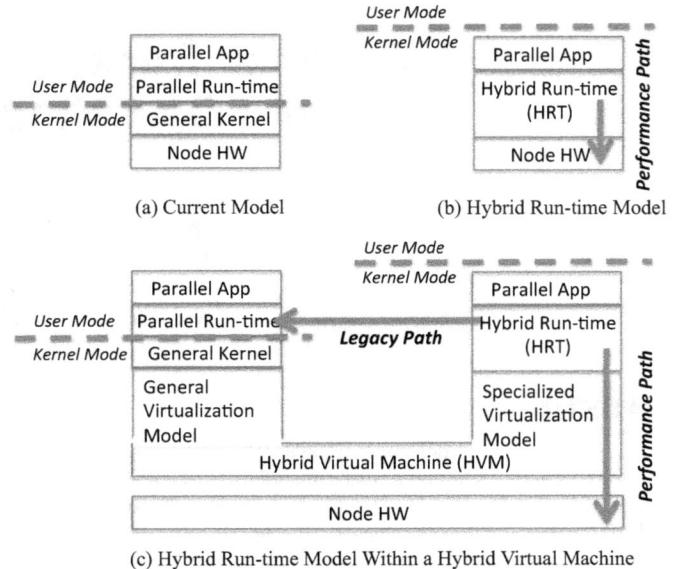

(a) Current Model

(b) Hybrid Run-time Model

(c) Hybrid Run-time Model Within a Hybrid Virtual Machine

Figure 1: Overview of Hybrid Runtime (HRT) approach: (a) current model used by parallel runtimes, (b) proposed HRT model, and (c) proposed HRT model combined with a hybrid virtual machine (HVM).

2. ARGUMENT

A language's runtime is a system (typically) charged with two major responsibilities. The first is allowing a program written in the language to interact with its environment (at runtime). This includes access to underlying software layers (e.g., the OS) and the machine itself. The runtime abstracts the properties of both and impedance-matches them with the language's model. The challenges of doing so, particularly for the hardware, depend considerably on just how high-level the language is—the larger the gap between the language model and the hardware and OS models, the greater the challenge. At the same time, however, a higher-level language has more freedom in implementing the impedance-matching.

The second major responsibility of the runtime is carrying out tasks that are hidden from the programmer but necessary to program operation. Common examples include garbage collection in managed languages, JIT compilation or interpretation for compilers that target an abstract machine, exception management, profiling, instrumentation, task and memory mapping and scheduling, and even management of multiple execution contexts or virtual processors. While some runtimes may offer more or less in the way of features, they all provide the programmer with a much simpler view of the machine than if he were to program it directly.

As a runtime gains more responsibilities and features, the lines between the runtime and the OS often become blurred. For example, Legion manages execution contexts (an abstraction of cores or hardware threads), regions (an abstraction of NUMA and other complex memory models), task to execution context mapping, task scheduling with preemption, and events. In the worst case this means that the runtime and the OS are actually trying to provide the *same* functionality. In fact, what we have found is that in some cases this duplication of functionality is brought about by inadequacies of or grievances with the OS and the services it provides. A common refrain of runtime developers is that they want the kernel to simply give them a subset of the machine's resources and then leave them alone. They attempt to approximate this as best they can within the confines of user space and the available system calls.

That this problem would arise is not entirely too surprising. After all, the operating system is, *prima facie*, designed to provide adequate performance for a broad range of general-purpose applications. However, when applications demand more control of the machine, the OS can often get in the way, whether due to rigid interfaces or to mismatched priorities in the design of those interfaces. Not only may the kernel's abstractions be at odds with the runtime, it may also completely prevent the runtime from using hardware features that might otherwise significantly improve performance or functionality. If it provides access to these features, it does so through a system call, which—even if it has an appropriate interface for the runtime—nonetheless exacts a toll for use, as the system call mechanism itself has a cost. Similarly, even outside system calls, while the kernel might build an abstraction on top of a fast hardware mechanism, an additional toll is taken. For example, signals are simply more expensive than interrupts, even if they are used to abstract an interrupt.

A runtime that *is* a kernel will have none of these issues. It would have full access to all hardware features of the machine, and the ability to create any abstractions that it needs using those features. We want to support the construction of such runtimes, which we call Hybrid Runtimes (HRTs), as they are hybrids of parallel runtimes and kernels. To do so, we will provide basic kernel functionality on a take-it-or-leave-it basis to make the process easier. We also want such runtime kernels to have available the full functionality of the general-purpose OS for components not central to runtime operation.

Figure 1 illustrates three different models for supporting a parallel runtime system. The current model (a) layers the parallel runtime over a general-purpose kernel. The parallel runtime runs in user mode without access to privileged hardware features and uses a kernel API designed for general-purpose computations. In the Hybrid Runtime model (b) that we describe in this paper the parallel runtime is integrated with a specialized kernel framework such as Nautilus. The resulting HRT runs exclusively in kernel mode with full access to all hardware features and with kernel abstractions designed specifically for it. Notice that both the runtime and the parallel application itself are now below the kernel/user line. Figure 1(b) is how we run Legion, NESL, and NDPC programs in this paper. We refer to this as the *performance path*.

A natural concern with the structure of Figure 1(b) is how to support general-purpose OS features. For example, how do we open a file? We do not want to reinvent the wheel within an HRT or a kernel framework such as Nautilus in order to support kernel functionality that is not performance critical. Figure 1(c) is our response, the Hybrid Virtual Machine (HVM). In an HVM, the virtual machine monitor (VMM) or other software will partition the physical resources provided to a guest, such as cores and memory into two parts. One part will support a general purpose virtualization model suitable for executing full OS stacks and their applications, while the second part will support a virtual-

ization model specialized to the HRT and allowing it direct hardware access. The specialized virtualization model will enable the performance path of the HRT, while the general virtualization model and communication between the two parts of the HVM will enable a *legacy path* for the runtime and application that will let it leverage the capabilities of the general-purpose kernel for non-performance critical work.

An effort to build this HVM capability into the Palacios VMM [18] is currently underway in our group as part of the Hobbes exascale software project [9]. However, it is important to note that other paths exist. For example, Guarded Modules [17] could be used to give portions of a general-purpose virtualization model selective privileged access to hardware, including I/O devices. As another example, Dune [2] uses hardware virtualization features to provide privileged CPU access to Linux processes. The HVM could be built on top of Dune. The Pisces system [21] would enable an approach that could eschew virtualization altogether by partitioning the hardware and booting multiple kernels simultaneously without virtualization. Our focus in this paper is not on the HVM capability, but rather on the HRT.

3. NAUTILUS

Nautilus[1] is a small prototype kernel framework that we built to support the HRT model, and is thus the first of its kind. We designed Nautilus to meet the needs of parallel runtimes that may use it as a starting point for taking full advantage of the machine. We chose to minimize imposition of abstractions to support general-purpose applications in lieu of flexibility and small codebase size. As we will show in Sections 4–5, this allowed us to port three very different runtimes to Nautilus and the HRT model in a very reasonable amount of time. Note that while these initial ports were carried out manually, we are currently investigating how to automate this process.

As Nautilus is a prototype for HRT research, we targeted the most popular architecture for high-performance and parallel computing, x86_64. However, given the very tractable size of the codebase, introducing platform portability would not be too challenging. Nautilus currently has been tested on a range of Intel and AMD machines, as well as on the Palacios VMM. A port to the Intel Phi is underway. The machine used for performance evaluation in this paper is a 4 socket, 8 NUMA domain, 64 core server based on 2.1GHz AMD Opteron 6272 (Interlagos) processors and 128 GB of memory.

The design of Nautilus was heavily influenced by early research on microkernels [19, 6, 5] and even more by Engler and others' work on exokernels [12, 13]. Like Nautilus, the exokernel concept involves an extremely thin kernel layer that only serves to provide isolation and basic primitives. Higher-level abstractions are delegated to user-mode *library OSes*. Nautilus can be thought of as a kind of library OS for a parallel runtime, but we shed the notion of privilege levels for the sake of functionality and performance.

We stress that the design of Nautilus is, first and foremost, driven by the needs of the parallel runtimes that use it. Nevertheless, it is complete enough to leverage the full capabilities of a modern 64-bit x86 machine to support

---

[1]Named after the submarine-like, mysterious vessel from Jules Verne's Twenty Thousand Leagues Under the Sea.

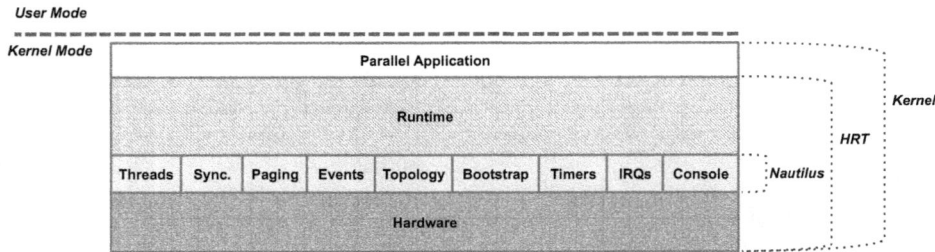

Figure 2: Structure of Nautilus.

Language	SLOC
C	22697
C++	133
x86 Assembly	428
Scripting	706

Figure 3: Source lines of code for the Nautilus kernel.

three runtimes, one of which (Legion) is quite complex and is used in practice today.

Currently, Nautilus is designed to boot the machine, discover its capabilities, devices, and topology, and immediately hand control over to the runtime. Figure 2 shows the core functionality provided by Nautilus. Current features include multi-core support, Multiboot2-compliant modules, synchronization primitives, threads, IRQs, timers, paging, NUMA awareness, IPIs, and a console. A port to the Intel Xeon Phi is currently underway.

We spent a good deal of time measuring the capabilities that affect the performance of the HRTs we built, and were pleased to find that the Nautilus can, in many cases, significantly outperform the only other viable OS for these runtimes, i.e. Linux. For example, Nautilus enjoys a speedup of 30x over Linux for light-weight thread creation. Some of the runtimes we investigated made heavy use of event notification mechanisms. We found that we could provide significantly lighter-weight event notification using hardware features, such as inter-processor interrupts (IPIs), that are not available in user-space. To give an idea of the magnitude of the difference, an event wakeup using an IPI to "kick" the processor waiting for the event produced an 8x speedup over the traditional condition variable implementation.

3.1 Complexity

We now make a case for the potential for Nautilus as a vehicle for HRTs, setting aside the attractive raw performance of its primitives and focusing on implementation complexity.

The process of building Nautilus as a minimal kernel layer with support for a complex, modern, many-core x86 machine took six person-months of effort on the part of seasoned OS/VMM kernel developers. Figure 3 shows that Nautilus is fairly compact at ~24,000 lines of code.

Building a kernel, however, was not our main goal. Our main focus was supporting the porting and construction of runtimes for the HRT model. The Legion runtime, discussed at length in the next section, was the most challenging and complex of the three runtimes to bring up in Nautilus. Legion is about double the size of Nautilus in

terms of codebase size, consisting of about 43000 lines of C++. Porting Legion and the other runtimes took a total of about four person-months of effort. Most of this work went into understanding Legion and its needs. Only about 800 lines of code needed to be added to Nautilus to support Legion and the other two runtimes. This is tiny considering the size of the Legion runtime and the others.

This suggests that exploring the HRT model for existing or new parallel runtimes, especially with a small kernel like Nautilus designed with this in mind, is a perfectly manageable task for an experienced systems researcher or developer. We hope that these results will encourage others to similarly explore the benefits of HRTs.

4. EXAMPLE: LEGION

The Legion runtime system is designed to provide applications with a parallel programming model that maps well to heterogeneous architectures [1, 22]. Whether the application runs on a single node or across nodes—even with GPUs—the Legion runtime can manage the underlying resources so that the application does not have to. There are several reasons why we chose to port Legion to the HRT model. The first is that the primary focus of the Legion developers is on the design of the runtime system. This not only allows us to leverage their experience in designing runtimes, but also gives us access to a system designed with experimentation in mind. Further, the codebase has reached the point where the developers' ability to rapidly prototype new ideas is hindered by abstractions imposed by the OS layer. Another reason we chose Legion is that it is quickly gaining adoption among the HPC community, including within the DOE's exascale effort. The third reason is that we have corresponded directly with the Legion developers and discussed with them issues with the OS layer that they found when developing their runtime.

Under the covers, Legion bears many similarities to an operating system and concerns itself with many issues that an OS must deal with, including task scheduling, isolation, multiplexing of hardware resources, and synchronization. As we discussed in Section 2, the way that a complex runtime like Legion attempts to manage the machine to suit its own needs can often conflict with the services and abstractions provided by the OS.

As Legion is designed for heterogeneous hardware, including multi-node clusters and machines with GPUs, it is designed with a multi-layer architecture. It is split up into the *high-level* runtime and the *low-level* runtime. The high-level runtime is portable across machines, and the low-level runtime contains all of the machine specific code. There is a separate low-level implementation called the *shared low-*

level runtime. This is the low-level layer implemented for shared memory machines. As we are interested in single-node performance, we naturally focused our efforts on the shared low-level Legion runtime. All of our modifications to Legion when porting it to Nautilus were made to the shared low-level component. Outside of optimizations using hardware access, and understanding the needs of the runtime, the port was fairly straight-forward.

Legion, in its default user-level implementation, uses pthreads as representations of logical processors, so the low-level runtime makes fairly heavy use of the pthreads interface. In order to transform Legion into a kernel-level HRT, we simply had to provide a similar interface in Nautilus. After porting Legion into Nautilus, we then began to explore how Legion could benefit from unrestricted access to the machine.

We now present a brief evaluation of our transformation of the user-level Legion runtime into a kernel using Nautilus, highlighting the realized and potential benefits of having Legion operate as an HRT. Our port is based on Legion as of October 4, 2014, specifically, commit e22962d, which can be found via the Legion project web site.[2]

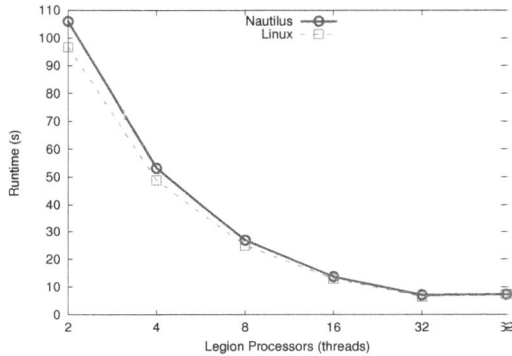

Figure 4: Run time of Legion circuit simulator versus core count.

The Legion distribution includes numerous test codes, as well as an example parallel application that is a circuit simulator. We used the test codes to check the correctness of our work and the circuit simulator as our initial performance benchmark. Legion creates an abstract machine that consists of a set of cooperating threads that execute work when it is ready. These are essentially logical processors. The number of such threads can vary, representing an abstract machine of a different size.

We ran the circuit simulator with a medium problem size (100000 steps) and varied the number of cores Legion used to execute Legion tasks. Figure 4 shows the results. The x-axis shows the number of threads/logical processors. The thread count only goes up to 62 because the Linux version would hang at higher core counts, we believe due to a livelock situation in Legion's interaction with Linux. Notice how closely, even with no hardware optimizations, Nautilus tracks the performance of Linux. The difference between the two actually increases when scaling the number of threads. They are essentially at parity, even though Nautilus and the Legion port to it are still in their early stages. Nautilus is slightly faster at 62 cores.

---

[2] http://legion.stanford.edu

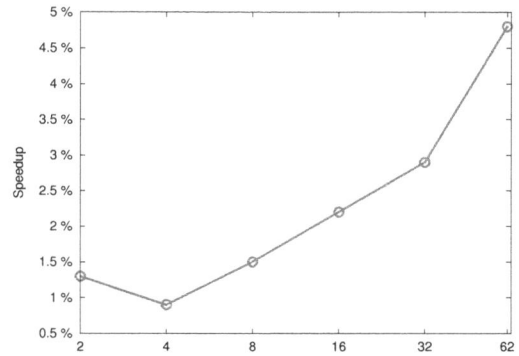

Figure 5: Speedup of Legion circuit simulator comparing the baseline Nautilus version and a Nautilus version that executes Legion tasks with interrupts disabled.

To experiment with hardware functionality in the HRT model, we wanted to take advantage of a capability that normally is not available in Linux at user-level. We decided to use the capability to disable interrupts. In the Legion HRT, there are no other threads running besides the threads that Legion creates, and so there is really no need for timer interrupts (or device interrupts). Observing that interrupts can cause interference effects at the level of the instruction cache and potentially in task execution latency, we inserted a call to disable interrupts when Legion invokes a task (in this case the task to execute a function in the circuit simulator). Figure 5 shows the results, where the speedup is over the baseline case where Legion is running in Nautilus but without any change in the default interrupt policy. While this extremely simple change involved only adding two short lines of code, we can see a measurable benefit that scales with the thread count, up to 5% at 62 cores.

We believe that this is a testament to the promise of the HRT model. While the Legion port to Nautilus is still in its early stages, there is a large opportunity for exploring other potential hardware optimizations to improve runtime performance.

5. EXAMPLE: NESL AND NDPC

NESL [7] is a highly influential implementation of nested data parallelism developed at CMU in the '90s. Very recently, it has influenced the design of parallelism in Manticore [14, 15], Data Parallel Haskell [10, 11], and arguably the nested call extensions to CUDA [20]. NESL is a functional programming language, using an ML-style syntax that allows the implementation of complex parallel algorithms in a very compact and high level way, often 100s or 1000s of times more compactly than using a low-level language such as C+OpenMP. NESL programs are compiled into abstract vector operations known as VCODE through a process known as flattening. An abstract machine called a VCODE interpreter then executes these programs on physical hardware. Flattening transformations and their ability to transform nested (recursive) data parallelism into "flat" vector operations while preserving the asymptotic complexity of programs is a key contribution of NESL [8] and very recent work on using NESL-like nested data parallelism for

GPUs [4] and multicore [3] has focused on extending flattening approaches to better match such hardware.

As a proof of concept, we have ported NESL's existing VCODE interpreter to Nautilus, allowing us to run any program compiled by the out-of-the-box NESL compiler in kernel mode on x86_64 hardware. We also ported NESL's sequential implementation of the vector operation library CVL, which we have started parallelizing. Currently, pointwise vector operations execute in parallel.

We have created a different implementation of a subset of the NESL language which we refer to as "Nested Data Parallelism in C/C++" (NDPC). This is implemented as a source-to-source translator whose input is the NESL subset and whose output is C++ code (with C bindings) that uses recursive fork/join parallelism instead of NESL's flattened vector parallelism. It ties specifically to a fast thread fork mechanism implemented in Nautilus.

We believe that our transformations of NESL and NDPC into the HRT model show that adapting a parallel language to this model does not require a monumental effort. This provides an opportunity for parallel runtime developers to quickly prototype their runtime implementation with unrestricted access to hardware using Nautilus.

6. CONCLUSIONS

We have summarized the case for transforming parallel runtimes into operating system kernels, forming hybrid runtimes (HRTs). The motivations for HRTs include the increasing complexity of hardware, the convergence of parallel runtime concerns and abstractions in managing such hardware, and the limitations of executing the runtime at user-level, both in terms of limited hardware access and limited control over kernel abstractions. We introduced Nautilus, a prototype kernel framework to facilitate the construction of HRTs. Using Nautilus, we were able to successfully transform three very different runtimes into HRTs. For the Legion runtime, we were able to exceed Linux performance with simple techniques that can only be done in the kernel. Building Nautilus was a six person-month effort, while porting the runtimes was a four person-month effort. It is somewhat remarkable that even with a fairly nascent kernel framework, *just* by dropping the runtime down to kernel level and taking advantage of a kernel-only feature in two lines of code, we can exceed performance on Linux, which has undergone far more substantial development and tuning.

7. REFERENCES

[1] M. Bauer, S. Treichler, E. Slaughter, and A. Aiken. Legion: Expressing locality and independence with logical regions. In *Proceedings of Supercomputing (SC 2012)*, Nov. 2012.

[2] A. Belay, A. Bittau, A. Mashtizadeh, D. Terei, D. Mazières, and C. Kozyrakis. Dune: Safe user-level access to privileged CPU features. In *Proceedings of the 10th USENIX Conference on Operating Systems Design and Implementation (OSDI 2012)*, pages 335–348, Oct. 2012.

[3] L. Bergstrom, M. Fluet, M. Rainey, J. Reppy, S. Rosen, and A. Shaw. Data-only flattening for nested data parallelism. In *Proceedings of the 18th ACM SIGPLAN Symposium on Principles and Practice of Parallel Programming (PPoPP 2013)*, pages 81–92, Feb. 2013.

[4] L. Bergstrom and J. Reppy. Nested data-parallelism on the GPU. In *Proceedings of the 17th ACM SIGPLAN International Conference on Functional Programming (ICFP 2012)*, pages 247–258, Sept. 2012.

[5] B. N. Bershad, S. Savage, P. Pardyak, E. G. Sirer, M. E. Fiuczynski, D. Becker, C. Chambers, and S. Eggers. Extensibility, safety and performance in the SPIN operating system. In *Proceedings of the 15th ACM Symposium on Operating Systems Principles (SOSP 1995)*, pages 267–283, Dec. 1995.

[6] D. L. Black, D. B. Golub, D. P. Julin, R. F. Rashid, R. P. Draves, R. W. Dean, A. Forin, J. Barrera, H. Tokuda, G. Malan, et al. Microkernel operating system architecture and Mach. In *Proceedings of the USENIX Workshop on Micro-Kernels and Other Kernel Architectures*, pages 11–30, Apr. 1992.

[7] G. E. Blelloch, S. Chatterjee, J. Hardwick, J. Sipelstein, and M. Zagha. Implementation of a portable nested data-parallel language. *Journal of Parallel and Distributed Computing*, 21(1):4–14, Apr. 1994.

[8] G. E. Blelloch and J. Greiner. A provable time and space efficient implementation of NESL. In *Proceedings of the International Conference on Functional Programming (ICFP)*, May 1996.

[9] R. Brightwell, R. Oldfield, D. Bernholdt, A. Maccabe, E. Brewer, P. Bridges, P. Dinda, J. Dongarra, C. Iancu, M. Lang, J. Lange, D. Lowenthal, F. Mueller, K. Schwan, T. Sterling, and P. Teller. Hobbes: Composition and virtualization as the foundations of an extreme-scale OS/R. In *Proceedings of the 3rd International Workshop on Runtime and Operating Systems for Supercomputers (ROSS 2013)*, June 2013.

[10] M. Chakravarty, G. Keller, R. Leshchinskiy, and W. Pfannenstiel. Nepal—nested data-parallelism in haskell. In *Proceedings of the 7th International Euro-Par Conference (EUROPAR)*, Aug. 2001.

[11] M. Chakravarty, R. Leshchinskiy, S. P. Jones, G. Keller, and S. Marlow. Data parallel haskell: A status report. In *Proceedings of the Workshop on Declarative Aspects of Multicore Programming*, Jan. 2007.

[12] D. R. Engler and M. F. Kaashoek. Exterminate all operating system abstractions. In *Proceedings of the 5th Workshop on Hot Topics in Operating Systems (HotOS 1995)*, pages 78–83, May 1995.

[13] D. R. Engler, M. F. Kaashoek, and J. O'Toole, Jr. Exokernel: An operating system architecture for application-level resource management. In *Proceedings of the 15th ACM Symposium on Operating Systems Principles (SOSP 1995)*, pages 251–266, Dec. 1995.

[14] M. Fluet, N. Ford, M. Rainey, J. Reppy, A. Shaw, and Y. Xiao. Status report: The manticore project. In *Proceedings of the 2007 ACM SIGPLAN Workshop on ML*, October 2007.

[15] M. Fluet, M. Rainey, J. Reppy, and A. Shaw. Implicitly threaded parallelism in manticore. In *Proceedings of the 13th ACM SIGPLAN International Conference on Functional Programming (ICFP)*, Sept. 2008.

[16] K. C. Hale and P. Dinda. Details of the case for transforming parallel runtimes into operating system kernels. Technical Report NU-EECS-15-01, Department of Computer Science, Northwestern University, Apr. 2015.

[17] K. C. Hale and P. A. Dinda. Guarded modules: Adaptively extending the VMM's privilege into the guest. In *Proceedings of the 11th International Conference on Autonomic Computing (ICAC 2014)*, pages 85–96, June 2014.

[18] J. Lange, K. Pedretti, T. Hudson, P. Dinda, Z. Cui, L. Xia, P. Bridges, A. Gocke, S. Jaconette, M. Levenhagen, and R. Brightwell. Palacios and kitten: New high performance operating systems for scalable virtualized and native supercomputing. In *Proceedings of the 24th IEEE International Parallel and Distributed Processing Symposium (IPDPS 2010)*, Apr. 2010.

[19] J. Liedtke. On micro-kernel construction. In *Proceedings of the 15th ACM Symposium on Operating Systems Principles (SOSP 1995)*, pages 237–250, Dec. 1995.

[20] NVIDIA Corporation. Dynamic parallelism in CUDA, Dec. 2012.

[21] J. Ouyang, B. Kocoloski, J. Lange, and K. Pedretti. Achieving performance isolation with lightweight co-kernels. In *Proceedings of the 24th International ACM Symposium on High-Performance Parallel and Distributed Computing (HPDC 2015)*, June 2015.

[22] S. Treichler, M. Bauer, and A. Aiken. Language support for dynamic, hierarchical data partitioning. In *Proceedings of the 2013 ACM SIGPLAN International Conference on Object-Oriented Programming, Systems, Languages, and Applications (OOPSLA 2013)*, pages 495–514, Oct. 2013.

A Multiplatform Study of I/O Behavior on Petascale Supercomputers

Huong Luu, Marianne Winslett,
William Gropp
Univ. of Illinois at Urbana-Champaign
{luu1, winslett, wgropp}@illinois.edu

Robert Ross, Philip Carns,
Kevin Harms
Argonne National Laboratory
{rross, carns}@mcs.anl.gov
harms@alcf.anl.gov

Mr Prabhat, Suren Byna,
Yushu Yao
Lawrence Berkeley Nat'l Laboratory
{Prabhat, sbyna,yyao}@lbl.gov

ABSTRACT

We examine the I/O behavior of thousands of supercomputing applications "in the wild," by analyzing the Darshan logs of over a million jobs representing a *combined* total of six years of I/O behavior across three leading high-performance computing platforms. We mined these logs to analyze the I/O behavior of applications across all their runs on a platform; the evolution of an application's I/O behavior across time, and across platforms; and the I/O behavior of a platform's entire workload. Our analysis techniques can help developers and platform owners improve I/O performance and I/O system utilization, by quickly identifying underperforming applications and offering early intervention to save system resources. We summarize our observations regarding how jobs perform I/O and the throughput they attain in practice.

Categories and Subject Descriptors

C.4 [**Performance of systems**]: *Performance attributes, Measurement techniques*

Keywords: Input/Output; Performance Analysis; HPC; Parallel I/O

1. INTRODUCTION

The 2014 TOP500 list includes over 40 deployed petascale systems, and the high-performance computing (HPC) community is working toward developing the first exaflop system by 2023. Scientific applications on such large-scale computers often read and write a lot of data. For example, an earth science code on an IBM Blue Gene/P system at Argonne National Laboratory read ~3.5 PB during two months in 2010 [1]. With such rapid growth in computing power and data intensity, I/O remains a challenging factor in determining the overall performance of HPC codes.

Analyzing I/O behavior of applications (apps) can help improve their performance and increase the utilization of supercomputing systems. By analyzing the runtime behavior of an individual job, we can identify its I/O bottlenecks and potential implementation inefficiencies and suggest improvements to its owner and users. By analyzing the I/O behavior of an app (i.e., the set of all its jobs), we can identify patterns in its behavior. By analyzing the I/O behavior of the workload of a *platform* (i.e., a supercomputer instance), we can give the platform owners insights into the usage of their storage systems and identify apps that consume I/O resources inefficiently, so that improvements to these apps may free up resources for other apps. By analyzing the changes in I/O behavior when apps migrate to similar or radically different platforms, we can help scientists avoid unexpected performance degradation. I/O behavior analysis can even show us how the behavior of individual apps evolves over time. To accomplish all these purposes, we need a systematic approach to app-specific, platform-wide, **and** cross-platform analysis of I/O behavior.

In this paper, we show how automated collection and analysis of I/O logs across multiple platforms can help accomplish these purposes. We used Darshan [1], a lightweight instrumentation tool, to capture application-level I/O behavior at production scale. Because Darshan's overhead is low, a number of platform owners[1] have deployed it as the default option for all apps, thus enabling workload-wide and cross-platform analysis.

This paper presents insights we gleaned by analyzing Darshan logs from three large-scale supercomputers: Intrepid and Mira at the Argonne Leadership Computing Facility (ALCF) and Edison at the National Energy Research Scientific Computing Center (NERSC). The logs span a substantial period of time—4 years on Intrepid, 18 months on Mira and 9 months on Edison—and capture the I/O behavior "in the wild" of about 1M jobs, representing thousands of apps and roughly a third of the workload on these platforms. This is the first study that has been able to compare and contrast the I/O behavior and evolution of many different apps at production scale across platforms.

Our contributions fall into two categories:

- The logs provide a broad portrait of the state of HPC I/O usage on three modern platforms. For example, *among Darshan-instrumented jobs*:

  o Every widely used I/O paradigm (file per process, global shared file, or subsetting I/O) is represented in the set of best-performing **and** worst-performing apps, in terms of aggregate I/O throughput. Thus, use of a particular paradigm does not in itself guarantee good or bad performance.

HPDC'15, June 15 - 19, 2015, Portland, OR, USA Copyright 2015 ACM
978-1-4503-3550-8/15/06...$15.00
http://dx.doi.org/10.1145/2749246.2749269

---

[1] In this paper, a *job* or *run* is a particular execution of an app. Unless otherwise noted, we consider two jobs to belong to the same app if and only if their executables have the same name. Someone who submits a job is a *user*; users may have to configure an app before they submit a job. Someone responsible for developing the source code of an app is its *owner*, or rather one of its owners. A widely used app may have a small set of owners and a much bigger set of users. A *platform* is a particular installation of a supercomputer. Someone responsible for configuring or administering a platform or for helping its users is an *owner* of that platform.

o Roughly a third of jobs have aggregate average I/O throughput no more than that of a single contemporary USB flash memory thumb drive (~256 MB/s [2]). Three-quarters of apps never exceed the throughput of four thumb drives in *any* of their jobs. Over a third of jobs spend more time in I/O metadata functions than in transfer of actual data.

o Roughly half of apps have low throughput because none of their jobs access more than 1 GB of data, so that file startup costs cannot be amortized across much data transfer; or because they rely on text files instead of binary files. Even on the most data-intensive platform we studied, half of apps wrote less than 10 GB of data in 99% or more of their jobs. On one platform we studied, roughly one-fifth of apps relied exclusively on text files, which almost certainly guarantee poor performance at scale.

o Three-quarters of jobs use only POSIX to perform I/O. This does not condemn a job to poor I/O throughput, but it does suggest a need to investigate why higher-level parallel I/O libraries are not more widely used.

- We discuss ways to address these problems, including a simple and effective analysis and visualization procedure for quickly identifying apps' I/O bottlenecks; criteria for system owners to identify potentially underperforming apps; and an I/O boot camp for users/owners of underperforming apps. The resulting performance improvements could raise the level of satisfaction of users, app owners, and platform owners. Two subtle points:

o The I/O performance of an app may satisfy its owners but not necessarily the platform owners, and vice versa. Thus analysis of I/O logs must address the needs of both populations.

o 90% of a platform's I/O usage comes from less than 10% of its apps, but some of these apps do not have many large jobs. The greatest potential resource savings for platform owners lies in identifying and correcting an app's I/O issues *before* it becomes a top consumer of I/O time. Automated analysis can be particularly helpful here, as smaller jobs are less likely to attract expert human scrutiny.

The remainder of this paper is organized as follows. Section 2 provides background on Darshan and summarizes related work. Section 3 describes the target platforms and collected data. Section 4 presents a three-dimensional analysis of the collected logs: app-specific, platform-wide, and cross-platform. Section 5 summarizes our findings and outlines future work.

2. BACKGROUND AND RELATED WORK

For over 20 years, researchers have sought to understand HPC I/O workloads. As the size, composition, and complexity of platforms and their workloads grow continuously, the topic must be revisited in each generation of platforms (see, e.g., [3][4] from the 1990s, [5][6] from the 2000s, and [7][8] from the 2010s). Many workload studies (e.g., [5][6][8], among more recent works) use popular scientific codes such as FLASH [11], GCRM [12], Nek5000 [13], CESM [14], and their associated benchmarks as representative of the entire I/O workload. Such benchmarks are widely used to tune and refine I/O libraries and storage systems. Since these apps are widely used in their fields, any improvements made to them can benefit many users. As important as they are, however, these well-studied apps and benchmarks are not necessarily representative of the long tail of apps that constitute the majority of submitted jobs. By considering a platform's entire

workload, we can gain additional insights into its I/O system usage. By considering multiple platforms and many apps, we can gain general insights into I/O performance portability.

I/O tracing is very helpful in capturing details of individual I/O functions and allowing in-depth analysis of application performance. Researchers have created many tools for generating app I/O traces, such as RIOT I/O [15], ScalaIOTrace [16], //TRACE [17], IPM [18], LANL-Trace [19], TraceFS [20], and Recorder [21]. After the traces have been generated, they can be used for app debugging, performance tuning, creating benchmarks, system analysis, or cross-platform studies. For example, the RIOT I/O tracing toolkit has been used to assess the performance of three I/O benchmarks on three platforms with GPFS and Lustre file systems. ScalaIOTrace, //TRACE and Recorder traces can be replayed to create app-specific benchmarks. I/O tracing provides very detailed information about app executions, which can be extremely useful in improving I/O performance. Such I/O tracing tools are ideal for investigating individual runs in full detail, but are too expensive to be used to find broader patterns at the scale of thousands of jobs and apps.

Kim et al. [7] characterized platform workloads by instrumenting the storage system. This approach does not provide app-specific information for analysis. In this paper, we rely on data captured for a general production workload, which can be used to characterize I/O behavior at both the app and workload levels.

Darshan [1] instruments I/O functions at multiple levels, primarily MPI-IO and POSIX I/O. Darshan collects about 30 pieces of summary data for each job, as well as 162 additional parameters for each file opened by a process of the job. Example job-level data include the numbers of processes, files accessed, and bytes read/written; aggregate I/O throughput; and total run time and I/O time [9]. After a run, users can employ Darshan's tools to parse their job's logs and summarize its I/O behavior.

Darshan's minimal collection of data (adding no more than a few seconds to job execution time for most apps [10][23]) allows it to be enabled for all jobs by default. This allows us to observe a platform at workload scale and to identify its jobs and apps that can most benefit from follow-up analyses with I/O tracing and other performance analysis tools. As Darshan captures all runs of the apps it observes, we can see the patterns of I/O behavior at scale and across platforms, rather than only for selected jobs.

Darshan logs have already been used for system-wide analysis. Carns et al. used two months of Darshan logs on Intrepid [1] and four months on Hopper [10] to explore how such logs can be used to improve storage system utilization and identify candidate apps for additional I/O tuning. We extend this approach to cover three platforms over a much longer period of time. To the best of our knowledge, this is the first study that compares and contrasts application I/O behavior across platforms at full scale.

3. TARGET PLATFORMS AND LOGS

Darshan is deployed and enabled by default for all users of ALCF and NERSC platforms, and Edison users automatically see Darshan's I/O summary report on a web page for their completed job. But Darshan does not see every job running on a platform. Apps are not logged if they do not call `MPI_Init()` and `MPI_Finalize()`, use nondefault build scripts, or run legacy executables that are not already linked to Darshan. Further, an issue in the F90 MPI wrapper on Mira prevents Darshan from observing F90 codes (a fix has been requested from IBM). Users can also choose to disable Darshan but do not normally do so.

On average, Darshan logs on Intrepid, Mira and Edison cover roughly *a third of jobs*. In the remainder of this paper we consider only those jobs and apps observed by Darshan, and we use the term *workload* to refer to the platform workload as observed by Darshan. We do not know whether Darshan's observations are typical of the I/O behavior of the unobserved part of the workload; but the observed fraction of the workload is large enough to interest platform owners in its own right.

Table 1 describes Intrepid, Mira, Edison, and their Darshan logs. Intrepid is an IBM Blue Gene/P computer at ALCF with 40,960 quad-core nodes, 557 TFlops peak performance, and 88 GB/s peak I/O throughput to its GPFS file system. Each set of 64 compute nodes has one of 640 dedicated I/O forwarding nodes (IONs). From Jan. 2010 to Dec. 2013, Darshan captured 239K jobs representing over 1K apps, 1405M core-hours, and up to 163K processes and moving as much as 218TB of data in one job.

Table 1. Target platforms and their Darshan logs

Platform	Intrepid	Mira	Edison
Architecture	BG/P	BG/Q	Cray XC30
Peak Flops	0.557 PF	10 PF	2.57 PF
Memory	80 TB	768 TB	357 TB
Cores per node	4	16	24
# of cores	160 K	768 K	130 K
Storage	6 PB	24 PB	7.6 PB
Peak I/O	88 GB/s	240 GB/s	168 GB/s
File system	GPFS	GPFS	Lustre
Period logged	Jan'10 – Dec'13	Apr'13 – Oct'14	Jan'14 – Sep'14
Jobs logged	239,304	137,311	703,647

Intrepid's successor at ALCF is Mira, an IBM Blue Gene/Q running GPFS. Mira has 48K 16-core nodes, a peak computing performance 20x faster than Intrepid, and peak I/O throughput 3x faster than Intrepid. Mira has 384 IONs, each serving 128 compute nodes. Mira entered production mode in April 2013, with Darshan enabled. The 137K jobs Darshan observed there used 1456M core-hours and up to 1.04M processes and 570 TB per job.

Edison is the newest supercomputer at NERSC, a Cray XC-30 of size and performance roughly halfway between Intrepid and Mira. Edison has 5,576 24-core nodes and a peak I/O bandwidth of 168 GB/s to its Lustre file system. Edison's cores are several times more powerful than Mira's, making up for their smaller number. Darshan observed 703K jobs consuming 75M core-hours, using up to 131K processes and moving up to 426 TB of data in one job.

Figure 1 shows that average Darshan coverage is 20% to 40% (Edison graph omitted here). For these three platforms Figure 2 compares the number of processes per job and the bytes each job read or wrote, showing quartiles and outliers in log scale. On all platforms, some jobs run at full system scale and/or transfer over 100 TB. However, most jobs transfer relatively little data and use few processes compared with the available number of cores. On Edison, 75% of jobs use under 100 processes and/or transfer no more than 3 GB of data. On Intrepid and Mira, 50% of jobs transfer less than 4 GB and/or use no more than 2K processes. Figure 3 shows that few apps ever use more than 4K processes or transfer more than a few gigabytes of data.

We imported Darshan's log files into a MySQL database and used SQL scripts to analyze the data. Script details are important for ensuring meaningful and reproducible results on other platforms, but due to space constraints, we only discuss the critical issue of computing the aggregate I/O throughput of a job. For each process

of the job, we consider the total time spent in Darshan-tracked POSIX IO or MPI-IO data and metadata function calls for all the files the process opened. We set the job's I/O time to be the largest I/O time among all its processes. We computed the job's (aggregate) I/O throughput as its total bytes moved in Darshan-tracked POSIX IO or MPI-IO calls, divided by its I/O time.

App-level I/O throughput could be computed in other ways, e.g., sum/median/average across processes, but we find the slowest process's viewpoint best for comparing throughput across many jobs/apps. Usually computation does not resume until the slowest process has finished its I/O, due to an explicit barrier or the need to exchange data with neighbors. Thus *from the app's point of view*, our formula approximates its I/O throughput, and avoids misleading statistics when I/O loads are skewed across processes.

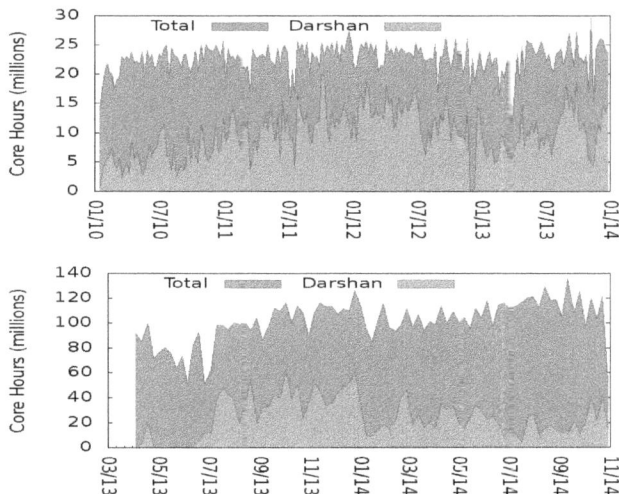

Figure 1: Darshan coverage in core hours on Intrepid (top) and Mira (bottom).

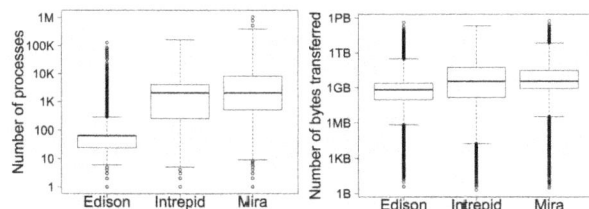

Figure 2: Cross-platform comparison of each *job's* number of processes (left) and number of bytes read/written (right).

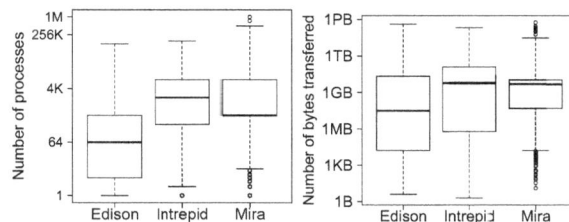

Figure 3: Cross-platform comparison of each *app's* maximum number of processes and maximum bytes read/written.

Darshan records the number of processes that a job runs on, but not the number of cores or nodes. The default Darshan configuration tracks most of the key POSIX IO or MPI-IO functions; condensing the wrapped functions' names, they are [l][f]*seek*[64], [ncmpi_][H5f]*creat*[e][64], [aio_][p][f]*read*[v][64], *lio_listio*[64], [aio_][p][f]*write*[v][64], [ncmpi_][[H5f]*open*[64], *mmap*[64], *aio_return*[64], __[l][f]*xstat*[64], f[data]*sync*, and [ncmpi_][[H5]f]*close*. Darshan's default configuration does not track character-oriented functions such as *getc* and *putc* and their higher-level analogs *scanf* and *printf*, all intended for text data transfer. (Such functions may choose to call *read* or *write* for data access, but POSIX IO does not require them to do so, and we have not observed them doing so on our platforms.) The Darshan developers did this to reduce overhead, assuming users would not spend much time performing character-oriented I/O.

4. ANALYSIS OF DARSHAN LOGS

4.1 Application-specific analysis

In this section, we present an analysis and visualization procedure that app users and owners can use to identify I/O bottlenecks and inefficiencies across all runs of their apps. Platform owners can use the same techniques to examine the apps that are their top users of I/O time (as identified by another set of scripts we wrote). The analysis consists of the following steps.

STEP 1. Identify where the job/app spends most of its I/O time, out of four possibilities:
  a) **Global metadata.** All metadata functions for *global* files (i.e., files accessed by all processes), such as file open, close, stat, and seek functions.
  b) **Nonglobal metadata.** Metadata functions for files that are not global (i.e., files accessed by a *proper subset* of the job's processes). These files may be *local*, that is, accessed by a single process; or *subset*, i.e., accessed by multiple processes, such as under a subsetting I/O paradigm.
  c) **Global data I/O.** Data transfer functions for global files. These include the read, write, and sync functions.
  d) **Non-global data I/O.** Data transfer for nonglobal files.

STEP 2. Identify which file(s) consume most of that time. We categorize the files along three dimensions: global, local or subset; MPI or POSIX; read-only, write-only, or read/write.

STEP 3. Examine Darshan's performance data for those files.

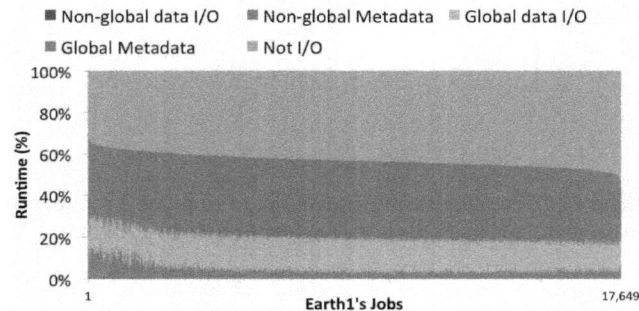

Figure 4: Breakdown of total run time for each Earth1 job.

As a case study, consider the app that consumed the most I/O time on Mira, an Earth science code we'll call "Earth1". Earth1 ran ~18K times in 4400 wall-clock hours and 36M core-hours. With Earth1's jobs ordered by their percentage of run time that is not I/O time (light blue), Figure 4 divides each job's remaining run time into the four categories in Step 1. Earth1 spent over half its time in I/O, most of which was for global file metadata.

To begin Step 2, we examined a randomly-selected Earth1 run. This job had 35 global shared files, including 24 using MPI for write-only files, 5 using POSIX for read-only files, and 6 using POSIX for write-only files. The total I/O time of the job was ~700 seconds, of which 567 seconds were spent on 6 POSIX write-only global files. Returning to the set of all Earth1 jobs, Figure 5 shows

how Earth1's I/O time relates to the number of POSIX write-only global files its jobs use, as computed by our scripts. Global data I/O time increases gracefully with the number of files, while global metadata time increases much faster – even though graphs not included here show that the amount of global data transferred differs *by a factor of 3* across runs with the same number of POSIX write-only global files. In other words, I/O throughput tracks the changes in file count. This result indicates that the app owner should take a closer look at those files.

In Step 3, an I/O expert would quickly notice that according to the per-file Darshan data, each process writes the POSIX global files in relatively small pieces (<256 KB) that do not align with file block boundaries, making I/O costs high. Common issues of this nature could be included in a checklist for users or automatically recognized.

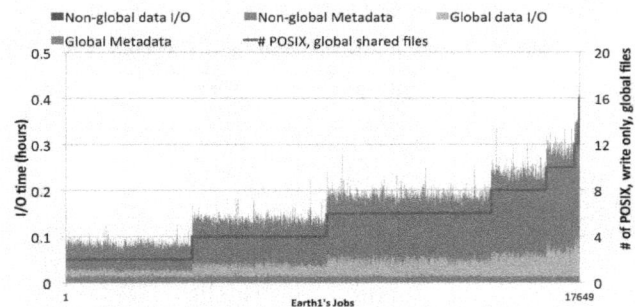

Figure 5: Earth1's I/O time and number of POSIX write-only global files (red line).

Job- and app-specific analysis can be done immediately after a run or a series of runs to help the app owner or user quickly locate an I/O bottleneck, avoiding a long-lasting inefficient implementation. Darshan's data is relatively high level, so it can give owners/users an idea about where their I/O problems may lie; owners/users may want to follow up with a tracing or debugging tool.

4.2 Platform-wide analysis

An app's inefficient use of shared system resources may impact other apps' ability to perform useful work. Platform owners can use platform-wide analyses to assess job performance, identify large underperforming apps, and offer early intervention to save system resources. In this section, we assess the performance of I/O workloads on Edison, Intrepid, and Mira and propose criteria for platform owners to quickly identify underperforming apps that consume lots of system resources.

4.2.1 Very low I/O performance is the norm for most apps on these platforms.

Even though these platforms' file systems have a peak throughput of hundreds of GB/s, few apps experience high I/O throughput.

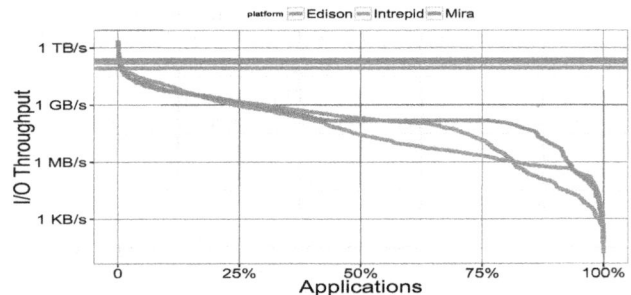

Figure 6: Maximum I/O throughput of each app across all its jobs on a platform, and platform peak I/O throughput.

For each app and platform, Figure 6 shows the *maximum* aggregate I/O throughput observed by Darshan, among all of the app's jobs on that platform. Horizontal lines show the platform's peak I/O bandwidth. (Apps exceed the platform peak when their data fits in the file system cache and reads/writes do not have to access the disk before I/O functions return.) Aggregate throughput for three-quarters of apps never exceeds 1 GB/s, roughly 1% of average peak platform bandwidth. As noted earlier, most apps are relatively small; and no one should expect a job running on a few nodes to approach peak platform I/O bandwidth. For example, the Mira owners told us that a 1K-node job cannot expect more than ~20 GB/s I/O throughput, less than 10% of the platform peak. Looking at the situation another way, however, three-quarters of apps never exceed the aggregate throughput of four modern USB thumb drives (writes average 239 MB/s and reads average 265 MB/s on the 64 GB Lexar P10 USB3.0 [2]).

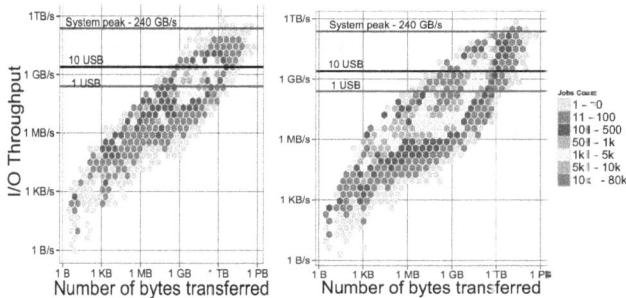

Figure 7: Number of jobs with a given I/O throughput and total number of bytes, on Mira (l) and Edison (r).

In Figure 7, each tile represents one or more *jobs*, with the tile color indicating the number of jobs. The figure shows that on Mira and Edison, a job's I/O throughput increases roughly linearly with its data size. Jobs that write very little data will not have high I/O throughput, because the fixed costs for accessing a file cannot be amortized across significant data transfer. Still, a third of jobs never reach the I/O throughput of a single modern thumb drive, and the vast majority of jobs never exceed the I/O bandwidth of 10 modern thumb drives. Intrepid (not shown) is similar.

Each vertical bar in Figure 8 represents all the jobs of one *app* on a platform. A bar's color indicates the total bytes accessed by its jobs. For example, a half-red, half-orange bar means that half the app's jobs accessed over 100 GB, and the other half accessed 10-100 GB (with perhaps a few smaller jobs not visible without magnification). Maximum and average I/O throughput for each app are indicated by squares and crosses, respectively, using the log-scale right-hand axis. The apps are sorted in decreasing order of importance for the storage system, as measured by the *total bytes transferred* across all the jobs of the app. Note that roughly half of apps do not transfer more than 1 GB of data in their jobs.

Darshan does not track text-oriented I/O functions, so apps that rely entirely on text files will register as having made metadata calls but transferring zero bytes, even if they access a lot of data and therefore are important to the storage system. Along with the apps that perform no I/O (e.g., a hello-world test), these text-only apps can be found at the far right-hand side of each graph, where there is a visible knee in the cloud of throughput dots. As the results indicate, 105 out of 1507, 201 out of 1032, and 42 out of 1183 apps open files but perform no binary I/O in *any* of their jobs on Intrepid, Mira, and Edison, respectively. Some of these apps are small by any measure, but others are not. For example, a third of the Mira text-only apps had an average job size of at least

1K processes, and a quarter of them averaged 16K or more processes per run. Some apps that heavily rely on text files also access binary files, so the counts listed above understate the extent of the usage of text files. Since we do not know how many bytes of text an app accesses, Figure 8 also understates the importance and impact on the storage system of text-based I/O. Since text-based I/O generally does not scale up well, we conclude that **text-based I/O is a more widespread practice than previously observed** and deserves further investigation.

I/O throughput for small jobs does not matter, in the sense that users and owners will be happy when a job's I/O time is only a second or so. But small jobs may be test runs for large jobs, such as the many Mira jobs in Figure 7 that transfer a terabyte of data and spend 10–20 minutes in I/O. Thus, small jobs may allow us to identify poor I/O practices before significant amounts of platform and user time have been wasted. Further, an app consisting entirely of relatively small jobs can still be a top user of I/O time on a platform. We consider these two points in the following discussions, which focus on apps that are heavy users of I/O time.

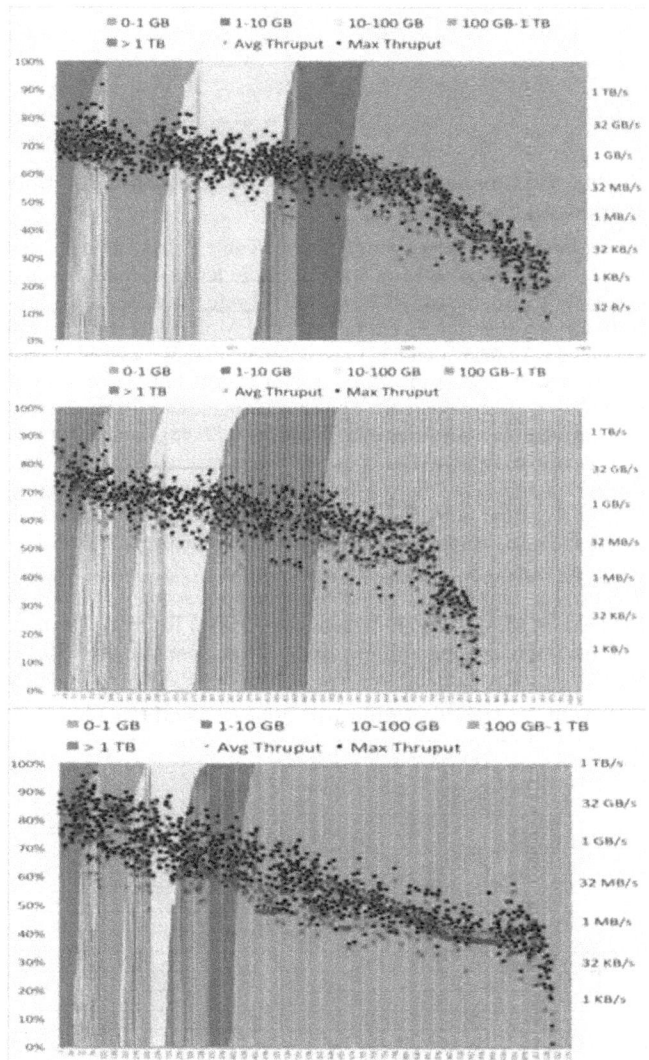

Figure 8: Breakdown of each app's jobs, by bytes written in each job, and average and maximum I/O throughput of each app's jobs. Intrepid is at the top, Mira in the middle, Edison at the bottom.

4.2.2 Platform I/O resource usage is dominated by a small number of jobs and apps.

On Edison, Intrepid, and Mira, the total I/O time consumed by all jobs observed by Darshan is 5,920 hours, 13,052 hours, and 5,335 hours, respectively. With jobs sorted by their total I/O time, Figure 9 shows the cumulative portion of platform I/O time that they use. On Edison, the top 10% of jobs consume 90% of the I/O time. On Intrepid and Mira, the top 25% of jobs consume 90% of the I/O time. The curve is even steeper for apps (not shown): 90% of I/O time goes to under 4% of apps on Intrepid, 3% on Mira, and 6% on Edison; each platform has approximately 1K–1.5K apps. These results echo the findings of [1], in which a single app dominated I/O time usage in a two-month study.

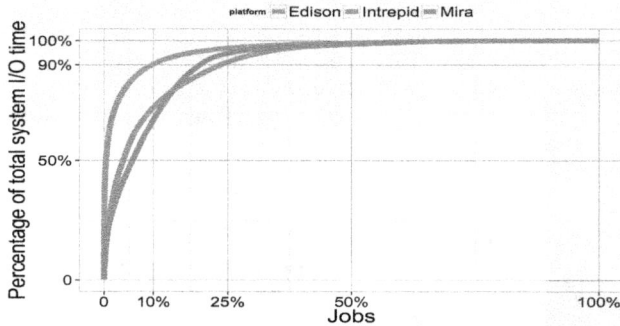

Figure 9: Cumulative percentage of platform I/O time consumed by jobs.

Let us look at these apps more closely. Table 2 and Table 3 show the 15 biggest apps on Mira and Edison, in terms of total I/O time across all their jobs. In what follows, we refer to these as the **big-time apps.** (Materials1, Turbulent1, and Molecular1 each merge two apps with near-identical executable names. We consider apps to be the same across platforms if their executables' names differ at most in version numbers). Apps whose names are in bold are on the big-time list for multiple platforms. Since Darshan is not configured to observe data accesses using character-oriented I/O, the I/O time for text-file-based apps is undercounted when picking out the big-time apps. To save space, we omit Intrepid's table, which includes Mira's Earth1, Physics2, Turbulence2, and Molecular2 at ranks 5, 7, 13, and 15, respectively, and Edison's Weather1 at rank 3. The top 15 big-time apps account for 83% of I/O time on Mira, 70% on Edison, and 73% on Intrepid. The total data read/written across all their jobs varies from a high of 10 PB for Earth1 and Materials3 to a low of 1 TB for PDE1.

Table 2: Mira's 15 Apps with Biggest Total I/O Time

#	App	Total I/O time (h)	Total run time (wall h)	# of jobs	Total bytes (TB)	Median job GB/s	Run time I/O %
1	**Earth1**	2,480	4,406	17,649	10,037	1.205	56%
2	**Materials1**	577	22,912	4,579	196	.103	3%
3	Turbulence1	428	4,121	972	153	.123	10%
4	Physics1	150	3,387	762	1,051	.475	4%
5	**Physics2**	133	6,262	1,966	1,115	.467	2%
6	Climate1	95	2,039	1,520	112	.291	5%
7	Molecular1	89	27,826	19,622	156	.571	0%
8	**Turbulence2**	83	671	335	251	.212	12%
9	Turbulence3	74	96	323	1,961	1.700	77%
10	Physics3	67	202	66	51	3.274	33%
11	**Molecular2**	67	1,686	2,480	34	.167	4%
12	PDE1	62	120	298	1	.098	52%
13	Plasma1	48	934	58	3,052	18.32	5%
14	Physics4	42	202	309	90	.186	21%
15	Aero1	41	61	151	359	2.505	67%

Improvements in big-time apps' throughput may free up resources for others to use and improve the satisfaction of all users. This

principle drives the attention given to important apps and their I/O benchmarks; and indeed, the I/O behavior of at least five of the apps in Table 2 and three in Table 3 is well studied and carefully tuned. However, apps with I/O bugs and with I/O paradigms that are suboptimal for their situation also appear in the tables. For example, as we discuss elsewhere, PDE1 used global text files with many processes, and Earth1 used relatively small POSIX writes to global files. Indeed, the apps in these tables are top in *usage* of I/O time, not top in terms of I/O throughput. Apps that are extremely successful in extracting I/O performance will not be listed in the tables unless their total data size is incredibly high.

Table 3: Edison's 15 Apps with Biggest Total I/O Time

#	App	Total I/O time (h)	Total run time (wall h)	# of jobs	Total bytes (TB)	Median job GB/s	Run time I/O %
1	Materials2	1,109	3,397	847	60	.016	33%
2	Materials3	505	7,329	78,302	10,351	.475	7%
3	Physics5	395	2,698	2,171	6	.005	15%
4	Physics6	322	3,353	6,687	15	.010	10%
5	Materials4	263	8,252	1,231	17	.038	3%
6	Molecular3	249	7,392	2,194	51	.036	3%
7	**Materials1**	219	11,671	16,221	44	.109	2%
8	Materials5	215	21,439	34,213	27	.061	1%
9	Materials6	213	983	926	16	.070	22%
10	Chem1	145	18,909	5,412	4	.013	1%
11	Materials7	129	453	5,769	18	.039	29%
12	**Weather1**	110	686	299	1,189	.660	16%
13	Materials8	103	1,011	1,383	2,477	7.993	10%
14	Materials9	93	175	12,344	266	.860	53%
15	Plasma2	89	102	41	246	2.265	87%

In the tables, the percentage of run time that big-time apps devote to I/O rises from ~0% for Molecular1 on Mira to 87% for Plasma2 on Edison. Owners and users of apps at the low end of this range are likely to be happy with their I/O throughput, even if platform owners are not. **Boosting the minimum aggregate throughput for all big-time apps to 1 GB/s would save platform owners 42% of total I/O time on Intrepid** (3758 hours out of 8920), **41% on Mira** (1803 hours out of 4435), **and 85% on Edison** (3542 hours out of 4158). Jobs running concurrently with big-time apps might also benefit from increased I/O resource availability.

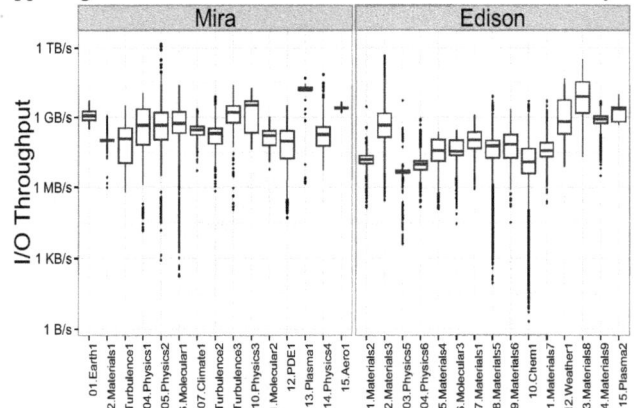

Figure 10: Big-time apps' throughput on Mira and Edison.

According to the tables, less than a quarter of Edison's and Mira's big-time apps get over 1 GB/s I/O throughput in their median job; only one gets over 10 GB/s in its median job (Plasma1, 18 GB/s on Mira). Figure 10 shows the quartiles and outliers for the I/O throughput of the big-time apps' jobs on Mira and Edison. As was true for the set of all jobs, big-time apps' jobs get better I/O throughput when they have more data. Figure 11 shows this with a four-category breakdown of the big-time apps' performance, based on whether they have *small data* (read/write under 10 GB) and/or *few processes* (under 2K). Figure 11 shows that most big-time apps' jobs with big data and processes get 1-16 GB/s of throughput on Mira. As we will see, each platform has apps with much higher median throughput than the big-time apps.

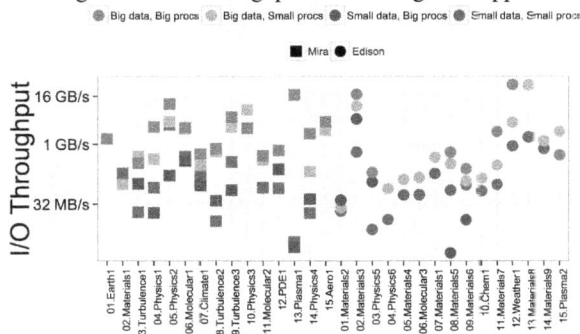

Figure 11: Average I/O throughput of Mira's (squares) and Edison's (circles) big-time apps' jobs, by job size.

4.2.3 *Early intervention by platform owners can identify apps with I/O problems, save I/O resources, and improve user satisfaction.*

Table 2 and Table 3 show that most of the big-time apps on Mira and Edison ran over a thousand times, and all but three ran over a hundred times. Clearly, early intervention where needed could have saved a huge amount of system resources. As Figure 12 shows, almost all big-time apps have small jobs, especially on Edison, which is the newest platform; early smaller jobs are the ideal point for recognizing and addressing problems.

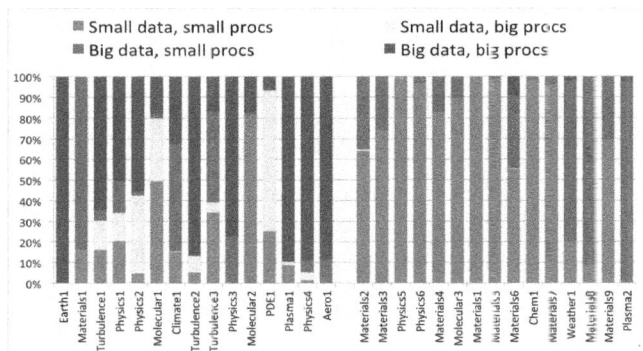

Figure 12: Job sizes for Mira (l) and Edison (r) big-time apps.

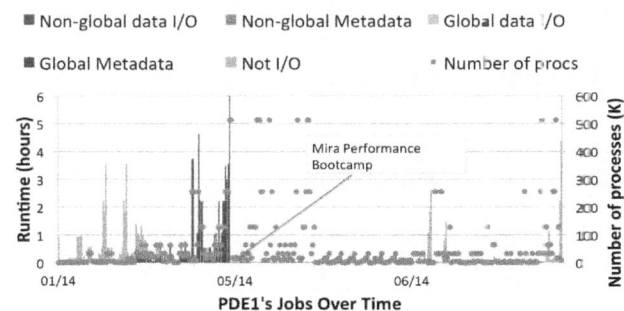

Figure 13: Evolution of PDE1's I/O paradigms. Red dots show the number of processes of each job (right-hand y-axis).

For example, PDE1 in Table 2 used ~13M core-hours on Mira and spent 52% of its run time in I/O. When PDE1 ran at scale (64K–128K processes) in its first implementation, I/O consumed almost all of its run time. For example, one job with 512K processes took

7 hours and over 3.5 million core-hours. Figure 13 includes a stacked bar for each successive PDE1 job, breaking down its total run time; the 7-hour run is excluded because it is off the chart. The clump of blue bars in Figure 13 shows that in its early runs at scale, PDE1's I/O time was devoted to metadata functions; in fact, the data transfer time for most files was zero. This tells us that the files are being read/written with functions not tracked by Darshan, namely, character-oriented functions for text files.

Conversations with PDE1's owner confirmed that the initial implementation used *fprintf* to write the output file accessed by all processes. After PDE1's owner attended Mira performance boot camp, the owner created an MPI-IO–based implementation that runs in 11 seconds with 512K processes. PDE1's owner would have benefited from automated analysis of the Darshan logs from its early jobs in Figure 13. Without extending Darshan to track character-oriented I/O functions, a script can still find apps that make heavy use of text files, by searching the logs for instances of files with high metadata time and zero data read/write time.

The logs also show how app I/O behavior evolves over time. PDE1's earliest runs used few processes, so its I/O paradigm was inexpensive relative to computation. As the number of processes went up, I/O dominated (purple bars). The purple bars disappear with the change to MPI-IO.

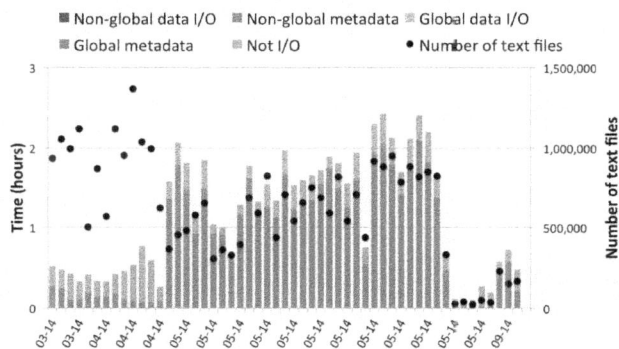

Figure 14: Earth2 read hundreds of thousands of text files.

As another example, consider "Earth2", an Earth science code that ran for 60 hours wall time on Mira and consumed about 100K core hours. It read from hundreds of thousands to over a million files and spent the vast majority of its time in I/O, as shown in Figure 14. Its I/O time breakdown reveals the tell-tale pattern of text files: high metadata time and zero data access time. Later, its owners identified a bug that put their read operations inside an unrelated nested loop, rather than outside. This costly bug persisted for a long time before it was noticed. The situation is another argument for automated early intervention.

We suggest the following four criteria to help platform owners identify apps whose I/O behavior makes them candidates for further investigation. The criteria are not absolute indicators of I/O problems, but rather help to narrow down the number of applications to consider.

- Apps using a text file I/O approach, such as PDE1 and Earth2. A query for jobs that use only text files finds 2121 jobs from 59 apps on Edison, 5561 jobs from 237 apps on Mira and 4725 jobs from 171 apps on Intrepid.

- Apps with many files and high metadata costs. For example, a query for Mira jobs with over 100k files and metadata time that is more than one third of run time finds 111 jobs from 11 apps, including Physics4 (discussed in Section 4.2.6).

- Apps with little data but large I/O time. For example, on Edison, a query for jobs with under 4 GB of data that spend over 5 minutes in I/O finds 4020 jobs from 79 apps. One of the apps has more than 500 jobs that match this criterion.

- Big time apps, such as the Top 15 discussed earlier.

The filtering capability further emphasizes the importance of having a central database about system workload that will enable early intervention from platform owners to save system resources and improve system utilization.

4.2.4 POSIX I/O is far more widely used than parallel I/O libraries.

The HPC community has worked hard to create a stack of parallel I/O libraries, including MPI-IO, HDF5, and NetCDF. But Figure 15 shows that users tend to stick with the POSIX I/O library (open, read, write). Nearly 95% of jobs visible to Darshan on Edison use POSIX exclusively. On Intrepid and Mira, the percentages are 80% and 50%, respectively. The remaining jobs use MPI-IO directly or use the libraries built atop MPI-IO (e.g., HDF5), for at least one of their files. MPI-IO is used most often among mid-sized jobs, in terms of their number of processes.

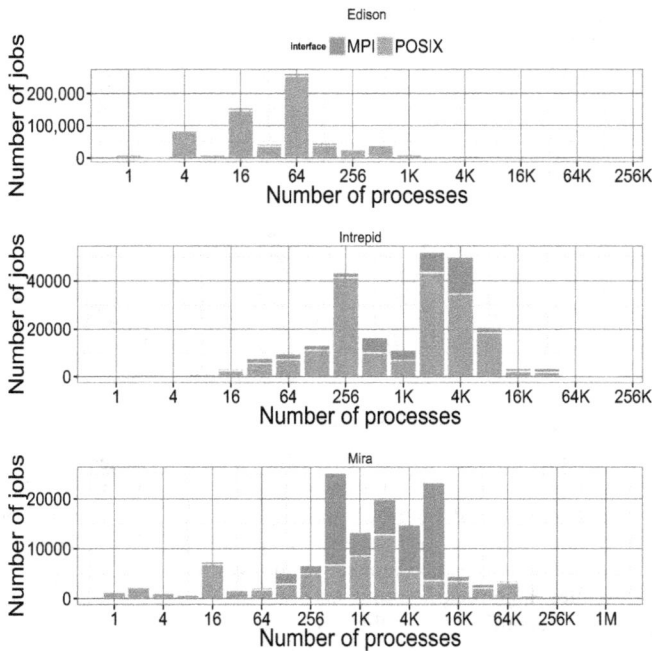

Figure 15: Number of jobs using POSIX IO only (teal) and using MPI-IO directly or indirectly for at least one file (red).

The POSIX-only approach does not necessarily mean low I/O performance; with care, POSIX apps can have high throughput. However, using MPI-IO offers more chances for decent I/O performance. As shown in Figure 16, on Mira and Intrepid, about 45% of jobs that used the MPI-IO library achieve more than 1 GB/s of aggregate I/O throughput, while less than 20% of POSIX-only jobs reach 1 GB/s. On Edison, most apps that used MPI-IO do not do so efficiently, although some have excellent throughput. We return to this point in our cross-platform analysis.

Carns et al. [1] analyzed the usage of different I/O interfaces and found that most jobs with few processors used POSIX I/O, while jobs with many processors used POSIX primarily for reads, if at all. MPI-IO prevailed among jobs with many processors and apps

that wrote more data than they read. We found that, in addition, POSIX is popular among many-processor jobs. This result agrees with another study in [26].

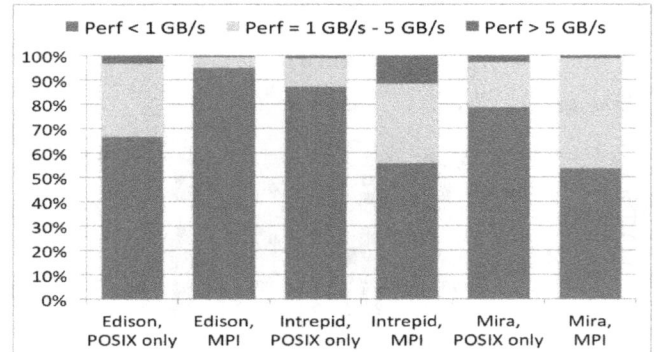

Figure 16: I/O throughput for apps that use only POSIX-IO and those that use MPI-IO for at least one file.

4.2.5 Metadata costs often exceed data I/O costs.

Metadata costs are a major factor in the I/O throughput of apps [10]. Averaging across the platforms in Figure 17, roughly 40% of jobs spend more time in metadata functions than in reading and writing data. We have already touched on a variety of reasons for this problem: the prevalence of small-data jobs and apps, which Figure 17 highlights; the hidden problem of overreliance on text files; and small data request sizes.

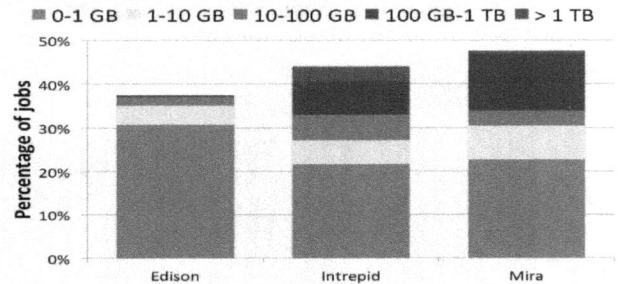

Figure 17: Breakdown of jobs by total data size, for jobs that spend more time in metadata functions than in data transfer.

4.2.6 No major I/O paradigm is always good or bad.

Text files almost guarantee poor throughput at scale; we do not consider apps using this minor I/O paradigm in this section.

As mentioned earlier, nonglobal files can be broken down into *local* files (i.e., accessed by one process) and *subset* files (i.e., accessed by more than one process but not all processes). An app uses the subset paradigm because it makes sense for the scientific problem and computational method—for example, adaptive mesh refinement—or because the owners want to put a subset of the processes (e.g., one process per node) in charge of all I/O. We call the latter *subsetting I/O*. Subsetting I/O can reduce contention and the number of files, but requires care for a good implementation. Taken to the extreme, subsetting turns into serial I/O, where one process does all the I/O, which never scales. In interpreting logs, we must distinguish between these three kinds of subset files.

Local files, often called file-per-process, are easy for users to implement, with no coordination between processes. But as the number of processes goes up, metadata costs can be high, and post-run data analysis and file management become painful. The use of global files, each accessed by all processes, can keep the job's input/result data tidy. But global files can have high metadata costs at scale, and contention can be an issue. Good implementations of this paradigm tend to require expertise, and the resulting parallel I/O libraries have a learning curve for users.

Some of these categories can be broken down further. For example, a sophisticated app might use subsetting I/O with files that are accessed by (and thus "global" to) all the processes allowed to perform I/O. And an app can use multiple paradigms in different jobs or inside one job. But the coarser breakdown suffices for our purposes. Each paradigm—global, local, and subset—has its pros and cons, and each is found among jobs with the worst *and* best I/O throughputs.

Local-file paradigm. If a job has enough data, it may be able to avoid the pitfall of excessive metadata costs at scale. An excellent example is the set of all jobs that access at least 1M files, grouped by app in Figure 18. Each job is represented by one vertical bar, subdivided into colors based on how it spends its I/O time. Each job also has a yellow dot indicating its throughput and a black X indicating its data size. Two apps are very tightly packed: Physics4 (116 jobs on Mira) and Plasma1 (1 subset-paradigm job on Intrepid and 41 local-file paradigm jobs on Mira). Figure 18 shows how fast the local file paradigm can be: Mira1 attains over 10 GB/s with ~25 TB of data, and Plasma1 attains about 20 GB/s for its many jobs with 60–80 TB of data. Plasma1 on Mira shows that even with millions of local files and metadata costs (red) exceeding transfer costs (blue), I/O throughput can reliably reach a level that would be the envy of most apps. But the I/O time of the vast majority of local-file jobs in the figure is almost totally dominated by metadata costs, resulting in extremely low throughput for example Physics4. The throughput closely tracks the data size, both of which use the same right-hand y-axis. Two of Plasma1's data points are off the chart: 174 TB and 100 TB of data.

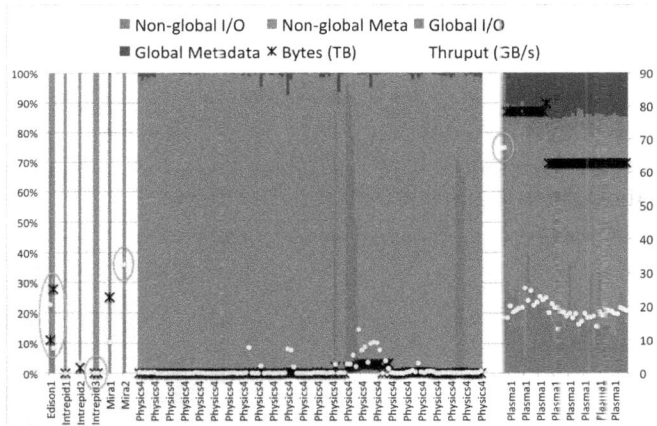

Figure 18: I/O throughput and I/O time breakdown for jobs that access over a million files.

Subset paradigm. In Figure 18, jobs that used the subset paradigm have pink circles around their yellow throughput dots. Two apps used the subset paradigm exclusively, and the figure shows that it can be very effective: Mira2 attained ~30 GB/s and Edison1 had 10–20 GB/s—far better than most apps. (Mira2's job has 165 TB of data, putting that data point off the chart.) But the third app, Plasma1, is the star, with over 60 GB/s in its lone subsetting job on Intrepid. The logs show that 1/8 of Plasma1's processes performed I/O in that job, and approximately 1/225 of Mira2's. Edison1 is using subset files, but not I/O subsetting; recall that subsetting serves other purposes too, such as AMR I/O.

Subsetting is not a panacea: Intrepid3 has poor I/O throughput, totally dominated by metadata costs. However, Intrepid3 was not doing *I/O* subsetting, as three-quarters of its processes wrote to the same file. For a better example of ineffective I/O subsetting, consider Turbulence1, which ran on Intrepid and Mira and is among Mira's big-time apps; its I/O time there averages 10% of run time. Figure 19 shows Turbulence1's Intrepid jobs, sorted by non-I/O time; the dark blue blocks are jobs using PCSIX IO with subsetting (ratio 1000:1), and the light green blocks use MPI-IO with global files. No matter what paradigm is used, the I/O time has little impact on total run time, so the owners would have little motivation to try other I/O approaches. (One way to achieve this insensitivity is to dedicate processes to I/O, so computation can resume once the output data has been sent to those processes.) Examining a randomly selected job, however, we see that 90% of Turbulence1's I/O requests are of size 8 B, which could be inefficient for the storage system and could impact other users.

Climate1 also offers I/O subsetting, along with interfaces to a variety of storage options. Figure 20 shows that users took advantage of these different options in its many jobs on Intrepid. Through other channels, we know that Climate1's owner worked very hard to tame metadata costs and reach its median job throughput on Mira, which Table 2 pegs at a low 0.3 GB/s. But Climate1's throughput may still be hurt by very small I/O request sizes. For example, in three randomly selected Mira and Intrepid jobs including both primarily POSIX and primarily MPI-IO runs, over half its I/O requests have size ~100 B. A randomly selected Intrepid job shows subsetting ratios ranging from 4:1 to 1000:1 during different parts of the job; each job subsets differently, with little visible impact on I/O throughput. With median job I/O time at just 5% of total run time on Mira, Climate1's owner has little incentive to refine its I/O approach further.

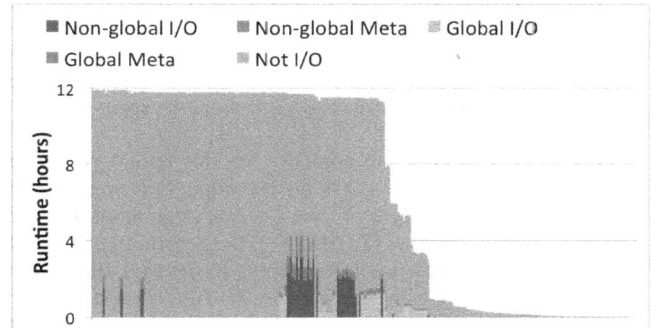

Figure 19: Turbulence1's 290 jobs on Intrepid.

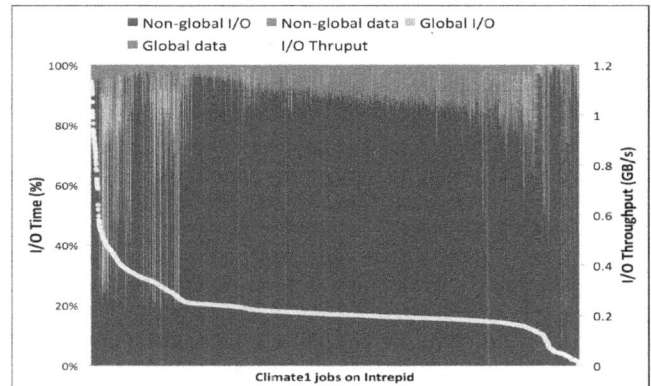

Figure 20: Climate1's 3578 Intrepid jobs, sorted by thruput.

Global files. Global files did not perform well for Earth1, which made small POSIX IO requests, or Climate1, which made small requests with both MPI-IO and POSIX. But Figure 21 shows that global MPI-IO files work well for the jobs of the "Physics7" app on Edison, shown sorted by throughput. The I/O throughput of Physics7's median job is 7 GB/s, helped along by its tendency to access data in 1 MB requests, well aligned with storage block boundaries. Also, Physics7 might not be using the default Lustre settings, which are slow for MPI-IO [24]. Physics7's users experimented twice with nonglobal files: once when they first arrived on Edison and then again after about a hundred jobs, always using a dozen or more processes. Both trials were quickly abandoned.

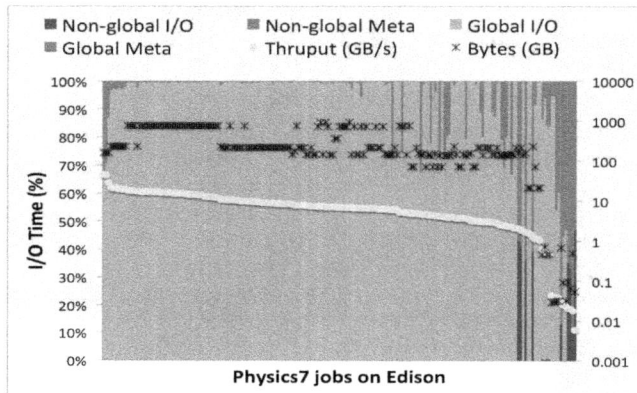

Figure 21: Physics7's 199 Edison jobs, sorted by throughput.

4.3 Cross-platform analysis

Supercomputer lifetimes are short; a new and faster platform is always on the way. But improved performance does not always come easily for users, as noted by Anantharaj et al.: "The high development and maintenance effort required to tune [applications] to multiple platforms is considered a large burden, taking time and resources that might otherwise be spent on other aspects of the projects" [25].

Migration to a new platform normally requires retuning of code for good performance, and I/O is no exception. Seemingly small details of the storage system can have a huge impact on a particular app's throughput [22]. Further, the general trend toward packing more cores into each node tends to increase file access contention for processes in the same node. Thus an app running with the same number of processes on a new platform might see throughput fall even if the new storage system is similar to the old and has higher peak throughput. Therefore, to maintain current throughput, app I/O may need retuning even when moving to a similar but faster platform. Case studies and I/O benchmarks have provided such insights in the past; Darshan can potentially help us examine the impact of migration at a larger scale.

Using the same naming methodology as in Table 2 and Table 3, we found the apps that ran on two or more of our platforms: 82 apps on both Intrepid and Mira, 39 on Mira and Edison, 27 on Intrepid and Edison, and 10 on all three platforms. For each such app, we compared the median aggregate I/O throughput of its jobs across platforms. However, most of these median jobs have small total data, as do most apps; Figure 22 illustrates this with a box plot of job data size for the ten apps that ran on all three platforms, with apps separated by vertical black bars. We have already observed that a small-data job will have well under 1 GB/s aggregate I/O throughput. Thus, the difference in median aggregate I/O throughput of jobs on different platforms is due

primarily to differences in a job's total data size. For a fair cross-platform comparison of these apps, we need to match job sizes across platforms. With over a hundred apps to match up, we present just three case studies here.

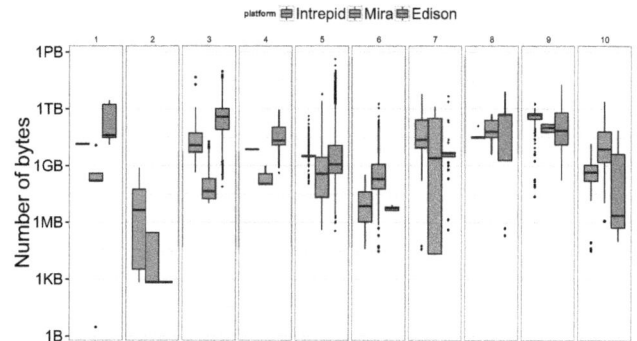

Figure 22: Quartiles and outliers of total bytes accessed by each job, for the ten apps that ran on all three platforms.

Case study 1: Earth1 is the number 1 big time app on Mira and number 4 on Intrepid. Figure 23 shows I/O throughput and data size of all Earth1 jobs on Mira and Intrepid. Median job throughput drops from 4.5 GB/s on Intrepid to 1.2 GB/s on Mira. Data size also declines but remains too big to explain the drop.

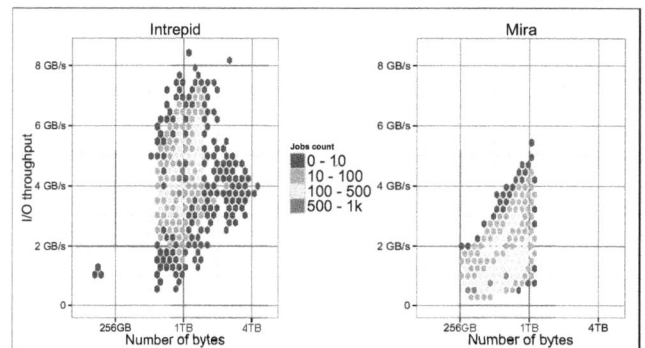

Figure 23: Earth1's jobs, broken down by data size and I/O throughput, on Intrepid (left) and Mira (right).

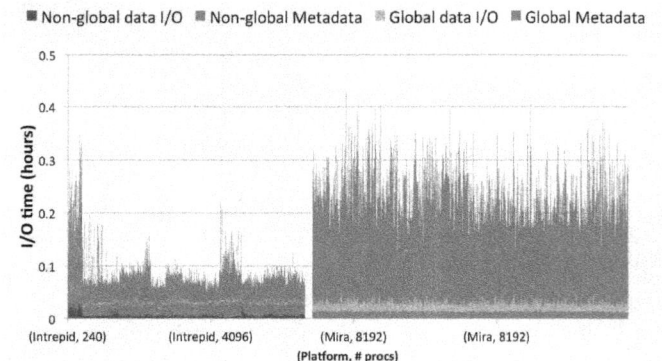

Figure 24: Earth1 jobs' I/O time on Intrepid (l) and Mira (r).

As shown in Figure 24, Earth1's main Mira bottleneck is metadata activity for global files. As discussed earlier, Earth1 uses POSIX to write to global shared files. Earth1's jobs on Mira use more processes, which are packed more tightly into nodes than on Intrepid. With more processes and less total data, request sizes drop. Tighter packing, more processes issuing requests, and smaller requests all increase contention, and throughput drops.

Case study 2: The "Crossplat1" physics code is the rightmost app in Figure 22. Figure 25 shows that in general, Crossplat1 scales well with increasing data on Mira and Edison, and with more processes on Edison. On Intrepid, Crossplat1 rarely exceeded 1 GB/s throughput.

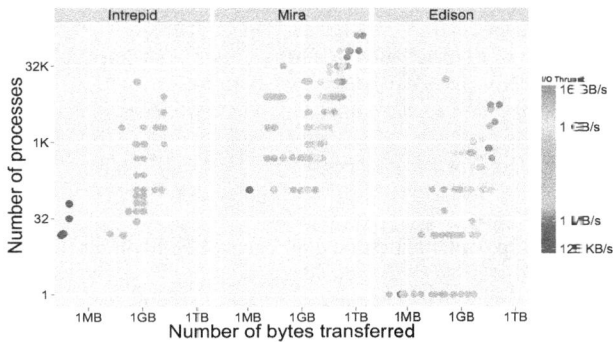

Figure 25: I/O throughput, data size, and number of processes for each of Crossplat1's jobs on three platforms.

We applied the three-step app-specific analysis procedure to Crossplat1 on Mira and Edison, and found that most I/O time was spent in non-global I/O of a number of local POSIX read/write files (*#lPrwf* for short). Figure 26 depicts this for Mira, with jobs sorted by #lPrwf. The log-scale right-hand y-axis is for the overlay variables: I/O throughput, total bytes and #lPrwf. For a fixed #lPrwf, I/O throughput increases nicely with data size. But when #lPrwf is 512 or more, metadata costs shoot up (tall red bars). This suggests that limiting #lPrwf may improve throughput for Crossplat1 on Mira. Crossplat1's behavior on Edison was similar (graph omitted) except that #lPrwf did not exceed 256, so metadata costs remained modest in almost all jobs on Edison.

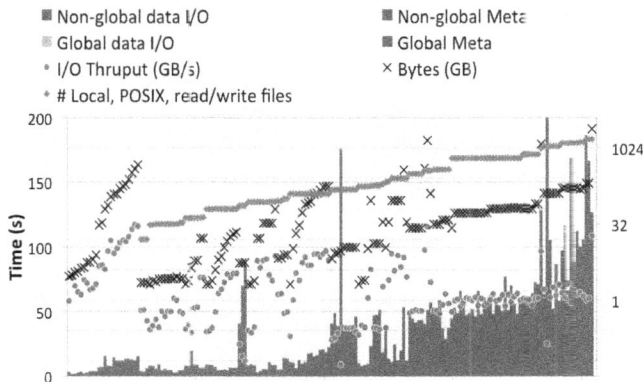

Figure 26: I/O time and throughput (green dot), bytes accessed (black X) and number of local POSIX read/write files (red diamond) for each of Crossplat1's jobs on Mira.

Case study 3: Weather1 is the ninth app in Figure 22 and a big-time app on Edison and Intrepid. Weather1 has few Mira runs, and we do not consider them here. Figure 27 shows that Weather1's I/O throughput was consistently low on Intrepid, but as high as 48 GB/s on Edison. The scaling pattern is unclear.

In Figure 28, each Weather1 job on Intrepid is represented by a vertical bar whose colors give a breakdown of the job's total I/O time (left-hand y-axis). The figure also shows each job's I/O throughput (black X), number of processes (yellow dot) and data size (blue plus) on the log-scale right-hand y-axis. The jobs are sorted by data size. Different I/O paradigms were used by different users, visible in the figure as four distinct blocks of

colors. Weather1 spent most of its I/O time in MPI global shared files and never reached 1 GB/s of throughput under any paradigm, even when accessing over 1 TB of data.

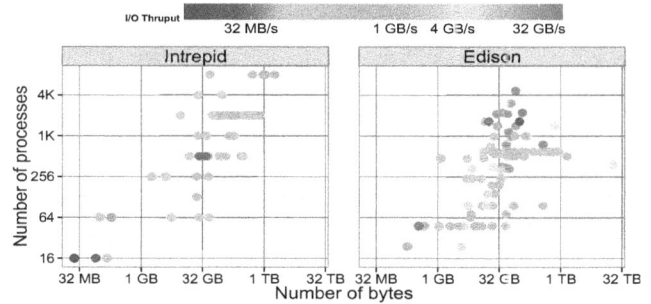

Figure 27: Breakdown of Weather1's jobs by I/O throughput, number of processes, total data size, and platform.

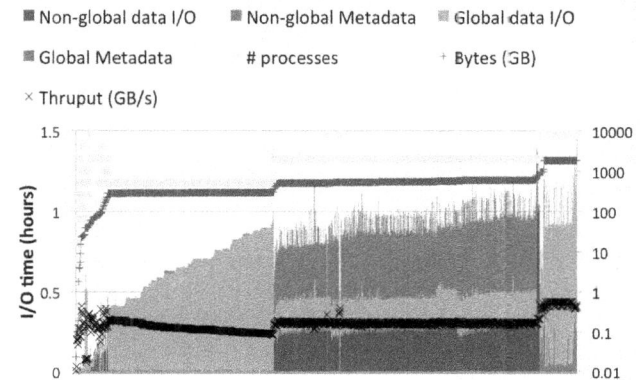

Figure 28: I/O time breakdown of Weather1 jobs on Intrepid.

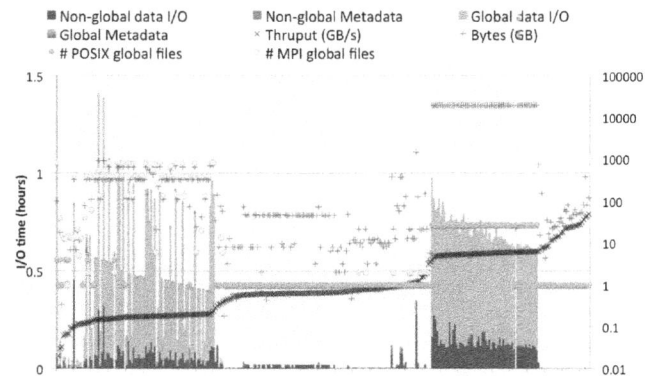

Figure 29: I/O time breakdown of Weather1 jobs on Edison.

Weather1 fares better on Edison, where a third of the jobs exceed 1 GB/s throughput, as shown in Figure 29 with jobs sorted by I/O throughput (black X). The figure also shows each job's data size (blue plus), number of POSIX global files (orange dot) and number of MPI global files (yellow dot) on the log-scale right-hand y-axis. Here, Weather1 jobs fall into three groups. The first group uses MPI-IO global shared files and has consistently low throughput (<0.2 GB/s). The second group uses local files and more modest data sizes (always under 1 TB) and throughput closely tracks data size, reaching as high as ~48 GB/s. The third group of jobs has extremely large data (over 10 TB), and uses POSIX global files; these jobs attain 3-6 GB/s. Darshan does not observe whether jobs tune Lustre parameter settings, but it is worth noting that these results are in line with others' observations that the default settings on Lustre lead to low MPI-IO performance [24], and that the local file I/O paradigm tends to perform relatively well on Edison.

5. CONCLUSIONS AND FUTURE WORK

Efficient I/O performance is a critical part of modern supercomputing. Lightweight tools such as Darshan can augment traditional benchmarking and tracing tools, and provide an overall understanding of the I/O behavior of apps, workloads, and platforms. This paper used Darshan I/O logs to provide a broad view of I/O behavior on three leading HPC platforms. Our results lead us to believe that while tremendous progress has been made in hardware and software research for HPC I/O, gaps remain in the adoption of best practices by scientific application developers. For instance, strategies such as usage of text files and raw, low-level POSIX I/O calls will be untenable on future platforms; adoption of higher-level I/O libraries can help increase the longevity of codes on future generations of supercomputers. HPC I/O specialists need to ensure that app developers understand the tradeoffs in different ways of performing I/O, perhaps through I/O boot camps and tutorials offered in cooperation with platform owners. Our results also lead us to believe that while much research effort is invested in extreme-scale testing and optimization, a large fraction of the HPC community has modest-scale metadata and data challenges; designers of HPC facilities must take these needs into account when designing and provisioning I/O resources. We believe that tools such as Darshan can give platform owners critical insights into system utilization; early and proactive intervention into suboptimal I/O behavior can greatly enhance the utilization of a platform's HPC resources.

Acknowledgments. We thank our application and platform owners and users for helpful discussions. This work was supported by NSF 0938064 and the U.S. Department of Energy, Office of Science, Advanced Scientific Computer Research, under contracts DE-AC02-06CH11357 and DE-AC02-05CH11231; the work used resources from ALCF and NERSC.

REFERENCES

[1] P. Carns, K. Harms, W. Allcock, C. Bacon, S. Lang, R. Latham, R. Ross, Understanding and improving computational science storage access through continuous characterization, ACM Trans. on Storage, 7(3):8, 2011.

[2] Fastest USB Thumb Drive, 14 February 2014. http://www.maximumpc.com/fast_usb_thumb_drive_2014.

[3] B. K. Pasquale, G. C. Polyzos, A static analysis of I/O characteristics of scientific applications in a production workload, Supercomputing, 1993.

[4] N. Nieuwejaar, D. Kotz, A. Purakayastha, C. S. Ellis, M. L. Best, File-access characteristics of parallel scientific workloads, IEEE Transactions on Parallel and Distributed Systems 7(10):1075–1089, Oct. 1996.

[5] F. Wang, Q. Xin, B. Hong, S. A. Brandt, E.L. Miller, D.D.E. Long, T. McLarty, File system workload analysis for large scale scientific computing applications, IEEE Conference on Mass Storage Systems and Technologies, 2005.

[6] S. Saini, D. Talcott, R. Thakur, P. Adamidis, R. Rabenseif-ner, R. Ciotti, Parallel I/O performance characterization of Columbia and NEC SX-8 superclusters, IPDPS, 2007.

[7] Y. Kim, R. Gunasekaran, G. M. Shipman, D.A. Dillow, Z. Zhang, B.W. Settlemyer, Workload characterization of a leadership class storage cluster, 5th Petascale Data Storage Workshop, 2010.

[8] S. Saini, J. Rappleye, J. Chang, D. Barker, P. Mehrotra, R. Biswas, I/O performance characterization of Lustre and NASA applications on Pleiades, HiPC, 2010.

[9] Darshan-util installation and usage, http://www.mcs.anl.gov/research/projects/darshan/docs/darshan-util.html.

[10] P. Carns, Y. Yao, K. Harms, R. Latham, R. Ross, K. Antypas, Production I/O characterization on the Cray XE6, Cray User Group Meeting, 2013.

[11] FLASH: http://www.flash.uchicago.edu/site/

[12] GCRM: https://svn.pnl.gov/gcrm

[13] Nek: http://nek5000.mcs.anl.gov/index.php/Main_Page

[14] CESM: http://www2.cesm.ucar.edu/

[15] S. A. Wright, S. D. Hammond, S. J. Pennycook, R. F. Bird, J. A. Herdman, I Miller, A. Vadgama, A. H. Bhalerao, S. A. Jarvis, Parallel File System Analysis Through Application I/O Tracing, http://eprints.dcs.warwick.ac.uk/1582/The Computer Journal, 56 (2), 2013.

[16] K. Vijayakumar, F. Mueller, X. Ma, and P. C. Roth, Scalable I/O tracing and analysis, Parallel Data Storage Workshop, 2009.

[17] M. P. Mesnier, M. Wachs, R.R. Sambasivan, J. Lopez, J. Hendricks, G. R. Ganger, D. O'Hallaron, //TRACE: Parallel trace replay with approximate causal events, File and Storage Technologies, 2007.

[18] N. J. Wright, W. Pfeiffer, A. Snavely, Characterizing parallel scaling of scientific applications using IPM, LCI International Conference on High-Performance Clustered Computing, 2009.

[19] LANL-Trace: http://institutes.lanl.gov/data/software/index.php#lanl-trace

[20] A. Aranya, C. P. Wright, E. Zadok, TraceFS: A file system to trace them all, File and Storage Technologies, 2004.

[21] H.V.T. Luu, B. Behzad, R. Aydt, M. Winslett, A multi-level approach for understanding I/O activity in HPC applications, Workshop on Interfaces and Abstractions for Scientific Data Storage, 2013.

[22] S. Langer, B. Still, D. Hinkel, B. Langdon, E. Williams, A pF3D case study of obtaining good I/O performance while running on over 100,000 processors, http://visitbugs.ornl.gov/attachments/43/Langer-pf3d-IO-study-Mar2011-final1.pdf

[23] P. Carns, R. Latham, R. Ross, K. Iskra, S. Lang, K. Riley, 24/7 characterization of petascale I/O workloads. IEEE CLUSTER, 2009.

[24] B. Behzad, S. Byna, S. M. Wild, Prabhat, M. Snir. Improving parallel I/O autotuning with performance modeling. High-performance Parallel and Distributed Computing, 2014.

[25] V. Anantharaj, F. Foertter, W. Joubert, J. Wells, Approaching exascale: Application requirements for OLCF leadership computing, Oak Ridge National Laboratory, July 2013. https://www.olcf.ornl.gov/wp-content/uploads/2013/01/OLCF_Requirements_TM_2013_Final1.pdf

[26] Hongzhang Shan, Katie Antypas, and John Shalf. Characterizing and predicting the I/O performance of HPC applications using a parameterized synthetic benchmark. In Proceedings of the 2008 ACM/IEEE conference on Supercomputing (SC), 2008.

CAST: Tiering Storage for Data Analytics in the Cloud

Yue Cheng*, M. Safdar Iqbal*, Aayush Gupta†, Ali R. Butt*

*Virginia Tech; †IBM Research – Almaden

{yuec,safdar,butta}@cs.vt.edu, {guptaaa}@us.ibm.com

ABSTRACT

Enterprises are increasingly moving their big data analytics to the cloud with the goal of reducing costs without sacrificing application performance. Cloud service providers offer their tenants a myriad of storage options, which while flexible, makes the choice of storage deployment not trivial. Crafting deployment scenarios to leverage these choices in a cost-effective manner — under the unique pricing models and multi-tenancy dynamics of the cloud environment — presents unique challenges in designing cloud-based data analytics frameworks.

In this paper, we propose CAST, a Cloud Analytics Storage Tiering solution that cloud tenants can use to reduce monetary cost and improve performance of analytics workloads. The approach takes the first step towards providing storage tiering support for data analytics in the cloud. CAST performs offline workload profiling to construct job performance prediction models on different cloud storage services, and combines these models with workload specifications and high-level tenant goals to generate a cost-effective data placement and storage provisioning plan. Furthermore, we build CAST++ to enhance CAST's optimization model by incorporating data reuse patterns and across-jobs interdependencies common in realistic analytics workloads. Tests with production workload traces from Facebook and a 400-core Google Cloud based Hadoop cluster demonstrate that CAST++ achieves 1.21× performance and reduces deployment costs by 51.4% compared to local storage configuration.

Categories and Subject Descriptors

D.4.2 [**Operating Systems**]: Storage Management—*Allocation/deallocation strategies*; D.4.8 [**Operating Systems**]: Performance—*Modeling and prediction*

Keywords

Cloud computing; MapReduce; Big data analytics; Storage tiering

Storage type	Capacity (GB/volume)	Throughput (MB/sec)	IOPS (4KB)	Cost ($/month)
ephSSD	375	733	100,000	0.218×375
persSSD	100	48	3,000	0.17×100
	250	118	7,500	0.17×250
	500	234	15,000	0.17×500
persHDD	100	20	150	0.04×100
	250	45	375	0.04×250
	500	97	750	0.04×500
objStore	N/A	265	550	0.026/GB

Table 1: Google Cloud storage details. `ephSSD`, `persSSD`, `persHDD` and `objStore` represent VM-local ephemeral SSD, network-attached persistent SSD and HDD, and Google Cloud object storage, respectively. The performance of `persSSD` and `persHDD` scale with volume capacity, whereas `ephSSD` volumes are multiples of 375 GB with a maximum of 4 volumes per VM. Tenants can provision `persSSD` and `persHDD` with a per-volume capacity of up to 10, 240 GB. `objStore` has no storage capacity limit. I/O performance of the local and network-attached block volumes is measured using `fio` and the performance of `objStore` is measured using `gsutil`. All the measured performance numbers match the information provided on [6] (as of Jan. 14, 2015).

1. INTRODUCTION

The cloud computing paradigm provides powerful computation capabilities, high scalability and resource elasticity at reduced operational and administration costs. The use of cloud resources frees tenants from the traditionally cumbersome IT infrastructure planning and maintenance, and allows them to focus on application development and optimal resource deployment. These desirable features coupled with the advances in virtualization infrastructure are driving the adoption of public, private, and hybrid clouds for not only web applications, such as Netflix, Instagram and Airbnb, but also modern big data analytics using parallel programming paradigms such as Hadoop [2] and Dryad [26]. Cloud providers such as Amazon Web Services, Google Cloud, and Microsoft Azure, have started providing data analytics platform as a service [1, 8, 12], which is being adopted widely.

With the improvement in network connectivity and emergence of new data sources such as Internet of Things (IoT) endpoints, mobile platforms, and wearable devices, enterprise-scale data-intensive analytics now involves terabyte- to petabyte-scale data with more data being generated from these sources constantly. Thus, storage allocation and management would play a key role in overall performance improvement and cost reduction for this domain.

While cloud makes data analytics easy to deploy and scale, the vast variety of available storage services with different persistence, performance and capacity characteristics, presents unique challenges for deploying big data analytics in the cloud. For example, Google Cloud Platform provides four different storage options as listed in Table 1. While `ephSSD` offers the highest sequential and random I/O performance, it does not provide data persistence (data stored in `ephSSD` is lost once the associated VMs are terminated). Network-attached persistent block storage services using `persHDD` or `persSSD` as storage media are relatively cheaper than `ephSSD`, but offer significantly lower performance. For instance, a 500 GB `persSSD` volume has about $2\times$ lower throughput and $6\times$ lower IOPS than a 375 GB `ephSSD` volume. Finally, `objStore` is a RESTful object storage service providing the cheapest storage alternative and offering comparable sequential throughput to that of a large `persSSD` volume. Other cloud service providers such as AWS EC2 [5], Microsoft Azure [4], and HP Cloud [10], provide similar storage services with different performance–cost trade-offs.

The heterogeneity in cloud storage services is further complicated by the varying types of jobs within analytics workloads, e.g., iterative applications such as `KMeans` and `Pagerank`, and queries such as `Join` and `Aggregate`. For example, in map-intensive `Grep`, the map phase accounts for the largest part of the execution time (mostly doing I/Os), whereas CPU-intensive `KMeans` spends most of the time performing computation. Furthermore, short-term (within hours) and long-term (daily, weekly or monthly) data reuse across jobs is common in production analytics workloads [18, 15]. As reported in [18], 78% of jobs in Cloudera Hadoop workloads involve data reuse. Another distinguishing feature of analytics workloads is the presence of workflows that represents interdependencies across jobs. For instance, analytics queries are usually converted to a series of batch processing jobs, where the output of one job serves as the input of the next job(s).

The above observations lead to an important question for the cloud tenants *How do I (the tenant) get the most bang-for-the-buck with data analytics storage tiering/data placement in a cloud environment with highly heterogeneous storage resources?* To answer this question, this paper conducts a detailed quantitative analysis with a range of representative analytics jobs in the widely used Google Cloud environment. The experimental findings and observations motivate the design of CAST, which leverages different cloud storage services and heterogeneity within jobs in an analytics workload to perform cost-effective storage capacity allocation and data placement.

CAST does offline profiling of different applications (jobs) within an analytics workload and generates job performance prediction models based on different storage services. It lets tenants specify high-level objectives such as maximizing tenant utility, or minimizing deadline miss rate. CAST then uses a simulated annealing based solver that reconciles these objectives with the performance prediction models, other workload specifications and the different cloud storage service characteristics to generate a data placement and storage provisioning plan. The framework finally deploys the workload in the cloud based on the generated plan. We further enhance our basic tiering design to build CAST++, which incorporates the data reuse and workflow properties of an analytics workload.

Specifically, we make the following contributions in this paper:

1. We employ a detailed experimental study and show, using both qualitative and quantitative approaches, that extant hot/cold data based storage tiering approaches cannot be simply applied to data analytics storage tiering in the cloud.

2. We present a detailed cost-efficiency analysis of analytics workloads and workflows in a real public cloud environment. Our findings indicate the need to carefully evaluate the various storage placement and design choices, which we do, and redesign analytics storage tiering mechanisms that are specialized for the public cloud.

3. Based on the behavior analysis of analytics applications in the cloud, we design CAST, an analytics storage tiering management framework based on simulated annealing algorithm, which searches the analytics workload tiering solution space and *effectively meets* customers' goals. Moreover, CAST's solver *succeeds in discovering non-trivial opportunities* for both performance improvement and cost savings.

4. We extend our basic optimization solver to CAST++ that considers data reuse patterns and job dependencies. CAST++ supports cross-tier workflow optimization using directed acyclic graph (DAG) traversal.

5. We evaluate our tiering solver on a 400-core cloud cluster (Google Cloud) using production workload traces from Facebook. We demonstrate that, compared to a greedy algorithm approach and a series of key storage configurations, CAST++ improves tenant utility by $52.9\% - 211.8\%$, while effectively meeting the workflow deadlines.

2. BACKGROUND AND RELATED WORK

In the following, we provide a brief background of storage tiering, and categorize and compare previous work with our research.

Hot/Cold Data Classification-based Tiering Recent research [28, 34, 43] has focused on improving storage cost and utilization efficiency by placing hot/cold data in different storage tiers. Guerra et. al.[22] builds an SSD-based dynamic tiering system to minimize cost and power consumption, and existing works handle file system and block level I/Os (e.g., $4 - 32$ KB) for POSIX-style workloads (e.g., server, database, file systems, etc.). However, the cost model and tiering mechanism used in prior approaches cannot be directly applied to analytics batch processing applications running in a public cloud environment, mainly due to cloud storage and analytics workload heterogeneity. In contrast, our work provides insights into design of a tiered storage management framework for cloud-based data analytics workloads.

Fine-Grained Tiering for Analytics Storage tiering has been studied in the context of data-intensive analytics batch applications. Recent analysis [23] demonstrates that adding a flash tier for serving reads is beneficial for HDFS-based HBase workloads with random I/Os. As opposed to HBase I/O characteristics, typical MapReduce-like batch jobs issues large, sequential I/Os [40] and run in multiple stages (map, shuffle, reduce). Hence, lessons learned from HBase tiering are not directly applicable to such analytics workloads. hatS [31] and open source Hadoop community [9] have taken the first steps towards integrating heterogeneous storage devices in HDFS for local clusters. However, the absence of task-level tier-aware scheduling mechanisms implies that these HDFS block granularity tiering approaches cannot avoid stragglers within a job, thus achieving limited performance gains if any. PACMan [15] solves this slow-tier straggler problem by using a memory caching policy for small jobs whose footprint can fit in the memory of the cluster. Such caching approaches are complementary to CAST as it provides a coarse-grained, static data placement solution for a complete analytics workload in different cloud storage services.

Cloud Resource Provisioning Considerable prior work has examined ways to automate resource configuration and provisioning process in the cloud. Frugal Cloud File System (FCFS) [39] is a cost-effective cloud-based file storage that spans multiple cloud storage services. In contrast to POSIX file system workloads, modern analytics jobs (focus of our study) running on parallel programming frameworks like Hadoop demonstrate very different access characteristics and data dependencies (described in Section 3); requiring a rethink of how storage tiering is done to benefit these workloads. Other works such as Bazaar [27] and Conductor [44], focus on automating cloud resource deployment to meet cloud tenants' requirements while reducing deployment cost. Our work takes a thematically similar view — exploring the trade-offs of cloud services — but with a different scope that targets data analytics workloads and leverages their unique characteristics to provide storage tiering. Several systems [14, 37] are specifically designed to tackle flash storage allocation inefficiency in virtualization platforms. In contrast, we explore the inherent performance and cost trade-off of different storage services in public cloud environments.

Analytics Workflow Optimization A large body of research [45, 35, 21, 36, 33] focuses on Hadoop workflow optimizations by integrating workflow-aware scheduler into Hadoop or interfacing Hadoop with a standalone workflow scheduler. Our workflow enhancement is orthogonal and complements these works as well — CAST++ exploits cloud storage heterogeneity and performance scaling property, and uses opportunities for efficient data placement across different cloud storage services to improve workflow execution. Workflow-aware job schedulers can leverage the data placement strategy of CAST++ to further improve analytics workload performance.

3. A CASE FOR CLOUD STORAGE TIERING

In this section, we first establish the need for cloud storage tiering for data analytics workloads. To this end, we characterize the properties of applications that form a typical analytics workload and demonstrate the impact of these properties on the choice of cloud storage services. We then argue that extant tiering techniques, such as hot/cold data based segregation and fine-grained partitioning within a single job, are not adequate; *rather a course-grained, job-level storage service tiering is needed for cloud-based data analytics.*

App.	I/O-intensive			CPU-intensive
	Map	Shuffle	Reduce	
Sort	✗	✓	✗	✗
Join	✗	✓	✓	✗
Grep	✓	✗	✗	✗
KMeans	✗	✗	✗	✓

Table 2: Characteristics of studied applications.

3.1 Characterization of Data Analytics Workloads

We characterize the analytics workloads along two dimensions. First, we study the behavior of individual applications within a large workload when executed on parallel programming paradigms such as MapReduce — demonstrating the benefits of different storage services for various applications. Second, we consider the role of cross-job relationships (an analytics workload comprises multiple jobs each executing an application) and show how these interactions affect the choice of efficient data placement decisions for the same applications.

3.1.1 Experimental Study Setup

We select four representative analytics applications that are typical components of real-world analytics workloads [18, 46] and exhibit diversified I/O and computation characteristics, as listed in Table 2. Sort, Join and Grep are I/O-intensive applications. The execution time of Sort is dominated by the shuffle phase I/O, transferring data between mappers and reducers. In contrast, Grep spends most of its runtime in the map phase I/O, reading the input and finding records that match given patterns. Join represents an analytics query that combines rows from multiple tables and performs the join operation during the reduce phase, and thus is reduce intensive. KMeans is an iterative machine learning clustering application that spends most of its time in the compute phases of map and reduce iterations, which makes it CPU-intensive.

The experiments are performed in Google Cloud using a n1-standard-16 VM (16 vCPUs, 60 GB memory) with the master node on a n1-standard-4 VM (4 vCPUs, 15 GB memory). Intermediate data is stored on the same storage service as the original data, except for objStore, where we use persSSD for intermediate storage. Unless otherwise stated, all experiments in this section are conducted using the same compute resources but with different storage configurations as stated.

3.1.2 Analysis: Application Granularity

Figure 1 depicts both the execution time of the studied applications and tenant utility for different choices of storage services. We define *tenant utility* (or simply "utility," used interchangeably) to be $\frac{1/execution\ time}{cost\ in\ dollars}$. This utility metric is based on the tenants' economic constraints when deploying general workloads in the cloud. Figure 1 (a) shows that ephSSD serves as the best tier for both execution time and utility for Sort even after accounting for the data transfer cost for both upload and download from objStore. This is because there is no data reduction in the map phase and the entire input size is written to intermediate files residing on ephSSD that has about 2× higher sequential bandwidth than persSSD. Thus, we get better utility from ephSSD than

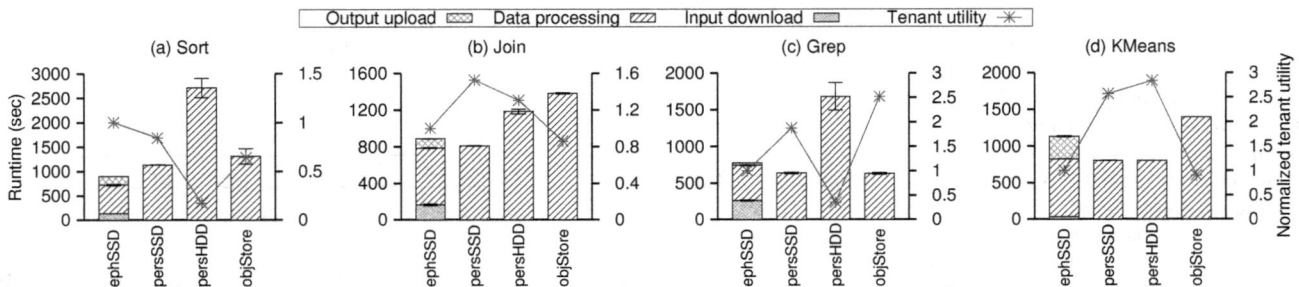

Figure 1: Application performance and achieved tenant utility on different cloud storage tiers. `ephSSD` does not offer persistence, so we account for data transfer time (i.e., input download time from `objStore` and output upload time to `objStore`) and break down the `ephSSD` runtime into three parts. Applications that run on `ephSSD` incur storage cost that includes both the cost of `ephSSD` and `objStore`. Applications that run on `objStore` require either a local ephemeral disk or network-attached persistent disk for storing intermediate data. For this set of experiments, we used a 100 GB `persSSD` as intermediate data store. Each bar represents the average from three runs. Tenant utility is normalized to that of `ephSSD`.

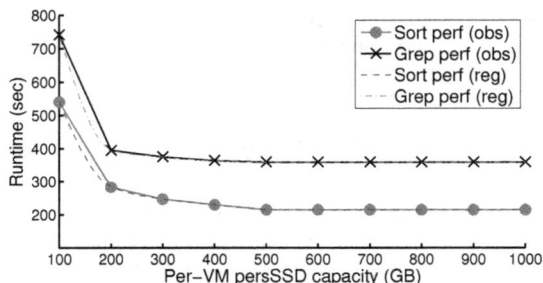

Figure 2: Impact of scaling `persSSD` volume capacity for `Sort` and `Grep`. The regression model is used in CAST's tiering approach and is described in detail in §4. These tests are conducted on a 10-VM `n1-standard-16` cluster.

`persSSD`, albeit at a slightly higher cost. On the other hand, Figure 1 (b) shows that, `Join` works best with `persSSD`, while it achieves the worst utility on `objStore`. This is due to high overheads of setting up connections to request data transfers using the Google Cloud Storage Connector (GCS connector) for Hadoop APIs [7] for the many small files generated by the involved reduce tasks. `Grep`'s map-intensive feature dictates that its performance solely depends on sequential I/O throughput of the storage during the map phase. Thus, in Figure 1 (c) we observe that both `persSSD` and `objStore` provide similar performance (both have similar sequential bandwidth as seen in Table 1) but the lower cost of `objStore` results in about 34.3% higher utility than `persSSD`. Similarly, for the CPU-bound `KMeans`, while `persSSD` and `persHDD` provide similar performance, the lower cost of `persHDD` yields much better utility as shown in Figure 1 (d).

Performance Scaling In Google Cloud, performance of network-attached block storage depends on the size of the volume, as shown in Table 1. Other clouds such as Amazon AWS offer different behavior but typically the block storage performance in these clouds can be scaled by creating logical volumes by striping (RAID-0) across multiple network-attached block volumes. In Figure 2, we study the impact of this capacity scaling on the execution time of two I/O-intensive applications, `Sort` and `Grep` (we also observe similar patterns for other I/O-intensive applications). For a network-attached `persSSD` volume, the dataset size of `Sort` is 100 GB and that of `Grep` is 300 GB. We observe that as the volume capacity increases from 100 GB to 200 GB, the run

time of both `Sort` and `Grep` is reduced by 51.6% and 60.2%, respectively. Any further increase in capacity offers marginal benefits. This happens because in both these applications the I/O bandwidth bottleneck is alleviated when the capacity is increased to 200 GB. Beyond that, the execution time is dependent on other parts of the MapReduce framework. These observations imply that it is possible to achieve desired application performance in the cloud without resorting to unnecessarily over-provisioning of the storage and thus within acceptable cost.

Key Insights From our experiments, we infer the following. (i) There is no one storage service that provides the best raw performance as well as utility for different data analytics applications. (ii) For some applications, slower storage services, such as `persHDD`, may provide better utility and comparable performance to other costlier alternatives. (iii) Elasticity and scalability of cloud storage services should be leveraged through careful over-provisioning of capacity to reduce performance bottlenecks in I/O intensive analytics applications.

3.1.3 Analysis: Workload Granularity

We next study the impact of cross-job interactions within an analytics workload. While individual job-level optimization and tiering has been the major focus of a number of recent works [31, 32, 44, 25, 24, 17], we argue that this is not sufficient for data placement in the cloud for analytics workloads. To this end, we analyze two typical workload characteristics that have been reported in production workloads [18, 15, 38, 23, 19], namely data reuse across jobs, and dependency between jobs, i.e., workflows, within a workload.

Data Reuse across Jobs As reported in the analysis of production workloads from Facebook and Microsoft Bing [18, 15], both small and large jobs exhibit data re-access patterns both in the short term, i.e., input data shared by multiple jobs and reused for a few hours before becoming cold, as well as in the long term, i.e., input data reused for longer periods such as days or weeks before turning cold. Henceforth, we refer to the former as reuse-lifetime (short) and the later as reuse-lifetime (long).

To better understand how data reuse affects data placement choices, we evaluate the tenant utility of each application under different reuse patterns. Figure 3 shows that the choice of storage service changes based on data reuse patterns for different applications. Note that in both reuse

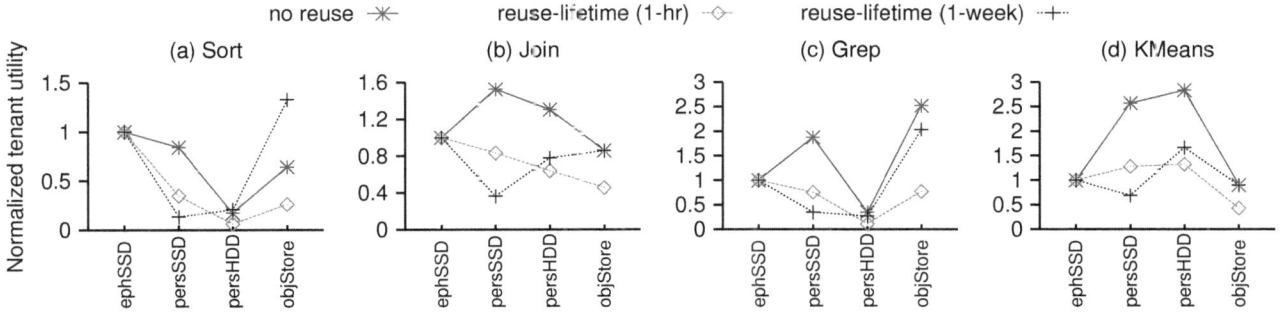

Figure 3: Tenant utility under different data reuse patterns. `reuse-lifetime (1 hr)` represents re-accesses of the same data over a period of 1 hour and `reuse-lifetime (1 week)` represents data re-accesses over 1 week. Tenant utility is normalized to that of `ephSSD`.

cases we perform the same number of re-accesses (i.e , 7) over the specified time period. For instance, in `reuse-lifetime (1 week)`, data is accessed once per day, i.e., 7 accesses in a week. Similarly, data is accessed once every 8 minutes in `reuse-lifetime (1 hr)` [1]. For `ephSSD`, the input download overheads can be amortized by keeping the data in the ephemeral SSD, since the same data will be re-accessed in a very short period of time. This allows `ephSSD` to provide the highest utility for `Join` (Figure 3 (b)) and `Grep` (Figure 3 (c)) for `reuse-lifetime (1 hr)`. However, if the data is re-accessed only once per day (`reuse-lifetime (1 week)`), the cost of `ephSSD` far outweighs the benefits of avoiding input downloads. Thus, for `Sort` (Figure 3 (a)), `objStore` becomes the storage service of choice for `reuse-lifetime (1 week)`. For similar cost reasons, `persSSD`, which demonstrates the highest utility for individual applications (Figure 1 (b)), becomes the worst choice when long term re-accesses are considered. Furthermore, as expected, the behavior of CPU-intensive `KMeans` (Figure 3 (d)) remains the same across reuse patterns with highest utility achieved with `persHDD`, and the storage costs do not play a major role in its performance.

Workflows in an Analytics Workload An analytics workflow consists of a series of jobs with inter-dependencies. For our analysis, we consider the workflows where the output of one job acts as a part of an input of another job. Thus, a workflow can be abstracted as Directed Acyclic Graph (DAGs) of actions [3]. Prior research [33, 35] has shown that not only overall completion times of individual jobs in a workflow an important consideration, but meeting completion time deadlines of workflows is also critical for satisfying Service-Level Objectives (SLOs) of cloud tenants.

Consider the following example to illustrate and support the above use case. Figure 4(a)[2] lists four possible tiering plans for a four-job workflow. The workflow consists of four jobs and represents a typical search engine log analysis. Figure 4(a) (i) and Figure 4(a) (ii) depict cases where a single storage service, `objStore` and `persSSD`, respectively, is used for the entire workflow. As shown in Figure 4(b), the complex nature of the workflow not only makes these two data placement strategies perform poorly (missing a hypothetical deadline of 8,000 seconds) but also results in high costs com-

pared to the other two hybrid storage plans. On the other hand, both the hybrid storage services meet the deadline. Here, the output of one job is pipelined to another storage service where it acts as an input for the subsequent job in the workflow. If the tenant's goal is to pick a strategy that provides the lowest execution time, then the combination `objStore+ephSSD` shown in Figure 4(b) provides the best result amongst the studied plans. However, if the tenant wants to choose a layout that satisfies the dual criteria of meeting the deadline and providing the lowest cost (among the considered plans), then the combination `objStore-ephSSD+persSSD` — that reduces the cost by 7% compared to the other tiering plan — may be a better fit.

Key Insights From this set of experiments, we infer the following. (i) Not only do data analytics workloads require use of different storage services for different applications, the data placement choices also change when data reuse effects are considered. (ii) Complex inter-job requirements in workflows necessitate thinking about use of multiple storage services, where outputs of jobs from a particular storage service may be pipelined to different storage tiers that act as inputs for the next jobs. (iii) Use of multiple criteria by the tenant, such as workflow deadlines and monetary costs, adds more dimensions to a data placement planner and requires careful thinking about tiering strategy.

3.2 Shortcomings of Traditional Storage Tiering Strategies

In this following, we argue that traditional approaches to storage tiering are not adequate for being used for analytics workloads in the cloud.

Heat-based Tiering A straw man tiering approach that considers the monetary cost of different cloud storage mediums is to place hot data on `ephSSD`; semi-hot data on either `persSSD` or `persHDD`; and cold data on the cheapest `objStore`. Heat metrics can include different combinations of access frequencies, recency, etc. But the performance–cost model for cloud storage for analytics workloads is more complicated due to the following reasons. (1) The most expensive cloud storage tier (`ephSSD`) may not be the best tier for hot data, since the ephemeral SSD tier typically provides no persistence guarantee — the VMs have to persist for ensuring that all the data on ephemeral disks stays available, potentially increasing monetary costs. `ephSSD` volumes are fixed in size (Table 1) and only 4 volumes can be attached to a VM. Such constraints can lead to both under-provisioning (requiring

---

[1] While re-access frequency can vary for different reuse-lifetimes, we selected these two cases to highlight the changes in data placement options for the same applications due to different data reuse patterns.

[2] We do not show utility results of `Pagerank` because it exhibits the same behavior as `KMeans` in §3.1.2.

(a) Four possible workflow tiering plans.

(b) Workflow tiering performance-cost trade-offs.

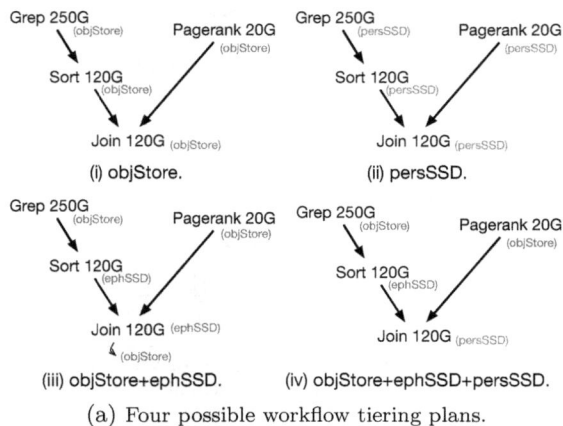

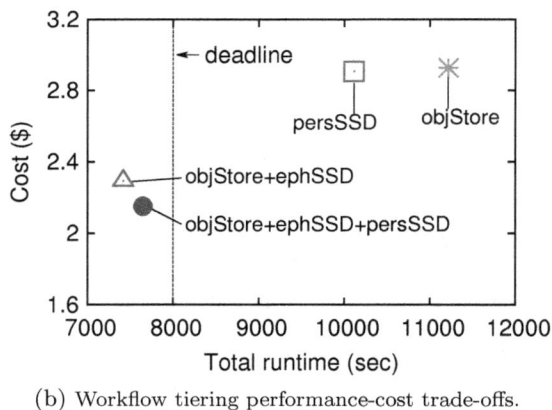

Figure 4: Possible tiering plans for a simple 4-job workflow. Storage medium in parentheses indicates where the input of the job is stored. For instance, `Pagerank 20G (objStore) -> Join 120G (persSSD)` means that the input and intermediate data of job `Pagerank` is stored on `objStore`, and the output is placed on `persSSD` and then consumed by the job `Join` as input. The output of `Pagerank` is 386 MB and consists of `pageIDs`, and hence is not shown being added to the input of `Join`.

more VMs to be started) and over-provisioning (wasting capacity for small datasets), in turn reducing utility. (2) Furthermore, analytics applications may derive better utility from cheaper tiers than their more expensive counterparts.

Fine-Grained Tiering Recently, hatS [31] looked at a tiered HDFS implementation that utilizes both HDDs and SSDs to improve single job performance. Such approaches focus on fine-grained tiering within a single job. While this can be useful for on-premise clusters where storage resources are relatively fixed and capacity of faster storage is limited [23], it provides few benefits for cloud-based analytics workloads where resources can be elastically provisioned. Furthermore, maintaining heat metrics at a fine-grained block or file level may be spatially prohibitive (DRAM requirements) for a big data analytics workload with growing datasets.

We contend that instead of looking at block or file-level partitioning, a more coarse-grained approach that performs job-level tiering, is needed for cloud-based analytics. To illustrate this, in Figure 5 we measure the performance of `Grep` under various placement configurations (using default Hadoop task scheduler and data placement policy) for a 6 GB input dataset requiring 24 map tasks scheduled as a single wave. As shown in Figure 5(a), partitioning data across a faster `ephSSD` and slower `persSSD` tier does not improve performance. The tasks on slower storage media dominate the execution time. We further vary the partitioning by increasing the fraction of input data on faster `ephSSD` (Figure 5(b)). We observe that even if 90% of the data is on the faster tier, the performance of the application does not improve, highlighting the need for job-level data partitioning. Such an "all-or-nothing" [15] data placement policy, i.e., placing the whole input of one job in one tier, is likely to yield good performance. This policy is not only simple to realize, but also maps well to both the characteristics of analytics workloads and elasticity of cloud storage services.

4. CAST FRAMEWORK

We build CAST, an analytics storage tiering framework that exploits heterogeneity of both the cloud storage and analytics workloads to satisfy the various needs of cloud

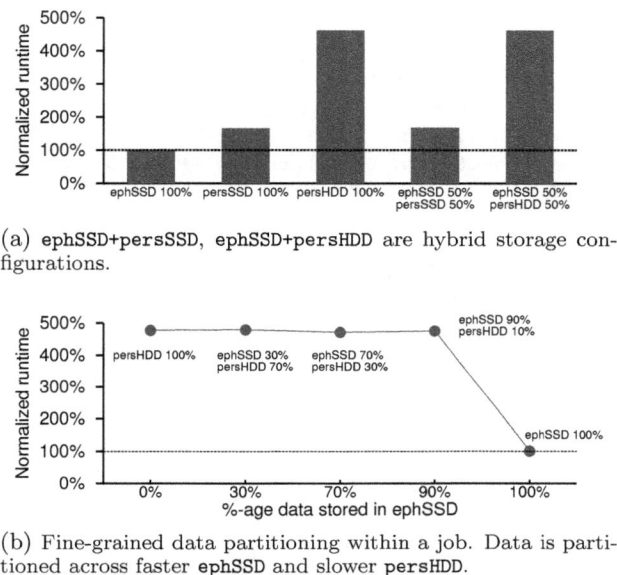

(a) `ephSSD+persSSD`, `ephSSD+persHDD` are hybrid storage configurations.

(b) Fine-grained data partitioning within a job. Data is partitioned across faster `ephSSD` and slower `persHDD`.

Figure 5: Normalized runtime of `Grep` under different HDFS configurations. All runtime numbers are normalized to `ephSSD` 100% performance.

tenants. Furthermore, CAST++, an enhancement to CAST, provides data pattern reuse and workflow awareness based on the underlying analytics framework. Figure 6 shows the high-level overview of CAST operations and involves the following components. (1) The analytics *job performance estimator* module evaluates jobs execution time on different storage services using workload specifications provided by tenants. These specifications include a list of jobs, the application profiles, and the input data sizes for the jobs. The estimator combines this with compute platform information to estimate application run times on different storage services. (2) The *tiering solver* module uses the job execution estimates from the *job performance estimator* to generate a tiering plan that spans all storage tiers on the specific cloud provider available to the tenant. The objective of the solver

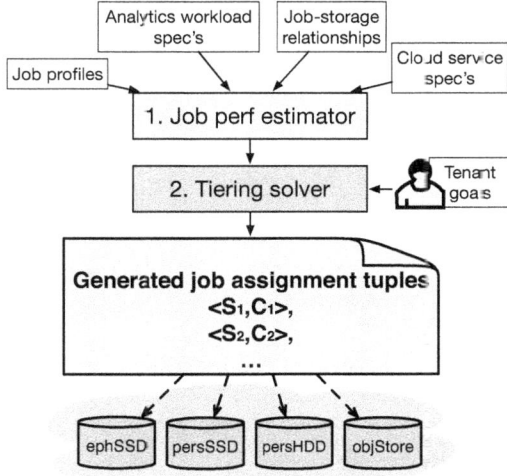

Figure 6: Overview of CAST tiering framework.

is to satisfy the high-level tenants' goals such as achieving high utility or reducing deadline miss rates.

4.1 Estimating Analytics Job Performance

The well-defined execution phases of the MapReduce parallel programming paradigm [20, 27] implies that the runtime characteristics of analytics jobs can be predicted with high accuracy. Moreover, extensive recent research has focused on data analytics performance prediction [42, 25, 24, 13, 41, 27]. We leverage and adapt MRCute [27] model in CAST to predict job execution time, due to its ease-of-use, availability, and applicability to our problem domain.

Equation 1 defines our performance prediction model. It consists of three sub-models — one each for the map, shuffle, and reduce phases — where each phase execution time is modeled as $\#waves \times runtime\ per\ wave$. A *wave* represents the number of tasks that can be scheduled in parallel based on the number of available slots. CAST places all the data of a job on a single storage service with predictable performance, and tasks (within a job) work on equi-sized data chunks. The estimator also models wave pipelining effects — in a typical MapReduce execution flow, the three phases in the same wave are essentially serialized, but different waves can be overlapped. Thus, the prediction model does not sacrifice estimation accuracy. The model simplifies the predictor implementation, which is another advantage of performing coarse-grained, job-level data partitioning.

$$EST\left(\hat{\mathcal{R}}, \hat{\mathcal{M}}(s_i, \hat{\mathcal{L}}_i)\right) = \underbrace{\left[\frac{m}{n_{vm} \cdot m_c}\right]}_{\#\ waves} \cdot \underbrace{\left(\frac{input_i/m}{bw_{map}^{s_i}}\right)}_{Runtime\ per\ wave}$$
$$+ \underbrace{\left[\frac{r}{n_{vm} \cdot r_c}\right] \cdot \left(\frac{inter_i/r}{bw_{shuffle}^{s_i}}\right)}_{shuffle\ phase}$$
$$+ \underbrace{\left[\frac{r}{n_{vm} \cdot r_c}\right] \cdot \left(\frac{output_i/r}{bw_{reduce}^{s_i}}\right)}_{reduce\ phase} . \tag{1}$$

The estimator $EST(.)$ predicts job performance using the information about (i) job configuration: number of map/reduce tasks, job sizes in different phases; (ii) compute configura-

tion: number of VMs, available slots per VM; and (iii) storage services: bandwidth of tasks on a particular storage service. Table 3 lists the notations used in the model.

Notation		Description
$\hat{\mathcal{R}}$	n_{vm}	number of VMs in the cluster
	m_c	number of map slots in one node
	r_c	number of reduce slots in one node
$\hat{\mathcal{M}}$	bw_{map}^f	bandwidth of a single map task on tier f
	$bw_{shuffle}^f$	bandwidth of a single shuffle task on tier f
	bw_{reduce}^f	bandwidth of a single reduce task on tier f
$\hat{\mathcal{L}}_i$	$input_i$	input data size of job i
	$inter_i$	intermediate data size of job i
	$output_i$	output data size of job i
	m	number of map tasks of job i
	r	number of reduce tasks of job i
solver	$capacity$	total capacities of different storage mediums
	$price_{vm}$	VM price (\$/min)
	$price_{store}$	storage price (\$/GB/hr)
	J	set of all analytics jobs in a workload
	J_w	set of all analytics jobs in a workflow w
	F	set of all storage services in the cloud
	D	set of all jobs that share the same data
	$\hat{P}$	tiering solution
decision vars	s_i	storage service used by job i
	c_i	storage capacity provisioned for job i

Table 3: Notations used in the analytics jobs performance prediction model and CAST tiering solver.

4.2 Basic Tiering Solver

The goal of the basic CAST tiering solver is to provide near-optimal specification that can help guide tenant's decisions about data partitioning on the available storage services for their analytics workload(s). The solver uses a simulated annealing algorithm [29] to systematically search through the solution space and find a desirable tiering plan, given the workload specification, analytics models, and tenants' goals.

4.2.1 CAST Solver: Modeling

The data placement and storage provisioning problem is modeled as a non-linear optimization problem that maximizes the tenant utility (U) defined in Equation 2:

$$max\ U = \frac{1/T}{(\$_{vm} + \$_{store})} , \tag{2}$$

$$s.t.\ c_i \geq (input_i + inter_i + output_i)\ (\forall i \in J) , \tag{3}$$

$$T = \sum_{i=1}^{J} REG\left(s_i, capacity[s_i], \hat{\mathcal{R}}, \hat{\mathcal{L}}_i\right), where\ s_i \in F , \tag{4}$$

$$\$_{vm} = n_{vm} \cdot (price_{vm} \cdot T) , \tag{5}$$

$$\$_{store} = \sum_{f=1}^{F} \left(capacity[f] \cdot \left(price_{store}[f] \cdot \lceil T/60 \rceil\right)\right) \tag{6}$$

$$where\ \forall f \in F : \left\{\forall i \in J,\ s.t.\ s_i \equiv f : capacity[f] = \sum c_i\right\} .$$

The performance is modeled as the *reciprocal* of the estimated completion time in minutes ($1/T$) and the costs include both the VM and storage costs. The VM cost[3] is defined by Equation 5 and depends on the total completion time of the workload. The cost of each storage service is determined by the workload completion time (storage cost is

---

[3] We only consider a single VM type since we focus on storage tiering. Extending the model to incorporate heterogeneous VM types is part of our future work.

charged on a hourly basis) and capacity provisioned for that service. The overall storage cost is obtained by aggregating the individual costs of each service (Equation 6).

Equation 3 defines the *capacity constraint*, which ensures that the storage capacity (c_i) provisioned for a job is sufficient to meet its requirements for all the phases (map, shuffle, reduce). We also consider intermediate data when determining aggregated capacity. For jobs, e.g., Sort, which have a selectivity factor of one, the intermediate data is of the same size as the input data. Others, such as inverted indexing, would require a large capacity for storing intermediate data as significant larger shuffle data is generated during the map phase [16]. The generic Equation 3 accounts for all such scenarios and guarantees that the workload will not fail. Given a specific tiering solution, the estimated total completion time of the workload is defined by Equation 4. Since job performance in the cloud scales with capacity of some services, we use a regression model, $REG(s_i, .)$, to estimate the execution time. In every iteration of the solver, the regression function uses the storage service (s_i) assigned to a job in that iteration, the total provisioned capacity of that service for the entire workload, cluster information such as number of VMs and the estimated runtime based on Equation 1 as parameters. After carefully considering multiple regression models, we find that a third degree polynomial-based cubic Hermite spline [30] is a good fit for the applications and storage services considered in the paper. While we do not delve into details about the model, we show the accuracy of the splines in Figure 2. We also evaluate the accuracy of this regression model using a small workload in §5.1.

4.2.2 CAST Solver: Algorithms

Algorithm 1: Greedy static tiering algorithm.

Input: Job information matrix: $\hat{\mathcal{L}}$,
Output: Tiering plan $\hat{P}_{greedy}$
begin
    $\hat{P}_{greedy} \leftarrow \{\}$
    foreach *job j in $\hat{\mathcal{L}}$* **do**
        $f_{best} \leftarrow f_1$ // f_1 represents the first of the
                               // available storage services in F
        foreach *storage service f_{curr} in F* **do**
            if $Utility(j, f_{curr}) > Utility(j, f_{best})$ **then**
                $f_{best} \leftarrow f_{curr}$
        $\hat{P}_{greedy} \leftarrow \hat{P}_{greedy} \cup \{ \langle j, f_{best} \rangle\}$
    return $\hat{P}_{greedy}$

Greedy Algorithm We first attempt to perform data partitioning and placement using a simple greedy algorithm (Algorithm 1). The algorithm takes the job information matrix J as the input and generates a tiering plan as follows. For each job in the workload, the utility (calculated using function $Utility(.)$) is computed using Equation 1 and Equation 2 on each storage service. The tier that offers the highest utility is assigned to the job. As astute readers will observe, while this algorithm is straightforward to reason about and implement, it does not consider the impact of placement on other jobs in the workload. Furthermore, as we greedily make placement decisions on a per-job basis, the total provisioned capacity on a tier increases. Recall that the performance of some storage services scales with capacity. Thus, the tiering decisions for some jobs (for which placement has already been done) may no longer provide maximum utility. We evaluate the impact of these localized greedy decisions in §5.1.

Algorithm 2: Simulated Annealing Algorithm.

Input: Job information matrix: $\hat{\mathcal{L}}$,
           Analytics job model matrix: $\hat{\mathcal{M}}$,
           Runtime configuration: $\hat{\mathcal{R}}$,
           Initial solution: $\hat{P}_{init}$.
Output: Tiering plan $\hat{P}_{best}$
begin
    $\hat{P}_{best} \leftarrow \{\}$
    $\hat{P}_{curr} \leftarrow \hat{P}_{init}$
    $exit \leftarrow False$
    $iter \leftarrow 1$
    $temp_{curr} \leftarrow temp_{init}$
    $U_{curr} \leftarrow Utility(\hat{\mathcal{M}}, \hat{\mathcal{L}}, \hat{P}_{init})$
    while *not exit* **do**
        $temp_{curr} \leftarrow Cooling(temp_{curr})$
        for *next $\hat{P}_{neighbor}$ in AllNeighbors($\hat{\mathcal{L}}, \hat{P}_{curr}$)* **do**
            if $iter > iter_{max}$ **then**
                $exit \leftarrow True$
                break
            $U_{neighbor} \leftarrow Utility(\hat{\mathcal{M}}, \hat{\mathcal{L}}, \hat{P}_{neighbor})$
            $\hat{P}_{best} \leftarrow UpdateBest(\hat{P}_{neighbor}, \hat{P}_{best})$
            $iter++$
            if $Accept(temp_{curr}, U_{curr}, U_{neighbor})$ **then**
                $\hat{P}_{curr} \leftarrow \hat{P}_{neighbor}$
                $U_{curr} \leftarrow U_{neighbor}$
                break
    return $\hat{P}_{best}$

Simulated Annealing-based Algorithm In order to overcome the limitations of the Greedy approach, we devise a simulated annealing [29] based algorithm. The algorithm (Algorithm 2) takes as input workload information ($\hat{\mathcal{L}}$), compute cluster configuration ($\hat{\mathcal{R}}$), and information about performance of analytics applications on different storage services ($\hat{\mathcal{M}}$) as defined in Table 3. Furthermore, the algorithm uses $\hat{P}_{init}$ as the initial tiering solution that is used to specify preferred regions in the search space. For example, the results from the greedy algorithm or the characteristics of analytics applications described in Table 2 can be used to devise an initial placement.

The main goal of our algorithm is to find a near-optimal tiering plan for a given workload. In each iteration, we pick a randomly selected neighbor of the current solution ($AllNeighbors(.)$). If the selected neighbor yields better utility, it becomes the current best solution. Otherwise, in the function $Accept(.)$, we decide whether to move the search space towards the neighbor ($\hat{P}_{neighbor}$) or keep it around the current solution ($\hat{P}_{curr}$). This is achieved by considering the difference between the utility of the current (U_{curr}) and neighbor solutions ($U_{neighbor}$) and comparing it with a distance parameter, represented by $temp_{curr}$. In each iteration, the distance parameter is adjusted (decreased) by a $Cooling(.)$ function. This helps in making the search narrower as iterations increase; reducing the probability of missing the maximum utility in the neighborhood of the search space.

4.3 Enhancements: CAST++

While the basic tiering solver improves tenant utility for general workloads, it is not able to leverage certain properties of analytics workloads. To this end, we design CAST++, which enhances CAST by incorporating data reuse patterns and workflow awareness.

Enhancement 1: Data Reuse Pattern Awareness To incorporate data reuse patterns across jobs, CAST++ ensures that all jobs that share the same input dataset have the same storage service allocated to them. This is captured by Constraint 7 where D represents the set consisting of jobs sharing the input (partially or fully).

$$s_i \equiv s_l \ (\forall i \in D, \text{\ss} \neq l, \in D) \qquad (7)$$

$$where \ D = \{all \ jobs \ which \ share \ input\}$$

Thus, even though individual jobs may have different storage tier preferences, CAST++ takes a global view with the goal to maximize overall tenant utility.

Enhancement 2: Workflow Awareness Prior research has shown that analytics workflows are usually associated with a tenant-defined deadline [33, 21]. For workloads with a mix of independent and inter-dependent jobs, the basic dependency-oblivious CAST may either increase the deadline miss rate or unnecessarily increase the costs, as we show in §3.1.3. Hence, it is crucial for CAST++ to handle workflows differently. To this end, we enhance the basic solver to consider the objective of minimizing the total monetary cost (Equation 8) and introduce a constraint to enforce that the total estimated execution time meets the predefined deadline (Equation 9). This is done for optimizing each workflow separately. Each workflow is represented as a Directed Acyclic Graph (DAG) where each vertex is a job and a directed edge represents a flow from one job to another (refer to Figure 4(a)).

$$min \ \$_{total} = \$_{vm} + \$_{store} \ , \qquad (8)$$

$$s.t. \ \sum_{i=1}^{J_w} REG\Big(s_i, s_{i+1}, capacity[s_i], \hat{\mathcal{R}}, \hat{\mathcal{L}}\Big) \leq deadline \ , \qquad (9)$$

$$c_i \geq \sum_{i=1}^{J_w} \big((s_{i-1} \neq s_i) \cdot input_i + inter_i \qquad (10)$$

$$+ (s_{i+1} \equiv s_i) \cdot output_i\big) \ , where \ s_0 = \phi \ .$$

Furthermore, Equation 10 restricts the capacity constraint in Equation 3 by incorporating inter-job dependencies. The updated approach only allocates capacity if the storage tier for the output of a job at the previous level is not the same as input storage tier of a job at the next level in the DAG. To realize this approach, we enhance Algorithm 2 by replacing the next neighbor search ($AllNeighbors(.)$) with a depth-first traversal in the workflow DAG. This allows us to reduce the deadline miss rate.

5. EVALUATION

In this section, we present the evaluation of CAST and CAST++ using a 400-core Hadoop cluster on Google Cloud. Each slave node in our testbed runs on a 16 vCPU n1-standard-16 VM as specified in §3. We first evaluate the effectiveness of our approach in achieving the best tenant utility for a 100-job analytics workload with no job dependencies. Then, we examine the efficacy of CAST++ in meeting user-specified deadlines.

5.1 Tenant Utility Improvement

5.1.1 Methodology

We compare CAST against six storage configurations: four without tiering and two that employ greedy algorithm based static tiering. We generate a representative 100-job work-

Bin	# Maps at Facebook	% Jobs at Facebook	% Data sizes at Facebook	# Maps in workload	# Jobs in workload
1				1	35
2	1—10	73%	0.1%	5	22
3				10	16
4	11—50	13%	0.9%	50	13
5	51—500	7%	4.5%	500	7
6	501—3000	4%	16.5%	1,500	4
7	> 3000	3%	78.1%	3,000	3

Table 4: Distribution of job sizes in Facebook traces and our synthesized workload.

load by sampling the input sizes from the distribution observed in production traces from a 3,000-machine Hadoop deployment at Facebook [18]. We quantize the job sizes into 7 bins as listed in Table 4, to enable us to compare the dataset size distribution across different bins. The largest job in the Facebook traces has 158,499 map tasks. Thus, we choose 3,000 for the highest bin in our workload to ensure that our workload demands a reasonable load but is also manageable for our 400-core cluster. More than 99% of the total data in the cluster is touched by the large jobs that belong to bin 5, 6 and 7, which incur most of the storage cost. The aggregated data size for small jobs (with number of map tasks in the range 1–10) is only 0.1% of the total data size. The runtime for small jobs is not sensitive to the choice of storage tier. Therefore, we focus on the large jobs, which have enough number of mappers and reducers to fully utilize the cluster compute capacity during execution. Since there is a moderate amount of data reuse throughout the Facebook traces, we also incorporate this into our workload by having 15% of the jobs share the same input data. We assign the four job types listed in Table 2 to this workload in a round-robin fashion to incorporate the different computation and I/O characteristics.

5.1.2 Effectiveness for General Workload

Figure 7 shows the results for tenant utility, performance, cost and storage capacity distribution across four different storage services. We observe in Figure 7(a) that CAST improves the tenant utility by 33.7% − 178% compared to the configurations with no explicit tiering, i.e., ephSSD 100%, persSSD 100%, persHDD 100% and objStore 100%. The best combination under CAST consists of 33% ephSSD, 31% persSSD, 16% persHDD and 20% objStore, as shown in Figure 7(c). persSSD achieves the highest tenant utility among the four non-tiered configurations, because persSSD is relatively fast and persistent. Though ephSSD provides the best I/O performance, it is not cost-efficient, since it uses the most expensive storage and requires objStore to serve as the backing store to provide data persistence, which incurs additional storage cost and also imposes data transfer overhead. This is why ephSSD 100% results in 14.3% longer runtime (300 minutes) compared to that under persSSD 100% (263 minutes) as shown in Figure 7(b).

The greedy algorithm cannot reach a global optimum because, at each iteration, placing a job in a particular tier can change the performance of that tier. This affects the *Utility* calculated and the selected tier for each job in all the previous iterations, but the greedy algorithm cannot update those selections to balance the trade-off between cost and performance. For completeness, we compare our approach with two versions of the greedy algorithm: Greedy exact-fit attempts to limit the cost by not over-provisioning extra storage space for workloads, while Greedy over-provisioned

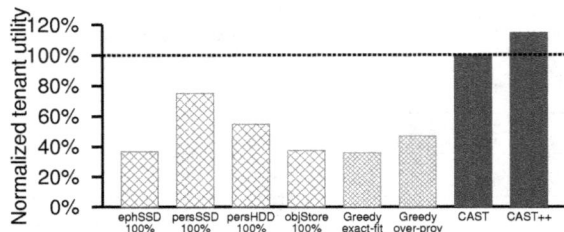

(a) Normalized tenant utility.

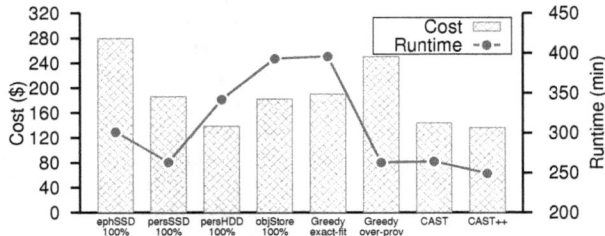

(b) Total monetary cost and runtime.

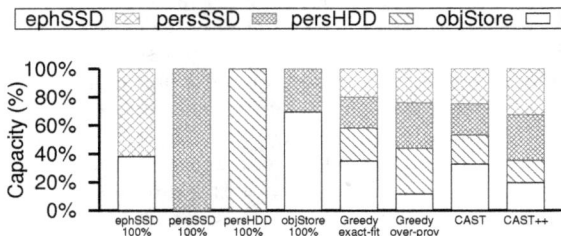

(c) Capacity breakdown.

Figure 7: Effectiveness of CAST and CAST++ on workloads with reuse, observed for key storage configurations. Note: Greedy over-prov represents **greedy over-provisioned**. Tenant utility is normalized to that of the configuration from basic CAST.

will assign extra storage space as needed to reduce the completion time and improve performance.

The tenant utility of Greedy exact-fit is as poor as objStore 100%. This is because Greedy exact-fit only allocates *just enough* storage space without considering performance scaling. Greedy over-provisioned is able to outperform ephSSD 100%, persHDD 100% and objStore 100%, but performs slightly worse than persSSD 100%. This is because the approach significantly over-provisions persSSD and persHDD space to improve the runtime of the jobs. The tenant utility improvement under basic CAST is 178% and 113.4%, compared to Greedy exact-fit and Greedy over-provisioned, respectively.

5.1.3 Effectiveness for Data Reuse

CAST++ outperforms all other configurations and further enhances the tenant utility of basic CAST by 14.4% (Figure 7(a)). This is due to the following reasons. (1) CAST++ successfully improves the tenant utility by exploiting the characteristics of jobs and underlying tiers and tuning the capacity distribution. (2) CAST++ effectively detects data reuse across jobs to further improve the tenant utility by placing shared data in the fastest ephSSD, since we observe that in Figure 7(c) the capacity proportion under CAST++ of objStore reduces by 42% and that of ephSSD increases by

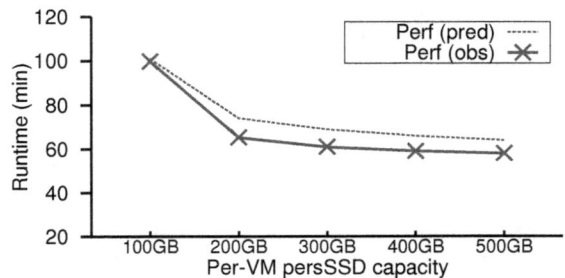

Figure 8: Predicted runtime achieved using CAST's performance scaling regression model vs. runtime observed in experiments by varying the per-VM persSSD capacity. The workload runs on the same 400-core cluster as in §5.1.2.

29%, compared to CAST. This is because CAST++ places jobs that share the data on ephSSD to amortize the data transfer cost from objStore.

5.1.4 Accuracy of the Regression Model

Figure 8 compares predicted runtime to observed runtime for a small workload consisting of 16 modest-sized jobs. The total dataset size of all jobs is 2 TB. Both the predicted and the observed runtime follow the same general trend, with an average prediction error of 7.9%, which demonstrates the accuracy of our cubic Hermite spline regression models. The margin of error is tolerable for our case, since the focus of CAST is to help tenants compare and choose among different tiering plans.

5.2 Meeting Workflow Deadlines

5.2.1 Methodology

In our next set of experiments, we evaluate the ability of CAST++ to meet workflow deadlines while minimizing cost. We compare CAST++ against four storage configurations without tiering and a fifth configuration from the basic, workflow-oblivious CAST. This experiment employs five workflows with a total of 31 analytics jobs, with the longest workflow consisting of 9 jobs. We focus on large jobs that fully utilize the test cluster's compute capacity.

We consider the completion time of a workflow to be the time between the start of its first job and the completion of its last job. The *deadline* of a workflow is a limit on this completion time, i.e., it must be less than or equal to the deadline. We set the deadline of the workflows between 15 – 40 minutes based on the job input sizes and the job types comprising each workflow. When a job of a workflow completes, its output is transferred to the input tier of the next job. The time taken for this cross-tier transfer is accounted as part of the workflow runtime by CAST++. However, since CAST is not aware of the intra-workflow job dependencies (treating all currently running workflows as a combined set of jobs), CAST cannot account for this transfer cost.

5.2.2 Deadline Miss Rate vs. Cost

Figure 9 shows the *miss rate* of workflow deadlines for the studied configurations. The miss rate of a configuration is the fraction of deadlines missed while executing the workflows using that configuration. CAST++ meets all the deadlines and incurs the lowest cost, comparable to that of

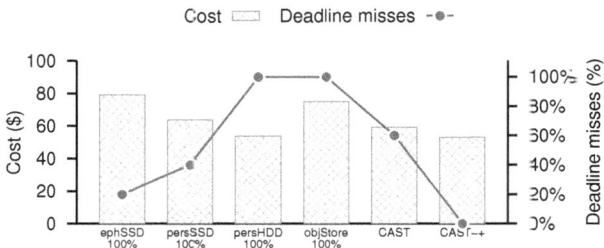

Figure 9: Deadline miss rate and cost of CAST++ compared to CAST and four non-tiered configurations.

persHDD that is the lowest-priced but the slowest tier and has a miss rate of 100%.

CAST misses 60% of the deadlines because of two reasons: (1) it selects slow tiers for several jobs in each workflow when trying to optimize for tenant utility; and (2) by not accounting for the cross-tier transfer time, it mis-predicts the workflow runtime. However, CAST incurs a lower cost compared to the non-tiered configurations, because it selects lower-priced tiers for many of the jobs.

Despite being the fastest tier, ephSSD misses 20% of the deadlines because of the need to fetch the input data for every workflow from objStore. persSSD misses 40% of the deadlines because it performs slightly worse than ephSSD for I/O intensive jobs. Finally, objStore misses all of the deadlines because it is slower than or as fast as persSSD. It incurs a higher cost because of the persSSD, which is needed for storing intermediate data.

In summary, CAST++ outperforms CAST as well as non-tiered storage configurations in meeting workflow deadlines, and does so while minimizing the cost of running the workflows on the cloud cluster.

6. DISCUSSION

In the following, we discuss the applicability and limitations of our storage tiering solutions.

Analytics Workloads with Relatively Fixed and Stable Computations Analytics workloads are known to be fairly *stable* in terms of the number of types of applications. Recent analysis by Chen et. al. [18] shows that a typical analytics workload consists of only a small number of common computation patterns in terms of analytics job types. For example, a variety of Hadoop workloads in Cloudera have four to eight unique types of jobs. Moreover, more than 90% of all jobs in one Cloudera cluster are Select, PigLatin and Insert [18]. These observations imply that a relatively fixed and stable set of analytics applications (or analytics kernels) can yield enough functionality for a range of analysis goals. Thus, optimizing the system for such applications, as in CAST, can significantly impact the data analytics field.

Dynamic vs. Static Storage Tiering Big data frameworks such as Spark [47] and Impala [11] have been used for real-time interactive analytics, where dynamic storage tiering is likely to be more beneficial. In contrast, our work focuses on traditional batch processing analytics with workloads exhibiting the characteristics identified above. Dynamic tiering requires more sophisticated fine-grained task-level scheduling mechanisms to effectively avoid the strag-

gler issue. While dynamic tiering in our problem domain can help to some extent, our current tiering model adopts a simple yet effective coarse-grained tiering approach. We believe we have provided a *first-of-its-kind* storage tiering methodology for cloud-based analytics. In the future, we plan to enhance CAST to incorporate fine-grained dynamic tiering as well.

7. CONCLUSION

In this paper, we design CAST, a storage tiering framework that performs cloud storage allocation and data placement for analytics workloads to achieve high performance in a cost-effective manner. CAST leverages the performance and pricing models of cloud storage services and the heterogeneity of I/O patterns found in common analytics applications. An enhancement, CAST++, extends these capabilities to meet deadlines for analytics workflows while minimizing the cost. Our evaluation shows that compared to extant storage-characteristic-oblivious cloud deployment strategies, CAST++ can improve the performance by as much as 37.1% while reducing deployment costs by as much as 51.4%.

8. ACKNOWLEDGMENTS

We thank the anonymous reviewers for their valuable feedback that helped us improve the paper. We also thank Taha Hasan for helpful discussions on the idea in its early stages, and Krishnaraj K. Ravindranathan for help in improving the presentation. This work was sponsored in part by the NSF under Grants CNS-1405697 and CNS-1422788.

9. REFERENCES

[1] Amazon EMR. http://aws.amazon.com/elasticmapreduce.

[2] Apache Hadoop. http://hadoop.apache.org.

[3] Apache Oozie. http://oozie.apache.org.

[4] Azure Storage. http://azure.microsoft.com/en-us/services/storage.

[5] EC2 Storage. http://docs.aws.amazon.com/AWSEC2/latest/UserGuide/Storage.html.

[6] Google Cloud Pricing. https://cloud.google.com/compute/#pricing.

[7] Google Cloud Storage Connector for Hadoop. https://cloud.google.com/hadoop/google-cloud-storage-connector.

[8] Hadoop on Google Compute Engine. https://cloud.google.com/solutions/hadoop.

[9] HDFS-2832. https://issues.apache.org/jira/browse/HDFS-2832.

[10] HP Cloud Storage. http://www.hpcloud.com/products-services/storage-cdn.

[11] Impala. http://impala.io.

[12] Microsoft Azure HDInsight. http://azure.microsoft.com/en-us/services/hdinsight.

[13] Mumak: MapReduce Simulator. https://issues.apache.org/jira/browse/MAPREDUCE-728.

[14] C. Albrecht, A. Merchant, M. Stokely, M. Waliji, F. Labelle, N. Coehlo, X. Shi, and C. E. Schrock. Janus: Optimal flash provisioning for cloud storage workloads. In *Proceedings of USENIX ATC 2013*.

[15] G. Ananthanarayanan, A. Ghodsi, A. Warfield, D. Borthakur, S. Kandula, S. Shenker, and I. Stoica.

PACMan: Coordinated memory caching for parallel jobs. In *Proceedings of USENIX NSDI 2012*.

[16] R. Appuswamy, C. Gkantsidis, D. Narayanan, O. Hodson, and A. Rowstron. Scale-up vs scale-out for hadoop: Time to rethink? In *Proceedings of ACM SoCC 2013*.

[17] S. Babu. Towards automatic optimization of MapReduce programs. In *Proceedings of ACM SoCC 2010*.

[18] Y. Chen, S. Alspaugh, and R. Katz. Interactive analytical processing in Big Data systems: A cross-industry study of MapReduce workloads. *PVLDB*, 5(12):1802–1813, Aug. 2012.

[19] B. F. Cooper, A. Silberstein, E. Tam, R. Ramakrishnan, and R. Sears. Benchmarking cloud serving systems with YCSB. In *Proceedings of ACM SoCC 2010*.

[20] J. Dean and S. Ghemawat. MapReduce: Simplified data processing on large clusters. In *Proceedings of USENIX OSDI 2004*.

[21] I. Elghandour and A. Aboulnaga. ReStore: Reusing results of MapReduce jobs. *PVLDB*, 5(6):586–597, Feb. 2012.

[22] J. Guerra, H. Pucha, J. Glider, W. Belluomini, and R. Rangaswami. Cost effective storage using extent based dynamic tiering. In *Proceedings of USENIX FAST 2011*.

[23] T. Harter, D. Borthakur, S. Dong, A. Aiyer, L. Tang, A. C. Arpaci-Dusseau, and R. H. Arpaci-Dusseau. Analysis of HDFS under HBase: A Facebook Messages case study. In *Proceedings of USENIX FAST 2014*.

[24] H. Herodotou and S. Babu. Profiling, what-if analysis, and cost-based optimization of MapReduce programs. *PVLDB*, 4(11):1111–1122, 2011.

[25] H. Herodotou, H. Lim, G. Luo, N. Borisov, L. Dong, F. B. Cetin, and S. Babu. Starfish: A self-tuning system for Big Data analytics. In *CIDR*, 2011.

[26] M. Isard, M. Budiu, Y. Yu, A. Birrell, and D. Fetterly. Dryad: Distributed data-parallel programs from sequential building blocks. In *Proceedings of ACM EuroSys 2007*.

[27] V. Jalaparti, H. Ballani, P. Costa, T. Karagiannis, and A. Rowstron. Bridging the tenant-provider gap in cloud services. In *Proceedings of ACM SoCC 2012*.

[28] H. Kim, S. Seshadri, C. L. Dickey, and L. Chiu. Evaluating Phase Change Memory for enterprise storage systems: A study of caching and tiering approaches. In *Proceedings of USENIX FAST 2014*.

[29] S. Kirkpatrick, C. D. Gelatt, and M. P. Vecchi. Optimization by simulated annealing. *SCIENCE*, 220(4598):671–680, 1983.

[30] E. Kreyszig. *Advanced Engineering Mathematics*. Wiley, 10th edition, August 2011.

[31] Krish K.R., A. Anwar, and A. R. Butt. hatS: A heterogeneity-aware tiered storage for Hadoop. In *Proceedings of IEEE/ACM CCGrid 2014*.

[32] Krish K.R., A. Anwar, and A. R. Butt. øSched: A heterogeneity-aware Hadoop workflow scheduler. In *Proceedings of IEEE MASCOTS 2014*.

[33] S. Li, S. Hu, S. Wang, L. Su, T. Abdelzaher, I. Gupta, and R. Pace. WOHA: Deadline-aware Map-Reduce workflow scheduling framework over Hadoop clusters. In *Proceedings of IEEE ICDCS 2014*.

[34] Z. Li, A. Mukker, and E. Zadok. On the importance of evaluating storage systems' $costs. In *Proceedings of USENIX HotStorage 2014*.

[35] H. Lim, H. Herodotou, and S. Babu. Stubby: A transformation-based optimizer for MapReduce workflows. *PVLDB*, 5(11):1196–1207, July 2012.

[36] M. Mao and M. Humphrey. Auto-scaling to minimize cost and meet application deadlines in cloud workflows. In *Proceedings of ACM/IEEE SC 2011*.

[37] F. Meng, L. Zhou, X. Ma, S. Uttamchandani, and D. Liu. vCacheShare: Automated server flash cache space management in a virtualization environment. In *Proceedings of USENIX ATC 2014*.

[38] M. Mihailescu, G. Soundararajan, and C. Amza. MixApart: Decoupled analytics for shared storage systems. In *Proceedings of USENIX FAST 2013*.

[39] K. P. Puttaswamy, T. Nandagopal, and M. Kodialam. Frugal storage for cloud file systems. In *Proceedings of ACM EuroSys 2012*. ACM.

[40] K. Shvachko, H. Kuang, S. Radia, and R. Chansler. The Hadoop Distributed File System. In *Proceedings of IEEE MSST 2010*.

[41] A. Verma, L. Cherkasova, and R. H. Campbell. Play it again, SimMR! In *Proceedings of IEEE CLUSTER 2011*.

[42] G. Wang, A. R. Butt, P. Pandey, and K. Gupta. A simulation approach to evaluating design decisions in MapReduce setups. In *Proceedings of IEEE MASCOTS 2009*.

[43] H. Wang and P. Varman. Balancing fairness and efficiency in tiered storage systems with bottleneck-aware allocation. In *Proceedings of USENIX FAST 2014*.

[44] A. Wieder, P. Bhatotia, A. Post, and R. Rodrigues. Orchestrating the deployment of computations in the cloud with Conductor. In *Proceedings of USENIX NSDI 2012*.

[45] D. Yuan, Y. Yang, X. Liu, and J. Chen. A data placement strategy in scientific cloud workflows. *Future Generation Computer Systems*, 26(8):1200 – 1214, 2010.

[46] M. Zaharia, D. Borthakur, J. Sen Sarma, K. Elmeleegy, S. Shenker, and I. Stoica. Delay scheduling: A simple technique for achieving locality and fairness in cluster scheduling. In *Proceedings of ACM EuroSys 2010*.

[47] M. Zaharia, M. Chowdhury, T. Das, A. Dave, J. Ma, M. McCauly, M. J. Franklin, S. Shenker, and I. Stoica. Resilient distributed datasets: A fault-tolerant abstraction for in-memory cluster computing. In *Proceedings of USENIX NSDI 2012*.

HPC System Lifetime Story: Workload Characterization and Evolutionary Analyses on NERSC Systems

Gonzalo P. Rodrigo, Per-Olov Östberg,
Erik Elmroth
Dept. Computing Science, Umeå University
SE-901 87, Umeå, Sweden
{gonzalo, p-o, elmroth}@cs.umu.se

Katie Antypas, Richard Gerber,
Lavanya Ramakrishnan
Lawrence Berkeley National Lab
Berkeley, CA 94720, USA
{kantypas, ragerber,
lramakrishnan}@lbl.gov

ABSTRACT

High performance computing centers have traditionally served monolithic MPI applications. However, in recent years, many of the large scientific computations have included high throughput and data-intensive jobs. HPC systems have mostly used batch queue schedulers to schedule these workloads on appropriate resources. There is a need to understand future scheduling scenarios that can support the diverse scientific workloads in HPC centers. In this paper, we analyze the workloads on two systems (Hopper and Carver) at the National Energy Research Scientific Computing (NERSC) Center. Specifically, we present a trend analysis towards understanding the evolution of the workload over the lifetime of the two systems.

Categories and Subject Descriptors

D4.1 [**Operating Systems**]: Process Management—*Scheduling*

Keywords

Scheduling; workload; trend analysis; HPC

1. INTRODUCTION

Traditionally, scientific applications running at HPC centers have been large monolithic MPI applications which require high bandwidth, low latency interconnects. However, large scientific computations that include high-throughput, data-intensive jobs, and stream-processing are increasingly becoming more common in HPC centers. These applications are assigned HPC resources through batch queue schedulers with objectives such as short wait times, high utilization, and selective prioritization [5].

The diversity of workloads in supercomputing centers requires us to investigate the right workload scheduling model for the next-generation systems addressing the needs of diverse workloads. As a first step, we need to understand the

Publication rights licensed to ACM. ACM acknowledges that this contribution was authored or co-authored by an employee, contractor or affiliate of the United States government. As such, the United States Government retains a nonexclusive, royalty-free right to publish or reproduce this article, or to allow others to do so, for Government purposes only.

HPDC'15, June 15 - 19, 2015, Portland, OR, USA.
DOI: http://dx.doi.org/10.1145/2749246.2749270 .

evolution of the workload on the current systems in depth. Previous works have analyzed workloads on various grid [6] and cloud [3] systems. However, these works and associated comparisons are based on single points in time of HPC workloads that are several years before the current trend in workloads.

In this paper, we analyze the workloads at the National Energy Research Scientific Computing Center (NERSC), a supercomputing center that supports the broad scientific workload of the Department of Energy Office of Science. We consider two systems: Carver and Hopper, selected due to differences in their hardware and timeline characteristics. Carver is a traditional high performance Linux cluster while Hopper is a specialized Cray supercomputer with a custom interconnect. These systems allow us to capture the workloads on high-end clusters and supercomputers over a period of four years.

Specifically, in this paper we provide an evolutionary analysis of the NERSC systems workloads. We study the trend in job geometry (i.e. allocated cores, wall clock time and consumed core-hours), job wait times, and wall clock time accuracy. Our analyses help in understanding the evolution of workload patterns over the lifetime of each system to facilitate short- and long-term decisions at HPC centers.

2. BACKGROUND

In this section, we present the background on workloads and current scheduling policies in HPC centers.

2.1 Evolution of HPC Workloads

Data-intensive applications are becoming increasingly more common in HPC workloads, partly following the increase of HPC use in scientific domains such as biology or astrophysics [8]. We are seeing an increase in the need for stream processing of large amounts of experimental data. For example, the Advanced Light Source is a particle accelerator that produces high quality energy beams. Large amounts of data produced are transferred to NERSC to be processed. A number of these experiments would benefit from processing the data in real-time to have low latency feedback [2]. To support this, advance resource reservations could be a means, but they are known to significantly reduce the overall utilization. Such changes in applications over time require us to analyze the workloads at supercomputers to understand their characteristics.

System	Vendor	Model	Built	Nodes	Cores/N	Cores	Memory	Network	TFlops/s	Service	Charging
Hopper	Cray	XE6	2010	6,384	24	154,216	212 TB	Gemini	144	Jan'10	Jan'10
Carver	IBM	iDataPlex	2010	1,120	8/12/32	9,984	147 TB	Infiniband	106.5	Apr'10	May'10

Table 1: Hopper and Carver characteristics

2.2 Scheduling

HPC systems are designed to run multiple jobs in parallel over large compute infrastructures. Their schedulers commonly use the FCFS (First-Come, First-Served) model [4], selecting jobs in arrival order. Additionally, they use backfilling [7] to avoid low resource utilization. Jobs submitted to the queue can have different priorities associated with them. Priority of a job is used by the scheduler in each scheduling pass to determine the speed at which a job makes its way through the queue (i.e. jobs belonging to higher priority users or projects are executed faster).

The quality of the results of backfilling algorithms depend on user wall clock estimations [4]. Under and overestimation of job execution times may lead to lower utilization of systems, motivating the need to study wall clock accuracy (relationship between estimated and actual wall clock, more in Section 4.3).

3. METHODOLOGY

In this section, we present the system and workloads in focus for our investigation and elaborate on the key parameters studied.

3.1 Systems Description

NERSC is a HPC center at the Lawrence Berkeley National Lab, that provides computing infrastructure and tools for scientists performing research of relevance to the United States Department of Energy (DOE). Over 5000 users and 700 distinct projects use the NERSC supercomputing infrastructures [1]. The workload is composed of applications that belong to a wide range of scientific fields including Chemistry, Material Science, Climate Research, Astrophysics, Life Sciences, and Nuclear Physics.

This work considers two systems at NERSC (summary of characteristics in Table 1): Hopper, built on multicore processors, packaged together on customized blades and connected with a high speed proprietary interconnect; and Carver, a high performance Linux cluster with a fat-tree Infiniband interconnect matrix. Both systems use the Moab scheduler and the Torque [9] resource manager.

NERSC users receive an allocation of compute hours that can be used to run on multiple NERSC systems, including Carver and Hopper. Each system has its own charging factor depending on its performance across a standard set of benchmarks. Both Carver and Hopper are heavily utilized systems ($\sim$ 90% for the years considered in this study)

During the deployment and initial testing phase, users run jobs without charges on their allocations. Users' behavior on the systems can be different during these times and hence it is important to note them: Hopper was deployed in December 2009 with a small Phase 1 system that was later upgraded to the full system in November 2010. Users started getting charged for running jobs in April 2011.

Carver was deployed in early 2010 and set into production in May 2010. Additionally, Carver was expanded in January 2012. Carver will be decommissioned in September 2015 and its jobs will be migrated to Edison, a new Cray system similar to Hopper. The staff at NERSC tweak scheduling and queuing policies a few times per year based on the characteristics of the system, user input, scientific requirements, DOE priorities, and observations of job backlog and usage across systems. Our analysis considers the period January 2010 to June 2014 for Hopper and Carver.

In addition to serving the typical workloads, Carver provides a *serial* queue: a special queue that allows users to submit and execute jobs with a very low degree of parallelism (i.e. one node). Since our analyses, serial queues have also been added to Hopper.

3.2 Data source

All workload analysis is performed on the job summary entries from the systems' Torque logs. The data includes 4.5 years and 4,326,870 jobs for Hopper and 4.5 years and 9,508,054 jobs for Carver. The raw data size is 45 GB, which, after filtering and parsing, is reduced to 6 GB of net data.

3.3 Analysis variables

Our analysis focuses on understanding the evolution of the two systems' lifetime workload. First, we try to understand the workload, i.e. the job geometry (wall clock time and degree of parallelism). The job geometry defines the upper bound of application resource requirements.

Second, we study the trend in job wait time and wall clock time accuracy. Job wait time represents the time a job spends in queue waiting to start its execution, and is a measure of the system's degree of overload. The wall clock estimation accuracy has an important impact on the scheduler decision quality.

The evolutionary trends of these variables are interesting as their characterization can help build more suitable future systems from the perspective of infrastructure and resource management.

3.4 Time Period of Trend Analysis

The trend analysis studies the workload in sequential time periods. The size of the periods is calculated using a Fourier transform analysis on the number of tasks submitted per hour, which identifies cycles in the job submission [10] and thus, the user behavior. The most powerful cycles correspond to the periods of one day, one week, three month and six months, matching calendar work periods and allocation year. Each project has a number of core hours to be consumed during a year, divided in four allocation quarters in which the project has to consume (or forfeit) the corresponding allocated time. The yearly allocation policy motivated the choice of one year as the analysis time period for the trend analysis.

4. TREND ANALYSIS

In this section, we present our trend analyses on job geometry, job wait time, and wall clock time accuracy.

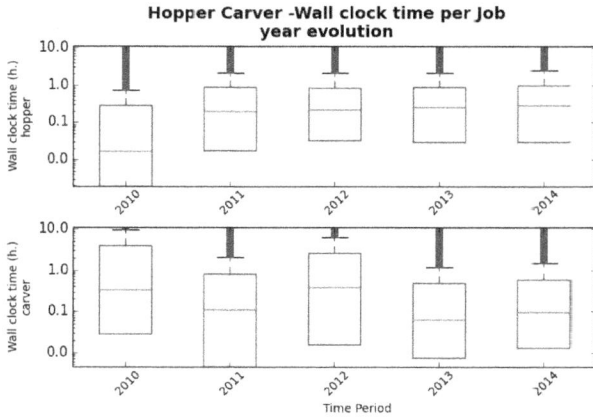

Figure 1: Job wall clock time for each each workload year. Trend: Hopper jobs become longer, Carver jobs shorter. Majority of jobs under one hour.

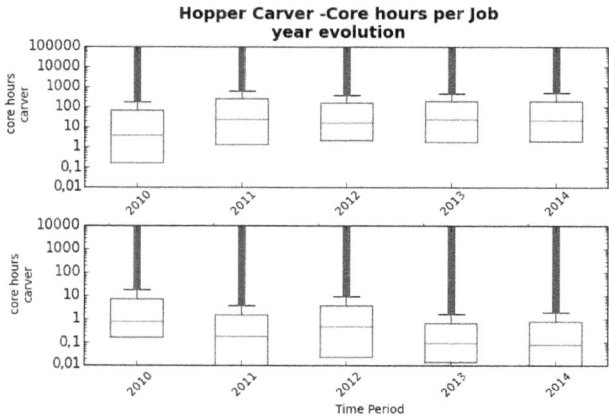

Figure 2: Allocated number of cores for each workload year. Trend: Hopper jobs allocate less cores. In 2011-2013, most Carver jobs used one core.

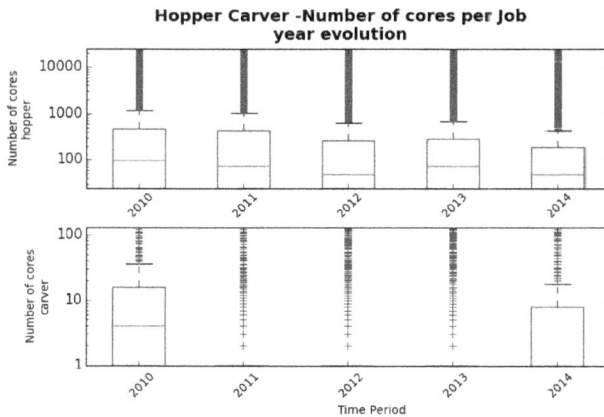

Figure 3: Allocated core hours for each workload year. Trend: No changes on Hopper. Carver jobs become smaller.

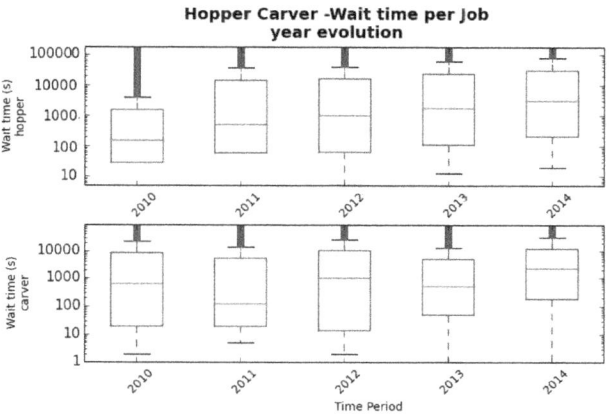

Figure 4: Jobs' wait time evolution for each workload year. Trend: All systems increase wait time. Carver lower wait time in 2011.

4.1 Job geometry

The evolution of the first job geometry variable is presented in Figure 1 as a box plot of job wall clock time for each system in each year. Hopper shows a significantly low wall clock median in 2010 (< 1 minute), which might be related to the fact that it was a smaller testbed system that year. In 2011, the median increased to ~ 5 minutes and subsequently increased to ~ 12 minutes by 2014. Carver shows a different trend: the median, upper and lower quartile decrease effectively over the period studied. The median decreased from ~ 20 minutes (2010) to ~ 6 minutes (2014). However, there is some variation from year to year: It is observed that in the first year in production, Carver ran longer jobs than Hopper, a fact that slowly changed in 2014 when Hopper ran longer jobs that Carver. More generally, Hopper presents fairly short jobs, as the highest upper quartile is around the one hour value. Carver presents a similar behavior as the upper quartiles of the last years are under one hour.

The evolution of the width of jobs (number of allocated cores per job) is shown in Figure 3. For Hopper, the median decreases from 100 cores (2010) to under 30 cores (2014).

Carver presents an opposite pattern. Except for 2010, the median of the rest of the years is one core, showing the predominance of single core serial jobs. In 2014 the upper quartile increased to 8 cores.

The core-time i.e., total clock time across all cores was also studied. In the case of Hopper, it remains nearly the same through time with a median of ~ 20 core hours and the upper quartile slightly under 200 core hours in most years. In the case of Carver, it slowly decreases from a median of almost 1 core hour to ~ 6 core minutes (and a last upper quartile of 1 core hour).

In summary, Hopper jobs (shorter jobs, with a higher degree of parallelism, bigger than Carver's) seem to be showing an increase in their wall clock time. As the effective job's core hours remain the same, they must be using fewer cores. Carver jobs (longer jobs, lower degree of parallelism, fewer core hours than Hopper's) have decreasing wall clock time and use more cores, but the increase is not sufficient to keep the job's core hours steady over the years.

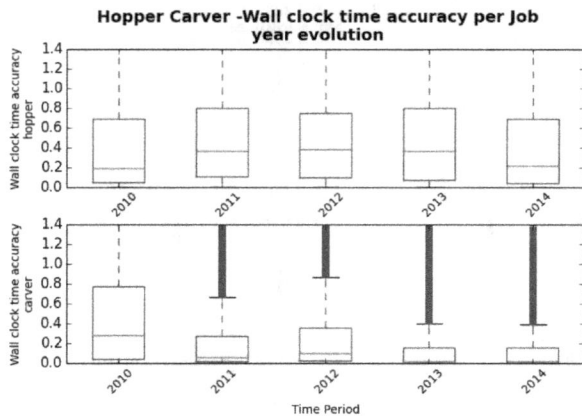

Figure 5: Jobs' wall clock time accuracy evolution for each workload year. In all systems wall clock time remains low.

4.2 Job wait time

According to Figure 4, for Hopper, the median of the wait time is steadily increasing from under 100 seconds to over 20 minutes (a pattern also present in the upper and lower quartiles). On Carver, the effective wait time increases over the four years from $\sim$ 10 minutes in 2010 to $\sim$ 20 minutes in 2014. However we notice a zigzag pattern trend in between. In 2011, Carver presented significantly shorter wait times, which could be attributed to a known increase of resources in the system. The steady increase of wait time over the lifetime fits with the growth of the user community of the systems.

4.3 Wall clock time accuracy

The wall clock accuracy is calculated as *real/estimated* wall clock time. The results are shown in Figure 5. Hopper does not show a clear trend: 2011 to 2013 presents a higher accuracy than 2010 and 2014, with a median variation between 0.2 and 0.4. For Carver, the median decreases over time, with significant changes between 2010 ($\sim$ 0.25) and 2011 (< 0.1). In 2014, the median is under 0.1 and the last quartile it is under 0.2. For Carver, there is a clear pattern of worse estimations as the time proceeds. In general, both systems present very low values with medians under 0.4.

Wall clock accuracy does not show a noticeable pattern beyond the fact that accuracy is low. On Hopper, 50% of all jobs run less than 40% of the estimated time. Similarly on Carver, 50% of all jobs less than 20% of the estimated time. These values indicate that the decisions made by the backfilling algorithms are based on inaccurate user estimations.

5. SUMMARY

Our work describes the evolution of jobs over the lifetime of two systems: Hopper and Carver. The results show that job wait times increased over time on both systems. Similarly, job size estimation accuracy was low on both systems. However, differences were found on the job geometry evolution. In the beginning of the time period analyzed, Carver's job run times were significantly higher than Hopper's. However, run time decreased on Carver and increased on Hopper. Thus the workloads became more similar towards the end of the period analyzed. Hopper jobs allocate significantly more

cores than Carver in all years, but the difference is slightly reduced over time. Core hours consumed by Hopper jobs did not change, but Carver's decreased over time.

In summary, this work shows that the systems were used differently at different points of their lifetimes. This can be attributed to the evolution of the user behavior as users adapt applications towards the most optimal configuration. Another possibility is that the results reflect user adaptation to policy changes over the lifetime. More detailed analyses and reasoning of these trends are topics for future work.

6. ACKNOWLEDGMENTS

Financial support has been provided in part by the Swedish Government's strategic effort eSSENCE, the European Union's Seventh Framework Programme under grant agreement 610711 (CACTOS), and the Swedish Research Council (VR) under contract number C0590801 for the project Cloud Control. This material is based upon work supported by the U.S. Department of Energy, Office of Science, Office of Advanced Scientific Computing Research (ASCR) and the National Energy Research Scientific Computing Center, a DOE Office of Science User Facility supported by the Office of Science of the U.S. Department of Energy under Contract No. DE-AC02-05CH11231.

7. REFERENCES

[1] K. Antypas, B. A. Austin, T. L. Butler, and R. A. Gerber. NERSC workload analysis on Hopper. Technical report, LBNL Report: 6804E, October 2014.

[2] M. A. Bauer, A. Biem, S. McIntyre, N. Tamura, and Y. Xie. High-performance parallel and stream processing of x-ray microdiffraction data on multicores. In *Journal of Physics: Conference Series*, volume 341, page 012025. IOP Publishing, 2012.

[3] S. Di, D. Kondo, and W. Cirne. Characterization and comparison of cloud versus grid workloads. In *2012 IEEE International Conference on Cluster Computing (CLUSTER)*, pages 230–238. IEEE, 2012.

[4] D. G. Feitelson, L. Rudolph, and U. Schwiegelshohn. Parallel job scheduling, a status report. In *Job Scheduling Strategies for Parallel Processing*, pages 1–16. Springer, 2005.

[5] I. Foster, Y. Zhao, I. Raicu, and S. Lu. Cloud computing and grid computing 360-degree compared. In *Grid Computing Environments Workshop, 2008. GCE'08*, pages 1–10. Ieee, 2008.

[6] A. Iosup, H. Li, M. Jan, S. Anoep, C. Dumitrescu, L. Wolters, and D. Epema. The grid workloads archive. *Future Generation Computer Systems*, 24(7):672–686, 2008.

[7] D. A. Lifka. The ANL/IBM SP scheduling system. In *Job Scheduling Strategies for Parallel Processing*, pages 295–303. Springer, 1995.

[8] S. N. Srirama, P. Jakovits, and E. Vainikko. Adapting scientific computing problems to clouds using MapReduce. *Future Generation Computer Systems*, 28(1):184–192, 2012.

[9] G. Staples. Torque resource manager. In *Proceedings of the 2006 ACM/IEEE conference on Supercomputing*, page 8. ACM, 2006.

[10] W. W.-S. Wei. *Time series analysis*. Addison-Wesley publ, 1994.

In-Situ Bitmaps Generation and Efficient Data Analysis based on Bitmaps

Yu Su
Computer Science and
Engineering
The Ohio State University
Columbus, OH 43210
su1@cse.ohio-state.edu

Yi Wang
Computer Science and
Engineering
The Ohio State University
Columbus, OH 43210
wayi@cse.ohio-state.edu

Gagan Agrawal
Computer Science and
Engineering
The Ohio State University
Columbus, OH 43210
agrawal@cse.ohio-
state.edu

ABSTRACT

Neither the memory capacity, memory access speeds, nor disk band-widths are increasing at the same rate as the computing power in current and upcoming parallel machines. This has led to considerable recent research on *in-situ* data analytics. However, many open questions remain on how to perform such analytics, especially in memory constrained systems. Building on our earlier work that demonstrated bitmap indices (bitmaps) can be a suitable summary structure for key (offline) analytics tasks, this paper develops an in-situ analysis approach that performs data reduction (such as time-steps selection) using just bitmaps, and subsequently, stores only the selected bitmaps for post-analysis. We construct compressed bitmaps on the fly, show that many kinds of in-situ analyses can be supported by bitmaps without requiring the original data (and thus reducing memory requirements for in-situ analysis), and instead of writing the original simulation output, we only write the selected bitmaps to the disks (reducing the I/O requirements). We also demonstrate that we are able to use bitmaps for key offline analysis steps. We extensively evaluate our method with different simulations and applications, and demonstrate the effectiveness of our approach.

Categories and Subject Descriptors

H.3.1 [**Information Systems**]: CONTENT ANALYSIS AND IN-DEXING—*Indexing Methods*; H.1.1 [**Information Systems**]: SYS-TEMS AND INFORMATION THEORY—*Information Theory*

Keywords

in-situ analysis; bitmaps; data reduction; time-steps selection; correlation analysis

1. INTRODUCTION

Data-driven discovery from scientific simulations is facing a major and *disruptive* challenge, due to the recent and emerging trends in high performance computing systems. Specifically, there is a shift towards architectures where memory and I/O capacities are not keeping pace with the increased computing power. There are

HPDC'15, June 15–20, 2015, Portland, Oregon, USA.
Copyright © 2015 ACM 978-1-4503-3550-8/15/06 ...$15.00.
http://dx.doi.org/10.1145/2749246.2749268.

many reasons for this constraint in high performance systems where science and engineering simulations are typically run. Most critically, the need for providing high computational power in a cost and power effective fashion is driving architectures with limited memory and severe data movement limitations [18, 24].

Examples of such designs can be seen from the architectures of accelerators and coprocessors like GPUs and Intel MIC, which have a large number of cores but only a small amount of memory per core. In fact, a detailed analysis of the supercomputers in the top 500 list has shown a clear decrease in the memory per Gflops in recent years [19]. A related issue is that the data movement costs have become the dominant consideration in design and operation of powerful parallel machines, and all indications are that they will be the bottleneck in the future. It needs to be noted that the memory-constrained powerful HPC systems are in contrast to the trend towards large main memory and memory-resident databases or analytics seen in 'big data' market. Servers with massive memory do not provide computing power in a cost and power effective fashion. Since the first order need of science and engineering simulations is large-scale computing, it is not a surprise that they are being increasing executed on systems with coprocessors and accelerators, and thus are facing memory and data movement bottlenecks.

Driven by the memory and data movement considerations, we can see that the only option for data-driven analysis of an engineering simulation on emerging (cost and power effective) systems involves: 1) Aggressive *reduction* of data soon after it is generated (so as to reduce the memory requirements for the next step), 2) Analyses performed in real-time over the reduced or summarized data, and possible further data reduction, 3) Long-term storage and/or movement of only the most critical and summarized data for future analyses, and 4) Aggressive analyses, visualization, and exploration, but using only the summarized data. The first two steps are referred to as *in situ* data reduction and data analysis, respectively [3, 16, 17, 20, 21, 28, 34].

Such in situ analysis, however, involves many open challenges. On one hand, memory and data movements considerations dictate that any summary structure be very compact, analyses be extremely memory efficient, and only a small fraction of the data generated be stored in the persistent memory or moved to a different device. On the other hand, it is also important that data analysis does not lose out on salient features – otherwise, the entire advantage of simulating the phenomenon at a high spatial and/or temporal granularity can be easily lost. Scientists often perform data reduction based on ad-hoc approaches, typically relying on their own insights into the simulation. However, in the process, they risk losing out on new insights into the phenomenon that can only be extracted by a more systematic analysis of data.

In our work, we propose a novel method that utilizes *bitmap index (bitmaps)* as a summarization of the data and showed that many kinds of analyses can be supported by bitmaps without requiring the original dataset. This work develops on top of our recent work

ID	Value	e_0	e_1	e_2	e_3	i_0	i_1
		=1	=2	=3	=4	[1, 2]	[3, 4]
0	4	0	0	0	1	0	1
1	1	1	0	0	0	1	0
2	2	0	1	0	0	1	0
3	2	0	1	0	0	1	0
4	3	0	0	1	0	0	1
5	4	0	0	0	1	0	1
6	3	0	0	1	0	0	1
7	1	1	0	0	0	1	0
Dataset		Low Level Indices				High Level Indices	

Figure 1: An Example of Bitmap Index

that demonstrated how bitmaps can be used as a compact summary of data and lead to efficient implementations of key (offline) analytics tasks [30]. This paper demonstrates how bitmaps can be used efficiently for in-situ analytics. Specifically, after the data is simulated in memory, we generate bitmaps, and subsequently, a number of different analysis steps are performed on bitmaps. Then, instead of writing the data, we only write the bitmaps (much smaller in size) back to disk, which greatly improves the I/O efficiency. We have also demonstrated how to use bitmaps for both online (in-situ) analysis (e.g., time-steps selection which focuses on selecting a subset of time-steps containing more *important* information out of simulated time-steps [22, 31, 35, 36]) and offline analysis (e.g., correlation mining which automatically finds data subsets with high correlations [5]) efficiently.

We have extensively evaluated our approach. We first show that although our method takes extra time for bitmaps generation, the time requirements for the entire in-situ analysis phase are lowered in most of the cases (the speedup is from 0.79x to 3.28x). This is because our method has much smaller online analyses and I/O time cost, and we also improved the bitmaps generation efficiency utilizing multi-core and many-core architectures. Besides efficiency improvement, another advantage of our method is that it has much smaller memory consumption because we only keep bitmaps (much smaller in size) instead of the original dataset in memory. This way, we can hold more time-steps in memory for more accurate online analysis. Second, we design different core allocation strategies and show how total time cost is affected by different strategies. Third, we show that the efficiency of in-situ bitmaps generation and online analysis can be improved in a parallel in-situ environment. Fourth, we show that our method can improve the efficiency for offline analyses such as correlation mining. Finally, we compared the in-situ sampling method with our in-situ bitmaps method and show that while our method does not incur any information loss for time-steps selection, in-situ sampling method incurs an average of 21.03% to 58.73% information loss depending on the sampling percentage.

2. IN-SITU BITMAPS GENERATION

This section first gives the background of bitmap index (bitmaps) and then describes our in-situ bitmaps generation method.

2.1 Background: Bitmap Index

An indexing method provides an efficient way to support value-based queries. Various methods have been extensively researched and used in the context of relational databases. Bitmap indexing, which utilizes the fast bitwise operations supported by the computer hardware, has been shown to be an efficient approach, and has been widely used in scientific data management [26, 43]. In particular, recent work has shown that bitmap index can help support efficient querying of scientific datasets stored in native formats [7, 29].

Figure 1 shows an example of a bitmap index. In this simple example, the dataset contains a total of 8 elements with 4 distinct values. The *low-level* bitmap index contains 4 bitvectors, where each bitvector corresponds to one value. The number of bits within each bitvector is the same as total number of elements in the dataset. In each bitvector, a bit is set to 1 if the value for the corresponding data element's attribute is equal to the *bitvector value*, i.e., the particular distinct value for which this vector is created. The *high-level* bitmap index can be generated based on either the value intervals or value ranges. From Figure 1, we can see two *high-level* bitvectors are built based on value intervals.

This simple example only contains integer values. Bitmap indexing also has been shown to be an efficient method for floating-point values [42]. For such datasets, instead of building a bitvector for each distinct value, we can first group a set of values together (*binning*) and build bitvectors for these bins. This way, the total number of bitvectors is kept at a manageable level.

From the example we can also see that the number of bits within each level of bitmap index is $n \times m$, where n is the total number of elements and m is the total number of bitvectors. This can result in sizes even greater than the size of the original dataset, causing high time and space overheads for bitmaps creation, storage, and query processing. To solve this problem, *run-length compression* algorithms such as Byte-aligned Bitmap Code (BBC) [4] and Word-Aligned Hybrid (WAH) [41] have been developed to reduce the bitmaps size. The main idea of these approaches is that for long sequences of 0s and 1s within each bitvector, an encoding is used to count the number of continuous 0s or 1s. Such encoded counts are stored, requiring less space. Another property of the run-length compression methods is that it supports fast bitwise operations without decompressing the data.

2.2 Summarizing Spatial Data with Bitmaps

The following observations can be made with respect to bitmap index and their suitability as a summary structure for multi-dimension arrays. There is no binning (and thus no loss of precision) with respect to dimensional attributes, unlike almost any other method, such as a histogram. This turns out to be a very important advantage, especially for any application where spatial precision is critical. The value distribution is also maintained (though this is also true for histograms). At the same time, because each point is represented by a single bit, compression is used, continuity of dimensional attributes is exploited, and due to the hardware support for bit operations, we can achieve space and time efficiency. Note that like other methods discussed above, there is binning with respect to value-based attributes, but it seems unavoidable when space efficiency is important.

The other advantages of bitmaps are as follows:

- Bitmaps are much smaller in size compared with the original dataset. In most of the cases, the size of bitmaps is less than 30% in size compared with the original dataset, which improves both data I/O and memory usage.

- Many kinds of analyses can be executed purely using bitmaps without the original dataset. In our previous work, we demonstrated that approximate data aggregation, data spatial join, correlation query, incomplete data analysis and subgroup discovery can be supported using bitmaps without touching the original dataset [2, 30, 38, 39]. In this work, we will further show that time-steps selection and correlation mining can be supported using bitmaps.

- Bitmaps can be generated efficiently in an in-situ setting with acceleration using multiple cores. More importantly, we observe that newer architectures have a large number of cores, which can be used to generate bitmaps without very high overheads. Moreover, the cost of bitmaps generation is easily offset by reduction in data movement times.

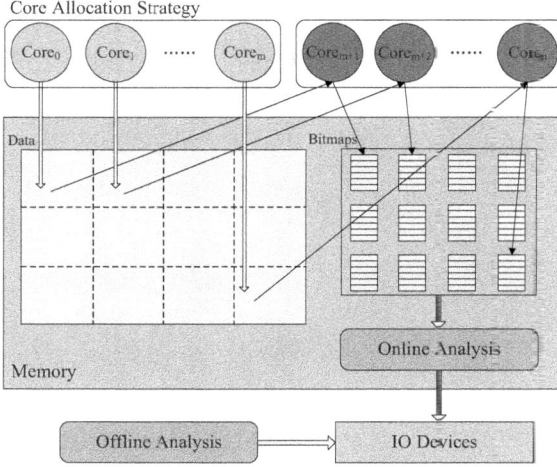

Figure 2: In-Situ Bitmaps Generation

2.3 In-Situ Bitmaps Generation

Recently, several others efforts [16, 20] demonstrate that the bitmap index generation speed can be greatly improved in an in-situ setting. Compared with these works, the main contribution of our work is that we design a WAH-based in-place bitmaps compression algorithm which has very small memory cost and hence is suitable for in-situ setting. We also propose different core allocation strategies for parallel bitmaps generation and discuss the advantage and disadvantage of each strategy.

Multi-Core Processing and Core Allocation: Figure 2 shows the process of generating distributed bitmaps from the data output using an ongoing simulation, and using multiple cores on a single node. The same algorithm can be applied if the data is simulated in a cluster environment where each machine simulates a portion of the data. A *Core Allocation Strategy* is pre-defined, and is used to decide how to allocate cores for simulation and bitmaps generation. Using the strategy, a set of cores ($core_0$ to $core_m$) is assigned for data simulation, while the remaining cores are responsible for bitmaps generation. Each simulation core will simulate a portion of the data and write the data into memory. After a time-step of data is ready, the data will be logically partitioned into $(n - m)$ sub-blocks based on a *pre-defined* partitioning algorithm. Then, each core among the cores assigned for bitmaps generation will access a sub-block of the data in memory and generate compressed bitvectors. This way, the bitmaps generation is performed in parallel without having any dependency among different cores. After bitmaps are generated, the original data can be discarded because bitmaps contain enough information for users to do certain kinds of online (e.g., time-steps selection) and offline analysis (e.g. correlation mining), which will be described in the next two sections.

In our work, two cores allocation strategies (*Shared Cores* and *Separate Cores*) are designed. The *Shared Cores* method assigns all the available cores for both data simulation and bitmaps generation. Each time after one time-step of data is generated (using all cores), the simulation program will be paused and all the cores will be switched for bitmaps generation. After that, the simulation continues to generate next time-step data when the bitmaps for current time-step are ready. The *Separate Cores* method divides the available cores into two separated sets. One set is always used for data simulation and another is responsible for bitmaps generation. In this case, the data simulation and bitmaps generation is performed in parallel, and a data queue is shared between simulation and bitmaps generation. Each time when a new time-step data is simulated, it will be added to the tail of the data queue if the queue is not full (the queue size is limited by the memory capac-

ity). And if the data queue is not empty, the data will be dequeued from the head of the queue and the cores for bitmaps generation will generate bitmaps based on the data. Using this method, the number of cores allocated between simulation and bitmaps generation becomes very important. Ideally, the average data simulation speed should be close to the average bitmaps generation speed after the core allocation. In our work, we use Equations 1 and 2 to decide core allocation. For each simulation, we first use an initial set of cores to run simulation and bitmaps generation and calculate the average simulation time ($Time_{simulate}$) and bitmaps generation time $Time_{bitmap}$. Then the number of cores of allocation depends on the ratio between $Time_{simulate}$ and $Time_{bitmap}$.

$$\text{Core}_{simulate} = \text{Core}_{total} \times \frac{\text{Time}_{simulate}}{\left(\text{Time}_{simulate} + \text{Time}_{bitmap}\right)} \quad (1)$$

$$\text{Core}_{bitmap} = \text{Core}_{total} - \text{Core}_{simulate} \quad (2)$$

Algorithm 1: Generate_Bitmaps($Data, DataSize, BinNum$)

```
 1:  id = 0;
 2:  allocate space for Segments with size BinNum;
 3:  allocate space for Result with size BinNum;
 4:  for i = 0; i < DataSize; i+ = 31 do
 5:     initialize elements in Segments to 0;
 6:     for j = 0; j < 31 AND j + i < DataSize; j+ = 1 do
 7:        VectorID = MapValueToID(Data[id + +);
 8:        Segments[VectorID] = Segments[VectorID] | (1UL ≪ (30 − j));
 9:     end for
10:     for j = 0; j < BinNum; j+ = 1 do
11:        &LastSeg = Result[j].back()
12:        if Segments[j] == 0x7FFFFFFF then
13:           if (LastSeg AND 0xC0000000) == 0xC0000000 then
14:              LastSeg+ = 31;
15:           else
16:              Result[j].push_back(0xC000001F);
17:           end if
18:        else if Segments[j] == 0 then
19:           if (LastSeg AND 0xC0000000) == 0x80000000 then
20:              LastSeg+ = 31;
21:           else
22:              Result[j].push_back(0x8000001F);
23:           end if
24:        else
25:           Result[j].push_back(Segments[j]);
26:        end if
27:     end for
28:  end for
29:  Return Result
```

Online Compression: For in-situ analysis, besides the efficiency, another important factor is the memory limitation. We do not want bitmaps to occupy a large amount of memory and thus affect the simulation process. From Subsection 2.1, we know that bitmaps before compression can require more memory than the original data. Hence, it is certainly unacceptable that we first generate all uncompressed bitvectors and then do a one-time compression. The problem, however, is that bitmap compression is normally based on identifying series of 0's or 1's, something that is hard if only small segments are available.

We address this problem through a novel algorithm. The basic idea of this algorithm is to fetch data segment by segment, generate bitvectors for each segment, and merge them into existing compressed bitvectors, while only needing to scan the data once. Moreover, because our goal is to only keep bitmaps instead of data for certain kinds of analysis, we can keep freeing the memory of the data we have already scanned and use it to hold bitmaps we generated. This way, the available memory actually keeps increasing as bitmaps are generating. Algorithm 1 shows the pseudocode of this method. The variable id is the index to iterate through the data, the variable $Segments$ contains the uncompressed bitvectors for the current segment, and the variable $Result$ contains the compressed bitvectors for all previous segments. The for loop in the line 4 shows that we generate the bitvectors segment by segment (we use WAH compression, where every 31 elements forms a segment). Line 5 to line 9 shows the process of generating uncompressed bitvectors ($Segments$) for current segment. $Segments$ is a 2D bit array (the first dimension is the number of bitvectors, the second dimension is 32 bits stored as one integer) and initially every bit is set to 0, as shown in line 5. Line 7 maps each element in current segment into corresponding bins (bitvectors) based on its value. Line 8 sets the corresponding bit of the mapped bitvector to 1 based on element position. Line 10 to line 28 shows the process of merging current uncompressed bitvectors ($Segments$) into existing compressed bitvectors ($Result$). Line 11 fetches the last compressed bitvector unit from $Result[j]$. If current $Segments[j]$ contains all 1-bits ($0x7FFFFFFF$), and if the previous compressed bitvector unit is a fill word containing 1-bits ($0xC0000000$), we update the last compressed unit by adding 31 new 1-bits, as shown from line 12 to line 14. Otherwise, we add a new fill word ($0xC000001F$) containing 31 bits into $Result[j]$, as shown from line 15 to line 17. Line 18 to line 23 shows the merging process when $Segments[j]$ is a fill word containing all 0-bits (0), and the logic is similar as 1-bit fill word. If $Segments[j]$ contains a mix of 0 and 1 bits, we treat it as a literal word, and directly add it to the tail of $Result[j]$, as shown from line 24 to line 26.

3. ONLINE ANALYSIS USING BITMAPS

Our claim is that bitmaps can be an effective summary of the original data. To this end, we show how some of the key data selection steps can be performed using only bitmaps (and after original data has been discarded). Performing such a step using only bitmaps greatly reduces memory requirements, a critical issue for today's accelerators and upcoming HPC architectures.

The specific data selection step we have implemented using bitmaps is *time-steps selection*. Specifically, for most of the simulations, the data is simulated time-step by time-step. Certain time-steps contain more *important* information over others, and can be one of the representative time-steps for a post analysis step. Thus, the goal of a *time-step* selection algorithm is to find K of the N given time-steps that represent the evolution of the phenomenon.

3.1 Importance Driven Time-steps Selection

Importance driven time-steps selection has been well studied [22, 31, 35, 36, 37]. The key question is how to measure the *importance* of a time-step – usually, the *importance* of a time-step is determined in two aspects: First, the output for the time-step itself may contain a high amount of *information*. Second, the time-step may convey a distinct type of information with respect to the other time-steps. Several correlation metrics from the information theory [6, 8, 32, 33] such as *Earth Mover's Distance*, *Shannon's Entropy*, *Mutual Information* and *Conditional Entropy* are applied to quantify the above two aspects.

The next question is selecting a subset of time-steps given a fixed number of time-steps. Wang *et al* [36] proposed a greedy algorithm, where the main steps are: 1) partition the time-steps into *intervals*, 2) calculate the *correlation* between the previous selected time-step (the one of the previous interval) and each time-step within this interval, and 3) select the time-step with the minimum correlation. Now, the key consideration is generating these partitions. One obvious method will be *fixed length partitioning*, i.e., each partition contains the same number of time-steps. However, more sophisticated method like *information-volume based partitioning* can also be used, where the time-steps within each partition contain the same total amount of accumulated importance values. Note that the above method is a greedy method, and there are

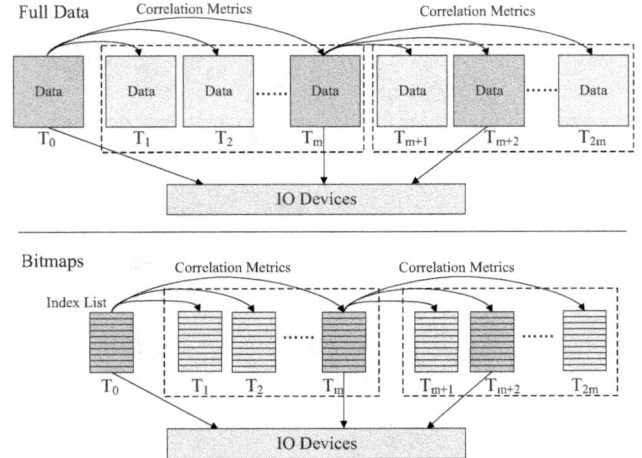

Figure 3: Time-Steps Selection Using Full Data and Bitmaps

other possibilities as well. For example, Tong *et al* [31] proposed a method that uses dynamic programming. Though bitmaps can be used to accelerate computation of almost any such algorithm, we have implemented a greedy algorithm, because efficiency is the most important consideration for us.

Figure 3 shows the process of supporting time-steps selection using both *full data* and *bitmaps*. We first look at the *full data* method. From the figure we can see that, there is a total number of $2m + 1$ time-steps, which are divided into three intervals. The first interval only contains one time-step (T_0), while the second and third interval contain m time-steps each. Initially we always choose the first time-step as the pre-selected time-step. To find the time-step in the second interval with minimum correlation with respect to the first time-step, we need to calculate different correlation metrics between the pre-selected time-step T_0 and each time-step in the second interval (T_1 to T_m). After the calculation, T_m contains the minimum correlation with respect to T_0. Hence, we only keep T_m for the second interval and discard others. Then, we use T_m as the preselected time-step and continue to select the time-step with minimum correlation in the third interval, and continue the process. This way, we are able to keep time-steps with maximum information with respect to each other. If we look at the *bitmaps* method, we can see that the calculation process is similar. However, instead of using the original data which is big in size, all the correlation metrics can be calculated using bitmaps. Because bitmaps is much smaller in size, this method has much smaller memory cost. And in the following subsection, we will also show that the calculation of different correlation metrics can be performed more efficiently using bitmaps.

The algorithm we have accelerated using bitmaps uses two important correlation metrics, the *Earth Mover's Distance* and *Conditional Entropy*. The calculation of *Conditional Entropy*, in turn, is based on two other metrics, which are *Mutual Information* and *Shannon's Entropy*. To be able to describe how these metrics can be computed using bitmaps, we first give mathematical definitions of these metrics, and how they are computed using original data.

Earth Mover's Distance: The earth mover's distance (EMD) is the measure of the distance between two probability distributions over a region D – it can be viewed as the cost of changing one distribution of the data to another distribution of the data. Let us say that we are looking at the difference of distribution between two time-steps A and B. Then, *EMD* is calculated by first dividing elements of attribute A and B into bins based on values (the binning range of different time-steps should be the same), then checking how many elements are different within each bin between A and B, and finally, taking a cumulative sum of these differences together,

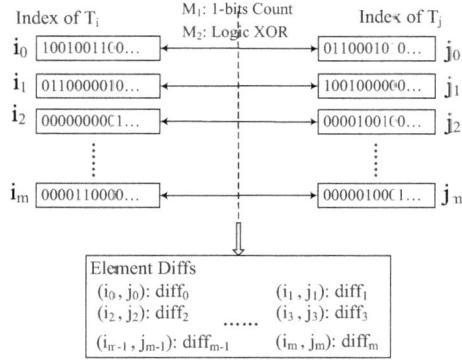

Figure 4: Calculating Earth Movers Distance Using Bitmaps

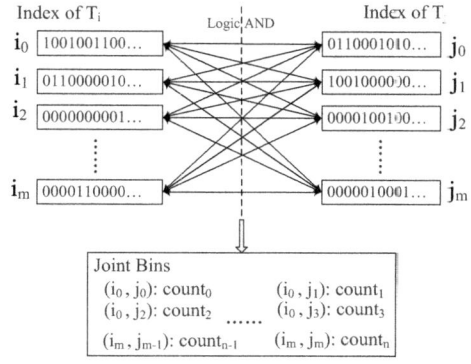

Figure 5: Calculating Conditional Entropy Using Bitmaps

as shown in Equation 3 below. Here, $CFP(j)$ indicates the differences between variable A and variable B when element values are smaller than the value range of the jth bin. The EMD calculation simply sums each $CFP(j)$ together.

$$\text{EMD} = \sum_{j=1}^{N} \text{CFP}(j),$$
$$\text{CFP}(j) = \text{CFP}(j-1) + Diff(\text{Bin}(A_j), \text{Bin}(B_j)), \qquad (3)$$
$$\text{CFP}(0) = 0.$$

Shannon's Entropy: In information theory, the information content of a random variable can be quantified by Shannon's entropy [11]. Constant data (easily predictable) has a low entropy, while apparently random data (uniform probability) has a high entropy. Equation 4 shows the expression to calculate the Shannon's entropy – here, N_A represents the number of distinct values of the attribute A, and the probability distribution functions P_A captures the probability of having each distinct value for A.

$$H(A) = - \sum_{j=1}^{N_A} P_A(x_j) \times log_2(P_A(x_j)) \qquad (4)$$

Mutual Information: Mutual information is the metric for computing the dependence between two random variables, and shows the amount of shared information between two variables in the number of bits. If the mutual information is low, then the two variables are independent. Conversely, if mutual information is high, one variable provides information about the other. Equation 5 shows the expression to calculate the mutual information. Here, we index the data in the variables or attributes A and B by j and k separately, and use x_j and y_k to represent each distinct value N_A and N_B represent the number of distinct values of each attribute, and three probability distribution functions, P_A, P_B and P_{AB}, capture the probability of having each distinct value for A, for B, and for a pair of values of A and B, respectively.

$$I(A; B) = \sum_{j=1}^{N_A} \sum_{k=1}^{N_B} P_{AB}(x_j, y_k) \times \log\left(\frac{P_{AB}(x_j, y_k)}{P_A(x_j) P_B(y_k)}\right) \quad (5)$$

Conditional Entropy: Conditional entropy is defined with the consideration of both self-contained information and the information with respect to others. It is calculated by Shannon's entropy minus mutual information, as shown in Equation 6. The bigger the conditional entropy value of A is, the more information A contains with the respect to B.

$$H(A|B) = H(A) - I(A; B) \qquad (6)$$

3.2 Time-steps Selection Using Bitmaps

This subsection describes how to select time-steps more efficiently using bitmaps.

Earth Mover's Distance: Recall that EMD is summed based on CFP of each bin, and each CFP, in turn, is calculated using the number of elements that are different within each bin pair (bins of two time-steps with the same value range). Hence, the calculation of EMD becomes the calculation of different number of elements for each bin pair between two time-steps. There are two methods to calculate the element differences. The first method is to simply count the number of elements of each bin pair and compute the count differences between them. The second method is to compute the element differences for each bin pair considering spatial information. Because most of the scientific data involves multi-dimensional spaces, calculating elements differences considering their spatial positions is necessary in many cases. For each bin pair, we need to scan each data element inside one bin and find if there is a match at the same position of another bin.

The question we focus on is of computing EMD accurately using only bitmaps, and not the original data. We have developed an algorithm, which we describe now (Figure 4 shows the algorithm pictorially). As a background, first consider the algorithm using full data. First, we have to scan data from both time-steps T_i and T_j to classify the data elements into bins. Then, we have to compare the elements of T_i and T_j inside each bin pair and compute the number of elements that are different. Both steps are time-consuming for large-scale data. In comparison, from Figure 4, we can see that with the help of bitmaps, we already have bitvectors (bits) of both T_i and T_j. For the first bin difference calculation method, we only need to perform 1-bits count operations on each bitvector pair of T_i and T_j. Because each 1-bit inside the bitvector indicates that there is one data element inside current bin, if we choose the same binning scale as when using the full data, we can get the same element differences for each bin pair and hence the same EMD result. For the second calculation method, we only need to perform m number of bitwise XOR operations between T_i and T_j to calculate the element differences for each bin pair. Logic XOR operation sets the target bit to 1 if the same position of the two inputs has different bit values (one bit is 1 which means there is a data element in current position of one bin, and another bit is 0 which means there is no matching element for the same position of another bin). Hence, we can quickly compute the different number of elements between bin pairs without scanning through each element inside the original data. Also, we are able to generate same element differences for each bin pair considering spatial differences compared with the full data method. This way, we can achieve much better efficiency compared to the full data method without any accuracy loss for the same binning scale.

Conditional Entropy: Now, consider the calculation of conditional entropy, which is the difference between Shannon's entropy and mutual information. Conditional entropy can be computed using the individual value distribution of time-steps T_i and T_j, and the joint value distribution of T_{ij}. Here, the key step is to generate the joint value distribution. Figure 5 shows the process of calculating conditional entropy using bitmaps. While using the original data, we need to scan through each element of both T_i and T_j at least twice to decide the binning scale and then to generate individual and joint value distributions. Using bitmaps, because each bitvector corresponds to one value or value range, the individual value distributions of T_i and T_j are already generated during the bitmaps generation process. From the figure we can see that, using bitmaps, we only need to perform fast bitwise *AND* operations between m bitvectors of T_i and m bitvectors of T_j to generate all the joint bins, which is efficient. Logic *AND* operation sets the target bit to 1 only if the same position of both inputs contain 1-bit values, which means that each time we count 1 for current joint bin T_{ij} only if both the value of T_i and the value of T_j in current position satisfy the value range of current joint bin. Hence, the joint value distribution generated by bitmaps is the same as that generated by the full data, assuming the same binning scale.

4. OFFLINE ANALYSIS USING BITMAPS

We can use bitmaps (only) to perform different kinds of offline analyses. In our previous work, we have demonstrated that we can perform approximate data aggregation, data spatial join, correlation query, incomplete data analysis and subgroup discovery using bitmaps [2, 30, 38, 39]. In this section, we will focus on correlation mining.

4.1 Motivation for Correlation Mining

There is often a need for complex analyses over datasets generated by scientific simulations. Such analyses can be classified into two categories: individual variable analysis and correlation analysis. Individual variable analysis involves analysis over each variable or attribute independently, and can take the form of data subsetting, data aggregation, data mining or visualization. Much of the existing work, especially in data visualization, has focused on individual variable analysis. However, more recently, several efforts [5, 35] have focused on studying the relationship among multiple variables and making interesting scientific discoveries based on such analysis.

In our previous work [30], we proposed an interactive framework to support correlation queries over multiple variables. Using our tool, users can submit different SQL queries to specify the data subsets (either value-based or dimension-based subsets) they are interested in for correlation analysis. Our tool is able to calculate correlations of the subsets among multi-variables and return the result to users. With the help of bitmaps, the entire process can be executed very efficiently.

However, one open challenge remaining in this work is that the users often do not know what subsets could provide interesting correlation results. Thus, there is a need for a *correlation mining* algorithm, and not just *correlation query processing*.

4.2 Correlation Mining Using Bitmaps

In this work, we focus on correlation mining between two variables. *Mutual Information*, discussed in the previous section, is used here as an indicator of correlations between two variables. Our goal is to find the data subsets (either value or spatial subsets) with a high value of mutual information.

$$I(A; B) = \sum_{j=1}^{N_A} \sum_{k=1}^{N_B} I(A_j; B_k), \quad I(A_j; B_k) \geq 0. \quad (7)$$

$$
\begin{aligned}
&P_A(x) = P_{A_1}(x) = P_{A_2}(x); \\
&P_B(y) = P_{B_1}(y) = P_{B_2}(y); \\
&P_{AB}(x, y) = \frac{P_{A_1 B_1}(x,y) + P_{A_2 B_2}(x,y)}{2}, \ P_{A_1 B_1} > P_{A_2 B_2}; \\
&I(A; B) < I(A_1; B_1).
\end{aligned}
\quad (8)
$$

In our solution, the mining process for value-based subsets and spatial-based subsets follows different orders. If we analyze the ex-

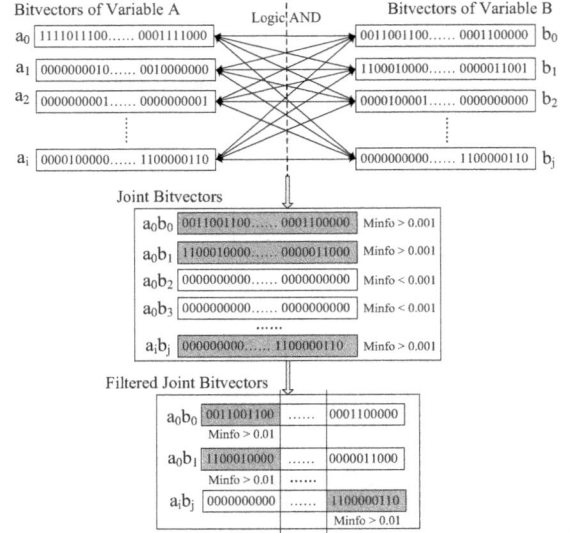

Figure 6: Correlation Mining Using Bitmaps

pression of mutual information in Subsection 3.1, we can see that mutual information is accumulated based on the probabilities of value subsets. If the mutual information of a bigger value range is low, all its value subsets must contain lower mutual information. As shown in Equation 7, the mutual information $I(A, B)$ is summed by the mutual information of each value subset $I(A_j; B_k)$. Because $I(A_j; B_k)$ is non-negative, we can see that $I(A, B)$ is always larger than or equal to the value of any subset $I(A_j; B_k)$. Hence, we use a top-down method for efficient value-based subsets mining, exploiting multiple levels of bitmaps. However, the situation is different for spatial subsets. We cannot draw the same conclusion if a bigger spatial area contains low mutual information. This is because it is highly possible that one spatial sub-area contains high mutual information while other sub-areas contain low mutual information, which make the final result low. A simple example is shown using Equation 8. Here we divide the data into two sub-spatial areas. To simplify the scenario, we assume these two sub-areas contain the same number of elements and also the same individual value distributions for both variable A and B ($P_A(x) = P_{A_1}(x) = P_{A_2}(x), P_B(y) = P_{B_1}(y) = P_{B_2}(y)$). The difference is that one sub-area has bigger joint value distribution than another ($P_{A_1 B_1} > P_{A_2 B_2}$). In such case, we can easy see that while the individual value distribution is the same, the joint distribution of entire area P_{AB} value is the average of two sub-areas $P_{A_1 B_1}$ and $P_{A_2 B_2}$. Because the mutual information is proportional to the joint value distribution, and P_{AB} is smaller than $P_{A_1 B_1}$, we can easily find that the mutual information of $I(A; B)$ is smaller than its sub-area $I(A_1; B_1)$. Hence, for spatial subsets, we follow a bottom-up order to calculate mutual information.

Without bitmaps, we have to manually divide the entire dataset into a huge number of values and spatial units and then calculate the mutual information between each unit pair, which is extremely time-consuming. With the help of bitmaps, although we follow different orders for value and spatial subsets mining, we do not need to process them separately. Figure 6 shows the process of correlation mining using one-level bitmaps, which comprises three steps. In the first step, we generate joint bitvectors based on logic *AND* operations between bitvectors of A and B. We also count the number of 1-bits for each joint bitvectors during the bitwise *AND* operations. The total number of bitwise operations are $i \times j$, where i is the number of bitvectors of variable A and j is the number of bitvectors of variable B. The second step is a pruning step. Although we generate $i \times j$ number of joint bitvectors, the 1-bits are distributed sparsely over the joint bitvectors. A pruning step is necessary to filter those joint bitvectors with small correlations. Here we calculate the mutual information for each joint bitvector and filter the joint bitvector if the result is smaller than a threshold T. The rule to decide T here is that even if all the 1-bits of the joint bitvector is located within the same spatial unit, we still consider it as uncorrelated. In such a case, we assume all elements inside this joint bitvector (corresponding to the value subsets of two variables) are uncorrelated and further processing is not required. In the third step, for the remaining joint bitvectors, we partition each bitvector into basic sub-spatial units and generate the 1-bits distribution over all units. We keep only those units with mutual information larger than another threshold T' and filter the others. All the remaining units are considered as spatial subsets with high correlations. Hence, with the help of bitmaps, we only need the bitwise *AND* and *Count* operations to detect all the interesting value or spatial subsets with high correlations.

Algorithm 2: Correlation_Mining($bitVectorsA, bitVectorsB$)

```
1:  for each vectorA in bitVectorsA do
2:    for each vectorB in bitVectorsB do
3:      jointBitVector = LogicAND(vectorA, vectorB);
4:      valueMutualInfo =
          CalMutualInfo(vectorA, vectorB, jointBitVector)
5:      if valueMutualInfo >= THRESHOLD1 then
6:        for unitBegin = 0; unitBegin < dataSize
             unitBegin+ = unitSize do
7:          spatialMutualInfo =
              CalMutualInfo(jointBitVector, unitBegin, unitSize);
8:          if spatialMutualInfo >= THRESHOLD2 then
9:            AddResult(unitBegin, unitSize, jointBitVector);
10:         end if
11:       end for
12:     end if
13:   end for
14: end for
```

Algorithm 2 shows the pseudo-code of correlation mining between two variables. Line 1 to line 3 iterates each bitvector of variable A and B, perform logic *AND* operation between each bitvector pair and generate joint bitvectors. Line 4 calculates the mutual information for the current joint bitvector. If the current mutual information is larger than a threshold (shown in line 5), we iterate each spatial unit of the joint bitvector and calculate the mutual information within each spatial unit (line 6 to line 11). Finally those spatial units with mutual information larger than another threshold are kept in the final result. All the other values and spatial units are treated as uncorrelated.

There are two optimizations in our work. For multi-dimensional dataset, to keep the multi-dimensional feature of each spatial unit, we use the Z-order curve [27] to iterate over the dataset during the bitmaps generation process. This way, when we partition the joint bitvectors, the basic spatial unit is the size of the smallest unit of Z orders. We can also choose different Z order granularity to match our efficiency goals. Moreover, because usually bitmaps are constructed at multiple levels, the higher level bitmaps contain smaller number of bins with bigger bin ranges, whereas, it is the other way around for the lower level. For efficiency consideration, we begin with high-level bitmaps to quickly filter the low correlated value subsets. Then we only look at the low-level bitvectors belonging to the high-correlated bitvectors of high-level bitmaps.

5. EXPERIMENTAL RESULTS

In this section, we report results from a number of experiments conducted to evaluate our in-situ bitmaps generation and bitmaps based data analysis algorithms. We designed a series of experiments with the following goals: (1) We compare the in-situ analyses time cost and memory consumption between *bitmaps* and the

full data method, and show that our method can achieve better efficiency and less memory cost for different simulations on different multi-core systems. (2) We compare the efficiency of two cores allocation strategies (*Shared Cores* and *Separate Cores*) and show that a good core allocation strategy can generate bitmaps efficiently. (3) We show that bitmaps can also improve the data analyses efficiency in a parallel in-situ scenario. (4) We show that bitmaps based correlation mining (offline analyses) has much smaller time cost than the *full data* method. (5) We compare the efficiency and accuracy between in-situ sampling and in-situ bitmaps methods and discuss the scenarios where in-situ bitmaps is a better method than in-situ sampling.

We use two simulation programs and one scientific dataset for our experiments. Heat3D simulation [1] is developed to estimate the effect of different geologic structures on heat flow. A 3D mesh can be created to simulate heat flows. The variable generated by the Heat3D application is *temperature*. Livermore Unstructured Lagrangian Explicit Shock Hydrodynamics (Lulesh) simulation [15] is an application which calculates the motion of materials relative to each other when subject to forces. It approximates the hydrodynamics equations discretely by partitioning the spatial problem domain into a collection of volumetric elements defined by a mesh. It is built on the concept of an unstructured hex mesh, and a node on the mesh is a point where mesh lines (edges) intersect. The variables of each node include *coordinates*, *force*, *velocity vector*, and *acceleration*. Lulesh simulation is a complex simulation with more time and memory cost (to hold mesh lines). The dataset we used for correlation mining is generated by the Parallel Ocean Program (POP) [14], which is an ocean circulation model (the simulation code for POP was unavailable to us). The reason we use this dataset here is it contains multiple variables and some of them have strong correlations within either the value or spatial subsets. POP has a grid resolution of approximately 10 km (horizontally) and vertically it has a grid spacing close to 10 m near the surface increasing up to 250 m in the deep ocean. The total number of variables in the dataset is 26, and each variable is modeled with either two dimensions (longitude and latitude) or three dimensions (longitude, latitude and depth). The data is stored in the NetCDF format.

For our single node experiments, we use two machines with large number of cores. One machine contains 32 Intel Xeon x5650 CPUs and 1 TB memory, and is located at the Ohio Super-computing Center (OSC). The second machine (Intel MIC) contains 60 Intel Xeon Phi coprocessors and 8 GB memory. Both these machines were chosen because they have a large number of cores on each node, a characteristic that will be common in the near future. In addition, the Intel MIC node has a small amount of memory per core, which is another expected feature for nodes of future supercomputers. For experiments in a distributed memory (cluster) environment, we used 32 nodes with 12 Intel Xeon x5650 CPUs and 48 GB memory from Oakley Cluster of OSC.

5.1 Efficiency and Memory Cost Comparison for In-Situ Analysis

The experiments in this subsection compare the efficiency and memory cost of in-situ analysis between the *full data* method and the *bitmaps* method.

Figures 7 and 8 compare the in-situ analysis efficiency between *full data* and *bitmaps* methods for Heat3D simulation. In our experiment, the simulation generates 100 time-steps and we select 25 time-steps from them using the *Fixed Length Partitioning* method, as described in Section 3.1. The selection metric used here is *conditional entropy*. Figure 7 shows execution on machine with the Intel Xeon and 1 TB memory. The dimension scale of Heat3D is $800 \times 1000 \times 1000$ and the output data size per time-step is 6.4 GB. Figure 8 shows execution on the Intel MIC with 8 GB memory. Because of the memory limitation, the dimension scale here is set as $200 \times 1000 \times 1000$, and the output data size per time-step is 1.6 GB.

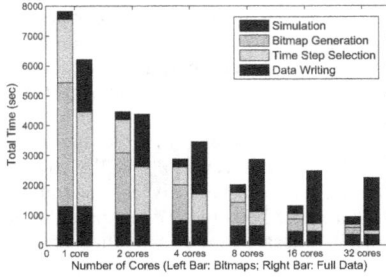

Figure 7: Heat3D: Selecting 25 Time Steps from 100 - Xeon

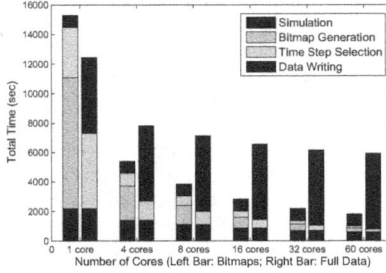

Figure 9: Lulesh: Selecting 25 Time Steps from 100 - Xeon

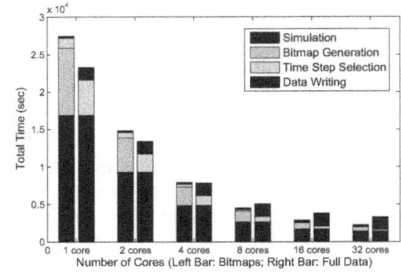

Figure 8: Heat3D: Selecting 25 Time Steps from 100 - MIC

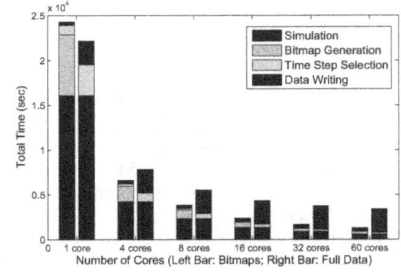

Figure 10: Lulesh: Selecting 25 Time Steps from 100 - MIC

Heat3D simulation has regular temperature changes but the number of distinct values is relatively low. The number of bitvectors (bins) we used ranged from 64 to 206, depending on the temperature range of different time-steps. The binning scale is set to retain 1 digit after the decimal point for each element. The execution time reported for the *bitmaps* method includes the simulation time, the in-situ bitmaps generation time (include both binning time and bitvector compression time), the time-steps selection time using bitmaps, and the time spent outputting bitmaps for the selected time-steps. The execution time reported for the *full data* method includes the simulation time, the time-steps selection time using full data, and the output time for the data from the selected time-steps.

From Figure 7 we can see that the *bitmaps* method has the additional bitmaps generation step, and it has a larger time cost than *full data* method if we only use 1 or 2 cores. However, it greatly reduces the time for time-steps selection and data writing. With the help of bitmaps, we achieved a speedup from 1.38x to 1.50x for time-steps selection (we support fast bitwise operations instead of scanning through 12.8 GB data for each calculation), and achieved a speedup around 6.78x for data writing (the bitmaps size is much smaller than the data size) compared with the *full data* method. The critical observation is that as an increasing number of cores are used, both bitmaps generation time and time-steps selection time is reduced almost linearly, whereas the data output time remains the same. From the figure we can see, the data writing time becomes the major bottleneck after we use 4 cores. If we consider the total execution time, our method can achieve a speedup from 0.79x to 2.37x compared with the *full data* method. More broadly, considering that nodes in current and future HPC machines have large number of cores but limited I/O bandwidth, we can see the clear advantage of bitmaps based approach.

Figure 8 compares the efficiency between the two methods on Intel MIC. Intel MIC contains a larger number of cores for computing, but the I/O bandwidth is even lower. As a larger number of cores are used, we are able to achieve a significant speedup. As a result, our method can achieve a speedup from 0.81x to 3.28x compared with the *full data* method on MIC.

Figures 9 and 10 compare the in-situ analysis efficiency between *full data* and *bitmaps* method for the Lulesh simulation. We select

25 time-steps out of 100 time-steps using the *Fixed Length Partitioning* method, and the selection metric here is *Earth Mover's Distance*. Lulesh is a more complex simulation which generates nodes and edges among nodes. Each node is formed by four variables *Coordinates*, *Force*, *Acceleration* and *Velocity*, and each variable contains data value in three scales *X*, *Y* and *Z*. There are a total of 12 data arrays (each array size is equal to the number of data nodes) for each time-step, and we support in-situ analysis based on all of them. Figure 9 shows execution on the machine with Intel Xeon and 1 TB memory. The total number of nodes generated by Lulesh is 64 MB and the total data size for analysis is 6.14 GB (Edges are used to help calculate nodes value, so we do not include edge data here). Figure 10 shows execution on Intel MIC with 8 GB memory. Because of the memory limitation, the total number of nodes is 8 MB here and the data size for analysis is 768 MB. The number of bitvectors (bins) ranges from 89 to 314, depending upon the number of distinct values in the output at each time-step.

From Figure 9 we can see that, compared with Heat3D simulation, Lulesh is a more complex simulation and has much larger simulation time. For all the cases, the bitmaps generation time and the time-steps selection time is much smaller than the simulation time. Moreover, we are able to achieve a good speedup for time-steps selection using *Earth Mover's Distance*. We only need to perform hundreds of *XOR* operations instead of scanning 12.28 GB data for each calculation. The speedup compared with *full data* method for time-steps selection is from 3.45x to 3.81x. As was the case with Heat3D simulation, our method achieves better efficiency as we use more cores, and the speedup ranges from 0.84x to 1.47x. Figure 10 compares the efficiency between the two methods using Intel MIC. As we had observed in our experiments with the Heat3D simulation, because the MIC system has a larger number of cores and slower disk I/O speed, we are able to achieve even better speedup compared with the *full data* method. The speedup here is from 0.92x to 2.62x.

Figure 11 compares the memory cost between the two methods. In this experiment we kept 10 time-steps in memory for selection. The major memory cost for *Heat3D* using *full data* method is 1 previous selected time-step, 1 intermediate time-step (designed by the simulation) and 10 current time-steps. In comparison, the memory

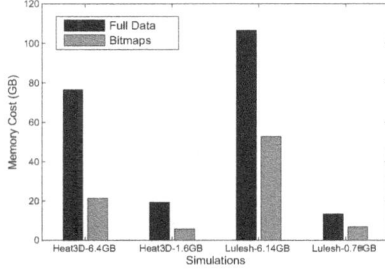

Figure 11: Memory Cost Comparison

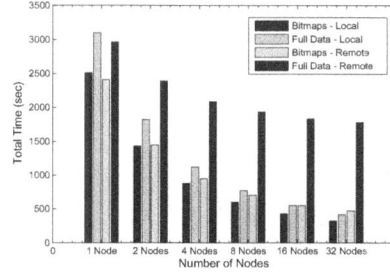

Figure 13: Scalability of Bitmaps (Heat3D on Xeon)

cost using *bitmaps* method is 1 intermediate time-step, 1 current time-step (to simulate next time-step), 1 previous selected bitmap, and 10 current bitmaps. Because bitmaps have much smaller size than the original data, the bitmaps method requires 3.59x (6.4 GB data) and 3.39x (1.6 GB data) smaller memory than the *full data* method. Lulesh is a more complex simulation. Beside the node storage cost, a large amount of memory is used to store the edges, which are used to calculate nodes. However, even with the extra memory cost, our method still has much smaller memory cost, which is 2.02x (6.14 GB) and 1.99x (0.76 GB).

5.2 Comparing Core Allocation Strategies

The experiments compare the simulation and bitmaps generation time between two core allocation strategies, which are the *shared cores* and *separate cores* strategies. Recall that the *shared cores* method involves assigning all the available cores to simulation and bitmaps generation in sequence, whereas the *separate cores* method involves dividing the total cores into two sets and assigning one set to simulation and another to bitmaps generation.

Figure 12 shows the execution times with these two strategies for Heat3D simulation and Lulesh simulation using Intel Xeon and Intel MIC systems. Sub-figure 12(a) compares the total time cost (simulation time plus bitmaps generation time) over 100 time-steps for the Heat3D simulation. The total number of cores used here is 28 (Intel Xeon), and the data size is 6.4 GB. From the figure, we can see that the left bar c_{all} indicates the *shared cores* method. All 28 cores are first used for simulation and then bitmaps generation, and the process is repeated. The right bar group ($c_i\_c_j$) indicates the *separate cores* method. Here i is the number of cores used for simulation, and j is the number of cores used for bitmaps generation. With the allocation $c_{12}\_c_{16}$, which indicates that we use 12 cores for simulation and 16 cores for bitmaps generation, the average time cost of simulation and bitmaps generation is the closest to each other and hence we are able to achieve the best efficiency. As indicated previously, Heat3D is a very simple numerical program, which also does not scale well with increasing number of cores. Thus, best results are obtained when more cores are dedicated to bitmaps generation than the simulation itself. The time cost of c_{all} is larger than $c_{12}\_c_{16}$. This is because of limited scaling of the simulation program – for example, the speedup is only 1.3x when we use 28 cores compared with 12 cores. This shows that it is not necessary to use all the cores for simulation. When we have a large number of cores, we can use the extra cores for bitmaps generation, which will not have a significant impact on the simulation speed.

Sub-figure 12(b) compares the total execution time using Heat3D simulation on Intel MIC system (using 56 cores). The data size is 1.6 GB. From this figure we can see that when we allocate 32 cores for simulation and 24 cores for bitmaps generation ($c_{32}\_c_{24}$), we can achieve the best efficiency. Again time cost of c_{all} allocation is bigger than $c_{32}\_c_{24}$. Sub-figure 12(c) compares the total time cost using Lulesh simulation on Intel Xeon system. We still use 100 time-steps here and the data size is 6.14 GB. Recall that Lulesh simulation has much bigger simulation time. From the figure we

can see that, $c_{20}\_c_8$ achieved the best efficiency, which means we only need to use 8 cores for bitmaps generation. Since most simulation programs involve a large amount of computing, we can expect to see good results by dedicating only a small fraction of the resources for bitmaps generation.

5.3 Efficiency Improvement in Parallel In-Situ Environment

The experiment in this subsection shows that our bitmaps based in-situ analyses method can scale quite well in a cluster setting. Moreover, in clusters or distributed memory machines where data has to be stored to disks that are not local to the node, we show how the bitmaps based method further improves efficiency.

Figure 13 shows the scalability of our method compared with the *full data* method. Same as the previous experiments, the time cost of *full data* method includes the simulation time, the time-steps selection time, and the data I/O time (either writing data to local disk or transferring data to a remote server). The time cost of *bitmaps* method includes the simulation time, the bitmaps generation time, the time-steps selection time, and the data I/O time (writing or transferring bitmaps instead). Here we used 32 computing servers from Oakley Cluster of OSC and 1 remote data server with around 100 MB/sec bandwidth connected to the compute cluster.

The simulation used here is Heat3D, which requires communication (MPI) among machines to update the boundary information. The data size is 6.4 GB. The number of machines varies from 1 to 32, and each machine uses 8 cores for parallel processing. We generate a total of 100 time-steps and select 25 out of them. The selection metric is *Conditional Entropy*. From the figure we can see that, although our method has an extra step for bitmaps generation, we can still achieve better speedup than the *full data* method. Our method saves both time-steps selection and data I/O time cost, and it also scales quite well. The *Bitmap - Local* and *Full Data - Local* methods directly write the data or bitmaps to the local disk of each machine. We can see that our method achieved a 1.24x to 1.29x speedup here. In many cases, the simulated data from multiple computing servers need to be sent to one remote data server for storage, which makes our method achieve further speedup as we have much smaller data transfer size. Using network with around 100 MB/s bandwidth, the *Bitmaps - Remote* method can achieve a 1.24x to 3.79x speedup compared to *Full Data - Remote* method.

5.4 Efficiency Improvement for Offline Analysis

In this experiment, we compares efficiency of correlation mining between *bitmaps* and *full data* method. Here we used the *ocean* dataset generated by the Parallel Ocean Program (POP).

Figure 14 compares the two methods using different data sizes. The two variables we used here are *temperature* and *salinity*. The data size of each variable varies from 1.4 GB to 11.2 GB. From the figure we can see that for all the cases, the *bitmaps* method has smaller execution time than the *full data* method. This is because of a number of reasons. First, our method has much smaller

(a) Heat3D - Xeon   (b) Heat3D - MIC   (c) Lulesh - Xeon

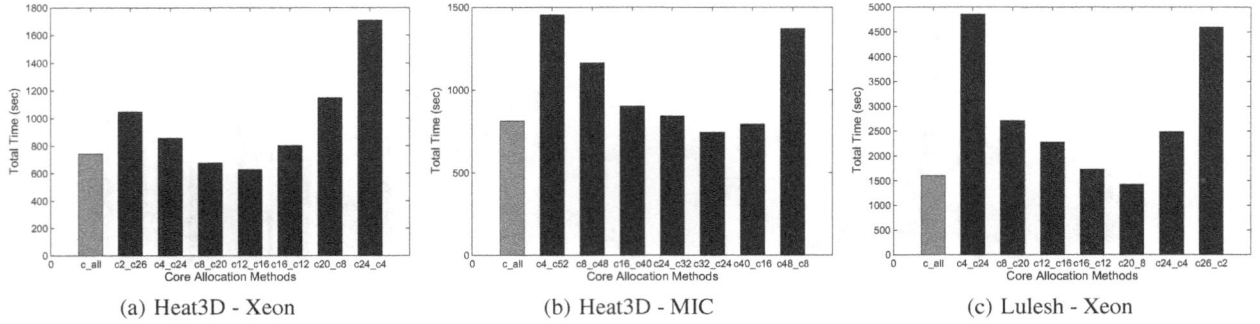

Figure 12: Efficiency Comparison between Shared Cores and Separate Cores Allocation Strategies

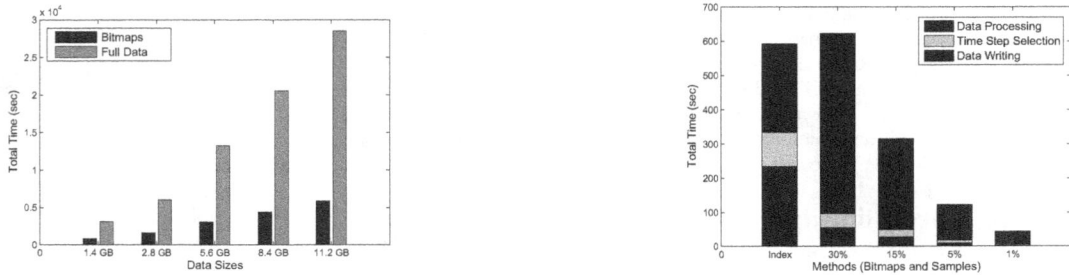

Figure 14: Efficiency of Correlation Mining - POP

Figure 15: Efficiency Comparison between Sampling and Bitmaps - Heat3D

data loading time and memory cost compared with the *full data* method because bitmaps are much smaller in size. Moreover, the mining process of our method involves performing $m \times n$ bitwise AND operations (m is the number of bitvectors of *temperature* and n is the number of bitvectors of *salinity*), filtering the uncorrelated units, and followed by 1-bits count operations based on partitioned spatial units. Both logic *AND* operations and 1-bits count operations can be executed very efficiently. On the other hand, the *full data* method needs to reorganize the entire data into small value and spatial units and then do an exhaustive calculation within each unit (The same filter rule is also applied to *full data* method, but it still has much bigger calculation cost). Also multi-level indices can further improve the efficiency, while building different scales of value range based on original data is time consuming. As a result, our method is able to achieve a 3.83x to 4.91x speedup compared with the *full data* method. The larger the dataset size, the better speedup we can achieve. It is also important to note that there is no accuracy loss compared with the *full data* method. This is because both methods use the same binning scale to calculate mutual information. Note that number of bins can be varied with either of the methods, but larger (smaller) number of bins will lead to higher (lower) execution time for both methods.

5.5 Comparing Bitmaps and Sampling

Bitmaps can be viewed as a data reduction method. One simple approach for data reduction is sampling – i.e., simply selecting a smaller number of output elements for further processing. The experiments in this subsection compare the efficiency and accuracy between in-situ sampling and in-situ bitmaps based analyses. The machine we used here are Intel Xeon with 32 cores.

Figure 15 compares the execution time between *bitmaps* and *sampling* method. We used Heat3D simulation here, which selects 25 time-steps out of 100 and the size of each time-step is 6.4 GB. The number of cores used here is 32. The *Bitmaps* method includes simulation, bitmaps generation, time-step selections using

bitmaps and outputting bitmaps. The *Sampling* method includes simulation, down-sampling, time-steps selection using sample and sample writing.

The left bar shows the time cost of bitmaps method and the right bar group shows the time cost of sampling method with different sampling levels (from 30% to 1%). From the figure we can see that the sampling method, which only selects a subset of the data from the original dataset, can generate different sample levels efficiently, while bitmaps generation, which requires binning and compression, has much bigger time cost than sampling. Moreover, the data size after sampling is effectively reduces, which also greatly improved the efficiency for the time-steps selection. However, from the figure we can see that the *bitmaps* method still achieves better efficiency than the *sampling* method using 30% samples. This is because the major bottleneck here is still the disk I/O speed. With the help of multiple cores within the node, we can significantly reduce the time differences for data processing (bitmaps generation or sampling) and time-steps selection between these two methods.

Besides the time cost, another big advantage of bitmaps method is that, using bitmaps for time-steps selection and correlation calculation does not incur any accuracy loss. In comparison, sampling involves loss of accuracy. Figure 16 shows the accuracy loss with different sampling levels, when sampling is performed before time-steps selection. For bitmaps method, the accuracy is the same as using the original dataset if we choose the same binning scales. For sampling method, we calculate the conditional entropy values between each time-step pairs and then compute the absolute value differences between the sample result and the original result. Then, we use a *Cumulative Frequency Plot* (CFP) to represent the absolute conditional entropy differences for all pairs. In CFP, a point (x,y) indicates that the fraction y of all calculated relative value differences are less than x. Because the value differences should be as small as possible, it implies that a method with the curve to the left has a better accuracy than the method with the curve to

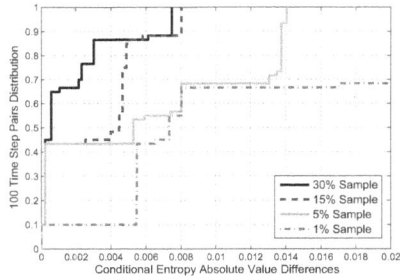

Figure 16: Accuracy Lost for Time Step Selection - Heat3D

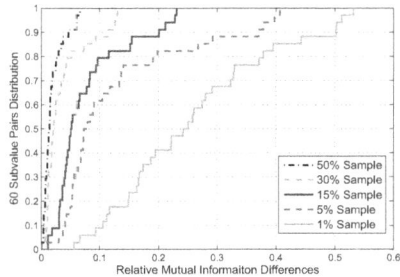

Figure 17: Accuracy Lost for Correlation Mining - POP

the right. From the figure, we can see that the smaller the sample level we use, the more accuracy loss we incur, which is not surprising. If we calculate the relative accuracy loss using the expression $(original\_result - sample\_result)/original\_result$ for each pair, using 30%, 15%, and 5% sample size incurs an average of 21.03%, 37.56%, and 58.37% information loss, respectively. Hence, we can see that although the sampling method can achieve better efficiency than our method if we use a small sample level (less than 30%), the information loss is very significant. On the other hand, 30% of the sample does not help the performance, but still involves a measurable loss of accuracy.

Figure 17 shows the accuracy loss with different sampling levels for offline analyses (Correlation Mining). For correlation mining, we continued to use POP data. The variables used here are *temperature* and *salinity* with 1.4 GB data size for each variable. Here we first divided the variables into 60 spatial and value subsets. Then we calculate the *mutual information* between these two variables within each subset. The value differences between the original dataset and samples are also shown in CFP plot. From the figure, we can also see that while bitmaps method does not have any information loss, the smaller sample level we use the more accuracy loss we incur. Compared with the original result, using 50%, 30%, 15%, and 5% sample size incurs an average of 3.14%, 7.56%, 10.15%, and 17.03% accuracy loss, respectively

6. RELATED WORK

In this section, we will first describe the existing in-situ analysis work and then discuss pertinent work on correlation analysis.

In-situ analysis frameworks have been developed by several groups in recent years. ADIOS [17, 23] makes it possible to independently select the I/O methods for each grouping of data in an application (based on both I/O patterns and the underlying hardware). GoldRush [45], which is built over ADIOS, uses fine-grained scheduling methods to harvest the otherwise idle resources to run in-situ data analytics efficiently. Several other efforts [12, 25] focus on improving I/O efficiency by identifying and leveraging I/O access patterns. GLEAN [34] is a flexible and extensible framework which takes application, analysis, and system characteristics into account to facilitate simulation-time data analysis and I/O acceleration. The

DIY [28] is an in-situ analyses prototype library of scalable core components for the decomposition and movement of data. The Damaris/Viz [10] studied different core allocation strategies (*time partitioning* vs *space partitioning*) with the consideration of memory constraints for in-situ data visualization, while our work is more focused on bitmap generation.

A recent effort [16] has demonstrated that the bitmap index generation efficiency can be greatly improved in an in-situ parallel environment. In their work, they analyzed the index comression and IO time and demonstrated that bitmap index compression efficiency can be greatly improved using multi-core. As we stated earlier, our contributions are in developing strategies for core allocation, and use of bitmaps as a data profile for various analytics steps. A potentially different in-situ compression method is presented in another recent paper [20]. Specifically, the DIRAQ framework provides a parallel *in-situ*, in network data encoding and reorganization technique that enables the transformation of simulation output into a query-efficient form. To the best of our knowledge, the method will not allow steps such as entropy or mutual information calculation or correlation analysis.

Analysis of multiple variables and their relationships in scientific simulation outputs has been an ongoing topic of research. In a very recent work, Biswas *et al.* [5] presented an information theoretic framework for exploring multivariate datasets in a *top-down* manner, where they divide the variables into groups based on their information overlap, and then identify representative variables from each group to conduct further relationship analysis. Wang *et al.* [35] used information theory for exploring the causal relationship among the variables of a time-varying multivariate dataset. In an earlier work, Jänicke *et al.* [13] applied the dimensionality reduction on the high dimensional data where each dimension was analogous to a variable in the multivariate context. Another well-known multivariate exploration technique was developed by Di Yang *et al.* [44]. They use a Nugget Management System (NMS), where the nuggets represent the information that the users are interested in. Several authors have surveyed existing multivariate data analysis techniques [9, 40]. Almost none of these efforts have focused on in-situ analyses and scalability limitations, especially, the challenges associated with a memory-constraint platform.

Our recent work demonstrated how bitmaps can be used to accelerate computation of correlations, in both parallel and distributed setting [30]. In comparison, this work makes several contributions. First, we have demonstrated the feasibility (and even benefits of) bitmap generating in in-situ settings. Second, we have presented novel algorithms for using bitmaps for time-step selection (which includes steps like computation of entropy and Earth Mover Distance). Next, we have used developped a novel algorithm for correlation mining using bitmaps. Finally, we have experimentally demonstrated how the use of bitmaps for summarization can be benefitial in architectures that are memory and I/O constraint.

7. CONCLUSIONS

Dealing with I/O and memory constraints is rapidly becoming the most critical challenge for data analytics associated with scientific data. In this paper, we have proposed an approach, which uses bitmaps as a compact representation of data that can be used for various in-situ and offline analyses steps. The key algorithmic contributions of the paper include a method for generating in-situ bitmaps with different core allocation strategies, methods for computing correlation metrics and Earth Mover's Distance (EMD) using only bitmaps, and a correlation mining algorithm using bitmaps. Because binning is used for these steps even when the original data is used, use of bitmaps does not lead to any loss of accuracy, whereas memory, I/O, and computational costs are reduced.

Our future efforts will focus on extending this work in at least two directions. First, we will like to evaluate this approach on other architectures like GPUs. Second, we will consider other in-situ and offline analytics tasks for acceleration using bitmaps.

Acknowledgements

This work was supported by DOE Office of Science, Advanced Scientific Computing Research, under award number DE-DC0012495, program manager Lucy Nowell, and by NSF under the award ACI-1339757.

8. REFERENCES

[1] Heat3d simulation.
http://http://dournac.org/info/parallel_heat3d.

[2] Sameh Abdulah, Yu Su, and Gagan Agrawal. Accelerating data mining on incomplete datasets by bitmaps-based missing value imputation. In *Proceedings of the 7th International Conference on Advances in Databases, Knowledge, and Data Applications*, 2015.

[3] James Ahrens, Sébastien Jourdain, Patrick OÂŠLeary, John Patchett, D Rogers, and M Peterson. An imagebased approach to extreme scale in situ visualization and analysis. In *Proceedings of the International Conference for High Performance Computing, Networking, Storage and Analysis*. IEEE Press, 2014.

[4] G. Antoshenkov. Byte-aligned bitmap compression. In *Data Compression Conference, 1995. DCC'95. Proceedings*, page 476. IEEE, 1995.

[5] Ayan Biswas, Soumya Dutta, Han-Wei Shen, and Jonathan Woodring. An information-aware framework for exploring multivariate data sets. *IEEE Transactions on Visualization and Computer Graphics*, 19(12):2683–2692, 2013.

[6] Udeepta D Bordoloi and H-W Shen. View selection for volume rendering. In *Visualization, 2005. VIS 05. IEEE*, pages 487–494. IEEE, 2005.

[7] J. Chou, K. Wu, O. Rübel, M.H.J.Q. Prabhat, B. Austin, E.W. Bethel, R.D. Ryne, and A. Shoshani. Parallel index and query for large scale data analysis. In *SC*, 2011.

[8] Thomas M Cover and Joy A Thomas. *Elements of information theory*. John Wiley & Sons, 2012.

[9] M.C.F. de Oliveira and H. Levkowitz. From visual data exploration to visual data mining: a survey. *Visualization and Computer Graphics, IEEE Transactions on*, 9(3):378–394, 2003.

[10] Matthieu Dorier, Roberto Sisneros, Tom Peterka, Gabriel Antoniu, and Dave Semeraro. A nonintrusive, adaptable and user-friendly in situ visualization framework. In *Proceedings of the third international symposium on Large-Scale Data Analysis and Visualization*. IEEE, 2013.

[11] Stefan Gumhold. Maximum entropy light source placement. In *Visualization, 2002. VIS 2002. IEEE*, pages 275–282. IEEE, 2002.

[12] Jun He, John Bent, Aaron Torres, Gary Grider, Garth Gibson, Carlos Maltzahn, and Xian-He Sun. I/o acceleration with pattern detection. In *Proceedings of the 22nd international symposium on High-performance parallel and distributed computing*, pages 25–36. ACM, 2013.

[13] H. Jänicke, M. Bottinger, and G. Scheuermann. Brushing of attribute clouds for the visualization of multivariate data. *Visualization and Computer Graphics, IEEE Transactions on*, 14(6):1459–1466, 2008.

[14] PW Jones, PH Worley, Y. Yoshida, JB White III, and J. Levesque. Practical performance portability in the parallel ocean program (pop). *Concurrency and Computation: Practice and Experience*, 17(10):1317–1327, 2005.

[15] Ian Karlin, Jeff Keasler, and Rob Neely. Lulesh 2.0 updates and changes. Technical Report LLNL-TR-641973, August 2013.

[16] Jinoh Kim, Hasan Abbasi, Luis Chacon, Ciprian Docan, Scott Klasky, Qing Liu, Norbert Podhorszki, Arie Shoshani, and Kesheng Wu. Parallel in situ indexing for data-intensive computing. In *Large Data Analysis and Visualization (LDAV), 2011 IEEE Symposium on*, pages 65–72. IEEE, 2011.

[17] Scott Klasky, Hasan Abbasi, Jeremy Logan, Manish Parashar, Karsten Schwan, Arie Shoshani, Matthew Wolf, Sean Ahern, Ilkay Altintas, Wes Bethel, et al. In situ data processing for extreme-scale computing. In *Proc. Conf. Scientific Discovery through Advanced Computing Program (SciDAC.11)*, 2011.

[18] Peter M Kogge and Timothy J Dysart. Using the top500 to trace and project technology and architecture trends. In *Proceedings of 2011 International Conference for High Performance Computing, Networking, Storage and Analysis*, page 28. ACM, 2011.

[19] Peter M. Kogge and John Shalf. Exascale computing trends: Adjusting to the "new normal"' for computer architecture. *Computing in Science and Engineering*, 15(6):16–26, 2013.

[20] Sriram Lakshminarasimhan, David A Boyuka, Saurabh V Pendse, Xiaocheng Zou, John Jenkins, Venkatram Vishwanath, Michael E Papka, and Nagiza F Samatova. Scalable in situ scientific data encoding for analytical query processing. In *Proceedings of the 22nd international symposium on HPDC*, pages 1–12. ACM, 2013.

[21] Aaditya G Landge, Valerio Pascucci, Attila Gyulassy, Janine C Bennett, Hemanth Kolla, Jacqueline Chen, and Peer-Timo Bremer. In-situ feature extraction of large scale combustion simulations using segmented merge trees. In *Proceedings of the International Conference for High Performance Computing, Networking, Storage and Analysis*, pages 1020–1031. IEEE Press, 2014.

[22] Teng-Yok Lee and Han-Wei Shen. Visualization and exploration of temporal trend relationships in multivariate time-varying data. *Visualization and Computer Graphics, IEEE Transactions on*, 15(6):1359–1366, 2009.

[23] Jay F Lofstead, Scott Klasky, Karsten Schwan, Norbert Podhorszki, and Chen Jin. Flexible io and integration for scientific codes through the adaptable io system (adios). In *Proceedings of the 6th international workshop on Challenges of large applications in distributed environments*, pages 15–24. ACM, 2008.

[24] Robert McLay, Doug James, Si Liu, John Cazes, and William Barth. A user-friendly approach for tuning parallel file operations. In *Proceedings of the international conference on SC*, pages 229–236. IEEE, 2014.

[25] James Oly and Daniel A Reed. Markov model prediction of i/o requests for scientific applications. In *Proceedings of the 16th international conference on Supercomputing*, pages 147–155. ACM, 2002.

[26] P. O'Neil and D. Quass. Improved query performance with variant indexes. In *ACM Sigmod Record*, volume 26, pages 38–49. ACM, 1997.

[27] V. Pascucci and R.J. Frank. Global static indexing for real-time exploration of very large regular grids. In *Supercomputing, ACM/IEEE 2001 Conference*, pages 45–45. IEEE, 2001.

[28] Tom Peterka, Robert Ross, Attila Gyulassy, Valerio Pascucci, Wesley Kendall, Han-Wei Shen, Teng-Yok Lee, and Abon Chaudhuri. Scalable parallel building blocks for custom data analysis. In *Large Data Analysis and Visualization (LDAV), 2011 IEEE Symposium on*, pages 105–112. IEEE, 2011.

[29] Yu Su, Gagan Agrawal, and Jonathan Woodring. Indexing and parallel query processing support for visualizing climate datasets. In *Proceedings of the 41th IEEE/ACM International Conference on Parallel Processing*, pages 249–258. IEEE, 2012.

[30] Yu Su, Gagan Agrawal, Jonathan Woodring, Ayan Biswas, and Han-Wei Shen. Supporting correlation analysis on scientific datasets in parallel and distributed settings. In *Proceedings of the 23rd international symposium on High-performance parallel and distributed computing*, pages 191–202. ACM, 2014.

[31] Xin Tong, Teng-Yok Lee, and Han-Wei Shen. Salient time steps selection from large scale time-varying data sets with dynamic time warping. In *Large Data Analysis and Visualization (LDAV), 2012 IEEE Symposium on*, pages 49–56. IEEE, 2012.

[32] Pere-Pau Vázquez, Miquel Feixas, Mateu Sbert, and Wolfgang Heidrich. Automatic view selection using viewpoint entropy and its application to image-based modelling. In *Computer Graphics Forum*, volume 22, pages 689–700. Wiley Online Library, 2003.

[33] Ivan Viola, Miquel Feixas, Mateu Sbert, and Meister Eduard Groller. Importance-driven focus of attention. *Visualization and Computer Graphics, IEEE Transactions on*, 12(5):933–940, 2006.

[34] Venkatram Vishwanath, Mark Hereld, and Michael E Papka. Toward simulation-time data analysis and i/o acceleration on leadership-class systems. In *Large Data Analysis and Visualization (LDAV), 2011 IEEE Symposium on*, pages 9–14. IEEE, 2011.

[35] Chaoli Wang, Hongfeng Yu, Ray W Grout, Kwan-Liu Ma, and Jacqueline H Chen. Analyzing information transfer in time-varying multivariate data. In *Pacific Visualization Symposium (PacificVis), 2011 IEEE*, pages 99–106. IEEE, 2011.

[36] Chaoli Wang, Hongfeng Yu, and Kwan-Liu Ma. Importance-driven time-varying data visualization. *Visualization and Computer Graphics, IEEE Transactions on*, 14(6):1547–1554, 2008.

[37] Jim Jing-Yan Wang, Xiaolei Wang, and Xin Gao. Non-negative matrix factorization by maximizing correntropy for cancer clustering. *BMC bioinformatics*, 14(1):107, 2013.

[38] Yi Wang, Yu Su, and Gagan Agrawal. A novel approach for approximate aggregations over arrays. In *Submission to the 18th International Conference on Extending Database Technology*, 2015.

[39] Yi Wang, Yu Su, Gagan Agrawal, and Tantan Liu. Scisd: Novel subgroup discovery over scientific datasets using bitmap indices. In *Proceedings of Ohio State CSE Technical Report*, 2015.

[40] Pak Chung Wong and R. Daniel Bergeron. 30 years of multidimensional multivariate visualization. In *Scientific Visualization, Overviews, Methodologies, and Techniques*, pages 3–33, Washington, DC, USA, 1997. IEEE Computer Society.

[41] K. Wu, E.J. Otoo, and A. Shoshani. Compressing bitmap indexes for faster search operations. In *Scientific and Statistical Database Management, 2002. Proceedings. 14th International Conference on*, pages 99–108. IEEE, 2002.

[42] K. Wu, K. Stockinger, and A. Shoshani. Breaking the curse of cardinality on bitmap indexes. In *Scientific and Statistical Database Management*, pages 348–365. Springer, 2008.

[43] Kesheng Wu, W. Koegler, J. Chen, and A. Shoshani. Using bitmap index for interactive exploration of large datasets. In *15th International Conference on Scientific and Statistical Database Management, 2003*, pages 65–74. IEEE, July 2003.

[44] Di Yang, E.A. Rundensteiner, and M.O. Ward. Analysis guided visual exploration of multivariate data. In *Visual Analytics Science and Technology, 2007. VAST 2007. IEEE Symposium on*, pages 83–90, 2007.

[45] Fang Zheng, Hongfeng Yu, Can Hantas, Matthew Wolf, Greg Eisenhauer, Karsten Schwan, Hasan Abbasi, and Scott Klasky. Goldrush: resource efficient in situ scientific data analytics using fine-grained interference aware execution. In *Proceedings of SC13: International Conference for High Performance Computing, Networking, Storage and Analysis*, page 78. ACM, 2013.

Automated Characterization of
Parallel Application Communication Patterns

Philip C. Roth, Jeremy S. Meredith, Jeffrey S. Vetter
Oak Ridge National Laboratory
One Bethel Valley Road
Oak Ridge, TN 37831 USA
{rothpc,jsmeredith,vetter}@ornl.gov

ABSTRACT

A concise description of an application's communication pattern is often useful, for example, as an efficient way to communicate application behavior to a system vendor. Several existing performance analysis tools can capture aspects of an application's communication behavior such as which processes communicated with which others and the communications operations they used. However, a human with a high degree of expertise is still required to recognize and characterize common communication idioms within the performance data collected by those tools. To simplify this characterization for non-experts, we have developed an approach for automatically characterizing a MPI application's communication behavior. We use the mpiP profiling tool to collect information about an application's communication topology and message volume. We then use a post-mortem search-based analysis to compare the application's observed communication pattern against a library of common communication patterns. By comparing the result of the various search paths, our approach identifies the combination of patterns that best matches the observed behavior. To evaluate our approach, we applied it to a synthetic example communication matrix and communication matrices obtained from two scientific applications. We determined that our automated approach was highly effective in characterizing the communication patterns represented in the matrices.

This manuscript has been authored by UT-Battelle, LLC under Contract No. DE-AC05-00OR22725 with the U.S. Department of Energy. The United States Government retains and the publisher, by accepting the article for publication, acknowledges that the United States Government retains a non-exclusive, paid-up, irrevocable, world-wide license to publish or reproduce the published form of this manuscript, or allow others to do so, for United States Government purposes. The Department of Energy will provide public access to these results of federally sponsored research in accordance with the DOE Public Access Plan (http://energy.gov/downloads/doe-public-access-plan). This research is sponsored by the Office of Advanced Scientific Computing Research in the U.S. Department of Energy.

Categories and Subject Descriptors

I.5.0 [**Pattern Recognition**]: General; D.2.8 [**Software Engineering**]: Metrics

Keywords

Application characterization; communication patterns; Message Passing Interface (MPI)

1. INTRODUCTION

Contemporary extreme-scale computing systems use a variety of interconnection networks [30, 8, 2, 1] that represent different design choices in terms of performance, manufacturability, reliability, power, and cost. These design points are realized with balanced choices in multiple factors: component integration, optical and electrical communication technologies, and topology complexity. Recent reports [18, 6] predict that future system architectures must continue to make tradeoffs in these factors, so it is more important than ever to make judicious choices to ensure that future networks match the requirements of their applications. Clearly, knowing these requirements is a critical first step to this design process, and being able to communicate these requirements among stakeholders greatly increases the likelihood that the final design will truly satisfy application requirements.

In this regard, researchers including application developers, computer architects, and performance engineers need accurate, concise, scalable, and flexible methods and metrics to describe application communication patterns [33, 25, 31]. Without such concise descriptions, architects are typically forced to use overly-simplistic descriptions of communication workloads, or use massive communication trace files on small scale systems to represent application workloads. Producing these concise descriptions is often difficult, however. Tools like the Tuning and Analysis Utilities [26] (TAU), SCALASCA [9], and mpiP [20, 32] capture performance data about an application's communication behavior in event traces or profiles and may even be able to visualize the captured data, but recognizing even common communication patterns in these visualizations requires a high degree of user expertise.

1.1 Contributions

To address this challenge, we have developed an approach for automatically characterizing an application's communication behavior. Our approach focuses on HPC applications that use the Message Passing Interface [10, 11] (MPI); we use the mpiP performance tool [32, 31] to capture information about how an application communicates, including its communication topology and message volume. We, then, use object recognition algorithms to compare the captured data against a library of common communication patterns to identify the pattern (or combination of patterns) that best explains the target application pattern. In addition to identifying these pattern(s), our approach reports a residual metric describing how closely the reported patterns match the observed behavior.

Specifically, the contributions of this work include the following:

- A novel approach for automatically characterizing a MPI application's communication behavior;

- A prototype implementation that works on scalable, real-world applications;

- A thorough discussion of a communication pattern characterization example using a synthetic communication pattern matrix; and

- Case studies of communication pattern characterization of the empirical behavior of two scientific applications.

The primary benefit of this work is in easing the recognition of common communication idioms exhibited in parallel applications, but in doing so we also define a concise language for representing these idioms and combinations thereof.

1.2 Approach Overview

Our approach for automatically recognizing parallel application communication patterns is inspired by object recognition strategies used in astronomy. When astronomers seek to identify a new object in the sky, or to see how a known object has moved, they sometimes use a technique called *sky subtraction*. In this technique, a known pattern is removed from an original image in the hopes that it will be easier to recognize interesting objects in the resulting image. For instance, given an image of the sky in the visual spectrum, an astronomer might remove the ambient background light by subtracting a constant amount of brightness from every pixel in the image. In the resulting image, objects that were only slightly brighter than the ambient background are often more easy to detect than in the original image.

We adopt this sky subtraction idea to recognize common patterns in an application's observed communication data. Starting with a communication matrix M such as the example shown in Figure 1a that contains data about an application's observed message volume and communication pattern, the approach searches for a combination of patterns that best explains the matrix data. In these matrix visualizations, the block at row i and column j is colored according to the amount of data that the process with MPI rank i transferred to the process with rank j. The approach attempts to recognize each pattern from its pattern library in the matrix M. If a pattern is recognized, such as the 8×8 two-dimensional nearest neighbor pattern shown in Figure 1b, its contribution is removed from M to produce a matrix M' (Figure 1c), and the pattern recognition step is repeated upon M'. Because multiple patterns might be recognized at each search step, the search produces a *results tree* such as the one shown in Figure 2 that displays the results of characterizing the matrix from Figure 1a. In this

results tree, a matrix is associated with each node and a communication pattern with each edge, such that the pattern associated with the edge between node N and N' was recognized in node N's matrix, and removing the pattern produced node N''s matrix. If no pattern can be recognized in a matrix, its node is a leaf, and the path from the tree root to that leaf defines a collection of patterns that can be removed from the original matrix to produce the leaf's matrix. Once the search is complete (i.e., no more patterns can be recognized in any of the matrices associated with tree nodes), the approach identifies a leaf node whose matrix exhibits the smallest residual value. The patterns along the path from the root to this leaf are the combination of patterns that best explains the original communication matrix. Figure 3 shows the intermediate matrices produced when recognizing and removing the patterns that best explain the Figure 1a matrix. These matrices correspond to the path drawn using thick red lines in the search results tree of Figure 2. Our approach identified six of the seven patterns used to produce the original matrix. The only pattern it did not recognize was the "garbage" pattern we used to place values randomly throughout the communication matrix. We have not yet implemented pattern recognition for this type of random pattern.

2. BACKGROUND

Our work on automatically recognizing common communication patterns builds on previous work on MPI performance tools and the characterization of scientific applications.

2.1 Oxbow

We recently began a multi-year application characterization activity. Our characterization approach uses a collection of tools we call the *Oxbow* tool set, and mpiP is one of the tools in this set. In our initial study [31], we characterized the computation and communication behavior of twelve scientific applications and benchmarks. We were especially interested in the proxy applications being developed within the United States Department of Energy (DOE)'s Co-design Centers. When run, a "proxy app" is intended to mimic part (but not all) of a full application that is either not able to be distributed widely or is too expensive to run in its full form. For instance, the Nekbone proxy app is intended to mimic some aspects of the Nek5000 [21] fluid dynamics solver. Whereas Nek5000 is more general, Nekbone only includes a basic conjugate gradient solver. In our initial study, we considered how well the proxy applications represented their associated full applications. More generally, we considered which metrics describing an application's behavior were most useful for characterizing the application, and how to obtain those metrics efficiently.

2.2 mpiP

To collect information about an application's communication behavior, we use a modified version of the mpiP [20] lightweight profiling tool. This tool was originally developed to support an approach for analyzing the scalability of an application's communication [32]. The tool is implemented as a library containing functions that are interposed between an application and the MPI library at that library's profiling interface. The tool's versions of MPI functions collect statistics about the application's use of MPI operations

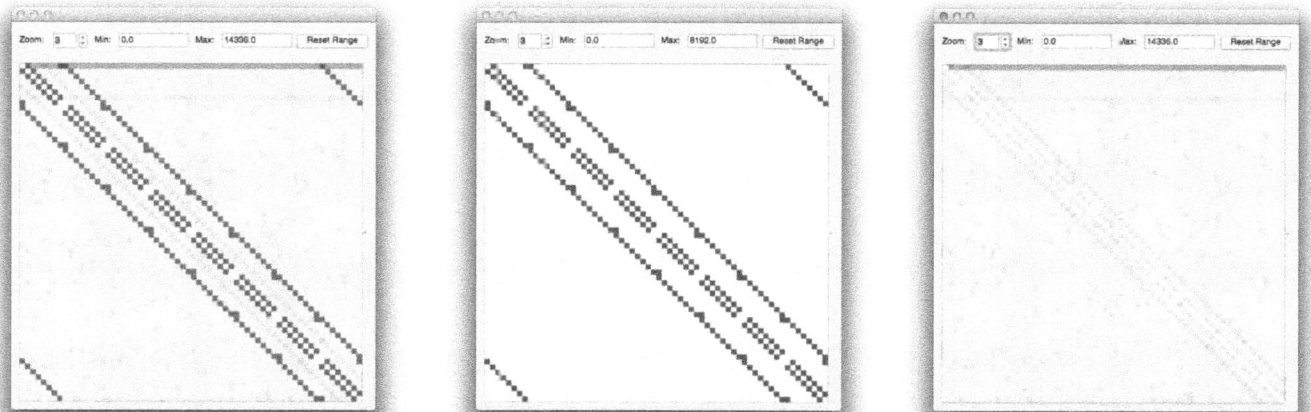

(a) Example communication matrix.

(b) 2D nearest neighbor pattern recognized in communication matrix.

(c) Resulting communication matrix.

Figure 1: Recognizing and removing the contribution of a communication pattern from a communication matrix. *The synthetic example communication matrix represents a 64 process run of an application that exhibits several diverse communication patterns. This recognition/removal is only one step in the recognition of the six communication patterns of the original matrix.*

that are reported when the application terminates. These reports can also be produced at other times to support collecting performance data for specific phases of the program's execution.

Until recently, mpiP collected and reported statistical data about an application's communication from only a *code-centric* perspective. The tool tracked how much data was sent and received at each application call site and how long those operations took. This information was useful, but not sufficient, for our Oxbow application characterizations. For the Oxbow study, we modified mpiP so that its MPI interposition functions also track how much data is transferred from each application process to each other process. For example, when the application calls `MPI_Send`, our version of mpiP tracks not only how long the send operation took and how much data was transferred, but also the destination process. In addition to mpiP's traditional report, our mpiP version also generates several additional output files containing:

1. A matrix indicating the number of times each process sent data to each other process using MPI point-to-point operations;

2. A matrix indicating the number of bytes each process sent to each other process using MPI point-to-point operations;

3. A histogram of the number of bytes involved in each collective communication operation;

4. A matrix indicating the number of bytes each process contributed to MPI collective operations; and

5. A matrix indicating the number of bytes each process received from MPI collective operations.

In file 1, the value at (i, j) indicates the number of times MPI rank i sent data to MPI rank j, and in file 2, the value

at (i, j) indicates the amount of data sent from rank i to rank j. Taken together, these matrices can be used to compute the average number of bytes per transfer between any pair of processes. Figure 4 shows a visualization produced by VisIt [5] that displays average point-to-point communication volume information collected during a 96-process run of the Large-scale Atomic/Molecular Massively Parallel Simulator [23] (LAMMPS) on the Keeneland Initial Delivery System [29] with the EAM benchmark problem inputs. Also, the matrices in files 2, 4, and 5 can be combined to produce a single matrix that represents the amount of data transferred from each process to the others using any kind of MPI operation. Our automated communication pattern characterization approach can work on each file individual, or on the combined matrix as illustrated in Section 4. The count and volume information that mpiP represents using a matrix can also be represented as a directed graph whose vertices represent application processes and whose edges represent data transfers between processes. Because the application's communication pattern can be represented using these graphs, this data may be said to express the application's *communication topology*.

3. AUTOMATIC CHARACTERIZATION OF COMMUNICATION PATTERNS

Algorithm 1 shows the pseudocode for our approach for automatic characterization of application communication patterns. As presented here, the algorithm operates on a message volume matrix, but the algorithm is nearly identical when operating on an operation count matrix. For input, the algorithm takes a communication matrix M and a library L of communication patterns. The algorithm outputs the set of patterns and scaling factors that best account for the observed communication topology and message volume data in M, or a message indicating that the algorithm could

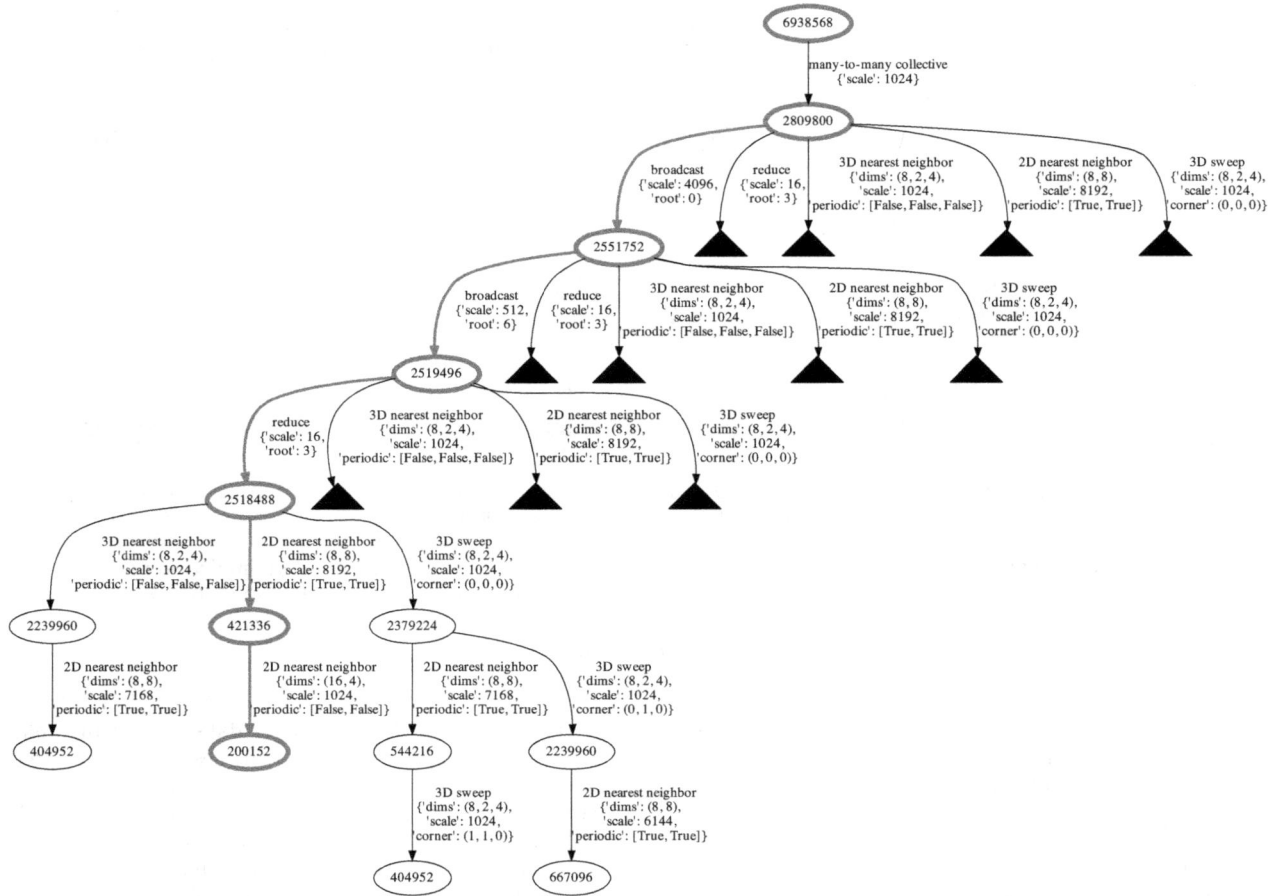

Figure 2: Pattern recognition results for the example matrix shown in Figure 1a. *Each node is labeled with the residual metric computed for the matrix associated with that node. Each edge is labeled with the pattern recognized within the parent node's matrix and removed to produce the child node's matrix. Black triangles indicate subtrees elided due to space constraints. Nodes and edges drawn in thick red lines indicate the combination of patterns that best explain the original communication matrix data.*

not identify any of its known patterns in the input matrix. In this section, we describe the algorithm and our initial implementation of it in detail.

First, the algorithm uses search to determine which combinations of patterns it can recognize in the input matrix, maintaining the results of this search in a tree. It creates a tree root node for the input matrix (line 3) and calls the recursive **Refine** function on that root node to complete the search (line 4). Given a node, the **Refine** function (lines 17–30) attempts to recognize patterns in that node's matrix. If a pattern is recognized, the **Refine** function generates a "pure" pattern matrix (line 22). This pattern matrix is the matrix that would result if an application only exhibited the recognized pattern. Pattern recognition and pattern matrix generation is described in more detail in Section 3.1. The **Refine** function then subtracts the pattern matrix from the node's matrix (line 23), and the resulting matrix is associated with a new node (line 24) that will become a child of the current node. The child node is attached to the parent node using an edge, to which the recognized pattern is asso-

ciated (lines 25–26). Finally, the **Refine** function is called recursively on the new child node. Our prototype implementation of the search (see Section 3.4) is sequential, but because there are no dependencies between the search refinements rooted at each child, the search could be parallelized.

After building the search results tree, the algorithm traverses the tree to identify the tree leaf node whose associated matrix has the smallest residual (line 5; the FindSmallestResidual function is not presented here due to space limitations). This residual metric is discussed further in Section 3.2. Once a leaf with the smallest residual is identified, the algorithm walks the path from the leaf to the search results tree's root, collecting the recognized patterns from the edges along this path (lines 7–13) into a set that it outputs as the algorithm's result (line 14). Note that the patterns in this set can be removed from the original communication matrix in any order to produce the matrix with the minimal residual.

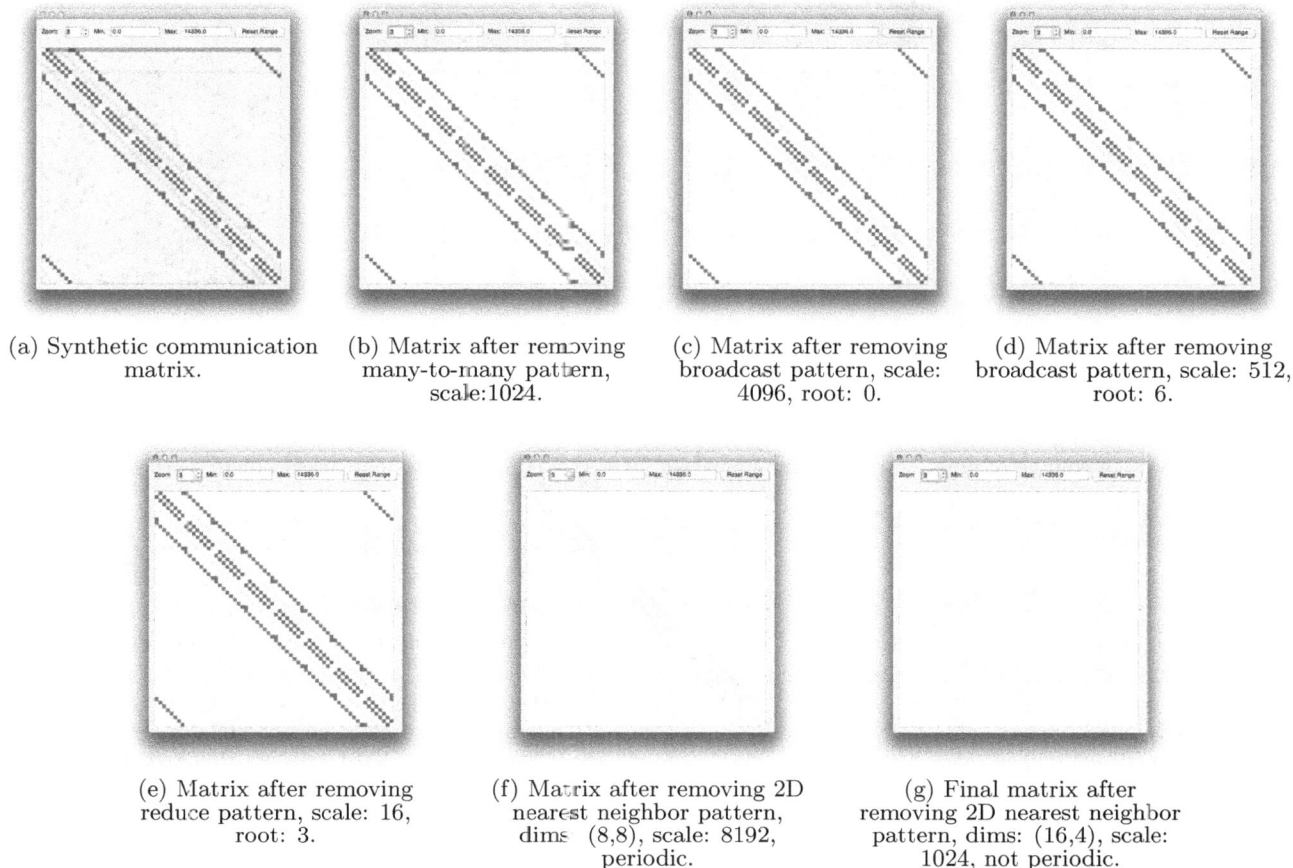

(a) Synthetic communication matrix.

(b) Matrix after removing many-to-many pattern, scale:1024.

(c) Matrix after removing broadcast pattern, scale: 4096, root: 0.

(d) Matrix after removing broadcast pattern, scale: 512, root: 6.

(e) Matrix after removing reduce pattern, scale: 16, root: 3.

(f) Matrix after removing 2D nearest neighbor pattern, dims (8,8), scale: 8192, periodic.

(g) Final matrix after removing 2D nearest neighbor pattern, dims: (16,4), scale: 1024, not periodic.

Figure 3: Sequence of recognized patterns and intermediate matrices for a synthetic communication matrix.

3.1 Patterns

Our automated communication pattern characterization approach uses a library of common communication patterns. For each pattern, the library entry contains the following information:

- Its name.

- A function `Recognize(M)` that attempts to recognize the pattern in the matrix M. If the pattern is recognized, the function returns the pattern's parameters. The parameters returned depend on the pattern. For instance, the Broadcast pattern returns the MPI rank of the Broadcast operation's root process and the amount of data that was broadcast. In contrast, the 2D Nearest Neighbor pattern returns the dimensions of the 2D Cartesian topology the application used, whether the application used periodic boundaries, and the amount of data transferred between pairs of processes. If the pattern is not recognized in the given matrix, this function returns an empty pattern parameter set.

- A function `Generate(n, pattern_params)` that generates a communication matrix that represents the "pure" pattern for n processes and the given *pattern_params*. It is this pure pattern matrix that is subtracted from

a search results tree node's matrix when a pattern is recognized within the `Refine` function.

The pattern library uses generator functions so that a pattern description is independent of the number of processes used to run the application. The collection of pattern names in the library define a language that can be used to describe the communication behavior of an application, in much the same way as the "Berkeley Dwarfs" [3] can be used to describe the algorithmic behavior of an application.

The approach used for recognizing a pattern varies depending on the pattern. Recognizing some patterns is fairly easy. For instance, the broadcast pattern's `Recognize` function looks for a row in the matrix M whose elements are all non-zero, except for the element on M's diagonal. If the function identifies such a row, it indicates the row number as the broadcast operation's root, and the minimum non-zero value of the row as the operation's *scale*–the amount of data broadcast. The pattern uses the minimum non-zero value as the scale because the scaled pure pattern, when removed from M, would produce a matrix M' with negative values that are invalid given our definition of a communication matrix.

Other patterns are more challenging to recognize. For example, the 2D nearest neighbor pattern's `Recognize` function looks for the following criteria in the input matrix M:

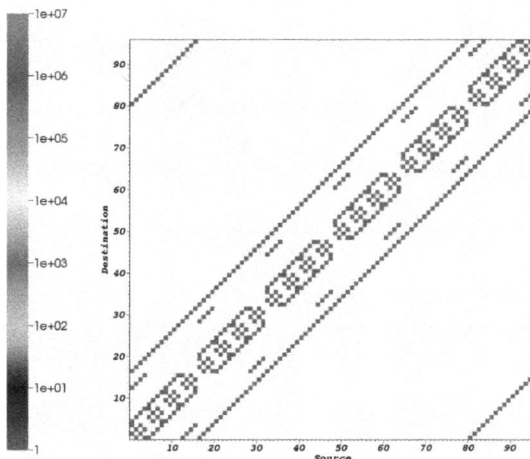

Figure 4: Average volume of point-to-point communication for LAMMPS, EAM benchmark problem, with 96 processes.

Algorithm 1 Communication Pattern Characterization

1: **procedure** CHARACTERIZE(M, L)
2:     $nprocs \leftarrow GetNumberProcesses(M)$
3:     $results\_tree \leftarrow CreateNode(M)$
4:     $Refine(L, nprocs, results\_tree)$
5:     $min\_leaf \leftarrow FindSmallestResidual(results\_tree)$
6:     $best\_patterns \leftarrow \emptyset$
7:     $curr\_node \leftarrow min\_leaf$
8:     **while** $Parent(curr\_node) \neq \emptyset$ **do**
9:         $curr\_edge \leftarrow curr\_node.GetParentEdge()$
10:        $curr\_pat \leftarrow curr\_edge.GetPattern()$
11:        $best\_patterns.Add(curr\_pat)$
12:        $curr\_node \leftarrow curr\_node.GetParent()$
13:     **end while**
14:     **return** $best\_patterns$
15: **end procedure**
16:
17: **procedure** REFINE(L, $nprocs$, $node$)
18:     $node\_M \leftarrow node.GetMatrix()$
19:     **for all** $pat \in L$ **do**
20:         $pat\_params \leftarrow pat.Recognize(node\_M)$
21:         **if** $pat\_params \neq \emptyset$ **then**
22:            $pat\_M \leftarrow pat.Generate(nprocs, pat\_params)$
23:            $child\_M \leftarrow node\_M - pat\_M$
24:            $new\_child\_node \leftarrow CreateNode(child\_M)$
25:            $new\_edge \leftarrow CreateEdge(pat, pat\_params)$
26:            $node.AddChild(new\_edge, new\_child\_node)$
27:            $Refine(new\_child\_node)$
28:         **end if**
29:     **end for**
30: **end procedure**

- The ± 1 diagonals (i.e., the diagonals just above and just below the matrix's main diagonal) are mostly non-zeros, but not entirely.

- There is a pair of $\pm x$ diagonals that are entirely non-zeros.

- The x identified by the previous criteria divides the number of processes evenly. This x is the number of columns in the 2D Cartesian topology, and $nprocs/x$ is the number of rows.

- If the $\pm(nprocs - x)$ diagonals are entirely non-zeros, the pattern uses periodic boundaries.

Some of these criteria are intentionally vague, such as the requirement for diagonals to be *mostly* non-zeros, because they are used as lightweight checks to rule out the pattern as early as possible. These lightweight criteria also provide potential values for the pattern's parameters, such as the dimensions of the 2D Cartesian topology used. If all of these lightweight criteria are satisfied, the **Recognize** function uses these potential parameters and the pattern's **Generate** function to produce a pure pattern matrix to be used as a *mask* against M. For every non-zero value in the mask, **Recognize** checks whether the value at the same $(row, column)$ coordinates in M is also non-zero. During this check, the **Recognize** function also tracks the minimum non-zero masked element in M, to be used as the pattern's scale if it is recognized successfully. If and only if all non-zero elements in the mask are also non-zero in M, the **Recognize** function returns the recognized dimensions, scale, and boundary periodicity as the pattern parameters.

3.2 Residual Metric

Algorithm 1 determines whether one collection of recognized patterns is better than another by comparing a residual metric computed for the resulting communication matrices. When computed for a matrix, this residual metric must indicate the amount of data that is not yet accounted for using known communication patterns. For our prototype implementation of Algorithm 1, we use a simple definition of the residual metric: the total data volume indicated by the matrix (i.e., the sum of the matrix elements). As evidenced by Figure 2, the values of this residual metric can be quite large even for application runs with a modest number of processes, so to improve the user-friendliness of our implementation's interface these residual values may be expressed as percentages of the original matrix's residual value.

3.3 Recognition Order

The order in which patterns are recognized matters, both in terms of the quality of the algorithm's results and as a performance optimization. The approach attempts to recognize each pattern during each search step because the recognition and removal of one pattern's contribution can preclude the recognition of another pattern later. For example, the synthetic example matrix shown in Figure 1a was constructed by combining seven communication patterns, including two different 2D nearest neighbor patterns. However, the combination of these patterns also matches a 3D nearest neighbor pattern. If the characterization algorithm recognizes and removes the 3D pattern first, the algorithm is no longer able to recognize a 2D pattern in the resulting matrix. On the other hand, if it recognizes a 2D pattern first, it is able to recognize the second 2D pattern. The residual metric of the matrix produced by recognizing both 2D patterns is smaller than that of the matrix produced by recognizing only the 3D pattern. Situations like this are the reason our algorithm attempts to recognize all patterns at each step in the search and compares the residual metric for the resulting methods only when the algorithm can no longer recognize further patterns along each search path.

Although recognizing a pattern P_1 instead of pattern P_2 may preclude later recognition of pattern P_3 as described in the example above, if both P_1 and P_2 are recognized, it makes no difference in which order they are recognized (P_1 then P_2 or vice versa). The algorithm as shown in Algorithm 1 does not attempt to optimize the search by eliminating search paths that represent permutations of paths that have already been searched, and explains why the search results tree shown in Figure 2 contains several paths that are permutations of each other. We leave this performance optimization for future work.

The quality and performance of the search are also affected in situations where a given pattern can be recognized in multiple ways. For example, if the communication matrix M includes an all-to-all communication pattern (called "many-to-many" in our prototype implementation), it is equally valid to recognize the pattern as one many-to-many operation, the combination of *nprocs* broadcast operations each rooted at a different application process, or the combination of *nprocs* reduce operations. The communication matrix itself does not contain enough information to determine which of these approaches were actually used in the application. However, recognizing this pattern as *nprocs* broadcast or reduce operations greatly increases the amount of time required to search for pattern combinations, and greatly increases the number of constituent patterns output by the algorithm, so we prefer to recognize and remove the many-to-many pattern first. Although line 19 of Algorithm 1 does not indicate that the **Refine** function attempts to recognize patterns in any order, our prototype implementation attempts to recognize the many-to-many pattern first. This is why the many-to-many pattern was recognized first in the search results shown in Figure 2.

3.4 Implementation

We have implemented our automated communication characterization algorithm in a Python command line tool called *AChax* (with pronunciation similar to "Ajax"), for Automated Characterization. Each pattern is implemented as a Python class with instance methods **Recognize**, and **Generate**. To date, we have implemented the classes for the following patterns:

- Many-to-Many (i.e., all-to-all);
- Broadcast;
- Reduce;
- 2D Nearest Neighbor;
- 3D Nearest Neighbor;
- 3D Wavefront (i.e., sweep) from a corner; and
- Random (**Generate** only).

A class named AChaxer implements Algorithm 1. The program's singleton instance of this class builds its pattern library by creating an instance of each of the known pattern classes, and placing them in a Python list. The AChaxer object's implementation of the **Refine** method attempts to recognize the patterns in the order they appear in this list, so as described in Section 3.3, the many-to-many pattern instance is placed first in the list. The AChaxer object's **Characterize** method uses its **Refine** method to build the search results tree, and implements the **FindSmallestResidual** method to identify the leaf node whose matrix has the smallest residual metric value. Although the ordering of the patterns recognized to produce this smallest residual matrix does not matter, to support debugging the AChaxer object reverses the order obtained by walking from leaf to root before outputting its results, so that the output matches the order in which the patterns were actually recognized. The AChaxer object can optionally write output files that contain:

- The matrix identified as having the smallest residual;
- A log of the actions performed during the automated search, including which patterns were tried and the pattern parameters of recognized patterns;
- A DOT representation of the search results graph that can be visualized using the Graphviz dot command; and
- A sequence of matrices showing the intermediate result of removing each recognized pattern until achieving the matrix with minimal residual.

An AChaxApp object implements the user interface to the tool. This object parses the command line, reads the input communication matrix, and outputs results. The NumPy [27] and SciPy [28] Python packages are used to implement matrix operations including the reading and writing of matrices to files, and both dense and sparse matrix representations are supported and used internally by the tool. Although this implementation is serial and the algorithm performs redundant work as described earlier in this section, the performance of this prototype implementation is still satisfactory. For instance, characterizing the communication patterns from a 216-process application run (detailed in Section 4.3) took less than 90 seconds on a four-year-old Macintosh laptop with 2.66 GHz dual core with 4 GB memory.

4. CASE STUDIES

4.1 Test System

We used the Keeneland Initial Delivery System [29] (KIDS) for our case studies. KIDS is a Georgia Institute of Technology cluster deployed at Oak Ridge National Laboratory. The system contained 120 HP ProLiant SL390 G7 compute nodes. Each compute node contained 24 GB memory, two Intel Xeon X5660 processors running at 2.80 GHz, and three NVIDIA M2090 GPUs. The nodes were connected with an Infiniband QDR interconnection network. The system used the CentOS 6.3 Linux distribution on its compute nodes. We used the Intel Composer XE 2013 SP1.1.106 (also reported as version 14.0.1) compilers to build and run the test applications, and OpenMPI 1.6.1 as the MPI library and runtime.

4.2 LAMMPS

LAMMPS is a molecular dynamics simulator, written in C++, that uses MPI for interprocess communication and synchronization. We obtained the LAMMPS source code from the project's Git repository, and used revision 42bb280c dated 2014-04-15. We modified the LAMMPS makefile to build on KIDS, and to link in our version of the mpiP library that produces communication topology matrix files. We ran LAMMPS with the EAM benchmark problem input file using 96 processes in a $4 \times 4 \times 6$ 3D Cartesian process topology.

When solving the EAM benchmark problem, LAMMPS uses MPI point-to-point operations in a 3D nearest neighbor communication pattern, and the MPI broadcast, allreduce, and scan collective operations. The broadcast operations are all rooted at MPI rank 0. The version of mpiP we used for this study models the rootless MPI allreduce operation as a reduce operation to rank 0, followed by a broadcast from 0 to all other operations. It also models the scan operation as a gather operation of data from all processes to rank 0, which then computes the scan result and scatters the result to all processes. This may not be how the underlying MPI implements these collective operations, but because mpiP operates at the MPI profiling interface, it has no information about the underlying implementation.

Figure 5 shows visualizations of the communication matrix produced by mpiP for the 96-process LAMMPS run, the patterns recognized by AChax in this matrix, and the matrices produced by removing those patterns. To expose detail that would be hidden if the blue saturation color map of Figure 3 were used, this figure uses a heat map color palette with "hotter" colors (e.g., yellow, orange) indicating larger values and "cooler" colors (e.g., blue, purple) indicating smaller values. Zero values in the communication matrix are indicated using white blocks. As shown in the figure, AChax recognized the 3D nearest neighbor communication pattern, including the correct dimensions of the 3D Cartesion topology used. Because of the way mpiP models MPI_Scan and MPI_Allreduce, AChax cannot distinguish between these operations and MPI_Bcast and MPI_Reduce, and has recognized the communication as the latter pair of patterns. Lacking more information about how the MPI library implements its rootless communication operations, and having mpiP expose that information, the resulting patterns reported by AChax are equivalent as far as their usefulness. We can express the LAMMPS communication be-

havior using the following expression, using the scale of each recognized pattern as a coefficient:

$$
\begin{aligned}
C_{LAMMPS} = {} & 13354 \cdot Broadcast(root:0) + \\
& 700 \cdot Reduce(root:0) + \\
& 19318888 \cdot 3DNearestNeighbor(\\
& \quad dims:(4,4,6), \\
& \quad periodic:True)
\end{aligned}
$$

The error in this expression, visualized as a communication matrix, is shown in Figure 5d.

At first glance, the residual matrix produced by removing all recognized patterns (Figure 5d) makes it appear as if AChax did not correctly determine the scale of the 3D nearest neighbor pattern, because the residual pattern appears to match the pure 3D nearest neighbor pattern. In fact, AChax *did* recognize the scale correctly: after removing the recognized pattern, there is a zero element (circled in the figure) in one of the diagonals that must be non-zero for a 3D nearest neighbor pattern. The residual matrix produced by AChax after removing recognized patterns provides the interesting insight that not only does LAMMPS use a 3D nearest neighbor communication pattern, the amount of data LAMMPS communicates between neighbors varies. The coloration of Figure 5d indicates that for the input problem we used, the LAMMPS nearest neighbor communication transferred more data in some dimensions than others. More data was sent by process with rank i to its neighbors with rank $i \pm 1$ (yellow blocks in the figure) than to its neighbors along the next dimension (blue blocks in the figure), and that more than to its neighbors along the final dimension (purple blocks in the figure). Furthermore, the amount of data sent by each proces to its neighbor along that third dimension varies, as indicated by the fact that removing the recognized pattern with its constant scale caused only one of the would-be-purple blocks to have a zero value. If all processes communicated the same amount along this dimension, the resulting matrix would have no non-zeros in these diagonals, and the purple-colored blocks in Figure 5d would not be there.

4.3 LULESH

The Livermore Unstructured Lagrangian Explicit Shock Hydrodynamics application [13] (LULESH) is a proxy application meant to approximate a typical hydrodynamics model such as ALE3D [22]. LULESH is one of the applications being used for hardware/software co-design within the U.S. Department of Energy's Exascale Co-Design Center for Materials in Extreme Environments [7]. Unlike a full application, LULESH solves a specific, hard-coded problem. We used LULESH version 2.0.3 [14]. This version is written in C++ and can be built for serial execution or parallel execution using MPI or MPI+OpenMP. We ran LULESH on KIDS with 216 processes in a $6 \times 6 \times 6$ 3D process topology.

LULESH uses a limited number of MPI communication operations: non-blocking point-to-point sends and receives, and the reduce and allreduce collective operations. Nevertheless, LULESH exhibits interesting communication patterns for AChax to characterize.

Figure 6 shows visualizations of the communication matrix produced by mpiP for the 216-process LULESH run, the patterns recognized by AChax in this matrix, and the intermediate matrices produced by removing the recognized

(a) Communication matrix produced by mpiP.

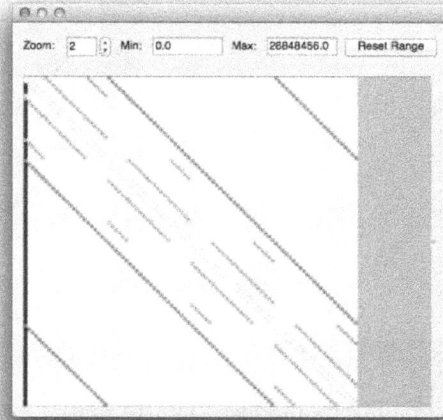

(b) Matrix after removing broadcast, root: 0, scale: 13354.

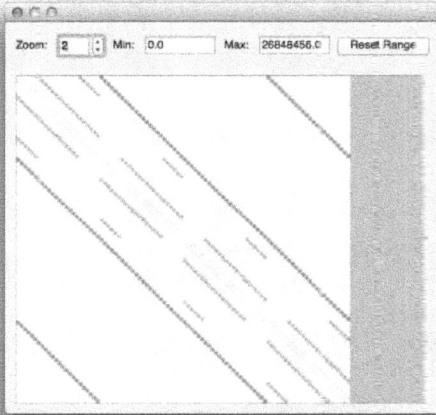

(c) Matrix after removing reduce, root: 0, scale: 700.

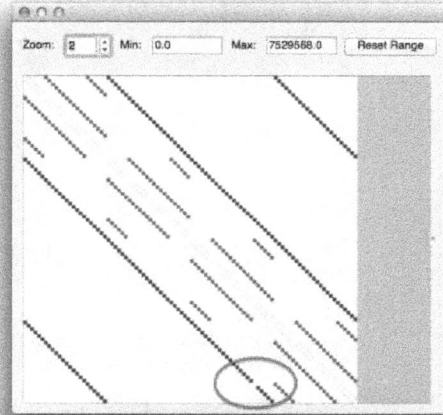

(d) Matrix after removing 3D nearest neighbor, dims: (4,4,6), scale: 19318888, periodic: True. Note the different scale compared to the other matrices in the figure, and the zero value indicated with a red oval that precludes the recognition of a 3D nearest neighbor pattern in this matrix.

Figure 5: Initial communication matrix produced by mpiP, and intermediate and final communication matrices produced by AChax for a 96-process LAMMPS run solving the EAM benchmark problem.

patterns. As with Figure 5 showing LAMMPS communication matrices, this figure uses a heat map color pallette with white blocks indicating zero values in the underlying matrix. As shown in the figure, AChax recognized 3D nearest neighbor and 3D sweep patterns with the correct Cartesian process topology dimensions, and recognized LULESH's use of Allreduce as combinations of broadcast and reduce as described in Section 4.2. The AChax-characterized expression

for LULESH's communication pattern is:

$$
\begin{aligned}
C_{LULESH} = \; &51984 \cdot Broadcast(root:0) + \\
&51992 \cdot Reduce(root:0) + \\
&290279024 \cdot 3DNearestNeighbor(\\
&\qquad dims:(6,6,6), \\
&\qquad periodic:False) + \\
&299785872 \cdot 3DSweep(\\
&\qquad dims:(6,6,6), \\
&\qquad corner:(5,5,5))
\end{aligned}
$$

(a) Communication matrix produced by mpiP.

(b) Matrix after removing broadcast, root: 0, scale: 51984.

(c) Matrix after removing reduce, root: 0, scale: 51992.

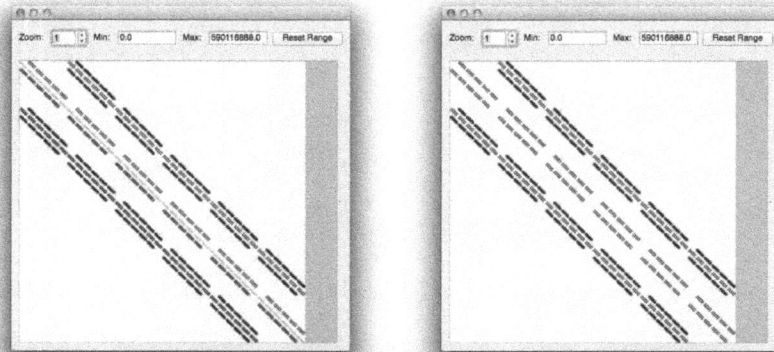

(d) Matrix after removing 3D nearest neighbor, dims: (6,6,6), scale: 290279024, periodic: False.

(e) Matrix after removing 3D sweep, dims: (6,6,6), scale: 299785872, originating corner: (5,5,5).

Figure 6: Initial communication matrix produced by mpiP, and intermediate and final communication matrices produced by AChax for a 216-process LULESH run.

Interestingly, the residual matrix (Figure 6e) exhibits a communication pattern for which there is not yet a pattern in AChax's pattern library. The pattern is regular and has hallmarks of a near-neighbor (but not necessarily nearest) pattern. The AChax pattern library is not considered complete, and identifying this pattern and adding a pattern recognizer and generator for it is one of our near-term future AChax work activities.

5. RELATED WORK

Researchers have long recognized the need to characterize communication patterns. For example, Kim and Lilja [17] characterized the communication patterns of several message passing applications and benchmarks from the NAS Parallel Benchmark suite, to study whether the benchmarks' behavior was similar to that of the applications. Karlsson and Brorsson [15] performed a similar study of a few applications to contrast their communication behavior when implemented using message passing and shared memory. More recently, Raponi et al [24] performed a similar study of applica-

tions and benchmarks from the Sequoia benchmark suite and from Argonne National Laboratory's workload. Although each of these studies produced useful information about the communication behavior of scientific applications, none used automated methods to characterize the communication behavior.

The communication pattern characterization approach that is most similar to ours is described by Kerbyson and Barker [16]. Both approaches perform automated characterization of application communication patterns by matching observed communication data against a library of known communication patterns. Both approaches dynamically produce a pattern mask and compare it to the observed communication data when attempting to match a pattern, and neither approach has support (yet) for identifying the patterns produced when a subset of all application processes communicate. Nevertheless, there are several substantial differences between the two approaches. Whereas their work considers only point-to-point communication, ours supports patterns produced using both point-to-point and collective operations. Their approach indicates only that a pattern was matched, whereas ours identifies how much data was transferred for each matched pattern. Their approach matches patterns on a per-call-site basis, and requires manual application instrumentation to identify those call sites. In contrast, our approach uses an automated search through a pattern space to identify the *combination* of patterns that best explains the application's communication behavior. Our approach does not require source code modification, but the mpiP application programming interface can be used to limit the collected communication data, and thus the communication pattern characterization, to a specific application phase or even a specific call site if desired.

Our approach draws on techniques used in automated performance analysis. For example, Miller et al [19] presented a search-based approach for automatically analyzing the computation and communication behavior of a running application to identify performance bottlenecks. Bhatia et al [4] presented an automatic analysis of application communication behavior, but their analysis sought to identify the cause of communication performance problems rather than to characterize the communication patterns used by the application. Unlike our work whose goal is to characterize application behavior (specifically communication behavior), this earlier research focuses on the complementary goal of automatically identifying the causes of application performance problems. He et al [12] presented an automated compiler-based approach for recognizing *performance idioms*, or common scientific computing patterns, in several of the NAS Parallel Benchmark suite. Although that work suggests detection of idioms that include both computation and communication, the paper provides no detail about recognition of communication patterns, whereas that is the focus of the work presented in this paper.

6. SUMMARY

In this paper, we described a novel approach for automatically characterizing a parallel application's communication behavior. Our approach uses a search algorithm with a library of known communication patterns to identify the pattern, or combination of patterns, that best explain the application's communication behavior. AChax, our implementation of the approach, applies our characterization algorithm on files produced by mpiP that contain information about an application's topology and message volume in the form of a communication matrix. In case studies using a complex synthetic communication matrix and matrices captured from the LAMMPS and LULESH scientific applications, we demonstrated the efficacy of our approach in automatically identifying the applications' communication patterns.

Going forward, we plan to improve the efficacy of our automated characterization approach by implementing support for the recognition of more types of communication patterns such as wavefront patterns, by researching whether image recognition techniques can improve or simplify pattern recognition, and by adding support for applications that use sub-communicators. We also plan to improve the performance of our search by implementing techniques for pruning the search when it determines it is attempting to search a permutation of patterns that have already been attempted, and by parallelizing the search.

7. REFERENCES

[1] Y. Ajima, S. Sumimoto, and T. Shimizu. Tofu: A 6D mesh/torus interconnect for exascale computers. *IEEE Computer*, 42(11):36–40, 2009.

[2] B. Arimilli, R. Arimilli, V. Chung, S. Clark, W. Denzel, B. Drerup, T. Hoefler, J. Joyner, J. Lewis, L. Jian, N. Nan, and R. Rajamony. The PERCS high-performance interconnect. In *High Performance Interconnects (HOTI), 2010 IEEE 18th Annual Symposium on*, pages 75–82, 2010.

[3] K. Asanovic, R. Bodik, B. C. Catanzaro, J. J. Gebis, P. Husbands, K. Keutzer, D. A. Patterson, W. L. Plishker, J. Shalf, S. W. Williams, and K. A. Yelick. The landscape of parallel computing research: A view from berkeley. Technical Report UCB/EECS-2006-183, EECS Department, University of California, Berkeley, Dec 2006.

[4] N. Bhatia, F. Song, F. Wolf, J. Dongarra, B. Mohr, and S. Moore. Automatic experimental analysis of communication patterns in virtual topologies. In *Parallel Processing, 2005. ICPP 2005. International Conference on*, pages 465–472, June 2005.

[5] H. Childs, E. Brugger, B. Whitlock, J. Meredith, S. Ahern, D. Pugmire, K. Biagas, M. Miller, G. H. Weber, H. Krishnan, T. Fogal, A. Sanderson, C. Garth, E. W. Bethel, D. Camp, O. Rübel, M. Durant, J. Favre, and P. Navratil. VisIt: An end-user tool for visualizing and analyzing very large data. In E. W. Bethel, H. Childs, and C. Hansen, editors, *High Performance Visualization—Enabling Extreme-Scale Scientific Insight*, Chapman & Hall, CRC Computational Science, pages 357–372. CRC Press/Francis–Taylor Group, Boca Raton, FL, USA, Nov. 2012. http://www.crcpress.com/product/isbn/9781439875728, LBNL-6320E.

[6] J. Dongarra, P. Beckman, T. Moore, P. Aerts, G. Aloisio, J.-C. Andre, D. Barkai, J.-Y. Berthou, T. Boku, B. Braunschweig, F. Cappello, B. Chapman, X. Chi, A. Choudhary, S. Dosanjh, T. Dunning, S. Fiore, A. Geist, B. Gropp, R. Harrison, M. Hereld, M. Heroux, A. Hoisie, K. Hotta, Z. Jin, Y. Ishikawa, F. Johnson, S. Kale, R. Kenway, D. Keyes, B. Kramer, J. Labarta, A. Lichnewsky, T. Lippert, B. Lucas, B. Maccabe, S. Matsuoka, P. Messina, P. Michielse, B. Mohr, M. S. Mueller, W. E. Nagel, H. Nakashima, M. E. Papka, D. Reed, M. Sato, E. Seidel, J. Shalf, D. Skinner, M. Snir, T. Sterling, R. Stevens, F. Streitz, B. Sugar, S. Sumimoto, W. Tang, J. Taylor, R. Thakur, A. Trefethen, M. Valero, A. van der Steen, J. Vetter, P. Williams, R. Wisniewski, and K. Yelick. The international exascale software project roadmap. *International Journal of High Performance Computing Applications*, 25(1):3–60, 2011.

[7] DoE Exascale Co-Design Center for Materials in Extreme Environments. http://www.exmatex.org, 2014.

[8] G. Faanes, A. Bataineh, D. Roweth, T. Court, E. Froese, B. Alverson, T. Johnson, J. Kopnick, M. Higgins, and J. Reinhard. Cray cascade: a scalable HPC system based on a dragonfly network. In

Proceedings of the International Conference on High Performance Computing, Networking, Storage and Analysis, pages 1–9, Salt Lake City, Utah, 2012. IEEE Computer Society Press.

[9] M. Geimer, F. Wolf, B. J. N. Wylie, E. Ábrahám, D. Becker, and B. Mohr. The Scalasca performance toolset architecture. *Concurrency and Computation: Practice and Experience*, 22(6):702–719, Apr. 2010.

[10] W. Gropp, E. Lusk, and A. Skjellum. *Using MPI: portable parallel programming with the message-passing interface*. Scientific and engineering computation. MIT Press, Cambridge, MA, 2nd edition, 1999.

[11] W. Gropp, R. Thakur, and E. Lusk. *Using MPI-2: Advanced Features of the Message Passing Interface*. MIT Press, Cambridge, MA, USA, 1999.

[12] J. He, A. Snavely, R. van der Wijngaart, and M. Frumkin. Automatic recognition of performance idioms in scientific applications. In *Parallel Distributed Processing Symposium (IPDPS), 2011 IEEE International*, pages 118–127, May 2011.

[13] I. Karlin, A. Bhatele, J. Keasler, B. L. Chamberlain, J. Cohen, Z. DeVito, R. Haque, D. Laney, E. Luke, F. Wang, D. Richards, M. Schulz, and C. Still. Exploring traditional and emerging parallel programming models using a proxy application. In *27th IEEE International Parallel & Distributed Processing Symposium (IEEE IPDPS 2013)*, Boston, USA, May 2013.

[14] I. Karlin, J. Keasler, and R. Neely. Lulesh 2.0 updates and changes. Technical Report LLNL-TR-641973, Lawrence Livermore National Laboratory, August 2013.

[15] S. Karlsson and M. Brorsson. A comparative characterization of communication patterns in applications using MPI and shared memory on an IBM SP2. In D. Panda and C. Stunkel, editors, *Network-Based Parallel Computing Communication, Architecture, and Applications*, volume 1362 of *Lecture Notes in Computer Science*, pages 189–201. Springer Berlin Heidelberg, 1998.

[16] D. J. Kerbyson and K. J. Barker. Automatic identification of application communication patterns via templates. In *Proceedings of the 5th international conference on Software engineering*, pages 114–121. ISCA, September 2005.

[17] J. Kim and D. J. Lilja. Characterization of communication patterns in message-passing parallel scientific application programs. In *Proceedings of the Second International Workshop on Network-Based Parallel Computing: Communication, Architecture, and Applications*, CANPC '98, pages 202–216, London, UK, UK, 1998. Springer-Verlag.

[18] P. Kogge, K. Bergman, S. Borkar, D. Campbell, W. Carlson, W. Dally, M. Denneau, P. Franzon, W. Harrod, K. Hill, J. Hiller, S. Karp, S. Keckler, D. Klein, R. Lucas, M. Richards, A. Scarpelli, S. Scott, A. Snavely, T. Sterling, R. S. Williams, and K. Yelick. Exascale computing study: Technology challenges in achieving exascale systems. Technical report, DARPA Information Processing Techniques Office, 2008.

[19] B. P. Miller, M. D. Callaghan, J. M. Cargille, J. K. Hollingsworth, R. B. Irvin, K. L. Karavanic, K. Kunchithapadam, and T. Newhall. The Paradyn parallel performance measurement tool. *Computer*, 28(11):37–46, Nov. 1995.

[20] mpiP: Lightweight, Scalable MPI Profiling. http://mpip.sourceforge.net, 2013.

[21] Nek5000. http://nek5000.mcs.anl.gov, 2014.

[22] A. Nichols. User's manual for ALE3D: An arbitrary lagrange/eulerian 3d code system. Technical Report UCRL-MA-152204 Rev 6, Lawrence Livermore National Laboratory, 2007.

[23] S. Plimpton. Fast parallel algorithms for short-range molecular dynamics. *Journal of Computational Physics*, 117:1–19, 1995.

[24] P. G. Raponi, F. Petrini, R. Walkup, and F. Checconi. Characterization of the communication patterns of scientific applications on blue gene/p. In *Parallel and Distributed Processing Workshops and Phd Forum (IPDPSW), 2011 IEEE International Symposium on*, pages 1017–1024, May 2011.

[25] J. Shalf, S. Kamil, L. Oliker, and D. Skinner. Analyzing ultra-scale application communication requirements for a reconfigurable hybrid interconnect. In *2005 ACM/IEEE conference on Supercomputing*, page 17. IEEE Computer Society, 2005.

[26] S. Shende and A. Malony. The TAU parallel performance system. *International Journal of High Performance Computing Applications*, 20(2):287–311, 2006.

[27] The NumPy Community. *NumPy reference, release 1.8.1*, March 2014.

[28] The SciPy Community. *SciPy reference guide, release 0.13.0*, October 2013.

[29] J. Vetter, R. Glassbrook, J. Dongarra, K. Schwan, B. Loftis, S. McNally, J. Meredith, J. Rogers, P. Roth, K. Spafford, and S. Yalamanchili. Keeneland: Bringing heterogeneous GPU computing to the computational science community. *Computing in Science Engineering*, 13(5):90–95, 2011.

[30] J. S. Vetter, editor. *Contemporary High Performance Computing: From Petascale Toward Exascale*, volume 1 of *CRC Computational Science Series*. Taylor and Francis, Boca Raton, 1 edition, 2013.

[31] J. S. Vetter, S. Lee, D. Li, G. Marin, C. McCurdy, J. Meredith, P. C. Roth, and K. Spafford. Quantifying architectural requirements of contemporary extreme-scale scientific applications. In *International Workshop on Performance Modeling, Benchmarking and Simulation of HPC Systems (PMBS13)*, Denver, Colorado, 2013.

[32] J. S. Vetter and M. O. McCracken. Statistical scalability analysis of communication operations in distributed applications. *SIGPLAN Not.*, 36(7):123–132, June 2001.

[33] J. S. Vetter and F. Mueller. Communication characteristics of large-scale scientific applications for contemporary cluster architectures. *Journal of Parallel and Distributed Computing*, 63(9):853–865, 2003.

Cache Line Aware Optimizations for ccNUMA Systems

Sabela Ramos
Computer Architecture Group
University of A Coruña
Spain
sramos@udc.es

Torsten Hoefler
Scalable Parallel Computing Lab
ETH Zurich
Switzerland
htor@inf.ethz.ch

ABSTRACT

Current shared memory systems utilize complex memory hierarchies to maintain scalability when increasing the number of processing units. Although hardware designers aim to hide this complexity from the programmer, ignoring the detailed architectural characteristics can harm performance significantly. We propose to expose the block-based design of caches in parallel computers to middleware designers to allow semi-automatic performance tuning with the systematic translation from algorithms to an analytic performance model. For this, we design a simple interface for cache line aware (CLa) optimization, a translation methodology, and a full performance model for cache line transfers in ccNUMA systems. Algorithms developed using CLa design perform up to 14x better than vendor and open-source libraries, and 2x better than existing ccNUMA optimizations.

Categories and Subject Descriptors

C.4 [**Performance of Systems**]: Modeling techniques

General Terms

Design, Algorithms, Performance

Keywords

Cache coherence, multi-cores, performance modeling.

1. MOTIVATION

Today's multi- and many-core architectures provide the illusion of coherent shared memory to simplify the initial design of parallel programs from a serial specification. Cache coherence protocols guarantee that there is exactly one value in each memory location in the system, even when several threads write simultaneously. To achieve the highest performance, programmers need to design highly-scalable parallel algorithms to utilize the exponentially growing number of cores. While cache coherence simplifies the initial design,

the complexity of the protocol's performance characteristics often leads to poorly-scalable solutions. This is mainly because the complex interactions in the cache coherence protocol are hidden from programmers, essentially forming an *abstraction barrier for performance-centric programming*. To overcome this, we propose the use of a Cache Line aware (CLa) design, a simple abstraction that considers cache coherence hardware during algorithm-design and implementation. The main features of CLa's abstract machine model are detailed cost functions for accesses in coherent hierarchical non-uniform memory access (ccNUMA) computers.

In summary, the specific contributions of our work are: (1) we propose Cache Line aware (CLa) optimization, a method for performance-centric programming of ccNUMA systems; (2) we show how to systematically model the performance of algorithms analytically; (3) we design a methodology to translate shared memory communication algorithms directly into an analytical performance model; and (4) we conduct a practical study with a dual-socket architecture yielding speedups between 1.8x and 14x over optimized libraries.

We start with a brief discussion of a performance model for cache-coherence protocols in ccNUMA systems. In Section 3 we introduce the rules for translating an algorithm into the performance model. Section 4 describes and exemplifies the application of our principles for CLa design.

2. CLA PERFORMANCE MODELS

Modern multi- and many-core processors provide cache coherence as a means to hide the management of data-sharing among cores. Yet, we show that performance engineers need to reason explicitly about cache coherence transfers in order to obtain highest performance. We propose a performance model based on a set of building blocks that enables programmers to analyze algorithms in terms of (cache) line transfers. We identify two main primitives which we parametrize through benchmarking considering thread location and coherence state: single-line and multi-line transfers. However, various interactions between threads may introduce additional overheads. Some interactions, such as contention (several threads accessing the same cache lines) and congestion (several threads accessing different lines) can be benchmarked and modeled accurately. Other interactions depend on the real-time order in which operations are performed and are not predictable (see Section 2.3).

Although our conclusions and methods are not limited to a specific architecture, we now briefly describe the NUMA system on which we developed and executed our benchmarks, a dual-socket eight-core processor Intel Sandy Bridge Xeon

E5-2660, at 2.20GHz with Hyper Threading activated and Quick Path Interconnect (QPI, 8 GT/s). Each socket has three levels of cache. L1 (32 KB data and 32 KB instructions) and L2 (256 KB unified) caches are private to each core. An L3 cache (or LLC) of 20 MB is shared by all cores within a socket and divided in eight slices. The internal components of the chip, including the LLC slices, are connected via a ring bus. All cores can use every LLC's cache slices, thus having access to data stored in any of them. The chip uses the MESIF cache coherence protocol [13], based on the classic MESI (Modified-Exclusive-Shared-Invalid) protocol. It adds a *Forward* state to optimize the management of shared states. Although it globally behaves like a snooping protocol, cache coherence within each socket is kept by the LLC, that holds a set of bits indicating the state of the line and which cores have a copy. Among sockets, the QPI implements the cache coherence protocol. It is in this scenario when the F state avoids multiple answers from different sockets to a snooping request.

2.1 Single-line Transfers

The basic block in our model is the transfer of a cache line between two cores. Line transfers are caused by two operations: *read* and *RFO* (Read For Ownership). Both involve fetching lines, but the latter indicates the intention to write. We estimate the cost of both as a *read* (R) although there could be some differences, e.g., an *RFO* of a shared line means that all copies must be invalidated. But we first analyze transfers between two threads where this difference is not significant.

We implemented a pingpong data exchange to analyze the impact of thread location and coherence state. Results show that there are significant differences when varying the location of threads and lines. But there are only minor variations for different cached states, hence, we cluster the costs for line transfers in five classes: (1) L if the line is in local cache, (2) R if it is in another core from the same socket, (3) Q if it is in another socket, (4) I if it is in memory in a local NUMA region, and (5) QI if it is in a remote NUMA region. Such a model would need to be generated for each microarchitecture. We parametrize the cost of a line transfer for each class with BenchIT [13], obtaining the following latencies: (1) $R_L \simeq 2.3ns$, (2) $R_R \simeq 35ns$, (3) $R_Q \simeq 94ns$, (4) $R_I \simeq 70ns$, and (5) $R_{QI} \simeq 107ns$.

Sandy Bridge supports loading half lines [1, §2.2.5.1] which is cheaper than always loading full lines. However, other architectures always transfer entire lines, thus, we will work with full lines for generality and clarity.

We use two benchmarks to evaluate contention (threads accessing the same CL) and congestion (threads accessing different lines). In these benchmarks, threads read an external send buffer and copy it into a local receive buffer. We did not observe contention in any scenario and results show no congestion for intra-socket transfers. We further analyze QPI congestion together with multi-line cache transfers.

2.2 Multi-line Transfers

We evaluate multi-line transfers with two benchmark strategies: pingpong and one-directional transfers (similar to those used for contention and congestion). Pingpong times exhibit significant variability when using invalid lines, especially for QPI transfers. This variability stems from the use of DRAM and different NUMA regions and we devel-

oped approximate models to simplify algorithm optimization and comparison. Without loss of generality, we work with cached multi-line transfers for which we empirically parametrize the model in Equation (1). N is the number of lines, n is the number of simultaneously accessing threads, and q, o, c are architecture-specific parameters (cf. Table 1). The term cnN represents congestion in the QPI link (it is zero in intra-socket scenarios).

$$T_m(n, N) = q + oN + cnN \qquad (1)$$

Table 1: Parameters for multi-line transfer of cached lines

	$\mathbf{q}$ $[ns]$	$\mathbf{o}$ $[\frac{ns}{line}]$	$\mathbf{c}$ $[\frac{ns}{line \cdot thread}]$	$\mathbf{R}^2$
Intra socket	63.4	11.1	0	0.8
Inter socket	180.65	7.5	3.0	0.91

2.3 Invalidation and Cache Line Stealing

The described building blocks can be used to model algorithms in terms of line transfers but we need to consider two additional sources of overhead due to interactions between threads or cores. First, an *RFO* of a shared line involves invalidation at its n owners (on our test system, it costs nR_R instead of R_R). Second, *cache line stealing* appears when several threads write one line where another thread is polling (*n-writers*), or when several threads poll a line that another thread writes (*n-readers*). Both scenarios get more complex with more than one reader or writer, respectively. To capture all these variations, we use *min-max* models [15] that provide performance bounds by estimating the best and worst stealing scenario. We represent a CLa algorithm in terms of line transfers and thread interactions, using the parametrized building blocks to derive models for the minimum (T_{min}) and maximum (T_{max}) scenarios.

3. A CANDIDATE CLA INTERFACE

In order to expose cache coherence interactions and apply our performance model, we propose a simple methodology that starts by expressing algorithms in a cache line centric manner using primitives that can be implemented in various ways in most languages. We implement them with direct load/store ISA instructions. When they are used for synchronization, we use atomic instructions for writing, but not for reading and polling, because atomics often force the eviction of lines from other caches. The cost of each operation is expressed in terms of location and state of the given lines. For more than one line, we use Equation (1). We define the following operations:

1. `cl_copy(cl_t* src,cl_t* dest,int N)` copies N lines from `src` to `dest`.
2. `cl_wait(cl_t* line,clv_t val,op_t comp=eq)` polls until `comp(*(line),val)` is true.
3. `cl_write(cl_t* line,clv_t val)` writes `val` in `line`.
4. `cl_add(cl_t* line,clv_t val)` adds `val` to `line`.

Once we have the CLa pseudo-code, we construct a graph in which nodes are the CLa operations performed by each thread, linked by four types of edges:

E1 A sequence of operations within a thread, represented by dotted directed edges.

E2 Logical dependencies between threads (i.e., reading or polling a line that has been written by others), represented by directed edges.

E3 Sequential restrictions between threads without order, represented by non-directed edges. We use them when several threads write the same flag (in any order), and a thread polls this flag waiting for all writes.

E4 Line stealing in non-related operations (e.g., a `wait` on a line that is written in two different stages of an algorithm), represented by dotted lines.

Next, we assign costs to the nodes using the following rules:

1. Flags are initially in memory. First fetch costs R_I.
2. An access to data in local cache costs R_L.
3. The access to the same line by the same thread in consecutive operations is counted once.
4. If the operation has an incoming edge from another thread, it costs R_R or R_Q depending on the location of threads.
5. Read operations with incoming edges from the same node can be simultaneous without contention. E.g., threads copying a line written by another.

In order to derive the T_{min} (cost of the critical path), we define a path as a sequence of nodes linked by E1, E2, and E3 edges, starting in a node with no incoming E1 and E2 edges, and finishing in a node with no outgoing edges. Regarding E3 edges, they link all sequential writes that have outgoing E2s towards the same `wait`. When searching for the critical path, we analyze reorderings of these writes, ensuring that the path visits once each of them before going towards the `wait`. When some E3s represent inter-socket communications, we select the reordering with less QPI transfers.

To identify QPI congestion, we look for directed arrows between sockets that have: (1) different start and end points (accesses to different addresses by different threads), and (2) previous paths of similar cost (simultaneous transfers). Finally, T_{max} is calculated by analyzing line stealing (the main cause is the `wait` operation) and we can refine it by considering which operations might not overlap. We optimize for T_{min} because T_{max} is usually too pessimistic. If an algorithm receives a communication structure as parameter, we analyze multiple structures to obtain the best one.

This set of rules is enough to derive graphs and performance models for multiple communication algorithms and it is easily extensible to cover other interactions.

4. SINGLE-LINE BROADCAST

Broadcast consists of transferring data from one thread (*root*) to n others. We designed a tree-based algorithm taking into account that all children of a given node copy the data without contention. However, the more children a parent has, the more costly the synchronization is: The parent notifies that data is ready (one-to-many, T_{o2m}) and children notify that they have copied so the parent can free the structure (many-to-one, T_{m2o}). We use notification with payload for the one-to-many synchronization. Regarding the many-to-one, we use one line in which children write and the parent polls. Although other analyzed variants have the same T_{min}, this version has lower T_{max}. Our algorithm (cf. Figure 1) uses a generic tree in which each node i has k_i children that copy the same data. We generate all structurally equivalent rooted trees [10], calculating the broadcast latency to select the best structure. This tree could change slightly in a scenario with contention in which we may have rounds of children accessing the same data at different stages.

```
Function OneLineBroadcast(int me, cl_t * mydata, tree_t tree)
       if tree.parent != -1 then
[S1]       cl_wait(tree.pflag[tree.parent],1);        //one-to-many
[S2]       cl_copy(tree.data[tree.parent],mydata,1);
       if tree.nsons > 0 then
[S3]       cl_copy(mydata,tree.data[me],1);
[S4]       cl_write(tree.pflag[me],1);                 //one-to-many
[S5]       cl_wait(tree.sflag[me],tree.nsons);         //many-to-one
       if tree.parent != -1 then
[S6]       cl_add(tree.sflag[tree.parent],1);          //many-to-one
       end
   end
```

Figure 1: One line broadcast in CLa pseudo-code. The first `if` block corresponds to children polling their parent's flag and copying the data. In the second one, a parent sets the data and the flag, and waits for its children to copy. Finally, children notify to their parent that they have copied.

For a given tree structure, we construct the CLa graph and search the critical path. Figure 2 shows an example of a four-node binary tree (the critical path has thicker edges and nodes with dotted circles). The E1s link operations within each thread and we use E2s in the synchronizations and data copies. Finally, there is an E3 because t_1 and t_2 write the same flag, where t_0 polls.

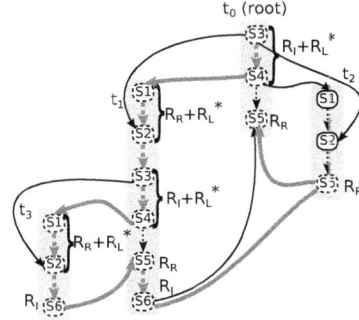

Figure 2: CLa graph for a one line broadcast using a four-node binary tree. Costs with '*' represent situations in which the same thread operates consecutively with the same line and the cost of accessing is counted only once.

Since we use tree structures, we observe regularities in the critical path: It includes the transfer of data from the root to its children plus the synchronizations ($T_{lev}(k_0) = T_{o2m}(k_0) + T_{data} + T_{m2o}(k_0)$), plus the cost of the most expensive subtree ($T_{bc}(stree_i)$, the left one in Figure 2). We generalize it in Equation (2)[1]. The minimization balances the number of simultaneous readers, and the notification cost. In a multi-socket broadcast some edges become QPI links. We generate permutations of the tree nodes to locate the QPI links in different edges[2] and we apply Equation (2) considering: (1) Inter-socket transfers cost R_Q. (2) To isolate QPI transfers and minimize line stealing, we use one synchronization line per socket. And (3) we do not consider QPI congestion caused by different subtrees because our experiments showed that the benefits are minimal.

$$\text{minimize}_{k_i} \quad T_{bc}(tree) = T_{lev}(k_0) + \max_{i=1,...,k_C} (T_{bc}(stree_i))$$
$$\text{subject to} \quad T_{bc}(leaf) = 0 \quad \sum_{i=0}^{n} k_i = r, \; k_i \geq 0 \tag{2}$$

Figure 3 shows the performance of our algorithm compared to two MPI libraries and the HMPI NUMA-aware

---

[1] If we use a global flag where the root sets the shared structure as occupied by this operation, we add R_I

[2] We do not need all permutations: there is no difference among threads from the same socket.

broadcast [12] (using a thread-based implementation to compare algorithms directly). We use `RDTSC` intervals [14] to synchronize threads before each iteration and we force synchronization data-structures and user-data in the desired cache states. The system used is described in Section 2, with CentOS 6.4. Compilers are Intel v.13.1.1 and GNU v.4.4.7, and MPI libraries Intel MPI v.4.1.4 and Open MPI 1.7.2. The shaded area represents the min-max model. The results of our algorithm include boxplots to represent the statistical variation of the measurements. We schedule up to eight threads in one socket and the rest of them in the second one. Broadcasts with an imbalanced number of threads per socket (e.g., ten threads) use different trees depending on the root is location. Our algorithm clearly outperforms both MPI libraries obtaining a speedup of up to 14x. HMPI uses a flat tree with synchronization based on barriers. We improve this approach by up to 1.8x.

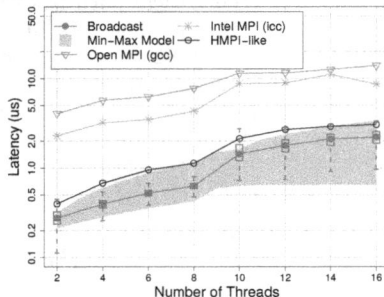

Figure 3: Single-line broadcast

5. RELATED WORK

Analytical performance models have been largely used to optimize parallel computation [3, 7], especially in distributed environments. Some of them were extended with memory concerns [5, 6] and multi-core features [11, 16]. Model-driven algorithm optimization has been tackled in multiple works [9, 12] but with almost no cache coherence concerns. And most cache coherence works focus on memory hierarchy and cache conflicts [2, 4]. David et al. [8] make an exhaustive analysis of lock synchronization for different multi-core architectures, evaluating the effect of cache states and memory operations. Our performance model significantly improves our previous work [15] on homogeneous many-core processors. We extend the model for hierarchical NUMA machines, generalizing its applicability and the algorithm design.

6. CONCLUSIONS

While cache coherence simplifies the use of multiple cores, it exhibits complex performance properties and thus complicates high-performance code design. We address this issue with cache line aware (CLa) optimizations, a semi-automatic design and optimization method that eases the translation of an algorithm to a performance model in a systematic manner. We exemplify its use improving broadcast performance up to 14x in comparison to highly-optimized vendor-provided communication libraries, and up to 1.8x when compared to the NUMA-aware HMPI collectives. Moreover, we expect higher improvements in future many-core systems. We expect that model-driven algorithm engineering will benefit high-performance low-level software engineering, and it will be necessary to address software and hardware complexity in the long run.

7. ACKNOWLEDGEMENTS

We thank the support from Alexander Supalov and Robert Blankenship from Intel. This work was supported by the Ministry of Economy and Competitiveness of Spain and FEDER funds of the EU (Project TIN2013-42148-P).

8. REFERENCES

[1] Intel® 64 and IA-32 Architectures Optimization Ref. Manual, 2014.

[2] A. Agarwal et al. An Analytical Cache Model. *ACM Trans. on Computer Systems*, 7(2):184–215, 1989.

[3] A. Alexandrov et al. LogGP: Incorporating Long Messages into the LogP Model - One Step Closer towards a Realistic Model for Parallel Computation. In *Proc. 7th ACM SPAA'95*, pages 95–105, S. Barbara, CA, USA, 1995.

[4] D. Andrade et al. Accurate Prediction of the Behavior of Multithreaded Applications in Shared Caches. *Parallel Computing*, 39(1):36 – 57, 2013.

[5] K. W. Cameron et al. lognP and log3P: Accurate Analytical Models of Point-to-Point Communication in Distributed Systems. *IEEE Trans. on Computers*, 53(3):314–327, 2007.

[6] K. W. Cameron and X. H. Sun. Quantifying Locality Effect in Data Access Delay: Memory logP. In *Proc. 17th IEEE IPDPS'03*, (8 pages),Nice, France, 2003.

[7] D. Culler et al. LogP: towards a Realistic Model of Parallel Computation. *SIGPLAN Not.*, 28(7):1–12, 1993.

[8] T. David et al. Everything You Always Wanted to Know About Synchronization but Were Afraid to Ask. In *Proc. 24th ACM Symp. SOSP'13*, pages 33–48, Farminton, PA, USA, 2013.

[9] R. M. Karp et al. Optimal Broadcast and Summation in the LogP Model. In *Proc. 5th ACM SPAA'93*, pages 142–153, Velen, Germany, 1993.

[10] G. Li and F. Ruskey. Advantages of Forward Thinking in Generating Rooted and Free Trees. In *Proc. 10th ACM-SIAM SODA'99*, pages 939–940, Baltimore, MD,USA, 1999.

[11] L. Li et al. mPlogP: A Parallel Computation Model for Heterogeneous Multi-core Computer. In *Proc. 10th IEEE/ACM Intl. CCGRID'10*, pages 679–684, Melbourne, Australia, 2010.

[12] S. Li et al. NUMA-aware Shared-memory Collective Communication for MPI. In *In Proc. 22nd Intl. Symp. HPDC'13*, pages 85–96, New York, NY, USA, 2013.

[13] D. Molka et al. Memory Performance and Cache Coherency Effects on an Intel Nehalem Multiprocessor System. In *Proc. 18th Intl. Conf. PACT'09*, pages 261–270, Raleigh, NC, USA, 2009.

[14] S. Ramos and T. Hoefler. Benchmark Suite for Modeling Intel Xeon Phi. http://gac.des.udc.es /~sramos/xeon_phi_bench/xeon_phi_bench.html.

[15] S. Ramos and T. Hoefler. Modeling communication in cache-coherent SMP systems: a case-study with Xeon Phi. In *Proc. of the 22nd Intl. HPDC'13*, pages 97–108, New York, New York, USA, 2013.

[16] Z. Wang and M. F. O'Boyle. Mapping Parallelism to Multi-cores: A Machine Learning Based Approach. In *Proc. 14th ACM SIGPLAN Symp. PPoPP'09*, pages 75–84, Raleigh, NC, USA, 2009.

XEMEM: Efficient Shared Memory for Composed Applications on Multi-OS/R Exascale Systems

Brian Kocoloski and John Lange
Department of Computer Science
University of Pittsburgh
{briankoco, jacklange}@cs.pitt.edu

ABSTRACT

Current trends in exascale systems research indicate that heterogeneity will abound in both the hardware and software layers on future HPC systems. It is our position that exascale environments are likely to be constructed from independent partitions of hardware and system software called *enclaves*, with multiple enclaves co-located on the same physical nodes and each executing an optimized operating system and runtime (OS/R) to support a particular application behavior. Fully utilizing these systems will require the ability to execute composed workloads, such as *in situ* applications, whereby HPC simulations execute synchronously with co-located analytic packages that in turn process simulation output via shared memory. In this work, we present the design and implementation of XEMEM, a shared memory system that can efficiently construct memory mappings across enclave OSes to support composed workloads while allowing diverse application components to execute in strictly isolated enclaves. By utilizing modifications to the Kitten lightweight kernel and Palacios lightweight virtual machine monitor, as well as leveraging our recent work on lightweight "co-kernels," we demonstrate that our approach can support a diverse range of native and virtualized environments likely to be deployed on future exascale systems. Finally, we demonstrate that a multi-enclave system can reduce cross-workload contention and improve performance for a sample composed benchmark compared to a single OS approach.

Categories and Subject Descriptors

B.3.2 [**Memory Structures**]: Shared Memory C.5.1 [**Computer System Implementation**]: Super (very large) computers; D.4.7 [**Operating Systems**]: Organization and Design

This project is made possible by support from the National Science Foundation (NSF) via grant CNS-1421585, and by the 2013 Exascale Operating and Runtime Systems Program under the Office of Advanced Scientific Computing Research in the DOE Office of Science.

Keywords

operating systems; shared memory; supercomputing; virtualization; exascale; application composition

1. INTRODUCTION

Historically, tightly-coupled and massively parallel HPC applications have enjoyed the luxury of single user operating environments devoted entirely to the forward progress of the application. However, as the HPC community ushers in the exascale era, a new and diverse set of challenges are emerging that will increase the amount of workload consolidation on exascale nodes, limiting the utility of single application environments. As systems become increasingly heterogeneous, new parallel programming paradigms and communication models [8] are likely to lead to the development of applications highly specialized for particular hardware and software environments which cannot be universally supported by a single system configuration [3, 1]. Furthermore, consolidating workloads to restrict data movement and communication will likely be needed to address power and performance constraints of exascale applications [12].

A key example of this type of workload consolidation can be seen in the emergence of composed workloads, such as *in situ* applications. Petascale-class and earlier generations of HPC applications generally employed models of computation whereby processing of simulation output was performed as a post-processing task on a separate I/O node or visualization cluster and as part of an entirely separate process [6]. However, this type of model becomes less feasible as the amount of data produced by simulations continues to increase, as it creates bottlenecks in networks and I/O subsystems, introduces contention on those resources for separate workloads, and unnecessarily consumes nontrivial amounts of power and memory to move data [23, 17]. These issues have driven the emergence of composed in situ models whereby the compute/memory intensive HPC simulation communicates via shared memory with a more general purpose, I/O intensive analytics package that executes on the same physical node.

While co-locating HPC simulation and analytics workloads provides the potential to increase the throughput of an exascale system, the individual workload components present different resource management and isolation requirements to the operating and runtime management systems (OS/R). In order to effectively consolidate exascale applications in such a system, it is necessary to support both the performance characteristics and strict isolation requirements of traditional HPC applications, while at the same time pro-

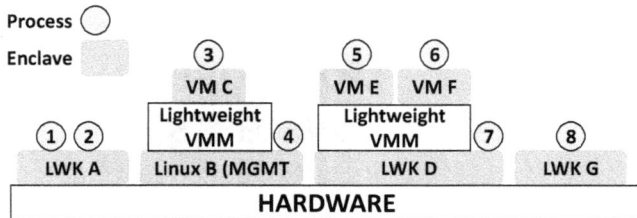

Figure 1: Exascale Enclave Partitioning

viding the full-featured environments required by analytic and visualization applications. Given these considerations, it is our position that exascale OS/Rs will be composed of a wide range of heterogeneous hardware and software environments, called *enclaves*, where each enclave is specialized in supporting a particular class of exascale workload, but still remains strictly isolated from the other enclaves on the system. Composed workloads executing in multi-enclave environments will be afforded high performance and consistent execution experience required by large-scale HPC applications, while at the same time having access to feature-rich runtimes and operating environments.

While the concept of a multi-enclave environment has been established for future exascale systems [3, 1], many details pertaining to enclave compositions are largely unresolved to this point. For example, previous work has shown the benefits of virtualization for high performance computing [13], and it is reasonable to consider virtualization to be a key component of an exascale system. Other work has identified techniques by which multiple operating systems can be deployed on partitioned hardware components without virtualization [16, 18, 20]. Our position, illustrated in Figure 1, is that many different software and hardware configurations, both native and virtualized, will be commonly deployed as exascale enclaves.

As Figure 1 illustrates, the individual OS/Rs of each enclave are capable of executing local processes, which by default are isolated from each other at both the system software and hardware layers. However, supporting composed workloads in these types of multi-enclave environments requires the ability to allow processes to communicate efficiently with other processes executing in separate enclaves. Thus, in this work, our key contribution is the design, implementation, and evaluation of XEMEM (Cross Enclave Memory), a system that can efficiently and dynamically provide inter-process shared memory mappings between separate OS/Rs to support the execution of composed workloads.

This paper makes the following main contributions:

- We present the design and implementation of XEMEM, a shared memory mechanism to enable composed workloads in a diverse set of multi-OS/R environments expected in exascale systems.

- We provide compatibility with existing applications by providing an implementation whose API is backwards compatible with the API exported by XPMEM [21], a shared memory implementation for large scale supercomputers. This allows unmodified applications to be deployed, without any knowledge of enclave topology or cross-enclave communication mechanisms.

- We demonstrate the scalability of our implementation, with respect to both the sizes of shared memory regions, as well as the number of enclaves concurrently executing on the system.

- By utilizing extensions to the Kitten lightweight kernel, Palacios virtual machine monitor, and a lightweight co-kernel architecture, we show that a multi-enclave system using shared memory allows an in situ workload to achieve superior and more consistent performance when compared to single OS/R configurations. Our results demonstrate the benefits of multi-OS/R configurations both on a single node as well as multiple nodes.

2. RELATED WORK

Prior research in shared memory for HPC workloads has focused on optimized memory mappings for single OS/R environments. SMARTMAP [4] allows sharing of coarse-grained regions through shared top-level tables between processes. However, utilizing this approach in a multi-enclave exascale environment would prove challenging, as different system software environments will likely utilize conflicting address space management routines that may not be easily negotiated in the same set of page tables. KNEM [10] provides single-copy shared memory designed to optimize intra-node MPI communication between processes as well as various communication devices, but again is designed to operate in a single OS/R environment and would require significant modifications to support a multi-enclave configuration.

Other research has focused on optimizing communication between co-located VMs. Fido [5] demonstrated that providing read-only inter-VM address space access can yield a high degree of performance suitable for many enterprise applications. More general inter-VM message passing techniques have been implemented via shared memory [19, 22]. However, exascale systems will require broader support for heterogeneous environments than these techniques support. For one, some exascale (co)processors may not support virtualization capabilities. Even those that do may still be required to support workload configurations requiring shared memory mappings between native processes and VM processes executing on different host OS/R environments.

Finally, projects such as FusedOS [16], McKernel [18], and mOS [20] have investigated the deployment of multi-enclave environments similar to the types of environments we envision in exascale systems. These approaches allow multiple system software configurations to exist on the same nodes by running lightweight environments on a partition of the system's cores and running fullweight environments like Linux on another partition. Threads executing in the lightweight environment request services, such as system calls and device management operations, by delegating these operations to threads running in the Linux environment. To support such a configuration, these systems use a memory mapping approach by which the Linux threads map the same memory as the lightweight threads, and thus can efficiently perform service operations without requiring memory copies. However, we envision that exascale systems will have greater needs for general purpose shared memory operations than are allowed by these systems, such as the sharing of address regions between virtual machines and native processes.

3. MULTI-OS/R SHARED MEMORY

To support the types of environments likely to be seen in exascale systems requires that our system, XEMEM, support arbitrary enclave topologies while at the same time provide scalability as the number of co-located enclave OS-/Rs increases. Furthermore, it is critical that the system scale to arbitrarily large shared memory regions as required by composed applications.

One of the key tenets of our approach is that, while meeting these requirements will require significant implementation effort in cross-enclave communication mechanisms and protocols, application programming for shared memory on an exascale system should not be more difficult than it is on current systems. Ideally, applications written for single OS/R systems should not need to be re-written or required to change at all to run in an multi-enclave environment. This section discusses how our system is built to maintain compatibility with existing shared memory applications while at the same time meeting the goals required for scalability and efficiency on future exascale architectures.

3.1 Common Global Name Space

Our approach to maintaining the simplicity of shared memory application programming centers around the ability to provision a single common global name space for shared memory registrations that provides two key features: unique naming and discoverability. In a single OS/R environment, shared memory regions can be readily named and tagged by a variety of basic mechanisms, such as using process IDs and virtual address ranges, which afford a simple way to maintain the unique addressability of each region. Furthermore, the OS/R has access to a plethora of shared IPC constructs, such as filesystems, to provide discoverability to processes.

In a multi-enclave environment, however, these operations are considerably more challenging. One approach to provide naming would be to eschew the requirement that the OS/R provide global uniqueness of identifiers, and instead force user applications to add an extra dimension to shared memory addresses by providing some form of unique enclave identifier. However, such an approach directly conflicts with our goal of maintaining application simplicity, as it would require applications to have knowledge of enclave configurations. Instead, our approach is to administer a common global name space by providing a centralized name server responsible for the allocation of segment identifiers for all shared address regions. This approach guarantees the uniqueness of all registered memory regions without requiring local OS/R environments to negotiate the availability of process IDs and virtual address regions, or adding complexity to application programming. This approach also allows our system to provide discoverability, as the name server can be queried for information regarding the existence and names of shared memory regions.

3.2 Arbitrary Enclave Topologies

One of the key requirements for an exascale shared memory system is the ability to support the construction of arbitrary enclave topologies. It is our vision that not only will exascale environments incorporate a variety of different enclave architectures, but also that an individual node's partitions are likely to be dynamic and will change in response to the node's workload characteristics. At any point in time, we refer to an enclave's architectural partitioning, including

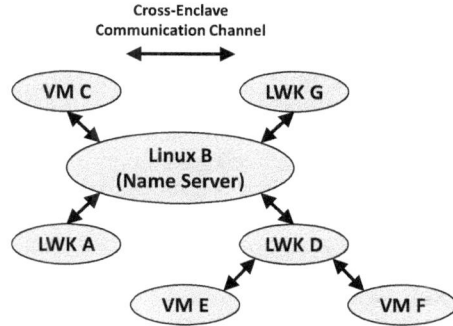

Figure 2: Exascale Enclave Topology

the hardware-supported inter-enclave communication interfaces, as the *enclave topology*. Figure 2 shows the topology for the example enclave partitions shown in Figure 1, for the configuration in which the name server discussed in the previous section is configured to run in the single native Linux enclave. As the figure demonstrates, our system assumes that enclave topologies will be organized in a hierarchical fashion such that communication channels between enclaves can be restricted. This means that enclaves will not necessarily have the ability to communicate directly with all other enclaves in the system, but rather will be required to communicate via an alternative mechanism that supports the routing of information based on the hierarchical configuration.

Our system supports communication in any arbitrary topology by utilizing a hierarchical routing algorithm that associates each enclave in the system with a unique identifier called an *enclave ID*. In order to route messages through the system, the algorithm requires each enclave to perform three main operations: (1) determine the local communication channel through which it can communicate with the name server, (2) request an enclave ID via this channel, and (3) maintain a mapping of enclave IDs to local communication channels. Initially, an enclave queries the location of the name server by broadcasting a message on each of its communication channels. When another enclave receives a broadcast message, it creates a response if it knows a path to the name server through one of its own channels. Once a response is received, the enclave remembers the communication channel through which the response came, and then sends a request through the link to allocate an enclave ID, which gets forwarded to the name server.

To maintain a mapping of enclave IDs to communication channels, each enclave is required to keep track of enclave IDs as they are allocated by the name server and forwarded through the system. For example, again referring to Figure 2, assuming *VM F* has determined it can reach the name server through *LWK D*, it sends a request through *LWK D* to allocate an enclave ID. *LWK D*, which has previously identified the name server location and allocated an enclave ID for itself, forwards the request to the name server and remembers that the request came from *VM F*. The name server receives the request, allocates an enclave ID, and updates its enclave map to map the new enclave ID to *LWK D*. Upon receiving the new enclave ID, LWK D queries its outstanding request list and finds that a request previously came from *VM F*. Thus, it forwards the enclave ID to *VM F* and updates its internal map accordingly.

By maintaining enclave ID mappings in this way, enclaves are able to make routing decisions for shared memory registration messages by using a simple algorithm. When an enclave receives a message, it searches its map for the destination enclave ID. If it finds the enclave ID, it forwards the message along the associated communication channel for that enclave. Otherwise, it forwards the message through the channel used to reach the name server. With this hierarchical architecture, our system is able to support any arbitrary enclave topology. It should be noted that the name server can be deployed in any enclave on the system, though we envision that most exascale systems will likely place the name server in a management enclave.

3.3 Dynamic Sharing of Memory Regions

Much of the previous work in high performance shared memory [4] has focused on efficiently creating large shared memory mappings between processes executing in single OS/R environments through the use of shared top-level page table entries. This approach is suitable for single-user environments such as the lightweight kernels it is currently deployed in.

Unfortunately, this approach is unsuitable in a multi-enclave environment for a variety of reasons. First, the sharing of page table entries across multiple heterogeneous processors may simply not be possible based on the hardware configurations in some exascale systems. Furthermore, heterogeneous software environments in different enclaves are likely to employ different address space management routines and operations. For example, full-featured environments such as Linux will require mechanisms such as page protections and page faulting semantics in order to support higher-level application behavior. Coalescing this type of behavior with a static, distributed shared memory approach is likely to be difficult to implement efficiently and correctly.

Our approach is to dynamically support more fine-grained memory mapping requests according to the individual memory sharing requirements of composed application processes. As such, our system provides shared memory mappings as they are created/requested by processes executing in different enclave environments. While this approach adds a small amount of overhead in the creation and attachment of shared memory mappings, it allows for a more efficient use of virtual and physical address space, and increases the number of heterogeneous enclave environments likely to be supported by our system.

3.4 Localized Address Space Management

Given the significant scale and level of heterogeneity that is likely to be found in the hardware and software environments on exascale systems, our system requires the enclave operating systems to perform memory mapping operations locally using the techniques required by the enclave's hardware configuration. These operations include walking page tables to generate physical address regions that map to segment identifiers, as well as performing page table modifications to modify process address spaces. While it may be possible to perform shared memory mappings by modifying enclave address spaces remotely, it would likely be difficult to provide such an implementation correctly, and would at least require complicated and inefficient address space synchronization mechanisms.

Function	Operation
xpmem_make	Export address region as shared memory. Returns *segid*.
xpmem_remove	Remove an exported region associated with a *segid*.
xpmem_get	Request access to shared memory region associated with a *segid*. Returns permission grant.
xpmem_release	Release permission grant.
xpmem_attach	Map a region of shared memory associated with a *segid*.
xpmem_detach	Unmap a region of shared memory.

Table 1: The XPMEM User-Level API

4. IMPLEMENTATION

The goals of the implementation of XEMEM are twofold. First, we seek to provide transparency to applications so that they are not required to have knowledge about the existence of enclaves or specific cross-enclave communication interfaces. Second, we seek to provide scalability with respect to the number of concurrently executing enclaves, as well as the amount of memory being shared in the system at any point in time.

Our implementation is largely based on our previous research in providing multi-OS/R system configurations. The implementation is based specifically on the Kitten lightweight kernel and the Palacios virtual machine monitor, as well as our recent work with lightweight "co-kernels" that leverage modifications to these systems to support the types of multi-enclave configurations proposed in Figure 1.

Kitten Lightweight Kernel.
Kitten [13] is a special-purpose OS kernel designed to provide an efficient environment for executing massively parallel HPC applications. Some of Kitten's unique characteristics are its modern code base that is partially derived from the Linux kernel and its use of virtualization to provide full-featured guest OS support when needed.

Palacios Virtual Machine Monitor.
Palacios [13] is a publicly available, open source, OS independent VMM that targets the x86 and x86_64 architectures with either ADM SVM or Intel VT extensions. Palacios is designed to be embeddable into multiple host OSes, and is currently supported in both the Linux and Kitten host environments. The combination of Palacios and Kitten acts as a lightweight hypervisor supporting full system virtualization.

Pisces Lightweight Co-Kernel Architecture.
Recently, we have proposed the use of lightweight "co-kernels" through the Pisces co-kernel architecture [15]. Co-kernels enable the decomposition of a node's hardware resources (cores, memory blocks, devices) into partitions that are fully managed by independent system software stacks. Pisces allows a node to deploy multiple co-located Kitten instances as co-kernels executing alongside an unmodified Linux host OS. By leveraging Palacios support, the enclave OSes managing these co-kernels may be virtualized, resulting in customizable OS/R configurations well-suited for the deployment of composed multi-enclave workloads.

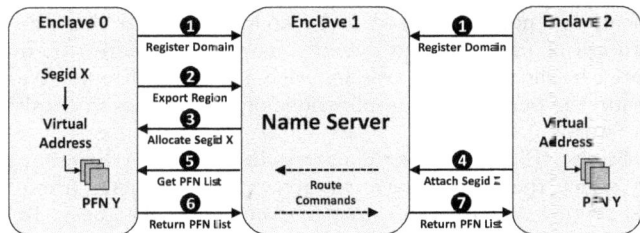

Figure 3: Shared Memory Protocol

4.1 XPMEM

To provide transparency to user processes executing in heterogeneous enclave environments, we leveraged an API that is backwards compatible with the XPMEM API for Linux systems developed by SGI/Cray [21]. XPMEM provides zero-copy shared memory to areas of a process' address spaces by allowing processes to selectively export address space regions and associate publicly visible segment identifiers (*segids*) with them. Given a valid *segid*, a process can create shared memory mappings with the source process. The XPMEM user-level API is shown in Table 1.

XPMEM also provides a kernel module responsible for providing shared memory mappings between multiple native Linux processes. We developed a similar XEMEM kernel module which implements the same functionality as XPMEM for Linux systems, but also supports sending memory attachment requests to remote enclaves, as well as serving attachment requests from remote enclaves by performing page table walks to generate page lists. We implemented the name server as a component of our XEMEM kernel module, which is responsible for the creation of unique *segids* for all enclaves in the system. We also implemented the routing protocol discussed in Section 3.2 to support arbitrary enclave topologies. Finally, we implemented the XEMEM service in both the Kitten lightweight kernel and Palacios Virtual Machine Monitor.

4.2 Shared Memory Protocol

While user-level processes are not required to have explicit knowledge of enclave topologies, they must still be able to discover exported memory regions created by external enclave processes. Our system provides a mechanism, illustrated in Figure 3, by which requests to create and attach to shared memory regions may be processed by the underlying enclave OS/R environments. As discussed in the previous section, XEMEM administers a common global name space for shared memory regions by utilizing a centralized name server responsible for assigning globally unique *segids* for all exported memory regions. Thus, to create a shared memory region, a local enclave's OS/R first sends a request to the name server to allocate a *segid*. The *segid* is then communicated to the user-level process according to the XEMEM API.

In order to attach to a shared memory segment, a process wishing to map the region must first discover the unique *segid* from the source process in some way. While single OS/R environments would likely resort to the IPC constructs provided by the local OS, our system provides an alternative mechanism for querying the name server using kernel-level inter-enclave messages.

Given a valid *segid*, the local OS/R for the attaching process first determines if the segment was created by a local process or not. If so, the attachment proceeds using the conventions of the local OS shared memory facilities. Otherwise, an attachment request is sent to the name server using the command routing protocol described in Section 3.2. Upon receiving the attachment request, the name server, which maps *segids* to enclaves, then forwards the command to the destination enclave which owns the *segid*. The destination enclave creates a list of the physical page frames that have been allocated to map the *segid*. A response message containing the list of frames is then forwarded back through the name server to the attaching enclave using the same routing mechanisms. Upon receiving the list of page frames, the attaching enclave maps them to user memory using the memory mapping constructs provided by the local OS.

4.3 OS Memory Mapping Routines

As discussed in the previous section, our system provides the ability to generate lists of page frames corresponding to *segids*, as well to map lists of page frames into destination enclave address spaces. Page frame lists are generated as enclaves receive remote requests for *segid* attachments. For Linux enclaves, memory must first be pinned in the user process' address space before a list can be generated. For this, we primarily rely on the `get_user_pages`[1] kernel function to allocate and pin physical memory for the process. Once the memory has been pinned, Linux provides a set of page table walking functions that allow the list to be easily generated. For mapping remote enclave page frame lists into Linux address spaces, we use the `vm_mmap` function to allocate an unused portion of virtual address space, and then use `remap_pfn_range` to map the page frames into the region.

For Kitten LWK enclaves, two existing design protocols complicate the dynamic creation of shared memory regions. First, the original shared memory mechanism in Kitten relies on the SMARTMAP [4] protocol, which uses page table sharing techniques to support local process shared memory in a way that would be difficult to extend to multi-enclave configurations. Furthermore, all virtual address space regions (heap, stack, etc.) for Kitten processes are mapped statically to physical memory as processes are created, and there was originally no support for dynamically expanding these regions. To address these issues, we added support for dynamic heap expansion, by which processes can map remote page frame lists in a way that does not sacrifice the ability to use SMARTMAP for shared memory with local processes, or negate the ability to map all other virtual regions with physical memory during process creation.

To implement page frame list generation for handling shared memory attachments from remote processes, we utilized existing page table walking functions already provided by the kernel.

4.4 Palacios Host/Guest Memory Sharing

Providing support for shared memory between Palacios virtual machine enclaves and the corresponding host enclave presents two main challenges. First, both the guest and host need to be able to initiate shared memory operations,

---
[1]Note that `get_user_pages` is a bit of a misnomer. Pages are generally already allocated when the function is invoked, with the main purpose being the pinning of memory to prevent paging out

(a) Guest Attachments to Host Enclave Memory

(b) Host Attachments to Guest Enclave Memory

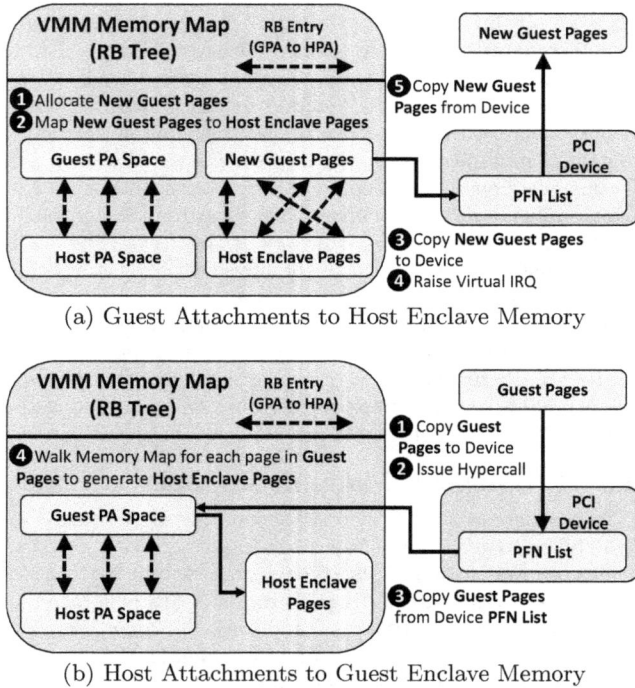

Figure 4: Palacios Memory Translations for Shared Memory Attachments

so our implementation must support efficient notifications of operations from host to the guest, as well as from the guest to the host. Additionally, Palacios should efficiently perform memory translations between host and guest page frame numbers for page lists that are passed during shared memory attachments.

To address these challenges, our approach, illustrated in Figure 4, consists of a virtual PCI device that allows efficient two-way notifications, as well as modifications to Palacios' internal memory management system to support the required memory translations. Figure 4(a) demonstrates the process by which a guest enclave completes an attachment to memory shared by the host. First, Palacios allocates a completely new region of guest physical address space that is equal in size to the amount of memory being shared. Then, Palacios updates its internal memory map to map this memory to the host page frames specified in the "Host Enclave Pages" list, which is supplied by the source enclave which exported the shared region. Once the memory map has been updated, Palacios copies the page frames corresponding to the new guest memory region to a list accessible through the virtual PCI device, and then issues an interrupt on the device. When the guest enters, it receives the interrupt, reads the page frame list from the device, and maps them into the attaching process' virtual address space.

It is important to note that Palacios' memory map is currently implemented as a red-black tree, where each entry in the tree maps a physically contiguous guest region to a physically contiguous host region. Palacios is usually configured to manage large blocks of physically contiguous memory, and thus is able to map all guest memory with a relatively small number of entries in this tree. However, the host enclave page frames that are mapped as part of XEMEM attach-

ments are not guaranteed to be contiguous, and thus the process of updating the memory map may require a new entry in the red-black tree for each host page frame. We study the performance implications of this process in detail in Section 5.4.

Figure 4(b) illustrates the process in the reverse direction, by which the host enclave can generate a host page frame list representing a memory region exported by the guest. To notify the host of the completion of an attachment operation, the guest copies the page frames to a list accessible through the PCI device, and then issues a hypercall to trigger an exit into the host. Using the pages frames specified by the guest, Palacios walks the memory map and generates the list of host page frames that correspond to the guest memory. The host enclave can then map the host page frames to the attaching process' virtual address space, or forward them according to the routing protocol if the attaching process exists in a separate enclave.

4.5 Cross-Enclave Communication Channels

Facilitating the shared memory protocol described in Section 4.2 requires the ability to send messages between enclaves. Messages generally compose one of the commands shown in Table 1, but also exist to support the routing protocol outlined in Section 3.2, such as sending or responding to the broadcasts needed to query the name server location. Our current system provides two separate mechanisms for cross-enclave messages: a channel leveraging the Palacios virtual machine monitor for allowing communication between virtual machines and a native host enclave, and a channel based on the Pisces co-kernel architecture, which allows communication between two native enclaves.

Palacios Host/Guest Channel.

The Palacios communication channel is implemented via a virtual PCI device, which is discussed at length in Section 4.4. In both transfer directions (host-to-guest or guest-to-host), if the message being transfered does not have an associated page frame list component (e.g., any of the operations in Table 1 except xpmem_attach), the mechanisms used are similar but simpler, as there is no need to translate page frame lists. For these operations, a simple command header located in the PCI device is set, and then either an interrupt into the guest or a hypercall into the host is used to signal the message notification.

Pisces IPI-Based Channel.

The other cross-enclave communication channel supported by our system is based on the Pisces co-kernel architecture. During the creation of a Kitten co-kernel enclave, the co-kernel creates a small shared memory region through which kernel-level messages can be transferred to/from the Linux management enclave. Both the Linux management enclave and the co-kernel enclave initialize special IPI (Inter-Processor Interrupt) vectors for negotiating access to this memory. To initiate a message transfer, an enclave sends an IPI to the destination enclave CPU using the indicated IPI vector. Upon receiving the IPI, the destination enclave sets a flag in the shared memory region indicating it is ready to receive data. The source enclave then copies the message into the shared memory region and waits for destination enclave to copy the message out into a separate locally allocated memory buffer.

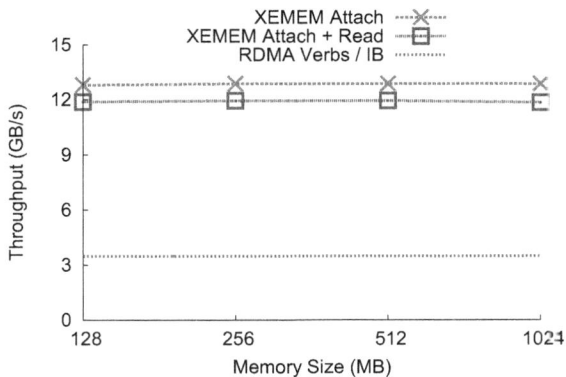

Figure 5: Cross-enclave throughput using shared memory and RDMA Verbs over Infiniband. Each XEMEM data point represents the throughput of 500 attachments for a given size

5. SHARED MEMORY EVALUATION

In this section, we present an experimental evaluation of our cross-enclave shared memory implementation. This evaluation will focus on the scalability of our implementation, with respect to the amount of memory shared across enclave partitions, as well as with respect to the number of enclaves running simultaneously on the system. These experiments will focus on performance measurements of shared memory attachment operations, as well as the performance implications for performing memory mappings in different enclave environments. We also compare our approach with an alternative approach to inter-enclave communication using RDMA.

5.1 System Configuration

This evaluation was carried out on a Dell PowerEdge R420 server configured with dual-socket 6-core Intel Xeon processors running at 2.10 GHz, with hyperthreading enabled for a total of 24 threads of execution. The memory layout consisted of two NUMA sockets with 16 GB of memory each, with memory interleaving disabled for a total of 32 GB of RAM. The system was also configured with a dual-port QDR Mellanox ConnectX-3 Infiniband device with SR/IOV enabled in order to demonstrate the potential for cross-enclave communication using RDMA. The system ran a stock Fedora 19 operating system.

For each of our experiments, the XEMEM name server was configured to run in the native Linux control enclave. Based on the individual details of the experiments, we created a set of enclaves using the Kitten lightweight kernel and Palacios virtual machine monitor to study both native and virtualized environments. In some configurations, the Palacios VMs were configured to run on the native Linux management enclave, while in others the VMs were deployed in isolated co-kernel enclaves managed by Kitten. In either case, all VMs ran a stock Centos 7 guest operating system. Furthermore, in each experiment, enclaves were only allocated memory and CPUs from a single NUMA socket in order to avoid overhead resulting from cross-NUMA domain memory accesses.

5.2 Shared Memory Attachment vs. RDMA Throughput

We first ran an experiment to demonstrate the potential throughput of cross-enclave communication using XEMEM compared to an alternative mechanism using RDMA. While these mechanisms are fundamentally different (byte-addressable memory operations versus block transfers over a peripheral bus), our goal was to demonstrate that our implementation does not add significant overhead, to the degree of diminishing throughout to the level of a simpler network-based approach. In this experiment, we created 1 Kitten enclave in addition to the Linux control enclave. A process in the Kitten enclave exported a single memory region of varying sizes, ranging from 128 MB to 1 GB. On the Linux enclave, a process repeatedly attached to the exported memory region, measuring the time it took to complete the attachment, as well as the time to read out the memory contents. Each memory region attachment was repeated 500 times. For the RDMA experiment, we configured the system's dual-port Infiniband device with 2 virtual functions and assigned each to a separate KVM virtual machine. We then performed a simple RDMA write bandwidth test using the recommended MTU supported by the device.

The results of this experiment are shown in Figure 5. As can be seen, for each memory size the shared memory implementation achieves a sustained throughput of around 13 GB/s for attachment operations, with around 12 GB/s when including the time to read out the memory contents. In comparison, the RDMA bandwidth test demonstrated that slightly less than 3.5 GB/s can be transferred across the Infiniband device using RDMA, showing that the overhead of XEMEM operations does not significantly reduce shared memory throughput. The experiment also demonstrates good scalability as XEMEM memory sizes increase, which bodes well for the prospects of applications hoping to make use of large shared memory regions.

5.3 Scalability of Multi-OS/R Shared Memory

Our next experiment was designed to demonstrate the ability of our implementation to scale to many enclave partitions running simultaneously on the same system, as well as the ability to support increasingly large shared memory regions in each enclave. In this experiment, we configured our system to create 1, 2, 4, or 8 Kitten enclaves using our co-kernel architecture. Each enclave was configured to run on a single core with 1.5 GB of memory, and to export memory regions ranging from 128 MB to 1 GB in size. Furthermore, for each enclave in the system a separate Linux process was created to attach to a single enclave's memory. In the case of 8 enclaves, this meant that up to 16 of the machine's 24 hardware threads were largely devoted to performing XEMEM operations. Note that although we chose a 1:1 communication model for this experiment, any arbitrary model is supported by our system.

The results of this experiment are illustrated in Figure 6. The figure demonstrates that the system scales well with respect to the amount of memory being shared at any point in time. This is a result of the fact that neither performing page table walks to generates page frame lists, nor subsequently communicating these lists across enclave communication channels, is a limit to the scalability of the memory sizes that can be shared. Furthermore, this figure also

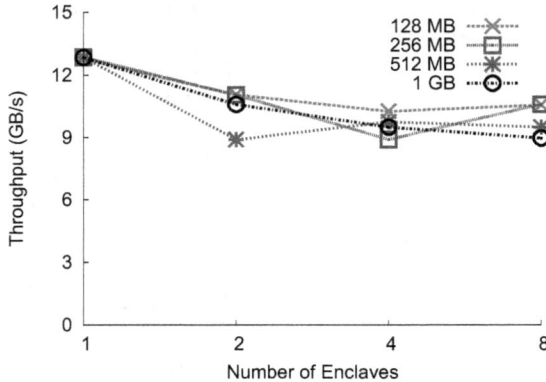

Figure 6: Cross-enclave throughput using shared memory between native Linux processes and native Kitten processes in co-kernel enclaves. Each data point represents the throughput of at least 500 attachments for a given size

Exporting Enclave	Attaching Enclave	GB/s (w/o rb-tree inserts)
Kitten	Linux	12.841 (N/A)
Kitten	Linux (VM)	3.991 (8.79)
Linux (VM)	Kitten	12.606 (N/A)

Table 2: Cross-enclave throughput using shared memory between a Linux process and a native Kitten process executing in a co-kernel enclave. Each value represents the throughput of at least 500 attachments to a 1 GB memory region

demonstrates that, beyond the initial configuration of only 1 enclave and 1 native Linux process, increasing the number of enclaves does not limit the scalability of the system. This indicates that our approach of using a centralized name server for allocating *segids*, as well as using a distributed routing protocol for performing shared memory attachments, are both suitable mechanisms for maintaining performance in the presence of high numbers of contending cores.

On the other hand, the figure does demonstrate slight performance degradation as the system scales from 1 to 2 enclaves. Given the good scaling demonstrated beyond 2 enclaves, we do not attribute this overhead to any scalability bottlenecks in our implementation, but rather attribute it to two main factors that are not fundamental limitations of our system. First, the co-kernel architecture used to perform cross-enclave message transfers (which are required for the transmission of XEMEM operations) currently restricts all IPI-based communication with the Linux management enclave to core 0 of the system, and thus the presence of multiple enclaves may cause contention for interrupt handlers on this core. The result is that even though the separate Linux processes performing XEMEM attachments may be running on separate cores, the low-level messages facilitating their operation must be handled on a single core. Future work in the design of the co-kernel architecture will investigate more intelligent mechanisms for interrupt handling. Additionally, we also attribute this overhead to contention for Linux data structures that are accessed when multiple processes concurrently update memory maps.

5.4 Performance of Shared Memory Using Virtual Machines

In addition to measuring the performance achievable in multi-enclave configurations with native OS/Rs, we also measured the throughput achievable when using the Palacios host/guest communication channel and memory translation mechanisms. We ran two separate experiments to measure both the host-to-guest and the guest-to-host performance as discussed in Section 4.4. In the first experiment, we launched a Linux VM running on the Linux management enclave, and we executed a single process in the VM that repeatedly attached to a 1 GB region of memory that was exported by

a native Kitten process executing in a co-kernel enclave. In the second experiment, we deployed the same enclave configuration, but instead configured the Linux VM process to export a 1 GB region to be attached by the Kitten process.

The results of these experiments can be seen in Table 2. The top row of the table shows the 1 GB result reported in Figure 5 for the native co-kernel configuration. The table demonstrates that moving the attaching process from the native Linux enclave to a virtualized Linux enclave causes a roughly 3x decrease in throughput when compared to the native configuration. In order to determine the source of this overhead, we measured the amount of time spent mapping remote enclave memory into the VM (those operations illustrated in Figure 4(a)), and we found that nearly 80% of the time was spent updating the guest's memory map. As discussed in Section 4.4, Palacios maintains a guest's memory map in the form of a red-black tree, and the process of mapping remote enclave memory generally requires as many updates to this tree as there are pages being shared. Thus, as the tree continues to grow, the cost for insertions and re-balancing operations increases, leading to performance degradation. Indeed, when removing the time spent updating the red-black tree, the throughput increases to 8.79 GB/s. In the future we intend to remove this overhead through the use of more intelligent radix tree based data structures that can more appropriately mimic a page table's organization.

Lastly, the bottom row of Table 2 shows that mechanisms for performing guest-to-host memory translations (illustrated in Figure 4(b)) are not nearly as costly, as the Kitten process is able to achieve over 12 GB/s throughput when attaching to the VM Linux process. This result indicates that performing page translations in Palacios does not add significant overhead to shared memory operations in the common case where the size of the Palacios memory map is limited.

5.5 Operating System Noise

The final experiment in the first part of our evaluation measured the impact of performing page frame lookups in Kitten enclaves on the Kitten noise profile. OS noise, which has been identified as a significant source of overhead for HPC applications particularly at large scales [9, 14], is largely non-existent in Kitten as a result of its feature-limited design. Thus, while shared memory attachments may not necessarily qualify as noise, given that they are directly enabled by the HPC application and necessary in some sense for the progress of a composed workload, measuring the impact of attachment operations on the Kitten noise profile can provide some insight on the types of syn-

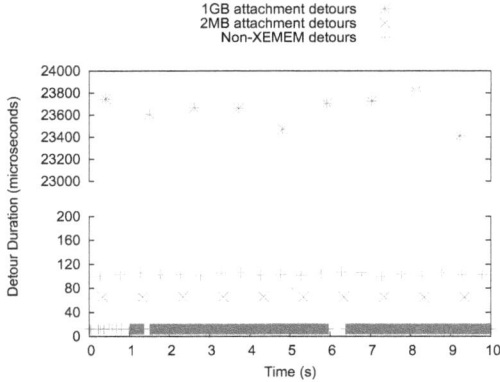

Figure 7: Noise profile of a Kitten enclave serving XEMEM attachment requests on a single core

Simulation Enclave	Analytics Enclave
Native Linux	Native Linux
Kitten Co-Kernel	Native Linux
Kitten Co-Kernel	Linux VM (Linux Host)
Kitten Co-Kernel	Linux VM (Kitten Host)

Table 3: Enclave configurations for the in situ workload in the single node experiments

chronization that may be needed to prevent attachments from perturbing simulations in future systems.

In this experiment, we configured a Kitten enclave on a single core to export memory regions of sizes 4 KB, 2 MB, and 1 GB, and ran the Selfish Detour benchmark [2] from Argonne National Lab, a noise detection benchmark that is designed to measure the fraction of time the CPU spends executing instructions that are not part of the user's application. We ran a process on the Linux enclave to attach to each region, sleep for one second, and repeat for a period of 10 seconds. Figure 7 presents the results of the experiment. The figure shows that Kitten experiences a baseline level of frequent hardware noise around the 12 microsecond mark, as well as a set of less frequent interruptions likely caused by periodic hardware events such as SMIs around the 100 microsecond mark. Interestingly, detours caused by 4 KB attachments are not noticeable in the figure, as they cause detours similar in length to the frequent noise baseline. Detours caused by 2 MB attachments are more noticeable, but still cause less of a disturbance than the periodic hardware interrupts. Finally, the 1 GB attachments cause much larger detours, creating noise events that are 2 orders of magnitude longer than any other events. For these memory sizes, only the 1 GB attachments seem likely to cause problems for large-scale HPC workloads on Kitten, and thus special care would be needed to synchronize their occurrence with respect to the application workflow.

6. SINGLE NODE BENCHMARK EVALUATION

The second part of our evaluation uses a set of HPC benchmark workloads to demonstrate our system's ability to support sample in situ workloads in multi-enclave environments. In this section, our experiments will focus on the single-node

performance implications of XEMEM in the presence of a wide range of enclave configurations and in situ workflow models. Then, in Section 7 we will evaluate a multi-node system configuration where each node employs XEMEM for local-node in situ execution, and demonstrate that the performance isolation benefits of multi-enclave configurations can lead to superior scaling behavior.

6.1 In Situ Workload

To present the performance characteristics of a composed in situ workload, we modified the HPCCG benchmark from the Mantevo suite [11] as well as the STREAM microbenchmark from the HPC Challenge suite [7] to synchronize their execution flows. Specifically, we modified the applications to use simple stop/go signals implemented on top of variables in shared memory. Throughout the evaluation sections, we refer to these modified benchmark components, respectively, as the HPC simulation and analytics program.

The HPC simulation executes an iterative conjugate gradient algorithm with collective operations in between iterations to gather intermediate results. We modified the benchmark to signal the analytics program at certain intervals during its execution to simulate an in situ workflow. During these intervals, the simulation sends a signal to the analytics program by writing to a variable in shared memory. The simulation then waits for a return signal by polling on another variable in shared memory, which is written by the analytics programs when it determines to resume the simulation. In all, we configured the HPC simulation to execute 600 iterations of the conjugate gradient algorithm, and to communicate with the analytics program every 40 intervals for a total of 15 communication points. Upon receiving a signal from the HPC simulation, the analytics program may or may not attach to a new exported region created by the simulation, a configuration option which we discuss below. In either case, the analytics program executes the STREAM benchmark over a 512 MB region specified by the simulation. The analytics program first copies the shared memory into a private array, and then executes STREAM over the array.

We note that currently the underlying enclave CS/Rs only support application communication through shared memory, and thus operations like event notifications must be supported via ad hoc techniques like polling on variables in memory. We plan to investigate techniques to support additional features in the OS/R environments as requirements of actual composed workflows become more evident.

6.2 Execution and Memory Registration Models

The simulation and analytics programs can be configured based on two different parameters to mimic different in situ communication behaviors: synchronous/asynchronous execution models, and one time/recurring shared memory attachments.

6.2.1 Synchronous vs. Asynchronous Execution

When using a synchronous execution model, the simulation and analytics programs do not simultaneously execute. Rather, when the analytics program receives a signal from the simulation, it (optionally) attaches to simulation data via shared memory, and executes the STREAM benchmark. Once the benchmark completes, it sends a signal to the HPC simulation to continue. When using an asynchronous execu-

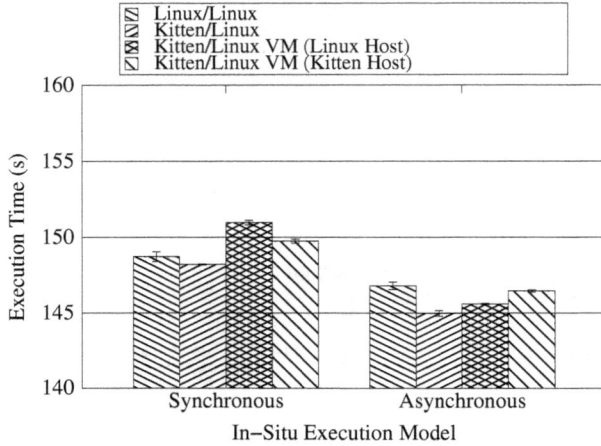

(a) One time shared memory attachment model

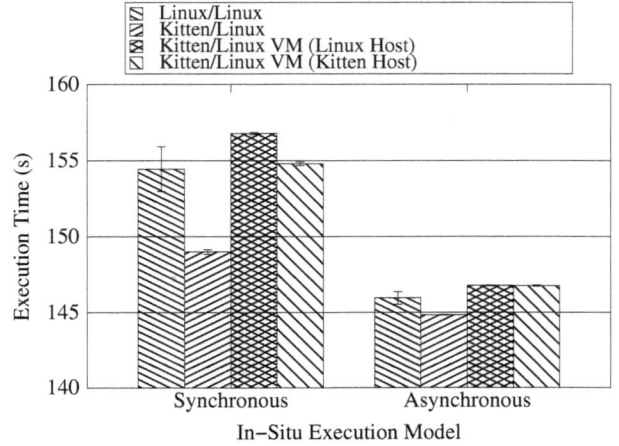

(b) Recurring shared memory attachment model

Figure 8: Performance of a sample in situ benchmark on a single node using various communication and execution workflows

tion model, the simulation and analytics programs may execute simultaneously. When the analytics program receives a signal from the simulation, it (optionally) attaches to the simulation data via shared memory, and then immediately signals the HPC simulation to continue. Then, it executes STREAM as the HPC simulation resumes simultaneously.

6.2.2 One time vs. Recurring Shared Memory Attachments

When using a one time shared memory attachment model, the HPC simulation exports a single region of memory at the start of the simulation. During communication intervals, the analytics program does not attach to new memory regions, but rather attaches a single time to shared memory region which persists over the benchmark duration. Conversely, when using the recurring attachment model, the simulation exports a new shared memory region during each communication interval, which is subsequently attached by the analytics program. Thus, for the former case, the overhead of setting up shared memory attachments is only experienced once at the beginning of the application; conversely, in the latter case, the overheads are experienced at each communication interval.

6.3 System Configuration

The system used for this evaluation was a Dell OptiPlex server with a single-socket 4-core Intel i7 processor running at 3.40 GHz, with hyperthreading enabled for a total of 8 threads of execution. The memory layout consisted of a single memory zone with 8 GB of RAM. This system ran a stock Centos 7 operating system. As in the previous experiments, for each experiment in this section we configured the XEMEM name server to run in the native Linux control enclave.

We varied the execution environments for the HPC simulation and analytics applications to study a variety of configurations. For a baseline comparison we configured the simulation and analytics applications to execute in the native Linux control enclave, using the XEMEM shared memory facilities provided for single Linux environments. In the remaining configurations, the HPC simulation was configured to execute in a Kitten co-kernel enclave, while the analytics application was deployed in Palacios virtual machines

executing on the host Linux control enclave as well as a separate Kitten co-kernel host. The configurations are shown in Table 3.

6.4 Results

In addition to varying the enclave configurations, we executed the in sample in situ workload in four separate configurations based on the four combinations of the workflow parameters discussed in Section 6.2. The completion times of the HPC simulation using a one time shared memory attachment model are shown in Figure 8(a), where each bar reports the average and standard deviation of 10 runs of the application. As expected, for each environment the HPC simulation completes in less time when executing asynchronously with respect to the analytics program than executing synchronously. Under both execution models, the configuration deploying the HPC simulation in the Kitten enclave and the analytics program natively on the Linux enclave outperforms all other configurations. When using the asynchronous execution model, each environment utilizing the Kitten enclave for the simulation outperforms the Linux-only configuration. Conversely, when using the synchronous execution model, any overheads experienced in processing the analytics directly impact the runtime of the HPC simulation. Given the lack of shared memory communication overhead in these experiments, it is clear that the native analytics program slightly outperforms the same program running virtualized, particularly in the Palacios on Linux case. However, in each multi-enclave configuration the performance is more consistent than exhibited by the Linux-only environment, demonstrating that our approach does not add variable delays to the runtime of the simulation.

The results of the experiments using a recurring shared memory attachment model can be seen in Figure 8(b). Given the overheads from repeated memory map updates identified in Section 5.4, it is clear that performing recurring shared memory attachments in addition to using a synchronous execution model represents the worst case configuration for the virtualized enclaves. However, interestingly the Linux-only environment also suffers significant overhead as well as a marked increase in runtime variance in this case. We attribute this overhead mainly to the page faulting semantics with which single environment XEMEM attachment

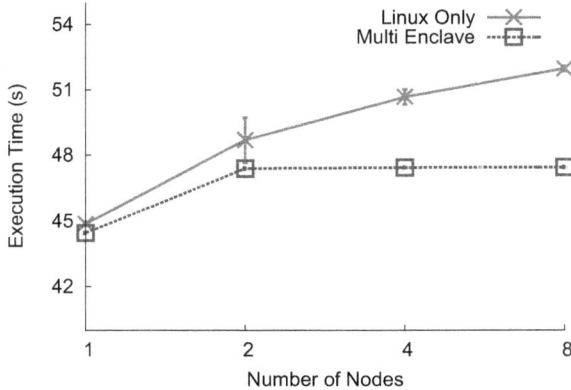

(a) One time shared memory attachment model

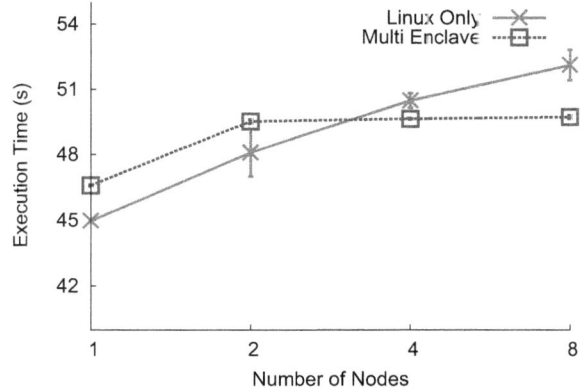

(b) Recurring shared memory attachment model

Figure 9: Performance of a sample in situ benchmark on a multi-node cluster using an asynchronous execution model. The benchmark is configured in weak-scaling mode

operations are performed in Linux. Indeed, when executing asynchronously, the overheads associated with both the virtualized and native Linux environments largely disappear. As in the previous cases, the performance in each multi-enclave configuration is very consistent, whereas the Linux-only configuration provides a lower degree of workload isolation leading to increased variance.

7. MULTI-NODE BENCHMARK EVALUATION

The final experiments for our evaluation were designed to demonstrate the benefits multi-enclave configurations provide for composed in situ applications executing on multiple nodes. As the previous section demonstrated, even on a single node, the performance isolation that isolated enclaves provide leads to a more consistent runtime experience for the composed workload. In this section, we show that providing multi-enclave shared memory for in situ components running on each node of a multi-node system leads to superior scalability, demonstrating the value of workload isolation.

7.1 Workload and System Configuration

For the experiments in this section, we used a local 8-node experimental research cluster. The nodes were each configured with dual-socket 6-core Intel Xeon processors running at 2.10 GHz, with hyperthreading enabled for a total of 24 threads of execution. The memory layout on each node consisted on two NUMA sockets with 16 GB of memory each, with memory interleaving disabled for a total of 32 GB of RAM. The nodes were interconnected with dual port QDR Mellanox ConnectX-3 Infiniband devices.

In these experiments we deployed two separate enclave environments in the system. In the default configuration, both in situ components were executed in the native Linux enclave with no other enclaves deployed in the system. The other configuration consisted of a Palacios VM enclave running on an isolated Kitten co-kernel host, in addition to the native Linux enclave. For this system composition we ran the HPC simulation in the Palacios VM, while the analytics program executed in the native Linux enclave. For each individual experiment, every node ran the same enclave configuration.

Finally, we executed the same in situ workload used in the single node experiments, with the exception that the HPC simulation was compiled to use OpenMPI over the Infiniband interconnect for multiple node deployment. The HPC simulation used 8 cores of each node, while the analytics program was parallelized using OpenMP threads to use 8 additional cores on each node. The HPC simulation was configured to execute 300 iterations of the conjugate gradient algorithm, and to communicate with the analytics program every 30 intervals for a total of 10 communication points on each node. The analytics program on each node then executes the STREAM benchmark over a 1 GB region specified by the simulation. As in the previous experiments, all workloads were explicitly pinned to NUMA domains in order to avoid the overheads on cross-domain contention. The benchmark was configured in weak-scaling mode, where the problem size of the HPC simulation scales with the number of nodes.

7.2 Results

In order to evaluate the benefits of performance isolation that our multi-enclave system provides, we ran the in situ benchmark using an asynchronous execution workflow, meaning that during the application's communication intervals, the HPC simulation and the analytics program are executing concurrently. This workload deployment is representative of the types of applications that we envision will be present on exascale systems in that it requires high performance local-node communication between its individual components, but at the same time requires that the components be strictly isolated from interference caused by contention for the node's resources.

As in the previous experiments, we ran these experiments with two separate shared memory models: one time and recurring attachments. The results of the experiments can be seen in Figure 9, where each data point reports the average and standard deviation of five runs of the benchmark. As Figure 9(a) demonstrates, the scaling behavior of the multi-enclave configuration is superior to that provided by the baseline Linux only environment for the experiments using a one time memory attachment model. This result is particularly interesting because the HPC simulation is running in a virtualized environment, which demonstrates two key results. First, it shows that performance isolation is a requirement for these types of applications, to the degree that the same workload running virtualized can outperform itself running natively if it is better isolated. Furthermore, this result demonstrates that the XEMEM implementation yields a consistent execution environment on each node, which can be seen by the low standard deviation and very good scaling behavior.

Finally, the results of the experiments using a recurring shared memory attachment model can be seen in Figure 9(b). As the overhead of shared memory attachments is experienced multiple times during the application, the Linux only configuration is able to outperform the multi-enclave configuration at a single node. However, both system configurations exhibit similar scaling behavior using this shared memory attachment model as they exhibited in Figure 9(a). Namely the lack of performance isolation in the single OS/R configuration leads to steady performance decline as each node has a different runtime experience, while the multi-enclave system shows almost no performance degradation past 2 nodes.

8. CONCLUSION

Research trends in the HPC community indicate that exascale systems will be constructed from multiple heterogeneous hardware and system software configurations, called *enclaves*. In this work, we presented the design, implementation, and evaluation of XEMEM, a shared memory system capable of supporting a wide variety of enclave configurations likely to be seen in exascale systems. We demonstrated that XEMEM is able to scale to a high number of enclaves simultaneously executing on a system, even while each enclave creates increasingly large shared memory mappings. We further evaluated our system's ability to support a sample *in situ* workload utilizing a set of different of execution and memory registration models. Finally, we demonstrated XEMEM's ability to support a multi-enclave in situ application, which can outperform the same application executing in a single OS/R environment.

9. REFERENCES

[1] P. Beckman et al. Argo: An Exascale Operating System and Runtime Reseach Project. [Online]. Available: http://www.argo-osr.org, 2014.

[2] P. Beckman, K. Iskra, K. Yoshii, S. Coghlan, and A. Nataraj. Benchmarking the Effects of Operating System Interference on Extreme-scale Parallel Machines. *Cluster Computing*, 11(1):3–16, 2008.

[3] R. Brightwell, R. Oldfield, A. Maccabe, and D. Bernholdt. Hobbes: Composition and Virtualization as the Foundations of an Extreme-scale OS/R. In *Proc. 3rd International Workshop on Runtime and Operating Systems for Supercomputers (ROSS)*, 2013.

[4] R. Brightwell, K. Pedretti, and T. Hudson. SMARTMAP: Operating System Support for Efficient Data Sharing Among Processes on a Multi-Core Processor. In *Proc. 21st. International Conference for High Performance Computing, Networking, Storage and Analysis (SC)*, 2008.

[5] A. Burstev et al. Fido: Fast Inter-Virtual-Machine Communication for Enterprise Appliances. In *Proc. Usenix Annual Technical Conference (ATC)*, 2009.

[6] D. Chen et al. The IBM Blue Gene/Q Interconnection Network and Message Unit. In *Proc. 24th International Conference for High Performance Computing, Networking, Storage and Analysis (SC)*, 2011.

[7] J. Dongarra et al. Introduction to the HPCChallenge Benchmark Suite. Technical report, University of Tennessee Knoxville, 2005.

[8] J. Dongarra et al. The International Exascale Software Project Roadmap. *International Journal of High Performance Computing Applications (IJHPCA)*, 25(1):3–60, 2011.

[9] K. Ferreira, P. Bridges, and R. Brightwell. Characterizing Application Sensitivity to OS Interference Using Kernel-Level Noise Injection. In *Proc. 21st. International Conference for High Performance Computing, Networking, Storage and Analysis (SC)*, 2008.

[10] B. Goglin and S. Moreaud. KNEM: a Generic and Scalable Kernel-Assisted Intra-node MPI Communication Framework. *Journal of Parallel and Distributed Computing (JPDC)*, 73(2):176–188, 2013.

[11] M. Heroux et al. Improving Performance via Mini-applications. Technical report, Sandia National Laboratories, 2009.

[12] P. Kogge et al. Exascale Computing Study: Technology Challenges in Achieving Exascale Systems. Technical report, University of Notre Dame CSE Department, 2008.

[13] J. Lange, K. Pedretti, T. Hudson, P. Dinda, Z. Cui, L. Xia, P. Bridges, M. Levenhagen, R. Brightwell, A. Gocke, and S. Jaconette. Palacios: A New Open Source Virtual Machine Monitor for Scalable High Performance Computing. In *Proc. 24th IEEE International Parallel and Distributed Processing Symposium (IPDPS)*, 2010.

[14] A. Morari, R. Gioiosa, R. Wisniewski, B. Rosenburg, T. Inglett, and M. Valero. Evaluating the Impact of TLB Misses on Future HPC Systems. In *Proc. 26th IEEE International Parallel and Distributed Processing Symposium (IPDPS)*, 2012.

[15] J. Ouyang, B. Kocoloski, J. Lange, and K. Pedretti. Achieving Performance Isolation with Lightweight Co-Kernels. In *Proc. 24th International ACM Symposium on High Performance Distributed Computing (HPDC)*, 2015. To Appear.

[16] Y. Park, E. Van Hensbergen, M. Hillenbrand, T. Inglett, B. Rosenburg, K. D. Ryu, and R. Wisniewski. FusedOS: Fusing LWK Performance with FWK Functionality in a Heterogeneous Environment. In *Proc. 24th IEEE International Symposium on Computer Architecture and High Performance Computing (SBAC-PAD)*, 2012.

[17] R. Stevens, A. White, et al. Architectures and Technology for Extreme Scale Computing. Technical report, U.S. Department of Energy, 2009.

[18] H. Tomita, M. Sato, and Y. Ishikawa. Japan Overview Talk. In *Proc. 2nd International Workshop on Big Data and Extreme-scale Computing (BDEC)*, 2014.

[19] J. Wang, K.-L. Wright, and K. Gopalan. XenLoop: A Transparent High Performance Inter-VM Network Loopback. In *Proc. 17th International Symposium on High Performance Distributed Computing (HPDC)*, 2008.

[20] R. Wisniewski, T. Inglett, P. Keppel, R. Murty, and R. Riesen. mOS: An Architecture for Extreme-Scale Operating Systems. In *Proc. 4th International Workshop on Runtime and Operating Systems for Supercomputers (ROSS)*, 2014.

[21] M. Woodacre, D. Robb, D. Roe, and K. Feind. The SGI Altix 3000 Global Shared-Memory Architecture. Technical report, Silicon Graphics International Corporation, 2003.

[22] X. Zhang, S. McIntosh, P. Rohatgi, and J. Griffin. XenSocket: A High Throughput Interdomain Transport for Virtual Machines. In *Proc. ACM/IFIP/USENIX International Conference on Middleware*, 2007.

[23] F. Zheng, H. Yu, C. Hantas, M. Wolf, G. Eisenhauer, K. Schwan, H. Abbasi, and S. Klasky. GoldRush: Resource Efficient In Situ Scientific Data Analytics Using Fine-Grained Interference Aware Execution. In *Proc. 26th. International Conference for High Performance Computing, Networking, Storage and Analysis (SC)*, 2013.

Transit: A Visual Analytical Model for Multithreaded Machines

Ang Li[*,†], Y.C. Tay[†], Akash Kumar[†], and Henk Corporaal[*]

[*]Eindhoven University of Technology, Eindhoven, Netherlands
[†]National University of Singapore, Singapore
ang.li@tue.nl, dcstayyc@nus.edu.sg, akash@nus.edu.sg, h.corporaal@tue.nl

ABSTRACT

With the extraordinary growth of cores and threads in today's multithreaded machines, analyzing and tuning the performance of such platforms becomes a challenging task. In this paper, we propose an intuitive and visualizable model for analyzing the performance of contemporary highly concurrent multithreaded machines. Based on flow balancing between service demand and service supply of the memory system, the model draws an intuitive figure to characterize machine state, identify bottlenecks and determine optimization directions. The tractability of the model is highlighted as it only requires two parameters from the workload. Our model achieves 90% and 83% prediction accuracy for computation throughput on Fermi and Kepler GPUs over the 16 applications from Rodinia benchmark.

Keywords

Performance modeling; Multithreaded machine; GPUs; Performance optimization

1. INTRODUCTION

Moore's Law has continued to show promise, but the end of clock-frequency scaling for uniprocessors has driven mainstream computation towards the multi-core era [1]. Multicore processors offer enormous computing power, but insufficient exploitable parallelism and long-latency remote communication, typically off-chip memory access, restrict the attainable performance [2]. Consequently, *multithreading* [3] has also been proposed as an effective solution. It raises processor utilization through thread-level parallelism (TLP) and hides memory delay via fast context switching. Later, with the rapid growth of cores in a processor, the number of threads has increased dramatically. Nowadays, a single GPU chip encapsulates up to 2,880 scalar cores and can accommodate over 30,000 active threads simultaneously.

Obviously, tuning performance for such massively multithreaded platforms becomes a difficult challenge. Although modest speedup could be attained through basic functional porting, programmers have to spend significant time and effort to identify and alleviate the system bottlenecks before fully extracting the hardware potential. This is especially the case when little is known about the underlying implementation of the target machine. Therefore, many programmers and designers have to search exhaustively via profilers or simulators in a huge design space, or rely entirely on empirical guidelines.

Analytical model offers an alternative approach. It either models a particular architecture that requires numerous parameters to grasp detailed machine features in order to predict performance precisely, e.g. [4, 5], or it models a general machine that is easy to understand and manipulate so as to highlight new behaviors, explain observed phenomena and derive intuition, e.g. [6, 7].

This paper falls into the second category – we propose a high-level, visualizable and throughput-oriented analytical model for general multithreaded machines. Based on flow balancing between service demand and supply of the memory system, our model clearly describes machine state, locates performance bottlenecks and indicates optimization directions. The major objective is to provide a visualizable modeling tool for gaining insight and deriving intuition.

2. TRANSIT MODEL

In this section, we present the **transit model**. We first describe how the components of the multithreaded machine system are organized. We then present how to construct the model and how to draw transit figures. Finally, we summarize the input and output of the model.

2.1 Model Components

In the transit model, a computer machine is decomposed into a *computation* and a *memory system*, denoted as **CS** and **MS**. CS refers to computation units including multiprocessors, coprocessors and special accelerators while MS refers to the memory hierarchy including local cache, shared cache, off-chip DRAM, etc. For flexibility, the scope of MS can be scaled along the memory hierarchy, from the top register level to the bottom hard-disk or Internet level, in a different context. For example, if MS refers to the off-chip DRAM, then CS refers to the entire processor chip.

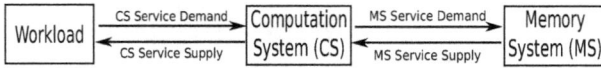

Figure 1: System Organization. A computer system is partitioned into double layers – MS stands isolated from the workload.

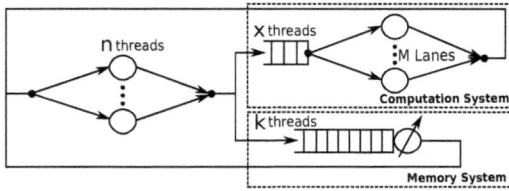

Figure 2: Multithreaded Machine Model

From the application's standpoint, it is CS that accomplishes the desired jobs; MS, however, plays an assistant role since the application logic does not impose any data movements among various memories – most of the time, the application logic postulates the memory space to be flat and unified. Therefore, the CS throughput is often viewed as the primary performance metric while MS throughput remains the secondary.

As depicted in Fig.1, MS stands isolated from the workload. Since it is CS that executes the user logic, the workload has service demand over CS, which is the theoretical attainable throughput of CS . However, due to performance bottlenecks inside the machine, the actual service supply is less or equal to such service demand. Meanwhile, CS requires MS to store the necessary data, so CS has service demand upon MS. Similarly, the actual service supply of MS to CS is less or equal to the service demand of CS.

2.2 Model Construction

With the system organization as a preamble, let us proceed to the model. As shown in Fig.2, the multithreaded machine is modeled as an *interactive queuing network* [8, 9], a special case of *closed networks* [10]. The reason for being "*closed*" is that the total number of threads is usually dictated by the availability of hardware resources or application configuration; while a new thread is only initiated when an in-flight thread terminates. The memory hierarchy is modeled as as an *aggregate queuing system* and the computation system is modeled as a *single-queue-multiple-server network*, inside which each server indicates a unique *execution lane* (also known as *thread slot* [11] or *logical processor* [12]) that is capable of performing a unit-cost operation in a single cycle or time slot. The n active threads are regarded as the users of the two systems, and is thus postulated to be independent of each other. Meanwhile, we also assume that the workload for each thread is roughly homogeneous, just like the GPU's single-instruction-multiple-threads (SIMT) kernels. However, this assumption could be relaxed if we emphasize average-value-analysis (AVA) [9].

A thread has two states: *thinking* and *waiting* by following the interactive model's terminology. It is thinking when being processed in CS. After an average of Z cycles[1], the thinking thread aborts CS and proposes a memory request. The thread is then suspended in MS for L cycles.

---

[1]Z is also known as *arithmetic intensity* [13] of the host application, which is a ratio of computation operations to memory operations.

Table 1: Symbol Table

n	Total threads in the machine
k	Threads in MS
x	Threads in CS
$f(k)$	Service supply of MS to CS
$g(x)$	Service demand from CS to MS
Z	Arithmetic intensity (thinking time)
R	Maximum MS throughput
M	Width of concurrent execution lanes
π	CS transition point
δ	MS transition point
L	Average memory access latency

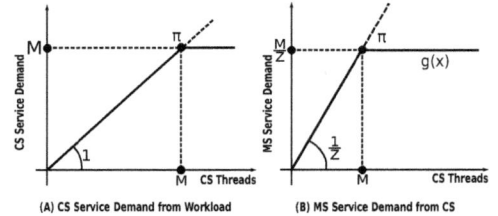

Figure 3: Computation System: Z acts as a scaling factor that transforms the service demand of the computation system to the service demand on the memory system.

Upon fulfillment of the memory request, the thread exits MS and enters CS again, starting a new *turnaround* ($Z + L$ cycles). Before actually being processed in CS, a thread might buffer in a waiting queue. It is assumed that both the waiting queue and the memory queue are sufficiently large to hold all the pending and outstanding threads. This assumption is justifiable as when threads are being blocked, it is equivalent to them waiting in an abstract queue.

Consider the CS service demand in Fig.1, if the throughput of a single thread being executed in one lane during a cycle is normalized as one unit, then for an M-lane system with x threads (Fig.2), the throughput is:

$$G(x) = \begin{cases} x & for\ x < M \\ M & for\ x \geq M \end{cases} \quad (1)$$

Such a shape (Fig.3-A) has been confirmed by several existing works on both multithreaded CPUs [14] and GPUs [15]. Now consider how CS service demand can be transformed to MS service demand in Fig.1. With computation intensity Z, we know that for each Z cycles on average, a memory fetch is prompted. Therefore, the MS service demand (from CS), or the average number of memory fetches with x threads in CS (Fig.2) is

$$g(x) = \begin{cases} \frac{x}{Z} & for\ x < M \\ \frac{M}{Z} & for\ x \geq M \end{cases} \quad (2)$$

as shown in Fig.3-B. Due to dependency, if such demand could not be fulfilled by MS, performance of CS suffers. Here, Z acts as a *scaling factor* that transforms CS service demand to MS service demand. We mark the special point $x = M$ as the *transition point* (π) of CS, beyond which CS saturates.

For MS, the service supply throughput in Fig.1 is generally similar to Fig.4-A: the beginning phase is nearly linear it is a closed network [9]; the ending phase flattens out as

102

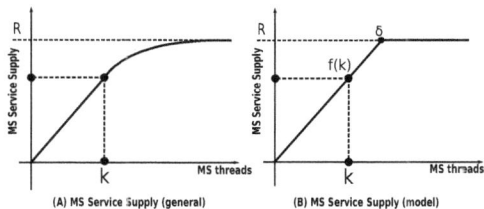

Figure 4: Memory System: the transition region is aggregated as a transition point.

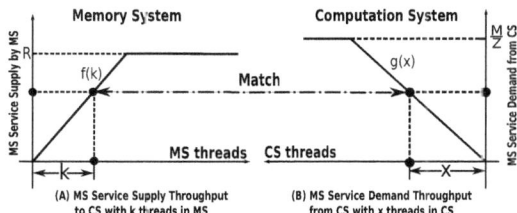

Figure 5: Memory system service supply (A) and demand (B). Note, (A) is the same as Fig.4-B. (B) is obtained by reversing the horizontal axis direction of Fig.3-B.

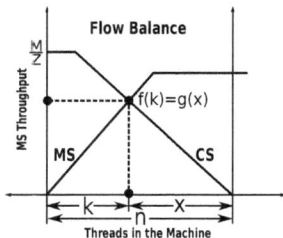

Figure 6: Transit Figure: the equilibrium between service demand and service supply of the memory system. It implies the current machine state: within the total n threads, k of them are in the memory system and x are in the computation system.

throughput approaches bottleneck capacity. However, for tractability, it is also modeled as a roofline shape (Fig.4-B). We argue that this abstraction is already sufficient to capture the characteristics of MS since only the transition region is aggregated as a *transition point* (δ). In fact, the roofline like MS throughput function has also been observed in real machines [16].

If we **reverse** the horizontal axis direction of MS service demand throughput function $g(x)$ (Fig.3-B), it becomes a figure like Fig.5-B. Now focus on MS, we have its *service supply curve* $\boldsymbol{f(k)}$ by itself (Fig.5-A) and *service demand curve* $\boldsymbol{g(x)}$ imposed by the CS (Fig.5-B). Based on the *flow balance property* [10], in a steady state of the machine,

$$f(k) = g(x) \tag{3}$$

Therefore, if the two figures are integrated as shown in Fig.6, their intersection is just the **equilibrium between service demand and supply** (or MS *inflow* and *outflow* [9]), which is exactly the current throughput of MS. Consequently, the CS throughput is $\boldsymbol{Zr}$. We label this visualization **transit figure** because it clearly illustrates the present bottlenecks of the machine and the corresponding optimization directions that are effective to mitigate or remove the bottlenecks.

2.3 Model Input & Output

Input – As aforementioned, in the transit model there are three architecture-related parameters R, L, M and two wor-

kload-related parameters Z and n (see Table.1). As the raw memory latency is generally very difficult to change, in the following optimization section, L is viewed as constant. The tuning of the other four parameters and their impact on the shape of the transit figures are shown in Fig.5.

Output – Given the five input parameters, the transit figure can show the tendency of MS throughput and CS throughput. In order see them directly from the figure, we propose the following principles:

- **Principle 1:** If the intersection of $f(k)$ and $g(x)$ goes up, then MS throughput increases.

- **Principle 2:** If the intersection goes up and Z is unchanged, then CS throughput increases.

- **Principle 3:** If Z is increasing and the intersection is on the right side of CS transition point, then CS throughput increases.

In the following subsection, we show how these principles can be leveraged to rapidly locate bottlenecks and determine optimization directions.

2.4 Performance Bound

In this subsection, we describe four types of performance bound. For each bound, we show the effective optimization approaches. Since CS throughput is the primary measure, we only discuss those approaches that can increase CS throughput.

2.4.1 Thread Bound

Identify – Thread bound addresses the state of the machine where insufficient threads are allocated. Therefore, neither CS nor MS can reach its maximum throughput: in the transit figure, the MS throughput function $f(k)$ and CS throughput function $g(x)$ intersect at their sloping parts, as shown in Fig.11.

Optimization – Based on Principle 2, to increase CS throughput, we could raise the intersection point of $f(k)$ and $g(x)$. To achieve this goal, we could push $g(x)$ to the right by enlarging thread volume n (via Fig.7), as described in Fig.11. Or based on Principle 3, we could also increase arithmetic intensity Z (via Fig.8) as the intersection is on the right side of the CS transition point π. The transit figure is shown in Fig.12.

2.4.2 Memory Bound

Identify – Memory bound models the state of the machine when the memory system obtains its maximum throughput: $f(k) = R$. It indicates that in the transit figure (Fig.13), $f(k)$ and $g(x)$ intersect at the flat part of $f(k)$ but the sloping part of $g(x)$.

Optimization – Obviously, tuning n does not affect the height of the intersection or Z. The feasible ways seem to lower the sloping part of $g(x)$ or lift the flat part of $f(k)$, which corresponds to upgrading Z (via Fig.8) and R (via Fig.9). The transit figures are shown in Fig.13 and Fig.14.

2.4.3 Computation Bound

Identify – Computation bound is the state of the machine that $g(x) = M/Z$, which implies that in the transit figure (Fig.15), $f(k)$ and $g(x)$ intersect at the flat part of $g(x)$ but at the sloping part of $f(k)$.

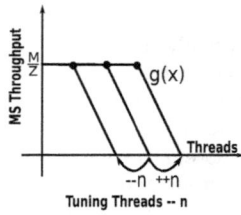

Figure 7: n is the thread volume in the machine. It dictates the relative position of $g(x)$.

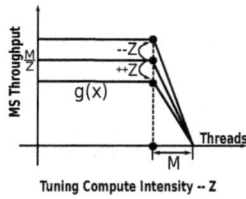

Figure 8: Z is the arithmetic intensity. It determines the scaling factor of $g(x)$.

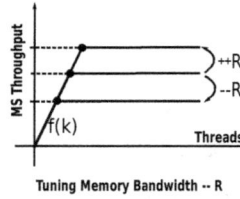

Figure 9: R is the maximum sustainable MS throughput. It determines the altitude of $f(k)$.

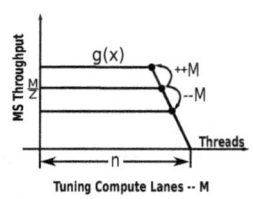

Figure 10: M is the width of concurrent execution lanes. It determines the altitude of $g(x)$.

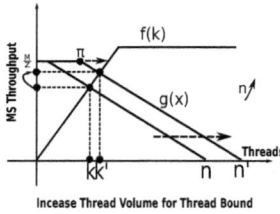

Figure 11: Thread Bound. $f(k)$ and $g(x)$ intersect at their sloping parts. If we slide $g(x)$ to the right by increasing n (via Fig.7) and draw a new curve, with the intersection goes up, by Principle 1, MS throughput increases. Meanwhile, as Z is unchanged, with Principle 2, CS throughput also increases. This method is effective until π touches $f(k)$ as then the machine becomes computation bound.

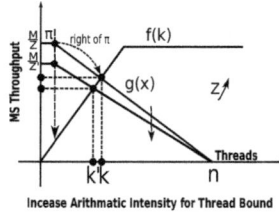

Figure 12: Thread Bound. $f(k)$ and $g(x)$ intersect at their sloping parts. If we tilt $g(x)$ by increasing arithmetic intensity Z (via Fig.8), as the intersection is on the right of π, with Principle 3, CS throughput is essentially rising albeit MS throughput is dropping. This approach fails when π reaches $f(k)$. At that moment, the machine becomes computation bound.

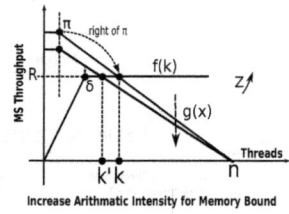

Figure 13: Memory Bound. $f(k)$ and $g(x)$ intersect at the flat part of $f(k)$ but the sloping part of $g(x)$. Since the intersection is on the right side of π, based on Principle 3, we can enhance CS throughput by increasing Z (via Fig.8). Since the height of the intersection is unchanged, by Principle 1, MS throughput keeps constant. The machine becomes thread bound when $g(x)$ coincides δ.

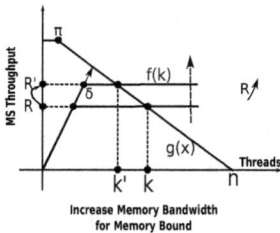

Figure 14: Memory Bound. $f(k)$ and $g(x)$ intersect at the flat part of $f(k)$ but the sloping part of $g(x)$. Based on Principle 2, we can raise the intersection point to increase CS throughput, which is equivalent to lifting the flat part of $f(k)$, or increasing R (via Fig.9). With Principle 1, it also promotes MS throughput. This approach is effective until δ arrives at $g(x)$, at which the machine becomes thread bound.

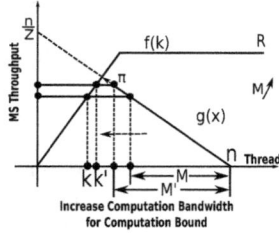

Figure 15: Computation Bound. $f(k)$ and $g(x)$ intersect at the flat part of $g(x)$ but the sloping part of $f(k)$. This is already a good state as all M lanes are leveraged albeit some memory bandwidth are wasted. To further increase CS throughput, we can lift the flat part of $g(x)$ by increasing M (via Fig.10) based on Principle 2. As the intersection goes up, by Principle 1, MS throughput also increases. This approach fails when π touches $f(k)$.

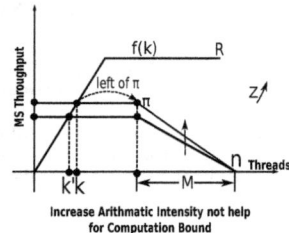

Figure 16: Computation Bound. $f(k)$ and $g(x)$ intersect at the flat part of $g(x)$ but the sloping part of $f(k)$. Here, increasing Z (via Fig.8) does not raise CS throughput because the interaction falls on the left side of the CS transition point π, which violates Principle 3. Also, since the height of the intersection is unchanged, by Principle 1, MS throughput keeps the same.

Optimization – Generally, this is the ideal state of the machine since CS throughput is already the maximum. However, we can still obtain a higher CS throughput by increasing M (via Fig.10), as shown in Fig.15. Note, it is not profitable to increase Z (via Fig.8), because in the scenarios of computation bound, the intersection point is on the left part of CS transition point π, which does not fulfill the requirement of Principle 3, see Fig.16.

2.4.4 Capacity Bound

Identify – Capacity bound describes a very special state of the machine when *workload balance* equals *machine balance* [17]. It requires $M/Z = R$, which is also the ridge point of the Roofline model [6]. In this condition (Fig.17), both $f(k)$ and $g(x)$ intersect at their flat parts. Here, the thread volume n is no longer important if it is sufficient to saturate both CS and MS.

Optimization – This is the **optimal state** for algorithm-architecture or software-hardware codesign regarding thread

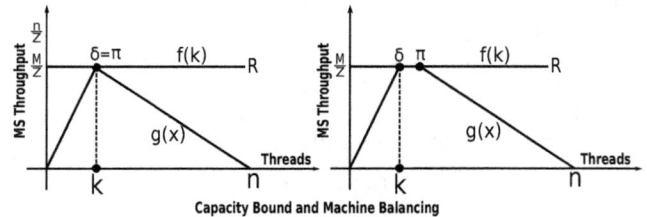

Figure 17: Capacity Bound or **Machine Balance**. This is the optimal case as both CS and MS attain its best performance. Meanwhile, due to capacity bound, some threads may be idle.

parallelism as both CS and MS bandwidth are fully leveraged ($f(k) = R, g(x) = M/Z$). Therefore, no more optimization is required. To break the balance and further improve performance, several factors have to be tuned simultaneously (e.g. M, n and R at the same time).

3. EXPERIMENT

We validate the transit model on a Fermi (Tesla-C2075) and a Kepler GPUs (GTX-690). Although we test on GPUs, the model can be applied on other multithreaded machines, e.g. UltraSPARC T2, Intel Xeon Phi, etc. The Rodinia Benchmark [18] is exploited for validation.

First we collect the machine-related input parameters L, M, R by profiling $f(k)$ and $g(x)$ via microbenchmarking. We view off-chip DRAM as MS. To plot $f(k)$, a CUDA version Stream Benchmark [19] is refined and utilized. In terms of $g(x)$, a microbenchmark is developed based on the method proposed by [20]. Due to space limitation, we cannot display the plots in the paper. However, we show the measured coordinates of δ and π, which can be used to determine $f(k)$ and $g(x)$ uniquely: For Tesla C2075, $\delta(SP) = (1536, 8.93)$, $\delta(DP) = (768, 9.29)$, $\pi(SP) = (576$, confirmed by [20], $24.8)$, $\pi(DP) = (384, 14)$; For GTX690, $\delta(SP) = (2048, 16.25)$, $\delta(DP) = (1024, 18.86)$, $\pi(SP) = (2048, 80)$, $\pi(DP) = (384, 8)$. SP stands for single precision while DP stands for double precision. The units are thread and GB/s.

Then we need the workload-related parameters Z and n. For simplicity, the CUDA command-line profiler is leveraged to gather and calculate. The equation is shown below:

$$\begin{cases} n = & occupancy * max\_resident\_threads \\ Z = & instruction\_issued/(dram\_read + dram\_write) \end{cases}$$

where the symbols on the right side are the names of the profiler counters.

We compare the predicted computation/memory throughput with the values measured by the profilers. A script is developed to gather n and Z, and plot the corresponding transit figure automatically. The results are shown in Fig.18 (for Tesla C2075) and Fig.19 (for GTX690).

As can be seen, for a majority of the applications, the dark star (measured memory throughput) is near the intersection (predicted by the model) except *gaussian*, *lavaMD* and *particlefilter*. We find that *gaussian* and *particlefilter* exhibit a very irregular memory access pattern so the actual memory throughput function $f(k)$ is far poorer than the ones we profiled. *lavaMD* is the only application that adopts double precision in Rodinia. Also, in the native machine code (SASS) generated by *cuobjdump*, we find that most of the stores are 128 bit-width while most of the loads are 64 bit-width. This explains why such few threads can generate extraordinary memory access performance. Finally, note that the abscissa value of $\delta(SP)$ is 1536 for Tesla C2075, which is also the maximum allowable threads per SM. This explains the linear behavior of $f(k)$ for most applications.

Overall, using the computation throughput (PCT & RCT in Fig.18) as the metric, our model achieves 90.4% prediction accuracy for Rodinia benchmarks on Tesla C2075 and 82.6% on GTX690 without the three outliers (*gaussian*, *lavaMD* and *particlefilter*). The major reason for Kepler showing a poorer accuracy than Fermi is the deviation of the profiled $f(k)$, as we did not consider coalescing degree to keep the model simple and general. However, Kepler is much more sensitive to memory efficiency than Fermi as the core number in Kepler SM is much larger than Fermi (192 vs. 32).

4. RELATED WORKS

Many performance models have been proposed for multithreaded machines [21, 22, 7, 23]. Saavedra-Barrera et al.

[21] set up a Markov-Chain to yield a formula for processor efficiency with respect to the number of threads. They characterize three operating regimes: linear (efficiency being proportional to thread volume), transition and saturation (efficiency depending only on remote reference rate and switch cost). The destructive impact on cache due to multithreading is also involved. Agarwal [22] presents an analytical model for a multithreaded machine that covers cache interference, interconnection network contention and context-switching overhead. He concludes that two to four threads are already sufficient to yield full processor utilization if the working-set size is much smaller than caches. Guz et al. [7] propose an analytical model targeting the trade-off between thread volume and the effectiveness of shared cache. A performance valley is identified between the cache efficiency zone and multithreaded efficiency zone for applications that are sensitive to cache efficiency. Chen et al. [23] focus on shared cache contention of multithreaded machines and construct a stochastic model based on circular sequence profiling of the threads.

All of these models, however, predominately focus on the temporal behavior of a *typical thread* or *average thread* (per-thread temporal behavior). Our model stays different in that it stresses on the spatial distribution of the thread population at a general state (all-thread spatial behavior). Meanwhile, most of the existing models (e.g. [4, 5]) are aimed at time prediction, so are mostly devoted to the precise modeling of low-level details. Such an effort requires large amount of parameters and the model itself can be time consuming to learn and implement. In comparison, our model is more straightforward as it focuses on providing high-level intuition and is visualizable as an intuitive figure.

The model that is most similar to the transit model is the Roofline model [6]. In comparison, both models utilize a roofline shape to describe system throughput. The major difference is that the transit model focuses specially on multithreaded machines. We add the thread volume, which is probability the most crucial parameter for a multithreaded machine, as a new dimension and emphasize the spatial distribution of the threads – the machine state. Secondly, in contrast to the Roofline model which attributes all optimizations as the impact to *operation intensity*, we separate a multithreaded machine into two parts so that each of them can be profiled, varied and analyzed independently.

5. CONCLUSIONS

This paper has introduced an intuitive, flexible and visualizable model for analyzing the performance of modern highly concurrent multithreaded machines. Motivated by the observation that the spatial distribution of threads between the computation and memory systems can also describe machine state and the fact that throughput performance is mostly proportional to the number of internal threads before saturation, we construct a **cross-roofline** like model called **transit** to illustrate the present machine state, identify performance bottlenecks and provide optimization intuition.

6. ACKNOWLEDGMENTS

This work was supported by Singapore Ministry of Education Academic Research Fund Tier 1 (No.R263-000-B02-112). The authors would like to thank Marissa E Kwan Lin from NUS for her useful comments on the draft paper.

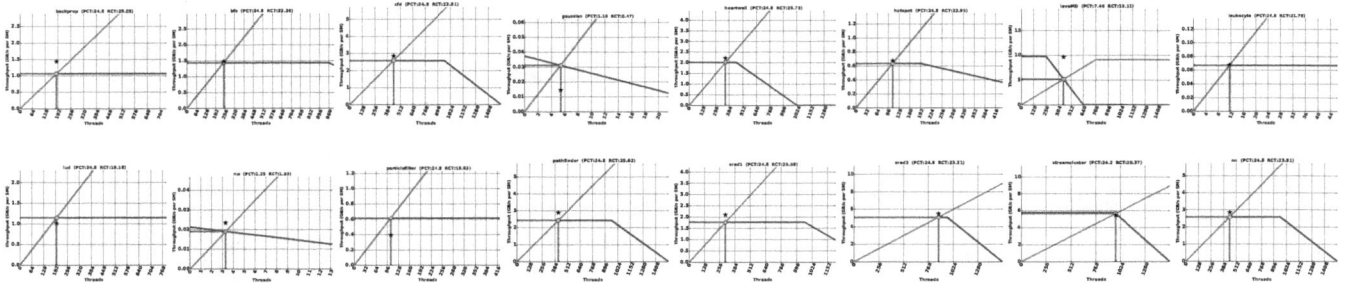

Figure 18: Testing Rodinia Benchmarks on NVIDIA Tesla C2075. The star denotes the measured memory throughput. "PCT" is the predicted computation throughput (GFLOPS) while "RCT" is the real measured computation throughput (GFLOPS).

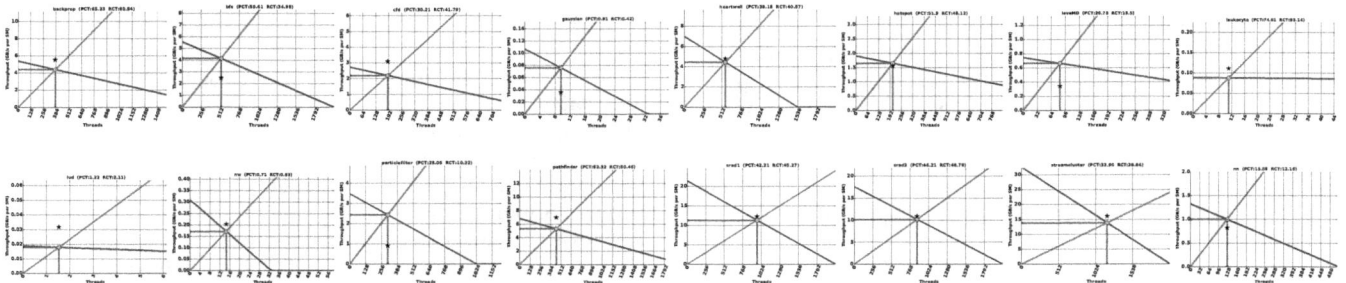

Figure 19: Testing Rodinia Benchmarks on NVIDIA Kepler GTX690. The star denotes the measured memory throughput. "PCT" is the predicted computation throughput (GFLOPS) while "RCT" is the real measured computation throughput (GFLOPS).

References

[1] S. W. Keckler et al. "GPUs and the future of parallel computing". In: *Micro, IEEE* 31.5 (2011), pp. 7–17.

[2] J. L. Hennessy and D. A. Patterson. *Computer architecture: a quantitative approach*. Elsevier, 2012.

[3] R. A. Iannucci. *Multithreaded computer architecture: A summary of the state of the art*. Springer, 1994.

[4] D. J. Sorin et al. "Analytic Evaluation of Shared-memory Systems with ILP Processors". In: *Proc.ISCA*. IEEE Computer Society, 1998, pp. 380–391.

[5] S. Hong and H. Kim. "An analytical model for a GPU architecture with memory-level and thread-level parallelism awareness". In: *ACM SIGARCH Computer Architecture News*. Vol. 37. 3. ACM. 2009, pp. 152–163.

[6] S. Williams, A. Waterman, and D. Patterson. "Roofline: an insightful visual performance model for multicore architectures". In: *Communications of the ACM* 52.4 (2009), pp. 65–76.

[7] Z. Guz et al. "Many-core vs. many-thread machines: stay away from the valley". In: *Computer Architecture Letters* 8.1 (2009), pp. 25–28.

[8] P.-S. Chen. "Queueing network model of interactive computing systems". In: *Proceedings of the IEEE* 63.6 (1975), pp. 954–957.

[9] Y. C. Tay. "Analytical performance modeling for computer systems". In: *Synthesis Lectures on Computer Science* 4.3 (2013), pp. 1–141.

[10] E. D. Lazowska et al. *Quantitative system performance: computer system analysis using queueing network models*. Prentice-Hall, Inc., 1984.

[11] H. Hirata et al. "An elementary processor architecture with simultaneous instruction issuing from multiple threads". In: *ACM SIGARCH Computer Architecture News*. Vol. 20. 2. ACM. 1992, pp. 136–145.

[12] K. Hwang. *Advanced computer architecture*. Tata McGraw-Hill Education, 2003.

[13] S. W. Williams. *Auto-tuning performance on multicore computers*. ProQuest, 2008.

[14] G. T. Byrd and M. A. Holliday. "Multithreaded processor architectures". In: *Spectrum, IEEE* 32.8 (1995), pp. 38–46.

[15] Y. Zhang and J. D. Owens. "A quantitative performance analysis model for GPU architectures". In: *High Performance Computer Architecture, 17th International Symposium on*. IEEE. 2011, pp. 382–393.

[16] J. Nieplocha et al. "Evaluating the potential of multithreaded platforms for irregular scientific computations". In: *Proceedings of the 4th International Conference on Computing Frontiers*. ACM. 2007, pp. 47–58.

[17] J. D. McCalpin. "A survey of memory bandwidth and machine balance in current high performance computers". In: *IEEE TCCA Newsletter* (1995), pp. 19–25.

[18] S. Che et al. "Rodinia: A benchmark suite for heterogeneous computing". In: *Workload Characterization. International Symposium on*. IEEE. 2009, pp. 44–54.

[19] NVIDIA. *CUDA port of the Stream benchmark*. 2010. URL: devtalk.nvidia.com/default/topic/381934/stream-benchmark/.

[20] V. Volkov. "Better performance at lower occupancy". In: *Proceedings of the GPU Technology Conference, GTC*. Vol. 10. 2010.

[21] R. Saavedra-Barrera, D Culler, and T. Von Eicken. "Analysis of multithreaded architectures for parallel computing". In: *Proceedings of the Second Annual ACM Symposium on Parallel Algorithms and Architectures*. ACM. 1990, pp. 169–178.

[22] A. Agarwal. "Performance tradeoffs in multithreaded processors". In: *Parallel and Distributed Systems, IEEE Transactions on* 3.5 (1992), pp. 525–539.

[23] X. E. Chen and T. Aamodt. "Modeling cache contention and throughput of multiprogrammed manycore processors". In: *Computers, IEEE Transactions on* 61.7 (2012), pp. 913–927.

DARE: High-Performance State Machine Replication on RDMA Networks

Marius Poke
Department of Computer Science
ETH Zurich
marius.poke@inf.ethz.ch

Torsten Hoefler
Department of Computer Science
ETH Zurich
htor@inf.ethz.ch

ABSTRACT

The increasing amount of data that needs to be collected and analyzed requires large-scale datacenter architectures that are naturally more susceptible to faults of single components. One way to offer consistent services on such unreliable systems are replicated state machines (RSMs). Yet, traditional RSM protocols cannot deliver the needed latency and request rates for future large-scale systems. In this paper, we propose a new set of protocols based on Remote Direct Memory Access (RDMA) primitives. To asses these mechanisms, we use a strongly consistent key-value store; the evaluation shows that our simple protocols improve RSM performance by more than an order of magnitude. Furthermore, we show that RDMA introduces various new options, such as log access management. Our protocols enable operators to fully utilize the new capabilities of the quickly growing number of RDMA-capable datacenter networks.

Categories and Subject Descriptors

C.4 [**Performance of Systems**]: Performance attributes; Fault tolerance

Keywords

Replicated State Machine; RDMA; Performance; Reliability

1. INTRODUCTION

The rapid growth of global data-analytics and web-services requires scaling single logical services to thousands of physical machines. Given the constant mean time between failures per server (≈ 2 years in modern datacenters [39]) the probability of a single-server failure grows dramatically; for example, a system with 1,000 servers would fail more than once a day if a single server failure causes a global system outage.

Replicated state machines (RSMs) prevent such global outages and can hide server failures while ensuring strong consistency of the overall system. RSMs are often at the core of global-scale services (e.g., in Google's Spanner [9]

or Yahoo!'s Zookeeper [20]). However, typical RSM request rates are orders of magnitude lower than the request rates of the overall systems. Thus, highly scalable systems typically utilize RSMs only for management tasks and improve overall performance by relaxing request ordering [11] which implicitly shifts the burden of consistency management to the application layer. Yet, many services, such as airline reservation systems, require a consistent view of the complete distributed database at very high request rates [41].

To ensure strong consistency, RSMs usually rely on a distinguished server—the leader—to order incoming requests [20, 29, 35]. Moreover, before answering a request, the leader must replicate the enclosed state machine update on the remote servers; thus, efficient replication is critical for high performance. Existing TCP or UDP-based RSMs perform these remote updates through messages; thus, the CPUs of the remote servers are unnecessarily involved into the replication process. A more fitting approach is to use remote direct memory access (RDMA): RDMA allows the leader to directly access the memory of the remote servers without involving their CPUs. The benefit of bypassing the remote CPUs is twofold: (1) the synchronization between the leader and the remote servers is reduced; and (2) while the leader handles requests, the remote servers can perform other operations, such as tacking checkpoints.

In this work, we utilize RDMA networking to push the limits of reliable high-performance RSM implementations by more than an order of magnitude. High-performance RDMA network architectures such as InfiniBand or RDMA over Converged Ethernet (RoCE) are quickly adopted in datacenter networking due to their relatively low cost and high performance. However, to exploit the whole potential of RDMA-capable networks, new algorithms need to be carefully designed for remote memory access. Indeed, simply emulating messages over RDMA (e.g., using the IPoIB protocol) leaves most of the performance potential untapped [16]. Our main contribution is a set of protocols for implementing high-performance RSMs by using RDMA techniques in unconventional ways.

We design a novel *wait-free* direct access protocol, called DARE (Direct Access REplication), that uses RDMA features such as QP disconnect (§ 3.2.1) and QP timeouts (§ 3.4, § 4), in atypical ways to ensure highest performance and reliability. For performance, DARE replicates state machine updates entirely through RDMA (§ 3.3.1); also, it proposes efficient RDMA algorithms for leader election and failure detection. For reliability, DARE builds on a detailed failure-model for RDMA networks that considers CPU, NIC, network, and memory failures separately (§ 5). Our implementation of DARE improves the latency compared to existing RSM protocols by up to 35 times and continues operation after a leader failure in less than $35ms$.

In summary, our work makes the following contributions:

- a complete RDMA RSM protocol and open-source reference implementation using InfiniBand (§ 3);

- an RDMA performance model of DARE in a failure-free scenario (§ 3.3.3);

- a failure model for RDMA systems in which we analyze both the availability and reliability of DARE (§ 5);

- a detailed performance analysis showing that our protocol has between 22 and 35 times lower latency than existing approaches (§ 6);

- a demonstration how DARE can be used to implement a strongly-consistent key-value store (§ 6).

2. BACKGROUND

Replicated state machines (RSMs) [40] provide reliable distributed services [24]. They replicate a (potentially infinite) state machine (SM), such as a key-value store, over a *group of servers*. A server consists of one or more processors that share the same volatile memory; also, it acts as an endpoint in the system's interconnection network. The servers update their SM replicas by applying *RSM operations*. Usually, they store the RSM operations into buffers—the local *logs*. Then, they apply each operation in order. For consistency, the logs must contain the same sequence of operations. Thus, the servers must agree on each RSM operation's position in the log; that is, they need to reach *consensus*.

2.1 Consensus

We consider a group of P servers out of which at most f are faulty. We assume a *fail-stop* model: A *faulty* server operates correctly until it fails and once it fails, it can no longer influence the operation of other servers in the group. A server that did not fail is called *non-faulty*.

In the consensus problem, each server has an *input* and an initially unset *output*. The servers propose their inputs; then, they irreversibly decide upon a value for the outputs such that three conditions are satisfied—agreement, validity and termination. Agreement requires any two non-faulty servers to decide the same; validity requires that if all the inputs are the same the value decided upon is the common input; and termination requires that any non-faulty server decides. The three conditions ensure the main properties of consensus: safety and liveness [26]. *Safety* is provided by agreement and validity; *liveness* is provided by termination. Also, it is common for consensus protocols to adopt a *leader-based* approach [20, 26, 29, 35]. Leader-based consensus protocols delegate the proposal and decision to a *distinguished leader*. The leader can both propose and decide upon values until the other servers decide to elect a new leader (§ 3.2).

The impossibility result of Fischer, Lynch, and Paterson, states that liveness cannot be ensured in an asynchronous model where servers can fail [14]. To overcome this result, we augment a synchronous model by a failure detector (FD)—a distributed oracle that provides (possible incorrect) information about faulty servers [6]. In particular, we use a $\diamond\mathcal{P}$ FD, which satisfies both *strong completeness* and *eventual strong*

$o_p = 0.07\mu s$		RDMA/rd	RDMA/wr		UD	
				inline		inline
o	$[\mu s]$	0.29	0.26	0.36	0.62	0.47
L	$[\mu s]$	1.38	1.61	0.93	0.85	0.54
G	$[\mu s/KB]$	0.75	0.76	2.21	0.77	1.92
G_m	$[\mu s/KB]$	0.26	0.25	-	-	-

Table 1: LogGP parameters on our system.

accuracy. Strong completeness requires that eventually every faulty server is suspected to have failed by every non-faulty server. Eventual strong accuracy requires that eventually every non-faulty server is trusted by every non-faulty server. A $\diamond\mathcal{P}$ FD guarantees the termination of leader-based consensus only if a majority of the servers are non-faulty [6]. Therefore, for the remainder of the paper, we consider a group of P servers, out of which up to $f = \lfloor \frac{P-1}{2} \rfloor$ can fail.

2.2 RDMA overview

Remote Direct Memory Access is an interface that allows servers to access memory in the user-space of other servers. To enable this mechanism, two user-space processes establish so called Queue Pairs (QPs) and connect them; each QP is a logical endpoint for a communication channel. The remote access is fully performed by the hardware (using a reliable transport channel) without any interaction with the OS at the origin or target of the access. In this way, the NIC can be seen as a separate but limited processor that enables access to remote memory. This mechanism is fundamentally different from existing message-passing mechanisms where messages are processed by the main CPU. Thus, RDMA changes the system's failure-characteristics: a CPU can fail but its memory is still remotely accessible (see Section 5).

Modern networks, such as InfiniBand, also offer unreliable datagram (UD) messaging semantics that support multicast. We use these to simplify non-performance-critical parts of our protocol such as setup and interaction with clients.

2.3 Modeling RDMA performance

We estimate the performance of RDMA operations through a modified LogGP model [2]. The LogGP model consist of the following parameters: the latency L; the overhead o; the gap between messages g; the gap per byte for long messages G; and the number of processes (or servers) P. We make the common assumption that $o > g$ [2]; also, we assume that control packets, such as write acknowledgments and read requests, are of size one byte. Moreover, we readjust the model to fit the properties of RDMA communication. In particular, we make the following assumptions: (1) the overhead of the target of the access is negligible; (2) the latency of control packets is integrated into the latency of RDMA accesses; (3) for large RDMA accesses, the bandwidth increases after transferring the first MTU bytes; (4) for RDMA write operations, L, G, and o depend on whether the data is sent inline; and (5) o_p is the overhead of polling for completion. Table 1 specifies the LogGP parameters for our system, i.e., a 12-node InfiniBand cluster (§ 6).

According to the assumptions above, the time of either writing or reading s bytes through RDMA is estimated by

$$\begin{cases} o_{in} + L_{in} + (s-1)G_{in} + o_p & \text{if inline} \\ o + L + (s-1)G + o_p & \text{if } s \leq m \\ o + L + (m-1)G + (s-m)G_m + o_p & \text{if } s > m, \end{cases} \quad (1)$$

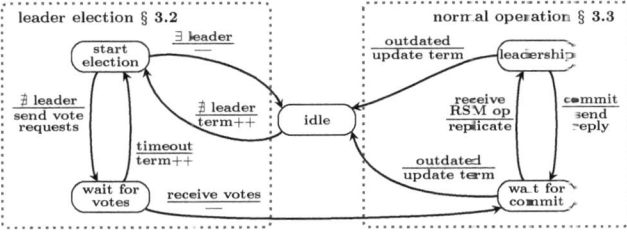

Figure 1: Outline of both leader election and normal operation protocols of DARE. Solid boxes indicate states; arrows indicate transitions. Each transition is described by its precondition (top) and postcondition (bottom).

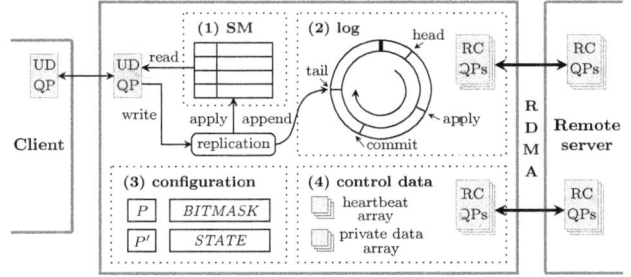

Figure 2: The internal state and interface of a DARE server.

where m is the MTU of the system, G is the gap per byte for the first m bytes, and G_m is the gap per byte after the first m bytes. Besides RDMA operations, DARE uses also unreliable datagrams (UDs). To estimate the time of UD transfers, we use the original LogGP model; thus, the time of sending s bytes over UD is

$$\begin{cases} 2o_{in} + L_{in} + (s-1)G_{in} & \text{if inline} \\ 2o + L + (s-1)G & \text{otherwise.} \end{cases} \quad (2)$$

Both RDMA and UD models fit the data on our system with coefficients of determination larger than 0.99.

3. THE DARE PROTOCOL

DARE is an RSM protocol that solves consensus through a leader-based approach: A distinguished leader acts as the interface between clients and the SMs. When the leader is suspected to have failed, the servers elect another leader. Each election causes the beginning of a new *term*—a period of time in which at most one leader exits. A server that wins an election during a term becomes the leader of that term. Furthermore, to make progress, DARE requires the existence of a *quorum*; that is, at least $q = \lceil \frac{P+1}{2} \rceil$ servers must "agree" on the next step. This ensures that after any $f = \lfloor \frac{P-1}{2} \rfloor$ failures there is still at least one non-faulty server that is aware of the previous step (since $q > f$). That server guarantees the safe continuation of the protocol.

Existing leader-based RSM protocols and implementations rely on message passing, often implemented over UDP or TCP channels [9,20,29,35]. DARE replaces the message-passing mechanism with RDMA; it assumes that servers are connected through an interconnect with support for RDMA, such as InfiniBand. To our knowledge, DARE is the first RSM protocol that can exploit the whole potential of RDMA-capable networks. All of the main sub-protocols (see below) entail the design of special methods in order to support remotely accessible data structures; we detail the design of these methods in the following subsections.

DARE outline. We decompose the DARE protocol into three main sub-protocols that contribute to the implementation of an RSM:

- **Leader election:** the servers elect a distinguished server as their leader (§ 3.2).

- **Normal operation:** the leader applies RSM operations in a consistent manner (§ 3.3).

- **Group reconfiguration:** either the group's membership or size changes (§ 3.4).

The first two sub-protocols—leader election and normal operation—are the essence of any leader-based RSM protocol; group reconfiguration is an extension that enables DARE to change the set of servers in the group. Figure 1 shows an outline of both leader election and normal operation.

All servers start in an idle state, in which they remain as long as a leader exists. When a server suspects the leader to have failed it starts a new election (left side of Figure 1). First, it proposes itself as the leader for the subsequent term by sending vote requests to the other servers. Then, the server either becomes leader after receiving votes from a quorum (itself included) or it starts a new election after timing out (§ 3.2). Note that if another server becomes leader, the server returns to the idle state.

Once a server becomes leader, it starts the normal operation protocol (right of Figure 1). In particular, it must ensure the consistency of the SM replicas. Thus, when it receives an RSM operation the leader replicates it on the other servers with the intention to *commit* it; for safety, an RSM operation is committed when it resides on at least a majority of servers. After an RSM operation is committed, the leader sends a reply to the client that sent the operation. Finally, a leader returns to the idle state if it is *outdated*. An outdated leader is a server that regards itself as leader, although another leader of a more recent term exists; for example, a temporary overload on the current leader can cause a majority of the servers to elect a new leader.

In the remainder of this section, we first present the basics of the DARE protocol (§ 3.1): we specify the internal state of a server; and we outline how both clients and servers interact with each other. Then, we describe in detail the three main sub-protocols of DARE: leader election; normal operation; and group reconfiguration.

3.1 DARE basics

3.1.1 Server internal state

The internal state of each server consists of four main data structures depicted in Figure 2: (1) the client SM; (2) the log; (3) the configuration; and (4) the control data. The *SM* is an opaque object that can be updated by the server through RSM operations received from clients. For consistency, servers apply the RSM operations in the same order; this is achieved by first appending the operations to the log.

The *log* is a circular buffer composed of entries that have sequential indexes; each entry contains the term in which it was created. Usually, log entries store RSM operations that need to be applied to the SM; yet, some log entries are used by DARE for internal operations, such as log pruning (§ 3.3.2) and group reconfiguration (§ 3.4). Similar to

RSM operations, log entries are called *committed* if they reside on a majority of servers. The log is described by four dynamic pointers, which follow each other clockwise in a circle:

- **head** points to the first entry in the log; it is updated locally during log pruning (§ 3.3.2);

- **apply** points to the first entry that is not applied to the SM; it is updated locally;

- **commit** points to the first not-committed log entry; it is updated by the leader during log replication (§ 3.3.1);

- **tail** points to the end of the log; it is updated by the leader during log replication (§ 3.3.1).

The *configuration* data structure is a high level description of the group of servers. It contains four fields: the current group size P; a bitmask indicating the active servers; the new group size P'; and an identifier of the current state. Section 3.4 describes in details the role of these fields in DARE's group reconfiguration protocol.

Finally, the *control data* consists of a set of arrays that have an entry per server. One such array is the *private data array* that is used by servers as reliable storage (§ 3.2.3). Another example is the *heartbeat array* used by the leader to maintain its leadership (§ 4). We specify the rest of the arrays as we proceed with the description of the protocol.

In-memory data structures: benefits and challenges. The internal state of a DARE server consists of in-memory data structures. The benefit of an in-memory state is twofold. First, accessing in-memory data has lower latency than accessing on-disk data. Second, in-memory data structures can be remotely accessed through RDMA. In particular, in DARE, the leader uses the commit and tail pointers to manage the remote logs directly through RDMA. Thus, since the target servers are not active, they can perform other operations such as saving the SM on stable storage for higher reliability. Also, RDMA accesses are performed by the hardware without any interaction with the OS; this often leads to higher performance as compared to message passing [16].

Yet, the in-memory approach entails that the entire state is volatile; thus, when high reliability is required, DARE uses *raw replication*. Raw replication makes an item of data reliable by scattering copies of it among different nodes. Thus, this approach can tolerate a number of simultaneous node failures equal to the numbers of copies. In Section 5, we discuss reliability in more details.

3.1.2 Communication interface

DARE relies on both unreliable and reliable communication. Unreliable communication is implemented over UD QPs, which support both unicast and multicast transfers. The multicast support makes UD QPs practical in the context of a dynamic group membership, where the identity of the servers may be unknown. Thus, we implement the interaction between group members and clients over UD QPs. Note that new servers joining the group act initially as clients and, thus, they also use the UD QPs to access the group (§ 3.4).

The InfiniBand architecture specification's Reliable Connection (RC) transport mechanism does not lose packets [21]; therefore, DARE implements reliable communication over RC QPs. Since the servers need remote access

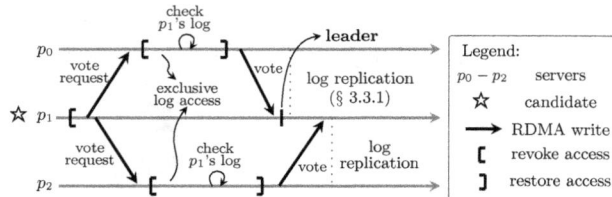

Figure 3: The voting mechanism during leader election.

to both the log and the control data, any pair of servers is connected by two RC QPs: (1) a control QP that grants remote access to the control data; and (2) a log QP that grants remote access to the local log (see Figure 2).

3.2 Leader election

We adopt a traditional leader election protocol to RDMA semantics: A server sends vote requests and it waits for votes from at least $\lfloor P/2 \rfloor$ servers, before it becomes the leader. In addition, a server cannot vote twice in the same term. Thus, DARE guarantees at most one leader per term.

In the remainder of this section, we describe our RDMA design of the voting mechanism. Figure 3 outlines this mechanism during a successful leader election in a group of three servers. Although our approach is similar to a message-passing one, it requires special care when managing the log accesses. In particular, by using RDMA semantics, the leader bypasses the remote CPUs when accessing their logs; as a result, the servers are unaware of any updates of their logs. This hinders the ability of a server to participate in elections. Thus, we first outline how DARE uses *QP state transitions* to allow servers to manage the remote access to their own memory; then, we describe the voting mechanism.

3.2.1 Managing log access

Once a QP is created, it needs to be transitioned through a sequence of states to become fully operational; moreover, at any time the QP can be locally reset to the original state, which is non-operational. Thus, DARE servers can decide on either exclusive local access or shared remote access. For exclusive local access, the QP is reset to the original non-operational state; while for remote log access, the servers move the QP in the ready-to-send state [21], which is fully-operational. Besides managing access to their logs, DARE servers use QP state transitions for both connecting and disconnecting servers during group reconfiguration (§ 3.4).

3.2.2 Becoming a candidate

The leader election protocol starts when a server suspects the leader to have failed. In Figure 3, server p_1 starts an election by revoking remote access to its log; this ensures that an outdated leader cannot update the log. Then, it proposes itself as a *candidate* for the leadership of the subsequent term. That is, it sends vote requests to the other servers: It updates its corresponding entry in the *vote request array* (one of the control data arrays) at all other servers by issuing RDMA write operations (see Figure 3). An entry in the vote request array consists of all the information a server requires to decide if it should vote for the candidate: the candidate's current term and both the index and the term of the candidate's last log entry (see Section 3.2.3).

Depending on the internal state of the candidate, we distinguish between three possible outcomes (depicted in the left side of Figure 1): (1) the candidate becomes leader if it receives the votes from at least $\lfloor P/2 \rfloor$ servers; (2) it decides to support the leadership of another candidate more suited to become leader (§ 3.2.3); or (3) otherwise, it starts another election after a timeout period. Note that the candidate restores remote log access for every server from which it received a vote; this ensures that a new leader can proceed with the log replication protocol (§ 3.3.1).

3.2.3 Answering vote requests

Servers not aware of a leader periodically check the vote request array for incoming requests. They only consider requests for the leadership of a higher (more recent) term than their own; on receiving a valid request, the servers increase their own term. In Figure 3, servers p_0 and p_2 receive vote requests from candidate p_1. Both servers grant their vote after first checking that the candidate's latests log entry is at least as recent as their own; an entry is more recent than another if it has either a higher term or the same term but a higher index [35]. Checking the candidate's log is essential for DARE's safety; it ensures that the log of a leader contains the most recent entry among a majority of servers. Also, note that while performing the check both servers need exclusive access to their own logs (see Figure 3).

A server's volatile internal state introduces an additional challenge. The server may fail after voting for a candidate, and then, recover during the same term. If after recovery, it receives a vote request from another candidate, but for the same term, the server could grant its vote. Thus, two servers may become leaders during the same term, which breaks the safety of our protocol. To avoid such scenarios, prior to answering vote requests, each server makes its decision reliable by replicating it via the private data array (§ 3.1.1).

RDMA vs. MP: leader election. Our RDMA design of leader election increases DARE's availability. When the leader fails, the RSM becomes unavailable until a new leader is elected. First, for leader election to start, the servers need to detect the failure (§ 4). Then, the election time depends on the period a candidate waits for votes before restarting the election. This period needs to be large enough for the vote requests to reach the servers and at least $\lfloor P/2 \rfloor$ votes to arrive back at the candidate. The RDMA-capable interconnect allows us to reduce this period; thus, our design increases the RSM's availability.

3.3 Normal operation

The normal operation protocol entails the existence of a sole leader that has the support of at least a majority of servers (including itself). The leader is responsible for three tasks: serving clients; managing the logs; and if needed, reconfiguring the group. In the remainder of this section, we describe the first two tasks; we defer the discussion of group reconfiguration to Section 3.4. First we specify how clients interact with DARE. Then, we present a log replication protocol designed entirely for RDMA (§ 3.3.1); also, we outline a log pruning mechanism that prevents the overflowing of the logs. Finally, we provide an RDMA performance model of DARE during normal operation.

Client interaction. Clients interact with the group of servers by sending requests through either multicast or unicast. To identify the leader of the group, clients send their first request via multicast. Multicast requests are considered only by the leader. Once the leader replies, clients send

subsequent requests directly to the leader via unicast. However, if the request is not answered in a predefined period of time, clients re-send the request through multicast. Also, the current implementation assumes that a client waits for a reply before sending the subsequent request. Yet, DARE handles different clients asynchronously: The leader can execute, at the same time, requests from multiple clients. This increases the protocol's throughput (see Figure 7b).

Write requests. Regardless of the nature of the SM, clients can send either write or read requests. *Write requests* contain RSM operations that alter the SM. Such operations need to be applied to all SM replicas in the same order. Therefore, when receiving a write request, the leader stores the RSM operation into an entry that is appended to the log. Then, it replicates the log entry on other servers with the purpose to commit it (see Section 3.3.1). As a safety requirement, each DARE server applies only RSM operations stored in committed log entries.

Write requests may contain RSM operations that are not idempotent (i.e., they change the SM replicas every time they are applied). DARE ensures that each RSM operation is applied only once by enforcing *linearizable semantics* [19] through unique request IDs (as other RSM protocols). Furthermore, to increase the throughput of strongly consistent writes, DARE executes write requests in batches: The leader first appends the RSM operations of all consecutively received write requests to the log; then, it replicates all the entries at once.

Read requests. *Read requests* contain RSM operations that do not alter the SM. For such operations, replication is not required: For efficiency, the leader answers read requests directly from the local SM. Yet, to ensure that reads do not return stale data, DARE imposes two constraints: (1) an outdated leader cannot answer read requests; and (2) a leader with an outdated SM cannot answer read requests.

First, to verify whether a leader is outdated, DARE uses a property of leader election—any successful election requires at least a majority of servers to increase their terms (cf. § 3.2.3). Therefore, before answering a read request, the leader reads the term of at least $\lfloor P/2 \rfloor$ servers; if it finds no term larger than its own, then it can safely answer the read request. As an optimization, the leader verifies whether it is outdated only once for a batch of consecutively received read requests; thus, DARE's read throughput increases.

Second, before answering a read request, the leader must ensure that all RSM operations stored in committed log entries are applied to the local SM. DARE guarantees that the leader's log contains all the committed entries that store RSM operations not yet applied by all non-faulty servers (§ 4). However, a new leader may not be aware of all the committed entries (§ 3.3.1); thus, the local SM is outdated. As a solution, a new leader appends to its log an entry with no RSM operation. This starts the log replication protocol that commits also all the preceding log entries.

3.3.1 Log replication

The core of the normal operation protocol is *log replication*—the leader replicates RSM operations on the other servers with the intention to commit them (see right side of Figure 1). In DARE, log replication is performed entirely through RDMA: The leader writes its own log entries into the logs of the remote servers. Yet, after a new leader is

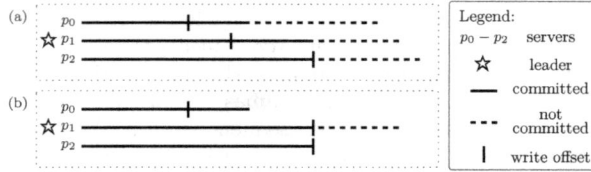

Figure 4: The logs in a group of three servers: (a) after server p_1 is elected leader; and (b) after log adjustment. For clarity, the apply pointers are omitted.

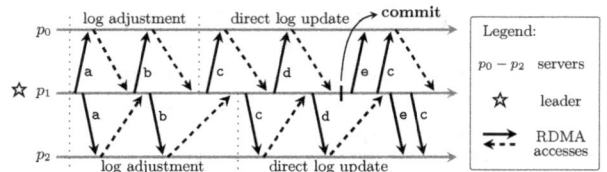

Figure 5: The RDMA accesses during log replication: (a) read the remote not-committed entries; (b) write the remote tail pointer; (c) write the remote log; (d) write the remote tail pointer; and (e) write the remote commit pointer.

elected, the logs can contain not-committed entries. These entries may differ from the ones stored at the same position in the leader's log; for example, Figure 4a shows the logs after server p_1 becomes the leader of a group of three servers. Before a newly elected leader can replicate log entries, it must first remove all the remote not-committed entries. Therefore, we split the log replication protocol into two phases: (1) log adjustment; and (2) direct log update.

Log adjustment. One naïve approach to adjust a remote log is to set its tail pointer to the corresponding commit pointer. However, this may remove committed entries (see server p_0's log in Figure 4a); as a result, a committed entry may no longer be replicated on a majority of servers, which breaks the safety of our protocol. A correct approach sets the remote tail pointer to the first not-committed entry; note that due to the "lazy" update of the commit pointers (see below), a server may not be aware of all its committed log entries. Thus, to adjust a remote log, the leader performs two subsequent RDMA accesses (labeled by a and b in Figure 5): (1) it reads the remote not-committed entries; and (2) it sets the remote tail pointer to the offset of the first non-matching entry when compared to its own log. In addition, the leader updates its own commit pointer. Figure 4b shows the logs of the three servers after the log adjustment phase is completed.

Direct log update. The second phase of log replication consists of three RDMA accesses (labeled by c, d and e in Figure 5). First, for each adjusted remote log, the leader writes all entries between the remote and the local tail pointers. Second, the leader updates the tail pointers of all the servers for which the first access completed successfully. To commit log entries, the leader sets the local commit pointer to the minimum tail pointer among at least a majority of servers (itself included). Finally, for the remote servers to apply the just committed entries, the leader "lazily" updates the remote commit pointers; by lazy update we mean that there is no need to wait for completion.

Asynchronous replication. During log replication, the leader handles the remote logs asynchronously. Figure 5 shows the RDMA accesses during log replication in a group of three servers. Once the leader receives the confirmation that server p_0's log is adjusted, it starts updating it, although it is not yet aware that server p_2's log is adjusted (the access is delayed). When the delayed access completes, the leader can also start the direct log update phase for server p_2. Furthermore, the leader commits its log entries after updating the tail pointer of server p_0 (since $P = 3$).

RDMA vs. MP: log replication. Replicating the logs through RDMA has several benefits over the more traditional message-passing approach. RDMA accesses remove the overhead on the target, which has two consequences:

first, the leader commits RSM operations faster; and second, the servers are available for other tasks, such as recovery (§ 3.4). Moreover, RDMA allows for servers with a faulty CPU, but with both NIC and memory working, to be remotely accessible during log replication, hence, increasing both availability and reliability (§ 5). Finally, RDMA allows for efficient log adjustment. In DARE, log adjustment entails two RDMA accesses regardless of the number of non-matching log entries; yet, in Raft [35] for example, the leader must send a message for each non-matching log entry.

3.3.2 Log pruning: removing applied entries

Every server applies the RSM operations stored in the log entries between its apply and commit pointers; once an operation is applied, the server advances its apply pointer. When an RSM operation is applied by all the non-faulty servers in the group, the entry containing it can be removed from the log. Thus, the leader advances its own head pointer to the smallest apply pointer in the group; then, it appends to the log an HEAD entry that contains the new head pointer. Servers update their head pointer only when they encounter a committed HEAD entry; thus, all subsequent leaders will be aware of the updated head pointer. Furthermore, when the log is full the leader blocks until the remote servers advance their apply pointers. To avoid waiting, the leader can remove the server with the lowest apply pointer on the grounds that it hinders the performance of the entire group (cf. [10]).

3.3.3 An RDMA performance model

DARE is designed as a high-performance RSM protocol. Its performance is given by the request latency—the amount of time clients need to wait for requests to be answered. Client requests have two parts: (1) the UD transfer, which entails both sending the request and receiving a reply; and (2) the RDMA transfer, which consist of the leader's remote memory accesses. We use Equations (1) and (2) from Section 2.3 to estimate the latency of both UD and RDMA transfers; for readability, we consider the gap per byte G only for the s bytes of either the read or written data.

The UD transfer entails two messages: one short that is sent inline (request for reads and replies for writes); and one long that transfers the data. Thus, the latency of the UD transfer is bounded (due to the above simplification) by

$$t_{UD} \geq 2o_{in} + L_{in} + \begin{cases} 2o_{in} + L_{in} + (s-1)G_{in} & \text{if inline} \\ 2o + L + (s-1)G & \text{otherwise} \end{cases}.$$

The latency introduced by RDMA accesses depends on the request type. For read requests, the leader needs to wait for at least $q - 1$ RDMA reads to complete ($q = \lceil \frac{P+1}{2} \rceil$). Thus, the latency of the RDMA transfer in case of read requests is bounded by

$$t_{RDMA/rd} \geq (q-1)o + \max\{fo, L\} + (q-1)o_p,$$

where f is the maximum number of faulty servers; also, the max function indicates the overlap between the overhead of issuing the last f reads and the latency of the $(q-1)$st one.

For write requests, the leader needs to go through the steps of log replication. Yet, the logs are adjusted only once per term; thus, assuming a fairly stable leader, the latency of log adjustment is negligible. During the direct log update phase, the leader accesses the logs of at least $q-1$ servers; for each, it issues three subsequent RDMA write operations (see Figure 5). Thus, the latency of the RDMA transfer in case of a write request is bounded by

$$t_{RDMA/wr} \geq 2(q-1)o_{in} + L_{in} + 2(q-1)o_p +$$

$$\begin{cases} (q-1)o_{in} + \max\{fo_{in}, L_{in} + (s-1)G_{in}\} & \text{if inline} \\ (q-1)o + \max\{fo, L + (s-1)G\} & \text{otherwise} \end{cases},$$

where similar to read requests, the max function indicates the overlap between the last f log update operations and the latency of the $(q-1)$st one. Figure 7a compares these bounds with measurements gathered on our system (§ 5).

3.4 Group reconfiguration

DARE is intended for dynamical environments where servers can fail at any time. Thus, the group of servers can modify both its membership and its size; we refer to this as *group reconfiguration*. DARE handles group reconfigurations through the configuration data structure (§ 3.1.1). A configuration can be in three states: a stable state that entails a group of P servers with the non-faulty servers indicated by a bitmask; an extended state used for adding servers to a full group (see below); and a transitional state that allows for the group to be resized without interrupting normal operation [35]. The last two states require the new group size P' to be set.

We define three operations that are sufficient to describe all group reconfiguration scenarios: (1) remove a server; (2) add a server; and (3) decrease the group size. For example, since a server's internal state is volatile, a transient failure entails removing a server followed by adding it back; also, increasing the size entails adding a server to a full group. The three operations can be initiated only by a leader in a stable configuration. Each operation may entail multiple phases. Yet, each phase contains the following steps: the leader modifies its configuration; then, it appends to the log an entry that contains the updated configuration (a CONFIG entry); and once the CONFIG entry is committed, the phase completes and a possible subsequent phase can start. Note that when a server encounters a CONFIG log entry, it updates its own configuration accordingly regardless of whether the entry is committed. In the remainder of this section, we first describe how DARE implements the three operations; then, we outline how a server recovers its internal state. If not stated otherwise, we assume all configurations to be stable.

Removing a server. A server may be removed in one of the following cases: the log is full and cannot be pruned (§ 3.3.2); the group size is decreased; or the leader suspects the server to have failed. The leader detects failed (or unavailable) servers by using the QP timeouts provided by the RC transport mechanism [21]. In all cases, removing

a server is a single-phase operation. First, the leader disconnects its QPs (§ 3.2.1) with the server. Then, it updates the bitmask of its configuration accordingly; also, it adds a CONFIG log entry with the updated configuration. Finally, once the log entry is committed, the server is removed.

Adding a server. Adding a server to a group is similar to removing a server; the only difference is that the QPs with the server must be connected instead of disconnected. Yet, if the group is full, adding a server requires first to increase the group size, which, without previously adding a server, decreases the fault-tolerance of the group. Intuitively, this is because the new group starts already with a failure since the new server is not yet added. Thus, adding a server to a full group is a three-phase operation: (1) adding the server; (2) increasing the group size; (3) stabilizing the configuration.

First, the leader establishes a reliable connection with the server; also, it creates an extended configuration with $P' = P + 1$. This configuration allows the added server to recover; yet, the server cannot participate in DARE's sub-protocols. Second, the leader increases the group size without interrupting normal operation [35]. In particular, it moves the configuration to a transitional state, in which all servers are participating in DARE's sub-protocols. The servers form two groups—the original group of P server and the new group of P' servers; majorities from both groups are required for both electing a leader and committing a log entry. Finally, the leader stabilizes the configuration: It sets P to the new size P' and it moves back into the stable state.

Decreasing the group size. Usually, adding more servers leads to higher reliability (see Figure 6); yet, it also decreases the performance, since more servers are required to form a majority. Thus, DARE allows the group size to be decreased. Decreasing the group size is a two-phase operation: first, the leader creates a transitional configuration that contains both the old and the new sizes; and then, it stabilizes it by removing the extra servers from the end of the old configurations.

Recovery. When added to the group, a server needs to recover its internal state before participating in DARE's sub-protocols; in particular, it needs to retrieve both the SM and the log. To retrieve the SM, the new server asks any server, except for the leader, to create a snapshot of its SM; then, it reads the remote snapshot. Once the SM is recovered, the server reads the committed log entries of the same server. After it recovers, the server sends a vote to the leader as a notification that it can participate in log replication. Note that the recovery is performed entirely through RDMA.

RDMA vs. MP: recovery. Our RDMA approach reduces the impact of recovery on normal operation. The reason for this is twofold. First, contrary to message-passing RSMs, in DARE, the leader manages the logs directly without involving the CPUs of the remote servers; thus, servers can create a snapshot of their SM without interrupting normal operation. Second, the new server can retrieve both the SM and the log of a remote server directly through RDMA.

4. DARE: SAFETY AND LIVENESS

Safety argument. In addition to the safety requirement of consensus (§ 2.1), DARE guarantees the *RSM safety* property: each SM replica applies the same sequence of RSM operations. DARE exhibits similar properties as existing RSM protocols. In particular, DARE satisfies two properties: (1) two logs with an identical entry have all the preceding entries identical as well; and (2) every leader's log contains all already-committed entries. The two properties are sufficient to argue the RSM safety property [35]. We omit the details because of space limitations; yet, they are available in an extended technical report [38].

Liveness argument. DARE guarantees liveness. Our argument relies on the following properties: (1) a quorum is always possible, since at most $\lfloor \frac{P-1}{2} \rfloor$ servers are faulty; and (2) faulty-leaders are detected through a $\diamond \mathcal{P}$ FD (i.e., eventual strong accuracy and strong completeness [6]). Thus, eventually, a non-faulty leader is not suspected for sufficiently long so that it can make progress. Also, a faulty-leader is eventually detected by all the non-faulty servers; thus, a leader election starts. By using randomized timeouts for restarting the election [35], DARE ensures that a leader is eventually elected. For details, we refer the reader to the technical report [38]. Further, we describe how we utilize InfiniBand's timeout mechanisms [21] to obtain a model of partial synchrony [6] required by a $\diamond \mathcal{P}$ FD. Also, we outline how to implement a $\diamond \mathcal{P}$ FD with RDMA-semantics.

Synchronicity in RDMA networks. Synchronicity in the context of processors implies that there is a fixed bound on the time needed by a processor to execute any operation; intuitively, this guarantees the responsiveness of non-faulty processors. Since DARE uses RDMA for log replication, the processors are the NICs of the servers. These NICs are special-purpose processors that are in charge solely of the delivery of network packets at line-rate; that is, NICs avoid nondeterministic behavior, such as that introduced by preemption in general-purpose CPUs. Therefore, we can assume a bound on the execution time of NIC operations.

Synchronous communication requires a bound on the time within which any packet is delivered to a non-faulty server. Time can generally not be bound in complex networks, however, datacenter networks usually deliver packets within a tight time bound. InfiniBand's reliable transport mechanism does not lose packets and notifies the user if the transmission experiences unrecoverable errors [21]: It uses Queue Pair timeouts that raise unrecoverable errors in the case of excessive contention in the network or congestion at the target. Thus, the RC service of InfiniBand offers a communication model where servers can ascertain deterministically if a packet sent to a remote server was acknowledged within a bounded period of time.

Leader failure detection. The $\diamond \mathcal{P}$ FD used by DARE to detect failed leaders is based on an heartbeat mechanism implemented with RDMA semantics. Initially, every server suspects every other server to have failed. Then, the leader starts sending periodic heartbeats by writing its own term in the remote heartbeat arrays (§ 3.1.1). Every other server checks its heartbeat array regularly, with a period Δ: First, it selects the heartbeat with the most recent term; then, it compares this term with its own. If the terms are equal, then the leader is non-faulty; thus, the server extends its support. If its own term is smaller, then a change in leadership occurred; thus, the server updates its own term to indicate its support. Otherwise, the server assumes the leader has failed; thus, the strong completeness property holds [6].

In addition, when a server finds an heartbeat with a term smaller than its own, it first increments Δ to ensure that eventually a non-faulty leader will not be suspected; thus, the eventual strong accuracy property holds [6]. Then, it

Component	AFR	MTTF	Reliability
Network [12, 17]	1.00%	876, 000	4-nines
NIC [12, 17]	1.00%	876, 000	4-nines
DRAM [18]	39.5%	22, 177	2-nines
CPU [18]	41.9%	20, 906	2-nines
Server [17, 39]	47.9%	18, 304	2-nines

Table 2: Worst case scenario reliability data. The reliability is estimated over a period of 24 hours and expressed in the "nines" notation; the MTTF is expressed in hours.

informs the owner of the heartbeat that it is an outdated leader, so it can return to the idle state (see Figure 1).

5. FINE-GRAINED FAILURE MODEL

As briefly mentioned in Section 2.2, RDMA requires a different view of a failing system than message passing. In message passing, a failure of either the CPU or OS (e.g., a software failure) disables the whole node because each message needs both CPU and memory to progress. In RDMA systems, memory may still be accessed even if the CPU is blocked (e.g., the OS crashed) due to its OS bypass nature.

To account for the effects of RDMA, we propose a failure model that considers each individual component—CPU, main memory (DRAM), and NIC—separately. We make the common assumption that each component can fail independently of the other components in the system [5,33]; for example, the CPU may execute a failed instruction in the OS and halt, the NIC may encounter too many bit errors to continue, or the memory may fail ECC checks. We also make the experimentally verified assumption that a CPU/OS failure does not influence the remote readability of the memory. Finally, we assume that the network (consisting of links and switches) can also fail.

Various sources provide failure data of systems and system components [12, 18, 31, 36]. Yet, systems range from very reliable ones with AFRs per component below 0.2% [31] to relatively unreliable ones with component failure log events at an annual rate of more than 40% [18] (here we assume that a logged error impacted the function of the device). Thus, it is important to observe the reliability of the system that DARE is running on and adjust the parameters of our model accordingly. For the sake of presentation, we pick the *worst case* for DARE, i.e., the highest component errors that we found in the literature. Table 2 specifies this for the main components over a period of one 24 hours.

Availability: zombie servers. We refer to servers with a blocked CPU, but with both a working NIC and memory as *zombie servers*. Zombie servers account for roughly half of the failure scenarios (cf. Table 2). Due to their non-functional CPU, zombie servers cannot participate in some protocols, such as leader election. Yet, DARE accesses remote memory through RDMA operations that consume no *receive request* on the remote QP, and hence, no *work completions* [21]. Therefore, a zombie server's log can be used by the leader during log replication increasing DARE's availability. Note that the log can be used only temporarily since it cannot be pruned and eventually the leader will remove the zombie server. Moreover, even in case of permanent CPU failures, zombie servers may provide sufficient time for recovery without losing availability.

Reliability. As briefly mentioned in Section 3.1.1, our design exploits the concept of memory reliability through

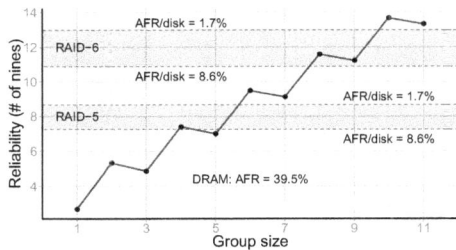

Figure 6: DARE's reliability over a period of 24 hours. Also, the reliability achieved by disks with RAID technologies.

raw replication. In particular, DARE uses raw replication in two situations: (1) explicitly by a server before answering a vote request during leader election; and (2) implicitly by the leader during log replication. In both situations, at least $q = \left\lceil \frac{P+1}{2} \right\rceil$ replicas are created. Thus, DARE's reliability is given by the probability that no more than $q - 1$ servers experience a memory failure (cf. Table 2, the failures probabilities of both NIC and network are negligible)

We propose a model that considers the components as part of non-repairable populations: Having experienced a failure, the same component can rejoin the system; yet, it is treated as a new individual of the population. We use basic concepts of probability to estimate the likelihood that no more than $q - 1$ out of P components are unavailable; for details see [38]. To estimate DARE's reliability, we use the data from Table 2 under the assumption that all components are modeled by exponential LDMs. Figure 6 plots the reliability as a function of the group size. Of particular interest is the decrease in reliability when the group size increases from an even to an odd value. This is expected since the group has one more server, but the size of a quorum remains unchanged. Also, Figure 6 compares the reliability of our in-memory approach with the one achieved by stable storage; the disk AFRs are according to [36]. We observe that for a group size of 7, DARE can achieve higher reliability than disks with RAID-5 [7], while 11 servers are sufficient to overpass the reliability of disks with RAID-6 [37].

6. EVALUATION

We evaluate the performance of DARE in a practical setting. We use a 12-node InfiniBand cluster; each node has an Intel E5-2609 CPU clocked at 2.40GHz. The cluster is connected with a single switch using a single Mellanox QDR NIC (MT27500) at each node. Moreover, the nodes are running Linux, kernel version 3.12.18. DARE is implemented[1] in C and relies on two libraries: *libibverbs*, an implementation of the RDMA verbs for InfiniBand; and *libev*, a high-performance event loop. Each server runs an instance of DARE; yet, each server is single-threaded. Finally to compile the code, we used GCC version 4.8.2.

We consider a key-value store (KVS) as the client SM: Clients access data through 64-byte keys. Moreover, since clients send requests through UD, the size of a request is limited by the network's MTU (i.e., 4096 bytes). Henceforth, we only state the size of the data associated with a key. The structure of this section is as follows: first, we evaluate both the latency and the throughput of DARE; then we

---

[1]DARE: http://spcl.inf.ethz.ch/Research/Parallel_Programming/DARE

analyze the throughput for different workloads; finally, we compare the performance of DARE with other protocols and implementations, such as ZooKeeper [20].

Latency. DARE is designed as a high-performance RSM. Figure 7a shows the latency of both write and read requests (gets and puts in the context of a KVS). In the benchmark, a single client reads and writes objects of varying size to/from a group of five servers. Each measurement is repeated 1,000 times; the figure reports the median and both the 2nd and the 98th percentiles. DARE has a read latency of less than $8\mu s$; the write latency is, with $15\mu s$, slightly higher because of the higher complexity of log replication. Also, Figure 7a evaluates the model described in Section 3.3.3. Of particular interest is the difference between our model and the measured write latency. In practice, the small RDMA overhead ($\approx 0.3\mu s$) implies that a slight computational overhead may cause more than $\lfloor P/2 \rfloor$ servers to go through log replication; as a result, the write latency increases.

Throughput. We analyze DARE's throughput in a group of three servers that receives requests from up to nine clients. We calculate the throughput by sampling the number of answered requests in intervals of $10ms$. For 2048-byte requests, DARE achieves a maximum throughput of 760 MiB/s for reads and 470 MiB/s for writes. Furthermore, Figure 7b shows how the throughput (for 64-byte requests) increases with the number of clients. The reason for the increase is twofold: (1) DARE handles requests from different clients asynchronously; and (2) DARE batches requests together to reduce the latency. Therefore, with 9 clients, DARE answers over 720.000 read requests per seconds and over 460.000 write requests per second.

Further, we study the effect of a dynamic group membership on DARE's performance. In particular, Figure 8a shows the write throughput (for 64-byte requests) during a series of group reconfiguration scenarios. First, two servers are subsequently joining an already full group causing the size to increase; this implies that more servers are needed for a majority; hence, the throughput decreases. Also, note that the two joins cause a brief drop in throughput, but no unavailability. Then, the leader fails causing a short period of unavailability (i.e., around $30ms$) until a new leader is elected; this is followed by a brief drop in performance when the leader detects and removes the previously failed leader.

Next, a server fails; the leader handles the failure in two steps, both bringing an increase in throughput. First, it stops replicating log entries on the server since its QPs are inaccessible; second, after a number of failed attempts to send an heartbeat (we use two in our evaluation), the leader removes the server. The removal of the failed server is followed by two other servers joining the group; note that these joins have similar effects as the previous ones. Once the group is back to a full size, the leader receives a request to decrease the size, which implies an increase in throughput.

In the new configuration, the leader fails again having a similar effect as the previous leader failure. After a new leader is elected, another server joins the group. Finally, the new leader decreases the group size to three. However, this operations entails the removal of two servers, one of them being the leader. Thus, the group is shortly unavailable until a new leader is elected.

Workloads. The results of Figure 7b are valid for either read-only or write-only client SMs; yet, usually, this is not the case. Figure 7c shows DARE's throughput when

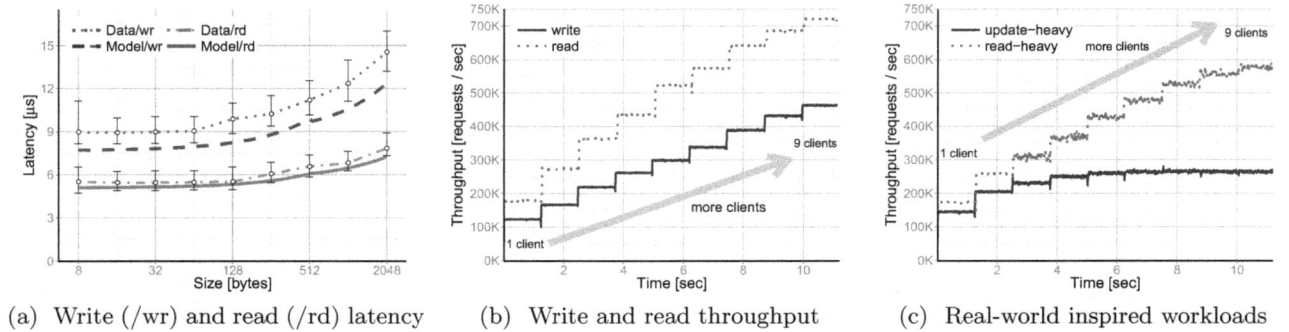

(a) Write (/wr) and read (/rd) latency   (b) Write and read throughput   (c) Real-world inspired workloads

Figure 7: Evaluation of DARE

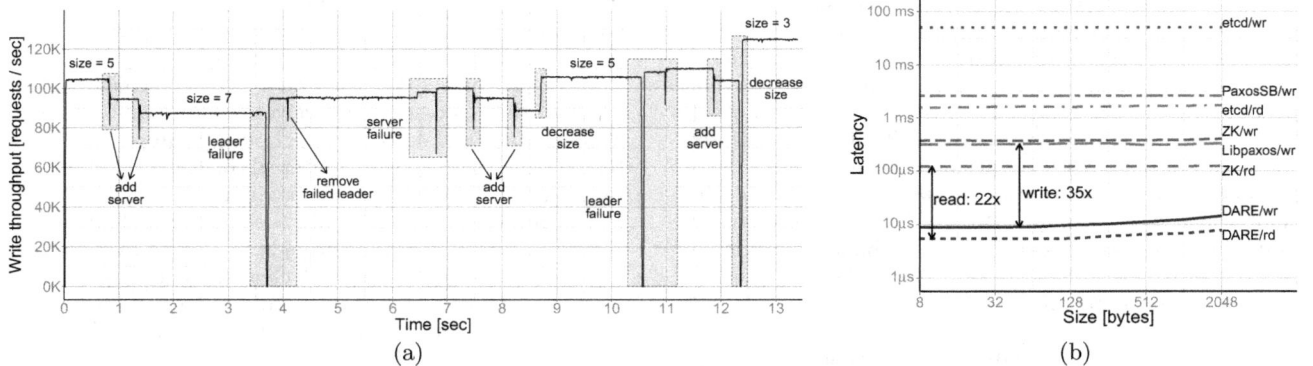

(a)   (b)

Figure 8: (a) DARE's write throughput during group reconfiguration. (b) DARE and other RSM protocols: write (/wr) and read (/rd) latency.

applying real-world inspired workloads to a group of three servers. In particular, we use two workloads: read-heavy and update-heavy [8]. The read-heavy workload consist of 95% reads; it is representative for applications such as photo tagging. The update-heavy workload consist of 50% writes; it is representative for applications such as an advertisement log that records recent user activities. For read-heavy workload, the throughput slightly fluctuates when more than one client sends requests. This is because DARE ensures linearizable semantics [19]; in particular, the leader cannot answer read requests until it answers all the preceding write requests. Also, by interleaving read and write requests, DARE cannot take advantage of batching; thus, for update-heavy workloads, the throughput saturates faster.

DARE vs. other RSMs. We conclude DARE's evaluation by comparing it with other state of the art RSM protocols and implementations. In particular, we measure the latency of four applications: ZooKeeper (ZK), a service for coordinating processes of distributed applications [20]; etcd[2], a key-value store that uses Raft [35] for reliability; and PaxosSB [23] and Libpaxos[3], both implementations of the Paxos protocol [25,26], providing support only for writes.

For each application, we implemented a benchmark that measures the request latency in a similar manner as for DARE—a single client sends requests of varying size to a group of five servers. All applications use TCP/IP for communication; to allow a fair comparison, we utilize TCP/IP

over InfiniBand ("IP over IB"). Also, for the applications that rely on stable storage, we utilize a RamDisk (an in-memory filesystem) as storage location. Figure 8b shows the request latency of the four applications on our system. For ZooKeeper, we observe a minimal read latency of $\approx 120\mu s$; the put performance depends on the disk performance, and with a RamDisk, it oscillates around $380\mu s$. In the case of etcd, a read requests takes around $1.6ms$, while a write request takes almost $50ms$. For both PaxosSB and Libpaxos, we measured only the write latency. While PaxosSB answers a write requests in around $2.6ms$, Libpaxos, with around $320\mu s$, attains a write latency lower than ZooKeeper.

In addition, Figure 8b compares our protocol against all four applications. The latency of DARE is at least 22 times lower for read accesses and 35 times lower for write accesses. Also, we evaluate DARE's write throughput against ZooKeeper; in particular, we set up an experiment were 9 clients send requests to a group of three servers. With a write throughput of ≈ 270 MiB/s, ZooKeeper is around $1.7x$ below the performance achieved by DARE. Finally, we compare DARE with the Chubby lock service [4]. Yet, since we cannot evaluate it on our system, we use the latency measurement from the original paper [4]. Chubby achieves read latencies of under 1 ms and write latencies of around 5-10 ms. Thus, DARE's performance is more than two orders of magnitude higher.

7. RELATED WORK

The importance of practical resilient services sparked numerous proposals for protocols and implementations so that

---

[2] etcd version 0.4.6: https://github.com/coreos/etcd

[3] Libpaxos3: https://bitbucket.org/sciascid/libpaxos.git

we can only discuss the most related approaches here. Starting from Lamport's original works on Paxos for solving consensus [25, 26], several practical systems have been proposed [9, 23]. Although the Paxos protocol ensures both safety and liveness, it is difficult both to understand and to implement. This led to a series of practical RSM protocols and implementations, that are at their heart similar to Paxos but simplify the protocol to foster understanding and implementability, such as Viewstamped Replication [29], Raft [35], ZooKeeper [20], and Chubby [4]. In general, DARE is different from these approaches in that it is designed for RDMA semantics instead of relying on messages. In this way, we achieve lowest latency in combination with high throughput which benefits client applications that cannot pipeline requests and require strong consistency.

Other attempts were made to increase the performance of key-value stores through RDMA; yet, they are using RDMA either as an optimization for message passing [22] or only for reading data [13, 32]. DARE uses RDMA for both read and write requests. In addition, unique features of RDMA, such as queue pair management, allow us to design wait-free protocols for normal operation.

Furthermore, a series of optimizations were proposed for solving consensus, such as distributing the load by allowing multiple servers to answer requests and answering not-interfering requests out-of-order [27, 30, 34]. While DARE does not consider these optimizations, we believe they could be added to our design with moderate effort. Also, highly scalable systems, such as distributed hash tables, offer high throughput by relaxing the consistency model [11, 28]. DARE's scalability is limited since it guarantees strong consistency for both reads and writes.

Finally, our fine-grained failure model, where remote CPUs can fail but their memory is still usable, is very similar to Disk Paxos [15]. Our work focuses on the fast implementation of this model with minimal overheads over realistic RDMA systems. Also, the idea of an in-memory RSM has been analyzed before [1, 29]. Yet, most practical systems utilize disks for saving the state on stable storage [20, 35], resulting in higher latency; while we can do this as well, we argue that it may not be necessary to achieve high reliability. Other systems reduce the latency by replacing disk storage with NVRAM; for example, CORFU uses a cluster of flash devices to offer a shared log abstraction [3]; however, it requires an RSM for reconfiguration.

8. DISCUSSION

Does it scale to thousands of servers? Leader-based RSM protocols are limited in scalability due to their dependency on consensus. Thus, DARE is intended to store metadata of more complex operations. A strategy to increase scalability would be partitioning data into multiple (reliable) DARE groups and delivering client requests through a routing mechanism [41]. Yet, routing requests that involve multiple groups would require consensus.

What about stable storage? Using stable storage, such as RAID systems, can further increase data reliability. Yet, waiting for requests to commit to disk would be too slow for normal latency-critical operations. While our protocol can easily be extended to facilitate this (one could even use additional InfiniBand disk storage or NVRAM targets directly), we currently only consider to periodically save the SM to disk. In case of a very unlikely catastrophic failure (more than half of the servers fail), one may still be able to retrieve from disk the slightly outdated SM. This is consistent with the behavior of most file-system caches today.

Can weaker consistency requirements be supported? DARE reads could be sped up significantly if any server could answer requests (not only the leader). This would also disencumber the leader who could process writes faster; yet, clients may read an outdated version of the data.

9. CONCLUSION

We demonstrate how modern RDMA networks can accelerate linearizable state machine replication by more than an order of magnitude compared to traditional TCP/IP-based protocols. Our RDMA-based RSM protocol and prototype DARE provide wait-free log replication and utilize RDMA features in innovative ways. For example, the queue pair connection management is extensively used to control log access during leader election and in failure situations.

An analysis of DARE's reliability shows that only five DARE servers are more reliable and 35x faster than storing the data on a RAID-5 system. This is mainly because an RDMA system is potentially more resilient—despite a fail-stop failure of the CPU or OS, a server is still accessible via RDMA. Our implementation allows operators to offer strongly consistent services in datacenters; we expect that RDMA-based protocols will quickly become a standard for performance-critical applications.

Acknowledgements. This work was supported by Microsoft Research through its Swiss Joint Research Centre. We thank our shepherd Jay Lofstead, the anonymous reviewers; Miguel Castro for his insightful feedback; Timo Schneider for helpful discussions; and the Systems Group at ETH Zurich for providing us the InfiniBand machine used for evaluation.

10. REFERENCES

[1] M. K. Aguilera, W. Chen, and S. Toueg. Failure detection and consensus in the crash-recovery model. *Distributed Computing*, 13(2):99–125, 2000.

[2] A. Alexandrov, M. F. Ionescu, K. E. Schauser, and C. Scheiman. LogGP: Incorporating Long Messages into the LogP Model—One Step Closer Towards a Realistic Model for Parallel Computation. In *Proc. 7th Annual ACM Symposium on Parallel Algorithms and Architectures*, SPAA '95, pages 95–105, New York, NY, USA, 1995. ACM.

[3] M. Balakrishnan, D. Malkhi, V. Prabhakaran, T. Wobber, M. Wei, and J. D. Davis. Corfu: A shared log design for flash clusters. In *Proc. 9th USENIX Conference on Networked Systems Design and Implementation*, NSDI'12, pages 1–1, Berkeley, CA, USA, 2012.

[4] M. Burrows. The Chubby Lock Service for Loosely-coupled Distributed Systems. In *Proc. 7th Symposium on Operating Systems Design and Implementation*, OSDI '06, pages 335–350, Berkeley, CA, USA, 2006.

[5] M. Castro and B. Liskov. Practical Byzantine Fault Tolerance. In *Proc. 3rd Symposium on Operating Systems Design and Implementation*, OSDI '99, pages 173–186, Berkeley, CA, USA, 1999.

[6] T. D. Chandra and S. Toueg. Unreliable Failure Detectors for Reliable Distributed Systems. *J. ACM*, 43(2):225–267, Mar. 1996.

[7] P. M. Chen, E. K. Lee, G. A. Gibson, R. H. Katz, and D. A. Patterson. RAID: High-performance, Reliable Secondary Storage. *ACM Comput. Surv.*, 26(2):145–185, June 1994.

[8] B. F. Cooper, A. Silberstein, E. Tam, R. Ramakrishnan, and R. Sears. Benchmarking Cloud Serving Systems with YCSB. In *Proc. 1st ACM Symposium on Cloud*

Computing, SoCC '10, pages 143–154, New York, NY, USA, 2010. ACM.

[9] J. C. Corbett, J. Dean, M. Epstein, A. Fikes, C. Frost, J. J. Furman, S. Ghemawat, A. Gubarev, C. Heiser, P. Hochschild, W. Hsieh, S. Kanthak, E. Kogan, H. Li, A. Lloyd, D. Melnik, D. Mwaura, D. Nagle, S. Quinlan, R. Rao, L. Rolig, Y. Saito, M. Szymaniak, C. Taylor, R. Wang, and D. Woodford. Spanner: Google's Globally-distributed Database. In *Proc. 10th USENIX Conference on Operating Systems Design and Implementation*, OSDI'12, pages 251–264, Berkeley, CA, USA, 2012.

[10] J. Dean and S. Ghemawat. MapReduce: Simplified Data Processing on Large Clusters. *Commun. ACM*, 51(1):107–113, Jan. 2008.

[11] G. DeCandia, D. Hastorun, M. Jampani, G. Kakulapati, A. Lakshman, A. Pilchin, S. Sivasubramanian, P. Vosshall, and W. Vogels. Dynamo: Amazon's Highly Available Key-value Store. *SIGOPS Oper. Syst. Rev.*, 41(6):205–220, Oct. 2007.

[12] J. Domke, T. Hoefler, and S. Matsuoka. Fail-in-place Network Design: Interaction Between Topology, Routing Algorithm and Failures. In *Proc. International Conference for High Performance Computing, Networking, Storage and Analysis*, SC '14, pages 597–608, Piscataway, NJ, USA, 2014. IEEE Press.

[13] A. Dragojević, D. Narayanan, O. Hodson, and M. Castro. FaRM: Fast Remote Memory. In *Proc. 11th USENIX Conference on Networked Systems Design and Implementation*, NSDI'14, pages 401–414, Berkeley, CA, USA, 2014.

[14] M. J. Fischer, N. A. Lynch, and M. S. Paterson. Impossibility of Distributed Consensus with One Faulty Process. *J. ACM*, 32(2):374–382, Apr. 1985.

[15] E. Gafni and L. Lamport. Disk Paxos. *Distrib. Comput.*, 16(1):1–20, Feb. 2003.

[16] R. Gerstenberger, M. Besta, and T. Hoefler. Enabling Highly-scalable Remote Memory Access Programming with MPI-3 One Sided. In *Proc. International Conference on High Performance Computing, Networking, Storage and Analysis*, SC '13, pages 53:1–53:12, New York, NY, USA, 2013. ACM.

[17] Global Scientific Information and Computing Center. Failure History of TSUBAME2.0 and TSUBAME2.5, 2014.

[18] E. Heien, D. Kondo, A. Gainaru, D. LaPine, B. Kramer, and F. Cappello. Modeling and Tolerating Heterogeneous Failures in Large Parallel Systems. In *Proc. of 2011 International Conference for High Performance Computing, Networking, Storage and Analysis*, SC '11, pages 45:1–45:11, New York, NY, USA, 2011. ACM.

[19] M. P. Herlihy and J. M. Wing. Linearizability: A Correctness Condition for Concurrent Objects. *ACM Trans. Program. Lang. Syst.*, 12(3):463–492, July 1990.

[20] P. Hunt, M. Konar, F. P. Junqueira, and B. Reed. ZooKeeper: Wait-free Coordination for Internet-scale Systems. In *Proc. 2010 USENIX Conference on USENIX Annual Technical Conference*, USENIX ATC'10, pages 11–11, Berkeley, CA, USA, 2010.

[21] InfiniBand Trade Association. *InfiniBand Architecture Specification: Volume 1, Release 1.2.1*. 2007.

[22] J. Jose, H. Subramoni, M. Luo, M. Zhang, J. Huang, M. Wasi-ur Rahman, N. S. Islam, X. Ouyang, H. Wang, S. Sur, and D. K. Panda. Memcached Design on High Performance RDMA Capable Interconnects. In *Proc. 2011 International Conference on Parallel Processing*, ICPP '11, pages 743–752, Washington, DC, USA, 2011.

[23] J. Kirsch and Y. Amir. Paxos for System Builders: An Overview. In *Proc. 2nd Workshop on Large-Scale Distributed Systems and Middleware*, LADIS '08, pages 3:1–3:6, New York, NY, USA, 2008. ACM.

[24] L. Lamport. The implementation of reliable distributed multiprocess systems. *Computer Networks (1976)*, 2(2):95 – 114, 1978.

[25] L. Lamport. The Part-time Parliament. *ACM Trans. Comput. Syst.*, 16(2):133–169, May 1998.

[26] L. Lamport. Paxos Made Simple. *SIGACT News*, 32(4):51–58, Dec. 2001.

[27] L. Lamport. Generalized Consensus and Paxos, 2005.

[28] T. Li, X. Zhou, K. Brandstatter, D. Zhao, K. Wang, A. Rajendran, Z. Zhang, and I. Raicu. ZHT: A Light-Weight Reliable Persistent Dynamic Scalable Zero-Hop Distributed Hash Table. In *Proc. 2013 IEEE 27th International Symposium on Parallel and Distributed Processing*, IPDPS '13, pages 775–787, Washington, DC, USA, 2013.

[29] B. Liskov and J. Cowling. Viewstamped Replication Revisited. Technical Report MIT-CSAIL-TR-2012-021, MIT, July 2012.

[30] Y. Mao, F. P. Junqueira, and K. Marzullo. Mencius: Building Efficient Replicated State Machines for WANs. In *Proc. 8th USENIX Conference on Operating Systems Design and Implementation*, OSDI'08, pages 369–384, Berkeley, CA, USA, 2008.

[31] C. D. Martino, F. Baccanico, Z. Kalbarczyk, R. Iyer, J. Fullop, and W. Kramer. Lessons Learned From the Analysis of System Failures at Petascale: The Case of Blue Waters. Jun 2014.

[32] C. Mitchell, Y. Geng, and J. Li. Using One-sided RDMA Reads to Build a Fast, CPU-efficient Key-value Store. In *Proc. 2013 USENIX Conference on Annual Technical Conference*, USENIX ATC'13, pages 103–114, Berkeley, CA, USA, 2013.

[33] A. Moody, G. Bronevetsky, K. Mohror, and B. R. d. Supinski. Design, Modeling, and Evaluation of a Scalable Multi-level Checkpointing System. In *Proc. 2010 ACM/IEEE International Conference for High Performance Computing, Networking, Storage and Analysis*, SC '10, pages 1–11, Washington, DC, USA, 2010.

[34] I. Moraru, D. G. Andersen, and M. Kaminsky. There is More Consensus in Egalitarian Parliaments. In *Proc. 24th ACM Symposium on Operating Systems Principles*, SOSP '13, pages 358–372, New York, NY, USA, 2013. ACM.

[35] D. Ongaro and J. Ousterhout. In Search of an Understandable Consensus Algorithm. In *2014 USENIX Annual Technical Conference*, USENIX ATC'14, Philadelphia, PA, June 2014.

[36] E. Pinheiro, W.-D. Weber, and L. A. Barroso. Failure Trends in a Large Disk Drive Population. In *Proc. 5th USENIX Conference on File and Storage Technologies*, FAST '07, pages 2–2, Berkeley, CA, USA, 2007.

[37] J. S. Plank, A. L. Buchsbaum, and B. T. Vander Zanden. Minimum Density RAID-6 Codes. *Trans. Storage*, 6(4):16:1–16:22, June 2011.

[38] M. Poke and T. Hoefler. DARE: High-Performance State Machine Replication on RDMA Networks (Extended Version). http://spcl.inf.ethz.ch/Research/Parallel_Programming/DARE, 2015.

[39] K. Sato, N. Maruyama, K. Mohror, A. Moody, T. Gamblin, B. R. de Supinski, and S. Matsuoka. Design and Modeling of a Non-blocking Checkpointing System. In *Proc. International Conference on High Performance Computing, Networking, Storage and Analysis*, SC '12, pages 19:1–19:10, Los Alamitos, CA, USA, 2012.

[40] F. B. Schneider. Implementing Fault-tolerant Services Using the State Machine Approach: A Tutorial. *ACM Comput. Surv.*, 22(4):299–319, Dec. 1990.

[41] P. Unterbrunner, G. Alonso, and D. Kossmann. High Availability, Elasticity, and Strong Consistency for Massively Parallel Scans over Relational Data. *The VLDB Journal*, 23(4):627–652, Aug. 2014.

High Impact Computing: Computing for Science and the Science of Computing

Ewa Deelman
Information Sciences Institute
University of Southern California

Abstract

Modern science often requires the processing and analysis of vast amounts of data in search of postulated phenomena, and the validation of core principles through the simulation of complex system behaviors and interactions. This is the case in fields such as astronomy, bioinformatics, physics, and climate and ocean modeling, and others. In order to support the computational and data needs of today's science, new knowledge must be gained on how to deliver the growing high-performance and distributed computing resources to the scientist's desktop in an accessible, reliable and scalable way. In over a decade of working with domain scientists, the Pegasus project has developed tools and techniques that automate the computational processes used in data- and compute-intensive research. Among them is the scientific workflow management system, Pegasus, which is being used by researchers to model seismic wave propagation, to discover new celestial objects, to study RNA critical to human brain development, and to investigate other important research questions.

This talk will review the conception and evolution of the Pegasus research program. It will touch upon the role of scientific workflow systems in advancing science, and will give specific examples of how the Pegasus Workflow Management System has done so. It will describe how the Pegasus project has adapted to changes in application needs and to advances in high performance and distributed computing systems. It will discuss the interleaving of Computer Science research and software development and how each benefits from the other while providing value to other science domains. The talk will also stress the importance of forming collaborations, both within Computer Science and with other disciplines, to help solve real-world problems and have fun along way.

HPDC'15, June 15–20, 2015, Portland, Oregon, USA.
ACM 978-1-4503-3489-1/15/06.
http://dx.doi.org/10.1145/2749246.2749247

Categories and Subject Descriptors:
D.1.0 [Software]: Programming Techniques

Keywords
Science workflows; distributed computing

Bio

Dr. Ewa Deelman is a Research Associate Professor at the USC Computer Science Department and the Assistant Director of Science Automation Technologies at the USC Information Sciences Institute. Dr. Deelman's research interests include the design and exploration of collaborative, distributed scientific environments, with particular emphasis on workflow management as well as the management of large amounts of data and metadata. In 2007, Dr. Deelman edited a book: "Workflows in e-Science: Scientific Workflows for Grids", published by Springer. She is also the founder of the annual Workshop on Workflows in Support of Large-Scale Science, which is held in conjunction with the Super Computing conference. In 1997 Dr. Deelman received her PhD in Computer Science from the Rensselaer Polytechnic Institute.

Acknowledgements

This work is funded by the National Science Foundation under grant # 1148515.

References

[1] Ewa Deelman, Karan Vahi, Gideon Juve, Mats Rynge, Scott Callaghan, Philip J Maechling, Rajiv Mayani, Weiwei Chen, Rafael Ferreira da Silva, Miron Livny and Kent Wenger, Pegasus: a Workflow Management System for Science Automation, Future Generation Computer Systems, 46, pp. 17-35, 2015.

[2] Ewa Deelman, Gurmeet Singh, Mei-Hui Su, James Blythe, Yolanda Gil, Carl Kesselman, Gaurang Mehta, Karan Vahi, G. Bruce Berriman, John Good, Anastasia Laity, Joseph C. Jacob and Daniel S. Katz, Pegasus: a Framework for Mapping Complex Scientific Workflows onto Distributed Systems, Scientific Programming Journal, 13:3, pp. 219-237, 2005.

Practical Resource Management in Power-Constrained, High Performance Computing

Tapasya Patki, David K. Lowenthal
University of Arizona
{tpatki,dkl}@email.arizona.edu

Anjana Sasidharan*
Amazon, Inc.
anjans@amazon.com

Matthias Maiterth
Ludwig Maximilian University
maiterth@nm.ifi.lmu.de

Barry L. Rountree, Martin Schulz, Bronis R. de Supinski
Lawrence Livermore National Laboratory
{rountree4,schulz6,bronis}@llnl.gov

ABSTRACT

Power management is one of the key research challenges on the path to exascale. Supercomputers today are designed to be worst-case power provisioned, leading to two main problems — limited application performance and under-utilization of procured power.

In this paper, we propose RMAP, a practical, low-overhead resource manager targeted at future power-constrained clusters. The goals for RMAP are to improve application performance as well as system power utilization, and thus minimize the average turnaround time for all jobs. Within RMAP, we design and analyze an adaptive policy, which derives job-level power bounds in a fair-share manner and supports *overprovisioning* and *power-aware backfilling*. Our results show that our new policy increases system power utilization while adhering to strict job-level power bounds and leads to 31% (19% on average) and 54% (36% on average) faster average turnaround time when compared to worst-case provisioning and naive overprovisioning respectively.

Categories and Subject Descriptors

C.4 [**Computer Systems Organization**]: Performance of Systems

Keywords

Power-constrained HPC, Resource Management

1. INTRODUCTION

The Department of Energy (DoE) has set an ambitious target of achieving an exaflop under 20 MW. While procur-

---

*This work was carried out when Ms. Sasidharan was a student at the University of Arizona and is not endorsed by Amazon, Inc.

ing this amount of power poses a problem, utilizing it efficiently is an even bigger challenge. Supercomputers today are typically targeted toward High Performance Linpack-like applications [34] and designed to be *worst-case provisioned*—all nodes in the system can run at peak power simultaneously, and thus applications are allocated all available power on a node. However, most real HPC applications do not use their allocated power, leading to inefficient use of both nodes and power.

An example of this can be found in data that we collected on Vulcan (see Figure 1), which is a high-end BlueGene/Q system located at Lawrence Livermore National Laboratory (LLNL). Vulcan is the ninth-fastest supercomputer in the world, and has procured power of 2.4 MW. However, our study shows that over a 16-month period, applications used only 1.47 MW on average with the only exception being the burn-in phase. This under-utilization of power has many negative ramifications, such as the use of lower water temperature than needed for cooling—which leads to additional power wasted on water chillers.

Ideally, supercomputing centers should utilize the procured power fully to accomplish more useful science. *Hardware overprovisioning* (or overprovisioning, for short) has recently been proposed as an alternative approach for designing power-limited supercomputers and improving performance [32,39]. The basic idea is to buy more compute capacity (nodes) than can be fully powered under the power constraint, and then reconfigure the system dynamically based on application characteristics such as scalability and memory intensity. Prior work has shown that on a dedicated cluster system, overprovisioning can improve individual application performance by up to 62% (32% on average) [32].

Initial research in the area explored managing resources on overprovisioned systems by deploying Integer Linear Programming (ILP) techniques to maximize throughput of data centers under a strict power budget [38]. While an interesting research approach, the proposed algorithm is not fair-share and is not sufficiently practical for deployment on a real HPC cluster. This is because each per-job scheduling decision involves solving an NP-hard ILP formulation, incurring a high scheduling overhead and limiting scalability. Additionally, ILP-based algorithms may lead to low resource utilization as well as resource fragmentation, which are major concerns for high-end supercomputing centers [13,17,18, 21]. While allowing jobs to be *malleable* (change node counts to grow/shrink at runtime) might help address some of these problems, less than 1% of scientific HPC applications are expected to support malleability due to the data migration, domain decomposition and scalability issues involved.

We present the design and implementation of *RMAP* (Resource MAnager for Power), a practical resource manager with minimal scheduling overhead ($O(1)$) that targets future power-constrained, overprovisioned systems. This paper focuses on the design, implementation, and comparison of three policies within *RMAP*: a baseline policy for safe execution under a power bound; a naive policy that uses overprovisioning; and an adaptive policy that is designed to improve application performance by using overprovisioning in a power-aware manner. The goal of the latter strategy is to provide faster job turnaround times as well as to increase overall system resource utilization. We accomplish this by introducing *power-aware backfilling*, a simple, greedy algorithm that allows us to trade some performance benefits of overprovisioning to utilize power better and to reduce job queuing times.

We make the following contributions in this paper:

- We design two novel policies with overprovisioning for which *RMAP* derives the job-level power bound based on a "fair share" strategy. The first is the *Naive* policy, which tries to find the best performing *configuration* under the derived job-level power bound. The second is an adaptive policy, which uses power-aware backfilling to optimize for average turnaround time as well as to improve power utilization. We refer to this policy as the *Adaptive* policy for the rest of this paper.

- We develop and validate a model to predict execution time and total power consumption for a given application configuration, in order to support overprovisioning within *RMAP*. Our model uses less than 10% of the data for training, and the average errors for both performance and power prediction are under 10%.

- We demonstrate that the *Adaptive* policy leads to better overall turnaround times, adjusts to different job trace types and varying global power bounds, and improves system power utilization. We also show that users can improve job turnaround times further by altruistically allowing some degradation in their execution time.

Our simple baseline policy, the *Traditional* policy, guarantees safe, correct execution under a power-constraint for systems that are not overprovisioned. The *Adaptive* policy provides 19% and 36% better average per-job turnaround time than the *Traditional* and *Naive* policies respectively. Since the *Naive* policy performs worse than the *Traditional* policy, power-constrained environments require policies such as the *Adaptive* policy.

The rest of the paper is organized as follows. Section 2 motivates our work. Sections 3 to 5 present the design and implementation of *RMAP* and our model. We discuss our results in Sections 6 and 7. We describe related work in Section 8 and summarize in Section 9.

2. MOTIVATION

This section motivates the need for overprovisioning-based scheduling. We discuss power profiles of HPC applications and show that applications do not use the allocated power efficiently. We then discuss hardware overprovisioning.

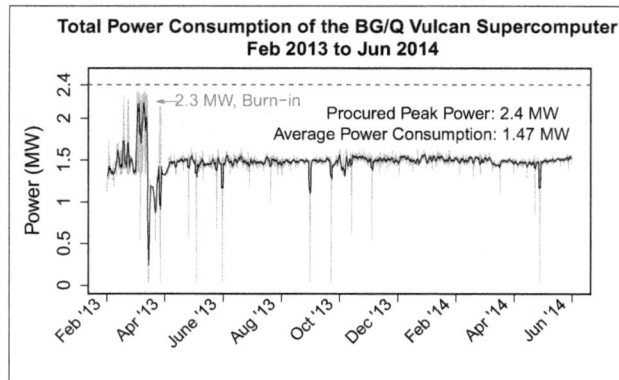

Figure 1: Power Consumption on Vulcan

2.1 HPC Application Power Profiles

In order to study HPC application power profiles, we selected eight strongly-scaled, load-balanced, hybrid MPI + OpenMP applications (described below) and gathered power and performance data for these at 64 nodes on the *Cab* cluster at LLNL. *Cab* is a 1,200-node, Intel Sandy Bridge cluster, with 2 sockets per node and 8 cores per socket. We measured per-socket power with Intel's *Running Average Power Limit* (RAPL) technology [23, 36]. The maximum power available on each socket was 115 W. We only measured socket power, as support to measure memory power was not available due to BIOS restrictions.

We used four real HPC applications for our study. These include SPhot [27] from the ASC Purple suite [26], and BT-MZ, SP-MZ and LU-MZ from the NAS suite [1]. SPhot is a 2D photon transport code that solves the Boltzmann transport equation. The NAS Multi-zone benchmarks are derived from Computational Fluid Dynamics (CFD) applications. BT-MZ is a the Block Tri-diagonal solver, SP-MZ is the Scalar Penta-diagonal solver, and LU-MZ is the Lower-Upper Gauss Seidel Solver. We used Class D inputs for NAS, and for SPhot, the NRuns parameter was set to 16,384.

We also used four synthetic benchmarks in our dataset to cover the extreme cases in the application space. These are (1) Scalable and CPU-bound (SC), (2) Not Scalable and CPU-bound (NSC), (3) Scalable and Memory-bound (SM), and (4) Not Scalable and Memory-bound (NSM). The CPU-bound benchmarks run a simple spin loop, and the memory-bound benchmarks perform a vector copy in reverse order. Scalability is controlled by adding `MPI_Alltoall` communication. We used MVAPICH2 version 1.7 and compiled all codes with the Intel compiler version 12.1.5. We used the scatter policy for OpenMP threads.

Figure 2 shows data for application power consumption for the eight applications running at 64 nodes, 16 cores per node, and maximum power per node. Each bar represents the average power consumption per socket (averaged over 128 sockets on 64 nodes) for an application. The minimum and maximum power consumed per socket by the application are denoted by error bars. While all applications were allocated 115 W per socket, they only used between 66 W (NSC) to 93 W (SPMZ). On average, they only used 81 W or 71% of the allocated socket power.

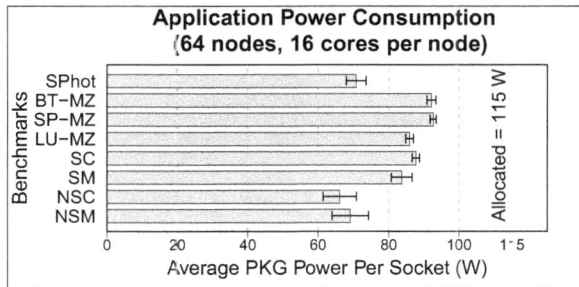

Figure 2: Application Power Consumption

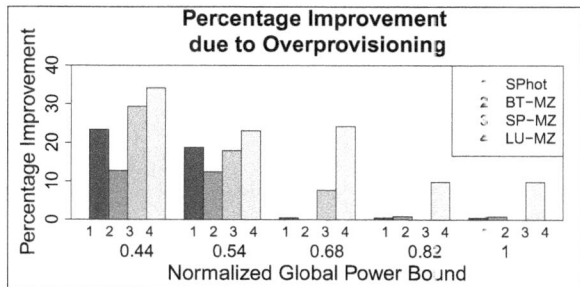

Figure 3: Performance with Overprovisioning

2.2 Hardware Overprovisioning

A cluster is *hardware overprovisioned* with respect to power if it has more nodes than it can fully power simultaneously. Such a cluster can essentially be "reconfigured" based on an application's memory-boundedness and scalability

The hardware cost for an overprovisioned system depends on the cost of the underlying processor architecture. For example, if more high-end processors are purchased, the hardware cost will increase; however, the system may be more efficient overall because more jobs will complete in its lifetime. The cost might *not* increase, though: power-inefficient processors typically have a lower unit price than power-efficient processors. Thus, a hardware cost budget provides a choice between more power-inefficient processors leading to better job throughput and performance under a power constraint, or fewer, power-efficient nodes on a non- overprovisioned cluster (which may lead to wasted power).

The benefits of overprovisioning rely on determining a *configuration*, $(n \times c, p)$ that leads to the best performance under a power bound, where n is the number of nodes, c is the number of cores per node, and p is the power per socket. This benefit requires that applications are somewhat flexible in terms of the number of nodes and/or the number of cores per node on which they can run (*moldable*).

We emulated overprovisioning by enforcing socket-level power caps with Intel's RAPL technology. The minimum RAPL socket power cap that we could enforce (within the processor's specification) was 51 W, and the maximum power cap was 115 W. We ran our applications with five package power values—51 W, 65 W, 80 W, 95 W, and 115 W. We gathered data for each configuration from 8 to 64 nodes (increments of 4) and 8 to 16 cores per node (increments of 2). We disabled Turbo Boost when we enforced power caps, except for the 115 W power bound, for which we enabled Turbo Boost. The highest non-Turbo frequency was 2.6 GHz, and the highest Turbo frequency was 3.3 GHz.

The maximum global power bound for our cluster was $64 \times 2 \times 115\ W$, which is 14,720 W. In order to analyze various degrees of overprovisioning, we chose five global power bounds for our study—6,500 W, 8,000 W, 10,000 W, 12,000 W and 14,720 W. These were determined by the product of (1) the number of nodes and (2) the minimum and maximum package power caps possible per socket (51 W and 115 W). With n_{max} being the maximum number of nodes that one can run at peak power without exceeding the power bound, the worst-case provisioned configuration is $(n_{max} \times 16, 115)$.

We measured execution time and total power consumed for each of the benchmarks in the configuration space discussed earlier. Figure 3 shows results of overprovisioning

when compared to worst-case provisioning for four HPC benchmarks at the five global power bounds discussed above. The x-axis is normalized to the worst-case provisioned power (14,720 W). For our dataset, we saw a maximum improvement of 34% (11% on average) in performance compared to worst-case provisioning. Note that choosing the correct application-specific configuration is important even when there is no global power bound, as shown by LU-MZ at 14,720 W and is increasingly critical under a power constraint. Previous results have indicated that overprovisioning can improve performance by up to 62% [32,39].

3. POWER-AWARE SCHEDULING

This section discusses HPC scheduling basics and backfilling. We then discuss the design challenges for *RMAP* and present the details of our three scheduling policies.

3.1 Basics

Users at HPC sites typically submit jobs by specifying a node count and an estimated runtime. The job executes when the resource manager acquires the specified number of nodes; the estimated runtime is used to set a deadline ($t_{deadline}$) for the job. The job is killed if it exceeds this deadline. Depending on the job-size, most HPC users are required to use specific partitions. For example, most high-end clusters have a *small* debug partition that specifically targets small-sized jobs, and a general-purpose *batch* partition for medium and large-sized jobs.

Resource requests are maintained in a *job queue*, and users are allocated dedicated nodes based on a scheduling policy. One such policy is First-Come First-Serve (FCFS), which services jobs strictly in the order they arrive. FCFS tends to cause a convoy effect when a job requesting more resources (large node count) ends up blocking several other smaller jobs. Policies that do not dedicate nodes to jobs, such as *gang scheduling* [4,15,40], are not feasible on supercomputers because memory demands for HPC applications are typically quite high—which leads to large paging costs[1].

3.2 Backfilling

Backfilling [24,29,30,42] addresses the convoy effect caused by FCFS by executing smaller jobs out of order on idle nodes and by improving utilization—in turn reducing the overall average turnaround time. Backfilling has two variants: *easy* and *conservative*. Easy backfilling allows short jobs to execute out of order as long as they do not delay the *first* queued job. Conservative backfilling, on the other hand, only lets

---

[1]Many HPC sites use operating systems that do not page.

short jobs move ahead if they do not delay *any* queued job. Easy backfilling performs better for most workloads [30].

Backfilling frequently uses a greedy algorithm that picks the *first-fit* from the job queue. The *first-fit* might not always be the *best-fit*, and a job further down the queue may fit the hole being backfilled better. Finding the *best-fit* involves scanning the entire job queue, which increases job scheduling overhead significantly [41].

3.3 Design Challenges

Power-aware schedulers must enforce job-level power bounds as they manage and allocate nodes. They need to optimize for overall system throughput as well as individual job performance under the job-level power bounds, which means they must minimize the amount of unused (leftover) power.

For simplicity, we assume that all jobs have equal priority, use MPI+OpenMP, and are moldable (not restrictive in terms of the number of nodes on which they can be executed). We also assume that the global power bound on the cluster is $P_{cluster}$, and that the cluster has $N_{cluster}$ nodes. We derive a power bound for each job fairly by allocating it a fraction of $P_{cluster}$ based on the fraction of $N_{cluster}$ that it requested (n_{req} being the number of requested nodes). Thus, $P_{job} = \frac{n_{req}}{N_{cluster}} \times P_{cluster}$.

This allocation for P_{job} can be extended easily to a priority-based system by using weights (w_{prio}) for the power allocation. Thus, $P_{job} = w_{prio} \times \frac{n_{req}}{N_{cluster}} \times P_{cluster}$. For example, higher priority jobs could be allocated more power by using $w_{prio} > 1$, and lower priority jobs could be allocated using $w_{prio} < 1$. This paper does not explore priorities further.

At any given point in time (say t), the available power in the cluster, P_{avail_t}, can be calculated by subtracting the total power consumption of running jobs from the cluster level power bound. P_{avail_t} is used to make power-aware scheduling decisions. Thus for r running jobs at time t,

$$P_{avail_t} = P_{cluster} - \sum_{j=1}^{r} P_{job\_j}$$

The performance of an individual job can be optimized by using overprovisioning with respect to the job-level power bound, P_{job}. To optimize system throughput and to minimize unused power, a scheduler could (1) dynamically redistribute the unused power to jobs that are currently executing, or (2) suboptimally schedule the next job with the unused (available) power and nodes.

Dynamically redistributing power to executing jobs to improve performance can be challenging, mostly because allocating more power per node may result in limited benefits (see Figure 2). In order to improve performance and to utilize power better, the system may have to change the number of nodes (or cores per node) at runtime. However, varying the node count at runtime (malleability) is not possible with the current MPI standard. In addition, dynamically changing the node and core counts of a job would incur data decomposition and migration overhead [25].

We explore extensions of traditional backfilling for a power-aware scenario. Traditional backfilling attempts to utilize as many nodes as possible in the cluster by breaking the FCFS order. Similarly, our new greedy approach, *power-aware backfilling*, attempts to use as much global power as possible by scheduling a job with currently available power. Most cases involve sacrificing some performance benefits attained from overprovisioning. The key idea is to schedule

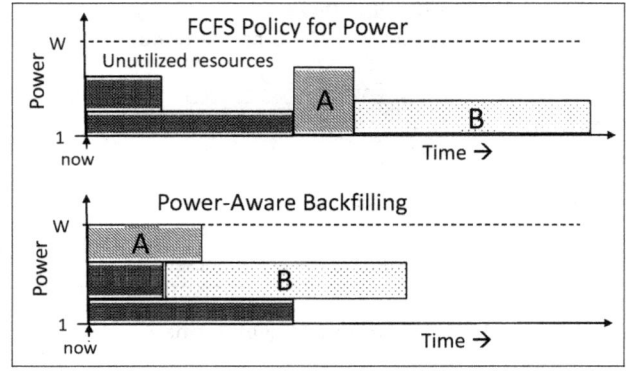

Figure 4: Advantage of Power-Aware Backfilling

a job with less power than was requested (derived using fair share) and schedule it with a suboptimal configuration, and to do so with execution time guarantees. Power-aware backfilling can adapt to extremely power-constrained scenarios and to scenarios with too much leftover power. Our approach builds on standard backfilling.

Figure 4 shows an example in which we assume that jobs A and B are currently waiting in the queue. Job A requested more power than is currently available in the system. Traditionally, Job A waits in the queue until enough power is available, which wastes resources. Our approach schedules Job A immediately with the *available* power. While we increase the execution time of Job A, our approach improves the overall turnaround time of Job A as well as the other jobs in the queue, and utilizes power better.

The key idea is to use power-aware backfilling while adhering to the user-specified time deadline for the job. Overprovisioning under a job-level power bound will often exceed the user's performance expectations. However, allowing users to specify a maximum slowdown for their job and thus trade their job's execution time for a faster turnaround time is an added incentive. We focus primarily on trading some of the benefits obtained from overprovisioning to utilize all available power to run jobs faster and to schedule more jobs.

Keeping cluster resources utilized (both nodes and power) via backfilling leads to better average turnaround times for the jobs, which in turn increases throughput. We thus focus on minimizing the average per-job turnaround time in this paper. The policy that we develop is called the *Adaptive* policy, and we discuss it in the next section.

3.4 Scheduling Policies

We now discuss the power-aware scheduling policies that we implemented in *RMAP*. Each of these policies needs to obtain job configuration information given a power bound. The details of how these configurations are determined are presented in Sections 4 and 5, which discuss the low level implementation details and the model.

Users specify nodes and time as input, along with an optional threshold value for the *Adaptive* policy. We derive, P_{job}, which is the job-level power bound based on the user input, as discussed in the previous subsection. This job-level power bound is an input to our scheduling policies (see Table 1). All three policies use basic node-level backfilling.

Policy	Input to Policy	Description
Traditional	(n_{req}, t_{req})	Pick the *packed* configuration $(c = 16, p = max = 115W)$
Naive	(P_{job}, t_{req})	Pick the optimal configuration under the derived job power limit
Adaptive	$(P_{job}, t_{req}, thresh)$	Use power-aware backfilling to select a configuration

Table 1: Job Scheduling Policies

ID	Configuration $(n \times c, p)$	Total Power (W)	Time (s)
C1	$(6 \times 16, max = 115)$	796.4	447.9
C2	$(8 \times 12, 65)$	783.8	415.3
C3	$(8 \times 10, 80)$	738.2	439.2

Table 2: List of Configurations for SP-MZ

3.4.1 The *Traditional* Policy

In this policy, the user is allocated a configuration with their requested node count that uses all available cores on a node at maximum possible power. A job that requests large node counts may exceed the system's global power bound. In this case, the *Traditional* policy allocates as many nodes (with all cores on the node and maximum power per node) as it can to the job without exceeding the system-wide budget (an unfair job-level power allocation). Alternatively, we could reject the job due to power constraints.

More formally, let c_{max} be the maximum number of cores per socket, p_{max} the maximum package power per socket, $P_{(n \times c, p)}$ the total power consumed by the job in the $(n \times c, p)$ configuration, and $P_{cluster}$ the global power bound on the cluster. Then, for a job requesting n_{req} nodes for time t_{req}, the *Traditional* policy allocates the $(n_{req} \times c_{max}, p_{max})$ configuration if $P_{(n_{req} \times c_{max}, p_{max})} \leq P_{cluster}$.

Otherwise, it allocates the $(n_{max} \times c_{max}, p_{max})$ configuration to the job, where n_{max} is the maximum n such that $P_{(n \times c_{max}, p_{max})} \leq P_{cluster}$.

Note that the job will have to wait in the queue if enough resources (nodes and power) are not available when the scheduling decision is being made (if $P_{avail_t} < P_{job}$).

3.4.2 The *Naive* policy

In this policy, we overprovision with respect to the job-level power bound. Given the derived job-level power bound, $P_{job} \leq P_{cluster}$, and an estimated runtime, t_{req}, the *Naive* policy allocates the $(n \times c, p)$ configuration that leads to the best time t_{act} under that power bound. Thus, $t_{act} = min(T)$, where $T = \{t_{(n \times c, p)} : P_{(n \times c, p)} \leq P_{job}\}$.

If $t_{act} > t_{req}$, the system sets the deadline $t_{deadline}$ for the job to t_{act} instead of t_{req} during job launch, so that the job does not get killed prematurely. This scenario occurs if the user's performance estimates are inaccurate and cannot be met with the derived power bound, and the best performance level that the *Naive* policy can provide under the specified power bound P_{job} is worse than t_{req}. In the scenario that $t_{act} < t_{req}$, $t_{deadline}$ is not updated until job termination. *RMAP* will kill the job after $t_{deadline}$. The main purpose for t_{req} is to have a valid deadline in case the job fails or crashes. User studies suggest that t_{req} is often over-estimated (by up to 20%) [44].

Again, note that the job may have to wait in the queue until enough power is available to schedule it.

3.4.3 The *Adaptive* policy

This policy's goal is to allow (1) users to receive better turnaround time for their jobs, and (2) the system to minimize the amount of unused power to achieve better average turnaround time for all jobs. Similar to the *Naive* policy,

the inputs are a (derived) job-level power bound and duration. However, the *Adaptive* policy considers these values as suggested and uses power-aware backfilling. It also trades the raw execution time of the application as specified by the user for potentially shorter turnaround times. The user can specify an optional *threshold (th)*, which denotes the percentage slowdown that the job can tolerate. When *th* is not specified, we assume that it is zero (no slowdown).

The *Adaptive* policy uses the suggested job-level power bound to check if the requested amount of power is currently available. If so, it obtains the best configuration under this power bound (similar to the *Naive* policy). If not, it determines a suboptimal configuration based on currently available power and the threshold value. The advantage for the user is that the job wait time may be significantly reduced. The administrative advantage is better resource utilization (in terms of nodes and overall power) and throughput.

More specifically, if $P_{avail_t} > P_{job}$, the *Adaptive* policy uses the same mechanism as the *Naive* policy. However, when $P_{avail_t} < P_{job}$, it determines $t_{act} = min(T)$, where $T = \{t_{(n \times c, p)} : P_{(n \times c, p)} \leq P_{avail_t}\}$, and schedules the job immediately with the $(n \times c, p)$ configuration with time t_{act} as long as $t_{act} <= (1 + th) \times t_{req}$. Thus, the job's wait time is reduced while meeting the performance requirement.

3.5 Example

As an example, consider SP-MZ from the NAS Multizone benchmark suite [1]. Some configurations for SP-MZ (Class C) are listed in Table 2. We now discuss three scenarios in which 750 W of power and 10 nodes are available in the cluster, and job A that is currently executing terminates in 1000s. Also, a user has requested 6 nodes for 450s, and, the derived job-level power bound is 800 W.

3.5.1 Scenario 1, Traditional Policy

Here, *RMAP* allocates configuration C1 to the job but it waits until job A terminates and enough power is available.

3.5.2 Scenario 2, Naive Policy

RMAP allocates configuration C2 to the job but also waits until job A terminates and enough power is available.

3.5.3 Scenario 3, Adaptive Policy (threshold=0%)

A threshold value of 0% means that the user cannot compromise on performance. Under the *Adaptive* policy, *RMAP* checks if enough power (800 W) is available in the system. It then determines that C3 does not violate the performance constraint (450s), and job A can be launched immediately with the currently available power (750 W). We distinguish this case from Scenario 2, which will *always* pick C2.

Picking C3 reduces the wait time of the job significantly (by 1000s). Also, in scenarios 1 and 2, 750 W of power is wasted for 1000s. In this scenario, power is utilized more efficiently and turnaround time for the job is reduced.

125

Field	Description
id	Unique Index (Primary)
job_id	Application ID
nodes	Number of nodes
cores	Number of cores per node
pkg_cap	PKG Power Cap
exec_time	Execution Time
tot_pkg	Total PKG Power

Table 3: Schema for Job Details Table

4. RMAP IMPLEMENTATION

We implemented *RMAP* within the widely-used, open source resource manager for HPC clusters, SLURM [45]. SLURM is used on several Top500 [2] supercomputers. It provides a standard framework for launching, managing and monitoring jobs on parallel architectures. The slurmctld daemon runs on the head node of a cluster and manages resource allocation. Each compute node runs the slurmd daemon for launching tasks. Slurmdbd, which also runs on the head node, collects accounting information with the help of a MySQL interface to the slurm_acct_db database.

As described earlier, *RMAP* supports overprovisioning and implements three power-aware scheduling policies that adhere to a global, system-wide power budget. We refer to our extension of SLURM as P-SLURM. RMAP can similarly be implemented within other resource managers.

Our scheduling policies require the ability to produce execution times for a given configuration under a job-level power bound. Table 3 shows the information that P-SLURM requires. We refer to this as the job_details_table, and we added this table to the existing slurm_acct_db. Values for exec_time and tot_pkg can be measured or predicted.

We developed a model to predict the performance and total power consumed for application configurations in order to populate this table. Section 5 presents the details of this model. Furthermore, to understand and to analyze the benefits of having exact application knowledge, we also included another table within the SLURM database (with the same schema) that contains an exhaustive set of empirically measured values (as per the details discussed in Section 2). For simplicity, we populated both tables in advance and the scheduler queried the database for information when making decisions, making the decision complexity O(1). The model can also be used to generate values dynamically without needing a database. However, this may incur scheduling overhead and call for advanced space-search algorithm implementations within the scheduler (such as hill climbing). We do not address this issue in this paper.

5. PREDICTING PERFORMANCE AND POWER

In this section, we discuss the models that *RMAP* deploys in its policies. The models predict execution time and total power consumed for a given configuration (number of nodes, number of cores per node, and power cap per socket). As discussed in Section 2, we first collected exhaustive power and performance information. We ranged the node counts from 8 to 64, core counts from 8 to 16, and power from 51 W to 115 W. The dataset that we built contained 2840

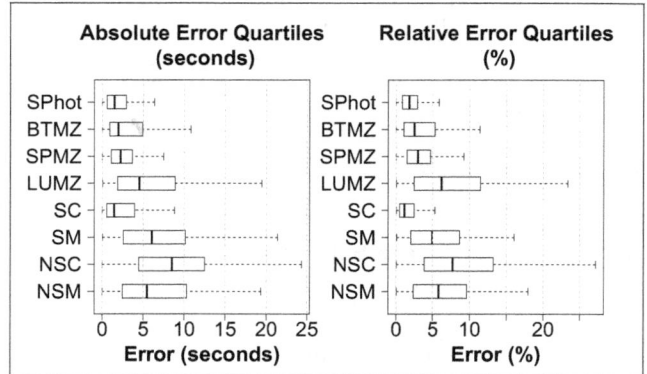

Figure 5: Error Quartiles of Regression Model

data points, with 5 different power caps, 15 different node counts, 5 different core counts per node and 8 applications.

We used 10% of this data for training and obtained application-specific linear regression parameters that allow us to predict application execution time and total package power consumption at a given configuration. We used a logarithmic polynomial regression of degree two. We limited our power predictions to package power only as memory power measurements were unavailable on our cluster.

We validated our models with our previously measured data. When using only 10% of the data for model training, the average error for execution time is below 10%, and the maximum error is below 33%. Figure 5 shows the absolute (seconds) and relative (percentage) error quartiles for all benchmarks when predicting execution time at arbitrary configurations. For all benchmarks, the third quartile is under 13%, and the median is below 8%.

If we over-predict the power consumed by a job, we may block the next job in the queue due to lack of enough power. On the other hand, under-predicting the power may lead us to exceed the cluster-level power bound (worst-case scenario). In our model, for 96% of our data, the under-prediction was no more than 10%, and the worst case was under 15%. This issue can be addressed by giving *RMAP* a conservative cluster-level power bound (15% less than the actual bound), or by relying on the common practice of designing supercomputing facilities to tolerate such surges [3].

6. EXPERIMENTAL DETAILS

In order to set up our simulation experiments for *RMAP*, we populate the job_details_table with application configuration information, as discussed in Section 4. In all our experiments, we consider the same architecture as *Cab*. We consider a homogeneous cluster with 64 nodes and global power bounds ranging from 6,500 W to 14,000 W, based on the product of the number of nodes and the minimum and maximum package power caps that can be applied to each socket (51 W and 115 W). Each node has two 8-core sockets.

We generate job traces from a random selection of our recorded configuration data as inputs for P-SLURM. Each trace has 30 jobs to ensure a reasonable simulation time. The total simulation time with all traces, power bounds, node counts and policies was about 3 days (approximately 30 minutes for each trace).

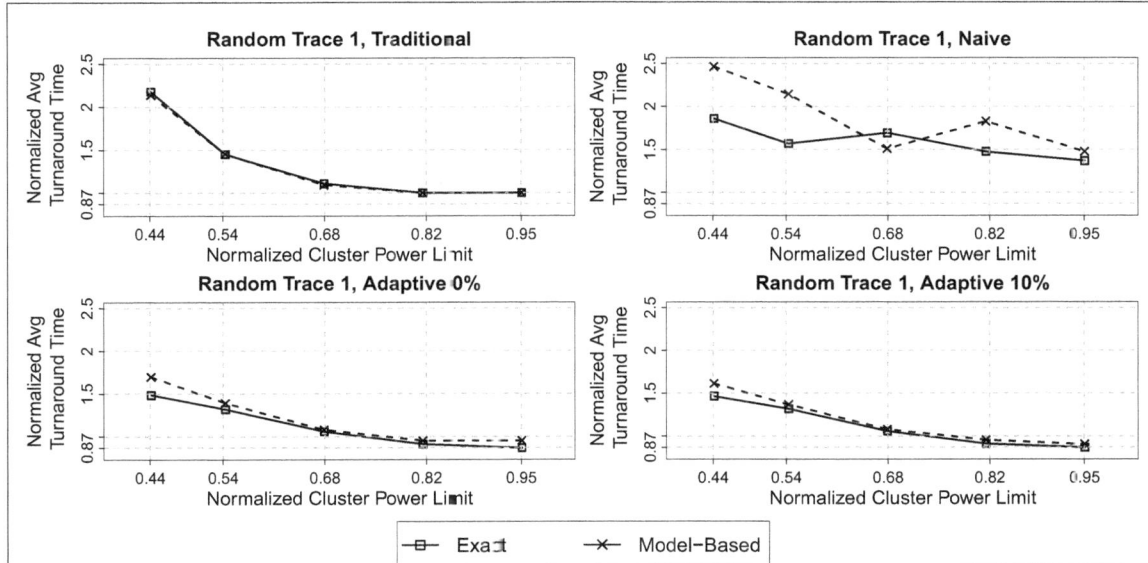

Figure 6: Model Results on the Random Trace

We use a Poisson process to simulate job arrival [14, 15]. Job arrival rate is sparse on purpose (to make queue times short in general), so we can be conservative in the improvements that we report with the *Adaptive* policy. We select the following types of job traces to evaluate our scheduling policies.

- Traces with *small-sized*[2] and *large-sized* jobs: To identify scenarios which may favor one power-aware scheduling policy over another, we create trace files with small-sized and large-sized jobs. Users could request up to 24 nodes in the former, and have to request at least 40 nodes for the latter.

- *Random* traces: For completeness, we also generate two random job traces. Users could request up to 64 nodes for these traces. We refer to these traces as *Random Trace 1* and *Random Trace 2*. The two traces differ in the job arrival pattern as well as job resource (node count) requests, thus exhibiting different characteristics. While both traces have the same number of jobs and used the same arrival rate parameter in the Poisson process, *Random Trace 1* has many jobs arrive early in the trace, whereas arrival times are more uniform in *Random Trace 2*.

7. RMAP RESULTS

In this section, we discuss our results and evaluate our scheduling policies on a Sandy Bridge cluster (which was described in Section 2) that we simulated with P-SLURM. In our experiments, we assume that all jobs have equal priority. For fairness and ease of comparison, in each experiment we assume that all users can tolerate the same slowdown

---

[2]Due to space limitations, we do not present the results on the small-sized trace in this paper. Our results indicate that the *Traditional* policy always does better for traces with several small jobs, as there is limited wait time [33].

(threshold value for the *Adaptive* policy). For readability, we do *not* center our graphs at the origin.

All figures in this section compare the *Traditional* and the *Naive* policies to the *Adaptive* policy when the global, cluster-level power bound is varied across the cluster. The x-axis is the global power limit enforced on the cluster (6,500 W–14,000 W), normalized to the worst-case provisioned power (in this case, that equals 64×115 W $\times 2$, which is 14,720 W). The y-axis represents the average turnaround time for the queue, normalized to the average turnaround time of the *Traditional* policy at 14,720 W (lower is better). The *Traditional* policy mimics worst-case provisioning, which unfairly allocates per-job power and always uses Turbo Boost, unlike the other two policies, which are fair-share and use power capping. Also, all three policies have O(1) decision complexity, so we do not compare their scheduling overheads.

We start by evaluating the model discussed in Section 5 when applied to *RMAP* and its policies. We then compare and analyze the three policies by applying them to different traces at several global power bounds. Finally, we analyze two traces in detail to explore how altruistic behavior on the part of the user can improve turnaround time, and how the *Adaptive* policy can improve system power utilization.

7.1 Model Evaluation Results within RMAP

This section explores the impact of using our model for predicting application configuration performance and power. Figure 6 compares average turnaround time for *Random Trace 1* at 5 different global power caps. Configuration performance and total power consumed are predicted for each job in the trace. The former is used for determining execution time, and the latter is used to determine available power. For the *Traditional* and *Adaptive* policies our model is accurate (error is always under 10%; and is 4% on average across the two policies). We observe similar results with the other traces.

While performance prediction introduces error and affects overall turnaround times, the errors introduced by overprediction of the total power consumed by a configuration propagates and impacts the turnaround time more. Scheduling and backfilling decisions can be significantly affected when they depend on available power. For example, at a lower cluster power bound, if we overpredict the power consumed by a small amount (even 3%), we might not be able to schedule the next job or backfill a job further down in the queue, resulting in added wait times for all queued jobs, particularly for the *Naive* policy at lower global power bounds.

In the subsections that follow, we conservatively establish the *minimum improvements* that the *Adaptive* policy can provide. For this purpose, we use oracular information for the *Traditional* and *Naive* policies, which are our baselines, and the model for the *Adaptive* policy.

7.2 Analyzing Scheduling Policies

In this subsection, we compare and analyze the power-aware scheduling policies on different job traces.

7.2.1 Trace with Large-sized Jobs

Each job in this trace file requests at least 40 nodes. For all enforced global power bounds, the *Adaptive* policy leads to faster turnaround times than the *Traditional* and *Naive* policies, primarily because it fairly shares power and uses power-aware backfilling to decrease job wait times. Figure 7 shows that the *Adaptive* policy with a threshold of 0% improves the turnaround time by 22% when compared to the *Naive* policy and by 14% when compared to the *Traditional* policy on average (up to 47% and 25%, respectively). The *Adaptive* policy with a threshold of 10% further improves the overall turnaround time by 16% on average when compared to the *Traditional* policy.

At lower global power bounds, the *Traditional* policy serializes the jobs, leading to longer wait times and larger turnaround times. The *Naive* policy always allocates the optimal configuration under the user-specified power bound, which can lead to longer wait times when the best configuration uses a large number of nodes.

7.2.2 Random Traces

Figure 6 (from the previous subsection) compares the three policies for *Random Trace 1*. The *Adaptive* policy with a threshold of 0% does 19% better than the *Traditional* policy and 36% better than the *Naive* policy on average (up to 31% and 54%, respectively), for both the random traces.

Policies may lead to larger turnaround times at higher global power bounds in some cases, such as the *Naive* policy at 10,000 W (a normalized value of 0.68 in Figure 6). This policy strives to optimize individual job performance, so it sometimes chooses configurations with large node counts under the power bound for minor gains in performance (less than 1% improvement in execution time). Thus, other jobs in the queue incur longer wait times.

Figure 8 depicts the impact of varying threshold values on the *Adaptive* policy for the large-sized and the random traces (*Random Trace 1*). We compare it to the baseline *Naive* policy, which does not exploit slowdown thresholds. We show threshold values that tolerate a slowdown of 0% to 30%. For large jobs, thresholding helps the user improve the turnaround time for their job by greatly decreasing queue time. However, when queue wait times are short, as with small-sized jobs, we expect that adding a threshold will lead to larger turnaround times. The random traces have a mix

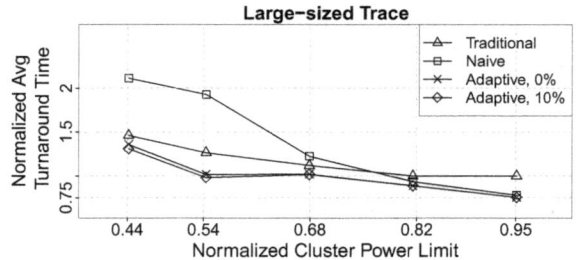

Figure 7: Large-sized Jobs

Policy	Average Turnaround Time (s)
Traditional	684
Naive	990
Adaptive, 0%	636
Adaptive, 10%	613
Adaptive, 20%	536
Adaptive, 30%	536

Table 4: Average Turnaround Times

of small-sized and large-sized jobs. For our traces, the *Adaptive* policy with thresholding up to 30% either improves average turnaround time (by up to 4%) or maintains the same turnaround time when compared to the *Adaptive* policy with a threshold of 0%. The unbounded *Adaptive* policy, which assumes that the job can be slowed down indefinitely, which we show for comparison, leads to worse turnaround times.

For the large trace, the *Adaptive* policy with a threshold of 0% does 34% better on average than the unbounded *Adaptive* policy. Slowing down by 10% to 30% improves the average turnaround time by 2% on average (up to 4%) when compared to the *Adaptive* policy with 0% thresholding. For the other three traces, the improvement obtained by slowing down the jobs is under 3% on average when compared to *Adaptive* policy with a threshold of 0%. This improvement depends on the power bound as well as the job mix. The numbers reported in this section are averaged across all global power bounds for the traces. We analyze per-job performance for a single trace at a fixed global power bound in the next subsection.

7.3 Analyzing Altruistic User Behaviour

We now present detailed results on the large-sized job trace in a power-constrained scenario, where only 6,500 W of cluster-level power is available (50% of worst-case provisioning). We pick this scenario because most important jobs in a high-end cluster typically have medium-to-large node requirements. Each job requests at least 40 nodes, so all jobs are allocated the entire 6,500 W ($P_{cluster}$) with the *Traditional* policy (as the scheduler runs out of power), leading to unfair power allocation, sequential schedules and no opportunity for backfilling. The trace contains 30 jobs.

Figure 9 shows individual job turnaround time for the *Traditional* policy, and for the *Adaptive* policy with 0% and 20% thresholding. Table 4 shows the absolute values of average turnaround times for the job trace for all policies. We limit the graph to our main policies.

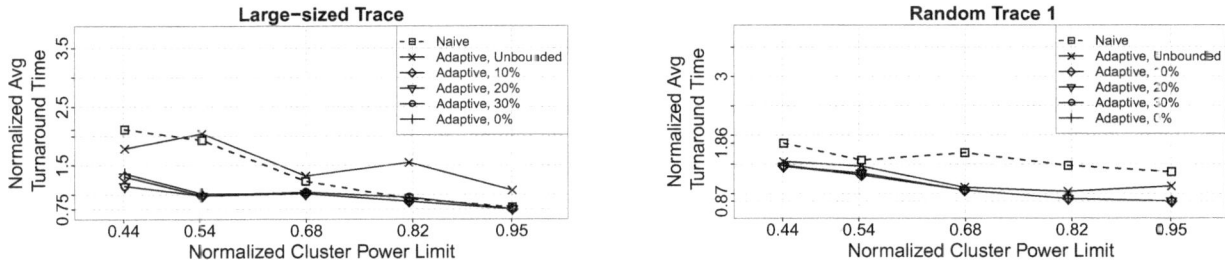

Figure 8: The *Adaptive* Policy with Varying Thresholds, Large and Random Traces

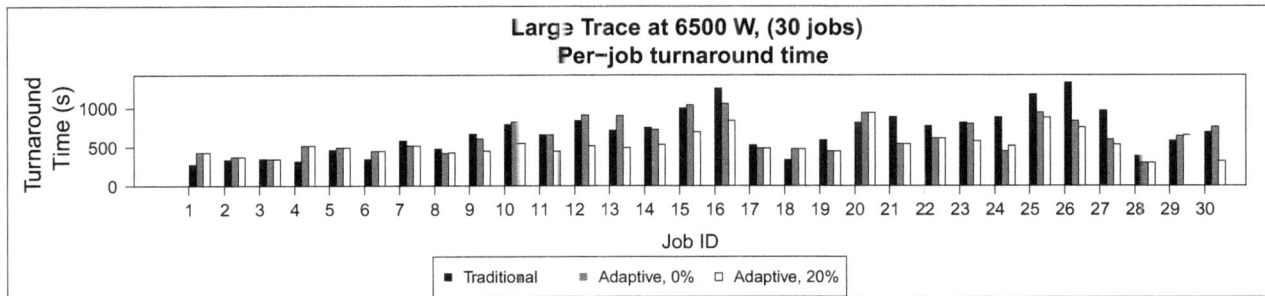

Figure 9: Benefits for Altruistic User Behavior

Allocating power fairly with the *Adaptive* policy with a threshold of 0% leads to better turnaround times for most users (17 out of 30), even though they are not altruistic. The average turnaround time improved by 7% for the job queue when compared to the *Traditional* policy in this case. For the *Adaptive* policy with 10% and 20% thresholding, 18 and 22 jobs resulted in better turnaround times, improving the average turnaround time of the job queue by 11% and 21% when compared to the *Traditional* policy, which demonstrates the benefits of altruistic behavior.

Altruistic users also get better turnaround times when compared to the *Adaptive* policy with a threshold of 0%. For example, when the threshold was set to 20%, 13 users got better turnaround times (up to 58% better, for job 30; and 13% on average) than they did with a threshold of 0%. 14 users had the same turnaround time, and for 3 users, the turnaround times increased slightly (by less than 2%). The average turnaround time for the queue improved by 21%, as discussed previously. These benefits come from power-aware backfilling as well as hardware overprovisioning.

In some cases, such as for the first 5 jobs in the queue, the turnaround times with the *Adaptive* policy increased when compared to the *Traditional* policy. Several reasons explain this increase. First, all jobs were allocated significantly more power with the *Traditional* policy (because no fair-share derived power bound was used, resulting in allocating the entire power budget to most jobs) and executed with Turbo Boost enabled (as no power capping was enforced) resulting in faster execution compared to the other policies. Also, depending on when a job arrived, it may have had zero wait time with the *Traditional* policy. In such a case, with the *Adaptive* policy, when the job's execution time increases, its turnaround time increases as well, because there is no queue wait time to trade for. Despite these issues, the *Adaptive*

policy with 0% thresholding improved the turnaround times for 17 out of 30 jobs, which shows the benefits of altruism. For this example, the utilization of system power by both the *Traditional* and *Adaptive* policies was high, leaving little unused power, mostly because the global power bound was tight (50% of peak) and the jobs were large-sized.

7.4 Power Utilization

We now analyze a random job trace (*Random Trace 2*) in detail in a scenario at 14,000 W, when the global power bound is 95% of peak power. We show that the *Adaptive* policy, even with a 0% threshold, improves system power utilization. Again, our results are conservative due to the sparse job arrival rate in our dynamic job queue (short queue times in general) so we can test the limits of our *Adaptive* policy. With a sparse arrival rate, we expect significant unused power.

Figure 10 shows the per-job allocated power and turnaround time for the *Traditional* policy, and for the *Adaptive* policy with 0% and 20% thresholding. The derived fair-share, job-level power bounds have been shown as well, which apply only to the *Adaptive* policy. The *Traditional* policy has job-level power bounds of 5% more power than that of the *Adaptive* policy in this scenario, as we are looking at 95% of peak power as the cluster power bound (14,000 W).

For this trace, 14 of the 30 jobs did not wait in the queue at all (even with the *Traditional* policy). Even with no wait time, the *Adaptive* policy improved the turnaround time for 28 of these 30 jobs (except Jobs 6 and 10). It tried to utilize all power without exceeding the job-level power bound to improve application performance. The average improvement in turnaround time was 13%, and by more than 2x for 8 jobs in the trace. The *Traditional* policy fails to utilize the power well, and leads to larger turnaround times. Also, at

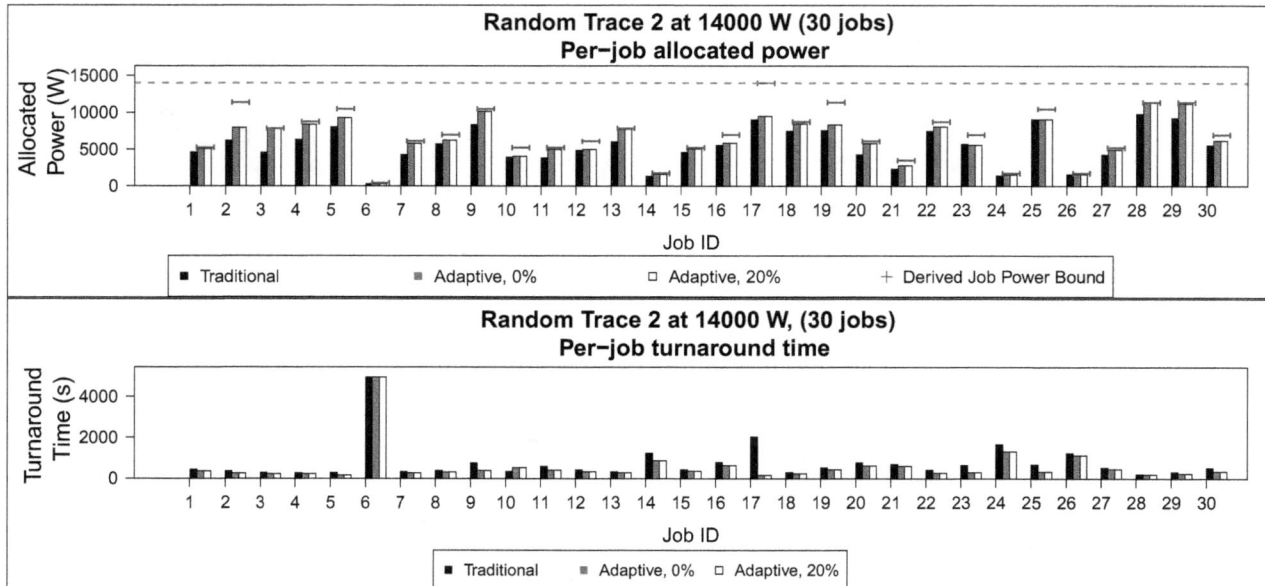

Figure 10: Power Utilization

higher global power bounds, as in this example, benefits of the *Adaptive* policy with thresholding (see *Adaptive*, 20% for example) are limited, which is expected as the system is not significantly power constrained.

7.5 Summary

Our results have yielded three important lessons for power-aware scheduling. First, our encouraging results with the *Adaptive* policy show that jobs can significantly shorten their turnaround time with power-aware backfilling and hardware overprovisioning. In addition, by being altruistic, most users will benefit further in terms of turnaround time.

Second, naive overprovisioning, as implemented by the *Naive* policy, can lead to significantly *worse* turnaround times than the non-fair-share policy (*Traditional*) for some job traces, as with the random job trace and the results that Figure 6 shows. Power-aware scheduling requires advanced policies or average turnaround time may actually *increase*.

Third, the node count requests made by jobs determine the best policy. The *Adaptive* policy targets the most important jobs in a high-end cluster, which are those jobs that request more resources. If most jobs are small, a simpler scheme such as the *Traditional* policy is often superior.

8. RELATED WORK

Job scheduling for parallel systems with a focus on backfilling algorithms has been studied widely [6, 16, 19, 20, 24, 29, 30, 41–44]. These studies have examined the advantages and limitations of various backfilling algorithms (conservative versus easy backfilling, lookahead-based backfilling, and selective reservation strategies). Early research in the domain of power-aware and energy-efficient resource managers for clusters involved identifying periods of low activity and powering down nodes when the workload could be served by fewer nodes from the cluster [28, 35]. The disadvantage of such schemes was that bringing nodes back up had a significant overhead.

DVFS-based algorithms can avoid this cost [7–12,31]. Fan et al. [12] looked at power provisioning strategies in data centers and proposed a DVFS-based algorithm to reduce energy consumption for server systems.

While most of this work identified opportunities for using power efficiently and reducing energy consumption, Etinski et al. [8–11] were the first to look at bounded slowdown of individual jobs and job scheduling under a power budget in the HPC domain. They proposed three DVFS-based policies; however, they did not consider application configurations or power capping and did not analyze overprovisioned systems. Zhou et al. [47] explored knapsack-based scheduling algorithms with a focus on saving energy on BG/Q architectures. Zhang et al. [46] further improved this work by using power capping and using leftover power to bring up more nodes when possible.

Recently, SLURM developers have looked at adding support for energy and power accounting [22]. However, this work does not discuss any new scheduling policies. Bodas et al. [5] explored a policy with dynamic power monitoring to schedule more jobs with stranded power. This work, however, has several limitations — the job queue is static and comprises three jobs, application performance is not clearly quantified, and overall job turnaround times are not discussed. Sarood et al. [37,38] developed an ILP-based policy for resource management under a power bound for over-provisioned systems for strongly-scaled applications. This work assumes a specific programming interface with malleability and focuses on maximizing power aware speedup for applications. As discussed earlier, this scheme has a high scheduling overhead, and less than 1% of real HPC codes are expected to support malleability. Our work, specifically the *Adaptive* policy, applies to general HPC applications, and improves system power utilization and overall job turnaround times. In addition, *RMAP* has significantly less scheduling overhead and derives job-level power bounds in a fair manner.

9. CONCLUSION AND FUTURE WORK

In this paper we discussed *RMAP*, a power-aware resource manager for hardware overprovisioned systems. We designed and implemented three batch scheduling algorithms within *RMAP* using the SLURM scheduler, the best of which is the *Adaptive* policy. The *Adaptive* policy leads to 19% faster average turnaround time when compared to the traditional algorithm that uses worst-case power provisioning. It also increases system power utilization.

We are currently working on extending *RMAP*. One direction is to look deeper into existing job queues and analyze them dynamically to determine which scheduling policy will best apply to upcoming jobs. We will also work towards handling different user priorities, which is essential for a production batch scheduler. Finally, we will look to integrate our work into realistic next-generation resource managers being developed at multiple sites that support real HPC users.

10. ACKNOWLEDGMENTS

We thank Livermore Computing and their support staff for providing us with the appropriate permissions required to access the MSRs. We also thank Dr. Ghaleb Abdulla for helping us gather data from Vulcan. This material is based upon work supported by the National Science Foundation under Grant No. 1216829. In addition, part of this work was performed under the auspices of the U.S. Department of Energy by Lawrence Livermore National Laboratory under Contract DE-AC52-07NA27344 (LLNL-CONF-669277).

11. REFERENCES

[1] NASA Advanced Supercomputing Division, NAS Parallel Benchmark Suite v3.3. 2006. http://www.nas.nasa.gov/Resources/Software/npb.html.

[2] Top500 Supercomputer Sites. November 2014. http://www.top500.org/lists/2014/11.

[3] NPFA 70. National Electric Code 2014. http://www.nfpa.org/codes-and-standards/document-information-pages?mode=code&code=70.

[4] Anat Batat and Dror Feitelson. Gang Scheduling with Memory Considerations. In *International Symposium on Parallel and Distributed Processing Symposium*, pages 109–114, 2000.

[5] Deva Bodas, Justin Song, Murali Rajappa, and Andy Hoffman. Simple Power-aware Scheduler to Limit Power Consumption by HPC System Within a Budget. In *Proceedings of the 2nd International Workshop on Energy Efficient Supercomputing*, pages 21–30. IEEE Press, 2014.

[6] Robert Davis and Alan Burns. A Survey of Hard Real-Time Scheduling Algorithms and Schedulability Analysis Techniques for Multiprocessor Systems. In *Technical Report YCS-2009-443, Department of Computer Science, University of York*, 2009.

[7] Elmootazbellah Elnozahy, Michael Kistler, and Ramakrishnan Rajamony. Energy-Efficient Server Clusters. In *Power-Aware Computer Systems*, volume 2325 of *Lecture Notes in Computer Science*, pages 179–197. Springer Berlin Heidelberg, 2003.

[8] Maja Etinski, Julita Corbalan, Jesus Labarta, and Mateo Valero. Optimizing Job Performance Under a Given Power Constraint in HPC Centers. In *Green Computing Conference*, pages 257–267, 2010.

[9] Maja Etinski, Julita Corbalan, Jesus Labarta, and Mateo Valero. Utilization Driven Power-aware Parallel Job Scheduling. *Computer Science - R&D*, 25(3-4):207–216, 2010.

[10] Maja Etinski, Julita Corbalan, Jesus Labarta, and Mateo Valero. Linear Programming Based Parallel Job Scheduling for Power Constrained Systems. In *International Conference on High Performance Computing and Simulation*, pages 72–80, 2011.

[11] Maja Etinski, Julita Corbalan, Jesus Labarta, and Mateo Valero. Parallel Job Scheduling for Power Constrained HPC Systems. *Parallel Computing*, 38(12):615–630, December 2012.

[12] Xiaobo Fan, Wolf-Dietrich Weber, and Luiz AndrÃl' Barroso. Power Provisioning for a Warehouse-sized Computer. In *The 34th ACM International Symposium on Computer Architecture*, 2007.

[13] Dror Feitelson. Job Scheduling in Multiprogrammed Parallel Systems, 1997.

[14] Dror Feitelson. Workload Modeling for Performance Evaluation. In *Performance Evaluation of Complex Systems: Techniques and Tools, Performance 2002, Tutorial Lectures*, pages 114–141, London, UK, UK, 2002. Springer-Verlag.

[15] Dror Feitelson and Morris Jette. Improved Utilization and Responsiveness with Gang Scheduling. In *Job Scheduling Strategies for Parallel Processing*, pages 238–261. Springer-Verlag LNCS, 1997.

[16] Dror Feitelson and Larry Rudolph. Parallel Job Scheduling: Issues and Approaches. *Job Scheduling Strategies for Parallel Processing*, pages 1–18, 1995.

[17] Dror Feitelson and Larry Rudolph. Towards Convergence in Job Schedulers for Parallel Supercomputers. In *Proceedings of the Workshop on Job Scheduling Strategies for Parallel Processing*, IPPS '96, pages 1–26, London, UK, UK, 1996. Springer-Verlag.

[18] Dror Feitelson, Larry Rudolph, and Uwe Schwiegelshohn. Parallel Job Scheduling: A Status Report. In *Job Scheduling Strategies for Parallel Processing*, volume 3277 of *Lecture Notes in Computer Science*, pages 1–16. Springer Berlin Heidelberg, 2005.

[19] Dror Feitelson, Larry Rudolph, Uwe Schwiegelshohn, Kenneth Sevcik, and Parkson Wong. Theory and Practice in Parallel Job Scheduling. *Job Scheduling Strategies for Parallel Processing*, pages 1–34, 1997.

[20] Dror Feitelson, Uwe Schwiegelshohn, and Larry Rudolph. Parallel Job Scheduling - A Status Report. In *In Lecture Notes in Computer Science*, pages 1–16. Springer-Verlag, 2004.

[21] Eitan Frachtenberg and Dror Feitelson. Pitfalls in Parallel Job Scheduling Evaluation. In *Proceedings of the 11th International Conference on Job Scheduling Strategies for Parallel Processing*, JSSPP'05, pages 257–282, Berlin, Heidelberg, 2005. Springer-Verlag.

[22] Yiannis Georgiou, Thomas Cadeau, David Glesser, Danny Auble, Morris Jette, and Matthieu Hautreux. Energy Accounting and Control with SLURM Resource and Job Management System. In *Distributed Computing and Networking*, volume 8314 of *Lecture Notes in Computer Science*, pages 96–118. Springer Berlin Heidelberg, 2014.

[23] Intel. Intel-64 and IA-32 Architectures Software Developer's Manual, Volumes 3A and 3B: System Programming Guide. 2011.

[24] David Jackson, Quinn Snell, and Mark Clement. Core Algorithms of the Maui Scheduler. In *Job Scheduling Strategies for Parallel Processing*, volume 2221 of *Lecture Notes in Computer Science*, pages 87–102. Springer Berlin Heidelberg, 2001.

[25] Ignacio Laguna, David F. Richards, Todd Gamblin, Martin Schulz, and Bronis R. de Supinski. Evaluating User-Level Fault Tolerance for MPI Applications. In *Proceedings of the 21st European MPI Users' Group Meeting*, EuroMPI/ASIA '14, pages 57:57–57:62, New York, NY, USA, 2014. ACM.

[26] Lawrence Livermore National Laboratory. The ASCI Purple benchmark codes. `http://www.llnl.gov/asci/purple/benchmarks/limited/code_list.html`.

[27] Lawrence Livermore National Laboratory. SPhot–Monte Carlo Transport Code. `https://asc.llnl.gov/computing_resources/purple/archive/benchmarks/sphot/`.

[28] Barry Lawson and Evgenia Smirni. Power-aware Resource Allocation in High-end Systems via Online Simulation. In *International onference on Supercomputing*, pages 229–238, June 2005.

[29] David Lifka. The ANL/IBM SP Scheduling System. In *Job Scheduling Strategies for Parallel Processing*, volume 949 of *Lecture Notes in Computer Science*, pages 295–303. Springer Berlin Heidelberg, 1995.

[30] Ahuva W. Mu'alem and Dror Feitelson. Utilization, Predictability, Workloads, and User Runtime Estimates in Scheduling the IBM SP2 with Backfilling. *Parallel and Distributed Systems, IEEE Transactions on*, 12(6):529–543, 2001.

[31] Trevor Mudge. Power: A First-class Architectural Design Constraint. *IEEE Computer*, 34(4):52–58, 2001.

[32] Tapasya Patki, David K. Lowenthal, Barry Rountree, Martin Schulz, and Bronis R. de Supinski. Exploring Hardware Overprovisioning in Power-constrained, High Performance Computing. In *International Conference on Supercomputing*, pages 173–182, 2013.

[33] Tapasya Patki, Anjana Sasidharan, Matthias Maiterth, David Lowenthal, Barry Rountree, Martin Schulz, and Bronis de Supinski. Practical Resource Management in Power-Constrained, High Performance Computing. TR 01-15, University of Arizona, January 2015. `http://www.cs.arizona.edu/people/tpatki/tr01-15.pdf`.

[34] Antoine Petitet, Clint Whaley, Jack Dongarra, and Andy Cleary. High Performance Linpack. `http://www.netlib.org/benchmark/hpl/`.

[35] Eduardo Pinheiro, Ricardo Bianchini, Enrique V. Carrera, and Taliver Heath. Load Balancing and Unbalancing for Power and Performance in Cluster-Based Systems. In *Workshop on Compilers and Operating Systems for Low Power*, 2001.

[36] Barry Rountree, Dong H. Ahn, Bronis R. de Supinski, David K. Lowenthal, and Martin Schulz. Beyond DVFS: A First Look at Performance under a Hardware-Enforced Power Bound. In *IPDPS Workshops (HPPAC)*, pages 947–953. IEEE Computer Society, 2012.

[37] Osman Sarood. *Optimizing Performance Under Thermal and Power Constraints for HPC Data Centers*. PhD thesis, University of Illinois, Urbana-Champaign, December 2013.

[38] Osman Sarood, Akhil Langer, Abhishek Gupta, and Laxmikant V. Kale. Maximizing Throughput of Overprovisioned HPC Data Centers Under a Strict Power Budget. In *Supercomputing*, November 2014.

[39] Osman Sarood, Akhil Langer, Laxmikant V. Kale, Barry Rountree, and Bronis R. de Supinski. Optimizing Power Allocation to CPU and Memory Subsystems in Overprovisioned HPC Systems. In *IEEE International Conference on Cluster Computing*, pages 1–8, Sept 2013.

[40] Sanjeev Setia, Mark S. Squillante, and Vijay K. Naik. The Impact of Job Memory Requirements on Gang-scheduling Performance. *SIGMETRICS Perform. Eval. Rev.*, 26(4):30–39, March 1999.

[41] Edi Shmueli and Dror Feitelson. Backfilling with Lookahead to Optimize the Performance of Parallel Job Scheduling. In *Job Scheduling Strategies for Parallel Processing*, volume 2862 of *Lecture Notes in Computer Science*, pages 228–251. Springer Berlin Heidelberg, 2003.

[42] Joseph Skovira, Waiman Chan, Honbo Zhou, and David Lifka. The EASY LoadLeveler API Project. In *Job Scheduling Strategies for Parallel Processing*, volume 1162 of *Lecture Notes in Computer Science*, pages 41–47. Springer Berlin Heidelberg, 1996.

[43] Srividya Srinivasan, Rajkumar Kettimuthu, Vijay Subramani, and P. Sadayappan. Selective Reservation Strategies for Backfill Job Scheduling. In *Scheduling Strategies for Parallel Processing, LNCS 2357*, pages 55–71. Springer-Verlag, 2002.

[44] Dan Tsafrir, Yoav Etsion, and Dror Feitelson. Backfilling using System-generated Predictions Rather than User Runtime Estimates. *Parallel and Distributed Systems, IEEE Transactions on*, 18(6):789–803, 2007.

[45] Andy Yoo, Morris Jette, and Mark Grondona. SLURM: Simple Linux Utility for Resource Management. In *Job Scheduling Strategies for Parallel Processing*, volume 2862 of *Lecture Notes in Computer Science*, pages 44–60. 2003.

[46] Ziming Zhang, Michael Lang, Scott Pakin, and Song Fu. Trapped Capacity: Scheduling under a Power Cap to Maximize Machine-room Throughput. In *Proceedings of the 2nd International Workshop on Energy Efficient Supercomputing*, pages 41–50. IEEE Press, 2014.

[47] Zhou Zhou, Zhiling Lan, Wei Tang, and Narayan Desai. Reducing Energy Costs for IBM Blue Gene/P via Power-Aware Job Scheduling. In *Job Scheduling Strategies for Parallel Processing*, Lecture Notes in Computer Science, pages 96–115. Springer Berlin Heidelberg, 2014.

Optimizing Grouped Aggregation in Geo-Distributed Streaming Analytics

Benjamin Heintz
University of Minnesota
Minneapolis, MN
heintz@cs.umn.edu

Abhishek Chandra
University of Minnesota
Minneapolis, MN
chandra@cs.umn.edu

Ramesh K. Sitaraman
UMass, Amherst & Akamai
Tech. Amherst, MA
ramesh@cs.umass.edu

ABSTRACT

Large quantities of data are generated continuously over time and from disparate sources such as users, devices, and sensors located around the globe. This results in the need for efficient geo-distributed streaming analytics to extract timely information. A typical analytics service in these settings uses a simple hub-and-spoke model, comprising a single central data warehouse and multiple edges connected by a wide-area network (WAN). A key decision for a geo-distributed streaming service is how much of the computation should be performed at the edge versus the center. In this paper, we examine this question in the context of *windowed grouped aggregation*, an important and widely used primitive in streaming queries. Our work is focused on designing aggregation algorithms to optimize two key metrics of any geo-distributed streaming analytics service: *WAN traffic* and *staleness* (the delay in getting the result). Towards this end, we present a family of optimal offline algorithms that *jointly minimize both staleness and traffic*. Using this as a foundation, we develop practical online aggregation algorithms based on the observation that grouped aggregation can be modeled as a *caching* problem where the cache size varies over time. This key insight allows us to exploit well known caching techniques in our design of online aggregation algorithms. We demonstrate the practicality of these algorithms through an implementation in Apache Storm, deployed on the PlanetLab testbed. The results of our experiments, driven by workloads derived from anonymized traces of a popular web analytics service offered by a large commercial CDN, show that our online aggregation algorithms perform close to the optimal algorithms for a variety of system configurations, stream arrival rates, and query types.

Categories and Subject Descriptors

C.2.4 [**Distributed Systems**]: Distributed Applications

Keywords

Geo-distributed systems, stream processing, aggregation, Storm

1. INTRODUCTION

Data analytics is undergoing a revolution: both the volume and velocity of analytics data are increasing at a rapid rate. Across a large number of application domains that include web analytics, social analytics, scientific computing, and energy analytics, large quantities of data are generated continuously over time in the form of posts, tweets, logs, sensor readings, etc. A modern analytics service must provide real-time analysis of these data streams to extract meaningful and timely information for the user. As a result, there has been a growing interest in streaming analytics with recent development of several distributed analytics platforms [2, 8, 28].

In many streaming analytics domains, data is often derived from disparate sources that include users, devices, and sensors located around the globe. As a result, the distributed infrastructure of a typical analytics service (e.g., Google Analytics, Akamai Media Analytics, etc.) has a hub-and-spoke model (see Figure 1). The data sources generate and send a stream of data to "edge" servers near them. The edge servers are geographically distributed and process the incoming data and send it to a central location that can process the data further, store the summaries, and present those summaries in visual form to the user of the analytics service. While the central location that acts as a hub is often located in a well-provisioned data center, the resources are typically limited at the edge locations. In particular, the available WAN bandwidth between the edge and the center might be limited.

A traditional approach to analytics processing is the *centralized model* where no processing is performed at the edges and all the data is sent to a dedicated centralized location. However, such an approach is often inadequate or suboptimal, since it can strain the scarce WAN bandwidth available between the edge and the center, cause longer delays due to the high volumes of unaggregated data to be sent over the network, and does not make use of the available compute and storage resources at the edge. An alternative is a *decentralized approach* [23] that utilizes the edge for much of the processing in order to minimize the amount of WAN traffic. In this paper, we argue that analytics processing must utilize *both* edge and central resources in a carefully coordinated manner in order to achieve the stringent requirements of an analytics service in terms of both network traffic and user-perceived delay.

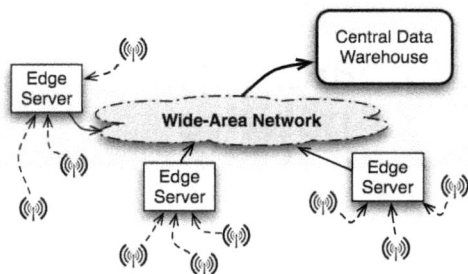

Figure 1: The distributed model for a typical analytics service comprises a single center and multiple edges, connected by a wide-area network.

An important primitive in any analytics system is *grouped aggregation*. Grouped aggregation is used to combine and summarize large quantities of data from one or more data streams. As a result, it is provided as a key operator in most data analytics frameworks, such as the Reduce operation in MapReduce, or GroupBy in SQL and LINQ. A common variant of the primitive in stream computing is *windowed grouped aggregation* where data produced within finite specified time windows must be summarized. Windowed grouped aggregation is one of the most frequently used primitives in an analytics service and underlies queries that aggregate a metric of interest over a time window. For instance, a web analytics user may wish to compute the total visits to his/her web site broken down by country and aggregated on an hourly basis to gauge the current content popularity. Similarly, a network operator may want to compute the average load in different parts of the network every 5 minutes to identify hotspots. In these cases, the user would define a standing windowed grouped aggregation query that generates results periodically for each time window (every hour, 5 minutes, etc.).

Our work is focused on designing algorithms for performing windowed grouped aggregation in order to optimize the two key metrics of any geo-distributed streaming analytics service: *WAN traffic* and *staleness* (the delay in getting the result for a time window). A service provider typically pays for the WAN bandwidth used by its deployed servers [3, 13]. In fact, bandwidth cost incurred due to WAN traffic is a significant component of the operating expense (OPEX) of the service provider infrastructure, the other key components being colocation and power costs. Therefore reducing WAN traffic represents an important cost-saving opportunity. In addition, reducing staleness is critical in order to deliver timely results to applications and is often a part of the SLA for analytics services. While much of the existing work on decentralized analytics [23, 25] has focused primarily on optimizing a single metric (e.g., network traffic), it is important to examine both traffic and staleness together to achieve both cost savings as well as higher information quality.

The key decision that our algorithms make is *how much of the data aggregation should be performed at the edge versus the center*. To understand the challenge, consider two alternate approaches to grouped aggregation: *pure streaming*, where all data is immediately sent from the edge to the center without any edge processing; and *pure batching*, where all data during a time window is aggregated at the

edge, with only the aggregated results being sent to the center at the end of the window. Pure batching results in a greater level of edge aggregation, resulting in a reduction in the edge-to-center WAN traffic compared to pure streaming. However, the edge must wait longer to collect more data for aggregation, risking the possibility of the aggregates reaching the center late, resulting in greater staleness. We have shown [15] that the decision about how much aggregation to be performed at the edge cannot be made statically; rather it depends on several factors such as the query type, network constraints, data arrival rates, etc. Further, these factors vary significantly over time (see Figure 2(b)), requiring the design of algorithms that can adapt to changing factors in a dynamic fashion.

Research Contributions

- To our knowledge, we provide the first algorithms and analysis for optimizing grouped aggregation, a key primitive, in a wide-area streaming analytics service. In particular, we show that simpler approaches such as pure streaming or batching do not jointly optimize traffic and staleness, and are hence suboptimal.
- We present a family of optimal offline algorithms that *jointly minimize both staleness and traffic*. Using this as a foundation, we develop practical online aggregation algorithms that emulate the offline optimal algorithms.
- We observe that grouped aggregation can be modeled as a *caching problem* where the cache size varies over time. This key insight allows us to exploit well known caching algorithms in our design of online aggregation algorithms.
- We demonstrate the practicality of these algorithms through an implementation in Apache Storm [2], deployed on the PlanetLab [1] testbed. Our experiments are driven by workloads derived from traces of a popular web analytics service offered by Akamai [19], a large content delivery network. The results of our experiments show that our online aggregation algorithms simultaneously achieve traffic within 2.0% of optimal while reducing staleness by 65% relative to batching. We also show that our algorithms are robust to a variety of system configurations (number of edges), stream arrival rates, and query types.

2. PROBLEM FORMULATION

System Model.

We consider the typical hub-and-spoke architecture of an analytics system with a center and multiple edges (see Figure 1). Data streams are first sent from each source to a proximal edge. The edges collect and (potentially, partially) aggregate the data. The aggregated data can then be sent from the edges to the center where more aggregation could happen. The final aggregated results are available at the center. Users of the analytics service query the center to visualize the data. To perform grouped aggregation, each edge runs a local aggregation algorithm: it acts independently to decide when and how much to aggregate the incoming data.

Data Streams and Grouped Aggregation.

A *data stream* comprises *records* of the form (k, v) where k is the *key* and v is the *value* of the record. Data records of a stream *arrive* at the edge over time. Each key k can be multi-dimensional, with each dimension corresponding to a data attribute. A *group* is a set of records that have the same key.

Windowed grouped aggregation over a *time window* $[t, t + W)$, where W is the user-specified window size, is defined as follows from an input/output perspective. The input is the set of data records that arrive within the time window. The output is determined by first placing the data records into groups where each group is a set of records with the same key. For each group $\{(k, v_i)\}, 1 \leq i \leq n$, that correspond to the n records in the time window that have key k, an aggregate value $\hat{v} = v_1 \oplus v_2 \cdots \oplus v_n$ is computed, where $\oplus$ is any associative binary operator[1]. Examples of aggregates include sums, histograms, and approximate data types such as Bloom filters. Customarily, the timeline is subdivided into non-overlapping intervals of size W and windowed group aggregation is computed on each such window[2]. Note that the aggregate record is typically of the same size as an incoming data record. Thus, grouped aggregation results in a reduction in the amount of data.

To compute windowed grouped aggregation, we consider aggregation at the edge as well as the center. The data records that arrive at the edge can be partially aggregated locally at the edge, so that the edge can maintain a set of partial aggregates, one for each distinct key k. The edge may transmit, or *flush* these aggregates to the center; we refer to these flushed records as *updates*. The center can further apply the aggregation operator $\oplus$ on incoming updates as needed in order to generate the final aggregate result. We assume that the computational overhead of the aggregation operator $\oplus$ is a small constant compared to the network overhead of transmitting an update.

Optimization Metrics.

Our goal is to *simultaneously* minimize two metrics: *staleness*, a key measure of information quality; and *network traffic*, a key measure of cost. Staleness is defined as the smallest time s such that the results of grouped aggregation for time window $[t, t + W)$ are available at the center at time $t + W + s$. In our model, staleness is simply the time elapsed from when the time window completes to when the last update for that time window reaches the center and is included in the final aggregate. Roughly, staleness is the delay measured from when all the data has arrived to when an analytics user views the results of her grouped aggregation query. The network traffic is measured by the number of updates sent over the network from the edge to the center.

Algorithms for Grouped Aggregation.

An aggregation algorithm runs on the edge and takes as input the sequence of arrivals for data records in a given time window $[t, t + W)$. The algorithm produces as output a sequence of updates that are sent to the center. For each distinct key k with n_k arrivals in the time window, suppose that the ith data record $(k, v_{i,k})$ arrives at time $a_{i,k}$, where $t \leq a_{i,k} < t + W$ and $1 \leq i \leq n_k$. For each key k, the output of the aggregation algorithm is a sequence of m_k updates where the ith update $(k, \hat{v}_{i,k})$ departs for the center at time

$d_{i,k}, 1 \leq i \leq m_k$. The updates must have the following properties:

- Each update for each key k aggregates all values for that key in the current time window that have not been previously aggregated.
- Each key k that has $n_k > 0$ arrivals must have $m_k > 0$ updates such that $d_{m_k,k} \geq a_{n_k,k}$. That is, each key with an arrival must have at least one update and the last update must depart after the final arrival so that all the values received for the key have been aggregated.

The goal of the aggregation algorithm is to minimize traffic which is simply the total number of updates, i.e., $\sum_k m_k$. The other simultaneous goal is to minimize staleness which is the time for the final update to reach the center, i.e., the update with the largest value for $d_{m_k,k}$, to reach the center[3].

3. DATASET AND WORKLOAD

To derive a realistic workload for evaluating our aggregation algorithms, we have used anonymized workload traces obtained from a real-life analytics service[4] offered by Akamai which operates a large content delivery network. The download analytics service is used by content providers to track important metrics about who is downloading their content, from where is it being downloaded, what was the performance experienced by the users, how many downloads completed, etc. The data source is a software called download manager that is installed on mobile devices, laptops, and desktops of millions of users around the world. The download manager is used to download software updates, security patches, music, games, and other content. The download managers installed on users' devices around the world send information about the downloads to the widely-deployed edge servers using "beacons"[5]. Each download results in one or more beacons being sent to an edge server containing information pertaining to that download. The beacons contain anonymized information about the time the download was initiated, url, content size, number of bytes downloaded, user's ip, user's network, user's geography, server's network and server's geography. Throughout this paper, we use the anonymized beacon logs from Akamai's download analytics service for the month of December, 2010. Note that we normalize derived values from the data set such as data sizes, traffic sizes, and time durations, for confidentiality reasons.

Throughout our evaluation, we compute grouped aggregation for three commonly-used queries in the download analytics service. Queries that are issued in the download analytics service that use the grouped aggregation primitive can be roughly classified according to *query size* that is defined to be the number of distinct keys that are possible for that query. We choose three representative queries for different size categories (see Table 1). The `small` query groups by two dimensions with the key consisting of the tuple of content provider id and the user's last mile bandwidth classified into four buckets. The `medium` query groups by three dimensions with the key consisting of the triple of the content provider id, user's last mile bandwidth, and the user's

---

[1]More formally, any binary operator that forms a semigroup can be used.

[2]Such non-overlapping time windows are often called *tumbling* windows in analytics terminology.

---

[3]We implicitly assume a FIFO ordering of data records over the network, as is typically the case with protocols like TCP.

[4]http://www.akamai.com/dl/feature_sheets/Akamai_Download_Analytics.pdf

[5]A beacon is simply an http `GET` issued by the download manager for a small GIF containing the reported values in its url query string.

Table 1: Queries used throughout the paper.

Name	Key	Value (aggregate type)	Description	Query Size
Small	`(cpid, bw)`	bytes downloaded (integer sum)	Total bytes downloaded by content provider by last-mile bandwidth.	$O(10^2)$ keys
Medium	`(cpid, bw, country_code)`	bytes downloaded (first 5 moments)	Mean and standard deviation of total bytes per download by content provider by bandwidth by country.	$O(10^4)$ keys
Large	`(cpid, bw, url)`	client ip (HyperLogLog)	Approximate number of unique clients by content provider by bw by url.	$O(10^6)$ keys

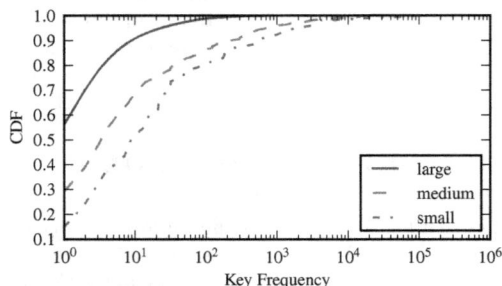

(a) CDF of the frequency per key at a single edge for the three queries.

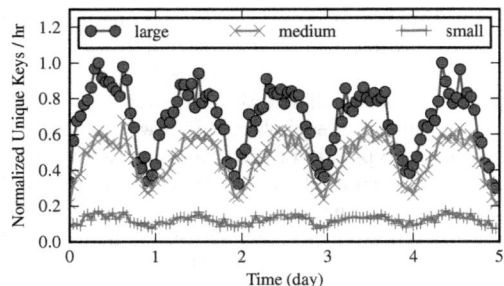

(b) The unique key arrival rate for three different queries in a real-world web analytics service, normalized to the maximum rate for the large query.

Figure 2: Akamai Web download service data set characteristics.

country code. The `large` query groups by a different set of three dimensions with the key consisting of the triple of the content provider id, the user's country code, and the url accessed. Note that the last dimension—url—can take on hundreds of thousands of distinct values, resulting in a very large query size.

The total arrival rate of data records across all keys for all three queries is the same, since each arriving beacon contributes a data record for each query. However, the three queries have a different distribution of those arrivals across the possible keys as shown in Figure 2(a). Recall that the large query has a large number of possible keys. About 56% of the keys for the large query arrived only once in the trace whereas the same percentage of keys for the medium and small query is 29% and 15% respectively. The median arrival rate per key was four (resp., nine) times larger for the medium (resp., small) query in comparison with the large query. Figure 2(b) shows the number of unique keys arriving per hour at an edge server for the three queries. The figure shows the hourly and daily variations and also the variation across the three queries.

4. MINIMIZING WAN TRAFFIC AND STALENESS

We now explore how to *simultaneously* minimize both traffic and staleness. We show that if the entire sequence of updates is known *beforehand*, then it is indeed possible to *simultaneously* achieve the optimal value for both traffic and staleness. While this offline solution is not implementable, it serves as a baseline to which any online algorithm can be compared. Further, it characterizes the optimal solution that helps us evolve the more sophisticated online algorithms that we present in Section 5. Due to space constraints, we

omit the proofs of lemmas and theorems here; more details can be found in our technical report [14].

LEMMA 1 (TRAFFIC OPTIMALITY). *In each time window, an algorithm is* traffic-optimal *iff it flushes exactly one update to the center for each distinct key that arrived in the window.*

Intuitively, this lemma states that multiple records for each key within a window can be aggregated and sent as a single update to minimize traffic. Note that a pure batching algorithm satisfies the above lemma, and hence is traffic-optimal, but may not be staleness-optimal.

We now present *optimal offline algorithms* that minimize *both* traffic and staleness, provided the *entire* sequence of key updates is known to our aggregation algorithm *beforehand*.

THEOREM 2 (EAGER OPTIMAL ALGORITHM). *There exists an optimal offline algorithm that schedules its flushes eagerly; i.e., it flushes exactly one update for each distinct key immediately after the last arrival for that key within the time window.*

Intuitively, this algorithm is traffic-optimal since it sends only one update per key, and is also staleness-optimal since it sends each update without any additional delay. We call the optimal offline algorithm described above the *eager optimal algorithm* due to the fact that it eagerly flushes updates for each distinct key immediately after the final arrival to that key. This eager algorithm is just one possible algorithm to achieve both minimum traffic and staleness. It might well be possible to delay flushes for some groups and still achieve optimal traffic and staleness. An extreme version of such a scheduler is the *lazy optimal algorithm* that flushes updates at the last possible time that would still provide the optimal value of staleness and is described below.

1) Let keys $k_i, 1 \leq i \leq n$ have their last arrival at times $l_i, 1 \leq i \leq n$ respectively. Order the n keys that require flushing in the given window in the increasing order of their last update, i.e., the keys are ordered such that $l_1 \leq l_2 \leq \cdots l_n$.

2) Compute the minimum possible staleness S using the eager optimal algorithm.

3) As the base case, schedule the flush for the last key k_n at time $t_n = S - \delta_n$, where δ_n is the time required to transmit the update for k_n. That is, the last update is scheduled such that it arrives at the center with staleness exactly equal to S.

4) Now, iteratively schedule k_i, assuming all keys $k_j, j > i$ have already been scheduled. The update for k_i is scheduled at time $t_{i+1} - \delta_i$, where δ_i is the time required to transmit the update for k_i. That is, the update for k_i is scheduled such that update for k_{i+1} is flushed immediately after the update of k_i completes.

THEOREM 3 (LAZY OPTIMAL ALGORITHM). *The lazy algorithm above is both traffic- and staleness-optimal.*

Further, consider a family of offline algorithms $\mathcal{A}$, where an algorithm $A \in \mathcal{A}$ schedules its update for key k_i at time t_i such that $e_i \leq t_i \leq l_i$, where e_i and l_i are the update times for key k_i in the eager and lazy schedules respectively. The following clearly holds.

THEOREM 4 (FAMILY OF OFFLINE OPTIMAL ALGORITHMS). *Any algorithm $A \in \mathcal{A}$ is both traffic- and staleness-optimal.*

5. PRACTICAL ONLINE ALGORITHMS

In this section, we explore practical online algorithms for grouped aggregation, that strive to minimize both traffic and staleness. To ease the design of such online algorithms, we first frame the edge aggregation problem as an equivalent *caching problem*. This formulation enables us to use insights gained from the optimal offline algorithms as well as the enormous prior work on cache replacement policies [21].

Concretely, we frame the grouped aggregation problem as a caching problem by treating the set of aggregates $\{(k_i, a_i)\}$ maintained at the edge as a cache. A novel aspect of our formulation is that the *number of items in this cache changes dynamically*, decreasing when an aggregate is flushed, and increasing upon arrival of a key that is not yet in the cache. Concretely, the cache works as follows:

• *Cache insertion* occurs upon the arrival of a record (k, v). If an aggregate with key k and value v_e exists in the cache (a "cache hit"), the cached value for key k is updated as $v \oplus v_e$ where $\oplus$ is the binary aggregation operator defined in Section 2. If no aggregate exists with key k (a "cache miss"), (k, v) is added to the cache.

• *Cache eviction* occurs as the result of a *decrease* in the cache size. When an aggregate is evicted, it is flushed downstream and cleared from the cache.

Given the above definition of cache mechanics, we can express any grouped aggregation algorithm as an equivalent caching algorithm where the key updates flushed by the aggregation algorithm correspond to key evictions of the caching algorithm. More formally:

THEOREM 5. *An aggregation algorithm A corresponds to a caching algorithm C such that:*

1. *At any time step, C maintains a cache size that equals the number of pending aggregates (those not sent to the center yet) for A, and*

2. *if A flushes an update for a key in a time step, C evicts the same key from its cache in that time step.*

Thus, any aggregation algorithm can be viewed as a caching algorithm with two policies: one for cache sizing and the other for cache replacement. In practice, we can define an online caching algorithm by defining online *cache size* and *cache eviction* policies. While the cache size policy determines *when* to send out updates, the cache eviction policy identifies *which* updates to send out at these times. Here we develop policies by attempting to emulate the behavior of the offline optimal algorithms using online information. We explore such online algorithms and the resulting tradeoffs in the rest of this section.

To evaluate the relative merits of these algorithms, we implement a simple simulator in Python. Our simulator models each algorithm as a function that maps from arrival sequences to update sequences. Traffic is simply the length of the update sequence, while staleness is evaluated by modeling the network as single-server queueing system with deterministic service times, and arrival times determined by the update sequence. Note that we have deliberately employed a simplified simulation, as the focus here is not on understanding performance in absolute terms, but rather to compare the tradeoffs between different algorithms. We use these insights to develop practical algorithms that we implement in Apache Storm and deploy on PlanetLab (Section 6). Also note that throughout this section, we present results for the `large` query due to space constraints, but similar trends also apply to the `small` and `medium` queries.

5.1 Emulating the Eager Optimal Algorithm

5.1.1 Cache Size

To emulate the cache size corresponding to that for an eager offline optimal algorithm, we observe that, at any given time instant, an aggregate for key k_i is cached only if: in the window, (i) there has already been an arrival for k_i, and (ii) another arrival for k_i is yet to occur. We attempt to compute the number of such keys using two broad approaches: analytical and empirical.

In our analytical approach, the eager optimal cache size at a time instant can be estimated by computing the *expected* number of keys at that instant for which the above conditions hold. To compute this value, we model the arrival process of records for each key k_i as a Poisson process with mean arrival rate λ_i. Then the probability $p_i(t)$ that the key k_i should be cached at a time instant t within a window $[T, T + W]$ is given by $p_i(t) = 1 - \hat{t}^{W\lambda_i} - (1 - \hat{t})^{W\lambda_i}$, where $\hat{t} = (t - T)/W$.[6]

We consider two different models to estimate the arrival processes for different keys. The first model is a *Uniform* analytical model, which assumes that key popularities are uniformly distributed, and each key has the same mean arrival rate λ. Then, if the total number of keys arriving during the window is k, the expected number of cached keys at time t is simply $k \cdot \left(1 - \hat{t}^{W\lambda} - (1 - \hat{t})^{W\lambda}\right)$.

---

[6]Note that $W\lambda_i > 0$ since we are considering only keys with more than 0 arrivals, and that $\hat{t} < 1$ since $T \leq t < T + W$.

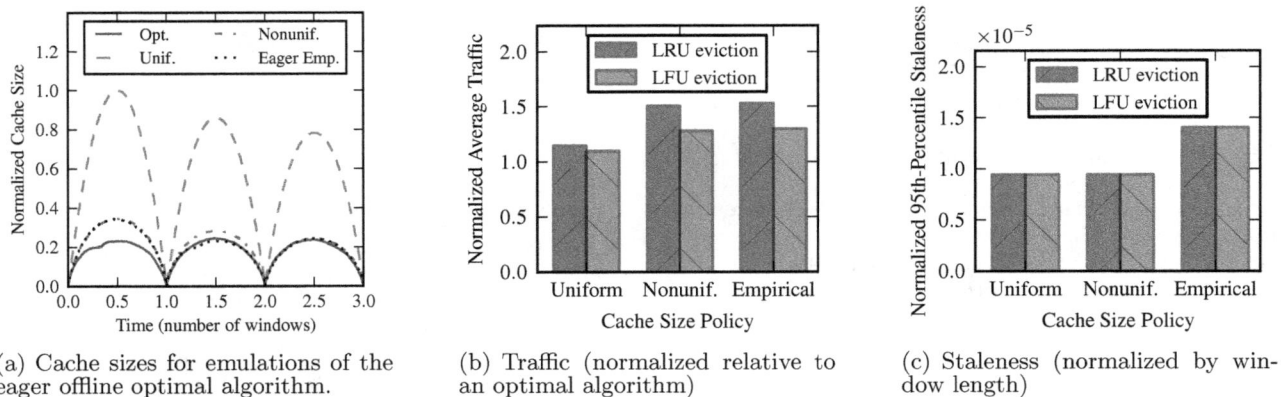

(a) Cache sizes for emulations of the eager offline optimal algorithm.

(b) Traffic (normalized relative to an optimal algorithm)

(c) Staleness (normalized by window length)

Figure 3: Eager online algorithms.

However, as Figure 2(a) in Section 3 demonstrated, key popularities in reality may be far from uniform. A more accurate model is the *Nonuniform* analytical model, that assumes each key k_i has its own mean arrival rate λ_i, so that the expected number of cached keys at time t is given by $\sum_{i=1}^{k} p_i(\hat{t})$.

An online algorithm built around these models requires predicting the number of unique keys k arriving during a window as well as their arrival rates λ_i. In our evaluation, we use a simple prediction: assume that the current window resembles the prior window, and derive these parameters from the arrival history in the prior window.

Our empirical approach, referred to as *Eager Empirical*, also uses the history from the prior window as follows: apply the eager offline optimal algorithm to the arrival sequence from the previous window, and use the resulting cache size at time $t - W$ as the prediction for cache size at time t.

Figure 3(a) plots the predicted cache size using these policies, along with the eager optimal cache size as a baseline. We observe that the Uniform model, unsurprisingly, is less accurate than the Nonuniform model. Specifically, it overestimates the cache size, as it incorrectly assumes that arrivals are uniformly distributed across many keys, rather than focused on a relatively small subset of relatively popular keys. Further, we see that the Eager Empirical model and the Nonuniform model both provide reasonably accurate predictions, but are prone to errors as the arrival rate changes from window to window.

5.1.2 Cache Eviction

Having determined the cache size, the next issue is which keys to evict when needed. We know that an optimal algorithm will only evict keys without future arrivals. However, determining such keys accurately requires knowledge of the future. Instead, to implement a practical online policy, we consider two popular practical eviction algorithms—namely least-recently used (LRU), and least-frequently used (LFU)—and examine their interaction with the above cache size policies.

Figures 3(b) and 3(c) show the traffic and staleness, respectively, for different combinations of these cache size and cache eviction policies. Here, we simulate the case where network capacity is roughly five times that needed to support the full range of algorithms from pure batching to pure streaming. In these figures, traffic is normalized relative to

the traffic generated by an optimal algorithm, while staleness is normalized by the window length.

From these figures, we see that the Eager Empirical and Nonuniform models yield similar traffic, though their staleness varies. It is worth noting that although the difference in staleness appears large in relative terms, the absolute values are still extremely low relative to the window length (less than 0.0015%), and are very close to optimal. We also see that LFU is the more effective eviction policy for this trace.

The more interesting result, however, is that the Uniform model, which produces the *worst* estimate of cache size, actually yields the *best* traffic: only about 9.6% higher than optimal, while achieving the same staleness as optimal. On the other hand, when combined with the most accurate model of eager optimal cache size (Nonuniform), even the best practical eviction policy (LFU) generates 28% more traffic than optimal. This result indicates that leaving more headroom in the cache size (as done by Uniform) provides more robustness to errors by an online cache eviction policy.

5.2 Emulating the Lazy Optimal Algorithm

5.2.1 Cache Size

To emulate the lazy optimal offline algorithm (Section 4), we estimate the cache size by working backwards from the end of the window, determining how large the cache should be such that it can be drained by the end of the window (or as soon as possible thereafter) by fully utilizing the network capacity. This estimation must account for the fact that new arrivals will still occur during the remainder of the window, and each of those that is a cache miss will lead to an additional update in the future. This leads to a cache size $c(t)$ at time t defined as: $c(t) = \max\left(\bar{b} \cdot (T - t) - M(t), 0\right)$, where $\bar{b}$ denotes the average available network bandwidth—in records per unit time—for the remainder of the window, T the end of the time window, and $M(t)$ the total number of cache misses that will occur during the remainder of the window.

Based on the above cache size function, an online algorithm needs to estimate the average bandwidth $\bar{b}$ and the number of cache misses $M(t)$ for the remainder of the window. We begin by focusing on the estimation of $M(t)$. We consider the bandwidth estimation problem in more detail in Section 5.3, and assume a perfect knowledge of $\bar{b}$ here. To estimate $M(t)$, we consider the following approaches. First,

138

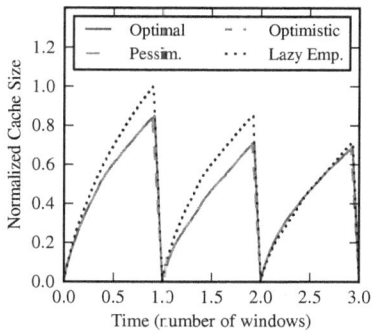

(a) Cache sizes for emulations of the lazy offline optimal algorithm.

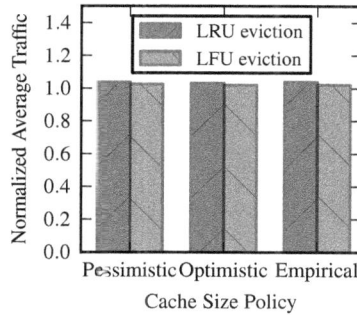

(b) Traffic (normalized relative to an optimal algorithm)

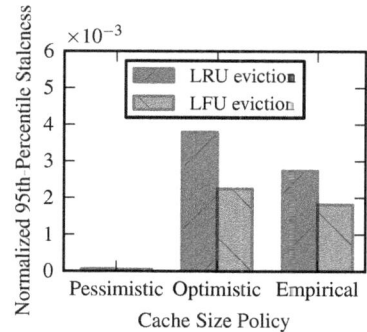

(c) Staleness (normalized by window length)

Figure 4: Lazy online algorithms.

we can use a *Pessimistic* policy, where we assume that *all* remaining arrivals in the window will be cache misses. Concretely, we estimate $M(t) = \int_t^T a(\tau) \, d\tau$ where $a(t)$ is the arrival rate at time t. In practice, this requires the prediction of the future arrival rate $a(t)$. In our evaluation, we simply assume that the future arrival rate is equal to the average arrival rate so far in the window.

Another alternative is to use an *Optimistic* policy, which assumes that the *current cache miss rate* will continue for the remainder of the window. In other words, $M(t) = \int_t^T m(\tau) a(\tau) \, d\tau$ where $m(t)$ is the miss rate at time t. In our evaluation, we predict the arrival rate in the same manner as for the Pessimistic policy, and we use an exponentially weighted moving average for computing the recent cache miss rate.

A third approach is the *Lazy Empirical* policy, which is analogous to the Eager Empirical approach. It estimates the cache size by emulating the lazy offline optimal algorithm on the arrivals for the prior window.

Figure 4(a) shows the cache size produced by each of these policies. We see that both the Lazy Empirical and Optimistic models closely capture the behavior of the optimal algorithm in dynamically decreasing the cache size near the end of the window.[7] The Pessimistic algorithm, by assuming that all future arrivals will be cache misses, decays the cache size more rapidly than the other algorithms.

5.2.2 Cache Eviction

We explore the same eviction algorithms here, namely LRU and LFU, as we did in Section 5.1.

Figures 4(b) and 4(c) show the traffic and staleness, respectively, generated by different combinations of these cache size and cache eviction policies. We see that LFU again slightly outperforms LRU. More importantly we see that, regardless of which cache size policy we use, these lazy approaches outperform the best online eager algorithm in terms of traffic. Even the worst lazy online algorithm produces traffic less than 4% above optimal.

The results for staleness, however, show a significant difference between the different policies. We see that by assuming that all future arrivals will be cache misses, the Pessimistic policy achieves enough tolerance in the cache size estimation, avoiding overloading the network towards the end of the window, and leading to low staleness (below 6×10^{-5} for both eviction policies).

Based on the results so far, we see that accurately modeling the optimal cache size does not yield the best results in practice. Instead, our algorithms should be lazy, deferring updates until later in the window, and in choosing how long to defer, they should be pessimistic in their assumptions about future arrivals.

5.3 The Hybrid Algorithm

In the discussion of the lazy online algorithm above, we assumed perfect knowledge of the future network bandwidth $\bar{b}$. In practice, however, if the actual network capacity turns out to be lower than the predicted value, then too much traffic may back up close to the end of the window, potentially resulting in high staleness.

Figure 5 shows how staleness increases as the result of overpredicting network capacity. Note that the predicted capacity remains constant, while we vary the actual network capacity. The top-most curve corresponds to a lazy online algorithm (Pessimistic + LFU) which is susceptible to very high staleness if it overpredicts network capacity (up to 9.9% of the window length for 100% overprediction).

To avoid this problem, recall Theorem 4, where we observed that the eager and lazy optimal algorithms are merely two extremes in a family of optimal algorithms. Further, our results from Sections 5.1 and 5.2 showed that it is useful to

Figure 5: Sensitivity of the hybrid algorithms with a range of α values to overpredicting the available network capacity. Staleness is normalized by window length.

---

[7]Note that we are primarily concerned with cache size while it is decreasing near the end of the window.

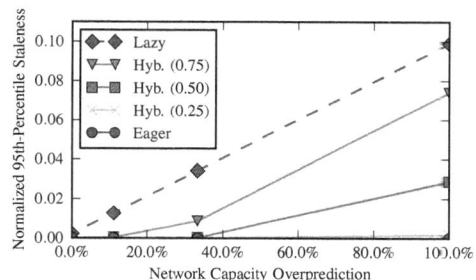

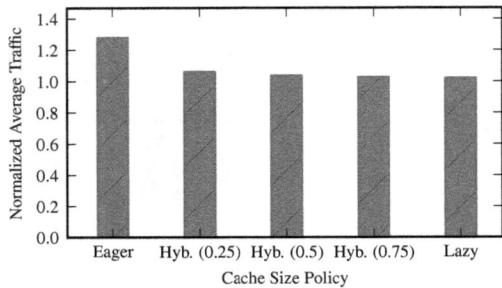

Figure 6: Average traffic for hybrid algorithms with several values of the laziness parameter α. Traffic is normalized relative to an optimal algorithm.

add headroom to the accurate cache size estimates: towards a larger (resp., smaller) cache size in case of the eager (resp., lazy) algorithm. These insights indicate that a more effective cache size estimate should lie somewhere between the estimates for the eager and lazy algorithms. Hence, we propose a *Hybrid* algorithm that computes cache size as a linear combination of eager and lazy cache sizes. Concretely, a Hybrid algorithm with a *laziness parameter* α—denoted by Hybrid(α)—estimates the cache size $c(t)$ at time t as: $c(t) = \alpha \cdot c_l(t) + (1 - \alpha) \cdot c_e(t)$, where $c_l(t)$ and $c_e(t)$ are the lazy and eager cache size estimates, respectively. In our evaluation, we use the Nonuniform model for the eager and the Optimistic model for the lazy cache size estimation respectively, as these most accurately capture the cache sizes of their respective optimal baselines.

Observing Figure 5 again, we see that as we decrease the laziness parameter (α) below about 0.5, and use a more eager approach, the risk of bandwidth misprediction is largely mitigated, and the staleness even under significant bandwidth overprediction remains small.

Note that since predicted network capacity is constant in this figure, traffic is fixed for each algorithm irrespective of the bandwidth prediction error. Figure 6 shows that as we use a more eager hybrid algorithm, traffic increases. This illustrates a tradeoff between traffic and staleness in terms of achieving robustness to network bandwidth overprediction. A reasonable compromise seems to be a low α value, say 0.25. Using this algorithm, traffic is less than 6.0% above optimal, and even when network capacity is overpredicted by 100%, staleness remains below 0.19% of the window length.

Overall, we find that a purely eager online algorithm is susceptible to errors by practical eviction policies, while a purely lazy online algorithm is susceptible to errors in bandwidth prediction. A hybrid algorithm that combines these two approaches provides a good compromise by being more robust to errors in both arrival process and bandwidth estimation.

6. IMPLEMENTATION

We demonstrate the practicality of our algorithms and ultimately their performance by implementing them in Apache Storm [2]. Our prototype uses a distinct Storm cluster at each edge, as well as at the center, in order to distribute the work of aggregation. We choose this multi-cluster approach rather than attempting to deploy a single geo-distributed Storm cluster for two main reasons. First, a single global

Storm cluster would require a custom task scheduler in order to control task placement. Second, and much more critically, Storm was designed and has been optimized for high performance within a single datacenter; it would not be reasonable to expect it to perform well in a geo-distributed setting characterized by high latency and high degrees of compute and bandwidth heterogeneity.

Figure 7 shows the overall architecture, including the edge and center Storm topologies. We briefly discuss each component in the order of data flow from edge to center.

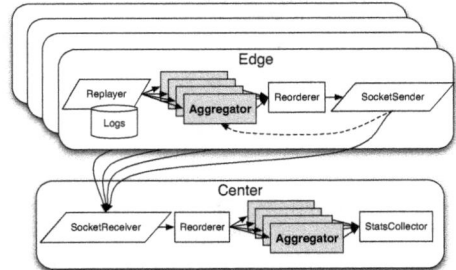

Figure 7: Aggregation is distributed over Apache Storm clusters at each edge as well as at the center.

6.1 Edge

Data enters our prototype through the `Replayer` spout. One instance of this spout runs within each edge, and it is responsible for replaying timestamped logs from a file, reproducing the original pattern of interarrival times. In order to allow us to explore different stream arrival rates, the `Replayer` takes a `speedupFactor` parameter, which dictates how much to speed up or slow down the log replay.

Each line of the logs is parsed using a query-specific parsing function, which produces a triple of (`timestamp`, `key`, `value`). We leverage Twitter's Algebird[8] library to generalize over a broad class of aggregations, so the only restriction on value types is that they must have an Algebird `Semigroup` instance. This is already satisfied for many practical aggregations (e.g., integer sum, unique count via HyperLogLog, etc.), and implementing a custom `Semigroup` is straightforward. The `Replayer` emits these records downstream, and also periodically emits punctuation messages. Carrying only a timestmap, these punctuation messages simply denote that no messages with earlier timestamps will be sent in the future. The frequency of these punctuations is user-specified, though it is required that one be sent to mark the end of each time window.

The next step in the dataflow is the `Aggregator` bolt, for which one or more tasks run at each cluster. Each task is responsible for aggregating a hash-partitioned subset of the key space, and applying a cache size and eviction policy to determine when to transfer partial aggregates to the center. Each task maintains an in-memory key-value map, and uses the Algebird library to aggregate values for a given key. We generalize over a broad range of *eviction policies* by ordering keys using a priority queue with an efficient `changePriority` implementation, and consulting this priority queue to determine the next victim key when it becomes necessary. By defining priority as a function of key, value, existing priority

---

[8]`https://github.com/twitter/algebird`

(if any) and the time that the key was last updated in the map, we can capture a broad range of algorithms including LRU and LFU.

The `Aggregator` also maintains a cache size function, which maps from time within the window to a cache size. This function can be changed at runtime in order to support implementing arbitrary dynamic sizing policies. Specifically, a concrete `Aggregator` instance can install callback functions to be invoked upon the arrival of records or punctuations. This mechanism can be used, for example, to update the cache size function based on arrival rate and miss rate as in our Lazy Pessimistic algorithm, or to record the arrival history for one window and use this history to compute the size function for the next window, as in the Eager Empirical algorithm. For our experiments, we use this mechanism to implement a cache size policy that learns the eager optimal eviction schedule after processing the log trace once.

The `Aggregator` tasks send their output to a single instance of the `Reorderer` bolt. This bolt is responsible for delaying records as needed in order to maintain punctuation semantics. Data then flows into the `SocketSender` bolt, which connects to the central cluster at startup, and has the responsibility of serializing and transmitting partial aggregates downstream to the center using TCP sockets. This `SocketSender` also maintains an estimate of network bandwidth to the center, and periodically emits these estimates upstream to `Aggregator` instances for use in defining their cache size functions. Our bandwidth estimation is based on simple measurements of the rate at which messages can be sent over the network. For a more reliable prediction, we could employ lower-level techniques [7], or even external monitoring services [26].

6.2 Center

At the center, data follows largely the reverse order. First, the `SocketReceiver` spout is responsible for deserializing partial aggregates and punctuations and emitting them downstream into a `Reorderer`, where the streams from multiple edges are synchronized. From there, records flow into the central `Aggregator`, each task of which is responsible for performing the final aggregation over a hash-partitioned subset of the key space. Upon completing aggregation for a window, these central `Aggregator` tasks emit summary metrics including traffic and staleness, and these metrics are summarized by the final `StatsCollector` bolt.

Note that our prototype achieves at-most-once delivery semantics. Storm's acking mechanisms can be used to implement at-least-once semantics, and exactly-once semantics can be achieved by employing additional checks to filter duplicate updates, though we have not implemented these measures.

7. EXPERIMENTAL EVALUATION

To evaluate the performance of our algorithms in a real geo-distributed setting, we deploy our Apache Storm architecture on the PlanetLab testbed. Our PlanetLab deployment uses a total of eleven nodes (64 total cores) spanning seven sites. Central aggregation is performed using a Storm cluster at a single node at `princeton.edu`[9]. Edge locations

include `csuohio.edu`, `uwaterloo.ca`, `yale.edu`, `washington.edu`, `ucla.edu`, and `wisc.edu`. Bandwidth from edge to center varies from as low as 4.5Mbps (`csuohio.edu`) to as high as 150Mbps (`yale.edu`), based on `iperf`. To simulate streaming data, each edge replays a geographic partition of the CDN log data described in Section 3. To explore the performance of our algorithms under a range of workloads, we use the three diverse queries described in Table 1, and we replay the logs at both low and high (8x faster than low) rates. Note that for confidentiality purposes, we do not disclose the actual replay rates, and we present staleness and traffic results normalized relative to the window length and optimal traffic, respectively.

7.1 Aggregation using a Single Edge

Although our work is motivated by the general case of multiple edges, our algorithms were developed based on an in-depth study of the interaction between a single edge and center. We therefore begin by studying the real-world performance of our hybrid algorithm when applied at a single edge. Following the rationale from Section 5.3, we choose a laziness parameter of $\alpha = 0.25$ for this initial experiment, though we will study the tradeoffs of different parameter values shortly.

Compared to the extremes of pure batching and pure streaming, as well as an optimal algorithm based on a priori knowledge of the data stream, our algorithm performs quite well. Figures 8(a) and 8(b) show that our hybrid algorithm very effectively exploits the opportunity to reduce bandwidth relative to streaming, yielding traffic less than 2% higher than the optimal algorithm. At the same time, our hybrid algorithm is able to reduce staleness by 65% relative to a pure batching algorithm.

7.2 Scaling to Multiple Edges

In order to understand how well our algorithm scales beyond a single edge, we partition the log data over three geo-distributed edges. We replay the logs at both low and high rates, and for each of the `large`, `medium`, and `small` queries[10]. As Figures 9(a) and 9(b) demonstrate, our hybrid algorithm performs well throughout. It is worth noting that the edges apply their cache size and cache eviction policies based purely on local information, without knowledge of the decisions made by the other edges, except indirectly via the effect that those decisions have on the available network bandwidth to the center.

Performance is generally more favorable for our algorithm for the `large` and `medium` queries than for the `small` query. The reason is that, for these larger queries, while edge aggregation reduces communication volume, there is still a great deal of data to transfer from the edges to the center. Staleness is quite sensitive to precisely when these partial aggregates are transferred, and our algorithms work well in scheduling this communication. For the `small` query, on the other hand, edge aggregation is extremely effective in reducing data volumes, so much so that there is little risk in delaying communication until the end of the window. For queries that aggregate extremely well, batching is a promis-

---

[9]We originally employed multiple nodes at the center, but were forced to confine our central aggregation to a single node due to PlanetLab's restrictive limitations on daily network bandwidth usage that was quickly exhausted by the communication between Storm workers.

[10]We do not present the results for `large`-high because the amount of traffic generated in these experiments could not be sustained within the PlanetLab bandwidth limits.

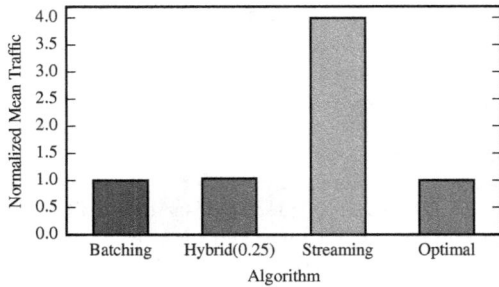

(a) Mean traffic (normalized relative to an optimal algorithm).

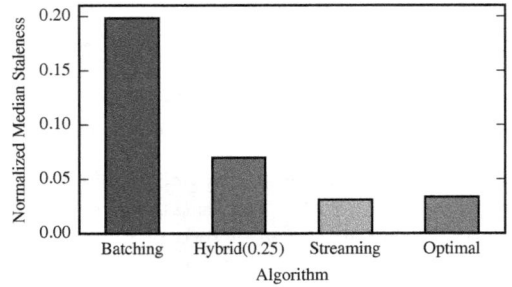

(b) Median staleness (normalized by window length).

Figure 8: Performance for batching, streaming, optimal, and our hybrid algorithm for the `large` query with a low stream arrival rate using a one-edge Apache Storm deployment on PlanetLab.

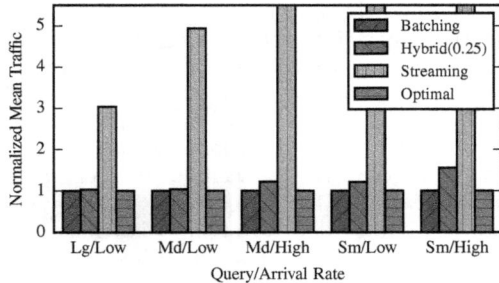

(a) Mean traffic (normalized relative to an optimal algorithm). Normalized traffic values for streaming are truncated, as they range as high as 164.

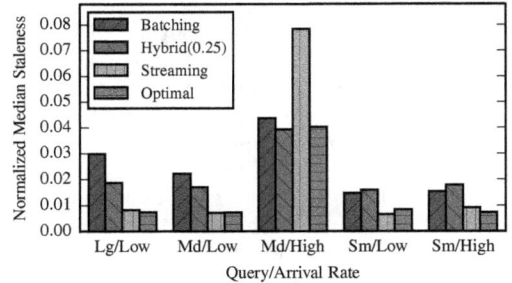

(b) Median staleness (normalized by window length).

Figure 9: Performance for batching, streaming, optimal, and our hybrid algorithm for a range of queries and stream arrival rates using a three-edge Apache Storm deployment on PlanetLab.

ing algorithm, and we do not necessarily outperform batching. The advantage of our algorithm over batching is therefore its broader applicability: the Hybrid algorithm performs roughly as well as batching for small queries, and significantly outperforms it for large queries.

We continue by further partitioning the log data across a total of six geo-distributed edges. Given the higher aggregate compute and network capacity of this deployment, we focus on the `large` query at both low and high arrival rates. From Figure 10(a), we can again observe that our hybrid algorithm yields near-optimal traffic. We can also observe an important effect of stream arrival rate: all else equal, a high stream arrival rate lends itself to more thorough aggregation at the edge. This is evident in the higher normalized traffic for streaming with the high arrival rate than with the low arrival rate.

In terms of staleness, Figure 10(b) shows that our algorithm performs well for the high arrival rate, where the network capacity is more highly constrained, and staleness is therefore more sensitive to the particular scheduling algorithm. At the low arrival rate, we see that our hybrid algorithm performs slightly worse than batching, though in absolute terms this difference is quite small. Our hybrid algorithm generates higher staleness than streaming, but does so at a much lower traffic cost. Just as with the three-edge case, we again see that, where a large opportunity exists, our algorithm exploits it, and where an extreme algorithm such

as batching already suffices, our algorithm remains competitive.

7.3 Effect of Laziness Parameter

In Section 5.3, we observed that a purely eager algorithm is vulnerable to mispredicting which keys will receive further arrivals, while a purely lazy algorithm is vulnerable to overpredicting network bandwidth. This motivated our hybrid algorithm, which uses a linear combination of eager and lazy cache size functions. We explore the real-world tradeoffs of using a more or less lazy algorithm by running experiments with the `large` query at a low replay rate over three edges with laziness parameter α ranging from 0 through 1.0 by steps of 0.25. As expected based on our simulation results, Figure 11(a) shows that α has little effect on traffic when it exceeds about 0.25. Somewhere below this value, the imperfections of practical cache eviction algorithms (LRU in our implementation) begin to manifest. More specifically, at $\alpha = 0$, the hybrid algorithm reduces to a purely eager algorithm, which makes eviction decisions well ahead of the end of the window, and often chooses the wrong victim. By introducing even a small amount of laziness, say with $\alpha = 0.25$, this effect is largely mitigated.

Figure 11(b) shows the opposite side of this tradeoff: a lazier algorithm runs a higher risk of deferring communication too long, in turn leading to higher staleness. Based on staleness alone, a more eager algorithm is better. Based on the shape of these trends, we have chosen to use $\alpha = 0.25$

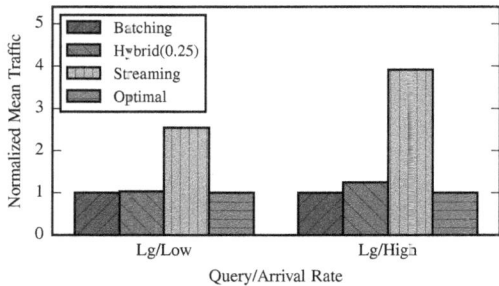

(a) Mean traffic (normalized relative to an optimal algorithm).

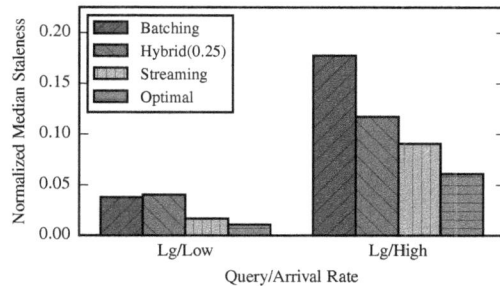

(b) Median staleness (normalized by window length).

Figure 10: Performance for batching, streaming, optimal, and our hybrid algorithm for the large query with low and high stream arrival rates using a six-edge Apache Storm deployment on PlanetLab.

throughout our experiments, but this may not be the optimal value. Further study would be necessary to determine an optimal value of α, and this optimal choice may in fact depend on the relative importance of minimizing staleness versus minimizing traffic.

8. RELATED WORK

Aggregation: Aggregation is a key operator in analytics, and grouped aggregation is supported by many data-parallel programming models [8, 12, 27]. Larson et al. [17] explore the benefits of performing partial aggregation prior to a join operation, much as we do prior to network transmission. While they also recognize similarities to caching, they consider only a fixed-size cache, whereas our approach uses a dynamically varying cache size. In sensor networks, aggregation is often performed over a hierarchical topology to improve energy efficiency and network longevity [18, 24], whereas we focus on cost (traffic) and information quality (staleness). Amur et al. [6] study grouped aggregation, focusing on the design and implementation of efficient data structures for batch and streaming computation. They discuss tradeoffs between eager and lazy aggregation, but do not consider the effect on staleness, a key performance metric in our work.

Streaming systems: Numerous streaming systems [5, 9, 22, 28] have been proposed in recent years. These systems provide many useful ideas for new analytics systems to build upon, but they do not fully explore the challenges that we've described here, in particular how to achieve high quality results (low staleness) at low cost (low traffic).

Wide-area computing: Wide-area computing has received increased research attention in recent years, due in part to the widening gap between data processing and communication costs. Much of this attention has been paid to batch computing [25]. Relatively little work on streaming computation has focused on wide-area deployments, or associated questions such as where to place computation. Pietzuch et al. [20] optimize operator placement in geo-distributed settings to balance between system-level bandwidth usage and latency. Hwang et al. [16] rely on replication across the wide area in order to achieve fault tolerance and reduce straggler effects. JetStream [23] considers wide-area streaming computation, but unlike our work, assumes that it is always better to push more computation to the edge.

Optimization tradeoffs: LazyBase [10] provides a mechanism to trade off increased staleness for faster query response in the case of ad-hoc queries. BlinkDB [4] and JetStream [23] provide mechanisms to trade off accuracy with response time and bandwidth utilization, respectively. Our focus is on *jointly* optimizing both network traffic and staleness. Das et al. [11] have studied the impact of batch intervals on latency and throughput. While their work focuses on setting batching intervals, we study scheduling at the much finer granularity of individual aggregates.

9. CONCLUSION

In this paper, we focused on optimizing the important primitive of windowed grouped aggregation in a wide-area streaming analytics setting on two key metrics: WAN traffic and staleness. We presented a family of optimal offline algorithms that *jointly minimize both staleness and traffic*. Using this as a foundation, we developed practical online aggregation algorithms based on the observation that grouped aggregation can be modeled as a *caching problem* where the cache size varies over time. We explored a range of online algorithms ranging from eager to lazy in terms of how soon they send out updates. We found that a hybrid online algorithm works best in practice, as it is robust to a wide range of network constraints and estimation errors. We demonstrated the practicality of our algorithms through an implementation in Apache Storm, deployed on the PlanetLab testbed. The results of our experiments, driven by workloads derived from anonymized traces of Akamai's web analytics service, showed that our online aggregation algorithms perform close to the optimal algorithms for a variety of system configurations, stream arrival rates, and query types.

10. ACKNOWLEDGMENTS

The authors would like to acknowledge NSF Grant CNS-1413998, and an IBM Faculty Award, which supported this research.

11. REFERENCES

[1] PlanetLab. http://planet-lab.org/, 2015.
[2] Storm, distributed and fault-tolerant realtime computation. http://storm.apache.org/, 2015.
[3] M. Adler, R. K. Sitaraman, and H. Venkataramani. Algorithms for optimizing the bandwidth cost of

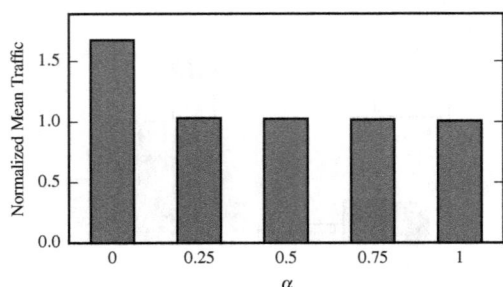

(a) Mean traffic (normalized relative to an optimal algorithm).

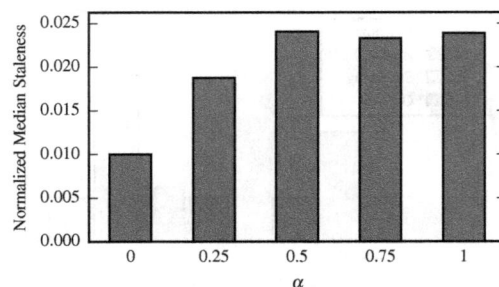

(b) Median staleness (normalized by window length).

Figure 11: Effect of laziness parameter α using a three-edge Apache Storm deployment on PlanetLab with query large.

content delivery. *Computer Networks*, 55(18):4007–4020, Dec. 2011.

[4] S. Agarwal et al. BlinkDB: queries with bounded errors and bounded response times on very large data. In *Proc. of EuroSys*, pages 29–42, 2013.

[5] T. Akidau et al. MillWheel: Fault-tolerant stream processing at internet scale. *Proc. of VLDB Endow.*, 6(11):1033–1044, Aug. 2013.

[6] H. Amur et al. Memory-efficient groupby-aggregate using compressed buffer trees. In *Proc. of SoCC*, 2013.

[7] J. Bolliger and T. Gross. Bandwidth monitoring for network-aware applications. In *Proc. of HPDC*, pages 241–251, 2001.

[8] O. Boykin, S. Ritchie, I. O'Connel, and J. Lin. Summingbird: A framework for integrating batch and online mapreduce computations. In *Proc. of VLDB*, volume 7, pages 1441–1451, 2014.

[9] S. Chandrasekaran et al. TelegraphCQ: Continuous dataflow processing for an uncertain world. In *CIDR*, 2003.

[10] J. Cipar, G. Ganger, K. Keeton, C. B. Morrey, III, C. A. Soules, and A. Veitch. LazyBase: trading freshness for performance in a scalable database. In *Proc. of EuroSys*, pages 169–182, 2012.

[11] T. Das, Y. Zhong, I. Stoica, and S. Shenker. Adaptive stream processing using dynamic batch sizing. In *Proc. of SoCC*, pages 16:1–16:13, 2014.

[12] J. Gray et al. Data cube: A relational aggregation operator generalizing group-by, cross-tab, and sub-totals. *Data Min. Knowl. Discov.*, 1(1):29–53, Jan. 1997.

[13] A. Greenberg, J. Hamilton, D. A. Maltz, and P. Patel. The cost of a cloud: Research problems in data center networks. *SIGCOMM Comput. Commun. Rev.*, 39(1):68–73, Dec. 2008.

[14] B. Heintz, A. Chandra, and R. K. Sitaraman. Optimizing grouped aggregation in geo-distributed streaming analytics. Technical Report TR 15-001, Department of Computer Science, University of Minnesota, 2015.

[15] B. Heintz, A. Chandra, and R. K. Sitaraman. Towards optimizing wide-area streaming analytics. In *Proc. of the 2nd IEEE Workshop on Cloud Analytics*, 2015.

[16] J.-H. Hwang, U. Cetintemel, and S. Zdonik. Fast and highly-available stream processing over wide area networks. In *Proc. of ICDE*, pages 804–813, 2008.

[17] P.-A. Larson. Data reduction by partial preaggregation. In *Proc. of ICDE*, pages 706–715, 2002.

[18] S. Madden, M. J. Franklin, J. M. Hellerstein, and W. Hong. TAG: A Tiny AGgregation service for ad-hoc sensor networks. In *Proc. of OSDI*, 2002.

[19] E. Nygren, R. K. Sitaraman, and J. Sun. The akamai network: a platform for high-performance internet applications. *SIGOPS Oper. Syst. Rev.*, 44(3):2–19, Aug. 2010.

[20] P. Pietzuch et al. Network-aware operator placement for stream-processing systems. In *Proc. of ICDE*, 2006.

[21] S. Podlipnig and L. Böszörmenyi. A survey of web cache replacement strategies. *ACM Comput. Surv.*, 35(4):374–398, Dec. 2003.

[22] Z. Qian et al. TimeStream: reliable stream computation in the cloud. In *Proc. of EuroSys*, pages 1–14, 2013.

[23] A. Rabkin, M. Arye, S. Sen, V. S. Pai, and M. J. Freedman. Aggregation and degradation in JetStream: Streaming analytics in the wide area. In *Proc. of NSDI*, pages 275–288, 2014.

[24] R. Rajagopalan and P. Varshney. Data-aggregation techniques in sensor networks: A survey. *IEEE Communications Surveys Tutorials*, 8(4):48–63, 2006.

[25] A. Vulimiri, C. Curino, B. Godfrey, K. Karanasos, and G. Varghese. WANalytics: Analytics for a geo-distributed data-intensive world. *CIDR 2015*, January 2015.

[26] R. Wolski, N. T. Spring, and J. Hayes. The network weather service: a distributed resource performance forecasting service for metacomputing. *Future Gener. Comput. Syst.*, 15(5-6):757–768, Oct. 1999.

[27] Y. Yu, P. K. Gunda, and M. Isard. Distributed aggregation for data-parallel computing: interfaces and implementations. In *Proc. of SOSP*, pages 247–260, 2009.

[28] M. Zaharia, T. Das, H. Li, T. Hunter, S. Shenker, and I. Stoica. Discretized streams: Fault-tolerant streaming computation at scale. In *Proc. of SOSP*, pages 423–438, 2013.

POW: System-wide Dynamic Reallocation of Limited Power in HPC

Daniel A. Ellsworth, Allen D. Malony
University of Oregon
Eugene, Oregon, USA
{dellswor,malony}@cs.uoregon.edu

Barry Rountree, Martin Schulz
Lawrence Livermore National Laboratory
Livermore, California, USA
{rountree4,schulzm}@llnl.gov

ABSTRACT

Current trends for high-performance computing systems are leading us towards hardware over-provisioning where it is no longer possible to run each component at peak power without exceeding a system or facility wide power bound. In such scenarios, the power consumed by individual components must be artificially limited to guarantee system operation under a given power bound. In this paper, we present the design of a power scheduler capable of enforcing such a bound using dynamic system-wide power reallocation in an application-agnostic manner. Our scheduler achieves better job runtimes than a naïve power scheduling approach without requiring a priori knowledge of application power behavior.

Categories and Subject Descriptors

D.4.m [**Operating Systems**]: Miscellaneous

Keywords

RAPL; hardware over-provisioning; HPC; power bound

1. INTRODUCTION

Scalable parallel applications have been the driving force behind the evolution of large-scale parallel systems with ever-increasing demands for processor, memory, and network performance. The evolution over the past decade has followed a "horizontal" scaling strategy to increase floating-point operations per second (*flops*) and I/O operations per second (*iops*) by adding more of the latest hardware. However, powering a massive cluster at the maximum simultaneous power draw of all hardware components is a major challenge, yet often unnecessary since few applications are able to fully exploit all components at peak capacity.

An alternative power strategy is *hardware over-provisioning*, where more hardware is available than can be powered at maximal draw at any time [4]. In this case, power provisioning and system scale can be designed for the common case,

but mechanisms are required to prevent the system from exceeding the predetermined maximal power draw. New technologies, such as Intel's Running Average Power Limit (RAPL), are a key enabling technology for hardware over-provisioning. However, while RAPL provides the necessary software configurable and hardware enforced power cap per CPU socket, an additional power distribution algorithm to spread the available power across the system is still required.

In this work, we present a dynamic power scheduler that monitors power consumption and reallocates power across a cluster. The power control system enforces the global power bound without requiring integration with the job scheduler. Using a simple heuristic our power scheduler reclaimes wasted power in the overall system to components restricted by their current power bound. This leads us to a dynamic power control system that enforces a global power budget while being completely opaque with respect to the particular applications in the workload, their power and performance characteristics, and their mix.

2. APPROACH

Our work targets large-scale high-performance computing (HPC) systems, primarily with an eye to future exascale platforms. HPC systems represent a substantial capital investment and are typically shared batch-scheduled resources. An HPC system is composed of many compute *nodes*, each with a number of processing elements, including CPUs and accelerators. Users of the system typically submit *jobs* with a desired number of nodes to a job scheduler where each job is queued. The scheduler will schedule a job to run when an adequate number of nodes become available. We will call a subset of the nodes assigned to a job a *partition* or *enclave*, and will assume that any particular node is a member of only one enclave at a time.

The HPC environment is highly parallel and concurrent. User jobs are typically multi-node highly-parallel applications and several jobs will run simultaneously on an HPC system. A job's start time is determined by node availability and a job's end time is based on the actual runtime (or maximum time allocation) of the job. Although the HPC machine is *space-partitioned*, in that each job has its own processing resources, certain shared resources (e.g. network, file system, power) are used by concurrently executing jobs, potentially impacting the runtime behavior across jobs.

One of the major challenges in the move from current petascale to future exascale computation is increasing computational power within realistic electrical power consumption. The current approach of designing power systems to

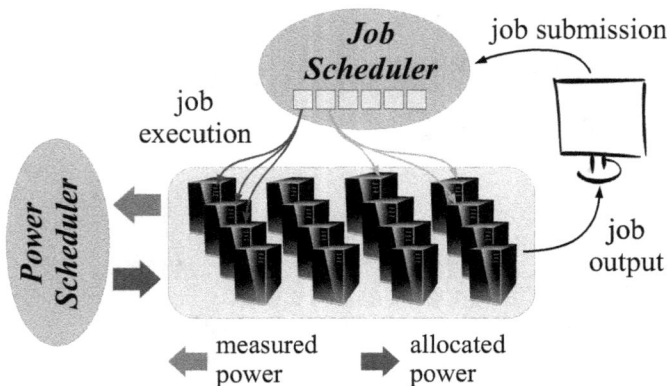

Figure 1: High-level model of system interactions

L	System-wide power limit
n	Number of sockets
t	A timestamp
c_i^t	Power consumed by socket i at time t
a_i^t	Power allocated to socket i at time t
w_i^t	Unused portion of socket i's allocation at time t
C_{min}	Min observable socket consumption
C_{max}	Max observable socket consumption
A_{min}	Min allocation for a socket according to the spec
A_{max}	Max allocation for a socket according to the spec

Table 1: Symbols use in the model

sustain peak power at all times, even though few jobs consume energy at that rate, is therefore unrealistic. Hardware over-provisioning is likely the only way to achieve the increase in computing power while maintaining the power budget, but requires new approaches to distribute the available power to components and to enforce that components stay within their assigned power limits.

We assume future hardware platforms will support an interface with properties similar to Intel's *Running Average Power Limit (RAPL)*. In current systems, components supporting RAPL can enforce a configurable maximum rate of energy consumption over a sliding temporal window. The particular techniques used to enforce the limit are selected and implemented completely by the hardware. The RAPL interface in our testbed uses *model-specific registers (MSRs)* (accessible via *libmsr* [3]) to allow software to interact with the hardware power management facilities.

A mechanism like RAPL alone, however, is insufficient for running in an over-provisioned environment, since it only enables the setting of power bounds for individual components. A global power scheduler is needed to control the individual power bounds for all components and ensure that the total sum of all bounds is below the total system bound. Exceeding the total system bound could damage the HPC cluster or the supporting power infrastructure.

Figure 1 shows a high-level view of the interaction between a potential power scheduler and an HPC cluster. The job scheduler is responsible for assigning jobs to hardware resources as well as starting and stopping the jobs. The power scheduler is solely responsible for analyzing power measurements from the cluster and providing updated power allocations to all cluster components. The HPC cluster itself is primarily concerned with executing jobs from the scheduler, but also provides the integrated infrastructure for power measurement and control used by the power scheduler.

2.1 Power Model

The system-wide power scheduler has the primary objective of enforcing a global power limit, L. We can think of the HPC system as having an infinite amount of energy but having a global maximum limit to the instantaneous rate at which energy can be used[1]. Power-optimization and energy-

---

[1]Energy and power are separate but related ideas. Energy is typically measured in joules. Power is a rate typically measured in watts, representing joules per second.

aware techniques reduce the energy consumed [1, 7, 6], often by reducing the power while maintaining the runtime, allowing more of the hardware over-provisioned system to be used concurrently. These techniques do not provide a guarantee that global rate of energy consumption remains within a fixed bound. Reduced energy consumption and optimal runtimes are secondary objectives for a power scheduler charged with enforcing the global power limit in a hardware over-provisioned system.

A global power limit L is set by facility limitations or administrative policy to protect the power infrastructure from damage due to exceeding capacity. A system is modeled as a set of n sockets. Every socket i has a power consumption, c_i, and a power allocation, a_i. The delta between c_i and a_i is the *wasted*[2] allocation and will be noted as w_i. It is assumed that the hardware enforces $c_i \leq a_i$ or equivalently $a_i = c_i + w_i$. Thus, the total power allocated to the system is $\sum a_i$ and the total power consumption is $\sum c_i$. Further, due to the hardware enforcement, $\sum c_i \leq \sum a_i$.

In the following sections, we will use the intuition that application runtime is roughly the same for any a_i such that $a_i > c_i$. Runtime should only be impacted when a_i is less than the amount an application would consume if there was no power bound. This conclusion is consistent with Fukazawa et al. [2] and our own experiments, which have been omitted for length.

2.2 Static Scheduling

A *static* power scheduler makes a decision about how to schedule power prior to the job launch. A naïve scheduling strategy would be to allocate an equal amount of power to each socket, $a_i = \frac{L}{n}$, over the lifetime of the machine. Since $\sum c_i \leq \sum a_i$, trivially this strategy maintains $L \geq \sum c_i$. Two existing systems at the Lawrence Livermore National Lab (LLNL) use this strategy presently.

While meeting the technical requirement of enforcing a global power bound, the naïve static strategy is expected to under perform. There are two reasons for this. First, prior work has shown a non-linear relationship between power allocation and application performance [5]. Setting each socket to the same level could degrade performance if that level is too low. Second, power consumption could be different on each socket used. A static, equal power setting for all sockets could disrupt performance non-uniformly.

A more refined static power scheduler could attempt some optimization of power distribution if it was aware at scheduling time of an application's characteristic power consump-

---

[2]The power is wasted in that power was allocated to the system but not used by the system.

tion. For instance, if w_i reflects performance behavior under an allocation a_i, then w_i could be used as a basic metric for optimization. Rather than allocating an equal amount of power to each socket, the static scheduler could allocate an equal amount of wasted allocation, w_i, to each socket. The allocation per socket for such a scheduler can be computed using $a_i = c_i + w_{avg}$ where $w_{avg} = \frac{1}{n}(L - \sum c_i)$.

For the more refined static approach, the scheduler must know a priori the corresponding c_i and w_{avg} values in the system. The behavior of a job can change based on the parameters used for execution and there is also an expectation of greater uncertainty in behavior as systems are scaled due to increasing runtime and interactions with other jobs. For long lived clusters, where numerous jobs of various sizes asynchronously enter and exit the system, $\sum c_i$ across the system is expected to vary greatly over time as jobs enter and leave the system. Even within a single job, different phases may consume energy at different rates. Knowledge of per socket power consumption in advance of execution is therefore not feasible in the general case.

2.3 Dynamic Scheduling

Static power scheduling at job launch time cannot maintain w_{avg} across the full machine in the presence of dynamic job power consumption and missing knowledge of future jobs. A dynamic approach to power scheduling is likely required to respond to the dynamic power consumption observed at runtime. Rather than attempting to set a_i once at job start time, a dynamic scheduler can periodically adjust any a_i in the system, even when there is an active job running on the socket.

Extending the model to include time, the scheduler must guarantee for all times t that $L \geq \sum c_i^t$. A basic dynamic scheduler strategy may assume that the power consumption of a running job remains fairly consistent over time, represented by the heuristic $c_i^t \approx c_i^{t-1}$. At time t, the scheduler can know the values c_i^{t-1} and a_i^{t-1}, as reported by the socket, as well as L. The updated per socket allocation can be computed as $a_i^t = c_i^{t-1} + w_{avg}^{t-1}$.

Using the formulation above, a dynamic power scheduler can maintain w_{avg} without any control of the job scheduling. If the scheduler is able to maintain $w_{avg} > 0$ then all applications are expected to complete with their unbounded runtime by the intuition that runtime is not degraded when $a_i^t > c_i^t$. The power scheduler only requires c_i^t and a_i^t for all sockets as input to set all a_i^{t+1} during runtime.

Up to this point in the discussion, there has been an assumption that there is sufficient power to run all scheduled jobs at the optimal power consumption, $c_i^t < \dot{c}_i^t$ for all i and t. This assumption requires a job scheduler that is guaranteed to never oversubscribe power. Due to the challenges discussed for static power scheduling, requiring the job scheduler to produce a schedule that never oversubscribes power and can consume the full system wide power allocation is not practical.

A dynamic scheduler reading where $c_i^t = a_i^t$ could indicate that the power is set to exactly what the application using the socket can consume. Alternatively, $c_i^t = a_i^t$ could indicate that a_i^t was too low and that the hardware reduced consumption on the socket, degrading application performance. The responsiveness of a dynamic power scheduler to increased consumption, using the formulation in this section, is expected to be impacted by both the scheduling interval

and the per socket wasted power allocation due to the assumption $c_i^t \approx c_i^{t+1}$ and hardware enforcement of $c_i^t \leq a_i^t$.

3. DESIGN

POWsched is a *dynamic* power scheduler based on the model and approach discussed in the previous section. Scheduling decisions in POWsched are per socket and are completely agnostic with respect to job, enclave, and node the socket is associated with. POWsched maintains a system-wide power bound without job scheduler coordination using only per socket observed power consumption to guide power scheduling across a cluster.

Pseudocode for the scheduler is provided in Algorithm 1. The scheduling task is performed in three phases during each scheduling interval. In Phase 1 POWsched collects recent consumption readings from all sockets. In Phase 2 power is greedily recovered from the existing allocations for later distribution. In Phase 3 additional power is given to sockets that may be able to use the power. At the end of Phase 3, POWsched sleeps the remainder of the scheduling interval.

Separation of power allocation into two phases is needed to guarantee that the system wide power limit is never exceeded due to communication delays. Recall that $a_i^t \leq L$ must be maintained for RAPL to successfully enforce $c_i^t \leq L$. Assume $a_0^t + a_1^t = L$. If the scheduler computes $a_0^t > a_0^{t+1}$ and $a_1^t < a_1^{t+1}$ and sends a_0^{t+1} and a_1^{t+1} at the same time, communication delays might cause socket 1 to update the allocation before socket 0. For a short interval the allocated power will be $a_0^t + a_1^{t+1} > L$, which is a violation of the system power bound. POWsched must be certain that all sockets receiving a lower allocation have been updated before any sockets receiving a higher allocation are updated.

POWsched does not compute w_{avg}. A target w_i is used to account for the measurement jitter and greedily reclaim power from under consuming sockets. POWsched assumes the system is oversubscribed and steals a percentage of the allocation for each socket allocated more than the system wide average per socket allocation ($a_i > \frac{L}{n}$) when no power can be reclaimed and very little surplus power is available. When adjusting allocations up, POWsched divides the surplus power evenly across the sockets consuming near their current allocation. When power is abundant, the allocation up behavior is expected to result in a lot of wasted power that can then be greedily collected in the next scheduling round. When power is scarce, the allocation up and power stealing behavior will eventually converge at a fair allocation across all sockets.

We implemented POWsched in C using libmsr to access the RAPL MSRs and MPI for collective communication. In our experiments with POWsched on the cab cluster at LLNL, POWsched is deployed as a separate process co-resident with the actual application workload[3]. This strategy allows us to use existing system setups within the constraints of the existing job scheduler. In future systems power scheduling is likely to be provided as part of the system stack by a global operating system.

Our preliminary results indicate overall runtime can be improved over naïve power scheduling. We have observed a 10% reduction in runtime versus naïve scheduling in most experiments where power is constrained.

---

[3] A workload in our experiments consist of several concurrent jobs.

Algorithm 1 POWsched logic in pseudocode

$q \leftarrow$ target w_i
C stores $\{c_0, \cdots, c_{n-1}\}$
A stores $\{a_0, \cdots, a_{n-1}\}$
M stores $\{m_0, \cdots, m_{n-1}\}$
numdown $\leftarrow$ count of nodes yielding power
interval $\leftarrow$ scheduling interval
reclaimfactor $\leftarrow$ power to reserve when stealing

procedure MAIN
    while *True* **do**
        GETREADINGS   ▷ Phase 1
        ALLOCDOWN   ▷ Phase 2
        ALLOCUP   ▷ Phase 3
        sleep rest of interval
    end while
end procedure

procedure GETREADINGS
    for all sockets **do**
        Update c_i with the current reading
    end for
end procedure

procedure ALLOCDOWN
    numdown $\leftarrow 0$
    for all sockets **do**
        if $c_i < a_i - q$ **then**
            Update a_i to $max\{c_i + q, A_{min}\}$
            numdown $\leftarrow$ numdown $+ 1$
            Update m_i to *False*
        else
            Update m_i to *True*
        end if
    end for
    if numdown$= 0$ and $\sum a_i + n \geq L$ **then**
        for all sockets **do**
            if $a_i > \frac{L}{n}$ **then**
                $a_i \leftarrow a_i - (a_i - \frac{L}{n}) \times (1-\text{reclaimfactor})$
                $m_i \leftarrow$ *True*
            end if
        end for
    end if
    for all sockets **do**
        Set the socket to limit a_i
    end for
end procedure

procedure ALLOCUP
    $u \leftarrow \frac{(L-\sum a_i)}{n-\text{numdown}}$
    for all sockets **do**
        if m_i **then**
            $a_i \leftarrow min\{a_i + u, A_{max}\}$
        end if
    end for
    for all sockets **do**
        Set the socket to limit a_i
    end for
end procedure

4. CONCLUSION

We have described a system-wide dynamic power scheduler that enforces a global power limit on an HPC system without requiring application specific profiling or application modification. POWsched monitors power consumption during the execution of multiple simultaneous applications and reallocates power to individual node sockets based on simple heuristic. We expect POWsched to out perform static fixed power allocation without a priori application analysis due to the ability to dynamically reallocate power from under consuming sockets to power bound sockets. Future work will focus on performance evaluation and assessing scalability issues in anticipation of next-generation exascale systems.

5. ACKNOWLEDGMENTS

Part of this work was performed under the auspices of the U.S. Department of Energy by Lawrence Livermore National Laboratory under Contract DE-AC52-07NA27344 (LLNL-CONF-669276). Work by the University of Oregon is supported by the DOE Office of Science, through a Sub-Contract No. 3F-32643 from the University of Chicago, Argonne, LLC (as operator of Argonne National Laboratory), under Prime Contract No. DE-AC02-06CH11357.

6. REFERENCES

[1] M. Bambagini, M. Bertogna, M. Marinoni, and G. Buttazzo. An energy-aware algorithm exploiting limited preemptive scheduling under fixed priorities. In *8th IEEE International Symposium on Industrial Embedded Systems (SIES)*, pages 3–12. IEEE, 2013.

[2] K. Fukazawa, M. Ueda, M. Aoyagi, T. Tsuhata, K. Yoshida, A. Uehara, M. Kuze, Y. Inadomi, and K. Inoue. Power consumption evaluation of an mhd simulation with cpu power capping. In *Cluster, Cloud and Grid Computing (CCGrid), 2014 14th IEEE/ACM International Symposium on*, pages 612–617. IEEE, 2014.

[3] L. L. N. S. LLC. libmsr. https://github.com/scalability-llnl/libmsr.

[4] T. Patki, D. K. Lowenthal, B. Rountree, M. Schulz, and B. R. de Supinski. Exploring hardware overprovisioning in power-constrained, high performance computing. In *27th ACM International Conference on Supercomputing*, pages 173–182. ACM, 2013.

[5] B. Rountree, D. H. Ahn, B. R. de Supinski, D. K. Lowenthal, and M. Schulz. Beyond dvfs: A first look at performance under a hardware-enforced power bound. In *IEEE 26th International Parallel and Distributed Processing Symposium Workshops (IPDPSW),*, pages 947–953. IEEE, 2012.

[6] B. Rountree, D. K. Lownenthal, B. R. de Supinski, M. Schulz, V. W. Freeh, and T. Bletsch. Adagio: making dvs practical for complex hpc applications. In *23rd ACM International Conference on Supercomputing*, pages 460–469. ACM, 2009.

[7] A. Tiwari, M. Laurenzano, J. Peraza, L. Carrington, and A. Snavely. Green queue: Customized large-scale clock frequency scaling. In *Second International Conference on Cloud and Green Computing (CGC)*, pages 260–267. IEEE, 2012.

Achieving Performance Isolation with Lightweight Co-Kernels

Jiannan Ouyang, Brian Kocoloski,
John Lange
Department of Computer Science
University of Pittsburgh
{ouyang, briankoco, jacklange}
@cs.pitt.edu

Kevin Pedretti
Center for Computing Research
Sandia National Laboratories
ktpedre@sandia.gov

ABSTRACT

Performance isolation is emerging as a requirement for High Performance Computing (HPC) applications, particularly as HPC architectures turn to *in situ* data processing and application composition techniques to increase system through-put. These approaches require the co-location of disparate workloads on the same compute node, each with different resource and runtime requirements. In this paper we claim that these workloads cannot be effectively managed by a single Operating System/Runtime (OS/R). Therefore, we present *Pisces*, a system software architecture that enables the co-existence of multiple independent and fully isolated OS/Rs, or *enclaves*, that can be customized to address the disparate requirements of next generation HPC workloads. Each enclave consists of a specialized lightweight OS co-kernel and runtime, which is capable of independently managing partitions of dynamically assigned hardware resources. Contrary to other co-kernel approaches, in this work we consider performance isolation to be a primary requirement and present a novel co-kernel architecture to achieve this goal. We further present a set of design requirements necessary to ensure performance isolation, including: (1) elimination of cross OS dependencies, (2) internalized management of I/O, (3) limiting cross enclave communication to explicit shared memory channels, and (4) using virtualization techniques to provide missing OS features. The implementation of the Pisces co-kernel architecture is based on the Kitten Lightweight Kernel and Palacios Virtual Machine Monitor, two system software architectures designed specifically for HPC systems. Finally we will show that lightweight isolated co-kernels can provide better performance for HPC applications, and that isolated virtual machines are even capable of outperforming native environments in the presence of competing workloads.

Categories and Subject Descriptors

D.4.7 [**Operating Systems**]: Organization and Design

Keywords

Operating Systems, Virtualization, Exascale

1. INTRODUCTION

Performance isolation has become a significant issue for both cloud and High Performance Computing (HPC) environments [6, 25, 9]. This is particularly true as modern applications increasingly turn to composition and *in situ* data processing [21, 32] as substrates for reducing data movement [18] and utilizing the abundance of computational resources available locally on each node. While these techniques have the potential to improve I/O performance and increase scalability, composing disparate application workloads in this way can negatively impact performance by introducing cross workload interference between each application component that shares a compute node's hardware and Operating System/Runtime (OS/R) environment. These effects are especially problematic when combined with traditional Bulk Synchronous Parallel (BSP) HPC applications, which are particularly prone to interference resulting from noise and other system-level overheads across the nodes of large scale deployments [24, 11, 13]. While previous work has identified shared hardware resources as a source of interference, we claim that workload interference can also result from shared resources residing inside a node's *system software*. Therefore, to fully prevent interference from affecting a given workload on a system, it is necessary to provide isolation features both at the hardware and system software layers.

In the last decade, HPC systems have converged to use Linux as the preferred node operating system. This has led Linux to emerge as the dominant environment for many modern HPC systems [31, 14] due to its support of exten-

This project is made possible by support from the National Science Foundation (NSF) via grant CNS-1421585, and by the 2013 Exascale Operating and Runtime Systems Program under the Office of Advanced Scientific Computing Research in the DOE Office of Science. Sandia National Laboratories is a multi-program laboratory managed and operated by Sandia Corporation, a wholly owned subsidiary of Lockheed Martin Corporation, for the U.S. Department of Energy's National Nuclear Security Administration under contract DE-AC04-94AL85000.

sive feature sets, ease of programmability, familiarity to application developers, and general ubiquity. While Linux environments provide tangible benefits to both usability and maintainability, they contain fundamental limitations when it comes to providing effective performance isolation. This is because commodity systems, such as Linux, are designed to maximize a set of design goals that conflict with those required to provide complete isolation. Specifically, commodity systems are almost always designed to maximize resource utilization, ensure fairness, and most importantly, gracefully degrade in the face of increasing loads. These goals often result in software level interference that has a significant impact on HPC application performance as these workloads are susceptible to system noise and overheads.

To address these issues we present *Pisces*, an OS/R architecture designed primarily to provide full system isolation for HPC environments through the use of *lightweight co-kernels*. [1] In our architecture, multiple heterogeneous OS/R instances co-exist on a single HPC compute node and directly manage independent sets of hardware resources. Each co-kernel executes as a fully independent OS/R environment that does not rely on any other instance for system level services, thus avoiding cross workload contention on system software resources and ensuring that a single OS/R cannot impact the performance of the entire node. Each co-kernel is capable of providing fully isolated OS/Rs, or *enclaves*, to local workloads. This approach allows a user to dynamically compose independent enclaves from arbitrary sets of local hardware resources at runtime based on a coupled applications' resource and isolation requirements.

While others have explored the concept of lightweight co-kernels coupled with Linux [23, 30, 28], our approach is novel in that we consider performance isolation to be the primary design goal. In contrast to other systems, where some or all system services are delegated to remote OS/Rs to achieve application compatibility, we explicitly eliminate cross OS dependencies for external services. Instead, each co-kernel must provide a self contained set of system services that are implemented internally. Second, we require that each co-kernel implement its own I/O layers and device drivers that internalize the management of hardware and I/O devices. Third, we restrict cross enclave communication to user space via explicit shared memory channels [17], and do not provide any user space access to in-kernel message passing interfaces. Finally, we support applications that require unavailable features through the use of fully isolated virtual machines hosted by the lightweight co-kernel. Taken together, these design requirements ensure that our system architecture can provide full isolation at both the hardware and software levels for existing and future HPC applications.

As a foundation for this work, we have leveraged our experience with the Kitten Lightweight Kernel (LWK) and the Palacios Virtual Machine Monitor (VMM) [19]. Previous work has shown the benefits of using both Palacios and Kitten to provide scalable and flexible lightweight system software to large scale supercomputing environments [20], as well as the potential of properly configured virtualized environments to outperform native environments for certain workloads [16]. In this paper we present a novel approach to achieving workload isolation by leveraging both Kitten and Palacios, deployed using the Pisces co-kernel framework, to

---

[1] http://www.prognosticlab.org/pisces

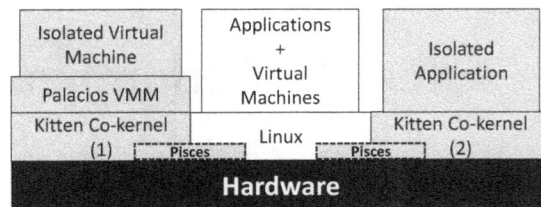

Figure 1: **The Pisces Co-Kernel Architecture**

provide lightweight isolation environments on systems running full featured OS/Rs.

We claim that our approach is novel in the following ways:

- Pisces emphasizes isolation as the primary design goal and so provides fully isolated OS instances, each of which has direct control over its assigned hardware resources (including I/O devices) and furthermore contains no dependencies on an external OS for core functionality.

- With Pisces, hardware resources are *dynamically* partitioned and assigned to specialized OS/Rs running on the same physical machine. In turn, enclaves can be created and destroyed at runtime based on application requirements.

- We leverage the Palacios VMM coupled with a Kitten co-kernel to provide fully isolated environments to arbitrary OS/Rs.

2. HIGH LEVEL APPROACH

At the heart of our approach is the ability to dynamically decompose a node's hardware resources into multiple partitions, each capable of supporting a fully independent and isolated OS environment. Each OS instance is referred to as an enclave, which is dynamically constructed based on the runtime requirements of an application. A high level overview of the Pisces system architecture is shown in Figure 1. In this environment a single Linux environment has dynamically created two separate enclaves to host a composed application, consisting of a traditional HPC simulation running natively on a co-kernel, and a coupled data visualization/analytic application running inside an isolated VM. Each enclave OS/R directly manages the hardware resources assigned to it, while also allowing dynamic resource assignment based on changing performance needs.

The ability to dynamically compose collections of hardware resources provides significant flexibility for system management. This also enables lightweight enclaves to be brought up quickly and cheaply since they can be initialized with a very limited set of resources, for example a single core and 128 MB of memory, and then dynamically expanded based on the needs of a given application. Furthermore, to fully ensure performance isolation for a given application, each enclave has direct control of the I/O devices that it has been assigned. This is in contrast to many existing OS/hypervisor architectures that incorporate the concept of a driver domain or I/O service domain to mediate access to shared I/O resources. Instead, we provide hosted workloads with direct access to the underlying hardware devices, relying on the hardware's ability to partition and isolate them from the different enclaves in the system.

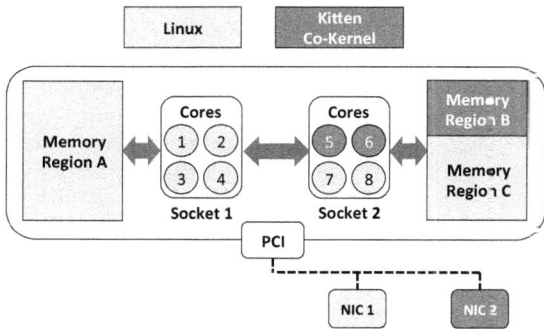

Figure 2: **Example Hardware Configuration with one Pisces Co-Kernel**

Figure 2 shows an example configuration of a co-kernel running on a subset of hardware resources. In this example case, a Linux environment is managing the majority of system resources with the exception of 2 CPU cores and half the memory in the 2nd NUMA domain, which are assigned to the co-kernel. In addition, the co-kernel has direct control over one of the network interfaces connected through the PCI bus. It is important to note that partitioning the hardware resources in the manner presented here is possible only if the hardware itself supports isolated operation both in terms of performance as well as management. Therefore, the degree to which we can partition a local set of resources is largely system and architecture dependent, and relies on the capabilities of the underlying hardware.

2.1 Background

Kitten Lightweight Kernel. The Kitten Lightweight Kernel [19] is a special-purpose OS kernel designed to provide an efficient environment for executing highly-scalable HPC applications at full-system scales (10's of thousands of compute nodes). [2] Kitten is similar in design to previous LWKs, such as SUNMOS [22], Puma/Cougar [29], and Catamount [15], that have been deployed on Department of Energy supercomputers. Some of Kitten's unique characteristics are its modern code base that is partially derived from the Linux kernel, its improved Linux API and ABI compatibility that allows it to fit in better with standard HPC toolchains, and its use of virtualization to provide full-featured OS support when needed.

The basic design philosophy underlying Kitten is to constrain OS functionality to the bare essentials needed to support highly scalable HPC applications and to cover the rest through virtualization. Kitten therefore augments the traditional LWK design [26] with a hypervisor capability, allowing full-featured OS instances to be launched on-demand in virtual machines running on top of Kitten. This allows the core Kitten kernel to remain small and focused, and to use the most appropriate resource management policies for the target workload rather than one-size-fits-all policies.

Palacios Virtual Machine Monitor. Palacios [19, 20] is a publicly available, open source, OS-independent VMM that targets the x86 and x86_64 architectures (hosts and guests) with either AMD SVM or Intel VT extensions. It is designed

---

[2]https://software.sandia.gov/trac/kitten

to be embeddable into diverse host OSes, and is currently fully supported in both Linux and Kitten based environments. When embedded into Kitten, the combination acts as a lightweight hypervisor supporting full system virtualization. Palacios can run on generic PC hardware, in addition to specialized hardware such as Cray supercomputer systems. In combination with Kitten, Palacios has been shown to provide near native performance when deploying tightly coupled HPC applications at large scale (4096 nodes on a Cray XT3).

3. PISCES CO-KERNEL ARCHITECTURE

The core design goal of Pisces is to provide isolated heterogeneous runtime environments on the same node in order to fulfill the requirements of complex applications with disparate OS/R requirements. Co-kernel instances provide isolated enclaves with specialized system software for tightly coupled HPC applications sensitive to performance interference, while a traditional Linux based environment is available for applications with larger feature requirements such as data analytics, visualization, and management workloads. Our work assumes that hardware level isolation is achieved explicitly through well established allocation techniques (memory/CPU pinning, large pages, NUMA binding, etc.), and instead we focus our work on extending isolation to the software layers as well.

The architecture of our system is specifically designed to provide as much isolation as possible so as to avoid interference from the system software. In order to ensure that isolation is maintained we made several explicit decisions while designing and implementing the Pisces architecture:

- Each enclave must implement its own complete set of supported system calls. System call forwarding is not supported in order to avoid contention inside another OS instance.

- Each enclave must provide its own I/O device drivers and manage its hardware resources directly. Driver domains are not actively supported, as they can be a source of contention and overhead with I/O heavy workloads.

- Cross enclave communication is not a kernel provided feature. All cross enclave communication is explicitly initialized and managed by userspace applications using shared memory.

- For applications with larger feature requirements than provided by the native co-kernel, we use a co-kernel based virtual machine monitor to provide isolated VM instances.

3.1 Cross Kernel Dependencies

A key claim we make in this paper is that cross workload interference is the result of both hardware resource contention and *system software* behavior. It should be noted that software level interference is not necessarily the result of contention on shared software resources, but rather fundamental behaviors of the underlying OS/R. This means that even with the considerable amount of work that has gone into increasing the *scalability* of Linux [5] there still remain a set of fundamental issues that introduce interference as the utilization of the system increases.

A common source of system software level interference are the system calls invoked by an application. Many of the control paths taken by common system calls contain edge cases in which considerably longer execution paths can be invoked under certain conditions. As an example, any system call that allocates memory from a slab allocator will with a certain (though small) probability be forced to undertake additional memory management operations based on the current state of the slab cache. The probability of these edge cases occurring increases along with the system utilization. As more workloads attempt to allocate memory from a slab cache, the probability of it being empty (and so requiring a more heavy weight allocation) increases. Operations such as this directly add overhead to an application, and must be avoided to ensure full isolation. It is for this reason that our architecture explicitly forbids reliance on another external OS/R for system call handling.

Our approach is in direct contrast to other co-kernel approaches that have been proposed [23, 28], and which make extensive use of system call forwarding and other inter-kernel communication. Our approach avoids not only the overhead associated with cross enclave messaging, but also ensures that interference cannot be caused by additional workloads in a separate OS/R instance.

	solitary workload (usecs)	w/ other workloads (usecs)
Linux	3.05	3.48
co-kernel fwd	6.12	14.00
co-kernel	0.39	0.36

Table 1: **Execution time of getpid() (in us).**

To demonstrate how system call forwarding can impact isolation, we conducted an experiment that measured the execution time of several implementations of the getpid() system call under different load conditions. These results, included in Table 1, show how additional workloads (parallel Linux kernel compilations) impact the performance of even simple system calls when they are executed in the same OS/R. For this experiment we evaluated the performance of getpid() natively on Linux as well as handled natively inside a co-kernel. In addition, we implemented a simple system call forwarding interface to measure the overheads associated with forwarding the system call to Linux (co-kernel fwd). For each of these cases we measured the execution time with and without a second workload. Each workload was isolated as much as possible at the hardware layer by pinning CPUs and memory to separate NUMA domains. Our results show that a native Linux environment adds an additional 14% overhead to the execution time of getpid() when running with additional workloads on the system. In contrast our isolated co-kernel shows no additional overhead, and in fact performs slightly better even when the other OS/R is heavily utilized. Finally, our system call forwarding implementation shows a drastic slowdown of 128% when handled by a highly utilized Linux environment. While our system call forwarding implementation is likely not as efficient as it could be, it does demonstrate the effect that cross workload interference can have on an application in a separate OS/R if it is not properly isolated.

3.2 I/O and Device Drivers

In addition to system call handling, device I/O represents another potential source of interference between workloads. The same issues discussed with system calls apply to the I/O paths as well, in which higher levels of utilization can trigger longer execution paths inside the I/O handling layers. Therefore, in order to further avoid software level interference, we require that each enclave independently manage its own hardware resources, including I/O devices. This requires that each independent OS/R contain its own set of device drivers to allow hosted applications access to the devices that have been explicitly assigned to that enclave. This prevents interference caused by other application behaviors, as well as eliminates contention on I/O resources that could be caused by sharing I/O devices or by routing I/O requests to a single driver domain. This approach does require that I/O devices either support partitioning in some way (e.g., SRIOV [7]) or that they be allocated entirely to one enclave. While this would appear to be inefficient, it matches our space sharing philosophy and furthermore it represents the same requirements placed on passthrough I/O devices in virtualized systems.

	solitary workload (ms)	w/ other workloads (ms)
Linux	231.69	312.66
co-kernel	212.75	212.38

Table 2: **Execution time of sequential reads from a block device**

Table 2 shows the benefits of isolated I/O in the case of a SATA disk. In this case we measured the performance differences between a local device driver implementation both on Linux and inside a co-kernel. For this experiment we evaluated the performance of sequential reads from a secondary SATA disk exported as a raw block device bypassing any file system layers. As with the first experiment additional workloads took the form of parallel kernel compilations occurring on the primary SATA disk hosting the main Linux file system. Accessing the SATA disk from Kitten required a custom SATA driver and block device layer which we implemented from scratch to provide zero-copy block access for our Kitten applications while also sharing a single SATA controller with other enclave OS/Rs. The results show that the optimized Kitten driver is able to outperform the Linux storage layer in each case, however more importantly the co-kernel is able to maintain isolation without meaningful performance degradation even in the face of competing workloads contending on the same SATA controller. Linux, on the other hand, demonstrates significant performance degradation when a competing workload is introduced even though it is accessing separate hardware resources.

3.3 Cross Enclave Communication

While full isolation is the primary design goal of our system, it is still necessary to provide communication mechanisms in order to support *in situ* and composite application architectures. Cross enclave interactions are also necessary to support system administration and management tasks. To support these requirements while also enforcing

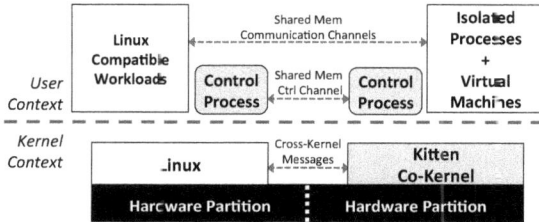

Figure 3: **Cross Enclave Communication in Pisces**

the isolation properties we have so far discussed, we chose to restrict communication between processes on separate enclaves to explicitly created shared memory regions mapped into a process' address space by using the XEMEM shared memory system [17]. While this arrangement does force user space applications to implement their own communication operations on top of raw shared memory, it should be noted that this is not a new problem for many HPC applications. Moreover this decision allows our architecture to remove cross enclave IPC services from the OS/R entirely, thus further ensuring performance isolation at the system software layer.

Due to the fact that communication is only allowed between user space applications, management operations must therefore be accomplished via user space. Each enclave is required to bootstrap a local control process that is responsible for the internal management of the enclave. Administrative operations are assumed to originate from a single management enclave running a full featured OS/R (in our case Linux), which is responsible for coordinating resource and workload assignments between itself and each locally hosted co-kernel. Administrative operations are therefore accomplished through control messages that are sent and received across a shared memory channel between the enclave control process and a global administrative service in the management enclave.

Figure 3 illustrates the model for communication between enclaves managed by a Linux environment and a Kitten co-kernel. While the purpose of our approach is to avoid unpredictable noise in the form of inter-core interrupts (IPIs) and processing delays that would necessarily accompany a kernel-level message-oriented approach, it is nevertheless necessary to allow some level of inter-kernel communication in some situations, specifically in the bootstrap phase and when dealing with legacy I/O devices. For these purposes we have implemented a small inter-kernel message passing interface that permits a limited set of operations. However this communication is limited to only the kernel systems where it is necessary, and is not accessible to any user space process.

3.4 Isolated Virtual Machines

The main limitation of lightweight kernels is the fact that the features they remove in order to ensure performance consistency are often necessary to support general purpose applications and runtimes. This is acceptable when the application set is tightly constrained, but for more general HPC environments and applications a larger OS/R feature set is required. For these applications we claim that we can still provide the isolation benefits of our co-kernel approach *as well as* their required feature set through the use of isolated virtual machine instances. For these applications our co-

kernel architecture is capable of providing a full featured OS/R inside a lightweight virtual environment hosted on the Palacios VMM coupled with a Kitten co-kernel, which we denote as a co-VMM. While past work has shown that Palacios is capable of virtualizing large scale HPC systems with little to no overhead, the isolation properties of Palacios (deployed as a co-VMM) actually provide *performance benefits* to applications. As we will show, a full featured Linux VM deployed on a co-VMM is capable of *outperforming* a native Linux environment when other workloads are concurrently executing on the same node.

4. PISCES IMPLEMENTATION

The Pisces architecture extends the Kitten Lightweight Kernel to allow multiple instances of it to run concurrently with a Linux environment. Each Kitten co-kernel instance is given direct control over a subset of the local hardware resources, and is able to manage its resources directly without any coordination with other kernel instances running on the same machine. Pisces includes the following components:

1. A Linux kernel module that allows the initialization and management of co-kernel instances.

2. Modifications to the Kitten architecture to support dynamic resource assignment as well as sparse (non-contiguous) sets of hardware resources.

3. Modifications to the Palacios VMM to support dynamic resource assignment and remote loading of VM images from the Linux environment.

As part of the implementation we made a significant effort to avoid any code changes to Linux itself, in order to ensure wide compatibility across multiple environments. As a result our co-kernel architecture is compatible with a wide range of unmodified Linux kernels (2.6.3x - 3.x.y). The Linux side components consist of the Pisces kernel module that provides boot loader services and a set of user-level management tools implemented as Linux command line utilities.

The co-kernel used in this work is a highly modified version of the Kitten lightweight kernel as previously described. The majority of the modifications to Kitten centered around removing assumptions that it had full control over the entire set of system resources. Instead we modified its operation to only manage resources that it was explicitly granted access to, either at initialization or dynamically during runtime. Specifically, we removed the default resource discovery mechanisms and replaced them with explicit assignment interfaces called by a user-space management process. Other modifications included a small inter-kernel message passing interface and augmented support for I/O device assignment. In total our modifications required ~9,000 lines of code. The modifications to Palacios consisted of a command forwarding interface from the Linux management enclave to the VMM running in a Kitten instance, as well as changes to allow dynamic resource assignments forwarded from Kitten. Together these changes consisted of ~5,000 lines of code.

In order to avoid modifications to the host Linux environment, our approach relies on the ability to *offline* resources in modern Linux kernels. The offline functionality allows a system administrator to remove a given resource from Linux's allocators and subsystems while still leaving the resource physically accessible. In this way we are able to dynamically remove resources such as CPU cores, memory blocks and PCI devices from a running Linux kernel. Once a resource has been offlined, a running co-kernel is allowed to assume direct control over it. In this way, even though both Linux and a co-kernel have full access to the complete set of hardware resources they are able to only assume control of a discontiguous set of resources assigned to them.

4.1 Booting a Co-kernel

Initializing a Kitten co-kernel is done by invoking a set of Pisces commands from the Linux management enclave. First a single CPU core and memory block (typically 128 MB) is taken offline, and removed from Linux's control. The Pisces boot loader then loads a Kitten kernel image and init task into memory and then initializes the boot environment. The boot environment is then instantiated at the start of the offlined memory block, and contains information needed to initialize the co-kernel and a set of special memory regions used for cross enclave communication and console I/O. The Kitten kernel image and init task are then copied into the memory block below the boot parameters. Pisces then replaces the host kernel's trampoline (CPU initialization) code with a modified version that initializes the CPU into long (64 bit) mode and then jumps to a specified address at the start of the boot parameters, which contains a set of assembly instructions that jump immediately into the Kitten kernel itself. Once the trampoline is configured, the Pisces boot loader issues a special INIT IPI (Inter-Processor Interrupt) to the offlined CPU to force it to reinitialize using the modified trampoline.

Once the target CPU for the co-kernel has been initialized, execution will vector into the Kitten co-kernel and begin the kernel initialization process. Kitten will proceed to initialize the local CPU core as well as the local APIC and eventually launch the loaded init task. The main difference is that instead of scanning for I/O devices and other external resources, the co-kernel instead queries a resource map provided inside the boot parameters. This resource map specifies the hardware that the co-kernel is allowed to access (offlined inside the Linux environment). Finally, the co-kernel activates a flag notifying the Pisces boot loader that initialization is complete, at which point Pisces reverts the trampoline back to the original Linux version. This reversion is necessary to support the CPU online operation in Linux, which is used to return the CPU to Linux after the co-kernel enclave has been destroyed.

4.2 Communicating with the co-kernel

Operation	Latency (ms)
Booting a Co-kernel	265.98
Adding a single CPU core	33.74
Adding a 128MB memory block	82.66
Adding an Ethernet NIC	118.98

Table 3: **Latency of various Pisces operations.**

To allow control of a Pisces co-kernel, the init task that is launched after boot contains a small control process that is able to communicate back to the Linux environment. This allows a Pisces management process running inside Linux to issue a set of commands to control the operation of the co-kernel enclave. These commands allow the dynamic assignment and revocation of additional hardware resources, as well as loading and launching VMs and processes inside the co-kernel. The communication mechanism is built on top of a shared memory region included in the initial memory block assigned at boot time. This shared memory region implements a simple message passing protocol, and is used entirely for communication with the control process in the co-kernel. Table 3 reports the latency for booting and dynamically assigning various hardware resources to a co-kernel.

In addition to the enclave control channel, an additional communication channel exists to allow the co-kernel to issue requests back to the Linux environment. The use of this channel is minimized to only routines that are strictly necessary and cannot be avoided, including the loading of VMs and applications from the Linux file system, configuration of the global IOMMU, and IRQ forwarding for legacy devices. Based on our design goals, we tried to limit the uses of this channel as much as possible to prevent the co-kernel from relying on Linux features. In particular, we did not want to rely on this channel as a means of doing system call forwarding, as that would break the isolation properties we were trying to achieve. For this reason, the channel is only accessible from inside kernel context and is hidden behind a set of constrained and limited APIs. It should be noted that this restriction limits the allowed functionality of the applications hosted by Kitten, but as we will demonstrate later, more full featured applications can still benefit from the isolation of a co-kernel through the use of virtualization.

4.3 Assigning hardware resources

The initial co-kernel environment consists of a single CPU and a single memory block. In order to support large scale applications, Pisces provides mechanisms for dynamically expanding an enclave after it has booted. As before, we rely on the ability to dynamically offline hardware resources in Linux. We have also implemented dynamic resource assignment in the Kitten kernel itself to handle hardware changes at runtime. Currently Pisces supports dynamic assignment of CPUs, memory, and PCI devices.

CPU Cores.

Adding a CPU core to a Kitten co-kernel is achieved in essentially the same way as the boot process. A CPU core is offlined in Linux and the trampoline is again replaced with a modified version. At this point Pisces issues a command to the control process running in the co-kernel, informing it that a new CPU is being assigned to the enclave. The control process receives the command (which includes the CPU and APIC identifiers for the new CPU) and then issues a system call into the Kitten kernel. Kitten then allocates the necessary data structures and issues a request back the Linux boot loader for an INIT IPI to be delivered to the target core. The CPU is then initialized and activated inside the Kitten environment. Reclaiming a CPU is done in a similar manner, with the complication that local tasks need to be migrated to other active CPUs before reclaiming a CPU.

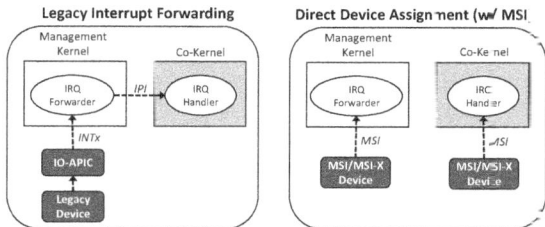

Figure 4: **Interrupt Routing Between Pisces Enclaves**

Memory.

Adding memory to Kitten is handled in much the same way as CPUs. A set of memory blocks are offlined and removed from Linux, and a command containing their physical address ranges is issued to the co-kernel. The control process receives the command and forwards it via a system call to the Kitten kernel. Kitten then steps through the new regions and adds each one to its internal memory map and ensures that identity mapped page tables are created to allow kernel level access to the new memory regions. Once the memory has been mapped in, it is added to the kernel allocator and is available to be assigned to any running processes. Removing memory simply requires inverting the previous steps, with the complication that if the memory region is currently allocated then it cannot be removed. While this allows the co-kernel to potentially prevent reclamation, memory can always be forcefully reclaimed by destroying the enclave and returning all resources back to Linux.

PCI devices.

Due to the goal of full isolation between enclaves, we expect that I/O is handled on a per enclave basis. Our approach is based on the mechanisms currently used to provide direct passthrough access to I/O devices for virtual machines. To add a PCI device to a co-kernel it is first detached from the assigned Linux device driver and then offlined from the system. The IOMMU (if available) is then configured by Pisces without involvement from the co-kernel itself. This is possible because Pisces tracks the memory regions assigned to each enclave, and so can update the IOMMU with identity mappings for only those regions that have been assigned. This requires dynamically updating the IOMMU as memory is assigned and removed from an enclave, which is accomplished by notifying the module whenever a resource allocation has been changed. Once an IOMMU mapping has been created, the co-kernel is notified that a new device has been added, at which point the co-kernel initializes its own internal device driver.

Unfortunately, interrupt processing poses a potential challenge for assigning I/O devices to an enclave. PCI based devices are all required to support a legacy interrupt mode that delivers all device interrupts to an IO-APIC, that in turn forwards the interrupt as a specified vector to a specified processor. Furthermore, since legacy interrupts are potentially shared among multiple devices a single vector cannot be directly associated with a single device. In this case, it is not possible for Pisces to simply request the delivery of all device interrupts to a single co-kernel since it is possible that it is not the only recipient. To address this issue, Pisces implements an IRQ forwarding service in Linux. When a device is assigned to an enclave any legacy interrupts origi-

nating from that device (or any other device sharing that IRQ line) are sent directly to Linux, which then forwards the interrupt via IPI to any enclave which has been assigned a device associated with that IRQ. This approach is shown in the left half of Figure 4. Fortunately, most modern devices support more advanced interrupt routing mechanisms via MSI/MSI-X, wherein each device can be independently configured to generate an IRQ that can be delivered to any CPU. For these devices Pisces is able to simply configure the device to deliver interrupts directly to a CPU assigned to the co-kernel, as shown in the right half of Figure 4.

4.4 Integration with the Palacios VMM

While our co-kernel architecture is designed to support native applications, the portability of our approach is limited due to the restricted feature set resident in Kitten's lightweight design. This prevents some applications from gaining the isolation and performance benefits provided by Pisces. While other work has addressed this problem by offloading unsupported features to Linux [23], we have taken a different approach in order to avoid dependencies (and associated interference sources) on Linux. Instead we have leveraged our work with the Palacios VMM to allow unmodified applications to execute inside an isolated Linux guest environment running as a VM on top of a co-VMM. This approach allows Pisces to provide the full set of features available to the native Linux environment while also providing isolation from other co-located workloads. As we will show later, Pisces actually allows a virtualized Linux image to *outperform* a native Linux environment in the face of competing workloads.

While Palacios had already been integrated with the Kitten LWK, in this work we implemented a set of changes to allow it to effectively operate in the Pisces environment. Primarily, we added support for the dynamic resource assignment operations of the underlying co-kernel. These modifications entailed ensuring that the proper virtualization features were enabled and disabled appropriately as resources were dynamically assigned and removed. We also added checks to ensure Palacios never accessed stale resources or resources that were not assigned to the enclave. In addition we integrated support for loading, controlling, and interacting with co-kernel hosted VMs from the external Linux environment. This entailed forwarding VM commands and setting up additional shared memory channels between the Linux and co-kernel enclaves. Finally, we extended Kitten to fully support passthrough I/O for devices assigned and allocated for a VM. This device support was built on top of the PCI assignment mechanisms discussed earlier, but also included the ability to dynamically update the IOMMU mappings in Linux based on the memory map assigned to the VM guest. Finally, we implemented a simple file access protocol to allow Palacios to load a large (multi-gigabyte) VM disk image from the Linux file system.

5. EVALUATION

We evaluated Pisces on an experimental 8 node research cluster at the University of Pittsburgh. Each cluster node consists of a Dell R450 server connected via QDR Infiniband. Each server was configured with two six-core Intel "Ivy-Bridge" Xeon processors (12 cores total) and 24 GB of RAM split across two NUMA domains. Each server was running CentOS 7 (Linux Kernel version 3.16). Performance isolation at the hardware level was achieved by pinning each workload to a dedicated NUMA domain. Our experiments used several different software configurations. The standard "CentOS" configuration consisted of running a single Linux environment across the entire machine and using the Linux resource binding APIs to enforce hardware level resource isolation. The KVM configuration consisted of assigning control of one NUMA domain to Linux, while the other was controlled by a KVM VM. Similarly, the "co-kernel" configuration consisted of one Linux managed NUMA domain while the other was managed by a Kitten co-kernel. Finally the "co-VMM" configuration consisted of a Linux guest environment running as a VM on Palacios integrated with a Kitten co-kernel.

5.1 Noise analysis

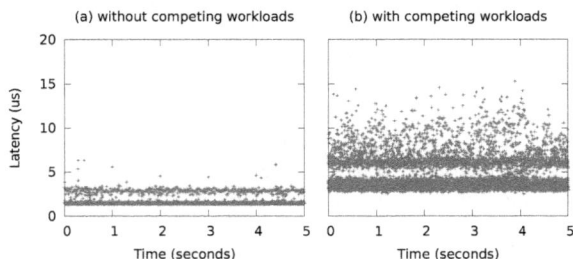

Figure 5: **Native Linux**

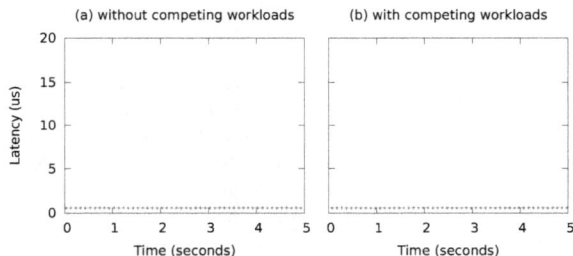

Figure 6: **Native Kitten (Pisces Co-Kernel)**

Our first experiments measured the impact that co-located workloads had on the noise profile of a given environment, collected using the Selfish Detour benchmark [4] from Argonne National Lab. Selfish is designed to detect interruptions in an application's execution by repeatedly sampling the CPU's cycle count in a tight loop. For each experiment we ran the benchmark for a period of 5 seconds, first with no competing workloads and then in combination with a parallelized Linux kernel compilation running on Linux. For each configuration the Selfish benchmark was pinned to the second NUMA domain while the kernel compilation was pinned to the first domain. Therefore changes to the noise profile are almost certainly the result of software level interference events, and not simply contention on hardware resources. The results of these experiments are shown in Figures 5 and 6. Each interruption (above a threshold) is plotted, and the length of the interruption is reported as the latency. As can be seen, the co-kernel predictably provides a dramatically lower noise profile, while the native Linux environment also exhibits a fairly low level of noise when no competing workloads are present. However, the native Linux configuration exhibits a significant increase in the number and duration of detour events once the competing workload is introduced.

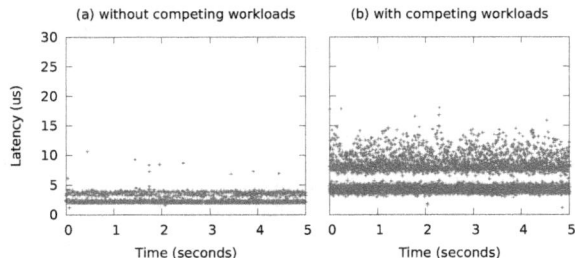

Figure 7: **Kitten Guest (KVM)**

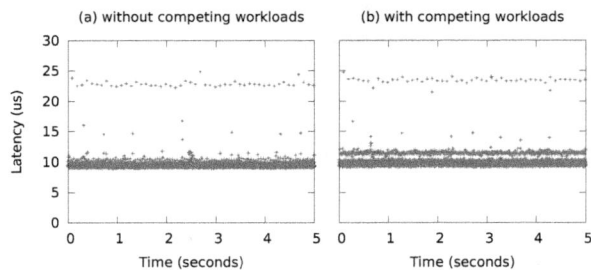

Figure 8: **Kitten Guest (Palacios/Linux)**

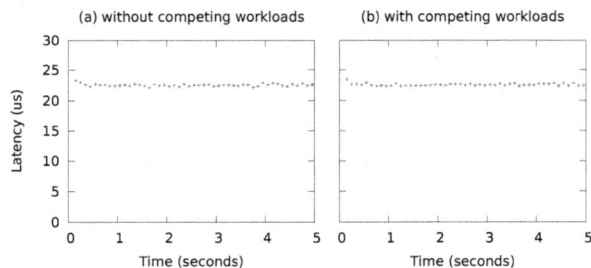

Figure 9: **Kitten Guest (Pisces Co-VMM)**

Next we used the same benchmark to evaluate the isolation capabilities of various virtualization architectures. The goal of these experiments were to demonstrate the isolation capabilities of our co-VMM architecture. For these experiments the Selfish benchmark was executed inside a VM running the Kitten LWK. The same VM image was used on 3 separate VMM architectures: KVM on Linux, Palacios integrated with Linux (Palacios/Linux), and Palacios integrated with a Kitten co-kernel (Palacios/Kitten). The results are shown in Figure 7, 8 and 9 respectively. While each of these configurations result in different noise profiles without competing workloads, in general the co-VMM environment shows considerably less noise events than either of the Linux based configurations. However when a second workload is added to the system KVM shows a marked increase in noise events, while Palacios/Linux shows a slight but noticeable increase in the amount of noise. Conversely, the Palacios/Kitten co-VMM environment shows no noticeable change to the noise profile as additional workloads are added to the system.

We note that the Palacios based environments do experience some longer latency noise events around the 23 microsecond mark (Figures 8 and 9), which are caused by Kitten's 10 Hz guest timer interrupts. The longer latency is a result of the fact that Palacios does not try to overly optimize common code paths, but instead is designed to prioritize consistency. For common events such as timer interrupts, this leads to slightly higher overhead and lower average case performance than demonstrated by KVM. However, as these figures demonstrate, the Palacios configurations provide more consistent performance, particularly as competing workloads are added to the system.

Taken together, these results demonstrate the effectiveness of a lightweight co-kernels in eliminating sources of interference caused by the presence of other co-located workloads running on the same local node. These results are important in analyzing the potential scalability of these C3/R configurations due to the noise sensitivity exhibited by many of our target applications [24, 11, 13]. Thus the ability of the Pisces architecture to reduce the noise effects caused by competing workloads indicates that it will provide better scalability than less isolatable OS/R environments.

5.2 Single Node Co-Kernel Performance

Figure 10 shows the results from a collection of single node performance experiments from the Mantevo HPC Benchmark Suite [1]. In order to evaluate the local performance characteristics of Pisces we conducted a set of experiments using both micro and macro benchmarks. Each benchmark was executed 10 times using 6 OpenMP threads across 6 cores on a single NUMA node. The competing workload we selected was again a parallel compilation of the Linux kernel, this time executing with 6 ranks on the other NUMA node to avoid overcommitting hardware cores. To eliminate hardware-level interference as much as possible, the CPUs and memory used by the benchmark application and background workload were constrained to separate NUMA domains. The NUMA configuration was selected based on the capabilities of the OS/R being evaluated: process control policies on Linux and assigned resources for the cc-kernel. For these experiments we evaluated two different OS/R configurations: a single shared Linux environment, a Kitten environment running in a KVM guest, and a Kitten co-kernel environment.

The top row of Figure 10 demonstrates the performance of several Mantevo mini-applications. In all cases, the Kitten co-kernel exhibits better overall performance. In addition the co-kernel environment also exhibits much less variance than the other system configurations. This can be seen especially with the CoMD benchmark, that has a large degree of variance when running on a native Linux environment. Collectively, these results suggest that Pisces is likely to exhibit

better scaling behavior to larger node counts than either alternate system configuration.

The bottom row of Figure 10 demonstrates memory microbenchmark performance with and without competing workloads in the different system configurations. The Stream results demonstrate that a Kitten co-kernel provides consistently better memory performance than either of the other system configurations, averaging 3% performance improvement over the other configurations, with noticeably less variance. Furthermore, the addition of a competing workload has a negligible effect on performance, whereas both of the other configurations show measurable degradation.

5.3 Co-Kernel Scalability

Next we evaluated whether the single node performance improvements would translate to a multi-node environment. For this experiment we deployed the HPCG [8] benchmark from Sandia National Labs across the 8 nodes of our experimental cluster. Because Kitten does not currently support Infiniband hardware, these experiments use a Linux environment running natively or as a VM hosted on either the Pisces co-VMM architecture or KVM. As in the previous sections, the workload configurations consist of an isolated configuration running only the HPCG benchmark, as well as a configuration with competing workloads consisting of parallel kernel compilations configured to run on all 6 cores of a single NUMA socket.

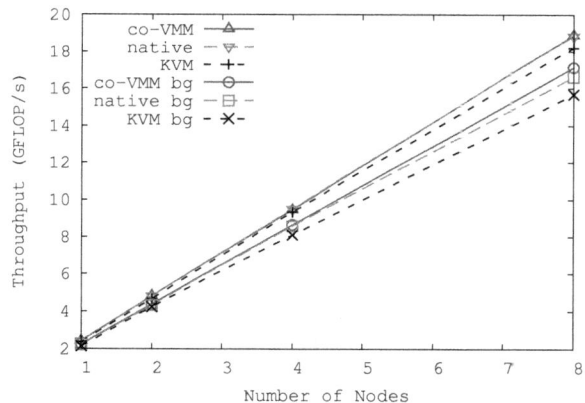

Figure 11: **HPCG Benchmark Performance.** Comparison between native Linux, Linux on KVM and Linux on Pisces co-VMM.

Figure 11 shows the results of these experiments. Without competing workloads, the co-VMM configuration achieves near native performance, while KVM consistently performs worse than both of the other configurations. When a background workload is introduced all of the configurations perform slightly worse. However, as the node count increases, the co-VMM configuration begins to actually *outperform* both the KVM instance as well as the native environment. These results demonstrate the benefits of performance isolation to an HPC class application, while also showing how cross workload interference can manifest itself inside system software and not just at the hardware level.

157

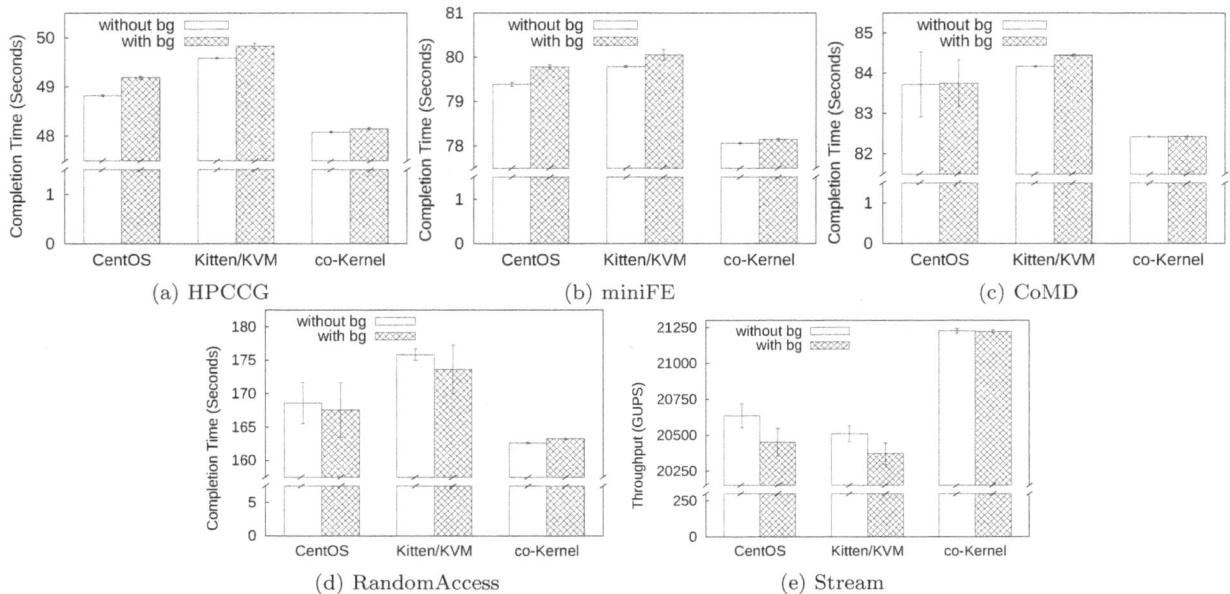

Figure 10: **Single Node Performance (Pisces Co-Kernel)**

5.4 Performance Isolation with Commodity Workloads

While Pisces is designed to target HPC environments running coupled application workloads, performance isolation has also become a key issue in large scale commodity cloud infrastructures [6]. The final set of experiments evaluate the performance isolation provided by the Pisces framework for an example cloud environment with traditional HPC applications co-located with more common cloud workloads on the same local resources. In this experiment, the experimental cluster was setup to co-locate cloud workloads with traditional HPC-class applications in separate Pisces enclaves.

The cloud workload used for these tests was the Mahout machine learning benchmark from the CloudSuite [10] benchmark suite. The HPC benchmarks were taken from the Mantevo benchmark suite, and consisted of HPCCG, Clover-Leaf, and miniFE. For these experiments we were focused on detecting performance outliers at small scale (8 nodes), as these would be indicative of scalability issues, given the tendency for small scale inconsistencies to result in lower average case performance as the node count increases [24, 11, 13]. Therefore, each benchmark was executed for a period of multiple hours, allowing the collection of a large number of total runtimes. The selected configurations consisted of both workloads running natively on Linux, the workloads running in separate KVM VMs, and the workloads running in separate co-VMM environments, where one VM was hosted by a Kitten co-kernel, while the other was hosted by the native Linux OS.

The results are presented using cumulative distribution functions (CDFs) of the benchmark completion times in Figure 12. We chose to present CDFs in order to demonstrate the tail behaviors of each configuration. Based on the results the co-VMM environment is again able to outperform both native and KVM based environments for each of the three benchmarks. In addition the number of outliers (rep-

resented by the length of the tails) is generally much smaller for the co-VMM configuration. While the tails only appear above the 95th percentile, it is important to note that as the number of nodes scales up significantly (to the order of thousands), the likelihood of encountering an outlier among any of the application's nodes will increase. Thus, given the tightly synchronized nature of these applications, these outliers are likely to lead be much poorer scalability for both native Linux and KVM.

6. RELATED WORK

Two separate philosophies have emerged over recent years concerning the development of operating systems for supercomputers. On the one hand, a series of projects have investigated the ability to configure and adapt Linux for supercomputing environments by selecting removing unused features to create a more lightweight OS. Alternatively, other work has investigated the development of lightweight operating systems from scratch with a consistent focus on maintaining a high performance environment.

Perhaps the most prominent example of a Linux-based supercomputing OS is Compute Node Linux (CNL) [14], part of the larger Cray Linux Environment. CNL has been deployed on a variety of Cray supercomputers in recent years, including the multi-petaflop Titan system at Oak Ridge National Laboratory. Additional examples of the Linux-based approach can be seen in efforts to port Linux-like environments to the IBM BlueGene/L and BlueGene/P systems [2, 3]. Alternatively, examples using non-Linux based OS deployment can be seen in IBM's Compute Node Kernel (CNK) [12] and several projects being led by Sandia National Laboratories, including the Kitten [19] project. While CNK and Kitten both incorporate lightweight design philosophies that directly attempt to limit OS interference by limiting many general-purpose features found in Linux environments, both CNK and Kitten address one of the primary weaknesses of previous LWK OSes by providing an environ-

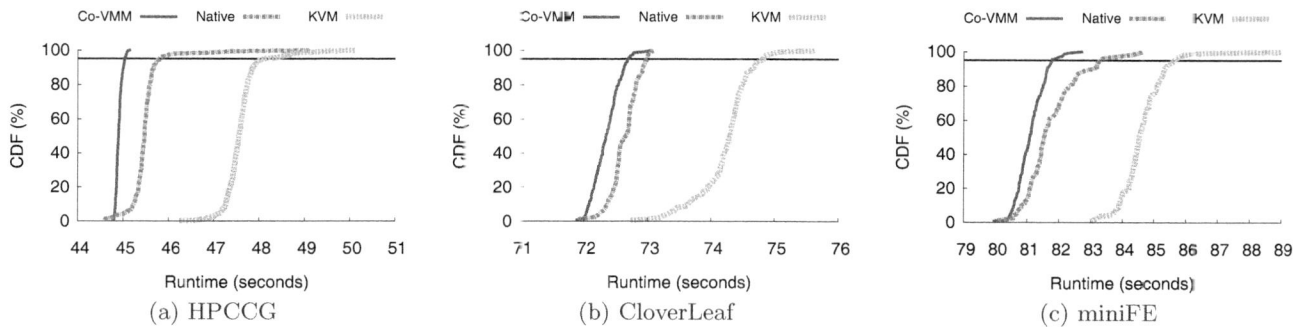

Figure 12: **Mantevo Mini-Application CDFs with Hadoop.** Solid horizontal lines shows 95th percentiles.

ment that is somewhat Linux-compatible and can execute a variety of applications built for Linux.

Deploying multiple operating systems on the same node has been explored previously with SHIMOS [27], whereby multiple modified Linux kernels can co-exist and manage partitioned hardware resources. However, this project was motivated by considerations such as physical device sharing between co-kernels and thus required significant effort in optimizing cross kernel communication with kernel-level message passing and page sharing, as well as shared resources such as page allocators that required kernel-level synchronization. Our approach is based more fundamentally on the concept of strict isolation between lightweight co-kernels that manage all resources assigned to them without cross dependencies.

The most relevant efforts to our approach are FusedOS from IBM [23], mOS from Intel [30], and McKernel from the University of Tokyo and RIKEN AICS [28]. FusedOS partitions a compute node into separate Linux and LWK-like partitions, where each partition runs on its own dedicated set of cores. The LWK partition depends on the Linux partition for various services, with all system calls, exceptions, and other OS requests being forwarded to Linux cores from the LWK partition. Similar to FusedOS McKernel deploys a LWK-like operating environment on heterogeneous (co)processors, such as the Intel Xeon Phi, and delegates a variety of system calls to a Linux service environment running on separate cores. Unlike FusedOS, the LWK environments proposed by mOS and McKernel allow for the native execution of some system calls, such as those related to memory management and thread creation, while more complicated system calls are delegated to the Linux cores. These approaches emphasize compatibility and legacy support with existing Linux based environments, to provide environments that are portable from the standpoint of existing Linux applications. In contrast to these approaches, Pisces places a greater focus on performance isolation by deploying co-kernels as fully isolated OS instances that provide standalone core OS services and resource management. In addition Pisces also supports dynamic enclave resource allocation and revocation, with the ability to grow and shrink enclaves at runtime, as well as virtualization capabilities through the use of the Palacios VMM.

7. CONCLUSION

In this paper we presented the Pisces lightweight co-kernel architecture as a means of providing full performance iso-

lation on HPC systems. Pisces enables a modified Kitten Lightweight Kernel to run as a co-kernel alongside a Linux based environment on the same local node. Each co-kernel provides a fully isolated enclave consisting of an independent OS/R environment capable of supporting a wide range of unmodified applications. Furthermore, we have shown that Pisces is capable of achieving better isolation than other approaches through a set of explicit design goals meant to ensure that isolation properties are maintained in the face of locally competing workloads. By providing superior isolation to applications, we have shown that applications can achieve superior performance as well as significant decrease in performance variability as their scale increases. Finally by utilizing the capabilities of the Palacios Virtual Machine Monitor we have demonstrated that virtual machines can actually outperform native environments in the face of competing or background workloads.

8. REFERENCES

[1] Mantevo Project
    https://software.sandia.gov/mantevo.

[2] ZeptoOS: The Small Linux for Big Computers
    http://www.mcs.anl.gov/research/projects/
    zeptoos/projects/.

[3] J. Appavoo, V. Uhlig, and A. Waterland. Project Kittyhawk: Building a Global-Scale Computer. *ACM Sigops Operating System Review*, Jan 2008.

[4] P. Beckman, K. Iskra, K. Yoshii, S. Coghlan, and A. Nataraj. Benchmarking the Effects of Operating System Interference on Extreme-scale Parallel Machines. *Cluster Computing*, 11(1):3–16, 2008.

[5] Boyd-Wickizer, A. Clements, Y. Mao, A. Festerev, F. Kaashoek, and N. Morris, Robert amd Zeldovich. An Analysis of Linux Scalability to Many Cores. In *Proc. 9th Symposium on Operating Systems Design and Implementation (OSDI)*, 2010.

[6] J. Dean and L. A. Barroso. The Tail at Scale. *Communications of the ACM*, 56(2), Feb. 2013.

[7] Y. Dong, Z. Yu, and G. Rose. SR-IOV Networking in Xen: Architecture, Design and Implementation. In *1st Workshop on IO Virtualization (WIOV)*, 2008.

[8] J. Dongarra and M. A. Heroux. Toward a New Metric for Ranking High Performance Computing Systems. *Sandia Report, SAND2013-4744*, 312, 2013.

[9] M. Dorier, G. Antoniu, R. Ross, D. Kimpe. and S. Ibrahim. CALCioM: Mitigating I/O Interference in HPC Systems Through Cross-Application

Coordination. In *Proc. 28th IEEE International Parallel and Distributed Processing Symposium (IPDPS)*, 2014.

[10] M. Ferdman, A. Adileh, O. Kocberber, S. Volos, M. Alisafaee, D. Jevdjic, C. Kaynak, A. D. Popescu, A. Ailamaki, and B. Falsafi. Clearing the Clouds: a Study of Emerging Scale-out Workloads on Modern Hardware. In *Proc. 17th International Conference on Architectural Support for Programming Languages and Operating Systems (ASPLOS)*, 2012.

[11] K. B. Ferreira, P. Bridges, and R. Brightwell. Characterizing Application Sensitivity to OS Interference Using Kernel-level Noise Injection. In *Proc. 21st International Conference for High Performance Computing, Networking, Storage and Analysis (SC)*, 2008.

[12] M. Giampapa, T. Gooding, T. Inglett, and R. Wisniewski. Experiences with a Lightweight Supercomputer Kernel: Lessons Learned from Blue Gene's CNK. In *International Conference for High Performance Computing, Networking, Storage and Analysis (SC)*, pages 1–10, Nov 2010.

[13] T. Hoefler, T. Schneider, and A. Lumsdaine. Characterizing the Influence of System Noise on Large-Scale Applications by Simulation. In *Proc. 23rd International Conference for High Performance Computing, Networking, Storage and Analysis (SC)*, pages 1–11, Washington, DC, USA, 2010. IEEE Computer Society.

[14] L. Kaplan. Cray CNL. In *FastOS PI Meeting and Workshop*, 2007.

[15] S. Kelly and R. Brightwell. Software Architecture of the Lightweight Kernel, Catamount. In *2005 Cray Users' Group Annual Technical Conference*. Cray Users' Group, May 2005.

[16] B. Kocoloski and J. Lange. Better Than Native: Using Virtualization to Improve Compute Node Performance. In *Proc. 2nd International Workshop on Runtime and Operating Systems for Supercomputers (ROSS)*, 2012.

[17] B. Kocoloski and J. Lange. XEMEM: Efficient Shared Memory for Composed Applications on Multi-OS/R Exascale Systems. In *Proc. 24th International ACM Symposium on High Performance Distributed Computing (HPDC)*, 2015.

[18] P. M. Kogge et al. ExaScale Computing Study: Technology Challenges in Achieving Exascale Systems . Technical report, University of Notre Dame CSE Department Technical Report, TR-2008-13, September 2008.

[19] J. Lange, K. Pedretti, T. Hudson, P. Dinda, Z. Cui, L. Xia, P. Bridges, A. Gocke, S. Jaconette, M. Levenhagen, and R. Brightwell. Palacios and Kitten: New High Performance Operating Systems For Scalable Virtualized and Native Supercomputing. In *Proc. 24th IEEE International Parallel and Distributed Processing Symposium (IPDPS)*, 2010.

[20] J. R. Lange, K. Pedretti, P. Dinda, P. G. Bridges, C. Bae, P. Soltero, and A. Merritt. Minimal-overhead Virtualization of a Large Scale Supercomputer. In *Proc. 7th ACM SIGPLAN/SIGOPS International Conference on Virtual Execution Environments (VEE)*, 2011.

[21] K.-L. Ma, C. Wang, H. Yu, and A. Tikhonova. In-Situ Processing and Visualization for Ultrascale Simulations. In *Journal of Physics: Proceedings of DOE SciDAC 2007 Conference*, June 2007.

[22] A. B. Maccabe, K. S. McCurley, R. Riesen, and S. R. Wheat. SUNMOS for the Intel Paragon - A Brief User's Guide. In *Proceedings of the Intel Supercomputer Users' Group*, Jul 1994.

[23] Y. Park, E. Van Hensbergen, M. Hillenbrand, T. Inglett, B. Rosenburg, K. D. Ryu, and R. Wisniewski. FusedOS: Fusing LWK Performance with FWK Functionality in a Heterogeneous Environment. In *Proc. 24th IEEE International Symposium on Computer Architecture and High Performance Computing*, Oct 2012.

[24] F. Petrini, D. J. Kerbyson, and S. Pakin. The Case of the Missing Supercomputer Performance: Achieving Optimal Performance on the 8,192 Processors of ASCI Q. In *Proc. 16th International Conference for High Performance Computing, Networking, Storage and Analysis (SC)*, New York, NY, USA, 2003. ACM.

[25] R. Phull, C.-H. Li, K. Rao, H. Cadambi, and S. Chakradhar. Interference-driven Resource Management for GPU-based Heterogeneous Clusters. In *Proc. 21st International Symposium on High-Performance and Distributed Computing (HPDC)*, 2012.

[26] R. Riesen, R. Brightwell, P. G. Bridges, T. Hudson, A. B. Maccabe, P. M. Widener, and K. Ferreira. Designing and Implementing Lightweight Kernels for Capability Computing. *Concurrency and Computation: Practice and Experience*, 21(6), 2009.

[27] T. Shimosawa and Y. Ishikawa. Inter-kernel Communication between Multiple Kernels on Multicore Machines. *IPSJ Transactions on Advanced Computing Systems*, 2(4):62–82, 2009.

[28] H. Tomita, M. Sato, and Y. Ishikawa. Japan Overview Talk. In *Proc. 2nd International Workshop on Big Data and Extreme-scale Computing (BDEC)*, 2014.

[29] S. R. Wheat, A. B. Maccabe, R. Riesen, D. W. van Dresser, and T. M. Stallcup. PUMA : An Operating System for Massively Parallel Systems. *Scientific Programming*, 3:275–288, 1994.

[30] R. Wisniewski, T. Inglett, P. Keppel, R. Murty, and R. Riesen. mOS: An Architecture for Extreme-Scale Operating Systems. In *Proc. 4th International Workshop on Runtime and Operating Systems for Supercomputers (ROSS)*, 2014.

[31] K. Yoshii, K. Iskra, P. Broekema, H. Naik, and P. Beckman. Characterizing the Performance of Big Memory on Blue Gene Linux. In *Proc. 2009 International Conference on Parallel Processing Workshops*, 2009.

[32] F. Zheng, H. Yu, C. Hantas, M. Wolf, G. Eisenhauer, K. Schwan, H. Abbasi, and S. Klasky. GoldRush: Resource Efficient In Situ Scientific Data Analytics Using Fine-Grained Interference Aware Execution. In *Proc. 26th. International Conference for High Performance Computing, Networking, Storage and Analysis (SC)*, 2013.

Accelerating Irregular Computations with Hardware Transactional Memory and Active Messages

Maciej Besta
Department of Computer Science
ETH Zurich
Universitätstr. 6, 8092 Zurich, Switzerland
maciej.besta@inf.ethz.ch

Torsten Hoefler
Department of Computer Science
ETH Zurich
Universitätstr. 6, 8092 Zurich, Switzerland
htor@inf.ethz.ch

ABSTRACT

We propose Atomic Active Messages (AAM), a mechanism that accelerates irregular graph computations on both shared- and distributed-memory machines. The key idea behind AAM is that hardware transactional memory (HTM) can be used for simple and efficient processing of irregular structures in highly parallel environments. We illustrate techniques such as coarsening and coalescing that enable hardware transactions to considerably accelerate graph processing. We conduct a detailed performance analysis of AAM on Intel Haswell and IBM Blue Gene/Q and we illustrate various performance tradeoffs between different HTM parameters that impact the efficiency of graph processing. AAM can be used to implement abstractions offered by existing programming models and to improve the performance of irregular graph processing codes such as Graph500 or Galois.

Categories and Subject Descriptors

D.1.3 [**Concurrent Programming**]: Parallel Programming

General Terms

Performance, Design

1. INTRODUCTION

Big graphs stand behind many computational problems in social network analysis, machine-learning, computational science, and others [26]. Yet, designing efficient parallel graph algorithms is challenging due to intricate properties of graph computations. First, they are often *data-driven* and *unstructured*, making parallelism based on partitioning of data difficult to express. Second, they are usually *fine-grained* and have *poor locality*. Finally, implementing synchronization based on locks or atomics is tedious, error prone, and typically requires concurrency specialists [26].

Recent implementations of hardware transactional memory (HTM) [14] promise a faster and simpler programming for parallel algorithms. The key functionality is that complex instructions or instruction sequences execute in *isola-*

tion and become visible to other threads *atomically*. Available HTM implementations show promising performance in scientific codes and industrial benchmarks [40, 36]. In this work, we show that the ease of programming and performance benefits are even more promising for fine-grained, irregular, and data-driven graph computations.

Another challenge of graph analytics is the size of the input that often requires distributed memory machines [27]. Such machines generally contain manycore compute nodes that may support HTM (cf. IBM Blue Gene/Q [36]). Still, it is unclear how to handle transactions accessing vertices on both local and remote nodes.

In this paper we propose a mechanism called *Atomic Active Messages* (AAM) that accelerates graph analytics by combining the active messaging (AM) model [35] with HTM. In AAM, fine units of graph computation (e.g., marking a vertex in BFS) are *coarsened* and executed as hardware transactions. While software-based coarsening was proposed in the past [18], in this paper we focus on developing high performance hardware-supported techniques to implement this mechanism on both shared- and distributed-memory machines, on establishing principles and practice of the use of HTM for the processing of graphs, and on illustrating various performance tradeoffs between different HTM parameters in the context of graph analytics. Figure 1 motivates AAM by showing the time to perform each phase in a synchronized BFS traversal using traditional fine-grained atomics and AAM based on coarser hardware transactions.

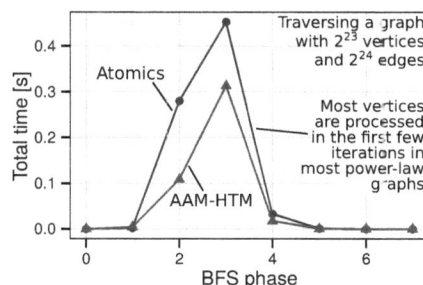

Figure 1: Comparison of the duration of an intra-node BFS traversal implemented with Blue Gene/Q fine-grained atomics and coarse hardware transactions (AAM-HTM). One transaction modifies 2^7 vertices. We use 64 threads and a Kronecker graph [23] with a power-law vertex degree distribution.

Another key insight of our work is that AAM constitutes a hierarchy of atomic actives messages that can be used to accelerate graph computations on both shared- and distributed-memory machines. We analyze this hierarchy in detail and conclude that AAM can be used to improve the performance of generic graph analytics tools such as Galois or Graph500. The key contributions of our work are:

- We design the generic AAM mechanism that uses state-of-the-art HTM implementations to accelerate both shared- and distributed-memory graph computations.

- We establish the principles and practice of the use of HTM for graph computations. Specifically, we develop protocols for spawning remote/distributed hardware transactions.

- We introduce a performance model and we conduct a detailed performance analysis of AAM based on Intel Haswell HTM [40] and IBM Blue Gene/Q HTM [36] to illustrate various performance tradeoffs between different HTM parameters in the context of graph analytics. Specifically, we find optimum transaction sizes for x86 and PowerPC machines that accelerate Graph500 [30] BFS code by >100%.

- We show that AAM accelerates the processing of various synthetic and real-world graphs.

2. BACKGROUND

We now describe active messages, atomics, transactional memory, and how they are used in graph computations.

2.1 Active Messages

In the active messaging (AM) model [35] processes exchange messages that carry: the address of a user-level handler function, handler parameters, and optional payload. When a message arrives, the parameters and the payload are extracted from the network and the related handler runs at the receiver [38]. Thus, AMs are conceptually similar to lightweight Remote Procedure Calls (RPCs).

Active messages are often used to implement low-level performance-centric libraries that serve as a basis for developing higher-level libraries and runtime systems. Example libraries are Myrinet Express (MX), IBM's Deep Computing Messaging Framework (DCMF) for BlueGene/P, IBM's Parallel Active Message Interface (PAMI) for BlueGene/Q, GASNet [2], and AM++ [38].

2.2 Active Messages in Graph Computations

A challenging part of designing a distributed graph algorithm is managing its data flow. One way is to use a distributed data structure (e.g., a distributed queue) that spans all of its intra-node instances. Such structures are often hard to construct and debug [8]. A BFS algorithm that uses a distributed queue is presented in Listing 1.

```
if (source is local) Q.push(source);
while (!Q.empty()) {
  for (Vertex v : Q)
    if (v.visited == false) {
      v.visited = true;
      for (Vertex w : v.neighbors()) {Q.add(w); } } }
```

Listing 1: Distributed BFS using a distributed queue [11] (§ 2.2)

Another approach uses active messages to express the data flow of the program dynamically. When a process schedules computation for a vertex, it first checks whether it is the *owner* of this vertex. If yes, it performs the computation. Otherwise, the computation is sent in an active message to a different node for processing in a remote handler [39]. Thus, no distributed data structures have to be used. We illustrate BFS using this approach in Listing 2.

```
struct bfs_AM_handler {
  bool operator()(const pair<Vertex, int>& x) {
    if (x.second < x.first.distance) {
      x.first.distance = x.second;
      send_active_message(x.first, x.second + 1); } } };
```

Listing 2: Distributed BFS using active messages [39] (§ 2.2)

2.3 Atomic Operations

Atomic operations appear to the rest of the system as if they occur instantaneously. Atomics are used in lock-free graph computations to perform fine-grained updates [11, 30]. Yet, they are limited to a single word and thus require complex protocols for protecting operations involving multiple words. We now present relevant atomics:

Accumulate(*target, arg, op) (ACC): it applies an operation op (e.g., sum) to *target using an argument arg.

Fetch-and-Op(*target, arg, op) (FAO): similar to Accumulate but it also returns the previous value of *target.

Compare-and-Swap(*target, compare, value, *result) (CAS): if *target == compare then value is written into *target and the function sets *result to true, otherwise it does not change *target and sets *result to false.

2.4 Transactional Memory

Transactional Memory (TM) [14] is a technique in which portions of code (*transactions*) are executed in isolation and their memory effects become visible atomically. Thus, such code portions are linearizable and easy to reason about. The underlying TM mechanism records all modifications to specific memory locations and commits them atomically. It also detects dependencies between transactions accessing the same memory locations and solves potential *conflicts* between such accesses by rolling back any changes to the data. TM can be based on software emulation [34] (software TM; STM) or native hardware support [14] (HTM).

Several vendors introduced HTM implementations: IBM, Sun, and Azul added HTM to Blue Gene/Q (BG/Q) machines [36], the Rock processor [6], and the Vega CPUs [5], respectively. Intel implemented two HTM instruction sets in the Haswell processor: Hardware Lock Elision (HLE) and Restricted Transactional Memory (RTM) that together constitute Transactional Synchronization Extensions (TSX) [40]. HLE allows for fast and simple porting of legacy lock-based code into code that uses TM. RTM enables programmers to define transactional regions in a more flexible manner than that possible with HLE [40].

There are few existing studies on STM in graph computations [16]. Using HTM in graph processing has been largely unaddressed and only a few initial works exist [7, 37].

3. ATOMIC ACTIVE MESSAGES

Atomic Active Messages (AAM) is a mechanism motivated by recent advances in deploying transactional memory in hardware. An atomic active message is a message that, upon its arrival, executes a user-specified handler called an *operator*. A *spawner* is a process (or a thread within this process, depending on the context) that issues atomic active messages. An *activity* is the computation that takes place as a result of executing an operator. Activities run speculatively, isolated from one another, and they either *commit* atomically or do not commit at all. We distinguish between operators and the activities to keep our discussion generic.

To use AAM, the developer specifies the operator code that modifies elements (vertices or edges) of the graph. We use single-element operators for easy and intuitive programming of graph algorithms. Still, multiple-element *coarse* operators can be specified by experienced users. The developer also determines the structure of a vertex or an edge and defines the *failure handler*, an additional piece of code executed in certain types of algorithms (explained in § 3.2).

Our runtime system executes algorithms by exchanging messages, spawning activities to run the operator code, running failure handlers, and optimizing the execution. An activity can be *coarse*: it may execute *several operators* atomically. Note that operators are (optionally) coarsened by the developer while activities are coarsened by the runtime.

The implementation determines how activities are isolated from one another. An activity can execute as a critical section guarded by locks, or (if it modifies one element) as an atomic operation (e.g., CAS in BFS). However, we argue that in many cases running activities as hardware transactions provides the highest speedup; we support this claim with a detailed performance study in Sections 5 and 6.

3.1 Definitions and Notation

Assume there are N processes $p_1, ..., p_N$ in the system. A process p_i runs on a compute node $n_i, 1 \geq i \geq N$ and it may contain up to T threads. Then, we model the analyzed graph G as a tuple (V, E); V is a set of vertices and $E \subseteq V \times V$ is a set of edges between vertices. Without loss of generality we assume that G is partitioned and distributed using a one-dimensional scheme [4]: V is divided into N subsets V_i and every $V_i \subseteq V$ is stored on node n_i. We call process p_i the *owner* of every vertex $v \in V_i$ and every edge (v, w) such that $v \in V_i, w \in V$. We denote the average degree in G as $\bar{d}$.

3.2 Types of Atomic Active Messages

AAM accelerates graph computations that run on a single ($N = 1$) or multiple ($N > 1$) nodes. If $N = 1$ then messages only spawn intra-node activities. If $N > 1$ then a message may also be sent over the network to execute a remote activity. Now, we identify two further key criteria of categorizing messages: *direction of data flow* and *activity commits*. They enable four types of messages; each type improves the performance of different graph algorithms.

3.2.1 Direction of Data Flow

This criteria determines if an activity has to communicate some data back to its spawner. In some graph algorithms the data flow is *unidirectional* and messages are *Fire-and-Forget* (FF): they start activities that do not return any data. Other algorithms require the activity to return some data to the spawner to run a failure handler. We name a message that executes such an activity a *Fire-and-Return* (FR) message (the flow of data is *bidirectional*).

3.2.2 Activity Commits

In some graph algorithms messages belong to the type *Always-Succeed* (AS): they spawn activities that have to successfully commit, even if it requires multiple rollbacks or serialized execution. An example such algorithm is PageRank [3] where each vertex v has a parameter *rank* that is augmented with the normalized ranks of v's neighbors. Now, if we implement activities with transactions, then such transactions may conflict while concurrently updating the rank of the same vertex v, but *finally each of them has to succeed*

to add its normalized rank. The other type are *May-Fail* (MF) messages that spawn activities that may also fail ultimately and not re-execute after a rollback. An example is BFS in which two activities, which concurrently change the distance of the same vertex, conflict and only one of them succeeds. Note that we distinguish between rollbacks of activities at the algorithm level, and aborts of transactions due to cache eviction, context switches, and other reasons caused by hardware/OS. In the latter case the transaction is reexecuted by the runtime to ensure correctness.

Our criteria entail four message types: FF&AS, FF&MF, FR&AS, FR&MF. We now show examples on how each of these types can be used to program graph algorithms.

3.3 Example Case Studies

In AAM, a single graph algorithm uses only one type of atomic active messages. This type determines the form of the related operator and the existence of the failure handler. Here, we focus on the operator as the most complex part of graph algorithms. We show C-like code to implement the operator in isolation. Our implementation utilizes system annotations to mark atomic regions in C. We present the code of four single-element operators (one per message type); more examples can be found in the technical report[1]. When necessary, we discuss the failure handlers. We describe multiple-element operators at the end of this section.

3.3.1 PageRank (FF & AS)

PageRank (PR) [3] is an iterative algorithm that calculates the *rank* of each vertex $v \in V$: $rank(v) = \frac{1-d}{|V|} + \sum_{w \in n(v)} (d \cdot \frac{rank(w)}{out\_deg(w)})$. $n(v)$ is the set of v's neighbors, d is the *dump factor* [3] and $out\_deg(w)$ is the number of links leaving w. Depending on the operator design, PR may be either *vertex-centric* and *edge-centric*.

The pseudocode of the vertex-centric variant is presented in Listing 3. The operator increases the ranks of v's neighbors with a factor $d \cdot \frac{rank(v)}{out\_deg(v)}$. It also adds $\frac{1-d}{|V|}$ to $rank(v)$. The copies of stale ranks from a previous iteration are kept and used for calculating new ranks. Assuming that each vertex v is processed by one activity, this PR variant uses AS messages: each activity has to successfully add the factors to the ranks of respective vertices (which may require serialization). Data flow is unidirectional (messages are FF) because activities do not have to communicate any results back to their spawners. Thus, the operator returns void.

```
void Operator(Vertex v) {
  v.rank += (1 - d) / vertices_nr;
  for(int i = 0; i < v.neighbors.length; i++) {
    v.neighbors[i].rank += d * v.old_rank/v.out_deg; } }
```

Listing 3: The operator in the vertex-centric PageRank variant (§ 3.3.1)

There exist other PR variants. Specifically, one can analyze incoming edges to dispose of conflicts. We will later (Section 6) show that a careful AAM design outperforms such approaches used in various codes such as PBGL.

3.3.2 Breadth First Search (FF & MF)

Breadth First Search (BFS) uses FF & MF messages. Spawners do not have to wait for any results, but some activities may fail when concurrently updating vertices using different distance values. Such a conflict is solved at the

---

[1] http://spcl.inf.ethz.ch/Research/Parallel_Programming/AAM/

node owning the vertex and no information has to be sent back to any of the spawners, thus the operator returns void. We present the operator pseudocode in Listing 4.

```
void Operator(Vertex v, int new_distance) {
  if(v.distance > new_dist) {v.distance = new_dist;} }
```

Listing 4: BFS operator (§ 3.3.2)

3.3.3 ST Connectivity (FR & AS)

ST connectivity [31] determines if two given vertices (s and t) are connected. First, the algorithm marks each vertex as "white". Then, it starts two concurrent BFS traversals from s and t. Both traversals use different colors ("grey" and "green") to mark vertices as visited. Each activity returns the information on the colors of visited vertices. In case of "white" no action is taken and the operator returns false. If the found color is used by the other BFS, then s and t are connected, the operator returns true, and the runtime executes a failure handler at the spawner that terminates the algorithm. The operator is presented in Listing 5.

```
bool Operator(Vertex v, Color new_col) {
  if(v.color != WHITE && v.color != new_col) return true;
  v.color = new_col; return false; }
```

Listing 5: ST Connectivity operator (§ 3.3.3)

3.3.4 Boman Graph Coloring (FR & MF)

Graph coloring proposed by Boman et al. [1] is a heuristic algorithm that minimizes the number of colors assigned to graph vertices. In this algorithm as expressed using AAM (see Listing 6), an activity changes the color or vertex v to X. Then, if any of v's neighbors has color X, either v or the neighbor has to change its color; the choice is random. Activities are spawned by MF & FR messages because multiple processes trying to update v's color may conflict and the spawners have to be notified if they need to assign new colors to v's neighbors in failure handlers.

```
int Operator(Vertex v, Color X) {
  v.Color = X;
  if(v.hasNeighborWithColor(X)) {
    //return the ID of a vertex to be recolored
    if(rand([0;1]) < 0.5) return v.neighborWithCol(X).ID;
    else return v.ID;
  } else { //NO_VERTEX_ID means no vertex is recolored
    return NO_VERTEX_ID; }
```

Listing 6: Boman graph coloring operator (§ 3.3.4)

3.4 Discussion

The introduced AAM operators modify single vertices. Thus, they enable intuitive developing and reasoning about graph computations that are also fine-grained by nature. Still, some users may want to specify coarser operators to use additional knowledge that they have about the graph structure for higher performance. Here, the user determines the number of elements to be modified in the operator and the policy of their selection (e.g., the operator may choose each vertex randomly, or try to modify elements stored in a contiguous block of memory to avoid HTM aborts).

Manual coarsening of operators may be challenging. Our runtime system automatically coarsens activities for easier AAM programming. We now discuss the implementation details of coarsening and other optimizations. While single-element operators can be implemented with atomics or fine-

grained locks, we argue that a more performant approach is based on coarse transactions.

4. IMPLEMENTING ACTIVITIES

We now discuss the details of implementing activities; we skip most of the issues related to the runtime as they were properly addressed in other studies [38, 8, 39].

4.1 Implementing Activities with HTM

In this paper we advocate for using HTM to implement activities. However, locks and atomics would also match the activity semantics (atomics can implement fine activities that modify single words). We thus compared the performance of all the three mechanisms to illustrate HTM's advantages. Locks consistently entailed generally lower performance and we thus skip them due to space constraints; a brief discussion can be found in the technical report.

Transactions can implement an activity of any size. We use Intel Haswell HLE and RTM ISAs[2] and IBM BG/Q HTM. RTM provides two key functions: XBEGIN that starts a transaction and XEND that performs a commit. As it does not guarantee progress, we manually repeat aborted transactions. The HTM in BG/Q automatically retries aborted transactions and it serializes the execution when the number of retries is equal to a certain value; we use the default value (10). HLE performs serialization after the first abort.

4.2 Optimizing the Execution of Activities

Two most significant optimizations applied by the runtime are *coarsening* and *coalescing* of activities. First, in the intra-node computations, the runtime coarsens activities by atomically executing more than one operator; an example is presented in Listing 7. We denote activities that are not coarse as *fine*. Coarsening amortizes the overhead of starting and committing an activity; it also reduces the amount of fine-grained synchronization. Second, activities targeted at the same remote node are sent in a single message, i.e., coalesced. This reduces the overhead of sending and receiving an atomic active message and saves bandwidth. Finally, we also use various optimizations that attempt to reduce the amount of synchronization even further. For example, the runtime avoids executing the BFS operator for each vertex by verifying if the vertex has already been visited.

```
void Activity(Vertex vertices[], int new_distance) {
  forall(Vertex v: vertices) {
    //call the BFS operator from Listing 5
    Operator(v, new_distance); } }
```

Listing 7: A BFS coarse activity (§ 4.2)

4.3 A Protocol for Distributed Activities

The *ownership protocol* enables activities implemented as hardware transactions that access or modify data from remote nodes. The basic idea behind the protocol is that a handler running such an activity has to first physically relocate all required vertices/edges to the memory of the node where the activity executes. This approach is dictated by the fact that a hardware transaction cannot simply send a message because it would not be able to rollback remote changes that this message caused. In addition, most HTM

---

[2]We verify the correctness of all the results to ensure that the limitations of TSX [15] do not affect our evaluation and the conclusions drawn.

implementations prevent many types of operations (e.g., system calls) from being executed inside a transaction [36].

Our protocol assumes that each graph element has an *ownership marker* that can be modified atomically by any process. Each marker is initially set to a value $\perp$ different from any process id. When a transaction from a node n_i accesses a remote graph element, it aborts and the runtime uses CAS or a different mechanism (e.g., an active message) to set the marker of this element to the id of process p_i. If the CAS succeeds, the marked element is transferred to node n_i and the transaction restarts. If the CAS fails, the handler sets all previously marked elements to $\perp$ and backs off for a random amount of time. If a local transaction attempts to access a marked element, it aborts. This mechanism is repeated until all remote elements are cached locally. Finally, after the transaction succeeds, the elements are sent back to their original nodes and their markers are set to $\perp$.

5. PERFORMANCE MODEL & ANALYSIS

We now introduce a simple performance model that shows the tradeoffs between atomics and HTM. Then, we analyze the performance of AAM and answer the following research questions: (1) what are HTM's advantages over atomics for implementing AAM activities, (2) what are performance tradeoffs related to various HTM parameters, and (3) what are the optimum transaction sizes for analyzed architectures that enable highest speedups in selected graph algorithms.

5.1 Experimental Setup

We compile the code with gcc-4.8 (on Haswell) and with IBM XLC v12.1 (on BG/Q). We use the following machines:

ALCF BG/Q Vesta (BGQ) is a supercomputing machine where each compute node contains 16 1.6 GHz PowerPC A2 4-way multi-threaded cores, giving the total of 64 hardware threads per node. Each core has 16 kB of L1 cache. Every node has 32 MB of shared L2 cache and 16 GB of RAM. Nodes are connected with a 5D proprietary torus network. This machine represents massively parallel supercomputers with HTM implemented in the shared last-level cache.

Trivium V70.05 (Has-C) is a commodity off-the-shelf server where the processor (Intel Core i7-4770) contains 4 3.4 GHz Haswell 2-way multi-threaded cores, giving the total of 8 hardware threads. Each core has 32 KB of L1 and 256 KB of L2 cache. The CPU has 8 MB of shared L3 cache and 8 GB of RAM. This option speaks for commodity computers with HTM operating in private caches.

Greina (Has-P) is a high-performance cluster that contains two nodes connected with InfiniBand FDR fabric. Each node hosts an Intel Xeon CPU E5-2680 CPU with 12 2-way 2.50GHz multi-threaded cores; the total of 24 hardware threads. Each core contains 64 KB of L1 and 256 KB of L2 cache. The CPU has 30 MB of shared L3 cache and 66 GB of RAM. This machine represents high-performance clusters deploying HTM in private caches.

5.2 Considered Hardware Mechanisms

For Haswell we compare the following mechanisms: RTM (Has-RTM), HLE (Has-HLE), GCC _sync_bool_compare_and_swap (Has-CAS), and GCC _sync_add_and_fetch (Has-ACC). We select CAS and ACC because they can be used in miscellaneous graph codes such as BFS (a FF&MF algorithm), PR (a FF&AS algorithm),

and ST Connectivity (a FR&AS algorithm) [30]. For BG/Q we analyze: IBM XLC _compare_and_swap (BGQ-CAS) and GCC _sync_add_and_fetch (BGQ-ACC). We compare two modes of HTM in BG/Q: the *short running mode* [36] (BGQ-HTM-S) that bypasses L1 cache and performs better for shorter transactions, and the *long running mode* [36] (BGQ-HTM-L) that keeps speculative states in L1 and is better suited for longer transactions [36].

5.3 Performance Model

Our performance model targets graph processing and we argue in terms of activities and accessed vertices. We predict that an activity implemented as a transaction that modifies one vertex is more computationally expensive than an equivalent single atomic. Yet, the transactional overheads (starting and committing) may be amortized with coarser transactions and respective activities would outperform a series of atomics for a certain number of accessed vertices.

We now model the performance to determine the existence of crossing points; our model includes both the execution of the operations and fetching the operands from the memory. The total time to execute an activity that modifies N vertices (using either atomics or HTM) can be modeled with a simple linear function with N as the argument. We denote the slope and the intercept parameters of a function that targets atomics as $\mathcal{A}_{AT}$ and $\mathcal{B}_{AT}$; the respective parameters for HTM are $\mathcal{A}_{HTM}$ and $\mathcal{B}_{HTM}$. We predict that $\mathcal{B}_{HTM} > \mathcal{B}_{AT}$ due to high transactional overheads. On the contrary, we conjecture that $\mathcal{A}_{HTM} < \mathcal{A}_{AT}$ because HTM overheads will grow at a significantly lower rate (determined by accesses to the memory subsystem) than that of atomics.

We illustrate the model validation for CAS in Figure 2; we plot only the results for RTM on Has-C and the long mode HTM on BGQ because all the other results differ marginally and follow similar performance patterns. We use linear regression to calculate $\mathcal{A}_{AT}$, $\mathcal{B}_{AT}$, $\mathcal{A}_{HTM}$, and $\mathcal{B}_{HTM}$. The analysis indicates that the model matches the data. While a more extended model is beyond the scope of this paper, our analysis illustrates that it is possible to amortize the transactional overhead with coarser activities. We now proceed to a performance analysis that illustrates various tradeoffs between respective HTM parameters.

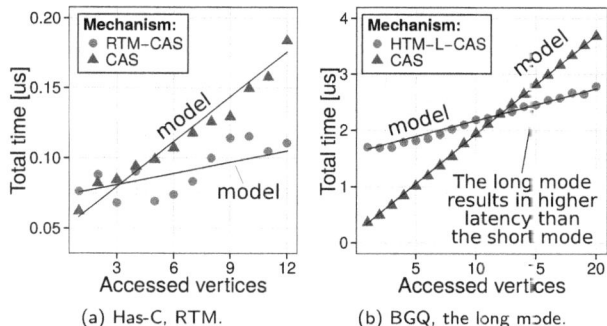

(a) Has-C, RTM. (b) BGQ, the long mode.

Figure 2: (§ 5.3) The validation of the performance model.

5.4 Single-vertex Activities

First, we analyze the performance of single-vertex activities. The results are illustrated in Figure 3. Has-C and Has-P follow similar performance trends and we show only the former (denoted as Has); we thus illustrate the results for both a multicore off-the-shelf system and a manycore high performance machine (BGQ).

166

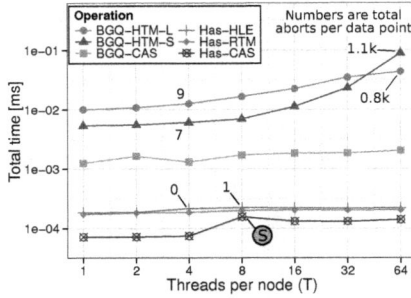

(a) Marking a vertex as visited 10 times (§ 5.4.1). (b) Marking a vertex as visited 100 times (§ 5.4.1).

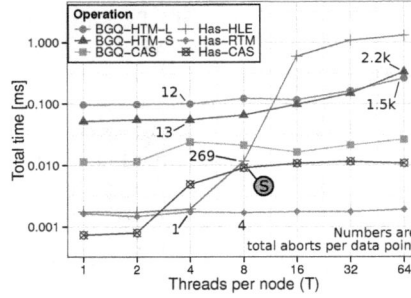

	Aborts due to:		
	Memory conflicts	Buffer overflows	Other reasons
10 ops			
Has-RTM	2	2	0
BGQ-HTM-L	802	3	1
BGQ-HTM-S	1,118	46	180
100 ops			
Has-RTM	2	2	0
BGQ-HTM-L	1,539	5	1
BGQ-HTM-S	2,242	13	2

(c) Marking a vertex as visited: details of the aborts in the HTM implementations (§ 5.4.1).

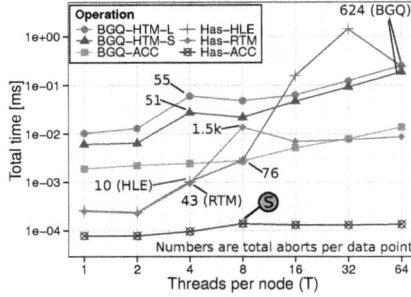

(d) Incrementing a vertex' rank 10 times (§ 5.4.2). (e) Incrementing a vertex' rank 100 times (§ 5.4.2).

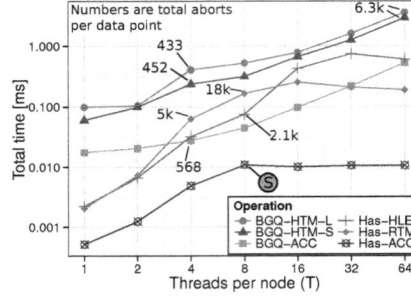

	Aborts due to:		
	Memory conflicts	Buffer overflows	Other reasons
10 ops			
Has-RTM	1,520	1	0
BGQ-HTM-L	624	62	614
BGQ-HTM-S	623	62	613
100 ops			
Has-RTM	18,952	33	0
BGQ-HTM-L	6,374	637	6,360
BGQ-HTM-S	6,392	639	6,380

(f) Incrementing a vertex' rank: details of the aborts in the HTM implementations (§ 5.4.2).

Figure 3: The analysis of the performance of intra-node activities implemented with atomics and HTMs (§ 5.4). Figures 3a and 3b illustrate the time it takes to mark a vertex as visited. Numbers in figures are sums of HTM aborts for a given datapoint (we report values for $T = 4$ for Has/BGQ; we also plot numbers for $T = 8$ (Has) and $T = 64$ (BGQ) to illustrate the numbers of aborts generated by all the supported hardware threads). Ⓢ indicates the point where the latency of Haswell atomics stops to grow. Table 3c shows the distribution of the reasons of aborts for $T = 64$ (BGQ) and $T = 8$ (Haswell). We skip Has-HLE as it does not provide functions to gather such statistics. A similar performance analysis for incrementing the rank of a vertex is presented in Figures 3d-3e and Table 3f.

5.4.1 Activity 1: Marking a Vertex as Visited

Here, each thread uses a CAS or an equivalent HTM code to atomically mark a single vertex; see Fig. 3a-3b, Table 3c. This activity may be used in BFS or any other related algorithm such as Single Source Shortest Path (SSSP). We analyze a negligibly contended scenario that addresses sparse graphs (Fig. 3a; a vertex is marked 10 times to simulate low contention) and a more contended case for dense graphs with high $\bar{d}$ (Fig. 3b; a vertex is marked 100 times). We repeat the benchmark 1000 times and derive the average total time to finish the operations.

Figure 3a shows that Has-CAS finishes fastest and is slightly impacted by the increasing T ($\approx 50\%$ of difference between the results for $T = 4$ and $T = 8$). This is because Has-CAS locks the respective cache line, causing contention in the memory system. Both Has-RTM and Has-HLE have 1.5-3x higher latency than Has-CAS, with Has-RTM being 5-15% faster than Has-HLE. Their performance is not influenced by the increasing T as they rarely abort. Then, BGQ-HTM-S and BGQ-HTM-L are more sensitive to the growing T and their performance drops 11x when switching from $T = 1$ to $T = 64$ due to expensive aborts. As expected, BGQ-HTM-S is faster than BGQ-HTM-L, but as T increases it also aborts more frequently, and becomes ≈ 2x less efficient ($T = 64$) with 37.5% more aborts. BGQ-CAS is least affected by the increasing T.

Figure 3b shows that Has-RTM, BGQ-CAS, BGQ-HTM-S, and BGQ-HTM-L follow similar performance patterns when threads access the vertex 100 times. The performance of Has-HLE drops rapidly as it always performs the costly serialization after the first abort and thus forces all other transactions to abort. The latency of Has-CAS grows proportionally to the contention in the memory system. It stabilizes at $T = 8$ as for $T > 8$ no more operations can be issued in parallel.

5.4.2 Activity 2: Incrementing Vertex Rank

This activity can be used to implement PR. Here, each thread increments the rank of a single vertex 10 times (Figure 3d) and 100 times (Figure 3e) with an ACC or an equivalent HTM code; see Table 3c for details. The most significant difference between the previous and the current benchmark is that the total time and the number of aborts of Has-RTM and Has-HLE grow very rapidly in both scenarios as T scales. This is because in the HTM implementation of ACC, the rank of the vertex is modified by each transaction, generating a considerable number of conflicts and thus aborts. On the contrary, the HTM implementation of CAS generates few memory conflicts: once the vertex id is swapped, other threads only read it and do not modify it. BGQ-HTM-S and BGQ-HTM-L follow a similar trend, with ≈ 3x more aborts than in the previous CAS benchmark.

Discussion We present the details of the above analysis in Tables 3c and 3f. We show that the considered single-vertex activities are in most cases best implemented with atomics. HTM is faster only in processing dense graphs with algorithms that use CAS (e.g., BFS) on Haswell. We also conclude that while atomic CAS is more expensive than ACC, HTM implementation of single ACC is slower (≈ 100x for RTM and ≈ 10x for BG/Q HTM) than that of CAS as it generates more memory conflicts and thus costly aborts.

5.5 Multi-vertex Activities

The performance analysis of single-vertex intra-node activities illustrates that in most cases a transaction modifying a single vertex is slower than an atomic operation. We now analyze if it is possible to amortize the cost of starting and aborting transactions by enlarging their size, i.e., *coarsening*. This section extends the model analysis (§ 5.3) by

(a) BFS runtime ($T = 1$) (§ 5.5.1).

(b) BFS runtime ($T = 16$) (§ 5.5.1).

(c) BFS runtime ($T = 64$) (§ 5.5.1).

(d) BG/Q events ($T = 64$) (§ 5.5.1).

(e) BFS runtime ($T = 1$) (§ 5.5.2).

(f) BFS runtime ($T = 4$) (§ 5.5.2).

(g) BFS runtime ($T = 8$) (§ 5.5.2).

(h) Has-C events ($T = 8$) (§ 5.5.2).

(i) BFS runtime ($T = 1$) (§ 5.5.3).

(j) BFS runtime ($T = 12$) (§ 5.5.3).

(k) BFS runtime ($T = 24$) (§ 5.5.3).

(l) Has-P events ($T = 24$) (§ 5.5.3).

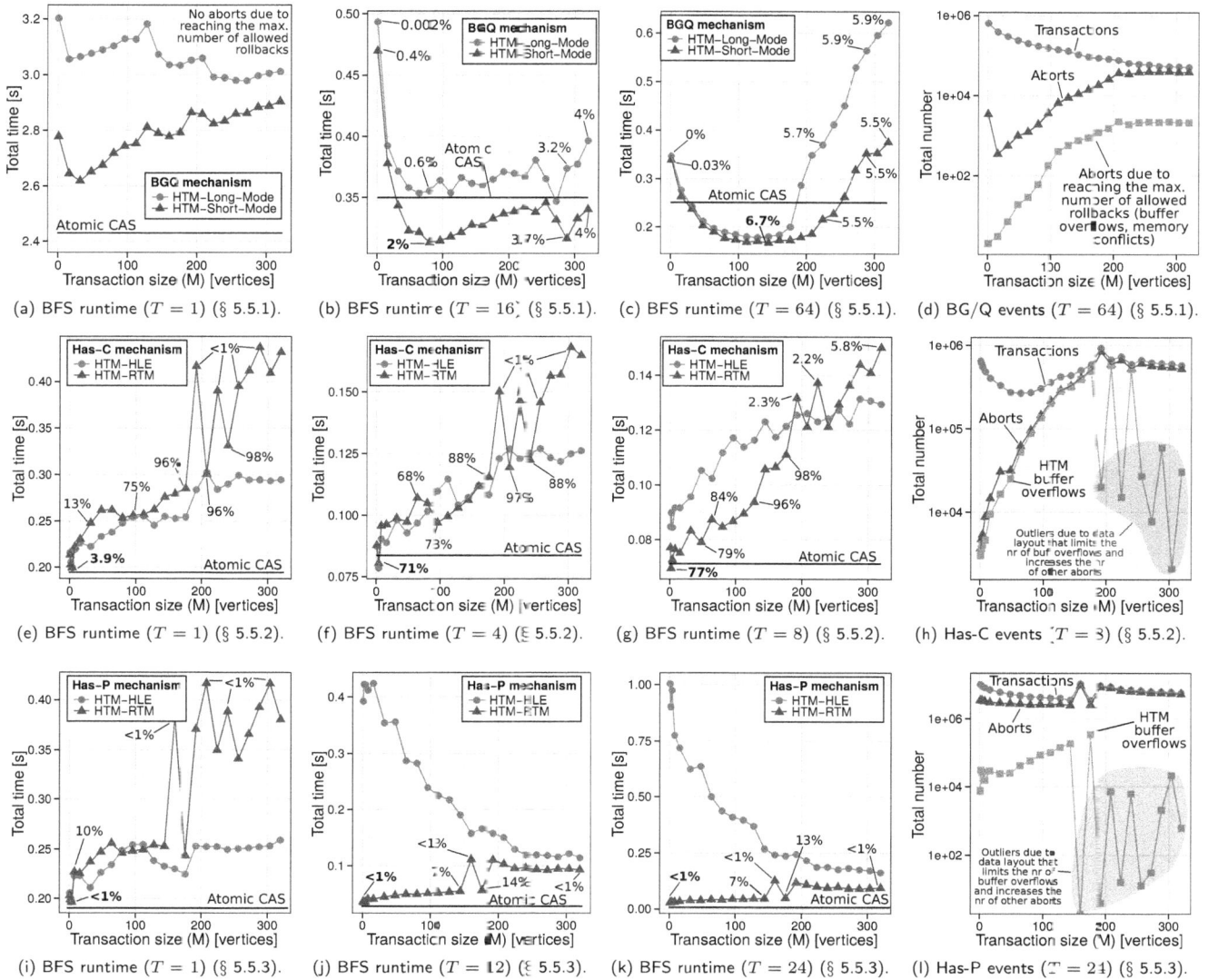

Figure 4: (§ 5.5) The analysis of the performance of Graph500 OpenMP BFS implemented with hardware transactions on BGQ (Figures 4a-4d), Has-C (Figures 4e-4h), and Has-P (Figures 4i-4l). In each figure we vary the size of the transactions M (i.e., the number of vertices visited). We also present the results for BFS implemented with atomics (horizontal lines). For BGQ, the percentages indicate the ratios of the numbers of serializations caused by reaching the maximum possible number of rollbacks to the numbers of all the aborts. For Haswell, the percentages are the ratios of the aborts due to HTM buffer overflows to all the aborts. Bolded numbers indicate the points with the minimum runtime per figure. We do not include the numbers for Haswell HLE because it does not enable gathering more detailed statistics [40]. Figures 4d, 4h, and 4l present the total number of HTM events (transactions, aborts, buffer overflows) for every analyzed M.

introducing effects such as memory conflicts or HTM buffer overflows. We perform the analysis for the highly-optimized OpenMP BFS Graph500 code [30]. We modify the code so that a single transaction atomically visits M vertices and we evaluate the modified code for M between 1 and 320 with the interval of 16. We present the results for three scenarios: a single-threaded execution ($T = 1$ for BGQ, Has-C, and Has-P), a single thread per core ($T = 16$ for BG/Q, $T = 4$ for Has-C, and $T = 12$ for Has-P), and a single thread per SMT hardware resource ($T = 64$ for BG/Q, $T = 8$ for Has-C, and $T = 24$ for Has-P). Other sets of parameters are illustrated in the technical report. We use Kronecker graphs [23] with the power-law vertex degree distribution and $|V| = 2^{20}$, $|E| = 2^{24}$. The results are shown in Figure 4.

5.5.1 BG/Q (Supercomputer)

Figures 4a-4d present the analysis for BG/Q. For $T = 1$ the runtime of both HTM-Long-Mode and HTM-Short-Mode is always higher than that of Atomic-CAS and it decreases ini-

tially with the increasing M because higher M reduces the number of transactions required to process the whole graph and thus amortizes the overhead of starting and committing transactions. The runtime of HTM-Short-Mode becomes higher with the increasing $M > 32$ because this mode is better suited for short transactions. The runtime of HTM-Long-Mode decreases as expected and it stabilizes at $M \approx 240$. For $T = 16$, initially the runtime drops rapidly for both HTM modes to reach the minimum (obtained for $M_{min} = 80$ in HTM-Short-Mode). Again, this effect is caused by amortizing the overheads of commits/aborts with coarser transactions. Beyond M_{min} the runtime slowly increases with M due to more frequent serializations caused by reaching the maximum number of allowed rollbacks (BGQ does not enable gathering more detailed statistics but we predict that these serializations are due to the higher number of HTM buffer overflows and memory conflicts). HTM-Long-Mode is never more efficient than Atomic-CAS. HTM-Short-Mode becomes more effi-

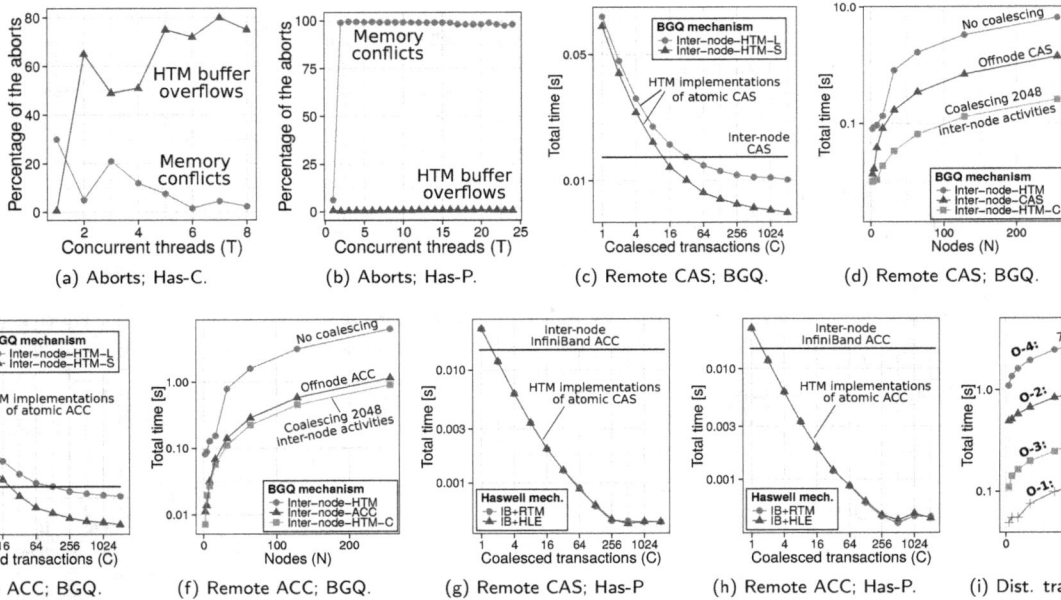

Figure 5: (§ 5.5 & § 5.6) The comparison of the percentage of the reasons of aborts on Has-C and Has-P (Figures 5a and 5b) and the analysis of the performance of inter-node activities on BG/Q and Has-P. The results for BG/Q are following: marking a remote vertex as visited (Figures 5c and 5d), incrementing a vertex' rank (Figures 5e and 5f), and executing distributed transactions (Figure 5i). The results for Haswell are following: marking a remote vertex as visited (Figure 5g) and incrementing a vertex' rank (Figure 5h).

cient than Atomic-CAS for $M = 32$ and achieves the speedup of 1.11 at $M_{min} = 80$. A similar performance pattern can be observed for $T = 64$; this time $M_{min} = 144$ in HTM-Short-Mode with the speedup of 1.49 over Atomic-CAS. The runtime becomes dominated by aborts for $M > 144$; cf. Figure 4d with more detailed numbers of aborts.

5.5.2 Has-C (Commodity Machine)

The results of the analysis for Has-C are presented in Figures 4e-4h. In each scenario ($T = 1, 4, 8$) the performance of both HTM-RTM and HTM-HLE decreases with increasing M. Several outliers are caused by disadvantageous graph data layouts that entail more aborts due to the limited associativity of L1 cache (8-way associative cache) that stores speculative states in Haswell [40]. We perform a more detailed analysis for $M \in \{1, ..., 16\}$ to find out that $M_{min} = 2$. HTM-RTM becomes less efficient than HTM-HLE at M≈200 because the cost of serializations due to the HTM buffer overflows dominates the runtime of HTM-RTM beyond this point (serializations in HTM-HLE are implemented in hardware [40], while in HTM-RTM they have to be implemented in software).

5.5.3 Has-P (High-Performance Server)

The analysis of Has-P is presented in Figures 4i-4l. The performance trends are partially similar to the observations for Has-C; especially for lower thread counts ($T \leq 4$). A distinctive feature is a significantly lower number of HTM buffer overflows than in Has-C. To gain more insight we performed an additional analysis to compare the number of memory conflicts and HTM buffer overflows with varying T for fixed $M = 2$. We present the results in Figures 5a-5b. Surprisingly, we observe Has-C has significantly more buffer overflows than memory conflicts for the increasing T; a reverse trend is observed on Has-P. This interesting insight may help improve the design of future HTM architectures. **Discussion** Our analysis shows that RTM is more vulnerable to aborts than BG/Q HTM. The difference between the number of transactions and aborts never drops below

25% for HTM in BG/Q for any analyzed M (cf. Figure 4d), while for RTM this threshold is achieved for $M = 144$ (Has-C). Another discovery is that Has-P is only marginally impacted by buffer overflows (<1% of all the aborts for $T = 24$ and $M = 320$). On the contrary, aborts in Has-C are dominated by HTM buffer overflows that constitute more than 90% of all the aborts for $M > 64$. The only exception are the data points where the number of overflows drops rapidly as aborts become dominated by the limited L1 cache associativity (a similar effect is visible for Has-P). This effect is not visible in BG/Q because it stores its speculative states in its L2 16-way associative cache [36], while both Has-P and Has-C have 8-way associative L1s.

We conclude that the coarsening of transactions provides significant speedups (up to 1.51) over the Atomic-CAS baseline on BGQ and Has-C; Has-P does not offer any speedups due to the overheads generated by memory conflicts. We find the following optimum transaction sizes for PowerPC in BG/Q: $M_{min} = 80$ ($T = 16$), $M_{min} = 144$ ($T = 64$). For x86 (Has-C) $M_{min} = 2$ for $T \in \{4, 8\}$. We present M_{min} for the remaining values of T in the technical report. We will use these values in Section 6 to accelerate Graph500 [30] for different types of graphs.

5.6 Activities Spawned on a Remote Node

We now analyze the performance of activities spawned on a remote node. We implement such activities as hardware transactions triggered upon receiving an atomic active message. We again test both the long and the short running mode (on BG/Q) and RTM/HLE (on Haswell). To reduce the overhead of sending and receiving an atomic active message and save bandwidth, we use *activity coalescing*: activities flowing to the same target are sent in a single message.

We run the benchmarks on BG/Q and Greina (Has-P); we skip Has-C because the Trivium server is not a distributed memory machine. On BG/Q, we compare inter-node activities to optimized remote one-sided CAS and ACC atomics provided by the generic function PAMI_Rmw in the IBM PAMI

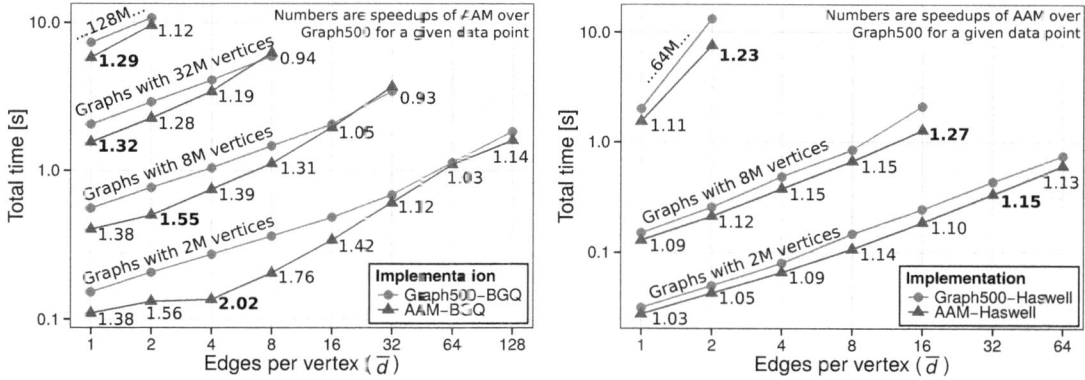

(a) The performance of BFS on BG/Q for Kronecker graphs.　(b) The performance of BFS on Haswell for Kronecker graphs.

Figure 6: (§ 6.1) The overview of the performance of intra-node Graph500 BFS implemented with atomics (Graph500-BGQ, Graph500-Haswell), AAM RTM (AAM-Haswell), and the short mode BG/Q HTM (AAM-BGQ). We vary $|V|$ and $\bar{d}$; $T = 64$ (on BG/Q) and $T = 8$ (on Has-C).

communication library [19]. On Has-P we compare activities to remote atomic operations provided by MPI-3 RMA [29] implemented over the InfiniBand fabric. We evaluate the performance of marking a remote vertex as visited (addressing distributed BFS computations) and incrementing the rank of a remote vertex (addressing distributed PageRank).

5.6.1　BG/Q (Supercomputer)

We first measure the time it takes a process p_i to mark 2^{13} vertices stored on a node n_j as visited (targeting distributed BFS). The results are presented in Figure 5c. Without coalescing, HTM activities (Inter-node-HTM-L for the long and Inter-node-HTM-S for the short mode) are ≈5× slower than PAMI atomics (Inter-node-CAS). Still, for $C_{cross} = 16$ Inter-node-HTM-S becomes more efficient. Second, we scale the number of nodes N. Figure 5d shows the time to mark a vertex stored in process p_N's memory by $N-1$ other processes. We use the short HTM mode. Coalesced AAMs (Inter-node-HTM-C) outperform Inter-node-CAS ≈5-7 times.

We also evaluate an inter-node activity that increments the rank of a vertex (targeting distributed PR). We perform analogous benchmarks as for the remote CAS; we present the results in Figures 5e-5f. Implementing ACC using HTM again generates costly aborts that dominate the runtime; however coalescing enables a speedup of ≈20% (for the short HTM running mode) over highly optimized PAMI atomics.

5.6.2　Has-P (High-Performance Server)

Here, we test the performance of inter-node activities implemented on Has-P. Our testbed has two nodes, thus we only vary C. We present the results in Figures 5g (CAS) and 5h (ACC). Setting $C = 2$ enables AAM to outperform remote atomics provided by MPI-3 RMA.

5.7　Distributed Activities

Finally, we test the ownership protocol for executing activities that span multiple nodes (see Figure 5i for BGQ results). Each process issues x transactions; each transaction marks a local and b remote randomly selected vertices. We compare four scenarios: O-1 ($x = 10^3, a = 5, b = 1$), O-2 ($x = 10^4, a = 5, b = 1$), O-3 ($x = 10^3, a = 7, b = 3$), and O-4 ($x = 10^4, a = 7, b = 3$). We measure the total time to execute transactions. O-1 finishes fastest, O-3 is slower as more remote vertices have to be acquired. O-2 and O-4 follow the same performance patterns; additional overheads are due to the backoff scheme. If no time is spent on backoff, then the protocol may livelock and may make no progress.

We conclude that AAM can be used in various environments (e.g., IBM networks or InfiniBand) to enable remote transactions and to accelerate distributed processing.

6.　EVALUATION

We now use AAM to accelerate the processing of large Kronecker [23] and Erdős-Renyi [10] (ER) graphs with different vertex distributions (power-law, binomial, Poisson). We also evaluate real-world SNAP graphs[3]. We evaluate BFS and PR because they are the basis of various data analytics benchmarks such as Graph500 and because they are proxies of many algorithms such as Ford-Fulkerson.

6.1　BFS: Massively-Parallel Manycores

We first evaluate the speedup that AAM delivers in highly-parallel multi- and manycore environments.

Comparison Baseline:　Here, we use the OpenMP Graph500 highly optimized reference code [30] (Graph500-BGQ, Graph500-Haswell) based on atomics as the comparison baseline. The baseline applies several optimizations; among others it reduces the amount of fine-grained synchronization by checking if the vertex was visited before executing an atomic.

We compare the Graph500 baseline with the coarsened variants that use the short mode HTM in BG/Q (AAM-BGQ) and RTM in Haswell (AAM-Haswell). We only use Has-C (denoted as Haswell) because it provides higher speedups over atomics than Has-P as we show in Figure 4. The long mode and HLE are omitted as they follow similar performance patterns and vary by up to 10%. We set $T = 64$ (for BG/Q) and $T = 8$ (for Haswell) for full parallelism.

6.1.1　Processing Kronecker Power-Law Graphs

Here, we use the results of the analysis in Section 5 and set $M_{min} \in \{2, 80, 144\}$ for the most advantageous size of transactions on BG/Q and Haswell. We present the results in Figure 6. We scale $|V|$ from 2^{20} to 2^{28}, and we use $\bar{d} \in \{1, 2, ..., 256\}$; highest values generate graphs that fill the whole available memory. For BG/Q, AAM-BGQ outperforms Graph500-BGQ by up to 102% for a graph with ≈2 millions vertices and $\bar{d} = 4$. For higher $\bar{d}$ AAM-BGQ becomes comparable to Graph500-BGQ. This is because adding more edges for fixed $|V|$ generates more transactions that conflict and abort more often. For Haswell, AAM consistently outperforms Graph500 by up to 27%. The speedup does not change significantly when increasing $\bar{d}$. This is because we use smaller transac-

---

[3] Available at https://snap.stanford.edu/data/index.html.

Input graph properties					BG/Q analysis			Haswell analysis					
Type	ID	Name	$|V|$	$|E|$	S over g500 ($M=24$)	M	S over g500	S over g500 ($M=2$)	S over Galois ($M=2$)	M	S over g500	S over Galois	S over HAMA
Comm. networks (CNs)	cWT	wiki-Talk	2.4M	5M	2.82	48	3.35	0.91	1.22	6	0.96	1.28	344
	cEU	email-EuAll	265k	420k	3.67	32	4.36	0.76	0.88	4	0.97	1.12	1448
Social networks (SNs)	sLV	soc-LiveJ.	4.8M	69M	1.44	12	1.56	1.05	1.1	3	1.07	1.12	$>10^4$
	sOR	com-orkut	3M	117M	1.22	20	1.27	1.06	0.69	4	1.13	0.74	$>10^4$
	sLJ	com-lj	4M	34M	1.44	12	1.54	1.03	1.03	4	1.04	1.04	603
	sYT	com-youtube	1.1M	2.9M	1.67	8	1.84	0.96	1.1	5	0.98	1.11	670
	sDB	com-dblp	317k	1M	1.33	8	1.80	≈ 1	2.5	2	≈ 1	2.53	2160
	sAM	com-amazon	334k	925k	1.14	8	1.62	1.04	1.64	2	1.04	1.64	1426
Purchase network (PNs)	pAM	amazon0601	403k	3.3M	1.45	8	1.91	≈ 1	1.25	3	1.03	1.30	618
Road networks (RNs)	rCA	roadNet-CA	1.9M	5.5M	≈ 1	2	1.59	1.33	1.74	8	1.38	1.80	$>10^4$
	rTX	roadNet-TX	1.3M	3.8M	≈ 1	2	1.53	1.29	1.89	6	1.42	2.08	$>10^4$
	rPA	roadNet-PA	1M	3M	≈ 1	2	1.52	≈ 1	2.00	9	1.07	2.16	$>10^4$
Citation graphs (CGs)	ciP	cit-Patents	3.7M	16.5M	1.16	8	1.57	1.01	1.26	2	1.01	1.26	1875
Web graphs (WGs)	wGL	web-Google	875k	5.1M	1.78	12	2.08	0.98	1.26	6	1.06	1.35	365
	wBS	web-BerkStan	685k	7.6M	1.91	24	1.91	0.93	1.31	5	1.07	1.40	755
	wSF	web-Stanford	281k	2.3M	1.89	24	1.89	0.98	1.54	5	1.07	1.58	1077

Table 1: (§ 6.1.2) The performance of AAM for real-world graphs. S and g500 denote speedup and Graph500. ≈ 1 indicates that the given $S \in (0.99; 1.01)$.

tions in AAM-Haswell ($M = 2$) than in AAM-BGQ ($M = 144$) and thus they do not incur considerably more memory conflicts when $\bar{d}$ is increased.

6.1.2 Processing Real-World Graphs

Next, we evaluate AAM for real-world graphs (see Table 1). For this, we extend Graph500 so that it can read graphs from a file. We selected directed/undirected graphs with $|V| > 250k$ that could fit in memory and we excluded graphs that could not easily be loaded into Graph500 framework (e.g., amazon0505).

BlueGene/Q: The tested graphs are generally sparser than the analyzed Kronecker graphs. We discovered that the optimum M is smaller than 144 (we set it to 24). This is because in dense graphs more data is contiguous in memory and thus can be processed more efficiently by larger transactions. The results show that graphs with similar structure entail similar performance gains. The highest S (speedup) is achieved for CNs (up to 3.67) and WGs (up to 1.91). SNs, PNs, and CGs offer moderate S (1.14-1.67). RNs entail no significant change in performance. We also searched for optimum values of M for specific graphs; this improves S across all the groups. The results indicate that respective groups have similar optimum values of M. The differences are due to the structures of the graphs that may either facilitate coarsening and reduce the number of costly aborts (CNs and WGs) or entail more significant overheads (RNs).

Haswell: We compare AAM to several state-of-the-art graph processing engines: Galois [18] (represents runtime systems that exploit amorphous data-parallelism), SNAP [22] (represents network analysis and data mining libraries), and HAMA [33] (an engine similar to Pregel [27] that represents Hadoop-based BSP processing engines). We do not evaluate these engines on BG/Q due to various compatibility problems (e.g., BG/Q does not support Java required by HAMA). BFS in Galois only returns the diameter. We modified it (with fine locks) so that it constructs a full BFS tree, analogously to AAM and Graph500.

First, we set $M = 2$. While AAM is in general faster than Graph500 (up to 33% for rCA), several inputs entail longer AAM BFS traversals. AAM is up to a factor of two faster than Galois but is slower for two inputs (cEU and sOR). There is some diversity in the results because AAM

on Haswell is significantly more sensitive to small changes of M than on BG/Q. Thus, we again searched for the optimum M for each input separately which resulted in higher AAM's speedups. The performance of HAMA and SNAP is generally much lower than AAM (results for SNAP are consistently worse than for HAMA and we exclude them due to space constraints). HAMA suffers from overheads caused by the underlying MapReduce architecture and expensive synchronization. The analyzed real-world graphs have usually high diameters (e.g., 33 for sAM) and thus require many BSP steps that are expensive in HAMA. This is especially visible for RNs that have particularly big diameters (554 for rCA) and accordingly long runtimes. As we will show in the next section, processing Kronecker graphs with lower diameters reduces these overheads. We also investigated SNAP and we found out that it is particularly inefficient for undirected graphs and it does not efficiently use threading. Our final discovery is that, similarly to BG/Q, respective groups of graphs have similar optimum values of M.

6.1.3 Evaluating the Scalability of AAM

Finally, we evaluate the scalability of AAM by varying T. The results are presented in Figure 7a (BG/Q) and 7b (Haswell). We use a Kronecker graph with 2^{21} vertices and 2^{24} edges. We vary T between 1 and the number of available hardware threads. The BG/Q results indicate that AAM utilizes onnode parallelism more efficiently than Graph500. For Haswell, the performance patterns for AAM and Graph500 are similar; both frameworks deliver positive speedups for any T and outperform other schemes by $\approx$20-50% (Galois) and $\approx$2 orders of magnitude (HAMA). We skip SNAP for clarity; it is consistently 2-3x slower than HAMA.

6.2 PR: Distributed Memory Machines

As the last step, we provide an initial large-scale evaluation of AAM in a distributed environment. We select PR to illustrate that expensive and numerous aborts generated by the HTM implementation of ACC (cf. § 5.4.2) can be amortized with the coalescing of activities. We compare AAM to a version of Parallel Boost Graph Library (PBGL) [11] based on active messages. The utilized variant of PBGL applies various optimizations; for example it processes incoming edges to reduce the amount of synchronization and

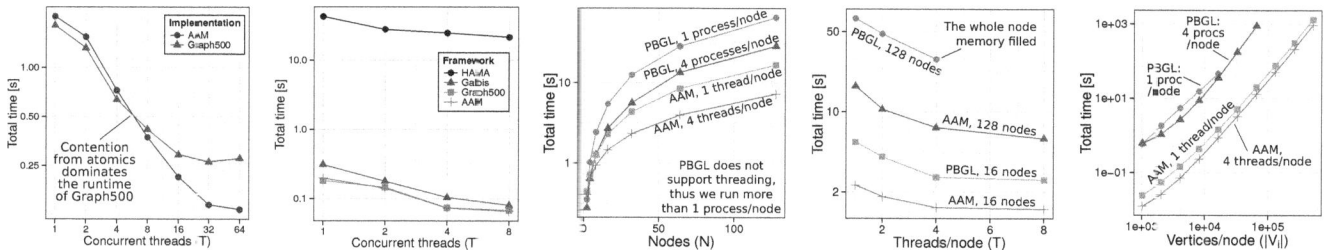

(a) Scalability of AAM; BG/Q. (b) Scalability of AAM; Haswell. (c) PageRank, $ER = 0.0005$. (d) PageRank, $ER = 0.0005$. (e) PageRank, $ER = 0.005$.

Figure 7: The analysis of the performance of: BFS (when varying T; § 6.1.3 and Figures 7a-7b) and distributed PR (§ 6.2, Figures 7c-7e).

to limit the performance overheads caused by atomics. We run the benchmarks on BG/Q to enable large-scale evaluation. We use ER graphs with the probability parameter $ER \in \{0.005, 0.0005\}$ and the number of vertices up to 2^{23}. PBGL does not support threading, we thus spawn multiple processes per node and an equal number of threads in AAM; we scale T until PBGL fills in the whole memory.

The results of the analysis are presented in Figure 7. We scale N (Figure 7c), T (Figure 7d), and $|V_i|$ (Figure 7e). In each scenario AAM outperforms PBGL $\approx$3-10 times thanks to the coalescing of activities and more efficient utilization of intra-node parallelism.

7. RELATED WORK AND DISCUSSION

The challenges connected with the processing of graphs are presented by Lumsdaine et al. [26]. Example frameworks for parallel graph computations are Pregel [27], PBGL [11], HAMA [33], GraphLab [24], and Spark [41]. There exist several comparisons of various engines [32, 12, 25, 9]. AAM differs from these designs as it is a mechanism that can be used to implement abstractions and to accelerate processing engines. It uses HTM to reduce the amount of synchronization and thus to accelerate graph analytics.

GraphBLAS [28] is an emerging standard for expressing graph computations in terms of linear algebra operations. AAM can be used to implement the GraphBLAS abstraction and to accelerate the performance of graph analytics based on sparse linear algebra computations.

The Galois runtime [17] optimizes graph processing by coarsening fine graph updates. AAM can be integrated with Galois. In AAM, we focus on scalable techniques for implementing coarsening with HTM. First, we provide a detailed performance analysis of HTM for graph computations, a core paper contribution. Instead, Galois mostly addresses locking [18]. Second, contrary to Galois, AAM targets both shared- and distributed-memory systems. Third, our work performs a holistic extensive performance analysis of coarsening. Instead, coarsening in Galois is not evaluated on its own. We conclude that AAM's techniques and analysis can be used to accelerate the Galois runtime.

Active Messages (AM) were introduced by Eicken et al. [35]. Various AM implementations were proposed [8, 38, 39, 19, 2]. Our work enhances these designs by combining AM with HTM. We illustrate how to program AAM and we conduct an extensive analysis to show how to tune AAM's performance on state-of-the-art manycore architectures.

Transactional memory was introduced by Herlihy et al. [14]. Several implementations of HTM were introduced, but their performance was not extensively analyzed [40, 36, 7, 6]. Yoo et al. [40] present performance gains from using Haswell HTM in scientific workloads such as simulated annealing. Our analysis generalizes these findings, proposes a simple performance model, and provides a deep insight into the performance of both BG/Q and Haswell HTM for a broad range of transaction sizes and other parameters in the context of data analytics.

AAM can be extended with a mechanism for the online selection of M. Such a mechanism would use the provided insights into the performance tradeoffs of the available HTM implementations. For example, the runtime system could prune the space of all the applicable values of HTM parameters depending on which HTM is utilized. In addition, our performance model can be combined with data mining techniques to enable more effective online decisions. We leave this study for future research.

Finally, we envision that the potential of AAM could be further expanded by combining it with some ideas related to code analysis. For example, one could envision a simple compiler pass that pattern-matches each single-vertex transaction against the set of atomic operations to transform it if possible to accelerate graph processing. However, such an analysis is outside the scope of this paper.

8. CONCLUSION

Designing efficient algorithms for massively parallel and distributed graph computations is becoming one of the key challenges for the parallel programming community [18]. Graph processing is fine-grained by nature and its traditional implementations based on atomics or fine locks are error-prone and may entail significant overheads [18].

We propose Atomic Active Messages (AAM), a mechanism that reduces the amount of fine-grained synchronization in irregular graph computations. AAM is motivated by recent advances towards implementing transactional memory in hardware. AAM provides several high performance techniques for executing fine-grained graph modifications as coarse transactions, it facilitates the utilization of state-of-the-art hardware mechanisms and resources, and it can be used to accelerate highly optimized codes such as Graph500 by more than 100%.

AAM targets highly-parallel multi- and manycore architectures and distributed-memory machines. It provides a novel classification of atomic active messages that can be used to design and program both shared- and distributed-memory graph computations. AAM enables different optimizations from both of these worlds such as coarsening intra-node transactions and coalescing inter-node activities. We illustrate how to implement AAM with HTM; however, other mechanisms such as distributed STM [21], flat-combining [13], or optimistic locking [20] could also be used.

Finally, to the best of our knowledge, our work is the first detailed performance analysis of hardware transactional memory in the context of graph computations and the first to compare HTMs implemented in Intel Haswell and IBM

Blue Gene/Q. Among others, we conjecture that implementing HTM in the bigger L2 cache (BG/Q) enables higher performance than in the smaller L1 cache (Haswell). We believe our analysis and data can be used by architects and engineers to develop a more efficient HTM that would offer even higher speedups for irregular data analytics.

Acknowledgements

We thank Hussein Harake and the CSCS and ALCF teams granting access to the Greina, Monte Rosa, and Vesta machines, and for their excellent technical support. MB is supported by the 2013 Google European Doctoral Fellowship in Parallel Computing.

References

[1] E. G. Boman, U. Catalyurek, A. Gebremedhin, and F. Manne. A scalable parallel graph coloring algorithm for distributed memory computers. In *Proc. of Euro-Par 2005 Par. Proc.*, pages 241–251, 2005.

[2] D. Bonachea. GASNet Specification, v1. *Univ. California, Berkeley, Tech. Rep. CSD-02-1207*, 2002.

[3] S. Brin and L. Page. The anatomy of a large-scale hypertextual Web search engine. In *Proc. of Intl. Conf. on World Wide Web*, WWW7, pages 107–117, 1998.

[4] A. Buluç and K. Madduri. Graph partitioning for scalable distributed graph computations. *Cont. Math.*, 588, 2013.

[5] C. Click. Azul's experiences with hardware transactional memory. In HP Labs' Bay Area Workshop on Trans. Mem.

[6] S. Chaudhry et al. Rock: A High-Performance Sparc CMT Processor. *IEEE Micro*, 29(2):6–16, Mar. 2009.

[7] D. Dice, Y. Lev, M. Moir, and D. Nussbaum. Early experience with a commercial hardware transactional memory implementation. In *Intl. Conf. on Arch. Support for Prog. Lang. and Op. Sys.*, ASPLOS XIV, pages 157–168, 2009.

[8] N. Edmonds, J. Willcock, and A. Lumsdaine. Expressing graph algorithms using generalized active messages. In *ACM Intl. Conf. on Supercomp.*, ICS '13, pages 283–292, 2013.

[9] B. Elser and A. Montresor. An evaluation study of BigData frameworks for graph processing. In *Big Data, Intl, Conf. on*, pages 60–67, 2013.

[10] P. Erdos and A. Rényi. On the evolution of random graphs. *Pub. Math. Inst. Hun. A. Sci.*, 5:17–61, 1960.

[11] D. Gregor and A. Lumsdaine. The parallel BGL: A generic library for distributed graph computations. *Parallel Object-Oriented Scientific Computing (POOSC)*, page 2, 2005.

[12] Y. Guo et al. How Well Do Graph-Processing Platforms Perform? An Empirical Performance Evaluation and Analysis. In *Intl. Par. and Dist. Proc. Symp.*, IPDPS '14, pages 395–404, 2014.

[13] D. Hendler, I. Incze, N. Shavit, and M. Tzafrir. Flat combining and the synchronization-parallelism tradeoff. In *Symp. on Par. in Alg. and Arch.*, SPAA '10, pages 355–364, 2010.

[14] M. Herlihy and J. E. B. Moss. Transactional memory: architectural support for lock-free data structures. In *Intl. Symp. on Comp. Arch.*, ISCA '93, pages 289–300, 1993.

[15] Intel. Intel Xeon Processor E3-1200 v3 Product Family, December 2014. Revision 009.

[16] S. Kang and D. A. Bader. An efficient transactional memory algorithm for computing minimum spanning forest of sparse graphs. In *Proc. of the Symp. on Prin. Prac. of Par. Prog.*, PPoPP '09, pages 15–24, 2009.

[17] M. Kulkarni et al. Optimistic parallelism requires abstractions. In *ACM SIGPLAN Conf. on Prog. Lang. Des. and Impl.*, PLDI '07, pages 211–222, 2007.

[18] M. Kulkarni et al. Optimistic Parallelism Benefits from Data Partitioning. In *Intl. Conf. on Arch. Sup. for Prog. Lang. and Op. Sys.*, ASPLOS XIII, pages 233–243, 2008.

[19] S. Kumar et al. PAMI: A Parallel Active Message Interface for the Blue Gene/Q Supercomputer. In *IEEE Par. Dist. Proc. Symp. (IPDPS)*, pages 763–773, 2012.

[20] H. T. Kung and J. T. Robinson. On optimistic methods for concurrency control. *ACM Trans. Database Syst.*, 6(2):213–226, June 1981.

[21] M. Lesani and J. Palsberg. Communicating memory transactions. In *Proc. of the Symp. on Prin. and Prac. of Par. Prog.*, PPoPP '11, pages 157–168, 2011.

[22] J. Leskovec. *Dynamics of large networks*. PhD thesis, Carnegie Mellon University, 2008.

[23] J. Leskovec et al. Kronecker Graphs: An Approach to Modeling Networks. *J. Mach. Learn. Res.*, 11:985–1042, Mar. 2010.

[24] Y. Low et al. Graphlab: A new framework for parallel machine learning. *preprint arXiv:1006.4990*, 2010.

[25] Y. Lu, J. Cheng, D. Yan, and H. Wu. Large-scale Distributed Graph Computing Systems: An Experimental Evaluation. *Proc. VLDB Endow.*, 8(3):281–292, Nov. 2014.

[26] A. Lumsdaine, D. Gregor, B. Hendrickson, and J. W. Berry. Challenges in parallel graph processing. *Par. Proc. Let.*, 17(1):5–20, 2007.

[27] G. Malewicz et al. Pregel: a system for large-scale graph processing. In *Proc. of the ACM SIGMOD Intl. Conf. on Manag. of Data*, SIGMOD '10, pages 135–146, 2010.

[28] T. Mattson et al. Standards for Graph Algorithm Primitives. *CoRR*, abs/1408.0393, 2014.

[29] MPI Forum. MPI: A Message-Passing Interface Standard. Version 3, September 2012.

[30] R. C. Murphy, K. B. Wheeler, B. W. Barrett, and J. A. Ang. Introducing the graph 500. *Cray User's Group (CUG)*, 2010.

[31] O. Reingold. Undirected ST-connectivity in Log-space. In *Proc. of the ACM Symp. on Theory of Comp.*, STOC '05, pages 376–385, 2005.

[32] N. Satish et al. Navigating the Maze of Graph Analytics Frameworks Using Massive Graph Datasets. In *ACM SIGMOD Intl. Conf. on Management of Data*, SIGMOD '14, pages 979–990, 2014.

[33] S. Seo et al. HAMA: An Efficient Matrix Computation with the MapReduce Framework. In *Intl. Conf. on Cloud Comp. Tech. and Science*, CLOUDCOM'10, pages 721–726, 2010.

[34] N. Shavit and D. Touitou. Software transactional memory. In *Proc. of ACM Symp. on Pr. of Dist. Comp.*, PODC '95, pages 204–213, 1995.

[35] T. von Eicken, D. E. Culler, S. C. Goldstein, and K. E. Schauser. Active messages: a mechanism for integrated communication and computation. In *Intl. Symp. on Comp. Arch.*, ISCA '92, pages 256–266, 1992.

[36] A. Wang et al. Evaluation of Blue Gene/Q hardware support for transactional memories. In *Intl. Conf. on Par. Arch. and Comp. Tech.*, PACT '12, pages 127–136, 2012.

[37] J.-T. W. S. Weigert. Dream: Dresden streaming transactional memory benchmark. 2013.

[38] J. Willcock, T. Hoefler, N. Edmonds, and A. Lumsdaine. AM++: A Generalized Active Message Framework. In *Proc. of the Intl. Conf. on Par. Arch. and Comp. Tech.*, pages 401–410, Sep. 2010.

[39] J. Willcock, T. Hoefler, N. Edmonds, and A. Lumsdaine. Active Pebbles: Parallel Programming for Data-Driven Applications. In *Proc. of the ACM Intl. Conf. on Supercomp. (ICS'11)*, pages 235–245, 2011.

[40] R. M. Yoo, C. J. Hughes, K. Lai, and R. Rajwar. Performance Evaluation of Intel Transactional Synchronization Extensions for High-Performance Computing. In *Proc. of the ACM/IEEE Supercomputing*, SC'13, 2013.

[41] M. Zaharia et al. Spark: Cluster Computing with Working Sets. In *Proc. of the USENIX Conf. on Hot Top. in Cl. Comp.*, HotCloud'10, pages 10–10, 2010.

Understanding Graph Computation Behavior to Enable Robust Benchmarking

Fan Yang and Andrew A. Chien*
Department of Computer Science
University of Chicago
Chicago, IL, U.S.A.
{fanyang, achien}@cs.uchicago.edu
*also Mathematics and Computer Science, Argonne National Laboratory

ABSTRACT

Graph processing is important for a growing range of applications. Current performance studies of parallel graph computation employ a large variety of algorithms and graphs. To explore their robustness, we characterize behavior variation across algorithms and graph structures at different scales. Our results show that graph computation behaviors, with up to 1000-fold variation, form a very broad space. Any inefficient exploration of this space may lead to narrow understanding and ad-hoc studies. Hence we consider constructing an ensemble of graph computations, or graph-algorithm pairs, to most effectively explore this graph computation behavior space. We study different ensembles of parallel graph computations, and define two metrics to quantify how efficiently and completely an ensemble explores the space. Our results show that: (1) experiments limited to a single algorithm or a single graph may unfairly characterize a graph-processing system, (2) benchmarks exploring both algorithm and graph diversity can significantly improve the quality (30% more complete and 200% more efficient), but must be carefully chosen, (3) some algorithms are more useful than others in benchmarking, and (4) we can reduce the complexity (number of algorithms, graphs, runtime) while conserving the benchmarking quality.

Categories and Subject Descriptors

C.4 [**Computer Systems Organization**]: Performance of systems – *Performance attributes.*

General Terms

Algorithms, Measurement, Performance, Experimentation.

Keywords

Graph processing, Graph-algorithms, Benchmarking.

1. INTRODUCTION

Rapid growth of WWW and social networking has given rise to massive graph datasets in domains such as social networks, recommender systems, web graphs, and more. These large-scale graphs along with complex algorithms create a critical need for graph-processing systems. In response, numerous graph-processing systems have been created (Pregel [13], Giraph [1], GraphLab [5], SNAP [17], TurboGraph [9], and GraphChi [11]).

Confounding factors are wide variation in both the properties of graphs and graph algorithms. For example, graph size can differ by 6 orders of magnitude [17, 19]. Compute and communication intensity usually vary a lot across vertices and algorithms. Hence, many performance studies of graph processing system, which employ various sets of graphs and algorithms, have produced incomparable results. For example, Elser [4] finds that GraphLab outperforms Giraph, Han [8] finds that their performance are comparable, and Guo [7] produces no overall conclusion. It is difficult to gain any clear perspective on which systems are preferable. Even experts cannot claim any deep understanding of graph computation performance. So, our goal is to provide a more systematic understanding of the impact of graph and algorithm on graph-processing systems, and enable robust evaluation.

To achieve this goal, we use GraphLab as an experimental vehicle on a cluster with 768 cores, and execute 11 graph algorithms over a collection of synthetic graphs of varying size and structure. We measure key properties ranging from vertex activity to compute intensity. Our results show that not only do algorithms behave differently, but also input graphs contribute a lot to behavior variation. Understanding performance over such broad space is challenging and also necessary for robust benchmarking of graph-processing systems. So, to systematically understand the behavior of parallel graph computation, we define a vector space using fundamental graph computation properties, and also define two metrics, *spread* and *coverage*, that capture how well a set of graph-algorithm pairs explores the behavior space. With these metrics, we evaluate the benchmarking quality of different ensembles of graph-algorithm pairs, and search for best-qualified ensembles. Our study suggests that a small set of carefully chosen experiments could sample the behavior space much more efficiently, which presents an opportunity to build a high-quality benchmark suite. Specific contributions of this paper include:

(1) We conduct a series of experiments varying algorithm and graphs on a 768-core cluster, which demonstrates 1000-fold variation across 5 dimensions of graph computation behavior.

(2) We define two ensemble metrics, *spread* and *coverage*, to measure how efficiently and thoroughly an *ensemble* of experiments explores the graph computation behavior space.

(3) We demonstrate that an ensemble drawn from a single algorithm or a single graph is a poor benchmark set, and an ensemble exploring both algorithm diversity and graph diversity gives 200% better *spread* and 30% better *coverage*.

HPDC'15, June 15 - 19, 2015, Portland, OR, USA
© 2015 ACM. ISBN 978-1-4503-3550-8/15/06...$15.00
DOI: http://dx.doi.org/10.1145/2749246.2749257

(4) Our insights into the best ensembles with high spread and coverage show that some algorithms, including K-Means, Alternating Least Squares, and Triangle Counting, are more useful than other algorithms in behavior space exploration.

(5) We find that careful reduction in algorithm diversity minimizes loss of *spread* and *coverage* with further optimization possible by reducing runtime.

The remainder of the paper is organized as follows. We detail our methodology in Section 2 and show the experimental results in Section 3. In Section 4, we consider how to best design ensembles for thorough graph system evaluation. Related work is discussed in Section 5, and Section 6 summarizes and suggests future work.

2. METHODS

We employ GraphLab v2.2 [5] as our graph-processing platform. We execute programs using the synchronous mode. Each graph algorithm is executed on a variety of graphs. All the experiments were performed on the Midway system in Research Computing Center of the University of Chicago. We used up to 48 nodes, connected by a fully non-blocking FDR-10 Infiniband network. Each node has two eight-core 2.6GHz Intel Xeon E5-2670 "Sandy Bridge" processors with 32GB of memory.

2.1 Workload

We use synthetic graph generators to create graphs for each application domain. We consider both graph size and degree distribution as main parameters of our generators, which have dominant impact on graph computation behavior. Graph size is measured in number of edges (*nedges*), which determines the scale of a graph problem. Assuming all graphs in our experiments are scale-free networks [22], the fraction $P(k)$ of vertices with degree k goes for large values of k as

$$P(k) \sim k^{-\alpha}, \qquad (1)$$

Where α is a constant typically ranging *2.0-3.0* in the real world. Hence, parameters of our graph generators include both *nedges* and α. We set *nedges* to different orders of magnitude (10^5 to 10^9). We also set α to match real-world scale-free graphs (2.0 to 3.0), accepting slight variation in the number of vertices. The vertex data and edge weights are generated randomly in Gaussian distribution. To limit the number of experiments, we use 4 different sizes, and 5 different degree distributions for each domain. The range of variables is shown in Table 1.

We selected graph algorithms from distinct application domains for their widely varying behaviors.

(1) *Graph Analytics (GA)* focuses on data mining, especially relationships from large graphs. We choose six algorithms, including Connected Components (CC), K-Core decomposition (KC), Triangle Counting (TC), Single-Source Shortest Path (SSSP), PageRank (PR), and Approximate Diameter (AD).

(2) *Clustering* classifies objects based on similarity. We choose

Table 1. Graph Feature Variables

Domains	Algorithms	Variables	Values
Graph Analytics	CC, TC, KC, SSSP, PR, AD	*nedges*	$10^6, 10^7, 10^8, 10^9$
		α	2.0, 2.25, 2.5, 2.75, 3.0
Clustering	KM	*nedges*	$10^6, 10^7, 10^8, 10^9$
		α	2.0, 2.25, 2.5, 2.75, 3.0
Collaborative Filtering	ALS, NMF, SGD, SVD	*nedges*	$10^5, 10^6, 10^7, 10^8$
		α	2.0, 2.25, 2.5, 2.75, 3.0

K-Means (KM) that partitions n vertices into k clusters such that each vertex belongs to the cluster with the nearest mean [21].

(3) *Collaborative Filtering (CF)* is used by recommender systems to predict the rating that user would give to an item, e.g. a movie or a book [20]. A general method for CF is to learn user-factor vectors and item-factor vectors through matrix factorization. We select four algorithms: Alternating Least Squares method (ALS), Non-negative Matrix Factorization (NMF), Stochastic Gradient Descent (SGD) and Singular Value Decomposition (SVD).

2.2 Computation Model

Our algorithms are implemented in the Gather-Apply-Scatter (GAS) model [5, 13]. Graph computation is expressed in a vertex-centric fashion. Each vertex can be active or inactive. Only active vertices can perform computation. In each iteration, vertices receive data through adjacent edges, called *edge reads*; then vertices perform user-defined computation and update their values, which are called *vertex updates*; finally vertices send signals to activate neighbors, which are called *messages* in this paper. In our experiments, all tested algorithms converge in finite number of iterations, except NMF and SGD. So we set a maximum 20 iterations for them.

There are also other computation models used in current graph-processing systems [14, 18], but the fundamental behavior of graph computation is conserved, such as transferring information through edges, performing computation on an independent unit (vertex/edge), and activations.

2.3 Performance Metrics

To characterize the fundamental behavior of parallel graph computations, we define five performance metrics.

On one hand, in order to capture the behavior variation over time, we define *active fraction*, which is the ratio of active vertices to all vertices in a single iteration that directly shows the activity of vertices across the whole lifecycle. For many algorithms, active fraction varies over time.

On the other hand, in order to capture the overall behavior, we define *{UPDT, WORK, EREAD, MSG}*, which reflect the compute intensity and communication intensity of a graph computation.

(1) *UPDT*: average number of vertex updates per iteration

(2) *WORK*: average CPU time for computing per iteration.

(3) *EREAD*: average number of edge reads per iteration

(4) *MSG*: average number of messages per iteration

Moreover, we divide each of these four metrics by the number of edges to capture the per-edge behavior. We also normalize these metrics to [0.0, 1.0] for highlighting the relative difference, rather than absolute values.

3. BEHAVIOR VARIATION IN PARALLEL GRAPH COMPUTATION

In this section, we present our experimental results. Due to paper length constraints, we present a selection of results. The full results are available in our technical report [23].

In our experiments, all algorithms have a characteristic shape of active fraction that varies significantly across algorithms (see Figure 1). The convergence rate also differs a lot across domains, by up to three orders of magnitude (TC vs. DD). Figure 2 shows

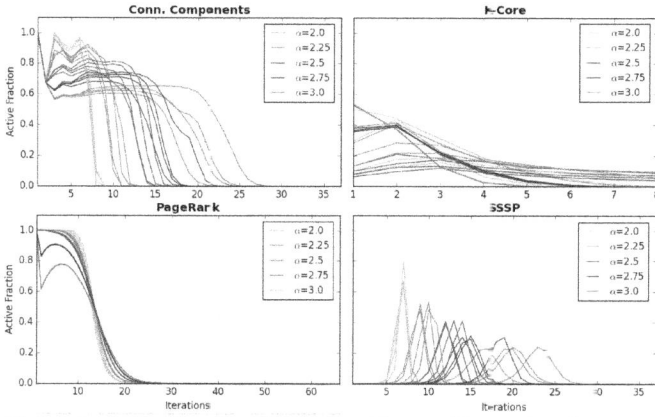

Figure 1. Active fraction for 4 algorithms x 20 graphs. Curves of same color correspond to graphs with same α but different size.

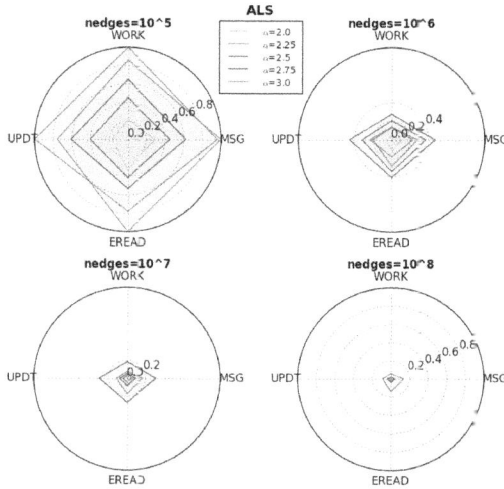

Figure 2. ALS metric values over 20 graphs.

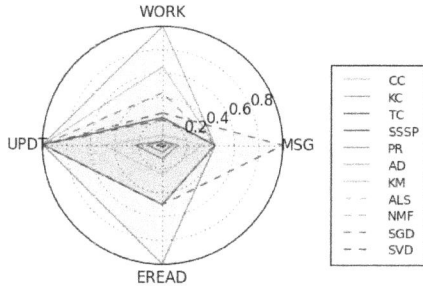

Figure 3. Metric values of 11 algorithms over same graph.

an interesting benchmark from our collection, ALS. Its behavior strongly depends on graph size and degree distribution. We observe high variation in all 4 metrics. Figure 3 shows the different shapes of 4 performance metrics for all algorithms. The values of all 4 metrics are much smaller in ALS. SSSP, KC, PR and LBP than in other algorithms. AD requires the most work for updating vertices, KM requires the most data transferring, and SGD requires the most message transferring.

Overall, graph computation behavior exhibits a wide diversity across algorithms and graphs, forming a very broad space. Any single experiment only samples a small part of that space, leading to ad-hoc performance studies that are unable to systematically understand the performance of graph-processing systems.

4. EXPLORING A BEHAVIOR SPACE

To systematically understand such wide variety of parallel graph computations, we define a behavior space that covers the fundamental properties we have measured in Section 3 as follows:

$$Behavior\ (GC_i) = <UPDT, WORK, EREAD, MSG> \quad (2)$$

Where GC_i is a graph computation represented as a *graph-algorithm* pair. While our behavior space is designed to capture fundamental graph computation behavior, doing so optimally is an open research challenge; we define only one[1] vector performance space, and evaluate its efficacy. Possible uses of our graph computation behavior characterization include basic algorithm analysis, algorithm comparison, performance analysis, graph computation optimization, performance prediction, system benchmarking, and even system design. Here we consider *how to use the behavior performance space to design efficient, high-quality benchmarking of graph-processing systems.*

We define an ensemble as a set of graph computations, $\{GC_1, GC_2, ...\}$ to model a benchmark suite and characterize any set of experiments. More formally we define:

$$Ensemble_k = \{GC_1, GC_2, ..., GC_N\} \quad (3)$$

Given this definition, then we would like to describe how well an ensemble characterizes graph computation behavior. To this end, we define two ensemble metrics, *spread* and *coverage*, that quantitatively characterize the quality of an ensemble to efficiently and thoroughly explore graph computation behavior.

Spread of an ensemble is defined as the mean pairwise distance between the *Behavior* vectors in an ensemble (see below).

$$Spread(Ensemble_k) = \frac{\sum_{i=1}^{N}\sum_{j=1}^{N} d(Behavior(GC_i), Behavior(GC_j))}{N(N-1)} \quad (4)$$

Where $d()$ is the Euclidean distance between two graph computation *Behavior* vectors. Intuitively, spread represents a form of "dispersion" of an ensemble. If the ensemble's elements are tightly clustered, then it will be low. If ensemble members are uniformly dispersed, it will be high.

Coverage of an ensemble is defined as average minimum distance from all points in the space to the nearest point in the ensemble.

$$Coverage(Ensemble_k) = \frac{N_S}{\sum_{i=1}^{N_S} \min_{k=1...N}\{d(Sample_i, Behavior(GC_k))\}} \quad (5)$$

Where sample points, $Sample_i$ ($i=1... N_S$), are taken randomly and uniformly throughout the space to compute the coverage. (We set N_S, the number of sample points to 1 million.) Intuitively, the notion of good coverage is the idea that no matter where a behavior falls in the space, it will be close to a point in the ensemble. For an ensemble, a high coverage indicates that we have sampled the behavior space thoroughly.

So, in order to construct an ensemble of graph computations with best benchmarking quality, for a given ensemble size, the goal is to maximize coverage. For a given coverage, the goal is to maximize spread to improve efficiency.

---

[1] Ours is the first formally defined behavior space for graph computations of which we are aware.

4.1 Ensembles of Single Algorithms/Graphs

Many studies assess graph computation performance with a single algorithm or a single graph, which seems to be a simple choice for benchmarking. So first, we consider the question: *How well can an ensemble using such a single origin explore the behavior space?*

A *single-algorithm ensemble* consists of experiments with one algorithm over a variety of graphs, and a *single-graph ensemble* consists of experiments over one graph with a variety of algorithms. We exhaustively test, and pick the best ensemble for both types and for each given ensemble size (5, 10, 15 and 20). In Figure 4 and 5, for both single-algorithm and single-graph ensembles, spread decreases steadily, and coverage increases very slowly. This indicates that additional runs of a single algorithm or a single graph tend to be clustered, and do not spread out to cover a larger behavior space. The achieved spread of single-graph ensembles is significantly higher than with single algorithms, which indicates that graph appears to be a more important factor in behavior variation than algorithm.

To understand the quality of the achieved spread and coverage, we also plot an empirical upper bound for each given ensemble size. These are computed assuming ensemble members uniformly and maximally distributed in the behavior space. Both the spread and coverage achieved by single-algorithm and single-graph ensembles fall well below our empirical upper bound.

Implications: If restricted to a single algorithm or a single graph, only limited graph computation behavior can be evoked. Adding more runs based on either the same algorithm or the same graph, generally leads to similar graph computation behavior. If we look at single-algorithm ensembles, they exhibit even less behavior variation than single-graph ensembles. In short, particular graph algorithms often behave similarly across graph structures and scales. Ensembles created with these properties (as used in numerous published graph computation system performance studies) risk unfair comparisons or incomplete results, and potentially erroneous conclusions.

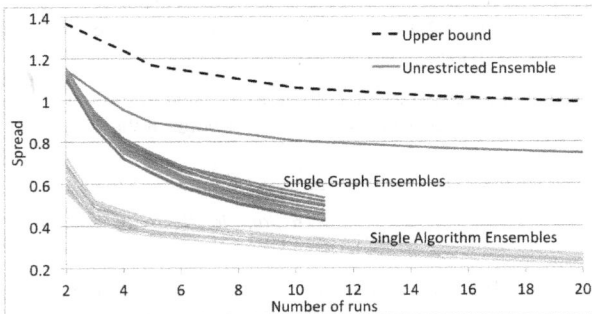

Figure 4. Spread for 3 types of ensembles.

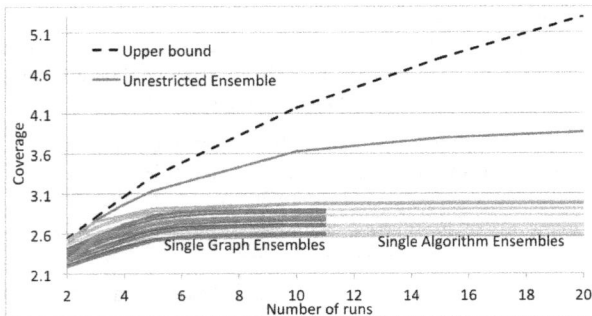

Figure 5. Coverage for 3 types of ensembles.

4.2 Unrestricted Diverse Ensembles

Given our broad exploration of graph computation behavior, we consider efficient and effective ensemble design retrospectively. Then we ask the question — *What are the ensembles we could have constructed? That is, the ensembles that would explore the behavior space most efficiently?* Intuitively, the best ensemble corresponds to the most efficient benchmark suite. We search all our 215 runs for the ensembles with best spread and coverage without any restriction on algorithms and graphs.

Allowed unrestricted choice across multiple algorithms and graphs, it is possible to sample the space much more efficiently and completely. Red curves in Figure 4 and 5 represent the achievable spread and coverage with unrestricted ensembles. Spread starts high (~1.2), and declines slowly to 0.75 for 20 members. Overall, there's a clear benefit in drawing richly from both algorithm and graph diversity, with as much as a three-fold greater spread. Considering coverage, ensembles that draw on both algorithm and graph diversity have clear advantage, delivering 30% better coverage than single-algorithm ensembles. The unrestricted ensembles achieve coverage that is significantly higher at as few as 5 runs, and the advantage grows even at 20 runs, achieving 3.9 overall.

Implications: Both algorithm diversity and graph diversity contribute to the behavior variation of graph computations. Hence, by exploiting both, we can identify multiple graph-algorithm pairs that exhibit diverse behaviors. We can use this information to construct an efficient and representative benchmark suite by carefully selecting graph-algorithm pairs that exhibit very different behavior and thoroughly sample the whole behavior space. In this way, this high-quality benchmark suite can exercise a broad graph computation behavior and systematically evaluate the performance of a graph processing system.

4.3 Understanding Diversity

While unrestricted diverse ensembles give much better results, we still want to understand *What aspects of diversity in algorithms and graphs contribute to this improvement?* Because algorithm usually dominants benchmarking complexity, we look into the representation of algorithms in the best ensembles (see Table 2).

Interestingly, some algorithms are consistently represented in the best ensembles, such as Alternating Least Squares for best spread, and K-Means for best coverage. The best ensembles are complicated – involving large numbers of algorithms and graphs. For example, the best 5-member ensemble for *spread* includes 4 algorithms and 5 different graphs. The best 5-member ensemble

Table 2. Ensembles Achieving Best Spread and Coverage (for ≥ 10, algorithms only).

Type	Size	Runs (Algorithm[, Graph Size, α])
Best spread	5	<ALS, 10^5, 3.0>, <SGD, 10^8, 2.0>, <TC, 10^9, 2.0>, <SSSP, 10^9, 3.0>, <ALS, 10^5, 2.75>
	10	ALS, SGD, TC, SSSP, ALS, TC, SGD, ALS, KM, SVD
	15	SSSP, ALS, KM, SGD, ALS, TC, SGD, ALS, TC, SSSP, ALS, SGD, TC, SVD, ALS
	20	SSSP, ALS, TC, SGD, ALS, TC, SGD, ALS, KM, SSSP, ALS, SGD, KM, SVD, ALS, TC, SGD, ALS, SGD, TC
Best coverage	5	<TC, 10^6, 2.5>, <KM, 10^6, 2.25>, <AD, 10^7, 3.0>, <ALS, 10^8, 2.0>, <KC, 10^6, 2.5>
	10	AD, SVD, KM, ALS, TC, KC, KM, ALS, KM, NMF
	15	KM, NMF, ALS, AD, SVD, KC, KM, ALS, KM, KM, SVD, PR, ALS, TC, NMF
	20	AD, SVD, KM, ALS, TC, KC, KM, ALS, KM, SGD, NMF, KM, ALS, NMF, PR, TC, NMF, SSSP, ALS, AD

for *coverage* includes 5 algorithms and 4 graphs. At the level of 10-member ensembles, the complexity already exceeds that of most comparative graph performance studies (6 algorithms for spread and 7 for coverage) [4, 7, 8, 9,15].

To reliably assess "diversity contribution" of an algorithm, we would like to minimize shadowing effects. That is, considering only the best ensembles, a particular algorithm that is useful for *spread* or *coverage* might be shadowed by others that are slightly better, but when they're removed, really contribute greatly to diversity. We consider the question: *Which algorithms contribute most often to the best ensembles for spread and coverage?* To minimize shadowing, we expand our consideration of the best ensemble of size *n* to the 100 best ensembles of size *n* for each – spread and coverage. Within the 100 best ensembles, we use the frequency of appearance of each algorithm as an indication of contribution to diversity (see Figure 6 and 7).

These results demonstrate that not all algorithms contribute significantly to a good spread or coverage. For example, K-Means, Alternating Least Squares, and Triangle Counting among our suite contribute to efficient and thorough behavior space exploration.

Implications: not all graph algorithms are equally useful in high-quality benchmarking. Some algorithms exhibit a greater diversity of behaviors across graphs (e.g. ALS appears several times in one best-spread ensemble), while others exhibit behaviors varying little and thus characterize a narrow class of behaviors. On the other hand, some algorithms explore a unique region of the behavior space, making them valuable and difficult to replace in a thorough benchmarking (e.g. KM appears in almost all best-coverage ensembles). Therefore, these "special" algorithms should be the first choice in the construction of a high-quality benchmark suite.

4.4 Reducing Ensemble Complexity

Because the best ensembles require complex combinations of algorithms and graphs, it is worthwhile to consider simpler combinations to reduce benchmarking complexity. So the next question is: *How does restricting our ensemble complexity impact*

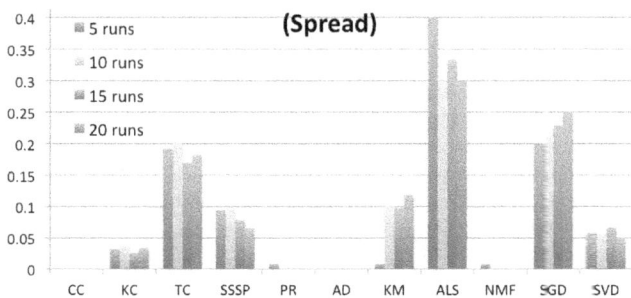

Figure 6. Frequency of algorithms in Top100 sets (spread).

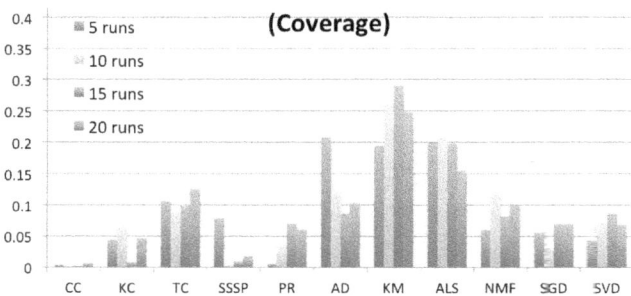

Figure 7. Frequency of algorithms in Top100 sets (coverage).

achievable spread and coverage? Here we consider three dimensions of constraints, limited algorithms, graphs, and runtime (see Figure 8 and 9).

First, we limit ensembles to three algorithms, selecting those that contribute most to both spread and coverage, including KM, ALS and TC. The algorithm-limited suites maintain a high spread, and a slight advantage over single algorithms.

Second, we limit ensembles to three graphs. The best ensembles use the graphs of size 10^7, 10^8 and 10^9 with $\alpha = 2.0$. The results indicate that limiting the number of graphs decreases spread rapidly and produces poor coverage – even lower than single algorithms like KC and CC.

Third, we consider shortening runtime. Some of our algorithms, including AD, KM, NMF, SGD, and SVD, have constant, repetitive behavior (i.e. a constant active fraction = 1.0). Their runs could be shortened, so ensembles using these 5 algorithms, can much more efficiently probe the behavior space. Because of the variety of these repetitive algorithms, these runtime-constrained suites still achieve high spread and coverage.

Implications: 1) A small collection of "special" algorithms can exercise a broad computation behavior. By employing these algorithms, we can reduce the number of algorithms used in benchmarking with minimal loss of quality. 2) Restricting graph selection significantly decreases benchmarking quality, because many algorithms exhibit similar behavior on the same graph structure. 3) Some algorithms that have unvaried behavior also have a high benchmarking quality, which enables us to further reduce runtime. Overall, by choosing these constrained runs to sample the behavior space efficiently, we can benchmark systems with minimum computational effort.

5. DISCUSSION AND RELATED WORK

General benchmark suites such as SPEC [16], NPB [3] and HPCC [10] employ a wide collection of programs, often with single inputs of varied sizes. Though these benchmarks are carefully selected, none are designed to systematically characterize performance, and efficient sampling of the full behavior space is beyond reach. Closer, there are also graph-oriented benchmarking efforts, including Graph 500 [6], LDBC [12], and LinkBench [2].

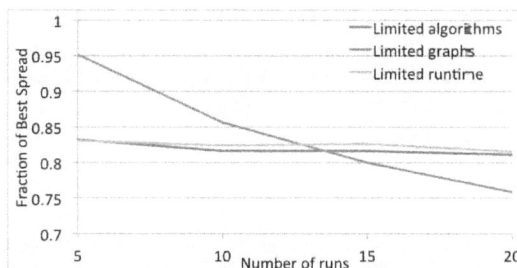

Figure 8. Spread for limited algorithms, graphs, runtime

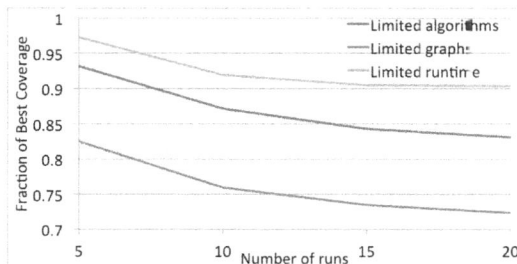

Figure 9. Coverage for limited algorithms, graphs, runtime

However, Graph 500 uses only a single program, on a single graph typically. LDBC is only emerging, and LinkBench provides general infrastructure, but not a specific benchmark.

Comparative graph processing systems studies are numerous. We summarize a few of the most complete efforts here. M. Han et al. [8] compare Giraph, GPS, Mizan, and GraphLab with 4 simple benchmarks and 5 real graphs. S. Salihoglu et al. [15] made similar study on Pregel-like systems. But neither Han nor Salihoglu give any clear rationale for benchmark selection, and no claims of thoroughness of behavior space exploration are made.

B. Elser et al. [4] compare 5 platforms using K-core program and 7 graphs. W. Han et al. [9] compare TurboGraph and GraphChi using simple benchmarks (PageRank, Connected Components, etc.) and 3 graphs. Our results show that, neither a single complex algorithm such as K-Core, nor several simple benchmarks such as PR and CC explore behavior thoroughly. For W. Han's experiments, the small number of graphs also narrows their study.

Y. Guo et al. [7] propose a comprehensive benchmarking method by exploring dataset, algorithm and platform diversity. They use 5 algorithms and 7 graphs to compare 6 platforms. Guo's work is perhaps closest to ours. They recognize the need to explore fully, and claim to do so. However, they present no clear framework of formal metric for assessing the thoroughness of exploration. In contrast, we have formulated a space and clear metrics for assessing thoroughness.

Our study suggests how to construct ensembles of graph computations that thoroughly explores the behavior space of graph computations. Beyond thoroughness, we describe how to further optimize an ensemble for efficiency and simplicity – limiting graphs, algorithms, etc. These ensembles can of course be used for benchmarking, and by exercising graph computing system behavior broadly, such a benchmark suite promises to give a comprehensive view of the performance of graph-processing systems, as well as an objective comparison between systems.

To the best of our knowledge, our study is the first and the only one that quantitatively characterize the behavior of parallel graph computation and to propose an evaluation methodology for systematic benchmarking.

6. SUMMARY AND FUTURE WORK
We have studied the behavior of a variety of graph algorithms (graph analytics, clustering, collaborative filtering, etc.) on a diverse collection of graphs (varying size and degree distribution). Our results characterize the variation of behavior across graph structures, application, domains, and graph algorithms. Given the broad range of graph computation behavior, we consider how well an ensemble of graph computations (algorithms and graphs) explores this space, in terms of spread and coverage. Since ad-hoc sets are unlikely to fairly characterize a graph-processing system, our study gives suggestions on systematically choosing a small set of algorithms and graphs to exercise broad computational behavior. We find that ensembles over single algorithms and single graphs are inefficient in sampling the behavior space, while a set of carefully selected runs exploring both algorithm diversity and graph diversity give significantly better results. We propose more efficient ensembles by considering constraints such as limited algorithms, graphs, and even runtime.

With understanding of how ensembles of experiments sample the behavior space, more ambitious goals are within reach. Can we design optimal ensembles? Can we model precisely a graph computation's behavior, and predict its performance?

7. ACKNOWLEDGEMENT
This work was supported in part by the Office of Advanced Scientific Computing Research, Office of Science, Department of Energy, under Award DE- SC0008603, as well as generous donations from HP Corporation and Agilent/Keysight Corporation. This work was completed in part with resources provided by: the University of Chicago Research Computing Center.

8. REFERENCES
[1] Apache, Apache Giraph, http://incubator.apache.org/giraph/.

[2] T.Armstrong et al. LinkBench: a Database Benchmark Based on Facebook Social Graph, *SIGMOD'13*, June 22-27, 2013.

[3] D. Bailey et al. THE NAS PARALLEL BENCHMARKS, Techical Report, NASA Ames Research Center, Jan 1991.

[4] B. Elser et al. An evaluation study of BigData frameworks for graph processing, *Big Data 2013*, pp. 60-67, 2013.

[5] J. E. Gonzalez et al. PowerGraph: Distributed Graph-Parallel Computation on Natural Graphs, *OSDI '12*, 2012.

[6] Graph500, Graph500 Benchmark, http://www.graph500.org/.

[7] Y. Guo et al. How Well do Graph-Processing Platforms Perform? An Empirical Performance Evaluation and Analysis, *IPDPS'14*, 2014.

[8] M.K. Han, Daudjee, et al. An Experimental Comparison of Pregel-like Graph Processing System, *the VLDB Endowment*, Vol. 7, No. 12, 2014.

[9] W. Han, et al. TurboGraph: A Fast Parallel Graph Engine Handling Billion-scale Graphs in a Single PC, *KDD'13*, 2013.

[10] HPCC, HPC Challenge Benchmark, http://en.wikipedia.org/wiki/HPC_Challenge_Benchmark.

[11] A. Kyrola, G. Blelloch, and C. Guestrin, "GraphChi: Large-scale Graph Computation on Just a PC," in OSDI, 2012.

[12] LDBC Organization, LDBC, http://www.ldbc.eu/.

[13] G. Malewicz, M. Austern, et al. Pregel: A system for large-scale graph processing, *SIGMOD'10*, pp. 135-146, 2010.

[14] A. Roy, et al. X-Stream: Edge-centric Graph Processing using Streaming Partitions, *SOSP'13*, Nov03-06, 2013.

[15] S. Salihoglu and J. Widom, Optimizing Graph Algorithms on Pregel-like Systems, Technical Report, Stanford, 2013.

[16] SPEC, SPEC CPU2006 benchmark suite, https://www.spec.org/cpu2006/Docs/readme1st.html.

[17] Stanford University, The Stanford Network Analysis Project (SNAP), http://snap.stanford.edu/index.html.

[18] Y. Tian, et al. From Think Like a Vertex to Think Like a Graph, *the VLDB Endowment*, Vol. 7, No. 3, 2014.

[19] Web Data Commons, Web Data Commons — Hyperlink Graphs. http://webdatacommons.org/hyperlinkgraph/.

[20] Wikipedia, Collaborative filtering, http://en.wikipedia.org/wiki/Collaborative_filtering.

[21] Wikipedia, K-means clustering, http://en.wikipedia.org/wiki/K-means_clustering.

[22] Wikipedia, Scale-free network, http://en.wikipedia.org/wiki/Scale-free_network.

[23] F. Yang and A. Chien, Understanding Graph Computation Behavior to Enable Robust Benchmarking, Technical Report, UChicago Computer Science, 2015.

Fast Iterative Graph Computation with Resource Aware Graph Parallel Abstractions

Yang Zhou[†], Ling Liu[‡], Kisung Lee[†], Calton Pu[‡], Qi Zhang[‡]
Georgia Institute of Technology
[†]{yzhou, kslee}@gatech.edu, [‡]{lingliu, calton.pu, qzhang90}@cc.gatech.edu

ABSTRACT

Iterative computation on large graphs has challenged system research from two aspects: (1) how to conduct high performance parallel processing for both in-memory and out-of-core graphs; and (2) how to handle large graphs that exceed the resource boundary of traditional systems by resource aware graph partitioning such that it is feasible to run large-scale graph analysis on a single PC. This paper presents GraphLego, a resource adaptive graph processing system with multi-level programmable graph parallel abstractions. GraphLego is novel in three aspects: (1) we argue that vertex-centric or edge-centric graph partitioning are ineffective for parallel processing of large graphs and we introduce three alternative graph parallel abstractions to enable a large graph to be partitioned at the granularity of subgraphs by slice, strip and dice based partitioning; (2) we use dice-based data placement algorithm to store a large graph on disk by minimizing non-sequential disk access and enabling more structured in-memory access; and (3) we dynamically determine the right level of graph parallel abstraction to maximize sequential access and minimize random access. GraphLego can run efficiently on different computers with diverse resource capacities and respond to different memory requirements by real-world graphs of different complexity. Extensive experiments show the competitiveness of GraphLego against existing representative graph processing systems, such as GraphChi, GraphLab and X-Stream.

Categories and Subject Descriptors

C.4 [**Performance of Systems**]: Reliability, availability, and serviceability; D.1.3 [**Concurrent Programming**]: Parallel Programming

Keywords

Graph Processing System; Large-scale Graph; Parallel Computing; 3D Cube Representation; Multigraph Processing

HPDC'15, June 15–20, 2015, Portland, Oregon, USA.
Copyright © 2015 ACM 978-1-4503-3550-8/15/06 ...$15.00.
http://dx.doi.org/10.1145/2749246.2749258.

1. INTRODUCTION

Scaling iterative computation on large graphs with billions of vertices and billions of edges is widely recognized as a challenging systems research problem, which has received heated attention recently [1–20]. We can classify existing research activities into two broad categories: (1) Distributed solutions and (2) Single PC based solutions. Most of existing research efforts are dedicated to the distributed graph partitioning strategies [2, 17–19] to distribute large graphs across a cluster of computer nodes. Several recent efforts [4, 11, 14, 16, 20] have successfully demonstrated huge opportunities for optimizing graph processing on a single PC through efficient storage organization and in-memory computation. However, most existing approaches rely on vertex-centric graph parallel computation model.

Many existing algorithms fail to work effectively under the vertex-centric computation model for several scenarios: (1) when the algorithms require to load the whole graph into the main memory but the graph and its intermediate results of computation together are too big to fit into the available memory; (2) when high degree vertices and their edges combined with the necessary intermediate results are too big to fit into the working memory; (3) when the time of computing on a vertex and its edges is much faster than the time to access to the vertex state and its edge data in memory or on disk; and (4) when the computation workloads on different vertices are significantly imbalanced due to the highly skewed vertex degree distribution.

To address the above issues, we propose to exploit computational parallelism by introducing three alternative graph parallel abstractions that offer larger level of granularity than vertex-centric model, with three complimentary objectives: (1) large graphs should be stored physically on disk using the right level of partition granularity to maximize sequential I/Os; (2) large graphs should be partitioned into graph parallel units such that each partition plus the necessary intermediate results will fit into the working memory and parallel computation on partitions generate well balanced workloads; and (3) different graph parallel abstractions are critical for scaling parallel processing of large graphs to computers with different capacities.

In this paper we present GraphLego, a resource aware graph processing system with multi-level programmable parallel abstractions. GraphLego by design has three novel features. First, to introduce graph parallel abstractions at different levels of granularity, we model a large graph as a 3D cube with source vertex, destination vertex and edge weight as the dimensions. This data structure enables us to introduce multi-level hierarchical graph parallel abstraction by slice, strip and dice based graph partitioning. Second, we dynamically determine the right level of graph parallel abstraction based on the available system resource and the characteristics of graph datasets for each of the iterative graph computation algorithms. By employing flexible and tunable graph parallel abstractions, GraphLego can run iterative graph computations efficiently on any single PC with different CPU and memory capacities. We show that by choosing the right level of parallel abstraction, we can maximize sequential access and minimize random access. Third but not the least, GraphLego uses dice-based data placement algorithm to store a large graph on disk by minimizing non-sequential disk access and enabling more structured in-memory access. By supporting multi-level programmable graph parallel abstractions and dynamic customization, GraphLego enables data scientists to tailor their graph computations in response to different real-world graphs of varying sizes/complexity and different computing platforms with diverse computing resources.

2. RELATED WORK

We classify existing research activities on graph processing system into two broad categories below [1–20].

Single PC based systems [4, 11, 14–16, 20] are gaining attention in recent years. GraphLab [4] presented a new sequential shared memory abstraction where each vertex can read and write data on adjacent vertices and edges. It supports the representation of structured data dependencies and flexible scheduling for iterative computation. GraphChi [11] partitions a graph into multiple shards by storing each vertex and its in-edges in one shard. It introduces a novel parallel sliding window based method to facilitate fast access to the out-edges of a vertex stored in other shards. Turbo-Graph [14] presented a multi-thread graph engine by using a compact storage of slotted page list and exploiting the full parallelism of multi-core CPU and Flash SSD I/O. X-Stream [16] is an edge-centric approach to the scatter-gather programming model on a single shared-memory machine. It uses streaming partitions to utilize the sequential streaming bandwidth of the storage medium for graph processing.

Distributed graph systems [1, 2, 5, 8, 10, 13, 17–19] have attracted active research in recent years, with Pregel [2], PowerGraph [10]/Distributed GraphLab [8], and GraphX [19] as the most popular systems. Pregel [2] is a bulk synchronous message passing abstraction where vertices can receive messages sent in the previous iteration, send messages to other vertices and modify its own state and that of its outgoing edges or mutate graph topology. PowerGraph [10] extends GraphLab [4] and distributed GraphLab [8] by using the Gather-Apply-Scatter model of computation to address the natural graphs with highly skewed power-law degree distributions. GraphX [19] enables iterative graph computation, written in Scala like API in terms of GraphX RDG, to run on the SPARK cluster platform, making the programming of iterative graph algorithms on Spark easier than PowerGraph and Pregel.

Iterative graph applications has been extensively studied in the areas of machine learning, data mining and information retrieval [21, 24–39]. Typical examples of real-world iterative graph applications include ranking, similarity search, graph classification, graph clustering, and collaborative filtering. Popular iterative graph applications can be catego-

rized into three classes in terms of the core computation used in the respective algorithms: (1) matrix-vector computation, such as PageRank [21], EigenTrust [28] and Random Walk with Restart [29]; (2) matrix-matrix computation, including Heat Diffusion Kernel [24, 30], Label Propagation [31], wvRN [32], Markov Clustering [33] and SA-Cluster [34]; and (3) matrix factorization, such as NMF [36], SVD++ [37], Social Regularization [38]. They often need to repeatedly self-interact on a single graph or iteratively interact among multiple graphs to discover both direct and indirect relationships between vertices.

To our best knowledge, GraphLego is the first one to support multi-level programmable parallel graph abstractions (slice, strip, dice) and to provide resource adaptive selection of the right level of graph parallel granularity for partitioning, storing and accessing large graphs.

3. GRAPHLEGO APPROACH

Real graphs often have skewed vertex degree distribution and skewed edge weight distribution. Partitioning a large graph in terms of vertex partitions without considering skewed vertex degree distribution or edges with skewed weight distribution may result in substantial processing imbalance in parallel computation. In addition, different types of iterative graph applications combined with different sizes of graphs often have different resource demands on CPU, memory and disk I/O. GraphLego is designed to address these issues by introducing resource-adaptive and multi-level programmable graph parallel abstractions.

3.1 Graph Processing with 3D Cube

3D Cube. GraphLego represents a given graph G as a 3D cube I with source vertices, destination vertices and edge weights as the three dimensions. Formally, a directed graph is defined as $G=(V, E, W)$ where V is a set of n vertices, E is a set of directed edges, and W is a set of weights of edges in E. Each vertex is associated with one or more states. Two vertices may be connected by multiple parallel edges. For an edge $e=(u, v) \in E$, we refer to e as the in-edge of v and the out-edge of u and we refer to u and v as the source vertex and the destination vertex of e respectively. In GraphLego, we model a graph G with a 3-dimensional representation of G, called **3D cube**, denoted as $I=(S, D, E, W)$ where $S=V$ represents the set of source vertices and $D=V$ specifies the set of destination vertices. Given a vertex $u \in S$ and a vertex $v \in D$, if $(u, v) \in E$ then $(u, v).weight=w \in W$ and (u, v, w) represents a cell with u, v, w as coordinates.

GraphLego by design provides three alternative graph parallel abstractions to partition a graph and to enable locality-optimized access to the stored graph using three different levels of granularity: slice, strip and dice. By utilizing different graph parallel abstractions based on memory resource capacity, GraphLego can process big graphs efficiently on a single PC with different resource capacity, by using a unified multi-level graph parallel abstractions based computation framework.

3.1.1 Dice-based Parallel Graph Abstraction

The dice partitioning method partitions a large graph G into dice-based subgraph blocks and store G in dices to balance the parallel computation tasks and maximize the advantage of parallel processing. Concretely, given $G=(V, E, W)$ and its 3D cube $I=(S, D, E, W)$, we first sort the vertices in

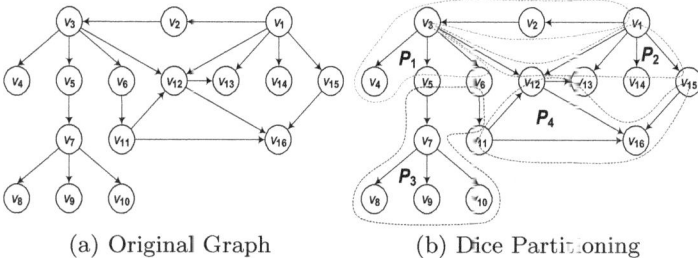

(a) Original Graph   (b) Dice Partitioning

Figure 1: Dice Partitioning: An Example

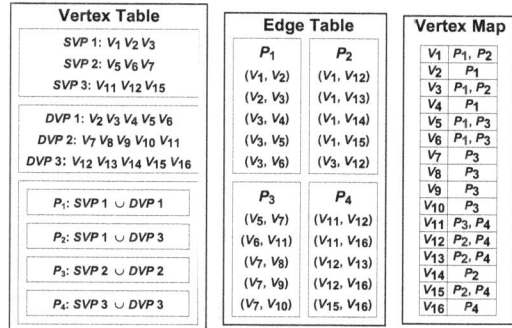

Figure 2: Dice Partition Storage (OEDs)

e.weight	(0, 0.1]	(0.1, 0.2]	(0.2, 0.3]	(0.3, 0.4]	(0.4, 0.5]	
edges(%)	59.90	18.79	6.99	6.61	5.14	
e.weight	(0.5, 0.6]	(0.6, 0.7]	(0.7, 0.8]	(0.8, 0.9]	(0.9, 1.0)	1.0
edges(%)	0.14	0.21	0.08	0.02	0.00	2.12

Table 1: Transition Distribution on DBLPS

S and D by the lexical order of their vertex IDs. Then we partition the destination vertices D into q disjoint partitions, called **destination-vertex partitions** (DVPs). Similarly, we partition the source vertices S ($|D|=|V|$) into r disjoint partitions, called **source-vertex partitions** (SVPs). A **dice** of I is a subgraph of G, denoted as $H=(S_H, D_H, E_H, W_H)$, satisfying the following conditions: $S_H \subseteq S$ is one of the SVP, denoting a subset of source vertices, $D_H \subseteq D$ is one of the DVP, denoting a subset of destination vertices, $W_H \subseteq W$ is a subset of edge weights, and $E_H=\{(u,v)|u \in S_H, v \in D_H, (u,v) \in E, (u,v).weight \in W_H\}$ is a set of directed edges, each with its source vertex from S_H and its destination vertex from D_H and its edge weight in W_H. Unlike a vertex and its adjacency list (edges), a dice is a subgraph block comprised of a SVP, a DVP and the set of edges that connect source vertices in the SVP to the destination vertices in the DVP. Thus, a high degree vertex u and its edges are typically partitioned into multiple dices. Figure 1 (a) gives an example graph and Figure 1 (b) shows a dice-based partitioning of this example graph. Each of four dice partitions is a dice-based subgraph satisfying the constraint defined by the specific SVP and DVP. Because in-edges and out-edges of a vertex are often applied to different application scenarios, we maintain two types of dices for each vertex v in G: one is **in-edge dice** (IED) containing only in-edges of v and another is **out-edge dice** (OED) containing only out-edges of v. Figure 2 shows the storage organization of the dice partitions in Figure 1 (b), consisting of a vertex table, an edge table (in-edges or out-edges), and a mapping of vertex ID to partition ID.

In GraphLego, dice is the smallest storage unit and by default the original graph G is stored on disk in unordered dices. To provide efficient processing for all types of iterative graph computations, GraphLego stores an original graph using two types of 3D cubes: in-edge cube and out-edge cube, each consists of unordered set of dices of the same type on disk (IEDs or OEDs). This provides efficient access locality for iterative graph computations that require only out-edges or only in-edges or both.

3.1.2 Slice-based Parallel Graph Abstraction

In contrast to dices, slices are the largest partition units in GraphLego. To address the skewed edge weight distribution, we provide the slice-based graph partitioning method, which partitions a 3D cube of graph into p slices along dimension W. p is chosen such that edges with similar weights are clustered into the same partition. Formally, given a 3D cube $I=(S,D,E,W)$, a **slice** of I is denoted as $J=(S,D,E_J,W_J)$ where $W_J \subseteq W$ is a subset of edge weights, and $E_J=\{(u,v)|u \in S, v \in D, (u,v).weight \in W_J, (u,v) \in E\}$ is a set of directed edges from S to D with weights W_J. A big advantage of slice partitioning along dimension W is that we can choose those slices that meet the utility requirement

to carry out the iterative graph computation according to application-dependent accuracy requirements.

An intuitive example for utilizing slice partitioning is to handle multigraphs. A multigraph is a graph that allows for parallel edges (multiple edges) between a pair of vertices. RDF graph is a typical example of multigraph, where a pair of subject and object vertices may have multiple edges with each annotated by one predicate. Similarly, the D-BLP coauthor graph can also be generated as a coauthor multigraph in terms of 24 computer research fields [46]: AI, AIGO, ARC, BIO, CV, DB, DIST, DM, EDU, GRP, HCI, IR, ML, MUL, NLP, NW, OS, PL, RT, SC, SE, SEC, SIM, WWW. A pair of coauthors in this multigraph can have up to 24 parallel edges, each weighted by the number of co-authored papers in one of the 24 computer science fields [27]. Figure 3 shows an illustrative example of slices. Consider the example co-author graph in Figure 3 (a) with three types of edges: AI, DB and DM, representing the number of coauthored publications on AI conferences (*IJCAI*, *AAAI* and *ECAI*), DB conferences (*SIGMOD*, *VLDB* and *ICDE*), and DM conferences (*KDD*, *ICDM* and *SDM*), respectively. By slice partitioning, we obtain three slices in Figure 3 (b), (c) and (d) respectively, one for each category. If we want to compute the coauthor based social influence among researchers in DB and DM area, we only need to perform iterative computation on the coauthor graph using joint publications in DB and DM conferences and journals.

Another innovative and rewarding usage of slice partitioning is to speed up the iterative graph algorithms on single graphs by performing parallel computation on p slices in parallel. Consider PageRank as an example, the edge weights in the original simple graph are normalized as probabilities in the transition matrix $\mathbf{M}$. Thus, the domain of W is defined on a continuous space over the range $[0,1]$. In each iteration, PageRank updates the ranking vector $\mathbf{R}$ by iteratively calculating the multiplication between $\mathbf{M}$ and $\mathbf{R}$. However, the transition matrix $\mathbf{M}$ often has skewed edge weight distribution. For instance, the transition matrix for the DBLPS dataset [44] has skewed distribution of transition probabilities (the percentage of edges in the specific weight range to total edges), as shown in Table 1. By introducing dimension W, GraphLego can partition the input DBLPS graph for PageRank into slices along dimension W based on its transition matrix $\mathbf{M}$ and execute the iterative computations at the slice level in parallel. This enables GraphLego to

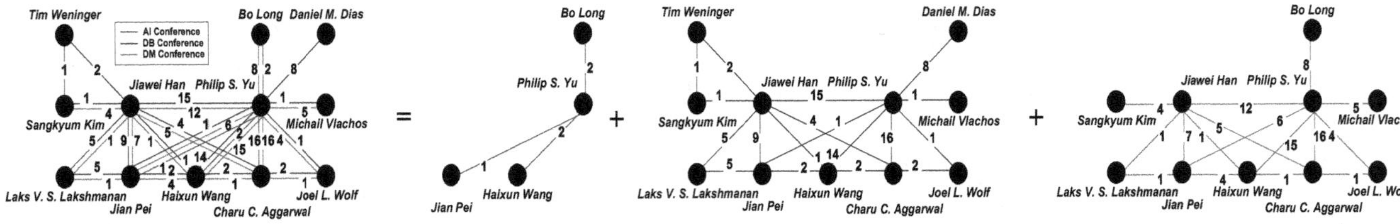

| (a) Coauthor Multigraph | (b) AI Slice | (c) DB Slice | (d) DM Slice |

Figure 3: Slice Partitioning: An Example from DBLP

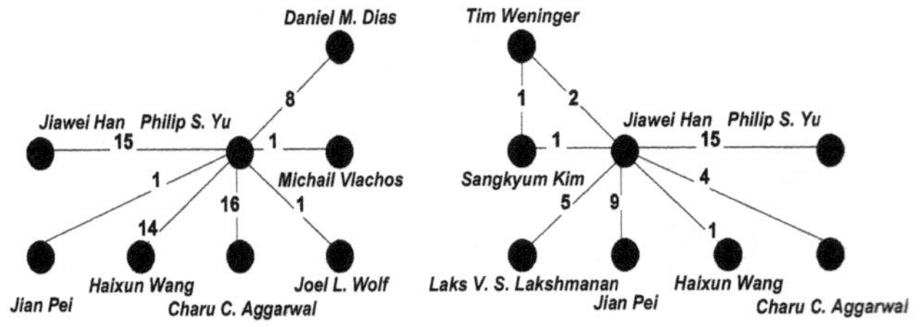

| (a) Strip 1 | (b) Strip 2 |

Figure 4: Strip Partitioning of DB Slice

address skewed edge weight distribution much more efficiently as demonstrated in our experiments reported in Section 4, where we set $p = 13, 10, 7, 7, 4$ and 4 for Yahoo, uk-union, uk-2007-05, Twitter, Facebook and DBLPS, respectively. We show that the iterative graph computation using the slice partitioning significantly improves the performance of all graph algorithms we have tested.

The slice partitioning can be viewed as an edge partitioning through clustering by the edge weights. However, when a slice-based subgraph (partition block) together with its intermediate results are too big to fit into the working memory, we further cut the graph into smaller graph parallel units such as dices (see Section 3.1.1) or strips (see Section 3.1.3).

3.1.3 Strip-based Parallel Graph Abstraction

For graphs that are sparse with skewed degree distribution, high degree vertices can incur acute imbalance in parallel computation, and lead to serious performance degradation. This is because the worker thread assigned to a high degree vertex takes much longer time to compute than the parallel threads computing on low degree vertices. To maximize the performance of parallel computation, and ensure better resource utilization and better work balance, in GraphLego we introduce the strip-based graph partitioning, which cuts a graph along either its source dimension or its destination dimension to obtain strips. Compared to the dice-based partitioning that cuts a graph (or slices of a graph) along both source and destination dimensions, strips represent larger partition units than dices. A strip can be viewed as a sequence of dices stored physically together. Similarity, we further cut a slice into strips when single slice can not fit into the working memory.

An efficient way to construct in-edge strips (out-edge strips) is to cut an in-edge cube or slice (out-edge cube or slice) along destination (source) dimension D (S). By cutting an in-edge slice of G, $J=(S, D, E_J, W_J)$, along D into q in-edge strips, each strip is denoted as $K=(S, D_K, E_K, W_J)$, where $D_K \subseteq D$ is a subset of destination vertices, and $E_K=\{(u,v)|u \in S, v \in D_K, (u,v).weight \in W_J, (u,v) \in E_J\}$ is a set of directed edges from S to D_K with weights in W_J. An in-edge strip contains all IEDs of a DVP. Similarly, an **out-edge strip**

can be defined and it has all OEDs of a SVP. Figure 4 gives an illustrative example of strip-based partitioning, where two strips are extracted from the DB slice in Figure 3 (c), i.e., all coauthored DB links of *Daniel M. Dias*, *Michail Vlachos* and *Philip S. Yu*, and all coauthored DB links of *Jiawei Han*, *Sangkyum Kim* and *Tim Weninger*. Another important feature of our graph partitioning methods is to choose smaller subgraph blocks such as dice partition or strip partition to balance the parallel computation efficiency among partition blocks and to use larger subgraph blocks such as slice partition or strip partition to maximize sequential access and minimize random access.

3.1.4 Graph Partitioning Algorithms

In the first prototype of GraphLego, we implement the three parallel graph abstraction based partitioning, placement and access algorithm using a unified graph processing framework with the top-down partitioning strategy. Given a PC, a graph dataset and a graph application, such as PageRank or SSSP, GraphLego provides the system default partitioning settings on p (#$Slices$), q (#$Strips$) and r (#$Dices$). We defer the detailed discussion on the settings of optimal partitioning parameters to Section 3.5. Based on the system-supplied default settings of the partitioning parameters, we first partition a graph into p slices, and then we partition each slice into q strips, and partition each strip into r dices. The partitioning parameters are chosen such that each graph partition block and its intermediate results will fit into the working memory. In GraphLego, we first partition the source vertices of a graph into SVPs, partition destination vertices of the graph into DVPs and then partition the graph into edge partitions slice by slice, strip by strip or dice by dice. Figure 2 gives an example of vertex partitioning and edge partitioning for the graph in Figure 1. Based on the system-recommended partitioning parameter, we store the graph in the physical storage using the smallest partition unit given by the system configuration. Dice is the smallest and most frequently used partition block in GraphLego (see Table 6).

GraphLego provides a three-level partition-index structure to access dice partition blocks on disk slice by slice, strip by strip or dice by dice. When the graph application has sufficient memory to host the entire index in memory, sequential access to dices stored in physical storage can be maximized. For example, PageRank algorithm requires computing the ranking score for every vertex using its incoming edges and its corresponding source vertices in each iteration. Thus, the PageRank implementation in GraphLego will start to access the graph by one in-edge strip at a time. For each strip, we check if there are multiple slices corresponding to this strip, For each strip and a corresponding slice, we access the dices corresponding to the strip and the slice. GraphLego provides a function library to

182

Algorithm 1 GraphPartitioning($G, app, p, q, r, flag$)

1: Sort source vertices by the lexical order of vertex IDs;
2: Sort destination vertices by the lexical order of vertex IDs;
3: Sort edges by source vertex ID, destination vertex ID and edge weight;
4: **switch**($flag$)
5:     **case** 0: select p, q, r input by user;
6:     **case** 1: detect resource, calculate p, q, r for app online;
7:     **case** 2: select the optimal p, q, r with offline learning;
8: Divide W into p intervals;
9: Split G into p in-edge slices;
10: Divide D into p DVPs; //partition destination vertices
11: Split p in-edge slices into $p \times q$ in-edge strips; //partition edges in each in-edge slice into q strip-based edge partitions
12: divide S into q SVPs; //partition source vertices
13: Split $p \times q$ in-edge strips into $p \times q \times r$ IEDs; //partition edges in each in-edge strip into r dice-based edge partitions
14: Compress DVPs, SVPs and IEDs, and write them back to disk; //compress vertex partitions and edge partitions
15: Build the indices for p slices, $p \times q$ strips and $p \times q \times r$ IEDs

support various iterative graph applications with a conventional vertex-oriented programming model. Algorithm 1 provides the pseudo code for an example function *Graph-Partitioning*. Given a graph G and a graph application, say PageRank, it constructs an in-edge cube representation of G and partitions its in-edge cube through slice, strip and dice abstractions. We do not build the out-edge cube of graph since PageRank does not use outgoing edges.

3.2   Access Locality Optimization

We describe two access locality based optimizations implemented in the first prototype of GraphLego: (1) graph index structure for indexing slices, strips and dices; and (2) graph partition-level compression for optimizing disk I/Os.

Partition Index. GraphLego stores a graph G in the physical storage as either dices or strips or slices. The iterative graph computation is performed in parallel at the partition level, be it a dice or a strip or a slice. Each partition block corresponds to a subgraph of G. In order to provide fast access to partition blocks of G stored on disk using slice or strip or dice specific conditions, and to ensure that each partition subgraph is loaded into the working memory only once or minimum number of times in each iteration, we design a general graph index structure to enable us to construct the slice index, the strip index or the dice index. The dice index is a dense index that maps a dice ID and its DVP (or SVP) to the chunks on disk where the corresponding dice partition is stored physically. The strip index is a two-level sparse index, which maps a strip ID to the dice index blocks and then map each dice ID to the dice partition chunks in the physical storage. Similarly the slice index is a three-level sparse index with slice index blocks at the top, strip index blocks at the middle and dice index blocks at the bottom, enabling fast retrieval of dices with a slice-specific condition. In addition, we also maintain a vertex index that maps each vertex to the set of subgraph partitions containing this vertex, as shown in Figure 2. This index allows fast lookup of the partitions relevant to a given vertex.

Partition-level Compression. It is known that iterative computations on large graphs incur non-trivial cost for the I/O processing. For example, the I/O processing of Twitter dataset on a PC with 4 CPU cores and 16GB memory takes 50.2% of the total running time for PageRank (5 iterations). In addition to utilize index, we employ partition-level compression to increase the disk I/O efficiency. Concretely, GraphLego transforms the raw graph data into par-

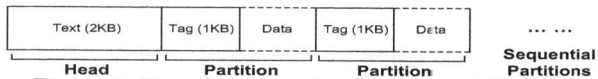

Figure 5: Data Structure for Compressed Graph

tition blocks and applies in-memory gzip compression to transform each partition block into a compressed format before storing them on disk. We maintain two buffers in memory, one for input graph data and another for in-memory compressed output graph data. As soon as a sequential read into the input stream buffer is completed, we start the in-memory gzip compression and append the compressed data to the output stream buffer. After finishing the compression, GraphLego sequentially writes the compressed chunks in the output stream buffer to disk. This one-time compression cost at the building time can provide quick access to stored graph partitions and reduce I/O time in each of the graph computation iteration. A gzip-compressed graph file consists of a 2KB head section and multiple partition sections, as shown in Figure 5. The head section stocks the descriptive information about the graph: the number of vertices, the number of edges, the edge type (undirected or directed), the domain of edge weights, the average degree, and the maximum degree. Each partition section consists of a 1KB metadata tag followed by the data in the partition. The tag provides the descriptive information about the specific partition: the data type, the size of partition, the number of edges, the source range, the destination range, the domain of edge weights.

3.3   Programmable GraphLego Interface

GraphLego provides a conventional programming interface to enable users to write their iterative graph algorithms using the vertex centric computation model. By supporting the vertex centric programming API, the users of GraphLego only need to provide their iterative algorithms in terms of vertex-level computation using the functions provided in our API, such as *Scatter* and *Gather*. For each iterative graph algorithm defined by users using our API, GraphLego will compile it into a sequence of GraphLego internal function (routine) calls that understand the internal data structures for accessing the graph by subgraph partition blocks. These routines can carry out the iterative computation for the input graph either slice by slice, strip by strip, or dice by dice. For example, PageRank algorithm can be written by simply proving the computation tasks, as shown in Algorithm 2.

For each vertex in a DVP to be updated, GraphLego maintains a temporary local buffer to aggregate received messages. Since each vertex v may contain both in-edges and out-edges, users only need to define two application-level functions to instruct the system-level scatter and gather routines to perform the concrete aggregations. Given a vertex, the *Scatter* function works on a selection of v's neighbors, say the destination vertices of the out-edges of v, to scatter its update based on its vertex state from the previous iteration. Similarly, the *Gather* function works on a selection of v's neighbors, e.g., the source vertices of the in-edges of v, to gather the information in order to update its vertex state, and pass this updated vertex state to the next iteration if the update commits and otherwise assign a partial commit to the gather task.

Vertices are accessed either by DVP or SVP depending on the specific graph algorithm. For each vertex to be updated, GraphLego maintains a temporary local buffer to aggregate

Algorithm 2 PageRank

```
1: Initialize(v)
2:    v.rank = 1.0;
3:
4: Scatter(v)
5:    msg = v.rank/v.degree;
6:    //send msg to destination vertices of v's out-edges
7:
8: Gather(v)
9:    state = 0;
10:   for each msg of v
11:   //receive msg from source vertices of v's in-edges
12:       state += msg; //summarize partial vertex updates
13:   v.rank = 0.15+0.85*state; //produce complete vertex update
```

received messages. We implement the *Scatter* API function as follows: First, an internal routine called *GraphScan* is invoked, which will access the graph dataset on disk by partition blocks (say dices). Then the *PartitionParallel* routine will be invoked to assign multiple threads to process multiple partitions in parallel, one thread per partition subgraph block. For each partition subgraph, the *VertexParallel* routine is called to execute multiple subthreads in parallel, one per vertex. At each vertex thread, the *Scatter* routine is performed. Given that the *Scatter* function at the system level intends to send the vertex state of v to all or a selection of its (out-edge) neighbor vertices, by utilizing the vertex-partition map (see Figure 2), each vertex thread will check if all partition blocks containing v as a source vertex have been processed. If so, then v finishes its scatter task with a commit status; Otherwise, v registers a partial commit.

Similarly, the *Gather* function in our API will be carried out by executing a sequence of four tasks with the first three routines identical to the implementation of the scatter function. The fourth routine is the *Gather* routine, which executes the gather task in two phases: (1) intra-partition gather, performing partial update of vertices or edges within a partition subgraph block, and (2) cross-partition gather, combining partial updates from multiple partition blocks. We call the vertices that belong to more than one subgraph partitions (e.g., dices) the *border* vertices. The cross-partition gather is only necessary for the *border* vertices. The *Gather* routine first records the messages that v has received from the source vertices of v's in-edges in the receive buffer, produces the count of the received messages, combines the update messages in the receive buffer using the local aggregation operation provided in the user-defined gather function, and then store the partial update as the new vertex state of v. At the end of the aggregation operation, if the received message count is the same as the in-degree of v, then we get the final update of v, and store it as the new state of v for this iteration. Otherwise, if the received message count is less than the in-degree of v, we mark this vertex as a *border* vertex, indicating that it belongs to more than one partition blocks and thus needs to enter the cross-partition gather phase. In the next subsection, we will discuss how GraphLego executes the cross-partition gather task to combine the partial updates from different edge partitions at different levels of granularity to generate the complete update.

3.4 Synchronization and Multi-threading

To maximize parallelism in iterative graph computations, GraphLego provides parallel processing at two levels: (1) parallel processing at the subgraph partition level (slice, strip or dice), and (2) parallel processing at the vertex level A number of design choices are made carefully to support ef-

fective synchronization and multi-threading, ensuring vertex and edge update consistency.

Parallel partial vertex update. As vertices in different dice or strip based subgraph partitions belong to different DVPs (or SVPs), and the DVPs (SVPs) from different strip or dice partitions are disjoint within the given graph or a slice of the graph, the vertex update can be executed safely in parallel on multiple strip or dice based partitions, providing partition-level graph parallelism. Furthermore, the vertex update can also be executed safely in parallel on multiple vertices within each strip or dice since each vertex within the same DVP (or SVP) is unique. Thus, GraphLego implements the two-level graph computation parallelism at the partition level and at the vertex level.

However, all the parallel vertex updates at both partition-level and vertex level are partial for two reasons: (1) although the edge sets in different in-edge subgraph partitions are disjoint, an edge may belong to one in-edge partition and one out-edge partition for strip or dice based partitions; thus concurrent edge update needs to be synchronized; (2) a vertex may belong to more than one partitions. Thus, the vertex updates performed within a strip or dice partition are partial and need to do cross-partition gather among strip or dice partitions; and (3) the associated edges of a DVP (or SVP) may lie in multiple slices. Thus, the vertex updates performed concurrently on strip or dice partitions within each slice are partial and need to do cross-partition gather among slices.

For cross-partition gather at slice level, for each vertex, there are at most p partial vertex update states, one per slice. We need to aggregate all the partial vertex update states for each vertex to obtain its final vertex update state before moving to the next iteration. To ensure the correctness and consistency of obtaining the final vertex updates via aggregating such partial vertex update states, during each iteration, GraphLego uses an individual thread to sequentially aggregate all partial vertex updates of a single DVP (or SVP) slice by slice.

Similarly, for cross-partition gather at strip or dice level, GraphLego divides the strip or dice based partitions that share the same DVP (or SVP) into DVP (or SVP) specific partition groups, and sets the number of DVPs (or SVPs) to be processed in parallel by the number of concurrent threads used (#threads) such that an individual memory block, i.e., partial update list is assigned to each partition group for cross-partition gather. Now each of the individual threads is dedicated to each edge partition within the DVP (or SVP) specific partition groups and execute one such partition at a time. In order to avoid conflict, GraphLego maintains a *counter* with an initial value of 0 for each specific partition group. When a thread finished the *Scatter* process of an edge partition within the partition group: put the partial update into the partial update list, this thread checks if *counter* is equal to the number of associated edge partitions for the specific partition group. If not, this thread performs *counter++* and the scheduler assigns an unprocessed edge partition within the same specific partition group to it. Otherwise, we know that GraphLego have finished the processing of all edge partitions within the partition group. Thus, this thread continues to perform the *Gather* process to aggregate all partial updates of this DVP (or SVP) in its partial update list to generate its complete update. Finally, the final update of this DVP (or SVP) in the current iteration are written back to disk. Then, this thread will start to fetch and process the next unfinished or unprocessed DVP (or SVP) and the set of subgraph partitions associated to this DVP (or SVP) in the same manner. We complete one round of iterative computation when vertices in all DVPs (or SVPs) are examined and updated.

Parallel edge update. In GraphLego each edge must belong to one in-edge dice (IED) and one out-edge dice (OED). Thus, edge update is relatively straightforward. GraphLego also implements a two-level parallelism at the strip level by strip threads and at the vertex level by vertex sub-threads. An individual strip thread is assigned to a single DVP (or SVP) to sequentially execute the updates of associated edges of this DVP (or SVP) slice by slice. When a DVP (or SVP) thread finishes the updates of all associated edges of a DVP (or SVP), this DVP (or SVP) thread will fetch and process the associated edges of the next unprocessed DVP (or SVP) in the same manner without synchronization.

3.5 Configuration of Partitioning Parameters

Given a total amount of memory available, we need to determine the best settings of the partitioning parameters for achieving the optimal computational performance. GraphLego supports three alternative methods to determine the settings of parameters: user definition, simple estimation, and regression-learning based configurations.

User Definition. We provide user-defined configuration as an option for expert users to modify the system default configuration.

Simple Estimation. The general heuristic used in simple estimation is to determine p (#Slices), q (#Strips) and r (#Dices) based on the estimation of whether each subgraph block for the given partition unit plus the intermediate results will fit into the available working memory. In GraphLego, we provide simple estimation from two dimensions: the past knowledge from regression-based learning and the simple estimation in the absence of prior experiences by estimating the size of the subgraph blocks and the intermediate results depending on the specific graph applications. GraphLego uses the parameter settings produced by simple estimation as the system-defined default configuration.

In summary, the decision of whether to use slice, strip or dice as the partition unit to access the graph data on disk and to process the graph data in memory should be based on achieving a good balance between the following two criteria: (1) We need to choose the partition unit that can best balance the parallel computation workloads with bounded working memory; and (2) we need to minimize excessive disk I/O cost by maximizing sequential disk access in each iteration of the graph algorithm.

Regression-based Learning. A number of factors may impact the performance of GraphLego, such as concrete applications, graph datasets, the number of CPU cores, the DRAM capacity. Thus, for a given graph application, a given dataset and a given server, we want to find the latent relationship between the number of partitions and the runtime. In order to learn the best settings of these partitioning parameters, we first utilize multiple polynomial regression [47] to model the nonlinear relationship between independent variables p, q or r and dependent variable T (the runtime) as an nth order polynomial. A regression model relates T to a function of p, q, r, and the undetermined coefficients α: $T \approx f(p,q,r,\alpha) = \sum_{i=1}^{n_p}\sum_{j=1}^{n_q}\sum_{k=1}^{n_r}\alpha_{ijk}p^i q^j r^k + \epsilon$ where

Application	Propagation	Core Computation
PageRank [21]	single graph	matrix-vector
SpMV [22]	single graph	matrix-vector
Connected Components [23]	single graph	graph traversal
Diffusion Kernel [24]	two graphs	matrix-matrix
Inc-Cluster [25]	two graphs	matrix-matrix
Matrix Multiplication	two graphs	matrix-matrix
LMF [26]	multigraph	matrix-vector
AEClass [27]	multigraph	matrix-vector

Table 2: Graph Applications

Graph	Type	#Vertices	#Edges	AvgDeg	MaxIn	MaxOut
Yahoo [40]	directed	1.4B	6.6B	4.7	7.6M	2.5K
uk-union [41]	directed	133.6M	5.5B	41.22	6.4M	22.4K
uk-2007-05 [41]	directed	105.9M	3.7B	35.31	975.4K	15.4K
Twitter [42]	directed	41.7M	1.5B	35.25	770.1K	3.0M
Facebook [43]	undirected	5.2M	47.2M	18.04	1.1K	1.1K
DBLPS [44]	undirected	1.3M	32.0M	40.67	1.7K	1.7K
DBLPM [44]	undirected	0.96M	10.1M	21.12	1.0K	1.0K
Last.fm [45]	undirected	2.5M	42.8M	34.23	33.2K	33.2K

Table 3: Experiment Datasets

n_p, n_q and n_r are the highest orders of variables p, q or r, and ϵ represents the error term of the model.

We then select m samples of (p_l, q_l, r_l, T_l) $(1 \leq l \leq m)$ from the existing experiment results, such as the points in Figure 15 (c)-(d), to generate the following m linear equations:

$$T_1 = \sum_{i=1}^{n_p}\sum_{j=1}^{n_q}\sum_{k=1}^{n_r}\alpha_{ijk}p_1^i q_1^j r_1^k + \epsilon$$
$$\cdots \quad \cdots \tag{1}$$
$$T_m = \sum_{i=1}^{n_p}\sum_{j=1}^{n_q}\sum_{k=1}^{n_r}\alpha_{ijk}p_m^i q_m^j r_m^k + \epsilon$$

We adopt the least squares approach [48] to solve the above overdetermined linear equations and generate the regression coefficients α_{ijk}. Finally, we utilize a successive convex approximation method (SCA) [49] to solve this polynomial programming problem with the objective of minimizing the predicted runtime and generate the optimal p, q and r. The experimental evaluation demonstrates that our regression-based learning method can select the optimal setting for the partitioning parameters, which gives GraphLego the best performance under the available system resource.

4. EXPERIMENTAL EVALUATION

We evaluate the performance of GraphLego using a set of well-known iterative graph applications in Table 2 on a set of large real world graphs in Table 3. DBLPS is a single heterogeneous graph with three kinds of vertices: 964,166 authors, 6,992 conferences and 363,352 keywords, and 31,962,786 heterogeneous links. By following the edge classification method in [27], we construct a coauthor multigraph, DBLPM, with 964,166 authors and 10,180,035 coauthor links. Each pair of authors have at most 24 parallel coauthor links, each represents one of the 24 computer research fields [46], as mentioned in Section 3.1.2. Similarly, we build a friendship multigraph of Last.fm with 2,500,000 highly active users and 42,782,231 parallel friendship links. All the experiments were performed on a 4-core PC with Intel Core i5-750 CPU at 2.66 GHz, 16 GB memory, and a 1 TB hard drive, running Linux 64-bit. We compare GraphLego with three existing representative single PC systems: **GraphLab** [4], **GraphChi** [11] and **X-Stream** [16].

We use regression-based learning described in Section 3.5 to choose the optimal setting for the GraphLego partitioning

Graph	GraphLab	GraphChi	X-Stream	GraphLego
Yahoo [40]	0	6073	28707	15343
uk-union [41]	0	4459	20729	10589
uk-2007-05 [41]	0	2826	13965	5998
Twitter [42]	6210	1105	5620	2066
Facebook [44]	31	4	25	9
DBLPS [43]	23	3	18	7

Table 4: Building Time (seconds)

parameters p, q and r_i or r_o. To show the significance of multi-level graph parallel abstraction powered by resource-adaptive customization, we evaluate and compare the following four versions of GraphLego: (1) **GraphLego** with the optimal setting of p, q and r; (2) **GraphLego-OSL** with only the optimal p (#*Slices*); (3) **GraphLego-OST** with only the optimal q (#*Strips*); and (4) **GraphLego-OD** with only the optimal r (#*Dices*).

4.1 Preprocessing Efficiency

Most of graph processing systems transform the raw graph text files into their internal graph representations through preprocessing. The preprocessing step typically performs three tasks: (1) read a raw graph dataset into memory block by block, (2) transform raw data blocks into the system-specific internal storage format, and (3) write the preprocessed data back to disk block by block. Table 4 compares the preprocessing time by four graph parallel systems. GraphLab can directly work on those raw graph text files with ordered edges, such as Yahoo, uk-union and uk-2007-05. Thus there is no building time for these datasets. However, for graph datasets with unordered edges, GraphLab needs to presort the graph text files. In this case, GraphLab tends to be the slowest in building time. The building time in X-Stream is usually 2-3 times slower than GraphLego since X-Stream uses a single thread to execute the import task line by line. GraphChi utilizes multiple threads to perform the transformation task and it only needs to build one copy of in-edges. GraphLego imports data faster than X-Stream and GraphLab, but slower than GraphChi, primarily due to the fact that GraphLego builds two copies of the raw graph: in-edge cube and out-edge cube and GraphLego executes in-memory gzip compression in parallel to reduce the total I/O cost for iterative graph computations.

4.2 Execution Efficiency on Single Graph

Figures 6-8 present the performance comparison of iterative algorithms on a single graph with different graph-parallel implementations. Figure 6 (a) shows the throughput ((#edges processed per second)) comparison of PageRank on six real graphs with different scales: Yahoo, uk-union, uk-2007-05, Twitter, Facebook and DBLPS with #*iterations*= 1, 2, 3, 5, 40, 30 respectively. GraphLego (with the optimal numbers of slices, strips and dices) achieves the highest throughput (around 1.53×10^7-2.27×10^7) and consistently higher than GraphLab, GraphChi and X-Stream and outperforms all versions of GraphLego with partial optimization on all six datasets, with the throughput values by GraphLego-OSL as the lowest (9.38×10^6-2.20×10^7), especially on the largest three graphs. Comparing among the three partial-optimization versions of GraphLego, GraphLego-OSL achieves the highest throughput on two smaller datasets (Facebook and DBLPS) but GraphLego-OD obtains the best performance on other four large-scale graphs (Facebook and D-BLPS). This demonstrates that, when handling large-scale graphs, we should focus more on the optimization of r_i (or

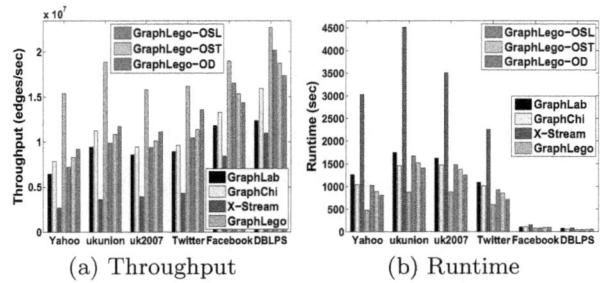

(a) Throughput   (b) Runtime

Figure 6: PageRank on Six Real Graphs

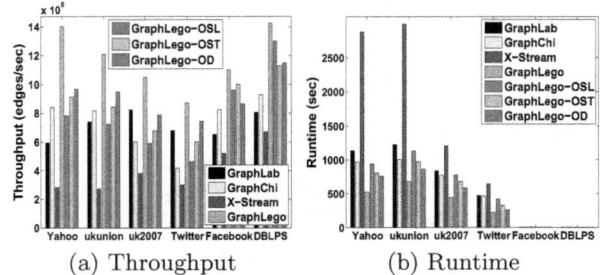

(a) Throughput   (b) Runtime

Figure 7: SpMV on Six Real Graphs

r_o) by drilling down to the lowest level of granularity in multi-level abstraction to ensure better work balance. On the other hand, the optimization of p should be emphasized for addressing small-scale graphs by rolling up to the highest level of granularity to maximize the sequential bandwidth.

Figure 6 (b) compares the running time by different graph-parallel models, including the loading time of preprocessed graph partitions from disk partition by partition, the in-memory decompression time (only for GraphLego and its variants), the computation time, and the time to write results back to disk. The runtime comparison is consistent with the throughput evaluation in Figure 6 (a). The GraphLego family outperforms GraphLab, GraphChi and X-Stream in all experiments. X-Stream achieves the worst performance on all six graph datasets. Although both Graph-Chi and GraphLab are slower than all versions of GraphLego, GraphChi is relatively faster than GraphLab, as it breaks the edges of large graph into small shards and sort edges in each shard for fast access.

Similar trends are observed for the performance comparison of SpMV and Connected Components (CC) in Figure 7 and Figure 8 respectively. Given that X-Stream failed to work on Yahoo and uk-union when running up to 36,000 seconds in the experiment of CC, we did not plot X-Stream for these two datasets in Figure 8. Compared to GraphLab, GraphChi and X-Stream, GraphLego (with the optimization of all parameters) doubles the throughput and runs twice faster in seconds.

4.3 Execution Efficiency on Multiple Graphs

Figures 9-11 present the performance comparison of iterative applications on multiple graphs with different graph-parallel models. Since GraphLab, GraphChi and X-Stream can not directly address matrix-matrix multiplications among multiple graphs, we thus modify the corresponding implementations to run the above graph applications. As the complexity of matrix-matrix multiplication ($O(n^3)$) is much larger than the complexity of matrix-vector multiplication and graph traversal ($O(n^2)$), we only compare the performance by different graph-parallel models on two s-

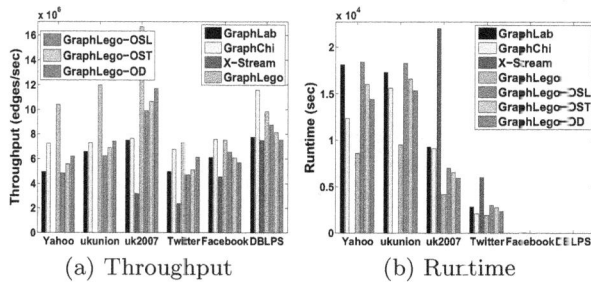

(a) Throughput (b) Runtime

Figure 8: Connected Components on Six Real Graphs

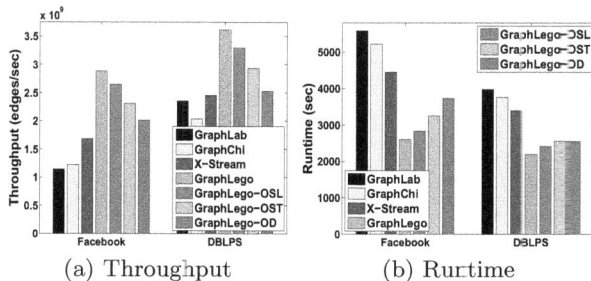

(a) Throughput (b) Runtime

Figure 9: Matrix Multiplication on Two Real Graphs

maller datasets: Facebook and DBLPS. We observe the very similar trends as those shown in Figures 6-8. All versions of GraphLego significantly prevail over GraphLab, GraphChi and X-Stream in all efficiency tests, and GraphLego (full optimization of partitioning parameters) obtains the highest throughput.

4.4 Effect of Partitioning on Dimension W

Figure 12 exhibits the efficiency comparison of PageRank on multiple graphs by GraphLego with different numbers of slices along dimension W. Although the above graphs are simple graphs (non-multigraphs) with the edge weights of 0 or 1, PageRank [21] needs to iteratively calculate the multiplication between the transition matrix M and the ranking vector R. Similar examples include Diffusion Kernel [24] which repeatedly computes the power of the generator E (real symmetric matrix), and Inc-Cluster [25] which iteratively calculates the power of the transition matrix P_A. To reduce the repeated cost of calculating the transition probabilities, instead of stocking the original simple graphs, we store the above graphs with their representations of transition matrix for PageRank in our current implementation. From the runtime curve (or the throughput curve) for each dataset, we have observed that the optimal #Slices on different graphs are quite different, depending on the graph size and the edge weight distribution: large-scale graphs contain more vertices and edges such that there exists more distinct edge weights. The optimal values of #Slices on Yahoo, uk-union, uk-2007-05, Twitter, Facebook and DBLPS are 13, 10, 7, 7, 4 and 4, respectively.

Figures 13-14 present the performance comparison of two multigraph algorithms with the GraphLego implementation. LMF [26] is a graph clustering algorithm based on multigraph in both unsupervised and semi-supervised settings, with the Linked Matrix Factorization (LMF) to extract reliable features and yield better clustering results. AEClass [27] transforms the problem of multi-label classification of heterogeneous information networks into the task of multi-label classification of coauthor (or friendship) multigraph based on activity-based edge classification. GraphLego

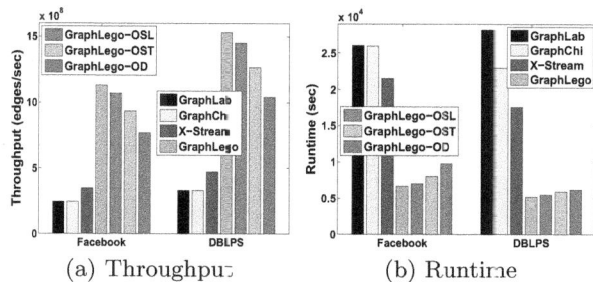

(a) Throughput (b) Runtime

Figure 10: Diffusion Kernel on Two Real Graphs

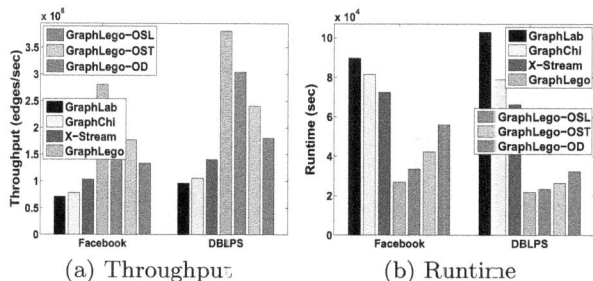

(a) Throughput (b) Runtime

Figure 11: Inc-Cluster on Two Real Graphs

partitions the 3D cube of a multigraph into p slices along dimension W. Each slice consists of parallel edges with a unique semantics. By hashing the parallel edges with the same semantics into the same partition, each slice corresponds to one partition, and represents a subgraph with only those edges that have the corresponding semantics included in the hash bucket for that partition. It is observed that the running time is relatively long when we ignore the slice partitioning, i.e, #Slices = 1. This demonstrates that GraphLego can deliver significant speedup for big multigraph analysis by running iterative computations on p slices with different semantics in parallel. In addition, we have observed that the optimal value of #Slices for a specific multigraph is related to the graph size, the edge weight distribution, and the graph algorithm.

4.5 Decision of #Partitions

Figure 15 measures the performance impact of different numbers of partition on GraphLego with PageRank running over Twitter, Diffusion Kernel and Inc-Cluster running on Facebook. The x-axis shows different settings of the number of partition units (slices, strips and dices). We vary the number of one partition unit, say slice, from 1 to 10,000 and fix the settings of other two units, say setting strips and dices as 5 in each figure. It is observed that the runtime curve (or the throughput curve) for each application in each figure follows a similar "U" curve (inverted "U" curve) with respect to the size of partition unit, i.e., the runtime is very long when the unit size is relatively small or very large and it is almost a stable horizontal line when the unit size stands in between two borderlines. This is because the bigger units often lead to substantial work imbalance in iterative graph applications. On the other hand, the smaller units may result in frequent external storage access and lots of page replacements between units lying in different pages. Among three partition units, the policy of dice partition achieves the best performance on large-scale graphs but the policy of slice partition achieves the best performance on small-scale graphs.

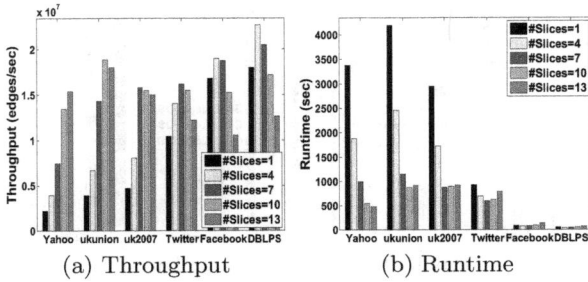

(a) Throughput (b) Runtime

Figure 12: PageRank: Vary #*Slices* on Dimension W

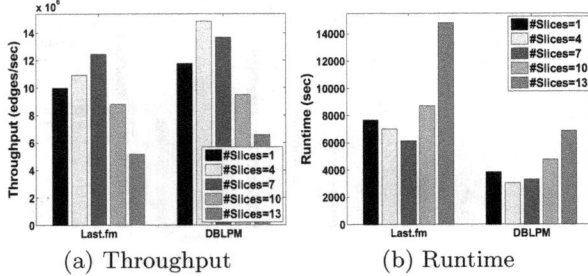

(a) Throughput (b) Runtime

Figure 13: LMF: Vary #*Slices* on Dimension W

Figures 15 (e)-(f) measures the CPU utilization by GraphLego for three real applications. The CPU utilization rate on each application increases quickly when the number of partitions (#Slices, #Strips, or #Dices) is increasing. This is because for the same graph, the larger number of partitions gives the smaller size per partition and the smaller partition units in big graphs often lead to better workload balancing when graph computations are executed in parallel. Figures 15 (g)-(h) show the memory utilization comparison. The memory utilization for each application is totally contrary to its CPU utilization when the number of partition units is increasing: the smaller the number of partitions, the larger size each partition will have, thus the larger the memory usage.

Figure 16 shows the effectiveness of the predicated runtime with regression-based learning method for PageRank over Twitter, Diffusion Kernel and Inc-Cluster on Facebook. Instead of the biased or incorrect decision made with experiential knowledge, GraphLego utilizes the multiple polynomial regression model and the successive convex approximation method to discover the optimal numbers of partition units to minimize the execution time. In spite of the common fixed partition scheme, GraphLego implements the 3D cube storage of graph and multi-level graph parallel abstraction to support access locality for various graph analysis algorithms, graphs with different characteristics, and PCs with diverse configurations by drilling down to the lowest level of granularity or by rolling up to the highest level of granularity in multi-level abstraction. The predication curve fits very well with the real execution curve on two settings of the optimal number of partition units (slices and dices) respectively, especially in data points corresponding to the optimal runtime (#Slices=75-250 and #Dices=50-500). Compared to the computational cost of iterative graph applications, the prediction cost is very small due to very small $n_p, n_q, n_{r_i}, n_{r_o} \ll |V|$ for large-scale graphs. In the current implementation, we set $n_p=n_q=n_{r_i}=n_{r_o}=3$ in Eq.(1). For the experiment of PageRank on Twitter by GraphLego in Figures 6, the computation time is 599 seconds but the prediction time is only 12 seconds.

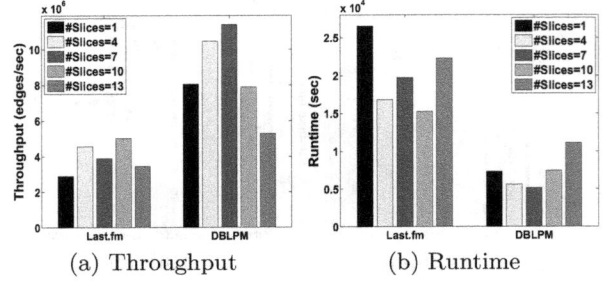

(a) Throughput (b) Runtime

Figure 14: AEClass: Vary #*Slices* on Dimension W

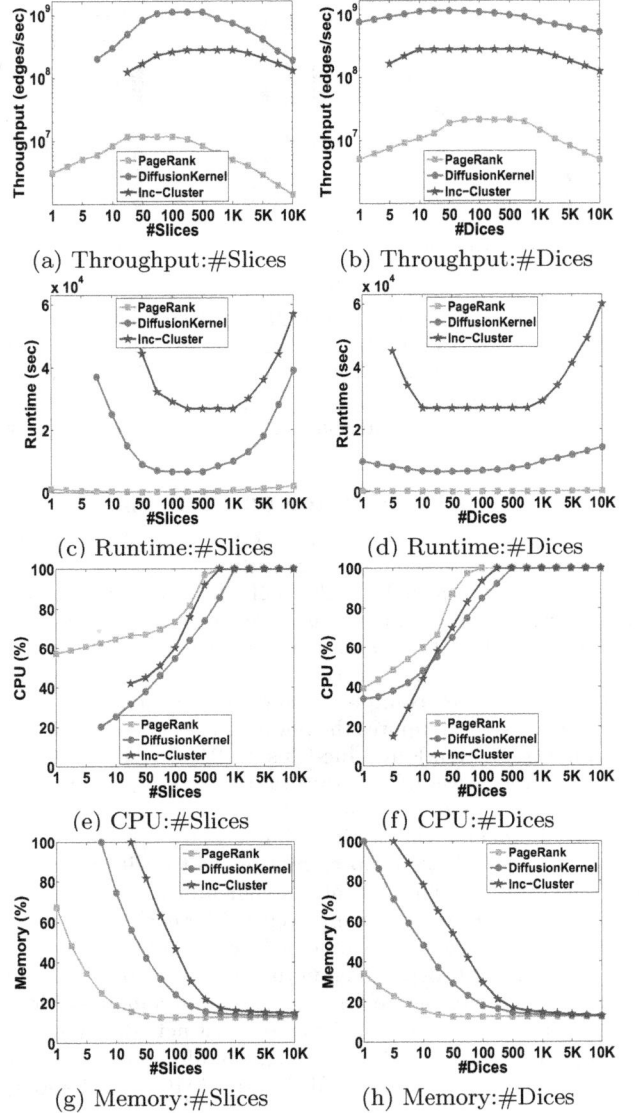

(a) Throughput:#Slices (b) Throughput:#Dices

(c) Runtime:#Slices (d) Runtime:#Dices

(e) CPU:#Slices (f) CPU:#Dices

(g) Memory:#Slices (h) Memory:#Dices

Figure 15: Impact of #Partitions

Tables 5 and 6 compare the optimal p (#*Slices*), q (#*Strips*), r (#*Dices*) generated by offline regression-based learning. Table 5 exhibits the optimal parameters by PageRank on three datasets using two PCs with different memory capabilities. From Table 5, we observe that the multiplications of $p*q*r$ on the 2-core PC are about 2.67-5.97 times than the multiplications of $p*q*r$ on the 4-core PC. This indicates that GraphLego can achieve good performance based on a simple estimation in terms of the optimal parameter setup

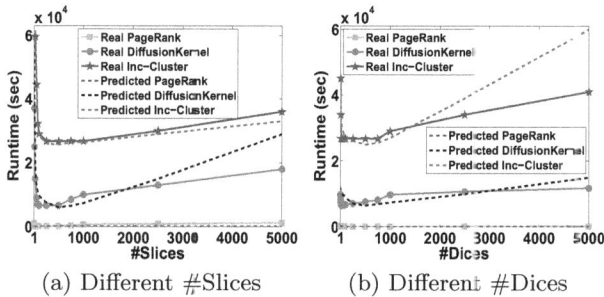

(a) Different #Slices (b) Different #Dices

Figure 16: Runtime Prediction

	PC (16 GB memory)			PC (2 GB memory)		
Dataset	Facebook	Twitter	Yahoo	Facebook	Twitter	Yahoo
p (#Slices)	4	7	13	4	8	9
q (#Strips)	3	5	4	4	10	12
r (#Dices)	0	4	8	2	7	23

Table 5: Optimal Partitioning Parameters for PageRank

on the existing machines as long as the simple estimation lies in the near-horizontal interval of the runtime "U" curve shown in Figure 15. Table 6 compares the optimal parameters recommended by regression-based learning for two applications over three different datasets on the 4-core PC. Clearly, the number of partitions grows as the graph dataset gets larger.

4.6 CPU, Memory and Disk I/O Bandwidth

Figure 17 compares three graph processing systems on CPU utilization, memory utilization and disk I/O bandwidth by PageRank on Twitter with 5 iterations. As shown in Figures 17 (a)-(b), GraphLego achieves the highest utilization rates in both CPU and memory. GraphChi has lower and stable CPU and memory utilization than X-Stream.

Figures 17 (c)-(d) report the I/O bandwidth comparison by three models. GraphLego incurs very small amount of updates but much larger number of reads compared to GraphChi and X-Stream. The I/O bandwidth curves (both I/O read and I/O write) by GraphChi and X-Stream are consistent with those in the X-Stream paper [16]. X-Stream consumes more I/O bandwidth than GraphChi. We observe that (1) Although Graphchi needs to load both in-edges (the shard itself) and out-edges (one sliding window of each of other shards) of a shard into memory, GraphChi updates this shard in memory and then directly write the update to disk. The size of a sliding window of one shard is much smaller than the size of the shard itself; (2) in X-Stream, the huge graph storage dramatically increases the total I/O cost. In addition, the two-phase implementation also doubles the I/O cost: for each streaming partition, the merged scatter/shuffle phase reads its out-edges from disk and writes its updates to disk, and the gather phase loads its updates from disk. When the graph is relatively dense or the edge update is very frequent at the beginning phase of computational iterations, the number of updates approximately equals to the number of edges. The parallelism of I/O processing may also result in higher disk seek time on the standard PC with a single disk; and (3) the gzip-compressed storage helps GraphLego dramatically reduce the total I/O cost At each iteration, GraphLego reads the in-edges of each DVP, calculates the updates of vertices in the DVP and writes the updates to the private buffer if the entire vertices can fit into the memory, or writes them back to disk if the working memory is limited. After completing the updating of a DVP,

	PageRank			Connected Components		
Dataset	Facebook	Twitter	Yahoo	Facebook	Twitter	Yahoo
p (#Slices)	4	7	13	4	6	8
q (#Strips)	3	5	4	2	6	7
r (#Dices)	0	4	8	0	4	12

Table 6: Optimal Parameters for PC with 16 GB DRAM

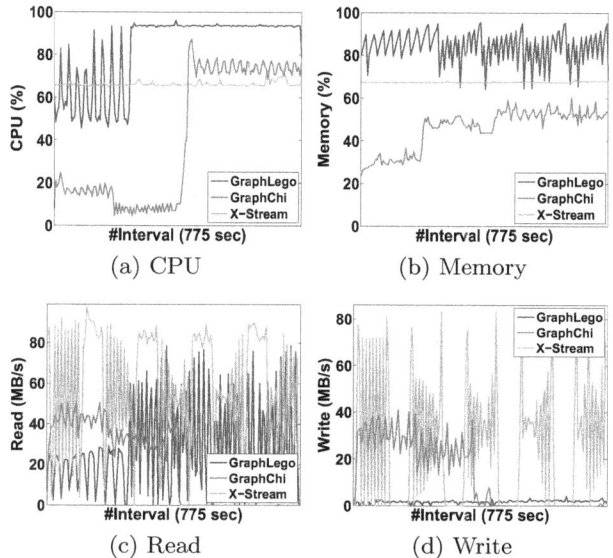

(a) CPU (b) Memory

(c) Read (d) Write

Figure 17: CPU, Memory and Disk I/O bandwidth

GraphLego never needs to read this DVP and its associated edges again until the algorithm enters the next iteration. Thus, GraphLego only has very few or no write I/O costs within each iteration.

5. CONCLUSIONS

We have presented GraphLego, a resource adaptive graph processing system with multi-level graph parallel abstractions. GraphLego has three novel features: (1) we introduce multi-level graph parallel abstraction by partitioning a large graph into subgraphs based on slice, strip and dice partitionings; (2) we dynamically determine the right abstraction level based on the available resource for iterative graph computations. This resource-adaptive graph partitioning approach enables GraphLego to respond to computing platforms with different resources and real-world graphs with different sizes through multi-level graph parallel abstractions; (3) GraphLego uses dice-based data placement algorithm to store a large graph on disk to minimize random disk access and enable more structured in-memory access.

Acknowledgement. This material is based upon work partially supported by the National Science Foundation under Grants IIS-0905493, CNS-1115375, IIP-1230740, and a grant from Intel ISTC on Cloud Computing.

6. REFERENCES

[1] U. Kang, C. E. Tsourakakis, and C. Faloutsos. Pegasus: A peta-scale graph mining system - implementation and observations. In *ICDM*, 2009.

[2] G. Malewicz, M. H. Austern, A. J. C. Bik, J. C. Dehnert, I. Horn, N. Leiser, and G. Czajkowski. Pregel: A system for large-scale graph processing. In *SIGMOD*, pages 135–146, 2010.

[3] R. Power and J. Li. Piccolo: Building fast, distributed programs with partitioned tables. In *OSDI*, 2010.

[4] Y. Low, J. Gonzalez, A. Kyrola, D. Bickson, C. Guestrin, and J. M. Hellerstein. Graphlab: A new framework for parallel machine learning. In *UAI*, 2010.

[5] U. Kang, H. Tong, J. Sun, C.-Y. Lin, and C. Faloutsos. Gbase: A scalable and general graph management system. In *KDD*, pages 1091–1099, 2011.

[6] A. Buluc and J. R. Gilbert. The combinatorial blas: Design, implementation, and applications. *IJHPCA*, 25(4):496–509, 2011.

[7] R. Cheng, J. Hong, A. Kyrola, Y. Miao, X. Weng, M. Wu, F. Yang, L. Zhou, F. Zhao, and E. Chen. Kineograph: Taking the pulse of a fast-changing and connected world. In *EuroSys*, pages 85–98, 2012.

[8] Y. Low, J. Gonzalez, A. Kyrola, D. Bickson, C. Guestrin, and J. M. Hellerstein. Distributed graphlab: A framework for machine learning and data mining in the cloud. In *PVLDB*, 2012.

[9] V. Prabhakaran, M. Wu, X. Weng, F. McSherry, L. Zhou, and M. Haridasan. Managing large graphs on multi-cores with graph awareness. In *ATC*, 2010.

[10] J. E. Gonzalez, Y. Low, H. Gu, D. Bickson, and C. Guestrin. Powergraph: Distributed graph-parallel computation on natural graphs. In *OSDI*, 2012.

[11] A. Kyrola, G. Blelloch, and C. Guestrin. Graphchi: Large-scale graph computation on just a pc. *OSDI'*12.

[12] Giraph. http://giraph.apache.org/.

[13] B. Shao, H. Wang, and Y. Li. Trinity: A distributed graph engine on a memory cloud. In *SIGMOD*, 2013.

[14] W.-S. Han, S. Lee, K. Park, J.-H. Lee, M.-S. Kim, J. Kim, and H. Yu. TurboGraph: A Fast Parallel Graph Engine Handling Billion-scale Graphs in a Single PC. In *KDD*, pages 77–85, 2013.

[15] W. Xie, G. Wang, D. Bindel, A. Demers, and J. Gehrke. Fast iterative graph computation with block updates. *PVLDB*, 2013.

[16] A. Roy, I. Mihailovic, and W. Zwaenepoel. X-Stream: Edge-centric Graph Processing using Streaming Partitions. In *SOSP*, 2013.

[17] K. Lee and L. Liu. Scaling Queries over Big RDF Graphs with Semantic Hash Partitioning. *PVLDB'*13.

[18] Y. Tian, A. Balmin, S. Andreas Corsten, S. Tatikonda, and J. McPherson. From "Think Like a Vertex" to "Think Like a Graph". *PVLDB*, 2013.

[19] J. E. Gonzalez, R. S. Xin, A. Dave, D. Crankshaw, M. J. Franklin, and I. Stoica. GraphX: Graph Processing in a Distributed Dataflow Framework. In *OSDI*, 2014.

[20] P. Yuan, W. Zhang, C. Xie, H. Jin, L. Liu, and K. Lee. Fast Iterative Graph Computation: A Path Centric Approach. In *SC*, 2014.

[21] S. Brin and L. Page. The anatomy of a large-scale hypertextual web search engine. In *WWW*, 1998.

[22] M. Bender, G. Brodal, R. Fagerberg, R. Jacob, and E. Vicari. Optimal sparse matrix dense vector multiplication in the i/o-model. *Theory of Computing Systems*, 47(4):934–962, 2010.

[23] X. Zhu and Z. Ghahramani. Learning from Labeled and Unlabeled Data with Label Propagation. In *CMU CALD Tech Report*, 2002.

[24] R. I. Kondor and J. D. Lafferty. Diffusion kernels on graphs and other discrete input spaces. In *ICML*, 2003.

[25] Y. Zhou, H. Cheng, and J. X. Yu. Clustering large attributed graphs: An efficient incremental approach. In *ICDM*, 2010.

[26] W. Tang, Z. Lu, and I. S. Dhillon. Clustering with multiple graphs. In *ICDM*, 2006.

[27] Y. Zhou and L. Liu. Activity-edge centric multi-label classification for mining heterogeneous information networks. In *KDD*, 2014.

[28] S. D. Kamvar, M. T. Schlosser, and H. Garcia-Molina. The eigentrust algorithm for reputation management in p2p networks. In *WWW*, pages 640–651, 2003.

[29] H. Tong, C. Faloutsos, and J.-Y. Pan. Fast random walk with restart and its applications. In *ICDM*, 2006.

[30] H. Ma, H. Yang, M. R. Lyu, and I. King. Mining social networks using heat diffusion processes for marketing candidates selection. In *CIKM*, pages 233–242, 2008.

[31] X. Zhu, Z. Ghahramani, and J. Lafferty. Semi-supervised learning using Gaussian fields and harmonic functions. In *ICML*, 2003.

[32] S. A. Macskassy and F. Provost. A simple relational classifier. In *MRDM*, pages 64–76, 2003.

[33] V. Satuluri and S. Parthasarathy. Scalable graph clustering using stochastic flows: Applications to community discovery. In *KDD*, 2009.

[34] Y. Zhou, H. Cheng, and J. X. Yu. Graph clustering based on structural/attribute similarities. *VLDB'*09.

[35] Y. Zhou and L. Liu. Social influence based clustering of heterogeneous information networks. In *KDD*, 2013.

[36] D. D. Lee and H. S. Seung. Algorithms for non-negative matrix factorization. In *NIPS*, 2000.

[37] Y. Koren. Factorization meets the neighborhood: a multifaceted collaborative filtering model. In *KDD'08*.

[38] H. Ma. An experimental study on implicit social recommendation. In *SIGIR*, pages 73–82, 2013.

[39] Y. Zhou, L. Liu, C.-S. Perng, A. Sailer, I. Silva-Lepe, and Z. Su. Ranking services by service network structure and service attributes. In *ICWS*, 2013.

[40] Yahoo Webscope. Yahoo! AltaVista Web Page Hyperlink Connectivity Graph, circa 2002. http://webscope.sandbox.yahoo.com/.

[41] P. Boldi, M. Santini, and S. Vigna. A Large Time-aware Web Graph. *SIGIR Forum*, 42(2):33–38, 2008.

[42] H. Kwak, C. Lee, H. Park, S. Moon. What is Twitter, a social network or a news media? In *WWW*, 2010.

[43] M. Gjoka, M. Kurant, C. T. Butts, A. Markopoulou. Walking in Facebook: A case study of unbiased sampling of OSNs. In *INFOCOM*, 2010.

[44] http://www.informatik.uni-trier.de/~ley/db/.

[45] http://www.last.fm/api/.

[46] T. Chakraborty, S. Sikdar, V. Tammana, N. Ganguly, and A. Mukherjee. Computer science fields as ground-truth communities: Their impact, rise and fall. In *ASONAM*, pages 426–433, 2013.

[47] J. Cohen, P. Cohen, S. G. West, and L. S. Aiken. *Applied Multiple Regression/Correlation Analysis for the Behavioral Sciences*. In *Routledge*, 2002.

[48] O. Bretscher. *Linear Algebra With Applications, 3rd Edition*. In *Prentice Hall*, 1995.

[49] F. Hillier and G. Lieberman. Introduction to Operations Research. In *McGraw-Hill College*, 1995.

Bidding for Highly Available Services with Low Price in Spot Instance Market

Weichao Guo[†] Kang Chen[‡] Yongwei Wu[‡] Weimin Zheng[‡]
Tsinghua National Laboratory for Information Science and Technology (TNLIST)
Department of Computer Science and Technology, Tsinghua University, Beijing 100084, China
Research Institute of Tsinghua University in Shenzhen, Shenzhen 518057, China
Technology Innovation Center at Yinzhou, Yangtze Delta Region Institute of Tsinghua University,
Ningbo 315000, Zhejiang
[†]gwc11@mails.tsinghua.edu.cn
[‡]{chenkang, wuyw, zwm-dcs}@tsinghua.edu.cn

ABSTRACT

Amazon EC2 has built the Spot Instance Marketplace and offers a new type of virtual machine instances called as spot instances. These instances are less expensive but considered failure-prone. Despite the underlying hardware status, if the bidding price is lower than the market price, such an instance will be terminated.

Distributed systems can be built from the spot instances to reduce the cost while still tolerating instance failures. For example, embarrassingly parallel jobs can use the spot instances by re-executing failed tasks. The bidding framework for such jobs simply selects the spot price as the bid. However, highly available services like lock service or storage service cannot use the similar techniques for availability consideration. The spot instance failure model is different to that of normal instances (fixed failure probability in traditional distributed model). This makes the bidding strategy more complex to keep service availability for such systems.

We formalize this problem and propose an availability and cost aware bidding framework. Experiment results show that our bidding framework can reduce the costs of a distributed lock service and a distributed storage service by 81.23% and 85.32% respectively while still keeping availability level the same as it is by using on-demand instances.

Categories and Subject Descriptors

C.2.4 [**Computer-Communication Networks**]: Distributed System—*client/server*; D.4.5 [**Operating System**]: Reliability—*fault-tolerance*; G.1.6 [**Numerical Analysis**]: Optimization—*Constrained optimization, Nonlinear programming*; G.3 [**Probability And Statistics**]: Markov processes

Keywords

Distributed service; high availability; bidding framework; spot instance failure model

1. INTRODUCTION

Virtual machines are widely used in cloud computing. A running virtual machine is usually called as an instance. An instance that supports the pay-as-you-use billing schema is called as an on-demand instance on Amazon Elastic Cloud Computing (EC2). Using on-demand instances can reduce users' cost comparing to owning dedicated physical clusters in house. Many users including startup companies as well as research institutes rely on cloud computing services. On the other hand, cloud providers are willing to provide virtual machines for improving the profits while keeping constant maintaining costs of underlying physical infrastructure.

To further increase the resource utilization, Amazon EC2 proposed a new type of virtual computing instances, the spot instances. Here are the descriptions from the website of introducing spot instances: "Spot Instances allow you to name your own price for Amazon EC2 computing capacity. You simply bid on spare Amazon EC2 instances and run them whenever your bid exceeds the current Spot Price, which varies in real-time based on supply and demand." [30]. From the providers' point of view, the utilization of idle periods of the infrastructure can be further improved. For users, spot instances are much cheaper and can be used to achieve economical computing. However, as with the characteristics of spot instances, they should not be considered as always available but failure-prone despite the practical underlying hardware status. It will become hard for analysing the availability level of services built on top of spot instances.

In distributed computing, some basic services are considered as 'should be highly available'. The lock service is an example. As a fundamental building block for applications, a lock service should be always on-line. Any failure of the lock service could hurt the running of applications. Another example is the storage service, which is a fundamental building block for providing data storage. These services are usually considered critical and should be as reliable as possible. They are different from the parallel batching processing jobs which can be fixed after actual failure occurrence [24, 36, 35]. For critical services, safety property, such as a lock cannot be assigned to more than one client, must be kept at any time. Such services do have their own fault tolerance mechanism such as Paxos-based state machine replication (SMR) [23]. The algorithms used can guarantee progress (eventually achieve the goal set forehand) if the majority number of the nodes are available for enough amount of time.

As a Paxos based mechanism can tolerate any minority of node failures in a distributed service, can we just replace normal nodes with spot instances to identically provide highly available distributed service? It is easy to just replace the on-demand instances with spot instances (maybe more spot instances) of the same distributed systems. However, it is non-trivial to analyze whether such a distributed service building on top of spot instances has the same availability level of the one bult on on-demand instances. The availability analysis becomes complicated because of the unique out-of-bid failure of spot instances. The failure probability is not fixed as it is in the traditional distributed model(usually a small constant). Thus, traditional way of using the number of available nodes for indicating the availability level should be amended by incorporating the probabilistic failure model.

To the best of our knowledge, there is no published solution to address this bidding problem, i.e., using spot instances to provide a distributed service while keeping the same availability level with another system using on-demand instances. In this paper, we will first formalize the model for describing the work of providing highly available system using spot instances. And based on this model, we propose a bidding framework to automatically make the bidding decisions for keeping appointed availability level and reducing the total cost of a distributed service.

It is feasible to achieve high availability with failure-prone spot instances when building distributed services. Take the distributed lock service as an example. The downtime of a distributed lock service using 5 geographical isolated on-demand instances should be less than 30 seconds in a whole month.[1] To achieve the same availablility level by using spot instances, we need to analyze the service availability based on the failure probability model of spot instances. As there are a large number of bidding decisions that satisfies the service availability requirement, it will be a question to decide which one is the most cost efficient. We think that this problem can be modeled as a non-linear programming problem. The objective is to minimize the total cost of spot instances for building a distributed service. The constraint is keeping the same availability level as using on-demand instances. The failure probability of a spot instance under a bid is correlative to the spot price. If the bid is lower than the spot price provided by Amazon EC2, the corresponding spot instance will not be available. As the spot prices sequence has Markovian property but the sojourn time between spot prices is not memoryless in the statistical inferences, we model the failure probability of a spot instance based on a semi-Markovian process of spot prices.

However, solving this non-linear programming is NP-hard. Exhaustive search is impractical for obtaining the optimal

solution. In this paper, we have built an availability and cost aware bidding framework for obtaining a near-optimal solution practically. The framework has two main components, one is online bidding module for getting spot instances and another is spot instance failure model for estimating failure probability of spot instances. The online bidding module employs an enumeration and greedy strategy based algorithm to bid spot instances. The spot instance failure model collects the spot price data continuously, and provides the estimated failure probability of a spot instance for the next hour under a bid.

To sum up, we have made the following contributions in this paper:

- We point out that the analysis of bidding for highly available service using spot instances is different from the bidding for batching processing jobs.

- The spot instance failure model is intrinsic different from the model in traditional distributed systems. It has been formalized according to the bid and price in the marketplace.

- We have built availability and cost aware bidding framework based on the formalization of spot instance failure model and non-linear programming model. The framework is effectively applied in two different highly available distributed systems.

The remainder of this paper is organized as follows. Section 2 introduces the spot instances in Amazon EC2 and the availability of distributed services. In Section 3, we model the failure probability of spot instances and formalize the optimization problem. Section 4 describes a bidding framework to obtain a near optimal solution. Section 5 gives evaluations with the two cases to demonstrate the effectiveness of the bidding framework. Section 6 discusses the related work and Section 7 concludes this paper.

2. BACKGROUND

2.1 Amazon EC2 Spot Instance

Same as on-demand instances, spot instances give tenants a wide selection of instance types [5], which comprise varying combinations of CPU, memory, storage, and networking capacity. Users can choose the instances for their applications based on the different characteristics provided. The instances are located on an increasing number of regions all over the world [4]. Each region is in a separated geographic area and the region number keeps increasing. To achieve the greatest possible fault tolerance and stability, each region has multiple, isolated locations known as "Availability Zones", which are shown in Table 1. We suppose the highly available services are built on top of spot instances from different availability zones. Thus, the failure model of the instances is independent identically distributed. The geographical replicated configuration is widely used in highly available services, such as Spanner [16], Dynamo [17] and Azure [14].

To use a spot instance, a user should place a spot instance request that specifies the instance type, the Availability Zone, and the maximum price he is willing to pay per hour, called as a spot bid. The current default upper limit of a spot bid is four times on-demand price [6]. The

---

[1]According to the Service Level Agreement (SLA) from Amazon EC2, the availability of an on-demand instance will be no less than 99% or otherwise users will have 30% fee as the compensation. The 5 on-demand instances are failure independent as launching from different locations. The availability of the lock service can be calculated by subtracting the probability that 3 or more instances are simultaneously unavailable from 100%.

Table 1: Amazon EC2 Regions and Availability Zones

Region	Location	Availability Zones
US East 1	Virginia	4
US West 2	Oregon	3
US West 1	California	3
EU West 1	Ireland	3
EU Central 1	Frankfurt	2
AP Southeast 1	Singapore	2
AP Northeast 1	Tokyo	3
AP Southeast 2	Sydney	2
SA East 1	Sao Paulo	2

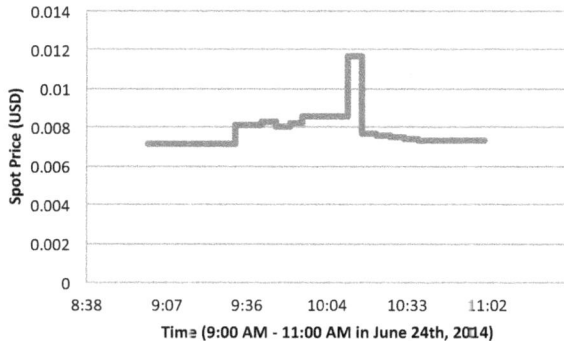

Figure 1: Spot price history for a "us-east-1a.linux.m1.small" spot instance

spot price is set by Amazon EC2, and fluctuates according to the supply and demand of the spot instance capacity. Figure 1 shows some spot price fluctuations for "us-east-1.linux.m1.small" instances during 9:00 AM - 11:00 AM on June 24th 2014. When a bid exceeds the spot price, the spot instance is launched and will run until the spot price rises above the bid(cut-of-bid failure) or the user chooses to terminate it. If the spot instance is terminated by Amazon EC2, the user will not be charged for any partial hour of usage. However, if the user terminates the spot instance, he will pay for any partial hour of usage as he would in occasions like using on-demand instances. Spot instances are charged with the spot price. Obviously, a higher spot bid returns a more reliable and available spot instance, and may also induce a higher charge.

2.2 The Availability of Distributed Service

To achieve high availability, state machine replication (SMR) is a general way for implementing a fault-tolerant service by replicating servers and coordinating client interactions with server replicas. Each operation should be a consensus value decided by SMR. Paxos [23] has been proved to be an effective consensus protocol in SMR to build highly available distributed services. Paxos family protocols have been widely used in varies of distributed services [13, 10, 26].

In fact, Paxos is one of the quorum based techniques [18] for building a highly available distributed system. Such protocols often use 'vote' like algorithms. A request has to obtain sufficient votes v by the nodes in the distributed system to perform an operation. In this context, the distributed sys-

tem will be unavailable when the live nodes have insufficient votes. A minimal number of v is called a quorum. If a quorum of nodes is available, the distributed system is available otherwise the system will be considered as unavailable.

Service availability can be defined as the probability that a request can get an appropriate response according to the specification. The availability is determined by the failure probabilities of nodes in the system. The availability of quorum systems is studied in [27]. For convenience, we introduce a definition of *Acceptance Set* [2] .

DEFINITION 1. *A collection $\mathcal{A}$ of sets over a finite universe U representing the nodes of a distributed system is called an acceptance set if*

1) $S \cap T \neq \emptyset$ for all $S, T \in \mathcal{A}$. (Intersection)

2) If $S \in \mathcal{A}$ then $T \in \mathcal{A}$ for all $T \supseteq S$. (Monotonicity)

The collection of minimal quorums is $\mathcal{S} = \mathcal{S}(\mathcal{A}) = \{S \in \mathcal{A} \mid S \setminus \{u\} \notin \mathcal{A} \text{ for all } u \in S\}$.

Let $\mathcal{A}$ be an acceptance set of a distributed system, for each set $S \in \mathcal{A}$, the probability of which the elements of S are alive and the rest are in failure is

$$\prod_{i \in S}(1 - p_i) \prod_{j \in \overline{S}} p_j,$$

where $\overline{S}$ denotes $U \setminus S$, $\mathbf{p} = (p_1, p_2, \cdots, p_n)$ denotes the failure probabilities of nodes in the distributed system over a period of time.

As S are different sets, the non-failure probability (the "availability") of $\mathcal{A}$ can be further extended as

$$A_{\mathcal{A}} = \sum_{S \in \mathcal{A}}(\prod_{i \in S}(1 - p_i) \prod_{j \in \overline{S}} p_j) \qquad (1)$$

Here, we introduce another definition of *Optimal Availability Acceptance Set*.

DEFINITION 2. *An acceptance set $\mathcal{A}$ over a finite universe U representing the nodes of a distributed service is called an optimal availability acceptance set if*

1) $A_{\mathcal{A}} \geq A_{\mathcal{B}}$ for all acceptance sets $\mathcal{B}$ over the same universe U.

For a distributed system, the non-failure probability of the optimal availability acceptance set $\mathcal{A}_o$ is equivalent to the expected availability of the distributed service. The acceptance set discussed here assumes the indepedent failure of spot instances. This is consistent to our discussion before that the highly available services are built over instances from different availability zones. As we have to estimate the availability of distributed service, acceptance set will be a constraint in the non-linear programming studied below.

3. PROBLEM FORMALIZE

Since configuring Paxos based SMR in a distributed system can tolerate a minority of node failures, it seems that we can replace the normal nodes in a distributed system with spot instances directly. In fact, the original high availability of the distributed service may no longer exist any more. This can be illustrated in the following example.

Supposing that a Paxos based distributed system has 5 nodes. The failure probability of each node is 0.01. This distributed system can tolerate any two-node simultaneous failures. According to Equation (1), the expected availability of the distributed service is 0.9999901494, which means that there should be only about 25.5 seconds downtime in one month. If replacing all the 5 nodes with Amazon EC2 spot instances and setting the bids same to spot price, a same availability level can not be achieved. Although the replaced distributed system can still tolerant the same number of node failures as before, the non-failure probability of the distributed system is much less than the original one. Taking 5 spot instances from different Amazon EC2 availability zones in June, 2014 as an example, the spot prices of availability zone US East 1a, US East 1c, US West 1b, US West 2a, US West 2b are \$ 0.008, \$ 0.008, \$ 0.009, \$ 0.009, \$ 0.009 at 0:00 AM on June 1st, 2014 respectively. If we bid a spot instance in each the availability zone with the aforementioned spot prices, node failures are encountered more often in such a distributed system. The downtime of the distributed service in June, 2014 may be more than 1500 seconds.

In essence, the number of tolerating simultaneous node failures with spot instances does not indicate the same availability with on-demand ones for a distributed system. Because the failure probability of spot instances are usually much higher than that of normal nodes. The failure values are in fact constantly changing with the fluctuation of spot prices. Therefore, we model the failure of spot instances from the spot bid and spot price.

Based on the failure model, we have to address the bidding decision problem i.e. how to keep a distributed service staying highly available and how to bid to minimize the cost of spot instance. We apply a non-linear programming to solve this optimization problem.

3.1 Spot Instance Failure Model

The availability of a distributed system is based on the availability of each component in the system. Considering Amazon EC2 instances, the availability of an instance can be estimated by its failure probability. Furthermore, let $MTBF$ (Mean Time Between Failures) denotes the average time between failures of an instance, $MTTR$ (Mean Time To Repair) denotes the average time for an instance to recover from a failure, the availability A of an Amazon EC2 instance can be measured as following.

$$A = \frac{MTBF}{MTBF + MTTR} \quad (2)$$

Diverse causes can bring down an Amazon EC2 instance including software and hardware errors. According to Amazon EC2's SLA [7], the measured availability of an on-demand instance is about 0.99. It means that the failure probability of an on-demand instance is about 0.01.

For a spot instance in Amazon EC2, the new and major type of failure is the out-of-bid failure as discussed in section 2.1. An out-of-bid failure is caused by the spot price fluctuates above the bid of the spot instance. Considering this type of failure only, the failure probability of a spot instance at time t can be represented by

$$Pr(p(t) > b) \quad (3)$$

Where $p(t)$ denotes the price at time t, and b denotes the bid.

As other kinds of failures are independent with the out-of-bid failure of Amazon EC2 spot instances, and the availability of a spot instance without out-of-bid failures will be the same as an on-demand instance, the failure probability of a spot instance $FP(t)$ can be further represented by

$$FP(t) = 1 - (1 - FP') \cdot (1 - Pr(p(t) > b)) \quad (4)$$

Where FP' denotes the failure probability of a corresponding on-demand instance. Here $FP' = 0.01$.

The total failure time of a spot instance is exactly the cumulative time of out-of-bid failures. Thus the failure probability of a spot instance in a time duration $d, d > 0$ can be further represented as

$$\int_0^d FP(t)dt \quad (5)$$

Amazon EC2 assigns spot instances to bidders in descending order of their bids until all available spot instances have been allocated or all spot instance requests have been satisfied. The spot price is equal to the lowest winning bid. And after a period of time, the spot price may or may not change depending on the changing of demand and supply. Figure 1 depicts the spot price history during 9:00AM - 11:00AM on June 24th, 2014 for the "us-east-1.linux.m1.small" spot instances. The spot price first remains at \$0.0071 before switching to \$0.0081, and reaches up to \$0.0117 after about half an hour. Thus, we should estimate the failure probability of a spot instance based on the spot price variations.

As shown in Figure 1, the spot price remains at a fixed value S_i for a time duration d_i before switching to another value S_{i+1}. In essence, spot price sequence $(S_i, i = 1, 2, \cdots, n)$ and sojourn time sequence $(d_i, i = 1, 2, \cdots, n)$ are both random process. Previous works [15] have proved that the spot price sequence has Markovian property with investigating the Chapman-Kolmogorov equation [19]. And the sojourn time sequence can be modeled as a temporal point process [12].

As the sojourn time between spot prices is not memoryless, we characterize the spot price variations by a semi-Markovian chain model, which is also employed in [31]. Denote the set of all unique spot prices as $\mathcal{S}$, where $\mathcal{S} = \{s_i, i = 1, \cdots, |\mathcal{S}|\}$, and denote the state space of sojourn time as $\mathcal{T}$, where $\mathcal{T} = \{\tau_i, i = 1, \cdots, |\mathcal{T}|\}$. The stochastic kernel of the semi-Markovian chain can be represented as

$$Q(i, j, k) = (q_{i,j,k}; s_i, s_j \in \mathcal{S}, k \in \mathcal{T}) \quad (6)$$

where

$$q_{i,j,k} = Pr(S_{n+1} = s_j, S_n = s_i, \tau_n = k) \quad (7)$$

i.e., the probability that at current state i, a transition will happen to state j after time k.

The detail statistical inference is in [31]. With this spot price model, we can calculated the transition probability of two spot prices in future, and then estimate the failure probability of a spot instance under a specific bid.

3.2 Cost Minimization Problem

We apply a non-linear programming model to this bidding problem. The objective is to minimize the cost of spot instances when building a distributed service. The constraint is that the availability of the distributed service built with spot instances is not worse than the one built with on-demand instances. We estimate the availability of the distributed service based on the spot instances failure probability estimation.

According to the spot pricing rules of Amazon EC2 mentioned in section 2.1, users need no payment for the partial hour of a spot instance that is terminated by Amazon EC2. If a user can precisely predict the price changing of a spot instance, it is possible to exploit this feature to reduce the cost or even free computation. However, it is difficult to take advantage of out-of-bid failure as an accurate prediction is required to notify when the price will change and what price it will be. Here we are not going to harness such Amazon EC2's spot pricing rule so as to simplify the cost minimization problem.

In Amazon EC2, not only varies of hardware or software failures of instances are isolated by different availability zones, but also the out-of-bid failure is isolated by pricing isolation of different availability zones. To ensure the failure independence of spot instances we bid, the distributed service should use only 0 or 1 instance in each availability zone as mentioned before. There are more than 20 availability zones in Amazon EC2. This is large enough for choosing moderate number of participants in a Paxos group in practical systems(usually 5 or 7).[13]. And performance requirements can be satisfied by launching multiple Paxos groups.

As Amazon EC2 charges for a spot instance hourly, the bidding interval should be n (a positive integer) hours. In each bidding interval, the cost minimization problem can be formalized using a non-linear programming. The decision variables in this model are the spot instance bids for different availability zones. Bidding decisions can be denoted as a variable vector $\mathbf{b} = (b_1, b_2, \cdots, b_n)$. The bid for a spot instance in the i-th Availability Zone is b_i, $i = 1, 2, \cdots, n$.

Unfortunately the cost for a spot instance in the next interval is still unknown when bidding. This is due to the way Amazon EC2 charges. Amazon EC2 charges hourly for a spot instance with the last price of a spot instance in the hour rather than the bid. For a system consist of multiple spot instances, the goal is to achieve minim the sum cost of each instance. As the spot prices in a future time point are random variables, we can minimize the expectation cost of spot instances under the given bids instead of minimizing the unknown cost. But the actual cost may be much higher than the expectation in some bidding intervals. We choose the sum of bids, an upper bound of the cost, instead of the expectation cost as the objective function in the non-linear programming.

The key constraint in the non-linear programming is to ensure that the availability of a distributed service with spot instances is comparable to that with on-demand ones. The availability of a distributed service can be represented as the availability of its optimal availability acceptance set. Denote the optimal availability acceptance set of a distributed service S as $\mathcal{A}_o(S, \mathbf{FP})$, $\mathbf{FP}$ is the node failure probability vector. Denote a distributed service built with spot instances as S_s, the spot price of availability zone i as p_i, and the failure probability vector of the spot instances under bids $\mathbf{b} = (b_1, b_2, \cdots, b_n)$ in S_s as $FP(\mathbf{b})$. Similarly, denote the associate distributed service built with on-demand instance as S_o, the number of on-demand instances in S_o as m. We finally can formalize the cost minimization problem as

$$\min \sum_{i=1}^{n} b_i \qquad (8)$$

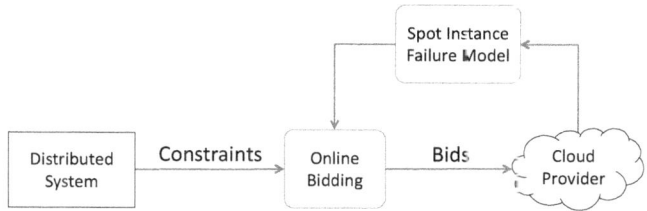

Figure 2: The bidding framework

s.t.

$$\sum_{i=1}^{n} \epsilon(b_i - p_i) \geq m \qquad (9)$$

and

$$A_{\mathcal{A}_o(S_o, \mathbf{FP'})} - A_{\mathcal{A}_o(S_s, FP(\mathbf{b}))} < \varepsilon \qquad (10)$$

The inequality (9) is a basic constraint that keeps the nodes are online at first to ensure that the distributed service built with spot instances initializes correctly. In the inequality (10), $\epsilon(u)$ equals 1 if $u > 0$ and 0 otherwise, and ε represents as an infinitesimal. It can be set to an acceptable availability variation in practice, e.g. 0.000001.

4. BIDDING FRAMEWORK

Solving the non-linear programming is NP-hard. All the possible candidates of bids $\mathbf{b}$ need to be traversed and verified with the availability constraint. The size of traverse space is m^n, where m is the number of possible prices and n is the number of availability zones. Using exhaustive search is not practical.

Fortunately, we just aim to reduce the cost of spot instances and do not have to get the optimal solution. As solving this optimization problem in an acceptable short time is impossible, we seek for a near-optimal solution rather than the optimal one. We have built a cost and availability aware bidding framework to make practical solutions. As illustrated in Figure 2, bidding decisions are made by online bidding module at the beginning of each bidding interval. And then the spot bids are issued to the cloud provider i.e. Amazon EC2. The spot instance failure estimation is used to estimate the failure probability of a spot instance for the next bidding interval under a specific bid. The estimated failure probability of a spot instance is then used to verify the availability requirement of the distributed system. With more and more spot prices data collected, the spot instance failure probability estimation can be improved.

In the bidding framework, the bidding decisions will change between two bidding intervals if spot prices fluctuate drastically. Some spot instances should be replaced by some new ones in different availability zone. To keep safety, i.e. the service availability level, the new spot instances are launched before the next bidding interval starts and added to the system, then the old spot instances that should be replaced are removed from the system at the beginning of the coming bidding interval. Adding and removing a spot instance is supported by the *view change* of Paxos. The startup time of a spot instance is usually 200~700 seconds and mainly varies in regions [25]. The actual time of a bidding interval is shortened by the startup time of spot instances. We give a discussion about the different choices of bidding interval in section 5.5.

4.1 Online Bidding

As we have illustrated, the failure probabilities of nodes are fixed to a same small constant in a traditional distributed system model. A quorum is a simple majority of the nodes in the distributed system. For a distributed system with nodes that have different failure probabilities, a calculated weighted voting assignment has been proved to be the optimal configuration. The optimal availability vote assignments for weighted voting mechanism are well studied in [33, 32, 2]. Denote all the failure probabilities of n nodes as $p_i, i = 1, 2, \cdots, n$, it has been proved that the optimal quorum system is a monarchy with one of the least unreliable processors as the king if $p_i \geq \frac{1}{2}$ for all i, and any node i with $p_i > \frac{1}{2}$ should be a dummy if only parts of nodes with $p_i \geq \frac{1}{2}$ in [2]. If $0 < p_i < \frac{1}{2}$ all i, the optimal weights are defined by the formula in [32, 33]

$$w_i = log_2(\frac{1 - p_i}{p_i}) \tag{11}$$

However, in a practical scenario, Formula (11) cannot be used in the case where the differences of p_i are significant. For example, suppose that the failure probabilities of nodes are respectively 0.01, 0.1, 0.1 in a distributed system with three nodes. Depending on Formula (11), the node with failure probability of 0.01 has a dominated vote that is larger than the sum of the other two nodes' votes. Ideally, this is reasonable because we should use a monachy system when one node is much more reliable than the other nodes. But in practical, the failure probability of a node is measured in a finite time period, and has a deviation away from the ideal value representing the steady state when the time period is infinite. The out-of-bid failure in the spot instance failure model just fits this case. Furthermore, some Paxos family protocols are designed without considering weighted voting assignment mechanism. To keep the bidding algorithm simple and compatible, we still use a simple majority of nodes as a quorum.

As the spot instances are fixed to an equal weighted vote, only same failure probabilities of spot instances meet the definition of optimal configuration. In our online bidding algorithm, we try to make failure probabilities be closed to each other. And enumeration and greedy strategy are used in the algorithm.

The pseudo code of the online bidding algorithm is shown in Figure 3. The algorithm gets the configurations of a distributed system as input, including the system availability requirement and instance type. The procedures of online bidding are simple: 1) For all possible number of nodes n, calculates the failure probability FP that satisfies the system availability requirement when each node has the same failure probability. 2) Under the configuration of n nodes, for all availability zones, gets the minimal bid of which the estimated failure probability is less than FP. The estimated failure probability depends on the spot instance failure model of the availability zone, the bid, the spot price and the sojourn time of the spot price. 3) Comparing the value of the bids, selects the availability zones in a greedy way. 4) By accumulating the selected bids, calculates the upper bound of the cost under each configuration of n nodes and returns the bids that have the lowest upper bound of the cost as the bidding decision. This algorithm does not always lead to an optimal bidding decision, but obtain a good and near optimal solution in practise.

Algorithm:Bidding

Input: *availability, type*
Output: *bids*
1: *zones ← get_availability_zones()*
2: $n \leftarrow 1$
3: **while** $n \not> zones.length$ **do**
4:     $FP \leftarrow node\_failure\_pr(n, availability)$
5:     **for all** *zone ∈ zones* **do**
6:        *spotprice ← get_spot_price(zone, type)*
7:        *bid ← spotprice.price*
8:        **while** *bid* $\not>$ *get_on_demand_price(zone, type)* **do**
9:           **if** *estimate_FP(zone, bid, spotprice)* $\not>$ *FP* **then**
10:             **break**
11:           **else**
12:             *bid ← bid + 1*
13:        *bids[n][zone] ← bid*
14:     *sort(bids[n])*
15:     *cost_upper_bound[n] ← sum(bids[n][1 : n])*
16:     $n \leftarrow n + 1$
17: $m \leftarrow min\_key(cost\_upper\_bound)$
18: **return** bids[m][1:m]

Figure 3: Bidding algorithm

4.2 Failure Probability Estimation

In the bidding framework, the spot instance failure model is employed by the online bidding module. To estimate the failure probability of a spot instance, a spot price model is embedded in the spot instance failure model. We use the semi-Markovian chain to model the spot price sequence as mentioned in section 3.1. Thus, a key task of spot instance failure probability estimation is to reconstruct the transition distribution from the observed spot price history data.

Wee [34] shows that the spot price sample cumulative distribution functions have significant increase around every hour in 2011. However, the spot prices data we collected in 2014 shows that the spot price change frequency has raised to many times each hour. For simplicity, we set the time unit of the semi-Markovian chain to 1 minute. The sojourn time d_i in the sample data is discretized as

$$\tau_i \triangleq \tau(S_i \rightarrow S_{i+1}) \triangleq \lfloor d_i \rfloor \tag{12}$$

We use an empirical estimator, which resembles a Maximum Likelihood Estimator (MLE) essentially [9]. The stochastic kernel $\mathbf{Q}$ is reconstructed by:

$$\widehat{q_{i,j,k}} = \frac{N_{i,j}^k}{N_i}, if N_i \neq 0 \tag{13}$$

otherwise, $\widehat{q_{i,j,k}} = 0$.

Where N_i denotes the number of occurrences of price $s_i \in \mathcal{S}$, $N_{i,j}^k$ denotes the number of transitions from price $s_i \in \mathcal{S}$ to $s_j \in \mathcal{S}$ with sojourn time of $k \in \mathcal{T}$.

Although we can make a bid for a spot instance as high as four times the on-demand price, we should choose an on-demand instance rather than a higher bid for a spot instance to avoid the potential higher charge. Thus, we force the bid of a spot instance lower than the corresponding on-demand instance in our bidding framework. In a time unit, the failure probability of a spot instance under a bid b as

$$FP(b) = \begin{cases} 1 & \text{if } 0 \leq b \leq p \\ 1 - (1 - FP') \cdot \sum_{j=p}^{b} \widehat{q_{p,j,k}} & \text{if } p < b < o \end{cases} \quad (14)$$

where b denotes a bid, p denotes the spot price, k denotes the sojourn time, o denotes the corresponding on-demand price, FP' denotes the failure probability of the corresponding on-demand instance, which is fixed to 0.01.

The failure probability of a spot instance in a bidding interval is the failure probability expectation of each time unit, which is a discretization of Formula (5).

5. EVALUATION

We have implemented a prototype of the bidding framework in Python. The prototype interacts with Amazon EC2 via boto [11], which is a Python interface library to Amazon Web Services. To evaluate our bidding framework we apply it to a distributed lock service and a distributed storage service on Amazon EC2. The experiments include a micro-benchmark, a one-week-long running on Amazon EC2 for feasibility verification and two 11-week-long trace replays for cost and availability evaluation.

5.1 Experimental Systems

5.1.1 Distributed Lock Service

A distributed lock service is intended for large-scale loosely coupled distributed systems. A representative distributed lock service is Google Chubby [13], which can help thousands of nodes to synchronize their activities and to agree on basic information about their environment such as system members.

Chubby provides an interface much like a file system with advisory locks and uses the Paxos protocol for practical distributed consensus to achieve high availability. A Chubby server is usually configured with 5 replicas. The Chubby clients communicate with Chubby server using a client library via RPC. The quorum in such a 5-node distributed system is a simple majority. Chubby follows the assumption here that the replicas are replicated in different regions i.e. similar to availability zones in Amazon EC2.

5.1.2 Erasure Code Based Distributed Storage Service

Distributed storage services usually provide an object store or key value store for clients while tolerating a portion of machine restarts and even permanent machine or disk failures. Using a distributed storage service across availability zones can provide better availability for tolerating data center crash or un-reachable problem. Instead of primary-backup techniques, Gaios [10] and Megastore [8] have employed Paxos based SMR for fault tolerance in the implementation of distributed storage service.

Erasure code [28] is a forward error correction (FEC) code in information theory and originally used to recover messages from independent packets loss in network transmission. And it has been widely adopted in distributed storage systems [21, 29] for reducing storage and network cost. In a common form of erasure coding, the original data object will be firstly divided into m equal-sized chunks and then k

parity chunks of the same size will be generated. The total number of chunks is $n = m + k$. The erasure code algorithm can reconstruct the original data from any m chunks out of total n chunks. This erasure coding can be denoted as $\theta(m, n)$.

Recently, Mu et al. [23] has proposed a Paxos based protocol, RS-Paxos, which can do erasure coding correctly in distributed services without the assumption of a "synchronous" network model. RS-Paxos can be employed in a distributed storage service for network transmission and disk writes reduction by sending coded data shards instead of full copy. We call such a distributed service as an erasure code based distributed storage service.

A standard configuration for RS-Paxos is also 5 nodes and a $\theta(3, 5)$ erasure coding. Notice that RS-Paxos can only tolerate one-node failure instead of two-node failures, which is very different from a distributed lock service. This is because the write quorum of the service is different from the one using a replication mechanism. To guarantee reconstruction of the original data, the intersection size of the acceptance set should be 3 instead of 1.

5.2 Experimental Setup

These two distributed services built with on-demand instances are set as the baseline in our experiments. Although using reserved instances can reduce $30\% \sim 40\%$ cost at most, it is inflexible and difficult to adapt to the changing of service load. The failure probability of an on-demand instance is 0.01 as illustrated in [7]. The distributed lock service used in the experiments is a simple implementation based on Paxos, and the distributed storage service is an implementation of RS-Paxos [26]. We configure the two systems both with 5 on-demand instances, which is the common configuration in practical systems [13, 26]. In such a configuration, the distributed lock service can tolerate any two-node failures. The distributed storage service can tolerate only any one-node failures instead of two-node failure as illustrated in section 5.1.2.

For comparison, we also pick a heuristic bidding strategy. In this strategy, the availability zones with the lowest $n + m$ spot prices are chosen, assuming that there are n nodes in the original distributed system configuration, m is the number of additional nodes. In these experiments, n is 5. For each availability zone, a spot instance bid is set as the spot price with an extra portion p, such as 10% or 20%. As there are various of selections of m and p, we use some typical configuration of m and p in the comparison experiments. For simplicity, we denote such a strategy with m additional nodes and p extra portion of bid as $Extra(m, p)$, and denote our bidding algorithm and framework as "Jupiter".

The experiments are run over 17 availability zones of Amazon EC2. The distributed lock service is built with the "linux.m1.small" instances. Each "linux.m1.small" on-demand instance is charged about \$ $0.044 \sim 0.061$ for one hour. The erasure code based distributed storage system is built on the "m3.large" instances, which have more CPU and memory capacity than "m1.small" ones. Each "linux.m3.large" on-demand instance is charged about \$ $0.14 \sim 0.201$ for one hour.

For each availability zone, the spot instance failure model is first trained with about three months of spot prices data. Such data training leads to convergence. In the experiments, we run the bidding framework for one week on Amazon EC2

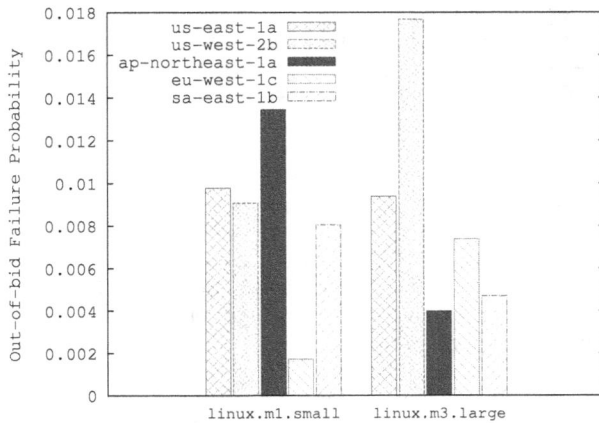

Figure 4: Measured out-of-bid failure probability of a spot instance under the estimation failure probability of 0.01

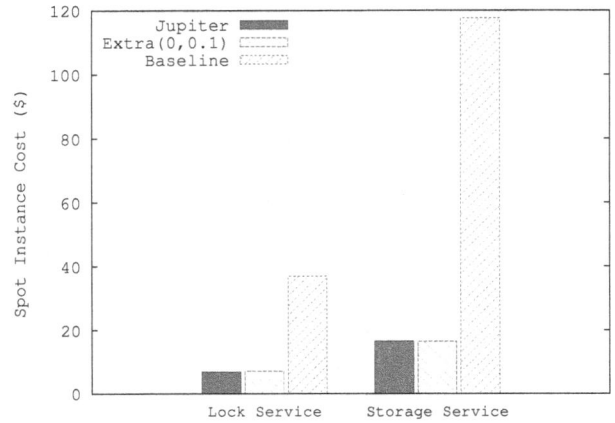

Figure 5: Spot instance cost of a distribued service under different bidding strategies from December 15th, 2014 to December 22th, 2014

and replay two 11-week-long spot price trace according to the Amazon EC2's spot pricing rule. The startup time of a spot instance is considered in the replay. It mainly varies in regions and usually 200∼700 seconds according to [25].

5.3 Micro-Benchmark

For the spot instance failure model, our major concern is the precision of spot instance failure probability estimation. Accordingly, we compare the measured failure probability of a spot instance and its expected failure probability in the spot instance failure model.

In this test, we first make a bid for each availability zone to keep the probability of out-of-bid failure no more than 0.01 in one month based on the spot instance failure model. Then we examined the out-of-bid failure probability by comparing the bids with the month's spot prices data. Figure 4 shows the measured failure probability of 5 availability zones.

For both "linux.m1.small" and "linux.m3.large" spot instances, the measured out-of-bid failure probability is less than 0.01 in most cases. There are two exceptions in all the test cases. One is in availability zone 'ap-southeast-1a', the out-of-bid failure probability is about 0.013553 for a 'linux.m1.small' instance. The other one is in availability zone 'us-west-2b', the out-of-bid failure probability of 'linux.m3.large' is about 0.017665. The test results show the spot instance failure model can estimate failure probability with minor deviation. And the failure probability estimation of spot instances can be more accurate with new spot prices data.

5.4 Feasibility

In December 2014, we performed a one-week-long running of the bidding framework on Amazon EC2. Our bidding framework functioned correctly and kept the two distributed services always available in the one-week experiment. The heuristic strategy $Extra(0, 0.1)$ is also tested in this experiment. The interval of each bidding is set to one hour in both strategies.

As shown in Figure 5, the cost of the distributed lock service under our bidding framework is about $ 6.91, only one sixth of the baseline and a little lower than the cost under

$Extra(0, 0.1)$. Both are always available in the one-week-long running. The cost of the distributed storage service under our bidding framework is about $ 16.53, close to the cost under $Extra(0, 0.1)$. The distributed storage service encountered no failure for one week. However, the distributed storage service under $Extra(0, 0.1)$ failed in the running. Our bidding framework outperformed the $Extra(0, 0.1)$ strategy on the whole. This experiment showed that our bidding framework is practical for reducing cost while still keeping the service highly available.

5.5 Cost and Availability

We evaluated our bidding framework in a long term by replaying the spot prices trace. As cost and availability of a spot instance are certained with the given spot prices data, the result is the same as real running the bidding framework on Amazon EC2. Two strategies, $Extra(0, 0.2)$ and $Extra(2, 0.2)$, are introduced for comparison. There are 11 weeks of "linux.m1.small" spot prices data and 11 weeks of "linux.m3.large" spot prices data from October 2014 to December 2014 in the trace replays. The distributed lock service is replayed with "linux.m1.small" trace and the distributed storage service is replayed with "linux.m3.large" trace. We mainly focus on the cost and availability of the two building cases. The bidding intervals of 3, 6, 9, and 12 hours are also tested besides 1 hour.

The cost of a distributed lock service for 11 weeks with 5 "linux.m1.small" on-demand instances in the cheapest availability zones is $406.56. For the erasure code based distributed storage service with 5 "linux.m3.large" on-demand instances, the value is $1293.6. These are the baselines in this experiment. The cost of distributed services under heuristic bidding strategies and our bidding framework are shown in Figure 6 and 8. The availability results are shown in Figure 7 and 9.

As shown in Figure 6, our bidding framework only cost about one-fifth of the baseline in the distributed lock service for the best case. The cost of our bidding framework with the bidding interval of 6 hours outperformed all the other solutions. In this case, the cost is about $ 77.3. For the bidding intervals of 1, 9, 12 hours, the cost of our bidding

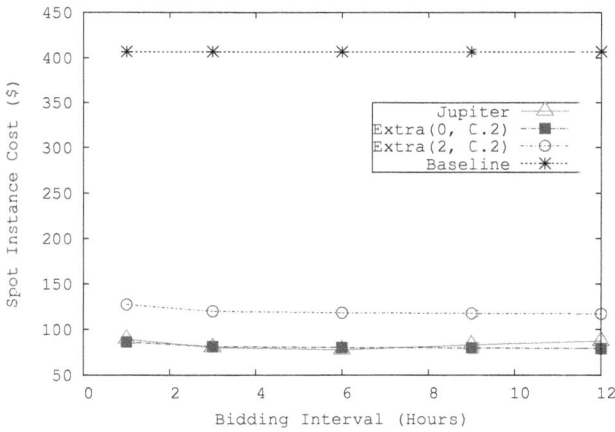

Figure 6: Spot instance cost of a distributed lock service under different bidding strategies from October 2014 to December 2014

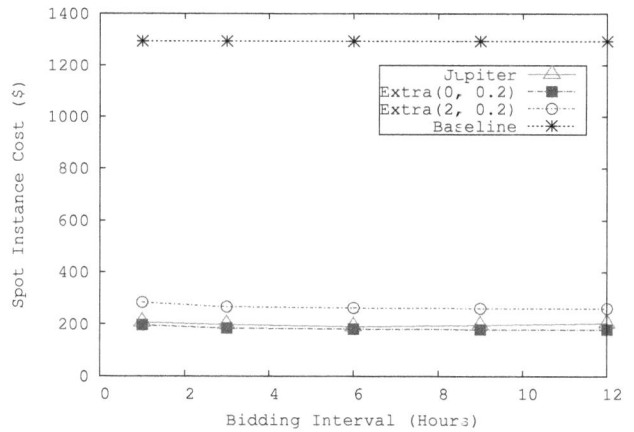

Figure 8: Spot instance cost of an erasure code based distributed storage service under different bidding strategies from October 2014 to December 2014

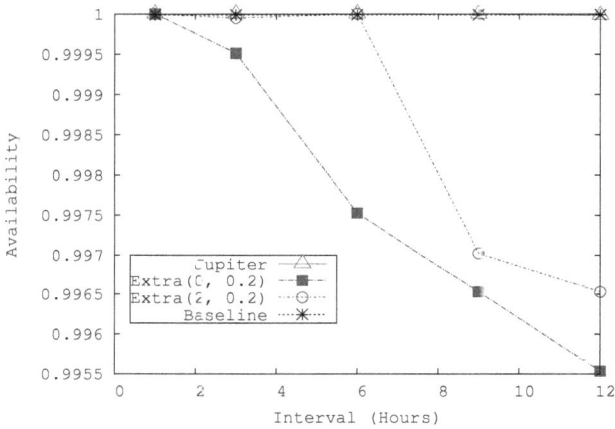

Figure 7: Availability of a distributed lock service under different bidding strategies from October 2014 to December 2014

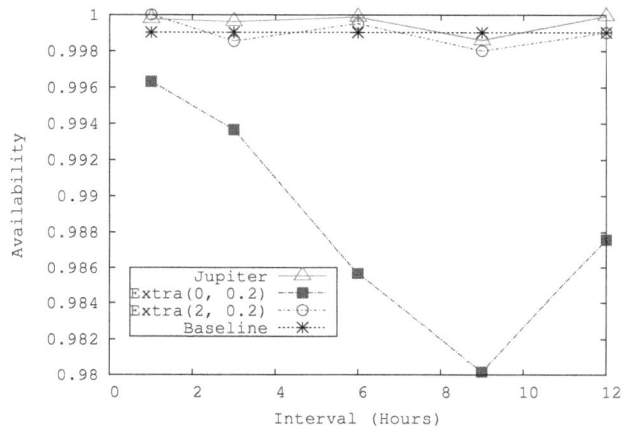

Figure 9: Availability of an erasure code based distributed storage service under different bidding strategies from October 2014 to December 2014

framework is a little higher than the strategy $Extra(0, 0.2)$. The cost of strategy $Extra(2, 0.2)$ is obviously higher than the other two bidding strategy.

There is no failure in the distributed lock service for our bidding framework besides the bidding interval of 12 hours (the availability is very close to 1.) as shown in Figure 7. The other two strategies cannot keep the same availability level at all. In the case of $Extra(0, 0.2)$, there are about 8 hours failure time in 11 weeks. This is far from the requirements of high availability. The availability of the distributed lock service under $Extra(2, 0.2)$ is higher than those under $Extra(0, 0.2)$. But it cannot always satisfy the constraints of service availability level in different bidding intervals.

For the $Extra(0, 0.2)$ strategy, the number of spot instances to bid is always 5. And $Extra(2, 0.2)$ strategy always bids 7 spot instances in each bidding interval. $Extra(2, 0.2)$ outperformed $Extra(0, 0.2)$ in the term of service availability level in all cases. This result demonstrates that system availability level is hard to keep without the failure probability of spot instances although the availability of distributed ser-

vices can be improved with additional spot instances. Furthermore, $Extra(2, 0.2)$ was charged about \$ 31 ∼ \$ 41 extra cost for the two additional spot instances. Our bidding framework outperformed the $Extra(2, 0.2)$ strategy in both cost and availability.

For the distributed storage service, Figure 8 shows that the cost of the distributed storage service under our bidding framework varies in different bidding interval. The best case is still the bidding interval of 6 hours. The cost of distributed storage service in this case is \$ 189.93. The cost of distributed storage service with on-demand instances is reduced by more than \$ 1000. The cost under the strategy $Extra(0, 0.2)$ is about \$ 183.5 in average. It is a littler lower than the cost under our bidding framework. This is mainly due to the too much out-of-bid failures of spot instances under $Extra(0, 0.2)$.

Our bidding framework kept the service availability level of the baseline except for the case of bidding interval of 9 hours. In this case, the failure time of the distributed storage service is a little longer than the requirements of the service availability level. Compared to our bidding framework, $Extra(0, 0.2)$ has a little lower cost but an unacceptable service availability level, and $Extra(2, 0.2)$ has a closed availability but much higher cost as shown in Figure 6 and 9.

In both Figure 6 and 8, the cost of our bidding framework changes a lot with different bidding intervals. A short bidding interval means launching new instances more frequently, which costs a lot on startup time. However, a long bidding interval loses some chance to change bidding with the spot prices. Our bidding framework should make higher bids for a longer bidding interval under availability consideration. The 6 hours bidding interval seems to be the most appropriate of all. An extension for our bidding framework is to detect the frequency of spot prices fluctuating and change the bidding interval correspondingly.

The "extra" strategies are simple and fixed. Without the knowledge of spot prices history data in each availability zone, making a same extra portion of bid is senseless. Furthermore, these strategies cannot keep high availability level as they have no spot instance failure probability estimation. Additional nodes and extra portion of bids reduce the failures potentially, but increase the cost. The results show that if using intuitive approaches, we cannot achieve both high availability and cost efficiency at the same time.

6. RELATED WORK

The advent of Spot Instance Market [30] has bring a new vision of cloud computing that computing instances can be traded like in a market where the price changes dynamically depending on the demand and supply. Research communities have shown a great interest on utilizing the spot instances for cost-efficient computing. Most of the current works focus on using spot instances for batch processing jobs such as MapReduce jobs. On the other hand, spot price models are proposed as the fluctuation of spot prices is fundamentally faced in the design of scheduling algorithms and fault tolerant mechanisms to be built over spot instance.

Chohan et al. [15] demonstrated that the execution of MapReduce jobs could speed up significantly by using spot instances as accelerators with an acceptable mount of monetary cost. Their work focused on bidding for performance using spot instances. There is no worry about the fault tolerance of computing jobs because the failures of spot instance have no impact on the execution of MapReduce jobs. The study of Chohan et al. revealed the possibility of using spot instances to speed up batching processing jobs. Instead of bidding for performance, our study mainly focuses on bidding for availability which is significantly different.

For MapReduce jobs, the failure of a task will not hurt the progress of the whole job. The tasks in such a job can be divided and scheduled to any available spot instance. As the bookkeeping task can run continuously by using normal on-demand instance during the lifetime of a job, all the tasks in the job will be scheduled and finished eventually. However, many MapReduce implementations, such as Hadoop [20], are not designed for the spot market environment. Even if the bookkeeping task does not run on a spot instance, several simultaneous spot instance terminations could cause all replicas of a data item to be lost. For fully taking advantage of spot instances, Spot Cloud MapReduce [24] was proposed as a MapReduce implementation that can make computing progress even if lots of nodes are in failure simultaneously.

By using the spot instance, the total cost of MapReduce job can be reduced while the completion time might be a little longer.

For compute-intensive, embarrassingly parallel jobs, adaptive checkpointing and work migration schemes were introduced to eliminate the impact of unexpected job terminations in [36, 35]. Checkpointing and work migration are two commonly used fault tolerance techniques for parallel computing jobs. These studies retrofitted these two fault tolerance mechanisms for reducing the job completion time with failure-prone spot instances. As the failures of such computing jobs can be fixed by re-execution like schemes, the fluctuation of spot prices do not need to be considered in these studies.

However, all these studies are targeted on the divisible computing jobs, which can shift the time of processing to when the computing resources are available. This is impossible for distributed services, which should be as available as possible and cannot delay users' request arbitrary. Moreover, as these works address the issue of frequent spot instance failures under a fixed bid, efficient bidding strategies based on statistical analysis of the spot price history are not considered.

Andrzejak et al. used a probabilistic model to capture the relations of continuous changing spot prices and job termination probabilities in [3], then a pre-computed and fixed optimum bid for a computing task can be given under SLA constraints. This simple approach is not suitable for the case of frequent fluctuation of spot prices. From a cloud service broker's perspective, Song et al. proposed a profit aware dynamic bidding algorithm based on Lyapunov optimization technique in [31]. These studies made statistical analysis of the spot prices, but do not involve the availability analysis of distributed services.

The design of bidding strategies and spot instance failure model rely on the spot price model. Although Amazon EC2 does not disclose the details of its underlying pricing algorithm, the spot price model has been studied from outside Amazon EC2. A statistical analysis for all spot instances in Amazon EC2 was provided in [22]. Ben-Yehuda et al. conjectured that the spot prices were usually not market-driven but determined by a pricing algorithm based on auto-regressive model in Amazon EC2 before October 2011 in [1]. The Markovian property of the spot price sequences had been verified in [15, 31], A discrete semi-Markovian chain was further applied to model the spot price variations in [31]. In our work, we embedded the semi-Markovian chain into the spot instance failure model and discretized the sojourn time of the semi-Markovian Chain into minutes as suggested by the spot prices data nowadays.

7. CONCLUSIONS

This paper addressed the problem of bidding for availability when building distributed service with the spot instances offered by Amazon EC2. We have pointed out several challenges of keeping service avilability level of a distributed system when using spot instances. The analysis is complicated because of the spot instance failure model. The out-of-bid failure is the main failure of spot instances. This is different from the node failure in traditional distributed systems. For estimating the failure probability of spot instances, we employed a semi-Markovian chain to model the fluctuation of spot prices. The availability of a distributed service built with spot instances can thus be estimated from the failure probabilities of instances instead of the number of simultaneous node failure that can be tolerant. The problem of bidding for availability is formalized as a non-linear programming model. The objective is to minimize the cost of spot instances and the constraint represents the availability requirements of the distributed service. However, solving this non-linear programming is NP-hard. Exhaustive search like methods is not practical at all. We presented a bidding framework to make practical solutions with a near-optimal bidding algorithm using enumerate and greedy strategy. Two fundamental distributed services, distributed lock service and erasure code based distributed storage service, are used to verify the effectiveness of the bidding framework. Our bidding framework can reduce the costs by 81.23% and 85.32% for lock service and storage service respectively while still keeping the availability level the same as it is by using on-demand instances.

8. ACKNOWLEDGMENTS

We would like to thank all the reviewers for their valuable comments and helpful suggestions. We also thank Yong Hu, Mingxing Zhang, Ce Guo for useful discussions about the spot price model and bidding framework. This work is supported by Natural Science Foundation of China (61433008, 61373145, 61170210, U1435216), National High-Tech R&D (863) Program of China (2012AA012600), Chinese Special Project of Science and Technology (2013zx01039-002-002).

9. REFERENCES

[1] O. Agmon Ben-Yehuda, M. Ben-Yehuda, A. Schuster, and D. Tsafrir. Deconstructing amazon ec2 spot instance pricing. *ACM Trans. Econ. Comput.*, 1(3):16:1–16:20, Sept. 2013.

[2] Y. Amir and A. Wool. Optimal availability quorum systems: Theory and practice. *Information Processing Letters*, 65(5):223 – 228, 1998.

[3] A. Andrzejak, D. Kondo, and S. Yi. Decision model for cloud computing under sla constraints. In *Proceedings of the 2010 IEEE International Symposium on Modeling, Analysis and Simulation of Computer and Telecommunication Systems*, MASCOTS '10, pages 257–266, Washington, DC, USA, 2010. IEEE Computer Society.

[4] https://aws.amazon.com/about-aws/globalinfrastructure/.

[5] http://aws.amazon.com/ec2/instance-types/.

[6] http://docs.aws.amazon.com/AWSEC2/latest/UserGuide/using-spot-limits.html.

[7] http://aws.amazon.com/ec2/sla/.

[8] J. Baker, C. Bond, J. C. Corbett, J. Furman, A. Khorlin, J. Larson, J.-M. Léon, Y. Li, A. Lloyd, and V. Yushprakh. Megastore: Providing scalable, highly available storage for interactive services. In *CIDR*, volume 11, pages 223–234, 2011.

[9] V. Barbu and N. Limnios. *Semi-Markov Chains and Hidden Semi-Markov Models Toward Applications: Their Use in Reliability and DNA Analysis*. Springer Publishing Company, Incorporated, 1 edition, 2008.

[10] W. J. Bolosky, D. Bradshaw, R. B. Haagens, N. P. Kusters, and P. Li. Paxos replicated state machines as

[11] the basis of a high-performance data store. In *Proceedings of the 8th USENIX Conference on Networked Systems Design and Implementation*, NSDI'11, pages 141–154, Berkeley, CA, USA, 2011. USENIX Association.

[11] https://github.com/boto/boto.

[12] D. R. Brillinger, P. M. Guttorp, and F. P. Schoenberg. Point processes, temporal. In *Encyclopedia of Environmetrics*. John Wiley & Sons, Ltd, 2006.

[13] M. Burrows. The chubby lock service for loosely-coupled distributed systems. In *Proceedings of the 7th Symposium on Operating Systems Design and Implementation*, OSDI '06, pages 335–350, Berkeley, CA, USA, 2006. USENIX Association.

[14] B. Calder, J. Wang, A. Ogus, N. Nilakantan, A. Skjolsvold, S. McKelvie, Y. Xu, S. Srivastav, J. Wu, H. Simitci, J. Haridas, C. Uddaraju, H. Khatri, A. Edwards, V. Bedekar, S. Mainali, R. Abbasi, A. Agarwal, M. F. u. Haq, M. I. u. Haq, D. Bhardwaj, S. Dayanand, A. Adusumilli, M. McNett, S. Sankaran, K. Manivannan, and L. Rigas. Windows azure storage: A highly available cloud storage service with strong consistency. In *Proceedings of the Twenty-Third ACM Symposium on Operating Systems Principles*, SOSP '11, pages 143–157, New York, NY, USA, 2011. ACM.

[15] N. Chohan, C. Castillo, M. Spreitzer, M. Steinder, A. Tantawi, and C. Krintz. See spot run: using spot instances for mapreduce workflows. In *Proceedings of the 2nd USENIX conference on Hot topics in cloud computing*, pages 7–7. USENIX Association, 2010.

[16] J. C. Corbett, J. Dean, M. Epstein, A. Fikes, C. Frost, J. J. Furman, S. Ghemawat, A. Gubarev, C. Heiser, P. Hochschild, W. Hsieh, S. Kanthak, E. Kogan, H. Li, A. Lloyd, S. Melnik, D. Mwaura, D. Nagle, S. Quinlan, R. Rao, L. Rolig, Y. Saito, M. Szymaniak, C. Taylor, R. Wang, and D. Woodford. Spanner: Google's globally-distributed database. In *Proceedings of the 10th USENIX Conference on Operating Systems Design and Implementation*, OSDI'12, pages 251–264, Berkeley, CA, USA, 2012. USENIX Association.

[17] G. DeCandia, D. Hastorun, M. Jampani, G. Kakulapati, A. Lakshman, A. Pilchin, S. Sivasubramanian, P. Vosshall, and W. Vogels. Dynamo: Amazon's highly available key-value store. In *Proceedings of Twenty-first ACM SIGOPS Symposium on Operating Systems Principles*, SOSP '07, pages 205–220, New York, NY, USA, 2007. ACM.

[18] D. K. Gifford. Weighted voting for replicated data. In *Proceedings of the Seventh ACM Symposium on Operating Systems Principles*, SOSP '79, pages 150–162, New York, NY, USA, 1979. ACM.

[19] G. Grimmett and D. Stirzaker. *Probability and random processes*, volume 2. Oxford Univ Press, 1992.

[20] http://hadoop.apache.org.

[21] C. Huang, H. Simitci, Y. Xu, A. Ogus, B. Calder, P. Gopalan, J. Li, and S. Yekhanin. Erasure coding in windows azure storage. In *Proceedings of the 2012 USENIX Conference on Annual Technical Conference*, USENIX ATC'12, pages 2–2, Berkeley, CA, USA, 2012. USENIX Association.

[22] B. Javadi, R. K. Thulasiramy, and R. Buyya. Statistical modeling of spot instance prices in public

cloud environments. In *Proceedings of the 2011 Fourth IEEE International Conference on Utility and Cloud Computing*, UCC '11, pages 219–228, Washington, DC, USA, 2011. IEEE Computer Society.

[23] L. Lamport. Paxos made simple. *ACM Sigact News*, 32(4):18–25, 2001.

[24] H. Liu. Cutting mapreduce cost with spot market. In *Proceedings of the 3rd USENIX Conference on Hot Topics in Cloud Computing*, HotCloud'11, pages 6–6, Berkeley, CA, USA, 2011. USENIX Association.

[25] M. Mao and M. Humphrey. A performance study on the vm startup time in the cloud. In *Cloud Computing (CLOUD), 2012 IEEE 5th International Conference on*, pages 423–430, June 2012.

[26] S. Mu, K. Chen, Y. Wu, and W. Zheng. When paxos meets erasure code: Reduce network and storage cost in state machine replication. In *Proceedings of the 23rd International Symposium on High-performance Parallel and Distributed Computing*, HPDC '14, pages 61–72, New York, NY, USA, 2014. ACM.

[27] D. Peleg and A. Wool. The availability of quorum systems. *Information and Computation*, 123(2):210 – 223, 1995.

[28] L. Rizzo. Effective erasure codes for reliable computer communication protocols. *SIGCOMM Comput. Commun. Rev.*, 27(2):24–36, Apr. 1997.

[29] M. Sathiamoorthy, M. Asteris, D. Papailiopoulos, A. G. Dimakis, R. Vadali, S. Chen, and D. Borthakur. Xoring elephants: novel erasure codes for big data. In *Proceedings of the 39th international conference on*

Very Large Data Bases, PVLDB'13, pages 325–336. VLDB Endowment, 2013.

[30] `http://aws.amazon.com/ec2/purchasing-options/ spot-instances/`.

[31] Y. Song, M. Zafer, and K.-W. Lee. Optimal bidding in spot instance market. In *INFOCOM, 2012 Proceedings IEEE*, pages 190–198. IEEE, 2012.

[32] M. Spasojevic and P. Berman. Voting as the optimal static pessimistic scheme for managing replicated data. *Parallel and Distributed Systems, IEEE Transactions on*, 5(1):64–73, Jan 1994.

[33] Z. Tong and R. Kain. Vote assignments in weighted voting mechanisms. In *Reliable Distributed Systems, 1988. Proceedings., Seventh Symposium on*, pages 138–143, Oct 1988.

[34] S. Wee. Debunking real-time pricing in cloud computing. In *Cluster, Cloud and Grid Computing (CCGrid), 2011 11th IEEE/ACM International Symposium on*, pages 585–590, May 2011.

[35] S. Yi, A. Andrzejak, and D. Kondo. Monetary cost-aware checkpointing and migration on amazon cloud spot instances. *IEEE Transactions on Services Computing*, 5(4):512–524, 2012.

[36] S. Yi, D. Kondo, and A. Andrzejak. Reducing costs of spot instances via checkpointing in the amazon elastic compute cloud. In *Cloud Computing (CLOUD), 2010 IEEE 3rd International Conference on*, pages 236–243, July 2010.

Planning and Optimization in TORQUE Resource Manager

Dalibor Klusáček*†
klusacek@cesnet.cz

Václav Chlumský†
vchlumsky@cesnet.cz

Hana Rudová*
hanka@fi.muni.cz

*Faculty of Informatics
Masaryk University
Brno, Czech Republic

†CESNET
Association of Legal Entities
Prague, Czech Republic

ABSTRACT

We presents a unique advanced job scheduler for the widely used TORQUE Resource Manager. Unlike common schedulers that are using queuing approach and heuristics, our solution uses planning (job schedule construction) and schedule optimization by a local search-inspired metaheuristic, achieving better predictability, performance and fairness with respect to common queue-based approaches. The suitability and good performance of our solution is demonstrated both by "synthetic" experiments as well as by our real-life performance results that are coming from the deployment of our scheduler in the production infrastructure of the Czech Centre for Education, Reasearch and Innovation in ICT (CERIT Scientific Cloud).

Categories and Subject Descriptors

D.4.1 [**OPERATING SYSTEMS**]: Process Management—*Scheduling*;
I.2.8 [**ARTIFICIAL INTELLIGENCE**]: Problem Solving, Control Methods, and Search—*Heuristic methods, Plan execution, formation, and generation, Scheduling*

General Terms

Algorithms, Performance

Keywords

Scheduler, Planning, Optimization, Metaheuristic

1. BACKGROUND AND MOTIVATION

Many studies in the past two decades focused on the problem of efficient job scheduling in large computational systems such as HPC clusters and grids [11]. For this purpose, advanced methods using *planning* [3] and/or some form of a *metaheuristic* [9, 10] have been frequently proposed, claiming better performance with respect to standard queue-based solutions. However, these works were often theoretical or used a (simplified) model together with a

HPDC'15, June 15–19, 2015, Portland, Oregon, USA.
Copyright is held by the owner/author(s). Publication rights licensed to ACM.
ACM 978-1-4503-3550-8/15/06 ...$15.00.
http://dx.doi.org/10.1145/2749246.2749266.

simulator, while realistic implementations in actual resource managers were not available for various reasons. Therefore, those promising results were *rarely reflected in the practice*. In fact, typical mainstream resource management systems/schedulers such as PBS Pro, TORQUE, SLURM or Moab/Maui are still using a rather limited set of scheduling policies [1, 4]. Neither metaheuristics nor other advanced optimization techniques are used in current mainstream systems. A notable exception represents the GORBA system [8], supporting planning along with nature-inspired optimization techniques. However, this system represents a proprietary solution and it is probably no longer operational.

This paper builds on the top of our earlier "theoretical" works [6, 5] which have proposed new methods for efficient use of metaheuristic algorithms for multi-criteria scheduling in grids. However, instead of a real resource manager, these works only used a simulator while considering simplified problem models. For example, job memory requirements were ignored [5] and precise job runtimes were used instead of more realistic inaccurate estimates [6].

The major contribution of this work is that *we bridge the gap between theory and practice*. We present a new unique job scheduler compatible with a production TORQUE Resource Manager, which supports planning and optimization. Importantly, this scheduler has been *successfully used in the practice* since July 2014 within a real computing infrastructure. The presented scheduler uses a job schedule which represents a preliminary job execution plan, such that an expected start time is known for every job prior its execution. Moreover, this plan can be easily evaluated in order to identify possible inefficiencies. Then, a local search-inspired metaheuristic is used to optimize the schedule with respect to considered optimization criteria. We use both *performance-related criteria* such as wait time and slowdown as well as *fairness-related criterion* that is used to manage user-to-user fairness. We emphasize realistic aspects by considering inaccurate job runtime estimates and complex job characteristics including, e.g., RAM memory and HDD storage requirements along with common CPU-related demands.

The suitability and good performance of our solution is demonstrated both by "synthetic" experiments that use historical workloads, as well as by *real-life performance results* that are coming from the deployment of our scheduler in the Czech Centre for Education, Reasearch and Innovation in ICT (CERIT Scientific Cloud), which is the largest partition of the Czech national grid and cloud infrastructure MetaCentrum, containing $\sim 5,000$ CPUs in 8 clusters.

2. PROPOSED SCHEDULER

The proposed advanced job scheduler has been built within the open source TORQUE Resource Manager system, which is an advanced open-source product providing control over batch jobs and distributed computing resources [1]. It consists of three main entities—the server (`pbs_server`), the job scheduler (`pbs_sched`) and the `pbs_mom` node daemons as shown in Figure 1.

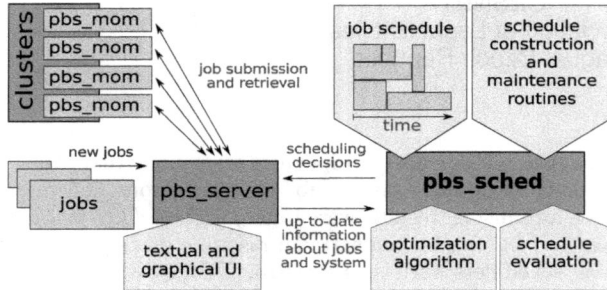

Figure 1: Extended TORQUE Resource Manager.

The scheduler makes the scheduling decisions and interacts with the server in order to allocate jobs onto available nodes. While the server and the node daemons are mostly unchanged, the original simple queue-based FCFS scheduler [1] available in the TORQUE's scheduler entity (`pbs_sched`) has been replaced with our own implementation. When using TORQUE, it is a common practice to use other than the default scheduler [1].

2.1 Major Extensions

As shown in Figure 1, the new scheduler contains four major parts. The first part is the data structure that represents the *job schedule*. The schedule is built using a default *schedule construction* algorithm, which is an optimized variant[1] of the well known *Conservative backfilling* [7], i.e., a newly incoming job is added at the earliest available time slot in the schedule. Also, auxiliary *maintenance routines* are used to adjust the schedule in time subject to dynamic events such as (early) job completions, machine failures, etc.

Remaining parts perform the *evaluation* and the *schedule optimization*. Since schedule is created, it can be periodically *evaluated* in order to identify possible inefficiencies. Then, a local search-inspired metaheuristic called *Random Search (RS)* [5] is used to find better schedules with respect to applied optimization criteria that cover both the performance and the fairness. We minimize the *avg. wait time* and the *avg. bounded slowdown* to improve the overall performance [2]. *User-to-user fairness* is optimized using the *Normalized User Wait Time (NUWT)* metric [6]. For a given user, NUWT is the total user wait time divided by the amount of previously consumed system resources by that user. Then, the user-to-user fairness is optimized by minimizing the variance of all NUWT values [6]. It follows the classical fair-share principles, i.e., a user with lower resource usage and/or higher total wait time gets higher priority over more active users and vice versa [4]. The calculation of NUWT reflects consumptions of multiple resources (CPU and RAM utilization), representing a solution suitable for

systems having heterogeneous workloads and/or infrastructures [4].

The *Random Search (RS)* optimization algorithm performs random changes in the existing schedule by moving a random job into a random position and then evaluates such changes using the above criteria. Only improving changes are accepted. RS is fully randomized and does not employ any "advanced" search strategy. In fact, in our earlier research [5] we have observed that such a simple randomized optimization is very robust and produces good results, often beating more advanced methods such as Simulated Annealing or Tabu Search. In addition, the advantage of RS is that—unlike, e.g., Simulated Annealing—its performance does not rely on additional (hand-tuned) parameters.

Beside the newly developed scheduler, we have also extended the `pbs_server` such that it can read job-related data from the schedule and then provide them to the users. For this purpose, the `pbs_server` queries the schedule and then displays the information obtained. We support both textual (`qstat` command) and graphical user interfaces (a web application called *PBSMon*[2]).

3. EXPERIMENTS AND DEPLOYMENT

Our solution has been evaluated both experimentally (Section 3.1) and in the practice (Section 3.2).

3.1 Experimental Evaluation

In our prior work [5], the proposed RS algorithm have been tested in a simulator demonstrating very good performance with respect to standard queue-based algorithms including popular First Come First Served (FCFS), EASY or Conservative backfilling. However, it was absolutely necessary to test the actual implementation within TORQUE prior deployment to see whether it will still perform reasonably. We present the main results in this section.

The experiments were performed on an Intel i5 3.1 GHz machine with 8 GB of RAM using publicly available workload traces from the Parallel Workloads Archive (HPC2N and KTH-SP2 logs) and our own workload (Zewura log[3]) collected in the Czech national grid and cloud infrastructure *MetaCentrum*. As we use an actual scheduler instead of a simulator we cannot use the whole workload "as is" since each of these three workloads lasted for several months and it would take too much time to use the whole log. Instead, we have extracted several job intervals from each workload where there was a significant contention lasting at least 5 days. Eight such sub-workloads were used—four of them from the Zewura workload, two from the HPC2N log and the two remaining came from the KTH-SP2. Each workload is described using the format `WORKLOAD_NAME [jobs: START_ID - END_ID]` where `START_ID` denotes the first job in the workload while `END_ID` is the identifier of the last job in the original workload log.

The proposed scheduler using RS metaheuristic has been evaluated against two scheduling algorithms: our optimized implementation of Conservative backfilling (BF) and the scheduling algorithm that was originally applied in Meta-Centrum (META). It is very appropriate to compare RS with plain Conservative backfilling (BF) to see the profit

---

[1]We have optimized the complexity of the *schedule-compression* routine applied in Conservative backfilling [5].

[2]http://www.metacentrum.cz/en/devel/pbsmon/

[3]The Zewura log and the detailed description is available at: http://www.fi.muni.cz/~xklusac/workload.

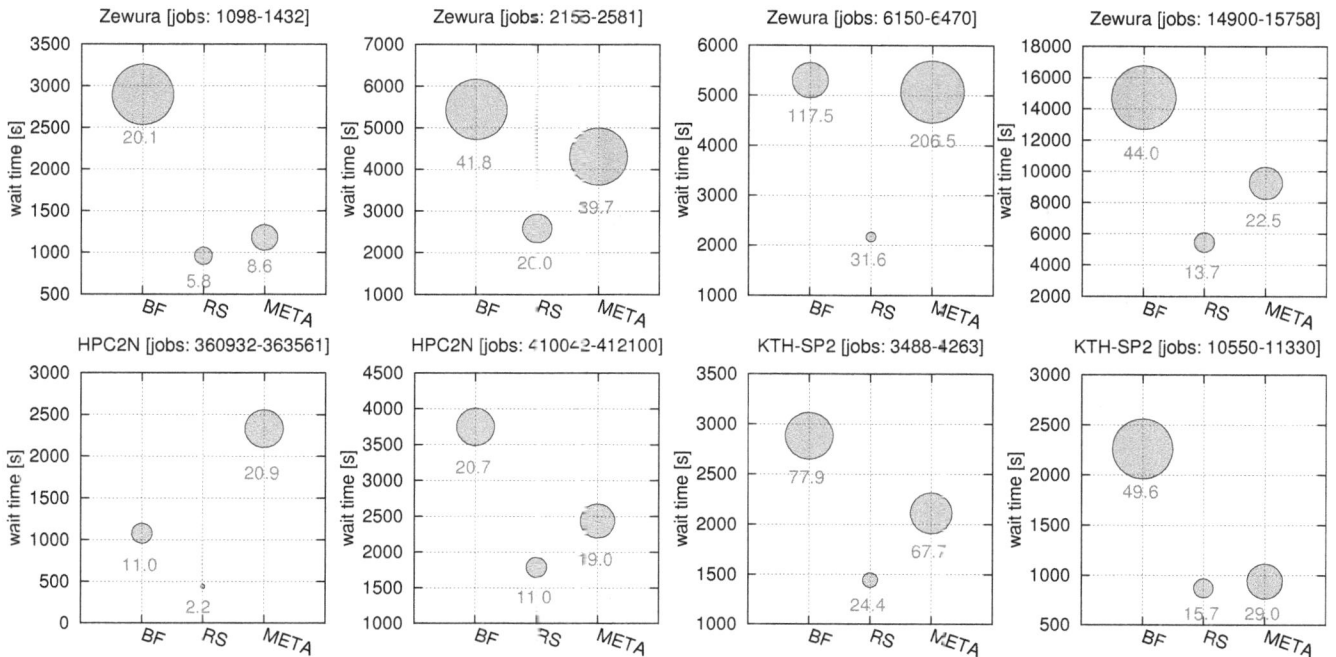

Figure 2: The avg. wait time (y-axis) and the avg. bounded slowdown (circle) for all eight data sets.

obtained via the RS metaheuristic.[4] META is a form of aggressive backfilling where waiting jobs get a reservation only when their waiting time reaches a given threshold. Then, these long waiting jobs obtain a full priority and cannot be further delayed to avoid starvation. Trivial FCFS was also tested but it performed very poor and we do not present it in the results. All simulations used the original inaccurate runtime estimates.

Figure 2 presents the main results for all eight data sets. We are using the *avg. wait time* and the *avg. bounded slowdown* criteria for comparison. Bubble charts are used to display wait times and corresponding slowdowns simultaneously — the y-axis depicts the avg. wait time while the size of the circle represents the avg. bounded slowdown. The actual value of bounded slowdown is shown as a label bellow each circle. In case of wait time criterion, the applied optimization algorithm (RS) is capable to significantly improve the overall performance as delivered by Conservative backfilling (BF). Moreover, in all eight data sets RS offers nontrivial improvement with respect to the META algorithm that represents the default solution applied in Meta-Centrum. It is important to notice that RS is able to improve both criteria simultaneously, i.e., also the slowdown is significantly better when RS is applied. As the slowdown represents the relation among the wait time and the job runtime, shorter slowdowns mean that short jobs are executed fluently without major delays which is very desirable.

Concerning fairness, we have used the NUWT metric (see Section 2.1) and RS again outperformed both BF and META. Compared to BF, the mean improvement of the average NUWT was 38%, while decreasing the variance of all NUWT values by 40%. Concerning META, those average improvements were 55% and 34%, respectively.

3.2 Real-Life Deployment

To further support our promising results we also present real-life data that were collected in the Czech Centre for Education, Research and Innovation in ICT (*CERIT Scientific Cloud*[5]), where our new scheduler has been operationally used since July 2014. CERIT Scientific Cloud shares its resources with the *MetaCentrum* national operator. Both MetaCentrum and CERIT use the same version of TORQUE resource manager. Before July 2014, CERIT was using the same scheduler (META) as MetaCentrum. Currently, CERIT contains eight computer clusters with ∼ 5,000 CPU cores that are managed by our new scheduler (RS).

Following results based on direct comparison are computed using historic workload data that were collected when either the original META scheduler or the new RS scheduler were used, respectively. In the former case (META), the data come from the January – June 2014 period while in the latter case (RS) the data cover the following six months period (July – December 2014).

The first example shown in Figure 3 (left) compares the average cluster utilization before (META) and after the new solution (RS) was introduced.[6] The new solution is more efficient with respect to machine usage as the average CPU utilization has increased significantly. When considering the average amount of used CPU hours per day (see the 2nd chart from the left in Figure 3), we have observed that — on average — the new scheduler was able to use additional 10,000 CPU hours per day compared to the previous scheduler. This represents 418 fully used CPUs (9.2% of all CPUs) that would otherwise remain idle.

Beside the utilization, we have also performed further data analysis focusing on additional performance indicators.

---

[4]Without the RS optimization, the scheduler uses our implementation of Conservative backfilling (BF) (see Section 2.1).

[5]http://www.cerit-sc.cz
[6]Only clusters available during both periods are considered.

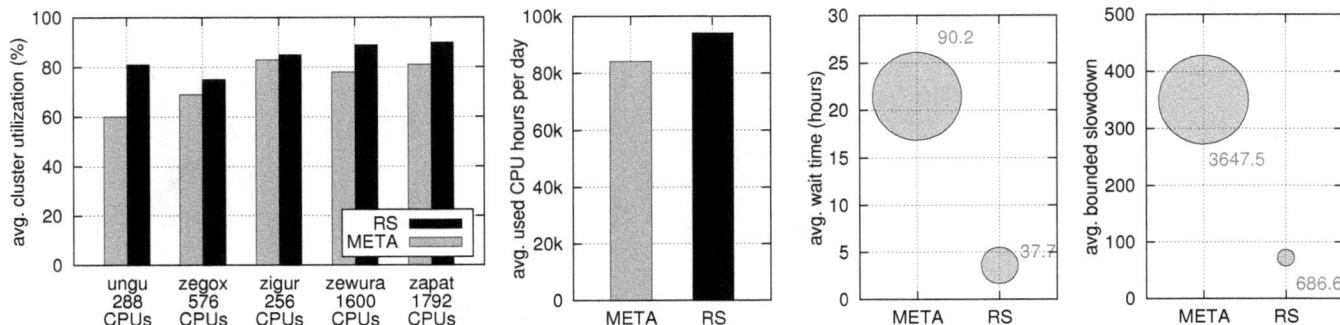

Figure 3: Real-life comparison: (from the left to right) the avg. cluster utilization, the avg. CPU hours used per day, the avg. wait time (with std. deviation) and the avg. bounded slowdown (with std. deviation).

First, we have compared the avg. wait time and the avg. bounded slowdown as well as their standard deviations for the two considered schedulers. The results are shown in Figure 3 (3rd and 4th chart from the left, respectively) using bubble charts — the y-axis depicts an average value while the size of the circle represents the standard deviation of a metric. The actual value of standard deviation is shown as a label next to each circle. As we have observed, the original META scheduler often produced very bad wait times and slowdowns for many jobs, causing high average values and large deviations. From this point of view, RS was much more efficient, significantly decreasing both the averages and the deviations. Given the increased utilization observed in Figure 3 (left), this is a very good result.

To sum up, our new RS scheduler has increased the utilization in CERIT Scientific Cloud system, without producing any significant undesirable side effect. In fact, also the avg. wait time and the avg. bounded slowdown have been significantly reduced compared to the original META scheduler.

4. CONCLUSION

This paper has presented a new scheduler for the widely used TORQUE Resource Manager, which uses planning, evaluation and a metaheuristic optimization algorithm to increase the quality of generated solutions with respect to both performance- and fairness-related criteria [6, 5]. Most importantly, the presented scheduler is used in a production computing system where it performs as expected, demonstrating that a complex scheduler using planning and advanced optimization techniques can be used in the practice. The proposed scheduler can be freely obtained at: http://www.metacentrum.cz/docs/pbts.

Acknowledgments

This work was kindly supported by the LM2010005 project funded by the Ministry of Education, Youth, and Sports of the Czech Republic and by the grant No. P202/12/0306 funded by the Grant Agency of the Czech Republic. Workload logs were kindly provided by Parallel Workloads Archive (KTH-SP2, HPC2N) and MetaCentrum (Zewura).

5. REFERENCES

[1] Adaptive Computing Enterprises, Inc. *TORQUE Admininstrator Guide, version 5.1.0*, April 2015. http://docs.adaptivecomputing.com.

[2] D. G. Feitelson, L. Rudolph, U. Schwiegelshohn, K. C. Sevcik, and P. Wong. Theory and practice in parallel job scheduling. In D. G. Feitelson and L. Rudolph, editors, *Job Scheduling Strategies for Parallel Processing*, volume 1291 of *LNCS*, pages 1–34. Springer Verlag, 1997.

[3] M. Hovestadt, O. Kao, A. Keller, and A. Streit. Scheduling in HPC resource management systems: Queueing vs. planning. In D. G. Feitelson, L. Rudolph, and U. Schwiegelshohn, editors, *Job Scheduling Strategies for Parallel Processing*, volume 2862 of *LNCS*, pages 1–20. Springer Verlag, 2003.

[4] D. Jackson, Q. Snell, and M. Clement. Core algorithms of the Maui scheduler. In D. G. Feitelson and L. Rudolph, editors, *Job Scheduling Strategies for Parallel Processing*, volume 2221 of *LNCS*, pages 87–102. Springer, 2001.

[5] D. Klusáček. *Event-based Optimization of Schedules for Grid Jobs*. PhD thesis, Masaryk University, 2011.

[6] D. Klusáček and H. Rudová. Performance and fairness for users in parallel job scheduling. In W. Cirne, editor, *Job Scheduling Strategies for Parallel Processing*, volume 7698 of *LNCS*, pages 235–252. Springer, 2012.

[7] A. W. Mu'alem and D. G. Feitelson. Utilization, predictability, workloads, and user runtime estimates in scheduling the IBM SP2 with backfilling. *IEEE Transactions on Parallel and Distributed Systems*, 12(6):529–543, 2001.

[8] W. Süß, W. Jakob, A. Quinte, and K.-U. Stucky. GORBA: A global optimising resource broker embedded in a Grid resource management system. In *International Conference on Parallel and Distributed Computing Systems, PDCS 2005*, pages 19–24. IASTED/ACTA Press, 2005.

[9] P. Switalski and F. Seredynski. Scheduling parallel batch jobs in grids with evolutionary metaheuristics. *Journal of Scheduling*, pages 1–13, 2014.

[10] F. Xhafa and A. Abraham. *Metaheuristics for Scheduling in Distributed Computing Environments*, volume 146 of *Studies in Comp. Intel.* Springer, 2008.

[11] F. Xhafa and A. Abraham. Computational models and heuristic methods for Grid scheduling problems. *Future Generation Computer Systems*, 26(4):608–621, 2010.

Cutting the Cost of Hosting Online Services Using Cloud Spot Markets

Xin He, Prashant Shenoy, Ramesh Sitaraman and David Irwin
University of Massachusetts Amherst
{xhe, shenoy, ramesh}@cs.umass.edu, irwin@ecs.umass.edu

ABSTRACT

The use of cloud servers to host modern Internet-based services is becoming increasingly common. Today's cloud platforms offer a choice of server types, including non-revocable on-demand servers and cheaper but revocable spot servers. A service provider requiring servers can bid in the spot market where the price of a spot server changes dynamically according to the current supply and demand for cloud resources. Spot servers are usually cheap, but can be revoked by the cloud provider when the cloud resources are scarce. While it is well-known that spot servers can reduce the cost of performing time-flexible interruption-tolerant tasks, we explore the novel possibility of using spot servers for reducing the cost of hosting an Internet-based service such as an e-commerce site that must *always* be on and the penalty for service unavailability is high.

By using the spot markets, we show that it is feasible to host an always-on Internet-based service at one-third to one-fifth the cost of hosting the same service in the traditional fashion using dedicated non-revocable servers. To achieve these savings, we devise a cloud scheduler that reduces the cost by intelligently bidding for spot servers. Further the scheduler uses novel VM migration mechanisms to quickly migrate the service between spot servers and on-demand servers to avoid potential service disruptions due to spot server revocations by the cloud provider. Our work provides the first feasibility study of using cloud spot markets to significantly reduce the cost of hosting always-on Internet-based services without sacrificing service availability.

Categories and Subject Descriptors

C.4 [**Performance of Systems**]: Reliability, availability, and serviceability

Keywords

Cloud computing; spot markets; cost optimization

HPDC'15, June 15–20, 2015, Portland, Oregon, USA.
Copyright is held by the owner/author(s). Publication rights licensed to ACM.
ACM 978-1-4503-3550-8/15/06 ...$15.00.
http://dx.doi.org/10.1145/2749246.2749275 .

1. INTRODUCTION

Cloud computing has become the paradigm of choice for building low-cost, scalable Internet-based services. Cloud providers such as Amazon AWS, Microsoft Azure [1], and Google Compute Engine [2] operate large, distributed computing infrastructures that provide computing and storage resources that can be leased by service providers. Cloud providers offer a number of benefits to service providers such as a pay-as-you-go model and flexible, on-demand allocation of resources to hosted services. A key business driver for the rapid adoption of cloud computing by service providers is the reduction in infrastructure costs. Unlike the traditional method of buying dedicated infrastructure, which must be provisioned in advance for the peak demand, leasing cloud servers enables the service provider to scale the service as it grows over time and also exploit just-in-time allocation of capacity to handle peak workloads. Consequently, leasing cloud servers is often more economical than building dedicated infrastructure, especially for services with dynamic or growing workloads.

Today's cloud platforms offer a variety of server types to meet the diverse needs of their hosted services. Cloud servers vary in the offered resource configurations, the leasing cost and the service model offered to customers. For instance, *on-demand* servers offer a fixed rental cost and a *non-revocable* model, where the customers pay a fixed cost and can voluntarily relinquish the server when they no longer need it. In contrast, *spot* servers offer a variable rental cost and a *revocable* model, where the customer bids an upper limit on the price they are willing to pay for a server. The cost of these spot servers fluctuates over time and an allocated spot server may be revoked by the cloud provider when its price rises above the bid price the customer is willing to pay for the server. Spot servers allow a cloud provider to offer unused server capacity at a lower price to customers, while allowing the cloud provider to revoke these servers at any time in order to fulfill requests for higher-priced on-demand servers.

Internet-based services that use the cloud vary significantly in their service requirements. At one end of the spectrum lie data-intensive cloud applications that use cloud servers to run large data analytics tasks (e.g., using MapReduce); such "big data" applications often run in batch mode with the results made available within a specified time period. As noted in Amazon's description of their cloud service [3], spot servers are a popular choice for reducing the cost of running "interruption-tolerant" and "time-flexible" tasks, such as data-intensive batch analytics and scientific computing. Indeed, there has been recent research [6] [19] [23] [13] on using spot markets to provide non-realtime services that can be performed in batch mode at a reduced cost.

At the other end of the spectrum are *always-on* Internet-based services that serve user requests in real-time. Providers of web content such as CNN, video content such as NetFlix, application portals such as Salesforce, e-commerce portals such as Walmart.com, and social networking sites such as Facebook all belong in this category. Traditionally always-on Internet-based services have relied on dedicated deployed servers owned by the service provider or a third-party content delivery network. Recently, in part to reduce costs, there has been a trend for always-on services to use non-revocable on-demand servers from the cloud markets to meet their infrastructure needs. For instance, Netflix uses Amazon's on-demand cloud services to operate their backend origin infrastructure that stores and serves out videos [4].

In this paper, we ask the intriguing question: *can an always-on Internet-based service utilize the cloud spot markets to host their service at a lower cost without sacrificing service availability?* We explore the feasibility of such a proposition and seek to quantify the cost reduction that is possible in comparison with using the more traditional option of non-revocable on-demand servers. Although the use of spot servers can lower the cost of hosting an Internet-based service, our approach raises new challenges since spot servers *can be revoked at any time.* Such a revocation can potentially cause unavailability of the service for which the penalty is high. It is worth noting that a widely-accepted industry requirement for an always-on Internet-based service such as an e-commerce site is to have *at least* four nines (99.99%) of availability. Alternately, the unavailability of the service can be at most one basis point (0.01%), which roughly translates to 4.3 minutes of downtime per month. The need to keep unavailability very low can be understood from the perspective of a large e-tailer, which could lose a significant amount of revenue if their website is down even for a few minutes during a peak hour [14]. To address this key challenge, we design a novel approach that combines intelligent bidding algorithms that reduce the frequency of revocations and combine it with intelligent migration mechanisms that can quickly migrate a service running on a spot server that is being revoked to an on-demand server. We show that as a result the service unavailability can be significantly reduced so as to be within an acceptable range.

Our Contributions: To our knowledge, our work is the first to examine the feasibility of using cloud spot markets to reduce the cost of always-on Internet-based services, while ensuring that service unavailability is acceptably small. Our work provides significant impetus for service providers to build systems that use the spot markets in a novel way to reduce their costs. We make the following specific contributions.

1. While VM migration mechanisms have been studied in other contexts, our work is the first to use clever migration in the cloud context to avoid service unavailability.

2. We propose proactive bidding algorithms that migrate a spot server before it is revoked by the cloud provider, in contrast with reactive algorithms that migrate *after* the spot server is revoked. We show that being proactive reduces both the service cost and unavailability in comparison with being reactive.

3. We compare three different migration mechanisms: memory checkpointing, memory checkpointing with lazy restore and live. We conclude that using checkpointing alone or using it in combination with live migration does not provide sufficiently low service unavailability. However, checkpointing in combination with lazy restore provides a service unavailability that is acceptable, so as to be a viable alternative for always-on Internet-based services. Further, the addition of live migration halves the unavailability even further.

4. We study multiple possible schemes for hosting Internet-based services on the spot market. First, we study hosting an Internet-based service using our cloud scheduler with the option to use only a single spot market in a single geographical region. In this case, the cost achieved by our scheduler is one-third to one-fifth of the baseline cost of hosting the same Internet-based service using only on-demand servers. If our scheduler has the ability to use multiple markets within the same region, the cost decreases further. And, if the scheduler has the ability to use multiple regions, the cost decreases even further. In the latter two cases, our scheduler exploits the lack correlation in the spot prices across different markets and different regions to achieve a lower cost.

Roadmap: The remainder of this paper is organized as follows. Section 2 presents background on cloud platforms and markets. Section 3 presents the design of our cloud scheduler, and Section 4 presents our experimental results. We present related work in Sec 7 and conclude in Sec 8.

2. BACKGROUND

In this section, we present background on cloud platforms and cloud markets and then describe the research problem addressed in this paper.

2.1 Cloud Platforms and Markets

Our work targets infrastructure clouds that lease server resources to service providers. An infrastructure cloud is a virtualized data center where the cloud provider allocates virtual machines (also referred to as virtual servers) to customers using the underlying physical servers. An infrastructure cloud typically supports different types of virtual servers that vary in their hardware configurations—for instance, Amazon's EC2 cloud supports over a dozen different virtual server configurations that differ in the amount of CPU, memory, disk and network allocations. The cost of a cloud server depends on the chosen configurations and is billed based on time of usage (e.g., hourly).

A cloud service provider can request any server type in one of two modes: on-demand and spot. On-demand cloud servers incur a fixed cost and are non-revocable. For instance, the fixed hourly price of on-demand server varies from 6 cents per hour for the small configuration to as much as $2.19 per hour for the double-extra large configuration. Importantly, once allocated, on-demand servers are non-revocable and the service provider is guaranteed availability to a server until it is no longer needed and voluntarily terminated. Since cloud platforms are provisioned with sufficient capacity to handle peak seasonal demands, they often have many unallocated and unutilized servers, which results in lost revenues due to lack of usage. Cloud providers such as Amazon have begun to offer this unused server capacity at significantly lower prices in the form of spot servers. Spot markets were first introduced by Amazon's EC2 cloud in

2009. Unlike on-demand servers, a spot server incurs a variable price and is revocable. A cloud-based service provider may request a spot server of any configuration by specifying the maximum hourly price they are willing to pay for such a server (also known as the bid price). Since the price of spot servers varies continuously, the request is granted only if the current price is below the customer's bid price. Furthermore, if the spot price rises above the bid price at any point in the future, the server is revoked. As shown in Figure 1, the price of a spot server fluctuates over time based on supply-demand considerations. Prices are low when there is plenty of unused capacity in relation to demand and the price rises when there is more demand for spot servers or increased demand for on-demand servers, both of which causes the customers with the low bid prices to lose these allocated servers (which are then re-allocated to higher paying on-demand customers).

Researchers have studied the dynamics of spot markets. Each server configuration has its own spot market with fluctuating prices. The different spot markets exhibit different types of dynamics and the price can also spike up during periods of extreme scarcity. As shown in Figure 1, the price of a large server can be as low as few cents per hour for long periods and can spike to as much as \$3/hr during high-demand periods. Other than the variable price and revocable nature, spot servers are identical to on-demand servers in all other respects such as their resource configurations. They are also billed on an hourly basis, based on the spot price (*not the bid price*) at the beginning of each hour. Partial hours are not billed if a spot server is revoked before the end of an hourly billing period. Researchers have also observed that upon being revoked, a spot server is given upto a 2 minute grace period to save all unsaved memory state to disk and execute a graceful shutdown (failing which it is forcibly terminated) [12]—while this was an "undocumented" feature of spot servers, Amazon has recently made this grace period official policy by providing an explicit two minute warning prior to revoking a spot server.

2.2 Problem Statement

Conventional wisdom has held that always-on services should be hosted using either dedicated hardware or non-revocable on-demand servers and that spot servers may not be suitable for this purpose due to potential service interruptions caused by server revocations. In contrast, batch jobs such as MapReduce-style data analytics tasks that have highly elastic deadlines can exploit spot servers to lower their costs while potentially increasing completion time; such tasks can employ checkpointing methods to periodically save their state to disk and resume from the most recent checkpoint if the computation was interrupted by the revocation of spot servers. Thus, as noted by Amazon, spot servers were designed for performing time-flexible and interruption-tolerant tasks.

In this paper, we study the feasibility and benefits of using spot servers for running always-on Internet services, which are *neither* time-flexible nor interruption-tolerant. We study how a service provider can exploit recent advances in OS and virtualization techniques such as nested virtualization and fast migration of virtual machine state to quickly move a service from spot servers to on-demand servers upon revocation and back to spot servers when they are available again. We seek to design clever bidding algorithms that exploit the low costs of spot servers and yet proactively migrate

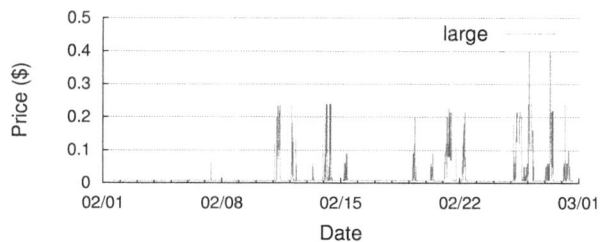

(a) Varying spot price of a small server

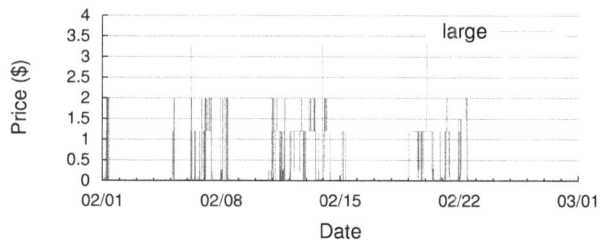

(b) Varying spot price of a large server

Figure 1: Spot prices over a month long period in Amazon's US East-1 region. The prices across markets even within the same region are not strongly correlated, a fact we use in our multi-market bidding algorithms.

the service to on-demand instances when faced with risk of revocation. We also seek to quantify the service unavailability due to downtimes when the cloud platform revokes spot servers. Our overall objectives are to quantify the cost savings and service unavailability and determine whether combining clever bidding and migration technique enable spot servers to be used in a novel fashion for always-on services.

3. A CLOUD SCHEDULER FOR ALWAYS-ON SERVICES

We design a cloud scheduler that procures servers in the cloud markets to host an always-on Internet-based service while minimizing both the cost and the unavailability of the service. A naive approach for using spot servers to host an always-on service is depicted in Figure 3. In this case, the service runs on a spot server for a period of time and the spot server is then revoked by the cloud provider, resulting in the service to be unavailable. Upon revocation, the cloud scheduler immediately requests an on-demand server to replace the revoked spot server. When the on-demand server is (eventually) allocated by the cloud provider, the Internet service is restarted on the new server. This naive baseline approach has two limitations: (i) any memory state of the spot server is lost upon revocation, and (ii) the service is unavailable from the time of revocation to the instant where the service is restarted on a new on-demand server. Note that even in this naive approach, the *disk state of the service is preserved*, since we assume that networked storage volumes are used by the service, so all data on the storage volume is preserved when the server is revoked and the volume can simply be re-attached to the new on-demand server (such networked storage volumes are referred to as EBS volumes in Amazon's EC2 cloud).

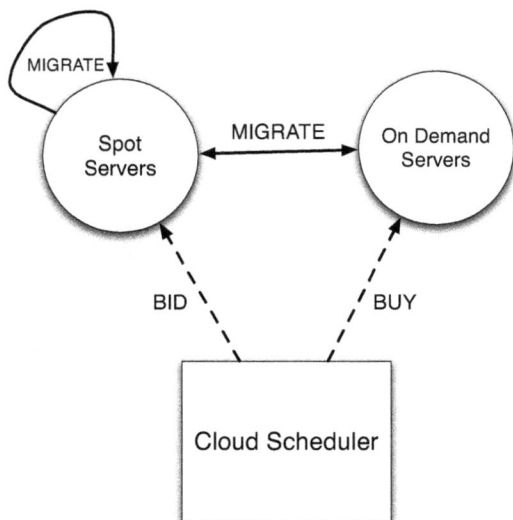

Figure 2: Interactions between the cloud scheduler and the cloud markets.

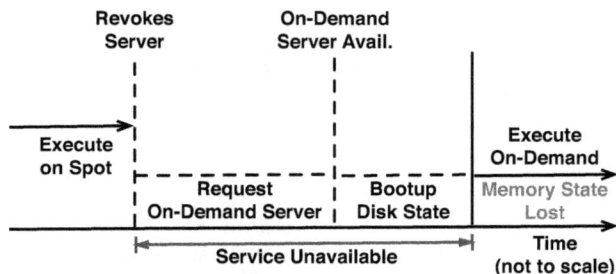

Figure 3: A naive approach to migrating from spot to on-demand server that involves substantial service unavailability and loss of memory state.

Our cloud scheduler uses a combination of intelligent bidding strategies and OS and virtualization-based techniques to address the two drawbacks of the naive approach. Our scheduler seeks to (i) eliminate any loss of memory state by migrating any such state to the new server, and (ii) reduce service unavailability or eliminate it completely in some scenarios. Figure 2 provides an overview of the server transitions implemented by the cloud scheduler. We next describe the two key components of the scheduler.

3.1 Bidding Algorithms

The cloud scheduler's bidding algorithm seeks to achieve two goals: (i) determine what prices to bid when acquiring spot servers so as to reduce the frequency of revocations and achieve cost savings over solely using on-demand servers, and (ii) determine when to transition from spot servers to on-demand servers and vice versa. As noted earlier, when requesting a spot server, the cloud platform requires a maximum price p_b to be specified by the service provider. Since the cost of a spot server fluctuates over time based on supply and demand considerations, this maximum price p_b, also known as the bid price, is the upper limit that the service provider is willing to pay for the spot server. Hence, when

the instantaneous spot price $p_{sp}(t)$ rises above the bid price p_b, the spot server is revoked by the cloud provider.

The bidding algorithm must intelligently choose the bid price p_b to achieve its goals. In general, a higher bid price reduces the chances that the spot price will rise above the bid and reduces the chances (and frequency) of server revocation. However, there is a risk that the spot price could increase but still stay below in the bid price, resulting in more cost and lower savings when compared to a pure on-demand model. In contrast, a lower bid price increases the chances of a revocation but can also lower costs.

The cloud scheduler implements two variants of the bidding algorithm. Note that whenever the spot price rises above the price of an on-demand servers, the cost savings vanish and it is more cost-effective to transition to an on-demand server and pay the fixed on-demand price over paying a even higher spot price. In the *reactive* version, the bid price is set to the price of an on-demand server i.e., $p_b = p_{on}$, where p_{on} denotes the cost of an on-demand server. Hence, setting $p_b = p_{on}$ ensures that the cloud platform will revoke the spot server whenever the spot price increases above the on demand price–forcing a migration (transition) to an on-demand server.

An alternative approach, which we refer to the *proactive* version, the bid price is set to a value that is higher than the on-demand price: $p_b = k \cdot p_{on}$, $k > 1$. In this case, the bidding algorithm continuously tracks the fluctuating spot price $p_{sp}(t)$ and whenever the spot price rises above the on-demand price, the algorithm *voluntarily and proactively* transitions to an on-demand server to pay the fixed on-demand price over paying the higher spot price. Since the migration to an on-demand server is voluntary, the cloud scheduler has more time and flexibility to make the transition, which in turn allows *service unavailability to be virtually eliminated*. Note that in the reactive approach, the transition must be made within a limited time duration before the server is revoked, while in the proactive case, the cloud scheduler can wait until the migration has completed before relinquishing the spot server. In the extreme case of the proactive version, the bidding algorithm can bid the highest bid that is allowed by the cloud platform (e.g., a large multiple k of the on-demand price) which gives the greatest flexibility[1] Regardless of the actual bid, a large sharp spike of the spot price above the bid price will cause the spot server to be revoked by the cloud platform before the proactive algorithm can begin (or finish) its voluntary migration.

After transitioning to an on-demand server, the bidding algorithm continues to monitor the spot price $p_{sp}(t)$ and can again request a spot server when $p_{sp}(t)$ falls below the on-demand price p_{on} and initiate a reverse migration from an on-demand to the spot server; such migrations are also voluntary and can take as long as needed to migrate the service.

Thus, both the reactive and proactive version of the bidding algorithms involve the following steps:

1. *Forced Migration.* If the $p_{sp}(t) > p_b$ and the algorithm holds a spot server, then the spot instance is terminated by the cloud provider. The algorithm is forced to migrate the spot server to an on-demand server.

---

[1] Note that cloud providers do not allow an infinite bid price. The largest bid price currently allowed by Amazon is four times the on-demand price which we use in our proactive algorithm.

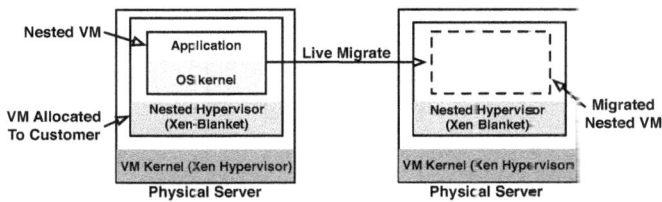

Figure 4: Nested virtualization and live migration of a nested virtual machine.

2. *Planned Migration.* If $p_b \geq p_{sp}(t) \geq p_{on}$ near the end of a billing period (i.e., billing hour) and the algorithm holds a spot server, it reduces cost by voluntarily migrating to an on-demand server.

3. *Reverse Migration.* If $p_{on} > p_{sp}(t)$ near the end of a billing hour and the algorithm currently holds an on-demand server, it reduces cost by re-procuring and migrating back to a spot server.

Note that planned migrations are more desirable than forced migrations, since there is more time to migrate the service in the former, resulting in less disruption to the service. Whereas with a forced migration there is only a short time window before the spot server is terminated.

3.2 OS Mechanisms

The cloud scheduler uses four well-known OS-level mechanisms to implement migrations from spot servers to on-demand servers and vice versa. While these OS-level mechanisms were proposed elsewhere, they have not been used in cloud platforms previously, nor has this novel combination been studied previously in the cloud context.

We assume that migrations from spot to on-demand servers and back is implemented at the virtual machine level. Virtual machine migration is transparent to the OS and the applications and does not require *any* modifications to either, allowing the technique to apply to all applications (here, cloud services) and operating systems unmodified. Our cloud scheduler employs three variants of virtual machine migration, as described below, to achieve different goals.

Nested virtualization. All common cloud platforms are virtualized and allocate virtual servers in the form of virtual machines. As a result, migration of virtual machines (VMs) is feasible in cloud platforms. Unfortunately, however, today's cloud platforms do not expose migration capabilities of virtual machines to customers and retain this control for themselves. Since the ability to migrate virtual machines from spot to on-demand servers and back is central to our approach, the cloud scheduler uses a mechanism called *nested virtualization* to achieve this goal in today's cloud platforms. Nested virtualization involves running a virtual machine *inside* another virtual machine and the application runs inside the nested virtual machine (see Figure 4). The advantage of nested virtualization is that it allows complete control of the nested virtual machine to the user without requiring any privileged access to the native virtual machine. Since cloud platforms allow a customer to run any OS kernel inside their virtual servers, a customer can easily run a nested virtual machine kernel, instead of a regular

OS kernel, and run the second, nested VM inside the virtual server. In such a scenario, we only need to migrate the nested virtual machine from one virtual server to another (e.g., spot to on-demand) without migrating the outside virtual machines. Nested virtualization was proposed in [20] and has been implemented in Xen, a widely used open-source virtualization platform, in the form of Xen-Blanket, which is compatible with Amazon's cloud servers that also use Xen. Experiments reported in [20] show only a modest overhead due to the second nested virtualization layer.

Live migration. Live virtual machine migration is a technique where an entire virtual machine is migrated from one physical server to another while the OS and resident applications continue to execute without requiring any downtime. Live VM migration techniques were proposed over a decade ago and are now supported by most common commercial and open-source virtual machine products (e.g., VMWare, Xen) [7]. Live migration is implemented by interactively copying the memory pages of the virtual machine from the source server to a destination server while the OS and applications continue to run. Since the VM is running during this migration process, memory pages will continue to be modified. Hence, live migration operates in rounds, where each round involves sending memory pages modified since the previous round. After several round of incremental transfers, the difference between the source and destination servers shrinks, and the virtual machine is momentarily paused to send the final set of changed memory pages. The VM at the destination is resumed and the source VM is terminated. This allows the application and its network connections to smoothly transition to the new server and no network reconfiguration is needed (the IP address remains unmodified when transferring the VM within a LAN). We note that VM migration techniques typically only transfer memory state of the virtual machine and do not transfer disk state since disk state is assumed to be stored on a network disk that can simply be re-attached to the destination server. By using nested virtualization, our cloud scheduler can live migrate nested virtual machines as shown in Figure 4. Further, the cloud scheduler uses techniques such as virtual private cloud [3] that allow customer control over the assignment of IP addresses to one's virtual machines to ensure that the address assigned to the nested VM on a spot server can be transparently reassigned to an on-demand server upon migration and vice versa.

Bounded memory checkpointing. Live migration is an attractive and straightforward method for transparently migrating a virtual machine from one server to another. The main limitation of the approach, however, is the latency involved in memory copying may be large, especially for larger server configurations that have substantial amount of memory (e.g., tens of GB of RAM). While these longer latencies can be easily accommodated during planned or reverse migrations initiated by the bidding algorithm, where there is flexibility in determining how much in advance to start the migration process, they may not be feasible for forced migrations. When a cloud platform revokes a spot server, there is a limited window of time to execute a graceful shutdown and this period may not suffice to live migrate a nested VM with large amounts of memory. Consequently a different approach is needed to quickly save memory state during forced migrations.

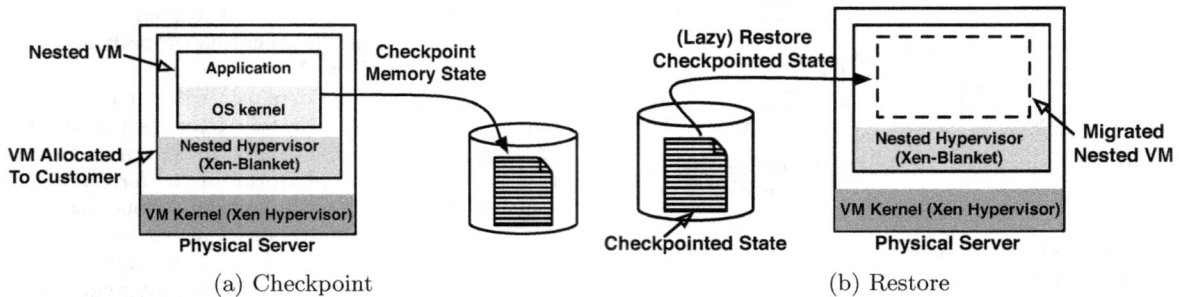

Figure 5: VM Memory checkpointing and restoration.

Memory checkpointing of a virtual machine in the form of *suspend-resume* involves writing out the entire memory contents of a VM to disk prior to suspending the virtual machine, and then resuming it at a later time by loading the checkpointed memory state (see Figure 5). Such suspend-resume support is already built into all virtual machine products and is an alternate approach to live migration for capturing memory state and resuming the VM on a different machine. However, writing of the memory contents of a virtual machine to a network disk can also involve a substantial latency for servers with substantial amounts of RAM. Fortunately, we need not wait to initiate memory checkpointing until a revocation is in progress and can instead run memory checkpointing periodically in the background on a continuous basis. In this case, memory contents are asynchronously written to disk in the background periodically and upon a renovation, only the incremental modified memory state since the most recent checkpoint needs to be written out, making the capturing of memory state very quick (and well suited to the limited time window available during a forced migration). Our cloud scheduler uses a recently proposed checkpointing technique called Yank [18] that provides an *upper bound* on the time needed to complement a checkpoint – given a bound τ, it dynamically adjusts the periodicity of the background checkpointing process to ensure that the incremental state does not exceed a threshold and can always be written out within the bound of τ seconds. By setting the bound to a small time window allowed by the cloud platform during a revocation, our cloud scheduler can ensure that all of the memory contents are safely captured to disk and the nested VM can be resumed on a different cloud server; we assume that network disks are used for the purpose of capturing memory state so that the disk is still available after a spot server has terminated.

Lazy VM restore. While bounded memory checkpointing allows suspension of the VM's memory state to complete within a small, bounded time period, the resume part of the suspend-resume process can still involve a latency of tens of seconds—since it requires reading the saved memory state from disk into RAM prior to the resumption of the nested VM. For larger cloud server configurations, this may involve reading tens of gigabytes of RAM state from disk. Hence, we employ an OS mechanism called lazy restore that substantially speeds up the resumption of a virtual machine from its saved memory state. Lazy restore [10, 24, 11] involves reading in only a small subset of the memory pages and resuming execution. The remaining memory state is read concurrently in the background as the VM executes. In the event the ex-

ecuting VM accesses a memory page that has not yet been read from disk, the corresponding memory page is fetched on-demand from disk (akin to how a page fault is handled in traditional operating systems). Lazy restore only requires a small fraction of the memory state to be read from disk before execution can be resumed, allowing for fast resumes and very small downtimes. Of course a downside is that the VM execution may be slower for a period of time due to the page faults that are seen while the remaining memory state is being loaded from disk in the background.

This novel combination of the four OS mechanisms makes it feasible to implement forced, planned and reverse migrations of our bidding algorithm in today's cloud platforms.

4. EVALUATION OF THE CLOUD SCHEDULER

We use empirical micro-benchmark measurements on Amazon's EC2 cloud as well as simulations seeded by Amazon's spot price traces to drive our evaluation. We evaluate the bidding algorithms and migration mechanisms employed by our cloud scheduler in three different scenarios. The simplest is the *single-region single-market* scenario where the cloud scheduler procures servers of a single size from a single spot market at a single geographical region, migrating to on-demand servers of the same size when necessary. More complex is the *single-region multi-market* scenario where the cloud scheduler has the option to buy servers of different sizes from different spot markets, though all of the servers are hosted at a single region. The most complex situation is the *multi-region multi-market* scenario where the cloud scheduler can procure servers of different sizes from different markets across any of the regions offered by the cloud provider. Intuitively, the cost reduction attainable should increase with each scenario since the cloud scheduler has more options for lowering the cost. However, the migration becomes more complex—a multi-market strategy involves packing multiple nested VMs onto a larger spot or on-demand server, while multi-region involves migration across regions that could be more complex and expensive.[2]

4.1 Microbenchmarks

We ran the XenBlanket nested hypervisor on Amazon's cloud servers and conduct a series of micro benchmark measurements to capture the overheads of various migration mechanisms; these measured values are then used to param-

---

[2]WAN VM migration across regions involves additional network reconfigurations [21] that also add to the overheads.

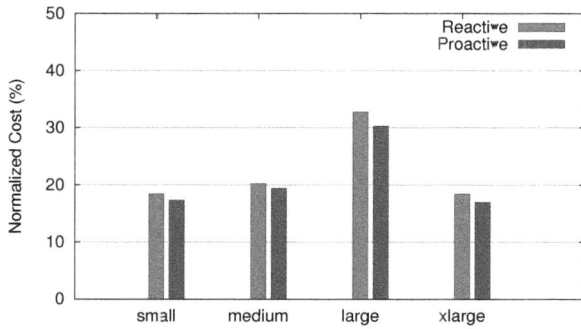

(a) Both proactive and reactive provide significantly smaller cost than the baseline.

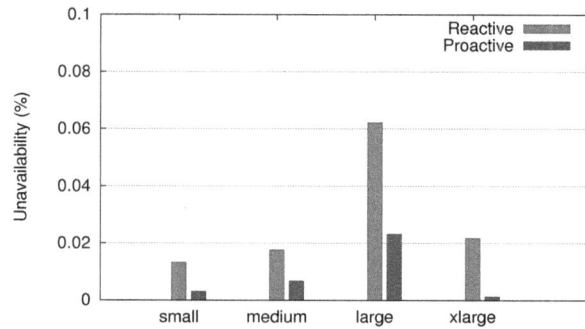

(b) Proactive mitigates service unavailability better than reactive.

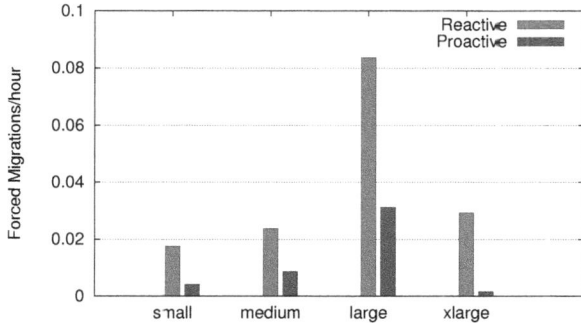

(c) Proactive has a smaller number of forced migrations per server per hour.

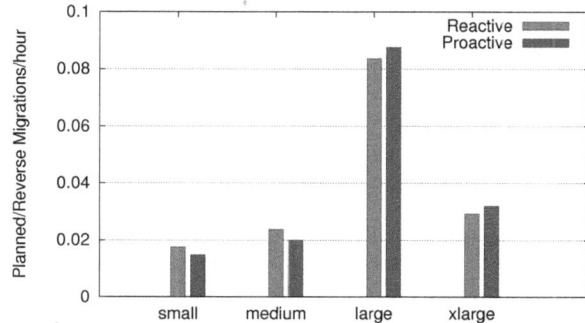

(d) Proactive and reactive have similar number of planned/reverse migrations per server per hour.

Figure 6: A comparison of proactive versus reactive bidding algorithms.

Instance type	US east (s)	US west (s)	EU west (s)
On-demand	94.85	93.63	98.08
Spot	281.47	219.77	233.37

Table 1: Average Start-up Time of On-demand and Spot instances

	Live migrate (s)	Memory checkpointing (s)	Disk copy (s)
Inside US East	58.5	28.9	–
Inside US West	57.1	28.8	–
Inside EU West	58.2	28.05	–
US East to US West	73.7	–	122.4
US East to EU West	74.6	–	141.5
US West to EU West	140.2	–	171.6

Table 2: Overhead of migration mechanisms.

eterize subsequent simulation experiments. We first measure the latency to allocate an on-demand and spot server of different sizes in different regions. Table 1 shows the mean measured values across multiple runs and shows that typical allocation times are around 1.5 minutes for an on-demand server and between 3.5 to 4.5 minutes for spot servers. Next, we measure the latency to live migrate a nested VM with 2GB of RAM within and across regions. Table 2 shows that live migration latency is around 1 minute for intra-data center migration and vary from 73 to 140 seconds for cross region migrations. While LAN migration can use networked storage and do not require disk state transfers, cross-region WAN migration do and the table shows that cross-

datacenter copying of disk state take between 2 to 3 minutes per GB of disk state. We also benchmark the latency of memory checkpointing, which involve writing memory pages sequentially to a network attached disk and observe a latency of 28s per GB of memory state (VM restoration latencies which read this data back from disk are similar). In contrast, we assume a lazy restoration latency of 20s, which is independent of memory size, based on measurements reported in [10].

In our microbenchmarks, we conducted multiple runs to obtain estimated startup times and migration times. In addition to these measured parameters, we also gathered published spot price history for Amazon's spot servers. In our simulations, we sampled the empirically observed distributions and used a different sample for each simulation run. We report results for small, medium, large and xlarge spot servers at four Amazon regions: US East 1A, US East 1B, US West 1A and Europe West 1A.

4.2 Proactive versus Reactive Bidding

We start with the simplest scenario where our bidding algorithm described in Section 3.1 uses a single market (either small, medium, or large) in a single region (us-east). The bidding algorithm alternately uses servers procured in the chosen spot market in the us-east region or an on-demand server obtainable at the same region. We study the two variants of the bidding algorithm described earlier, proactive and reactive, both using the bounded checkpointing with lazy restore for migration.[3] To estimate the cost savings from using the spot market, we use the cost of using only on-demand servers to host the service as the baseline. As shown in Figure 6(a), both proactive and reactive approaches show a significant reduction in cost achieving 17% to 33% of the baseline cost of not using the spot market at all. However, proactive does achieve a slightly smaller cost than reactive in all three markets. More importantly, the proactive algorithm achieves significantly less service unavailability than the reactive algorithm in *all* markets (cf. Figure 6(b)). Specifically, the unavailability of the proactive algorithm is smaller by a factor that ranges from 2.5 to 18 when compared to the reactive algorithm. The reason is that the proactive algorithm significantly reduces the number of forced migrations in comparison with the reactive algorithm as shown in Figure 6(c). Specifically, the proactive algorithm migrates its servers from the spot market to the on-demand market before it is forced to do so, giving it more time to perform the migration, in turn reducing the possibility of the service being unavailable during the migration process. Figure 6(d) shows that proactive and reactive algorithms have similar number of planned/reverse migrations.

The results for other regions are also similar to what we presented above for us-east. Thus, we conclude that it is better to be proactive rather be reactive, both from the perspectives of cost and unavailability. Henceforth, we will use the proactive bidding algorithm and its variants in all our subsequent evaluations.

4.3 Evaluating the Migration Mechanisms

We next evaluate the efficacy of four different combinations of migration mechanisms for the proactive bidding algorithm: memory checkpointing (with standard restore), memory checkpointing with lazy restore, live migration with checkpointing and live migration with checkpointing and lazy restore. The service unavailability of each combination is shown in Figure 7 for small servers in the US East 1a region; we report results for normal case as well as a pessimistic case where all migration mechanisms exhibit worst case behavior. Pure checkpointing alone has the worst unavailability of 0.018% due to the long latency needed to read the save memory state from disk prior to resuming the virtual machine. The unavailability improves significantly to 0.004% when lazy restore is used to speed up the resumption of a checkpointed VM. Similarly live migration with checkpointing has higher unavailability of 0.0095% since any forced migrations employ checkpointing with its longer downtimes. The final combination of using live migration when possible, and checkpointing with lazy restore for any forced migration has the smallest unavailability of 0.002% (roughly factor of two better than checkpointing with lazy restoration alone). According to [8] and [15], in the worst case, the downtime during migration of a 4GB virtual machine can be 10s, and migration of a 2GB VM causes down time of as much as 4s. The worst case of memory restore is copying the whole memory to the new VM while restoring. In our measurement, the time to copy a 2GB disk file which is less than 120s inside a region. The pessimistic scenarios, which assume pessimistic values of a 10s outage for live migration, and 120s latency for lazy restoration, see uniformly higher unavailability for all mechanisms, with the best unavailability of 0.017% for live migration with checkpointing and lazy restore. Thus we conclude that pure checkpointing is not desirable due to its higher unavailability, when used alone or in combination with live migration. However, when used with lazy restoration, the technique provides unavailability values that make it feasible for always-on services, with live migration further halving the unavailability of the service.

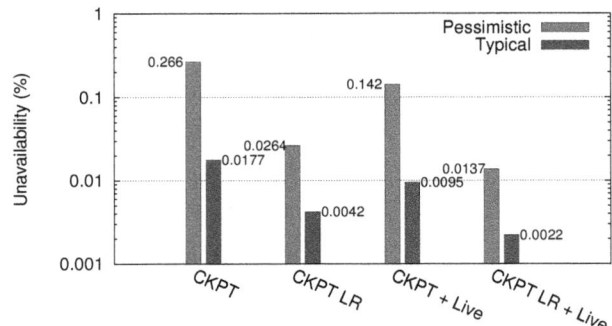

Figure 7: Comparison of different migration mechanisms using proactive bidding. (Unavailability percent is plotted in log-scale)

4.4 Multi-Market Bidding Strategies

We study the benefit of bidding in multiple spot markets in comparison with bidding in a single spot market within a given region. The intuitive reason why multiple markets can decrease the cost is that when one spot market has a price rise the other markets in the same region *may* not experience a similar rise. So, our cloud scheduler can move its servers from the pricier spot market to one of the cheaper ones.

We modified our proactive bidding algorithm of Section 3.1 to use multiple markets within the same region as follows. In the planned migration step, we look to see if there is *any* spot market in the same region that has a cheaper price than the on-demand price. If so, the algorithm bids in the cheapest available spot market in that region and migrates the spot server to that market. If not, the algorithm migrates the spot server to the on-demand server as it is currently cheaper than any of the spot servers. The forced and reverse migration steps work the same as before.

We evaluated our multi-market bidding algorithm in all regions and show the results in Figure 8. As shown in Figure 8(a), a multi-market scheme was able to reduce the cost by 8% for us-west-1a to 52% for us-east-1b in comparison with the average cost of the single-market schemes in those regions. The reason for the reduction is that price correlation between the different markets is low as shown in Figure 8(b), i.e., when the price spikes up in one of the spot markets, another of the spot markets in the same region may not have an equivalent increase. Our multi-market bidding algorithm exploits the lack of correlation to move servers from the costlier to the cheaper spot market.

4.5 Multi-Region Bidding Strategies

We study multi-region bidding algorithms that can move servers between spot markets both within a given region

---

[3]Results for planned live migrations are similar and omitted here.

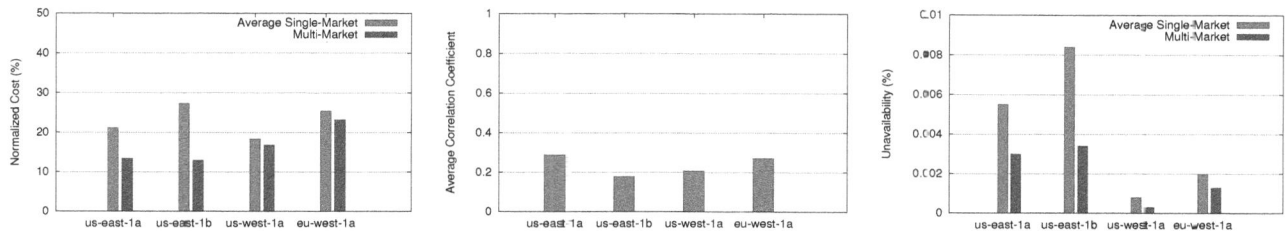

(a) Bidding in multiple markets decreases the cost in comparison with single-market schemes.

(b) The price correlation between the different spot markets within a region is low.

(c) Bidding in multiple markets decreases unavailability in comparison to single-market schemes.

Figure 8: The benefits of bidding in multiple markets within the same region.

as well as *across* different regions. Our multi-region algorithm is identical to the multi-market algorithm described in Section 4.4 except that the algorithm looks for the cheapest market both within and across regions for migration. We evaluate our multi-region bidding algorithm on pairs of regions and we show the results in Figure 9. To normalize the cost achieved by our multi-region algorithm, we use the lowest on-demand cost available in the two allowable regions as the baseline. As we show in Figure 9(a), our multi-region strategy achieves 12-17% of the baseline cost, resulting in a significant cost reduction in comparison to the baseline of not using the spot markets at all. Further our multi-region algorithm results in a normalized cost that is 5-28% smaller than the average cost achieved by the single-region bidding algorithm operating in each of the two regions. The reason for the additional cost savings is that the prices across two regions have a low correlation as shown in Figure 9(b). Therefore, when the spot price increases in one region, our multi-region algorithm is able find cheaper prices in the other region.

However, service unavailability can actually *increase* in some cases with multi-region bidding as can be seen in Figure 9(c). The reason is that regions such as us-east-1a and us-east-1b that tend to have cheaper prices, also have greater variability in those prices (cf. Figure 10). Whereas the eu-west region tends to be more expensive but the prices are more stable. Since our multi-region bidding algorithm migrates its servers to spot markets primarily based on a lower price, it can sometimes migrate to lower cost regions (such as us-east) with more volatile prices. Markets with larger price volatility can cause more migrations as the prices fluctuate making these markets more expensive at times than the other markets. The increased migration causes more unavailability. Bidding algorithms that also consider price stability instead of greedily opting for the cheapest price is a topic for future research.

5. COST AND AVAILABILITY ANALYSIS

In the previous section, we show that by using nested VMs and migrating between on-demand instances and spot instances, we can achieve a significant reduction in cost over using on-demand instances alone. In this section, we go a step further to show the advantage of our method over current spot market.

Figure 11 compares our proactive method to using spot instances alone. We find that although using spot instances reduce cost in some markets, its availability is quite bad.

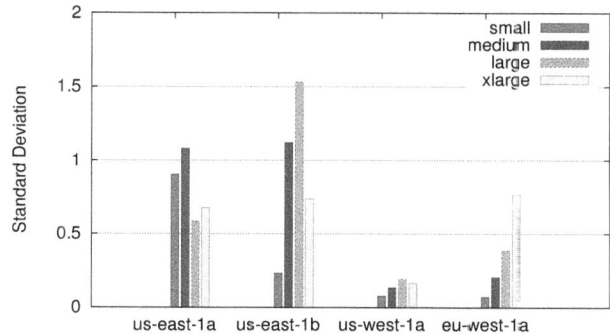

Figure 10: The prices of us-east are more variable than us-west or eu-west.

	Cost	Availability
Only On-demand	High	High
Only Spot	Low	Low
Using migration mechanisms	Low	High

Table 3: By using a combination of on-demand and spot servers, we can achieve low cost and high availability for online services

In small, medium and large markets, unavailability is over 1% which is not acceptable for always-on internet services. Further, since the price may be over bid limit for a long period, services can be unavailable for hours or even days. Hence, using spot instances alone are not a good choice for hosting always-on internet services, as conventional wisdom has held.

As table 3 shows, our method combines the advantage of on-demand and spot market and provides a solution with low cost and high availability to host always-on internet services in current cloud platforms.

6. IMPACT OF SYSTEM PERFORMANCE ON COST

Although nested VMs on spot instances provide good savings, nested virtualization can also impose system performance overheads. In this section, we quantify these system performance overheads and study their impact on the eventual cost savings.

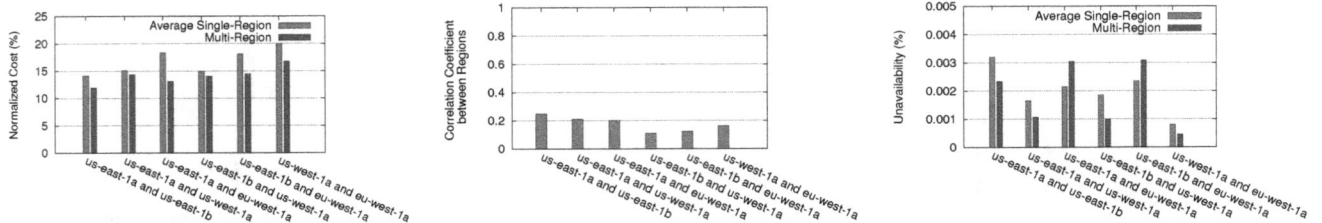

(a) Bidding in multiple regions decreases the cost in comparison with single-region schemes.

(b) The price correlation across regions is low, enabling the multi-region algorithm to avoid price hikes by switching to a cheaper alternate region.

(c) Multi-region unavailability can increase in cases when the lower-priced markets such as us-east happen to also be less stable.

Figure 9: A comparison of multi-region versus single-region bidding algorithms. Both algorithms bid in multiple markets within their allowable regions.

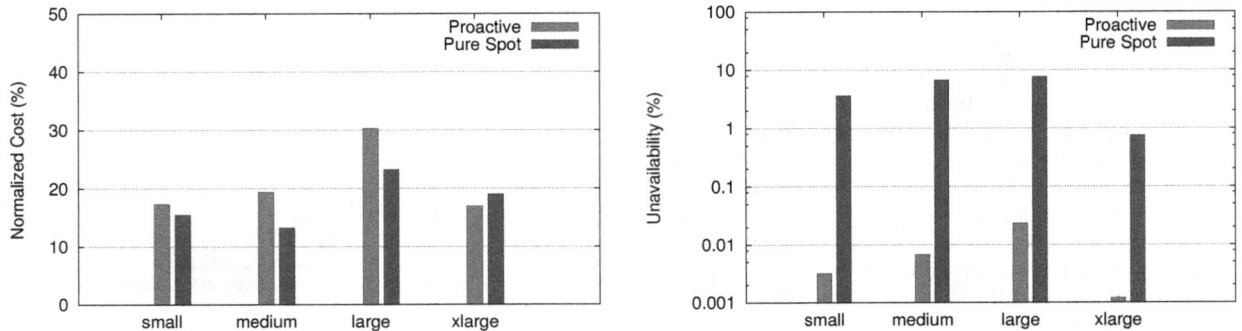

(a) Using pure spot instances can slightly reduce the total cost

(b) Using pure spot instances largely increases unavailability

Figure 11: A comparison of proactive method versus using only spot servers.

	Amazon VM (Mbps)	Nested VM (Mbps)
Network TX	304	304
Network RX	316	314
Disk Read	304.6	297.6
Disk Write	280.4	274.2

Table 4: Network and Disk I/O performance of nested VMs is comparable to Amazon's native VMs

6.1 Disk and Network I/O Overheads

Since we use a second hypervisor to host our nested VMs, our system will incur performance overheads. We compare the system performance of Amazon VMs and nested VMs (using the xen-blanket nested hypervisor). In our experiments, we use Amazon EC2 m3.medium VMs which has 1 virtual CPU and 3.75 GB memory, using HVM virtualization instances and Elastic Block Store (EBS). When creating a nested VM, we only distribute 3 GB memory to it because dom0 needs some memory to hold its service. Network address translation (NAT) is used to provide transparent network access to the nested VMs.

We first measure the network I/O and disk I/O overhead. We use iperf to get a measurement of network throughput. From Table 4 we can see that both the transmitting rate and receiving rate of nested VM matches the throughput of Amazon VM. Then we ran *dd* to measure disk I/O. System caches at all layers were flushed before reading and writing 2GB of data from the root file system. Table 4 shows that disk I/O performance is only degraded by 2%. These results show that disk and network I/O performance of nested virtual machine instances is close to Amazon's native VMs.

6.2 CPU Overhead Benchmarking

The original Xen-blanket paper [20] provided detailed results on the CPU overheads imposed by the Xen-blanket nested hypervisor. We use TPC-W as an example benchmark application to verify their results in Amazon's EC2 cloud. TPC-W is a web benchmark that emulates an online e-commerce store. We use a Java servlets-based multi-tiered configuration of the TPC-W shopping website. Our experiment injects an "ordering workload" where 50% of the clients only browse the website and the remaining 50% execute order transactions. TPC-W allows us to measure the influence of the extra xen-blanket hypervisor on the response time perceived by the clients of an interactive web application.

We perform the above experiment with two common configurations: 1) browsers fetch images from the server while browsing 2) browsers don't fetch images from the server while browsing. The first configuration emulates a case where the entire website, including the images, is served by our server VMs. The second configuration emulates a case where only the base web page is served by our server VMs and the embedded images are cached and served by a third-party content delivery service. Figure 12 shows

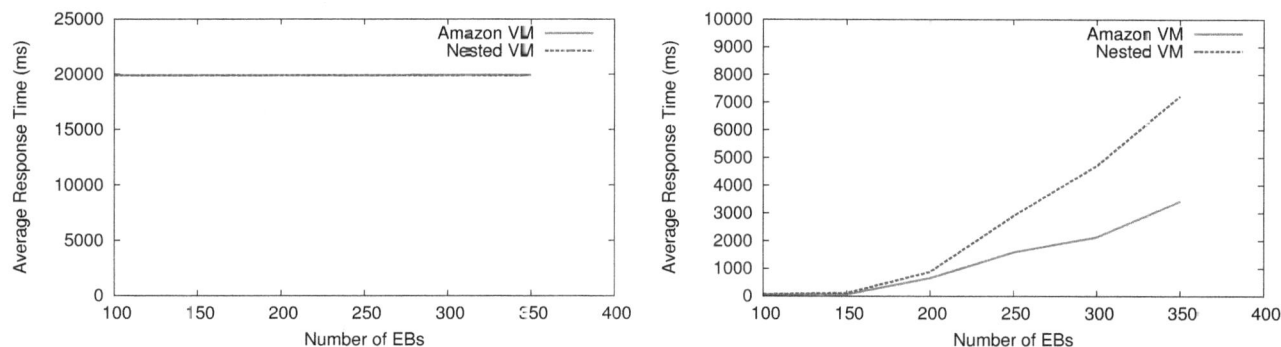

(a) If browsers fetch images while browsing, nested VM's performance is no worse than Amazon VM

(b) If browsers don't fetch images while browsing, nested VM's performance is upto 50% worse than Amazon VM

Figure 12: The overhead of nested VM depends on the type of service it provides

the response time under a varying load imposed by different number of emulated browsers. Figure 12(a) shows the result under the first configuration. We can see that nested VMs can achieve similar performance as Amazon VMs. This is because when browsers get images from the server, the benchmark is I/O bound and xen-blanket can provide efficient I/O. Figure 12(b) gives the result under the second CPU-intensive configuration; in this case, the CPU overhead depends on the load and in the worst case, we see that nested VMs incur up to a 50% overhead over Amazon VMs.

From our system measurements, we observe that disk and network intensive services will see close to native performance and achieve most of the cost savings. For CPU-intensive workloads, the overheads depends on the actual load and can reduce the cost savings (since additional capacity is needed to service a particular load). In the worst case, performance may be halved, yielding actual savings of 12%-34% of the baseline cost. Of course, Xen-Blanket is a research prototype of a nested hypervisor and a commercial ested hypervisor implementation may be able to optimize the performance overhead and yield better savings.

7. RELATED WORK

There has been recent research on cloud spot servers, but much of prior work has focused on interruption-tolerant batch jobs. The use of spot servers to reduce the cost of data-intensive MapReduce batch jobs has been studied in [12] and [6]. Optimal bidding strategies that minimize completion times of short batch jobs have also been studied in [23], [17], and [19]. Checkpointing techniques for batch jobs running on spot servers were studied in [22]. In contrast, our work focuses on using spot instances of always-on services that interact with users in real-time.

Our work builds on a large body of work in virtualization techniques [5]. Live migration of virtual machines was studied in [7], while checkpointing techniques for virtual machines have been studied in [9, 18]. Nested virtualization in the context of the Xen virtual machine platform was proposed in [20]. Lazy restoration methods have been studied in [24, 10, 11]. SpotCheck [16] is a system that uses nested virtualization and migration mechanisms to manage server pools based on spot and on-demand servers. Our work assumes the presence of such system level mechanisms and

examines a range of bidding and migration policies that use these mechanisms in the cloud context.

8. CONCLUSIONS

In this paper we studied the efficacy of using spot servers to lower the cost of hosting always-on Internet services. We proposed a cloud scheduler that combines bidding algorithms and migration techniques to reduce, or nearly eliminate, unavailability by migrating a spot server to an on-demand server when needed. Our results demonstrated the feasibility of using our proactive approach to provide availability levels that are close to levels desirable for always-on services, at nearly one-third to one-fifth of the cost of the traditional approach of using on-demand servers. As part of future work, we plan to design more sophisticated bidding strategies that take spot price stability into account to further reduce server revocation frequency, and hence, service unavailability.

9. ACKNOWLEDGMENTS

We thank all the reviewers for their insightful comments, which improved the quality of this paper. This work is supported in part by NSF grants CNS-1413998, CNS-1422245 and CNS-1229059.

10. REFERENCES

[1] https://azure.microsoft.com/.
[2] https://cloud.google.com/products/compute-engine/.
[3] http://aws.amazon.com/.
[4] http://aws.amazon.com/solutions/case-studies/netflix/.
[5] P. Barham, B. Dragovic, K. Fraser, S. Hand T. Harris, A. Ho, R. Neugebauer, I. Pratt, and A. Warfield. Xen and the art of virtualization. *ACM SIGOPS Operating Systems Review*, 37(5):164–177, 2003.
[6] N. Chohan, C. Castillo, M. Spreitzer, M. Steinder, A. Tantawi, and C. Krintz. See spot run: using spot

instances for mapreduce workflows. In *Proceedings of the 2nd USENIX conference on Hot topics in cloud computing*, pages 7–7. USENIX Association, 2010.

[7] C. Clark, K. Fraser, S. Hand, J. Hansen, E. Jul, C. Limpach, I. Pratt, and A. Warfiel. Live migration of virtual machines. In *Proceedings of Usenix NSDI Symp.*, May 2005.

[8] C. Clark, K. Fraser, S. Hand, J. G. Hansen, E. Jul, C. Limpach, I. Pratt, and A. Warfield. Live migration of virtual machines. In *Proceedings of the 2Nd Conference on Symposium on Networked Systems Design & Implementation - Volume 2*, NSDI'05, pages 273–286, Berkeley, CA, USA, 2005. USENIX Association.

[9] B. Cully, G. Lefebvre, D. Meyer, M. Feeley, N. Hutchinson, and A. Warfield. Remus: High availability via asynchronous virtual machine replication. In *Proceedings of the 5th NSDI Symp.*, pages 161–174. San Francisco, 2008.

[10] M. Hines and K. Gopalan. Post-copy based live virtual machine migration using adaptive pre-paging and dynamic self-ballooning. In *Proceedings of ACM VEE Conference*, March 2009.

[11] A. Lagar-Cavilla et al. Snowflock: rapid virtual machine cloning for cloud computing. In *Proceedings of ACM EuroSys*, pages 1–12, 2009.

[12] H. Liu. Cutting mapreduce cost with spot market. In *3rd USENIX Workshop on Hot Topics in Cloud Computing*, pages 1–5, 2011.

[13] A. Marathe, R. Harris, D. Lowenthal, B. R. de Supinski, B. Rountree, and M. Schulz. Exploiting redundancy for cost-effective, time-constrained execution of hpc applications on amazon ec2. In *Proceedings of the 23rd International Symposium on High-performance Parallel and Distributed Computing*, HPDC '14, pages 279–290, New York, NY, USA, 2014. ACM.

[14] E. Nygren, R. Sitaraman, and J. Sun. The Akamai Network: A platform for high-performance Internet applications. *ACM SIGOPS Operating Systems Review*, 44(3):2–19, 2010.

[15] F. Salfner, P. Troger, and A. Polze. Downtime analysis of virtual machine live migration. In *DEPEND 2011, The Fourth International Conference on Dependability*, pages 100–105, 2011.

[16] P. Sharma, S. Lee, T. Guo, D. Irwin, and P. Shenoy. Spotcheck: Designing a derivative iaas cloud on the spot market. In *Proceedings of the Tenth European Conference on Computer Systems*, 2015.

[17] X. Shi, K. Xu, J. Liu, and Y. Wang. Continuous double auction mechanism and bidding strategies in cloud computing markets. *arXiv preprint arXiv:1307.6066*, 2013.

[18] R. Singh, D. E. Irwin, P. J. Shenoy, and K. K. Ramakrishnan. Yank: Enabling green data centers to pull the plug. In *NSDI*, pages 143–155, 2013.

[19] Y. Song, M. Zafer, and K.-W. Lee. Optimal bidding in spot instance market. In *INFOCOM, 2012 Proceedings IEEE*, pages 190–198. IEEE, 2012.

[20] D. Williams, H. Jamjoom, and H. Weatherspoon. The xen-blanket: virtualize once, run everywhere. In *Proceedings of the 7th ACM european conference on Computer Systems*, pages 113–126. ACM, 2012.

[21] T. Wood, K. Ramakrishnan, P. Shenoy, and J. V. der Merwe. Cloudnet: Dynamic pooling of cloud resources by live wan migration of virtual machines. In *Proc. of ACM VEE*, March 2011.

[22] S. Yi, D. Kondo, and A. Andrzejak. Reducing costs of spot instances via checkpointing in the amazon elastic compute cloud. In *Cloud Computing (CLOUD), 2010 IEEE 3rd International Conference on*, pages 236–243. IEEE, 2010.

[23] M. Zafer, Y. Song, and K.-W. Lee. Optimal bids for spot vms in a cloud for deadline constrained jobs. In *Cloud Computing (CLOUD), 2012 IEEE 5th International Conference on*, pages 75–82. IEEE, 2012.

[24] I. Zhang, A. Garthwaite, Y. Baskakov, and K. C. Barr. Fast restore of checkpointed memory using working set estimation. In *ACM SIGPLAN Notices* volume 46, pages 87–98. ACM, 2011.

Towards Scalable Distributed Workload Manager with Monitoring-Based Weakly Consistent Resource Stealing

Ke Wang
Illinois Institute of Technology
kwang22@hawk.iit.edu

Xiaobing Zhou
Hortonworks Inc.
xzhou@hortonworks.com

Kan Qiao
Google
qiaokan.buaa@gmail.com

Michael Lang
Los Alamos National Laboratory
mlang@lanl.gov

Benjamin McClelland
Intel
benjamin.m.mcclelland@intel.com

Ioan Raicu
Illinois Institute of Technology
iraicu@cs.iit.edu

ABSTRACT

One way to efficiently utilize the coming exascale machines is to support a mixture of applications in various domains, such as traditional large-scale HPC, the ensemble runs, and the fine-grained many-task computing (MTC). Delivering high performance in resource allocation, scheduling and launching for all types of jobs has driven us to develop Slurm++, a distributed workload manager directly extended from the Slurm centralized production system. Slurm++ employs multiple controllers with each one managing a partition of compute nodes and participating in resource allocation through resource balancing techniques. In this paper, we propose a monitoring-based weakly consistent resource stealing technique to achieve resource balancing in distributed HPC job launch, and implement the technique in Slurm++. We compare Slurm++ with Slurm using micro-benchmark workloads with different job sizes. Slurm++ showed 10X faster than Slurm in allocating resources and launching jobs – we expect the performance gap to grow as the job sizes and system scales increase in future high-end computing systems

Categories and Subject Descriptors

C.5.1 [**Computer System Implementation**]: Large and Medium ("Mainframe") Computers – *Super (very large) computers.*

General Terms

Design, Algorithm, Performance.

Keywords

Workload manager; job launch; scheduling; resource balancing.

1. INTRODUCTION

With the predication that exascale supercomputers will have billion-way parallelism [1], one way of efficiently utilizing the whole machine is to support a mixture of applications in different domains that include traditional large-scale high performance computing (HPC), HPC ensemble runs, and fine-grained loosely coupled many-task computing (MTC) [2].

HPDC'15, June 15 - 20, 2015, Portland, Oregon, USA
Copyright © 2015 ACM 978-1-4503-3550-8/15/06…$15.00
DOI: http://dx.doi.org/10.1145/2749246.2749249.

Traditional **large-scale HPC applications** typically require many computing processors (e.g. half or full-size of the whole machine) for a long time (e.g. days or weeks). The jobs are tightly coupled, and use the message-passing interface (MPI) programming model [3] for communication and synchronization among all the processors. Although it is necessary to support HPC applications that demand the computing capacity of an exascale machine, it is also important to enable **ensemble runs** of applications that have uncertainty in high-dimension parameter space. Ensemble runs [4] decompose applications into many small-scale and short-duration coordinated jobs with each one doing a parameter sweep in a much lower-resolution parameter space using MPI in parallel, thus enabling a higher system utilization of exascale machines. Another domain of applications involves the **many-task computing (MTC)** [5] paradigm. MTC decomposes applications as orders of magnitude larger number (e.g. millions to billions) of embarrassingly parallel tasks with data-dependencies [6]. Tasks are fine-grained in both size (e.g. per-core) and duration (e.g. sub-second), and are represented as Direct Acyclic Graph (DAG) where vertices are tasks and the edges denote the data flows.

Running a mixture of applications in all domains on large-scale systems poses significant scalability challenges (e.g. grids [7][8], storage [9][10]) on workload managers (e.g. Slurm [11], PBS [12], and SGE [13]), which, up to date, have a centralized architecture where a controller manages all the compute daemons and are in charge of the activities, such as node partitioning, resource allocation, job scheduling and launching. This architecture cannot scale to exascale machines that will have system sizes one or two orders of magnitude larger for thousands of times more jobs with much wider distributions in both sizes and durations. Future exascale machines, along with a miscellaneous collection of applications, will demand orders of magnitudes higher job-delivering rates to make full utilization of the machine. The scalability challenge has driven us to develop the next generation distributed workload managers [14][15].

We have developed the Slurm++ [16] workload manager targeting all the applications at exascale. Slurm++ extends Slurm by applying multiple controllers with each one managing a partition of compute daemons and balancing resources among all the partitions through resource stealing techniques. Slurm++ utilizes ZHT [17], a distributed key-value store (KVS) [18][19], to keep the resource state information. In this paper, we propose a monitoring-based weakly consistent resource stealing technique to achieve dynamic resource balancing. We implement the technique in Slurm++, which shows 10X faster than Slurm in allocating resources and launching jobs. We expect the performance gap to grow as the job sizes and system scales increase in future high-end computing systems.

2. Slurm++ WORKLOAD MANAGER

Slurm++ is a distributed workload manager with a partition-based architecture, as shown in Figure 1. Slurm++ employs multiple controllers with each one managing a partition of compute daemons (*cd*). The partition size (the number of *cd* a controller managers) is configurable according to the application domains. We can also configure heterogeneous partition sizes to support workloads with a wide distribution of job sizes and with special requirements (e.g. only run on the partitions that have GPUs, InfiniBand, or SSDs). The users can submit jobs to arbitrary controller. Slurm++ deploys ZHT, a distributed key-value store (KVS), to manage the entire resource metadata and system state. One typical configuration is to co-locate a ZHT server with a controller forming 1:1 mapping, such as shown in Figure 1. Each controller is a ZHT client and uses the client APIs (e.g. *lookup*, *insert*) to communicate with ZHT servers to store, query and modify the metadata represented as (*key, value*) pair, for example, (*controllerId, free_node_list*), of resources of all the partitions.

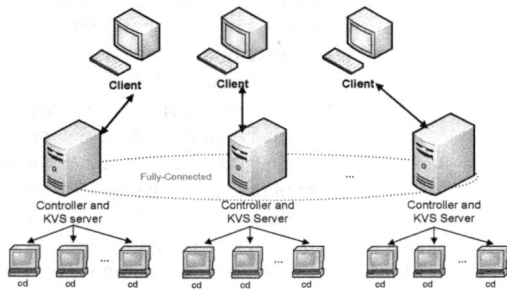

Figure 1: Slurm++ distributed workload manager

Note that Slurm also divides the system into multiple partitions. However, this is different from the partition management of Slurm++. Firstly, Slurm layers the partitions hierarchically up to the centralized controller, while Slurm++ is distributed by employing one dedicated controller to manage a partition independently from other partitions. The hierarchical layout leads to longer latency as a job may need to go through multiple hops. What's more, the root controller is still a central piece with limited capacity. Secondly, in Slurm, when a job is scheduled on one partition, it can only get allocation within that partition. This results in long job queueing time in over-loaded partitions, and poor utilization if loads are not balanced among the partitions.

3. RESOURCE STEALING TECHNIQUE

Resource balancing means to find the required number of free nodes in all the partitions as fast as possible to satisfy concurrent job submissions. It is trivial in the centralized architecture, as the controller has a global view of the system state. However, for the distributed architecture, resource balancing is a critical goal, and should be achieved dynamically in a distributed fashion by all the controllers, in order to maintain an overall high system utilization.

Inspired by the work stealing technique [20] that achieves distributed dynamic load balancing, we introduce the resource stealing concept to achieve distributed dynamic resource balancing. Resource stealing refers to a set of techniques of stealing free nodes from other partitions if the local one cannot satisfy a job in terms of job size. When a controller allocates nodes for a job, it first checks the local free nodes. If there are enough free nodes, then the controller directly allocates the nodes; otherwise, it allocates whatever resources the partition has, and queries ZHT for other partitions to steal resources from them. Our previous work [16] proposed a straightforward random resource

stealing technique, which has poor performance for big jobs. This section proposes a ***monitoring-based weakly consistent resource stealing technique*** that has better scalability than the random one. The proposed technique relies on a centralized monitoring service and each controller conducts a two-phase tuning procedure.

3.1 Monitoring Service

One of the reasons that the random technique is not scalable is because the controllers have no global view (even weakly consistent) of the system resource state. One alternative to enable all of the controllers to have global view is to alter the partition-based architecture to that the controllers know all the compute daemons. Then, there will be merely one (*key, value*) record of the global resource stored in a specific ZHT server. This method of strongly consistent global view is not scalable because all the frequent KVS operations on the resources are processed by a single ZHT server that stores the global resource (*key, value*) pair.

In order to keep a weakly consistent view of the global resources in each controller, we apply a monitoring service (MS) to query the free resources of all the partitions periodically. In each round, the MS looks up the free resource of each partition in sequence, and then gathers them together as global resource information and puts the global information as one (*key, value*) record in a ZHT server. This (*key, value*) record offers a global view of resource states for all the controllers.

This is different from the alternative mentioned above in that the frequency of querying this global (*key, value*) record is much less. Although the MS is centralized and queries all the partitions sequentially, we believe that it should not be a bottleneck. Because the number of partitions for large-scale HPC applications is not that many (e.g. 1K), and with the right granularity of frequency of updating and gathering the global resource information, the MS should be scalable. The MS could be implemented either as a standalone process on one compute node or as a separate thread in a controller. In Slurm++, the MS is implemented as the latter case.

3.2 Two-Phase Tuning

Each controller will conduct a two-phase tuning procedure of updating resources in the aid of allocating resources to jobs.

3.2.1 Phase 1: Pulling-based Macro-Tuning

As the MS offers a global view of the system free nodes (being kept in one ZHT server), each controller will periodically pull the global resource information by a ZHT *lookup* operation. In each round when the controller gets the global resources, it organizes the resources of different partitions as a binary-search tree (BST) data structure. Each data item of the BST contains the controller id (**char***) and the number of free nodes (**int**) of a partition. The data items are organized as a BST based on the number of free nodes of all partitions. The BST guides a controller to steal resources from the most suitable partitions.

We call this phase macro-tuning as it evicts the cached free resource information in BST, and updates the BST with the new information in each periodic query. This update is consistent for all the controllers as the resource information is pulled from a single place by all the controllers. Each controller pulls the information before it is too obsolete to offer valuable guidance.

3.2.2 Phase 2: Weakly Consistent Micro-Tuning

The controller uses the BST as a guide to choose the most suitable partitions to steal resources. The operations of the BST structure we implement to best serve the job resource allocation are:

BST_insert(BST*, char*, int): insert a data item to the BST data structure specifying the number of free nodes of a partition.

BST_delete(BST*, char*, int): delete a data item from the BST data structure for a partition.

BST_delete_all(BST*): evict all the data items from the BST data structure for all the partitions.

BST_search_best(BST*, int): for a given number of required compute nodes of a job, this operation searches for the most suitable partition to steal free nodes. There are 3 cases (1) multiple partitions have enough free nodes; (2) only one partition has enough free nodes; (3) none of the partitions have enough free nodes. For case (1), it will choose the partition that has the minimum number of free nodes among all the partitions that have enough free nodes. For case (2), it will choose the exact partition that has enough free nodes. For case (3), it will choose the partition that has the maximum number of free nodes.

BST_search_exact(BST*, char*): given a specific controller id, this operation searches the resource information of that partition.

The complete resource allocation procedure is described as follows. When a job is submitted to a controller, the controller first tries to allocate free nodes in local partition. As long as the allocation is not satisfied, the controller searches for the most suitable partition to steal resources from the BST. The controller then queries the actual free resource of that partition via a ZHT *lookup* operation. After that, the controller issues a ZHT *compare and swap* atomic operation to allocate resources. If the allocation succeeds, the controller will insert the updated free node list of that partition to the local BST. Otherwise, if the controller experiences several failures in a row, it releases the allocated free nodes for the job, waits some time, and tries this procedure again.

We call this the micro-tuning phase because only the data of the resource of one partition is changed during one attempted stealing. Every controller updates its BST individually. As time increases, the controllers would have inconsistent view of the free resources of all the partitions. In the meantime, the controller is updating the whole BST with the most current resources of all the partitions (macro-tuning phase). With both macro-tuning and micro-tuning, the resource stealing technique has the ability to balance the resources among all the partitions dynamically, to aggressively allocate the most suitable resources for big jobs, and to find the free resources quickly under high system utilization.

4. EVALUATION

We implement the monitoring-based weakly consistent resource stealing technique in the Slurm++ workload manager. The implementation source code is made open source on GitHub repository: https://github.com/kwangiit/SLURMPP_V2. The dependencies are Slurm [11], ZHT [17], and Google Protocol Buffer [21]. We evaluate Slurm++ by comparing it with Slurm using the micro-benchmark workloads up to 500 nodes.

4.1 Comparison between Slurm++ and Slurm

We run all the experiments on the Kodiak cluster from the PROBE environment at LANL [22]. Kodiak has 500 nodes, and each node has two 64-bit AMD Opteron processors at 2.6GHz and 8GB memory. For Slurm++, the partition size is set to be 50. At the largest scale of 500 nodes, there are 10 controllers. The workloads include the simplest possible NOOP "sleep 0" jobs that require various numbers of nodes per job with 3 different distributions: each controller runs 50 **one-node jobs**; each controller runs 50 jobs with sizes having uniform distribution that

has an average of half partition – 25 (1 to 50), referred to **half-partition jobs**; and each controller runs 20 jobs with sizes having uniform distribution that has an average of full partition – 50 (25 to 75), referred to **full-partition jobs**.

Figure 2 shows throughput speedups between Slurm++ and Slurm with the three workloads. We see that for all the workloads, Slurm++ is able to launch jobs faster than Slurm. The performance slowdown (9.3X from one-node to full-partition jobs) of Slurm due to increasingly large jobs is much more severe than that (2.3X from one-node to full-partition jobs) of Slurm++. This highlights the better scalability of Slurm++. In addition, the speedup is increasing as the scale increases for all the workloads, indicating that at larger scales, Slurm++ would outperform Slurm even more. Another important fact is that as the job size increases, the speedup also increases (2.61X for one-node, 8.5X for half-partition, and 10.2X for full-partition). This trend proves that the proposed technique has great scalability for big jobs.

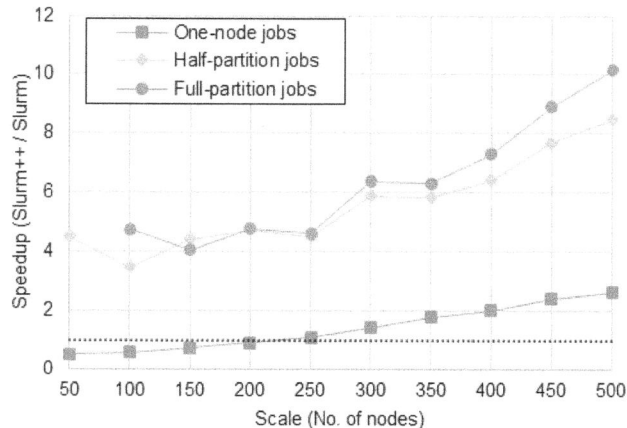

Figure 2: Speedup summary between Slurm++ and Slurm

5. RELATED WORK

Slurm [11] does scalable job launch via a tree based overlay network. But as we have evaluated, as scales grow, the scheduling cost per node increases, requiring coarser granularity workloads to maintain efficiency. BPROC [23] was a single system image and single process space clustering environment where all process ids were managed and spawned from the head node. BPROC moved virtual process spaces from the head node to the compute nodes via a tree spawn mechanism. However, BPROC was a centralized server with no failover mechanism. ALPS [24] is Cray's resource manager that constructs a management tree for job launch, and controls separate daemon with each one having a specific purpose. It is multiple single-server architecture, with many single-point of failures. ORCM [25] is an Open Resilient Cluster Manger originated from the Cisco runtime system for monitoring enterprise-class routers, and is under development in Intel to do resource monitoring and scalable job launching. Currently, the state management of ORCM is centralized in the top layer aggregator, which is not scalable. The use of KVS to manage the state similar to Slurm++ is an alternative for ORCM.

6. CONCLUSIONS AND FUTURE WORK

Exascale machine require next generation workload managers to deliver jobs with much higher throughput and lower latency for a mixture of applications. With the proposed resource stealing technique, Slurm++ showed performance 10X better than the Slurm production system, and the performance gap is expected to grow as the jobs and system scales increase. In the future, we will explore elastic resource allocation that could dynamically expand and shrink the allocated resources for the composed applications in Slurm++. This will help Slurm++ maintain high system utilization for a broader category of ensemble applications. Additions to this work would also include the investigations of distributed power-aware scheduling at the core level. Currently, Slurm++ allocates the whole node to a job, and doesn't consider the power effect. We will over-decompose a node, and launch jobs at the core level in order to save power. Another extension is to integrate Slurm++ with the MTC task execution fabric, MATRIX [26][27][28] (and the SimMatrix simulator [29][30][31]) and CloudKon [32], and study the scheduling of data-intensive HPC applications [33][10][34].

7. ACKNOWLEDGMENTS

This work was supported by the U.S. Department of Energy contract AC52-06NA25396, and in part by the National Science Foundation under award CNS-1042543 (PRObE). We thank Ralph Castain from Intel for his thoughtful comments.

8. REFERENCES

[1] V. Sarkar, S. Amarasinghe, et al. "ExaScale Software Study: Software Challenges in Extreme Scale Systems." ExaScale Computing Study, DARPA IPTO, 2009.

[2] Michael Wilde, et al. "Extreme-scale scripting: Opportunities for large task-parallel applications on petascale computers", SciDAC 2009.

[3] M. Snir, S.W. Otto, et al. "MPI: The Complete Reference." MIT Press, 1995.

[4] A. Basermann and K. Solchenbach. "Ensemble Simulations on highly Scaling HPC Systems (EnSIM)." CiHPC - Competence in High Performance Computing, June 2010.

[5] I. Raicu, Y. Zhao, et al. "Many-Task Computing for Grids and Supercomputers." IEEE MTAGS 2008.

[6] K. Wang, Z. Ma, I. Raicu. "Modelling Many-Task Computing Workloads on a Petaflop IBM BlueGene/P Supercomputer." IEEE CloudFlow 2013.

[7] Catalin Dumitrescu, Ioan Raicu, Ian Foster. "Experiences in Running Workloads over Grid3", GCC 2005

[8] Catalin Dumitrescu, Ioan Raicu, Ian Foster. "The Design, Usage, and Performance of GRUBER: A Grid uSLA-based Brokering Infrastructure", JGC 2007.

[9] Dongfang Zhao, Ioan Raicu. "Distributed File Systems for Exascale Computing", Doctoral Showcase, IEEE/ACM Supercomputing/SC 2012

[10] D. Zhao, Z. Zhang, et al. "FusionFS: Towards Supporting Data-Intensive Scientific Applications on Extreme-Scale High-Performance Computing Systems." IEEE International Conference on Big Data 2014.

[11] M. Jette, A. Yoo, M. Grondona. "SLURM: Simple Linux utility for resource management." JSSPP 2003.

[12] B. Bode, D. Halstead, et al. "The Portable Batch Scheduler and the Maui Scheduler on Linux Clusters." Usenix, 4th Annual Linux Showcase & Conference, 2000.

[13] W. Gentzsch, et al. "Sun Grid Engine: Towards Creating a Compute Power Grid." CCGrid 2001.

[14] K. Wang, I. Raicu. "Towards Next Generation Resource Management at Extreme-Scales." IIT, PhD Proposal, 2014.

[15] X. Zhou, H. Chen, et al. "Exploring Distributed Resource Allocation Techniques in the SLURM Job Management System." Tech Report, IIT, 2013.

[16] K. Wang, X. Zhou, et al. "Next generation job management systems for extreme-scale ensemble computing." ACM HPDC 2014.

[17] T. Li, X. Zhou, et al. "ZHT: A Light-weight Reliable Persistent Dynamic Scalable Zero-hop Distributed Hash Table." IEEE Conference on IPDPS, 2013.

[18] K. Wang, A. Kulkarni, et al. "Using Simulation to Explore Distributed Key-Value Stores for Extreme-Scale Systems Services." IEEE/ACM Supercomputing/SC 2013.

[19] A. Kulkami, K. Wang, et al. "Exploring Design Tradeoffs for Exascale System Services through Simulation." Tech Report, Los Alamos National Laboratory, 2013.

[20] J. Dinan, D.B. Larkins, et al. "Scalable work stealing." IEEE/ACM Supercomputing/SC, 2009.

[21] Google. "Google Protocol Buffers," available at https://github.com/google/protobuf/, 2015.

[22] G. Gibson, G. Grider, et al. "Probe: A thousand node experimental cluster for computer systems research." 2013.

[23] E. Hendriks. "BProc: The Beowulf distributed process space." ACM Proceedings of ICS, 2002.

[24] M. Karo, R. Lagerstrom, et al. "The application level placement scheduler." Cray User Group, pp. 1-7, 2006.

[25] Intel, ORCM, https://github.com/open-mpi/orcm, 2015.

[26] K. Wang, et al. "MATRIX: MAny-Task computing execution fabRIc at eXascale." Tech Report, IIT, 2013.

[27] K. Wang, I. Raicu. "Scheduling Data-intensive Many-task Computing Applications in the Cloud." NSFCloud Workshop, 2014.

[28] K. Wang, A. Rajendran, et al. "Paving the Road to Exascale with Many-Task Computing." Doctoral Showcase, IEEE/ACM Supercomputing/SC 2012.

[29] K. Wang, K. Brandstatter, I. Raicu, "SimMatrix: Simulator for MAny-Task computing execution fabRIc at eXascale." ACM HPC, 2013.

[30] K. Wang, J. Munuera, et al. "Centralized and Distributed Job Scheduling System Simulation at Exascale." Tech Report, IIT, 2011.

[31] D. Zhao, D. Zhang, et al. "Exploring Reliability of Exascale Systems through Simulations." ACM HPC 2013.

[32] I. Sadooghi, S. Palur, et al. "Achieving Efficient Distributed Scheduling with Message Queues in the Cloud for Many-Task Computing and High-Performance Computing." IEEE/ACM CCGrid, 2014.

[33] K. Wang, X. Zhou, et al. "Optimizing Load Balancing and Data-Locality with Data-aware Scheduling." IEEE International Conference on Big Data 2014.

[34] K. Ramamurthy, K. Wang, et al. "Exploring Distributed HPC Scheduling in MATRIX." Tech Report, IIT, 2013.

A Declarative Optimization Engine for Resource Provisioning of Scientific Workflows in IaaS Clouds

Amelie Chi Zhou
SCE, Nanyang Technological University
czhou1@ntu.edu.sg

Bingsheng He
SCE, Nanyang Technological University
bshe@ntu.edu.sg

Xuntao Cheng
LILY, IGS, Nanyang Technological University
xcheng002@ntu.edu.sg

Chiew Tong Lau
SCE, Nanyang Technological University
asctlau@ntu.edu.sg

ABSTRACT

Resource provisioning for scientific workflows in Infrastructure-as-a-service (IaaS) clouds is an important and complicated problem for budget and performance optimizations of workflows. Scientists are facing the complexities resulting from severe cloud performance dynamics and various user requirements on performance and cost. To address those complexity issues, we propose a declarative optimization engine named *Deco* for resource provisioning of scientific workflows in IaaS clouds. Deco allows users to specify their workflow optimization goals and constraints of specific problems with an extended declarative language. We propose a novel probabilistic optimization approach for evaluating the declarative optimization goals and constraints in dynamic clouds. To accelerate the solution finding, Deco leverages the available power of GPUs to find the solution in a fast and timely manner. We evaluate Deco with several common provisioning problems. We integrate Deco into a popular workflow management system (Pegasus) and show that Deco can achieve more effective performance/cost optimizations than the state-of-the-art approaches.

Categories and Subject Descriptors: C.4 [Computer Systems Organization]: Performance of Systems

Keywords: Cloud; Resource Provisioning; Scientific Workflow

1. INTRODUCTION

Workflow models have been widely used by scientists to manage and analyze large-scale scientific applications in many research fields. For example, Montage workflow [28] is an example in astronomical study for generating sky mosaics. Workflow management systems (WMSes) are often used to support the execution of scientific workflows, for example, deciding which task runs on which resource. Such resource orchestration is a major component of WMSes and is important to the performance of workflows. Most of the WMSes, such as Pegasus [13] and Kepler [23], are originally designed for grid and local cluster environments. Their resource orchestration components (or schedulers) are mainly designed for performance optimizations.

Due to the pay-as-you-go benefits, many scientific workflow applications are recently deployed and executed on the infrastructure-as-a-service (IaaS) clouds [4, 40]. "Science clouds' become an emerging and promising platform for next-generation scientific computing [39, 29, 19]. New resource orchestration methods have been proposed to decide which task runs on which *instance* (or virtual machine, VM) in order to optimize the execution time, monetary cost or both. Since an IaaS cloud provider offers different types of instances and pricing models, existing WMSes have to be redesigned for the cloud environment. Particularly, they did not well address the following features in the cloud: various user requirements and cloud dynamics.

User requirements: In the cloud environment, scientists can have different or evolving requirements on the budget/performance goals and constraints. A user may want to minimize the execution time of a workflow on a cloud C1 with a pre-defined budget. In another scenario, she may consider running the workflow on multiple clouds besides C1. At this point, the optimal solution depends on the offerings of the multiple clouds and the network performance across clouds. For different problems, custom-designed approaches with problem-specific heuristics are proposed to find a suitable solution [25, 26]. For example, Mao et al. [25] use a series of heuristics for minimizing the monetary cost while satisfying the performance requirement of individual workflows (denoted as Autoscaling). Later, they have proposed a very different set of heuristics to optimize the performance with the budget constraint [26]. New algorithms for workflow optimizations are still emerging as clouds and applications evolve.

Different resource provisioning schemes result in significant monetary cost and performance variations. Figure 1 shows the normalized average cost of running Montage workflow with deadline constraint using different instance configurations on Amazon EC2. More details about experimental setup can be found in Section 6. We consider seven scenarios: the workflow is executed on a single instance type only (m1.small, m1.medium, m1.large and m1.xlarge), on randomly chosen instance types, and using the instance configurations decided by Autoscaling [25] and by this paper (denoted as Deco). Although the configurations m1.small and m1.medium obtain low average cost, they can not satisfy the performance constraint of the workflow. Among the configurations satisfying the deadline constraint, Deco obtains the lowest monetary cost. The cost obtained by Deco is only 40% of the cost obtained by the most expensive configuration (i.e., m1.xlarge).

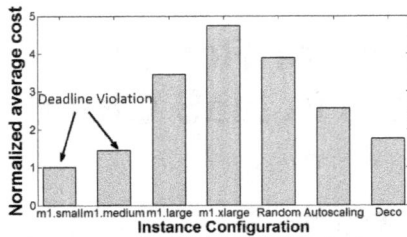

Figure 1: Average cost of running Montage workflows under different instance configurations on Amazon EC2.

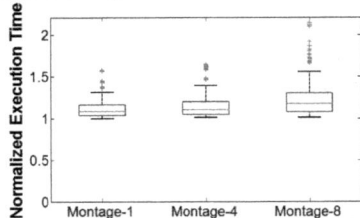

Figure 2: Execution time variances of running Montage workflows on Amazon EC2.

Cloud dynamics: As a shared infrastructure, the performance dynamics of the cloud have made the problem much complicated. Most resource provisioning approaches for scientific workflows in IaaS clouds [24, 7, 14] assume that the execution time of each task in the workflow is static on a given VM type. However, this assumption does not hold in the cloud, due to the performance dynamics in the cloud mainly caused by I/O and network interferences [33]. Figure 2 shows the quantiles of the normalized execution time of the Montage workflows in different scales running on Amazon EC2 for 100 times each. The instance configurations of each workflow are optimized by Deco. The execution time of the three workflows varies significantly. The variances are mainly from the interferences from disk and network I/O. In fact, scientific workflows may process input data of a large size. For example, an Epigenomics workflow typically processes input data of dozens of GB, and Montage and Ligo on hundreds of GB [18]. Due to the significant performance variance of scientific workflows in IaaS clouds, the deterministic notions of performance/cost constraints are not suitable, and a more rigorous notion is required.

In this paper, we address the above two problems in WMSes. Specifically, we propose a declarative optimization engine called *Deco*, which can automatically generate resource provisioning plan for scientific workflows in the cloud, considering the cloud performance dynamics. Many WMSes, such as Pegasus and Kepler, allow users to define their own resource scheduling policies. In this study, Deco works as an alternative to the user-defined *callouts* inside the WMS. With Deco, users only need to declaratively specify their performance/monetary cost goals and constraints and leave the rest to the optimization engine. Particularly, Deco uses a declarative language *WLog* which extends ProLog and supports a novel probabilistic notion of performance/monetary cost constraints to capture cloud dynamics. For example, a user can specify a probabilistic deadline requirement of $p\%$ so that the p-th percentile of the workflow execution time distribution in the target IaaS cloud is no longer than the pre-defined deadline. Similar probabilistic definitions have been used in computer networks and real-time systems [1]. Given a WLog program, Deco formulates the problem of finding a good solution as a search problem or even an $A^\star$ search problem for better efficiency (if users offer some application specific heuristics to prune optimization space).

Considering the features of our problem as well as the hardware features of modern accelerators, Deco leverages the power of the GPU to find the solution in a fast and timely manner. We implement Deco into a popular WMS (Pegasus [13]), although the design of this engine can be generally applied to other WMS.

We have applied Deco to three representative workflow optimization problems, which allow us to showcase the key features of Deco: 1) the workflow scheduling problem [25], 2) the workflow ensemble problem [24] and 3) the follow-the-cost problem across multiple clouds [36]. Our experiments show that, 1) Deco can significantly reduce the complexity of developing the three resource provisioning algorithms in the cloud; 2) Deco can achieve more effective performance/cost optimizations than state-of-the-art approaches; 3) The GPU-based acceleration improves the response time of getting the solution. As a result, the optimization overhead of Deco takes 4.3-63.17 ms per task for a workflow with 20-1000 tasks. That means, our optimization engine is practical for timely resource provisioning of workflows.

We summarize the main contributions of this paper as follows:

- *Declarative optimization engine.* Deco supports a novel declarative language for scientific workflow optimization problems in IaaS clouds, which combines special constructs of workflows and dynamics of cloud environment. Our engine supports both probabilistic and deterministic optimizations, while the existing approaches only support deterministic optimizations.

- *WMS integration.* We have developed a memory- and performance-optimized GPU-based implementation for Deco and integrated it into a popular WMS.

- *Use cases.* We have applied Deco to three representative use cases and the evaluation results have shown the effectiveness of Deco on these workflow optimization problems. Beyond these three use cases, we envision Deco has the potential to solve a wide class of workflow optimization problems.

The rest of this paper is organized as follows. Section 2 presents the overview of our system. We present three motivating examples in Section 3. Sections 4 and 5 present the major components of our system, including the declarative language and the GPU-accelerated solver. We evaluate the proposed optimization engine in Section 6 and review the related work in Section 7. We finally conclude this paper in Section 8.

2. SYSTEM OVERVIEW

WMSes [13, 23, 35] are often used by scientists to execute and manage scientific workflows. Those workflow management systems often have dependent software tools such as Condor and DAGMan [11], and require specific skills to implement the specific optimization algorithms in the cloud. All those software packages are interplayed with the resource provisioning problem in the cloud. It is desirable to abstract these complexities from users and shorten the development cycle. In this paper, we develop a declarative resource provisioning engine named Deco and integrate it into a popular WMS named Pegasus for executing scientific workflows in IaaS clouds. Figure 3 presents a system overview of Deco and its integration in the Pegasus WMS.

When using Pegasus to manage and execute workflows in the cloud, users submit workflows to Pegasus with DAX files, which describe workflows in the XML format. An example DAX file in Figure 4 describes a pipeline workflow. A job[1] XML element describes a task in the workflow, including its executable file (e.g., "process1" for task "ID01"), input and output files (e.g., "f.a" and "f.b1" respectively for task "ID01"). ⟨child⟩ and ⟨parent⟩ elements

---

[1] The term "job" is slightly misleading in the DAX file. This paper uses "task" to describe the minimum execution unit in a workflow, instead of "job".

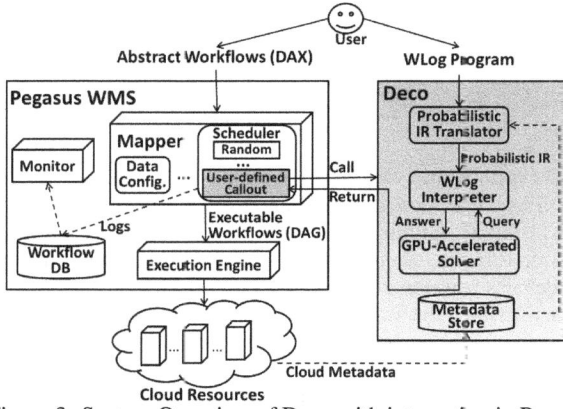

Figure 3: System Overview of Deco with integration in Pegasus

```
<!-- definition of all jobs -->
<job namespace="pipeline" name="process1" id="ID01">
<uses name="f.b1" link="output" />
<uses name="f.a" link="input" />
</job>
<job namespace="pipeline" name="process2" id="ID02">
<uses name="f.b2" link="output" />
 <uses name="f.b1" link="input" />
</job>
<!-- list of control-flow dependencies -->
<child ref="ID02"> <parent ref="ID01" /> </child>
```

Figure 4: An example DAX file.

show the dependency between tasks. For example, in the pipeline workflow, task "ID02" takes the output of task "ID01" (i.e., file "f.b1") as its input and thus is the child task of task "ID01". The mapper component of Pegasus takes the DAX file as input to generate executable workflows. An executable workflow contains information such as where to find the executable file of a task and which site the task should execute on. The execution engine of Pegasus distributes executable workflows to the cloud resources for execution.

In order to schedule the workflows in the cloud, users can alternatively choose from several traditional schedulers provided by Pegasus and our proposed Deco. For example, Pegasus provides a Random scheduler by default, which randomly selects the instance to execute for each task in the workflow. With Deco, we model the resource provisioning problem as a constrained optimization problem. Users can specify various optimization goals and constraints with *WLog* programs. WLog is a declarative language extended from ProLog, with special designs for scientific workflows and the dynamic clouds. Deco allows users to use *probabilistic* notions to specify their optimization requirements in the dynamic clouds. We model the dynamic cloud performance with probabilistic distributions, which is transparent to users. Deco automatically translates a WLog program submitted by users to probabilistic intermediate representation (IR) and interpret it using the WLog interpreter. We traverse the solution space to find a good solution for the optimization problem. For each searched solution, we evaluate it with the probabilistic IR, which requires a lot of computation [12]. To effectively and efficiently search for a good solution in a reasonable time, we implement a GPU-accelerated parallel solver to leverage the massive parallelism of the GPU. After the optimization process, Deco returns the found resource provisioning plan (indicating the selected execution site for each task in the workflow) to Pegasus for generating the executable workflow.

3. USE CASES

We present three use cases of resource provisioning problems for workflows in IaaS clouds, and demonstrate their common components to motivate our design of Deco. Those three use cases cover different aspects of typical workflow optimization problems. The first case addresses the resource provisioning for a single workflow, and the second case is for workflow ensembles (multiple workflows as a group). Both the first and the second cases can be performed in an offline setting. In the third case, we consider a dynamic workflow optimization problem, which makes workflow migration decisions across multiple clouds at runtime. Different from the former two cases, it assesses the efficiency of Deco. For each use case, we formally formulate the optimization goal and constraints of the problem. We present the declarative language specifications and detailed WLog programs of the use cases in later sections.

3.1 Workflow Scheduling Problem

In IaaS clouds, users rent instances to run workflows and pay for the instance hours accordingly. Since the cloud provides many types of instances with different capabilities and prices, the workflow scheduling problem is to select a good instance type for each task of the workflows, satisfying users' optimization requirements. While existing scheduling approaches use custom-designed heuristics for specific user requirements [25, 26], they are unlikely to work well upon changing optimization goals and constraints.

Different from the existing approaches, Deco takes the user requirements (i.e., optimization goals and constraints) as input and can adaptively work for a range of optimization problems. An example optimization goal is to minimize the average monetary cost of a workflow while satisfying its deadline requirement. Due to the cloud performance dynamics, we adopt the probabilistic deadline requirement notion for this problem. The probabilistic deadline requires that the p-th percentile of the workflow execution time distribution is no longer than D.

We assume the workflow has N tasks with IDs $0, 1, \ldots, N-1$, and the cloud provider offers K types of instances with IDs $0, 1, \ldots, K-1$. The optimization variable of this problem is vm_{ij}, which means assigning task i to instance type j. The value of vm_{ij} is 1 (i.e., task i is assigned to instance type j) or 0 (otherwise). Note, for each task i ($i = 0, 1, \ldots, N-1$), only one of the variables vm_{ij} ($j = 0, 1, \ldots, K-1$) can be 1. We denote the execution time distribution of task i on instance type j as $T_{ij}(t)$, which means $T_{ij}(t) = P(t_{ij} = t)$. That is, the probability that task i has execution time t on instance type j is $T_{ij}(t)$. The unit price of instance type j is U_j. We calculate the overall monetary cost of the workflow by summing up the average monetary cost of each task in the workflow, where the average monetary cost of a task is calculated using its mean execution time (M_{ij}) and the unit price of its assigned instance (see Equation (1)). We calculate the overall execution time of the workflow by summing up the execution time of all tasks on the critical path (denoted as CP) of the workflow (see Equation (3)). Formally, we express the problem as below:

$$\min \sum_i \sum_j (M_{ij} \times U_j \times vm_{ij}) \qquad (1)$$

$$M_{ij} = \sum_{t=0}^{D} (T_{ij}(t) \times t) \qquad (2)$$

subject to:

$$P(t_w \leq D) \geq p, \text{ where } t_w = \sum_{i \in CP} \sum_j (t_{ij} \times vm_{ij}) \qquad (3)$$

3.2 Workflow Ensemble

Many scientific workflow applications have a group of workflows with similar structure but different parameters (e.g., input data, number of tasks). These groups of workflows are called workflow ensembles [24], in which each workflow is associated with a priority to indicate its importance in the group and has a pre-defined deadline constraint. There is also an overall budget constraint for executing the entire ensemble. Such a resource provisioning problem aims to execute as many high-priority workflows as possible using limited resources. Given the budget and deadline constraints, the optimization goal is to maximize the total score of completed workflows in an ensemble e (see Equation (4)). The score of a workflow is proportional to its priority. We denote the priority of a workfow w as $Priority(w)$ (the highest-priority workflow has $Priority(w) = 0$, the next highest workflow has $Priority(w) = 1$, and so on). We use $CMP(e)$ to represent the set of completed workflows in the assemble e. Each workflow w in the ensemble has a probabilistic deadline constraint, which requires that the p_w-th percentile of the workflow execution time distribution is no longer than D_w (see Equation (6)). The budget constraint is set for the entire ensemble, which requires that the overall monetary cost of all workflows in ensemble e is smaller than the pre-defined budget B (see Equation (5)). We can formulate this problem as below:

$$\max \sum_{w \in CMP(e)} 2^{-Priority(w)} \qquad (4)$$

subject to:

$$\sum_{i \in w, w \in e} \sum_{j} (M_{ij} \times U_j \times vm_{ij}) \leq B \qquad (5)$$

$$\forall w \in CMP(e), \quad P(t_w \leq D_w) \geq p_w \qquad (6)$$

3.3 Follow-the-Cost

Our third use case is a dynamic workflow migration problem called follow-the-cost. We consider migrating multiple workflows among multiple cloud platforms to optimize the cost. We consider a task as the smallest migration unit. Different clouds may have different pricing schemes. Even within the same cloud provider, the pricing in multiple data centers may be different. For example, in Amazon EC2, prices of instances in the Singapore region are higher than those of the same type in the US East region. Migrating a partially executed workflow to another more cost-efficient cloud can reduce the monetary cost. However, the migrations induce extra cost on transferring intermediate data between clouds. We denote the monetary cost on the execution and migration of a task i as EC_i and MC_i, respectively. If a task is migrated from one cloud to another, the migration cost is the networking cost spent on transferring necessary data for executing the task. The goal of this problem is to minimize the overall monetary cost of all workflows while satisfying the deadline constraint of each individual workflow.

Due to cloud performance dynamics, the migration decisions have to be made at runtime for the trade-off between the monetary cost on execution and migration. Because of the light-weight characteristic of Deco, our engine is able to effectively handle this type of dynamic optimization problems. To assess runtime optimization, we use the traditional static deadline notion for this problem, which is that the expected execution time of each workflow w is no longer than a pre-defined deadline D_w. We denote the runtime execution time of a task i on instance type j as t_{ij}. $Unfinished(sw)$ denotes all unfinished tasks in the set of workflows sw. The optimization parameter of this problem is G_i^{mn}, meaning migrating a task i from a cloud m to another cloud n ($n \neq m$). We denote the transferred data size for task i as $data_i$, the network bandwidth between the original and migrated clouds as $Band_{mn}$ and the networking price between the two clouds as K_{mn}. Given the above variables, we formulate the problem as follows:

$$\min \sum_{i \in Unfinished(sw)} (EC_i + MC_i) \qquad (7)$$

$$EC_i = \sum_{j} (t_{ij} \times U_j \times vm_{ij}) \qquad (8)$$

$$MC_i = \sum_{n} (data_i \times K_{mn} \times G_i^{mn}) \qquad (9)$$

subject to:

$$\forall w \in sw, \sum_{i \in CP(w)} \left(\sum_{j} t_{ij} \times vm_{ij} + \sum_{n} \frac{data_i}{Band_{mn}} \times G_i^{mn} \right) \leq D \qquad (10)$$

Observations on Use Cases. We have the following observations. First, there are some common optimization requirements in the workflow optimization problems, such as the deadline and budget constraints. Second, the workflow structures and the data dependencies between tasks make the optimization problem much complex. Third, the various cloud offerings and dynamic cloud performance add another dimension for the resource provisioning problems. Thus, it is feasible and also desirable to attempt common constructs for different resource provisioning problems of workflows in IaaS clouds.

4. PROBABILISTIC SPECIFICATION LANGUAGE

WLog is designed as a declarative language for resource provisioning of scientific workflows in IaaS clouds. The major goal is to ease the programming effort of users. WLog is extended from ProLog [22]. ProLog is a powerful declarative language that allows users to define their constraint logics in a very convenient manner. We can leverage efficient techniques in ProLog such as ordering and cut pruning [30] to efficiently solve optimization problems. Users can also declare their own predicates to improve the search efficiency. For example, in Deco, we allow users to offer hints to our solver so that Deco can leverage the efficient A^* search. We model the cloud dynamics with probabilistic distributions and offer probabilistic notions for users to specify their optimization requirements. Some extensions of ProLog, such as the probabilistic extension [12], can be very useful for specifying the workflow optimization problems in dynamic clouds.

In the remainder of this section, we present the details on WLog language, by using a concrete example on the workflow scheduling problem. Additional examples on the workflow ensemble and follow-the-cost problems are presented in the appendix of our technical report [47].

4.1 ProLog Conventions

Following the conventions in ProLog, a WLog program consists of a set of declarative rules. Each rule has the form of `h :- c1, c2, ..., cn.`, which means that "clauses `c1` and `c2` and ... and `cn` implies `h`". Here, commas connecting the clauses represent logical "AND". `h` is the *head* of the rule and `c1`, `c2`, ..., `cn` constitutes the *body* of the rule. A rule with empty body is called a *fact*. Rules can refer to one another recursively until a fact is reached. The order of the rules appearing in a program as well as the order of the predicates in a rule are not semantically meaningful, but affect the efficiency of interpreting a program. Conventionally, the names of variables begin with upper-case letters while constant names start with lower-case letters.

Prolog offers many built-in predicates, such as the ones for arithmetic operations (e.g., `is`, `max` and `sum`) and the ones for list-based operations (e.g., `setof`, `findall`). These built-in predicates help users to write neat and concise WLog programs. We highlight the Prolog built-in predicates in blue color to differentiate from other terms. For example, one may write a rule in Example 1 (see Section 4.3):

```
cost(Tid,Vid,C) :- price(Vid,Up), exetime(Tid,Vid,T),
configs(Tid,Vid,Con), C is T*Up*Con.
```

where `price(Vid,Up)` stores the unit price of instance `Vid` into the unit price variable `Up`, `configs(Tid,Vid,Con)` indicates that task

Table 1: Workflow and cloud specific built-in functions and keywords in WLog.

Function/Keyword	Remark
`goal`	Optimization goal defined by the user.
`cons`	Problem constraint defined by the user.
`var`	Problem variable to be optimized.
`import(daxfile)`	Import the workflow-related facts generated from a DAX file.
`import(cloud)`	Import the cloud-related facts from the cloud metadata.
`budget(p, b)`	A probabilistic budget requirement that the p-th percentile of workflow monetary cost distribution is no larger than b.
`deadline(p, d)`	A probabilistic deadline requirement that the p-th percentile of workflow execution time distribution is no longer than d.
`enabled(astar)`	The A^* heuristic is enabled for efficiently finding solutions.

`Tid` runs on instance of type `Vid` and `exetime(Tid,Vid,T)` stores the execution time of task `Tid` on instance `Vid` into the execution time variable `T`. This rule calculates the monetary cost (`C`) of executing task `Tid` on instance `Vid`.

4.2 WLog Extensions

We extend ProLog in two major aspects to custom it for solving resource provisioning problems of scientific workflows. The first kind is to extend ProLog for workflow processing and IaaS clouds (i.e., cloud offerings and dynamic cloud performance). Given the dynamic cloud performance, WLog offers the probabilistic notion of specifying performance and budget goals. The second kind is to balance the design intentions on the expressive power and simplicity. For instance, WLog offers high-level workflow specific built-ins like `budget` and `deadline` to simplify the expressions.

WLog provides keywords for users to specify their optimization problems, as shown in Table 1. The `goal` keyword indicates the optimization goal. The `cons` keyword indicates the optimization constraints. The `var` keyword indicates the variables to be optimized. WLog also provides several workflow-specific and cloud-specific built-in functions and keywords.

Workflow- and cloud-specific facts. We allow users to "import" two kinds of facts from external workflow abstraction files (DAX files in this study), or by specifying which cloud to use. This functionality saves users a lot of time on writing the tedious facts related to workflows and clouds, and also makes the WLog programs neat and easy to read/maintain.

From the DAX file, Deco imports the common facts of the workflow, including workflow structure, input/output data of each task in the workflow, and the executable file of the task. For example, from the DAX file shown in Figure 4, a workflow structural fact `child(ID01, ID02)` (representing task "ID02" is the child task of task "ID01") can be imported.

The built-in predicate `import(cloud)` covers the cloud-related facts, such as the cloud provided instance types, the pricing for each type of instances and their capabilities. For example, we can construct a fact for an Amazon EC2 instance type, m1.small: ⟨ key="id1", cloud="ec2", instype="m1.small", price="0.044", cpu="1", mem="1.7", ...⟩. Some properties such as price and storage are constants, and other properties such as I/O and network performance can be modeled with some probabilistic distributions [48]. For example, the random I/O performance of the m1.medium instance type of Amazon EC2 can be modeled with a normal distribution (see Section 6 for details on the distributions and the way of obtaining them). For each dynamic performance component (i.e., network and I/O), we discretize the probabilistic

performance distributions as histograms, and store the histograms in the *metadata store*. We have developed some micro-benchmarks and periodically perform calibrations on the target cloud, which is totally transparent to users.

Constraint built-ins. We find that *budget* and *deadline* are the two most common constraints in workflow optimizations on IaaS clouds [25, 26, 24]. WLog supports built-in functions `budget` and `deadline` with probabilistic notions. For example, a user can submit a probabilistic deadline requirement that the 95-th percentile of the workflow execution time distribution is no longer than 10 hours. This requirement can be easily expressed as `deadline(95%, 10h)` in WLog.

We also support the `enabled` built-in function, which enables more efficient A^* search algorithm when searching for a good solution. We explain the usage and benefit of this function in Section 5.

4.3 A Concrete Example

In Example 1, the WLog program implements a workflow scheduling problem (described in Section 3.1) that aims at minimizing the total monetary cost of executing a Montage workflow in Amazon EC2 cloud while satisfying user's probabilistic deadline requirement `deadline(95%, 10h)`.

Example 1. WLog program for workflow scheduling.

```
        import(amazonec2).
        import(montage).
goal    minimize Ct in totalcost(Ct).
cons    T in maxtime(Path,T) satisfies deadline(95%,
        10h).
var     configs(Tid,Vid,Con) forall task(Tid) and
        vm(Vid).

        /*calculate the time on the edge from X to Y*/
r1      path(X,Y,Y,Tp) :- edge(X,Y), exetime(X,Vid,T),
        configs(X,Vid,Con), Con==1, Tp is T.
        /*calculate the time on the path from X to Y,
        with Z as the next hop for X*/
r2      path(X,Y,Z,Tp) :- edge(X,Z), Z\==Y,
        path(Z,Y,Z2,T1), exetime(X,Vid,T),
        configs(X,Vid,Con), Con==1, Tp is T+T1.
        /*calculate the time on the critical path from
        root to tail*/
r3      maxtime(Path,T) :- setof([Z,T1],
        path(root,tail,Z,T1), Set), max(Set, [Path,T]).
        /*calculate the cost of Tid executing on Vid,
        where T includes the instance up time for data
        transfer*/
r4      cost(Tid,Vid,C) :- price(Vid,Up),
        exetime(Tid,Vid,T), configs(Tid,Vid,Con), C is
        T*Up*Con.
        /*calculate the total cost of all tasks*/
r5      totalcost(Ct) :- findall(C, cost(Tid,Vid,C),
        Bag), sum(Bag, Ct).
```

Program description. The program takes `task(Tid)`, `vm(Vid)`, `edge(X,Y)`, `exetime(X,Vid,T)` and `price(Vid,Up)` as input, which are imported from the workflow DAX file and the cloud metadata. The first two lines of import clauses specify the cloud- and workflow-related facts. `import(amazonec2)` indicates that the workflow is executed in the Amazon EC2 cloud, and the Amazon EC2 related facts are imported. For example, the `vm` entry stores the unique identifier of a VM type `Vid`. The `price` entry stores the unit price `Up` of instance `Vid`. `import(montage)` imports the workflow-related facts from the Montage DAX file, such as `task` and `edge`. Each `task` entry stores the unique identifier of a task `Tid`. The `edge` entry stores pairs of connected tasks `X` and `Y` (i.e., task `X` is the parent of task `Y`). `exetime` stores the execution time `T` of a task `X` on a VM `Vid`. Given these input entries, the program expresses the following. The WLog program is essentially equivalent to the optimization problem that we have formulated in Section 3.1.

- **Optimization goal:** Minimize the monetary cost `Ct` of executing a workflow in `totalcost`.
- **Constraints:** Satisfy the probabilistic deadline constraint that the 95-th percentile of the workflow execution time distribution is no longer than 10 hours.
- **Variables:** `configs(Tid,Vid,Con)` means configuring task `Tid` to instance type `Vid`. The value of *Con* is 1 if `Tid` is assigned to `Vid` and 0 otherwise. A solution to the workflow scheduling problem is a list of instance configurations for each task in the workflow.
- **Derivation rules:** Rule `r1` to `r3` calculate the overall execution time (or makespan) of a workflow. `path(X, Y, Z, Tp)` calculates the execution time (`Tp`) from task `X` to task `Y`, with task `Z` as the next hop of `X`. `maxtime(Path,T)` stores the execution time on the critical path of the workflow, i.e., the makespan of the workflow, in `T` (as in Equation (3) in Section 3.1). Note, we add task `root` and `tail` as two virtual tasks to represent the start and end of the workflow, respectively. Rules `r4` and `r5` calculate the overall monetary cost by summing up the monetary cost of all the tasks (as in Equation (1) in Section 3.1).

5. PROVISIONING PLAN GENERATION

This section describes the process of generating resource provisioning plan from WLog programs. A WLog program represents a constrained optimization problem for the resource provisioning of scientific workflows. When a WLog program is submitted, Deco first translates it into a *probabilistic* intermediate representation (IR) to capture the dynamics of the IaaS clouds. A WLog interpreter and a solver are implemented, where the interpreter is used to evaluate each solution searched by the solver with the probabilistic IR. Each searched solution is a potential resource provisioning plan for the optimization problem and the best found solution is returned as the output.

The interpretation of the probabilistic IR can induce high runtime overhead due to the large solution space in the workflow resource provisioning problem. In order to balance the overhead and the solution optimality, we implement the interpreter and solver with massive parallel implementations to search for a good provisioning plan efficiently. Particularly, the solver performs generic search by default and more efficient $A^\star$ search if users have specified search heuristics in the WLog program. Despite the previous studies on formulating constrained optimization problem as a search problem [3, 21], Deco has the following unique features.

First, the generic search in Deco is specifically designed for workflows and IaaS cloud features. The state transition in the solution space is driven by some common workflow transformation operations [46]. Second, the evaluation of each solution is based on the probabilistic IR of WLog programs to capture the dynamic cloud performance. We also leverage the available GPU power to accelerate the probabilistic evaluations. Note, the previous engines (e.g., [13]) can only support deterministic optimizations.

5.1 Probabilistic IR Translation

Due to cloud dynamics, we adopt probabilistic notion for the optimization goals and constraints. To accurately evaluate the probabilistic goals and constraints, given a WLog program, we first translate it into a probabilistic IR.

In order to generate the probabilistic IR, we first obtain the performance dynamics of the target cloud from the metadata store. We collect the task-related profiles from the specified DAX file to estimate the execution time of each task in the workflow. In Deco, we use an existing task execution time estimation approach for workflows [43]. The basic idea is that, given the input data size,

the CPU execution time (we can define a scaling factor to scale the CPU time in multi-core system [31]) and the output data size of a task, the overall execution time of the task on a cloud instance can be estimated with the sum of the CPU, I/O and network time of running the task on this instance. Note, since the I/O and network performance of the cloud are dynamic, the estimated task execution time is also a probabilistic distribution.

With the obtained cloud performance dynamics, we generate the probabilistic IR by translating each rule in the WLog program following the syntax in ProbLog [12]. Each rule in the probabilistic representation of a WLog program is in the form `p : h :- c1, c2, ..., cn.`, where `p` states the probability of the rule being true. For example, with the cloud performance histogram metadata, the execution time of task `Tid` on instance type `Vid` is represented by p_j : `exetime(Tid,Vid,Tj)`, where $j = 1, \ldots, n$ and n is determined by the number of bins in the performance histogram. Consequently, the rule shown in Section 4.1 can be translated to the probabilistic representation as below:

`pj : cost(Tid,Vid,Cj) :- price(Vid,Up), exetime(Tid,Vid,Tj), configs(Tid,Vid,Con), Cj is Tj*Up*Con.`

Support for deterministic goals and contraints. Deco uses a WLog interpreter to evaluate each searched solution using the translated probabilistic IR, as we shall see later in this section. On the other hand, Deco also supports deterministic optimization goals and constraints, which are common in dynamic optimization problems such as Follow-the-cost. In order to provide a uniformed interface, we translate WLog programs with deterministic optimization requirements as follows: we obtain the runtime cloud performance from the metadata store and translate each WLog rule with probability of 1.0 in the same way as mentioned above.

5.2 Probabilistic IR Evaluation

The WLog interpreter answers the queries submitted by the solver to evaluate the quality of each solution found by the solver. There are two kinds of WLog queries, i.e., the ones on optimization goals (querying the value of the goals) and the ones on optimization constraints (querying whether a constraint is satisfied). Each WLog query is evaluated with the probabilistic IR, by calculating the probability that the query succeeds.

The probabilistic IR of WLog inherits many features from ProbLog [12], and we interpret the probabilistic IR in the way similar to the interpretation of ProbLog. Specifically, all rules in the probabilistic IR are denoted with an array Rule[1,...,n], where n is the number of rules in the program. The unification technique of ProLog [30] is adopted in the interpreter to find a series of proofs with certain succeeding probability for each submitted query. Exact inference for a query in ProbLog is quite complex or even impossible for large programs, as the number of proofs to be checked for the inference grows exponentially [20]. ProbLog provides several approximation methods [20] to reduce the inference time complexity and we adopt the Monte Carlo approximation which can benefit from the massive parallelism of GPU computations.

Given the probabilistic IR, Algorithm 1 describes the general process of answering a query q with WLog interpreter. In Line 1-4, we recursively look for the proofs of query q, using the unification policies defined in ProLog. Specifically, the *match* function uses the unification policies to find a match between the head of query q and the head of the rules in the probabilistic IR. If a match is found (Line 3), we generate a new query with the body of the matched rule and the body of q remaining to be matched. We recursively look for a match for the generated query. The function *append(X,Y)* concatenates two terms X and Y. When the newly generated query is nil, it means all terms of q have been answered.

In this way, we find a proof to query q. Given the found proofs and the probability p_i of each rule Rule[i], in Line 7-15, we use the Monte Carlo method [34] to calculate the approximate inference of the query. Specifically, *Max_iter* realizations are sampled from the found proofs. For each sample, we calculate the probability of the proof being true using the probabilities of the rules forming the proof. If query q is a query on constraint, we return the average probability of the constraint being true in the *Max_iter* samples. Otherwise, we return the mean value of the optimization goal as the answer to q.

GPU-accelerated evaluation implementation. GPUs can support a large number of threads running in parallel, but a single thread is not as powerful as a conventional CPU thread. GPU threads are grouped in *thread blocks*, where threads in the same block can cooperate via *shared memory*. Threads from different blocks communicate via the global memory and the data access bandwidth degrades a lot compared to the shared memory. We follow the following principles during the GPU implementation: 1) the work assigned to each thread should be light-weight; 2) threads in the same block should cooperate to reduce redundant computations; 3) communications across thread blocks should be avoided. Overall, our implementation features the GPU hardware features.

We adopt Monte Carlo approximation for the probabilistic IR evaluation. Since the work in one Monte Carlo iteration is light-weight, we use one GPU thread for each Monte Carlo iteration. We store the temporary results of each thread into the shared memory for fast synchronization.

Algorithm 1 Query evaluation function *WLogInterp*(q).

Require:
  Probabilistic IR with goal g, variable *var*;
  n rules: $p_i : Rule[i]$. where $i = 1, \ldots, n$;
  m probabilistic constraints: $Cons(1, \ldots, m)$;
  Query request: q.

1: **if** q is **not** *nil* **then**
2:   **for** $i = 1$ **to** n **do**
3:     **if** $match(head(Rule[i]), head(q))$ **then**
4:       $WLogInterp(append(body(Rule[i]), body(q)))$;
5: **else**
6:   $EvalResult = 0$;
7:   **for each** Monte Carlo iteration in *Max_iter* iterations **do**
8:     Randomly generate a realization from the found proofs and calculate the probability of the realization being true as α;
9:     **if** q is a probabilistic constraint of the program and the inference of q from the sampled realization is true **then**
10:       $EvalResult += \alpha$;
11:     **else**
12:       **if** q is a query on the optimization goal **then**
13:         Infer the result r of the query from the sampled realization;
14:         $EvalResult += r \times \alpha$;
15:   $EvalResult /= Max\_iter$;
16:   **return** $EvalResult$;

5.3 Parallel Solver Design

Generic Search. The key challenge of designing a generic search is how to have a generic representation on the state as well as state transitions. Each state is a solution to the optimization problem. We evaluate each state using the probabilistic IR and formulate the search as a traversal of the search tree from the initial state. In Example 1, a state in the search tree is an instance configuration plan, where `configs(Tid, Vid, Con)` stores the instance configuration of each task `Tid` in the workflow.

We need a systematic and generic approach to define the transition between states in order to explore all the feasible states. As a start, we adopt the transformation operations [46] as transitions to traverse the search tree. In our previous work, we propose six general transformation operations for workflows, including Move,

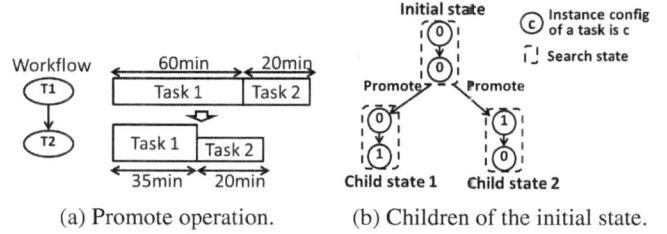

(a) Promote operation. (b) Children of the initial state.

Figure 5: Examples of using transformation operations in the generic search.

Merge, Promote, Demote, Split and Co-Scheduling. Suppose each task has an initial instance configuration (there are several ways to determine the initial configurations, see [46]). The transformation defines the change of instance configuration and the starting execution time of each task. We briefly describe the six transformation operations, and illustrate how we use them with an example.

The Move operation delays the execution of a task to a later time. The Merge operation merges two tasks with the same configuration onto the same instance to fully utilize the instance partial hour. The Promote/Demote operation changes the configuration of a task to a more/less powerful instance type. The Split operation suspends a running task and resumes its execution at a later time. The Co-scheduling operation assigns multiple tasks with the same instance configuration to the same instance. Figure 5a is an example of the Promote operation in the workflow scheduling problem. Consider a simple workflow with only two tasks. The deadline of the workflow is one hour and the execution time of the workflow under its initial instance configuration violates the deadline requirement. With the Promote operation, we can reduce the execution time of task 1 and satisfy the deadline constraint. Figure 5b shows the child states of the initial state generated by Promote. For example, the initial state configures each task with the cheapest instance type 0 (denoted as "0→0") and each child state configures one task with a better instance type 1 (denoted as "0→1" and "1→0"). Child state 2 is equivalent to the execution illustrated in Figure 5a.

Algorithm 2 General search process from initial state S to goal state D.

Require:
  WLog program P with user specified objective *goal* and constraints *cons*;

1: $CurBest = S$;
2: Create a FIFO queue Q and push the initial state into Q;
3: **for each** state *current* in Q **do**
4:   Assign the instance configurations in *current* to variables in P;
5:   Query *feasibility* = $WLogInterp(cons)$ and *cur_cost* = $WLogInterp(goal)$ from P, as in Algorithm 1;
6:   **if** *feasibility* is **true then**
7:     **if** *cur_cost* < *CurBest.cost* **then**
8:       $CurBest = current$;
9:       $CurBest.cost = cur\_cost$;
10:   Generate all child states of *current* that have not been visited;
11:   Add them into Q;
12: **return** $D = CurBest$;

Algorithm 2 shows the search process of the generic search. Deco evaluates each traversed state to check whether the target state is found. For evaluating a state, we first assign the values specified by the state to the variables in the WLog program and then submit queries regarding the goal and constraints (Line 5). The detailed algorithm of evaluating queries is shown in Algorithm 1.

We consider the balance between exploration and exploitation during the generic search. By exploitation, the depth first search is performed and the good partial solutions found are prioritized. By exploration, the breadth first search is performed and the threads traverse the search tree individually. A good partial solution does not guarantee global optimality. On the other hand, the parallelism of exploration offers a good opportunity to leverage the power of the GPU and accelerate the search process. Due to the above reasons, for the generic search, we choose exploration over exploitation for parallelism.

$A^\star$ **Search.** Deco allows users to define heuristic predicates on the good partial solutions. By calling `enabled(astar)` (as shown in Table 1), Deco utilizes $A^\star$ search to benefit from its pruning capability for better search performance. Particularly, users can specify two predicates $cal\_g\_score(s)$ and $est\_h\_score(s)$, which calculate the g score of state s and estimates the h score of state s, respectively. The $g(s)$ score and $h(s)$ score are the actual distance from the initial state to the state s and the estimated distance from the state s to the goal state, respectively. With the two heuristics, we can efficiently prune the solution space by not placing the states with high g and h scores into the candidate list.

Consider the workflow scheduling problem in Example 1, in order to enable $A^\star$ search, the user simply needs to add the following lines in her WLog program.

```
enabled(astar).
cal_g_score(C) :- totalcost(C).
est_h_score(C) :- totalcost(C).
```

In Example 1, both the g score and h score of a state s are the estimated monetary cost of state s. Since the optimization goal is to minimize monetary cost, if the monetary cost of a state is higher than the best found solution, all its child states can be pruned. Child states configure tasks with better instance types and thus always generate higher cost than their parent state, assuming the initial state to be all tasks on the cheapest instance type.

GPU-accelerated search implementation. According to our GPU implementation principles mentioned in Section 5.2, we use one thread block to handle each searched state since there is few data communication between two different states. We use N thread blocks to search the solution space at the same time, where N is the number of multiprocessors in the GPU. When evaluating a searched state, threads in the same block use the Monte Carlo method (see Algorithm 1) to verify the feasibility and calculate the optimization result of the state. Assume there are K threads in one block, ideally we can expect $K \times N$ times speedup comparing the parallel solver implementation to a single thread implementation. Note that, the GPU acceleration is transparent to users, which takes advantage of the available GPU computation power.

6. EVALUATION

We evaluate the performance dynamics observed on real clouds and then evaluate the effectiveness and efficiency of Deco.

6.1 Experimental Setup

We run Deco on a machine with 24GB DRAM, an NVIDIA K40 GPU and a 6-core Intel Xeon CPU. Workflows are executed on Amazon EC2 or a cloud simulator.

Clouds. We calibrate the cloud performance dynamics on Amazon EC2. The measurement results are used to model the probabilistic distributions of I/O and network performance, which are stored in the metadata store and used in `import(cloud)`. Specifically, we measure the performance of CPU, I/O and network for four frequently used instance types of Amazon EC2, namely m1.small, m1.medium, m1.large and m1.xlarge. We find that CPU performance is rather stable in the cloud, which is consistent with the previous studies [33]. In this paper, we focus on the calibration for I/O and network performance. We measure both sequential and random I/O performance for local disks. The sequential I/O reads performance is measured with hdparm. The random I/O

performance is measured by generating random I/O reads of 512 bytes each. Reads and writes have similar performance results, and we do not distinguish them in this study. We measure the network bandwidth between any two types of instances with Iperf [17]. In particular, we repeat the performance measurement under each setting once a minute, and each experiment lasts for 7 days (in total 10,000 times). When an instance has been acquired for a full hour, it is released and a new instance of the same type is created to continue the measurement.

Workflows. There have been some studies on characterizing the performance behaviors of scientific workflows [18]. In this paper, we consider three common workflow structures, namely Ligo, Montage and Epigenomics. The three workflows have different structures and parallelism.

We create three instances of Montage workflows with different sizes using Montage source code. Their input data are the 2MASS J-band images covering 1-degree by 1-degree, 4-degree by 4-degree and 8-degree by 8-degree areas retrieved from the Montage archive [27]. We denote them as Montage-1, Montage-4, and Montage-8 accordingly. Initially, the input data are stored in Amazon S3 storage. All intermediate data during workflow executions are stored on local disks and the final output data are stored in S3 for persistence.

Since Ligo and Epigenomics are not open-sourced, we construct synthetic Ligo and Epigenomics workflows using the workflow generator provided by Pegasus [41].

Implementation details. We conduct our experiments on both real clouds and simulator. These two approaches are complementary, because some scientific workflows (such as Ligo and Epigenomics) are not publically available. Specifically, when the workflows (including the input data and executables, etc.) are publically available, we run them on public clouds. Otherwise, we simulate the execution with synthetic workflows according to the workflow characteristics from existing studies [18].

On Amazon EC2, we create an AMI (Amazon Machine Image) installed with Pegasus and its prerequisites such as Condor. We acquire the four measured types of instances using the created AMI. We modify the Pegasus (release 4.3.2) scheduler to integrate Deco, such as scheduling the tasks onto instances of selected types. A script written with Amazon EC2 API is developed for acquiring and releasing instances at runtime.

We develop a simulator based on CloudSim [8]. We mainly present our new extensions, and more details on cloud simulations can be found in the original paper [8]. The simulator includes three major components, namely Cloud, Instance and Workflow. The Cloud component maintains a pool of resources which supports acquisition and release of Instance components. It also maintains the I/O and network performance histograms measured from Amazon EC2 to simulate cloud dynamics. The Instance component simulates cloud instances, with cloud dynamics from the calibration. We simulate the cloud dynamics in the granularity of seconds, which means the average I/O and network performance per second conform the distributions from calibration. The Workflow component manages the workflow structures and the scheduling of tasks onto the simulated instances.

We implemented three existing algorithms for the three use cases as state-of-the-art comparisons with Deco. Comparing the implementation of the existing algorithms and the WLog programs for the use cases, WLog significantly simplifies the programming for users to solve the workflow optimization problems, and brings the desirable features such as easy maintenance and code readability.

Workflow scheduling problem: We implement Autoscaling [25] as the comparison algorithm for this problem. This approach utilizes a series of heuristics such as deadline assignment to ensure the deadline while reducing the monetary cost.

Workflow ensemble: SPSS [24] is a state-of-the-art algorithm for scheduling workflow ensembles. SPSS is an offline provisioning and scheduling algorithm with heuristics to reduce resource waste on workflows that cannot be completed.

Follow-the-cost: Due to the large optimization overhead, most existing offline heuristics [21] can hardly solve this dynamic optimization problem at runtime. To make the workflow migration decisions, we design a simple and light-weight approach (denoted as Heuristic). At the offline stage, we consider the price differences among cloud data centers and determine the plan of migrating the workflows from their initial deployed data center to the more cost-efficient one. At runtime, we monitor the task execution time and make migration adjustments when the monitored execution time differs from the estimation by a threshold.

Parameter setting. We present the implementations in Deco and detailed experimental settings for each use case as follows.

Workflow scheduling problem: We study the average monetary cost and elapsed time for executing a workflow on Amazon EC2. Given the probabilistic deadline requirement, we run the compared algorithms for 100 times and record their monetary cost and execution time. For a fair comparison, we set the deadline of Autoscaling according to the QoS setting in Deco. For example, if user requires 90% of probabilistic deadline, the deadline setting for Autoscaling is the 90-th percentile of workflow execution time distribution. In the experiment, we consider the impact of different probabilistic deadline requirements of 90%, 92%, 94%, 96%, 98% to 99.9% (96% by default) on the optimization results. *All the results are normalized to those of Autoscaling [25].*

The deadline of workflows is an important factor for the candidate space of determining the instance configuration. We study the effectiveness of Deco under different deadline requirements. There are two deadline settings with particular interests: D_{min} and D_{max}, the expected execution time of all the tasks in the critical path of the workflow all on the m1.small and m1.xlarge instances, respectively. In the experiments, we vary the deadline parameter from $1.5 \times D_{min}$ (denoted as tight deadline), $\frac{D_{min}+D_{max}}{2}$ (denoted as medium deadline and used as the *default* setting) to $0.75 \times D_{max}$ (denoted as loose deadline) to study its impact on the optimization results. *All results are normalized to those of Autoscaling under the tight deadline.*

Workflow ensemble: In Deco, a state in the search space is implemented as an array of boolean values, where each dimension of the array indicates whether to execute a workflow in the ensemble. We enable the $A^\star$ search by specifying the g and h score of a search state s as the Score metric of s. Initially, all dimensions are set to false, meaning that none of the workflows in the ensemble is executed. For state transitions, we consider executing each of the uncompleted workflows in the ensemble to generate child states.

For a fair comparison, we follow the experimental setup in the previous study [24]. Like the previous study [24], we use simulation to perform the comparison studies. We generate in total 180 synthetic workflows with Ligo, Montage and Epigenomics application types, each type with 3 different workflow sizes from 20, 100 to 1000 tasks and 20 different workflow instances for each different setting. We construct five different ensemble types: constant, uniform sorted, uniform unsorted, Pareto sorted and Pareto unsorted. Each ensemble is composed of 30 to 50 workflows. We generate different deadline and budget parameters. We first identify the smallest budget and amount of time required to execute one/all of the workflows in the ensemble and denote them as MinBudget/MaxBudget and MinDeadline/MaxDeadline. We

generate 5 different budgets (denoted as Bgt1 to Bgt5, accordingly) and 5 different deadlines (denoted as D1 to D5, accordingly) equally distributed between the range [MinBudget, MaxBudget] and [MinDeadline, MaxDeadline], respectively. The default budget and deadline constraints are fixed at Bgt3 and Dl3, respectively. We perform sensitivity study on the probabilistic deadline requirement by varying it from 90% to 99.9% (96% by default). As for metrics, we compare the average monetary cost of workflows in the ensemble and the total score of completed workflows in ensembles. *All the metrics are normalized to those of SPSS.* Given each budget and deadline pair, we run the compared algorithms for 100 times.

Follow-the-Cost: In Deco, a state in the search space is implemented as an array of integers, where each dimension stands for a migration decision for a workflow. An integer in the array maintains the ID of the data center where the corresponding workflow will be migrated to. Generic search is used in the search engine of Deco. We make the migration decision periodically at runtime.

We consider two regions of the Amazon EC2, namely the US East Region and the Asia Pacific (Singapore) Region. These two regions have different instance prices. For example, the price difference of the m1.small instances is 33%. The number of workflows in each data center is randomly generated between 10 to 50. The threshold parameter for the runtime adjustment is set as 50% by default. We vary the threshold from 10%, 30%, 50%, 70% to 90% to show the trade-off between optimization results and overhead using Montage-8 workflows. As for metrics, we compare the overall monetary cost for workflow executions, including the operational cost spent on instance hours and the networking cost for transferring data across data centers. *All the metrics are normalized to those of Heuristic.*

6.2 Cloud Dynamics

We have observed performance dynamics on both I/O and network performances in the Amazon EC2 cloud. Figure 6a shows the network performance variance of m1.medium instances. The performance varies significantly, where the maximum variance can reach up to 50%.

Another important finding is that, we can model the performance dynamics with probabilistic distributions. Figure 6b shows the measurements of network performance of m1.medium instances. We verify the network performance with null hypothesis and find it can be modeled with a normal distribution.

We have also verified the performance of other instance types. Figure 7 shows the network performance between two m1.large instances and a m1.medium and a m1.large instance of Amazon EC2. The network performance dynamics of m1.medium instance type is much larger than that of m1.large instance type. Users can achieve better cloud performance by purchasing better types of instances.

On Amazon EC2, the sequential I/O performance of the four evaluated instance types follow Gamma distribution and the random I/O performance of the instance types follow Normal distribution. Table 2 presents the parameters of the distributions, which show that the I/O performance of the same instance type varies significantly, especially for m1.small and m1.medium instances. This can be observed from the θ parameter of Gamma distributions or the σ parameter of Normal distributions in Tables 2.

6.3 Evaluations on Use Cases

6.3.1 Workflow Scheduling Problem

We present the average monetary cost and execution time under different probabilistic deadline requirements in Figure 8. Note, the

Table 2: Parameters of I/O performance distributions on Amazon EC2.

Instance type	Sequential I/O (Gamma)	Random I/O (Normal)
m1.small	$k = 129.3, \theta = 0.79$	$\mu = 150.3, \sigma = 50.0$
m1.medium	$k = 127.1, \theta = 0.80$	$\mu = 128.9, \sigma = 8.4$
m1.large	$k = 376.6, \theta = 0.28$	$\mu = 172.9, \sigma = 34.8$
m1.xlarge	$k = 408.1, \theta = 0.26$	$\mu = 1034.0, \sigma = 146.4$

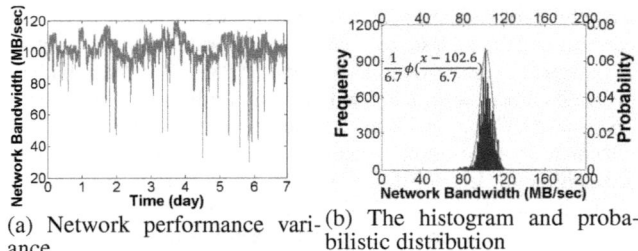

(a) Network performance variance

(b) The histogram and probabilistic distribution

Figure 6: Network performance dynamics of m1.medium instances in Amazon EC2 US East region.

optimization goal is to minimize the monetary cost. Deco obtains better cost optimization results than Autoscaling [25] under all cases, with the monetary cost reduction by 30%–50%. We have several major observations.

First, Deco reduces more monetary cost than Autoscaling on Montage workflows with larger sizes. The heuristics adopted in Autoscaling, such as deadline assignment, are not able to find the best instance configurations for tasks. On the other hand, our GPU-accelerated search engine can explore and exploit a large area of the search space in a reasonable time and thus is able to find better configurations. Second, when the probabilistic deadline requirement gets loose, Deco is able to save more cost compared to Autoscaling. This is because Autoscaling is static and thus cannot adjust the instance configurations accordingly. Although the average execution time optimized by Deco is larger than Autoscaling, all results can guarantee (be equal to or larger than) the probabilistic deadline requirement.

The optimization time of Deco is ignorable compared to the workflow execution time. Also, this use case is more for offline process. For comparison, we implement the CPU-based parallel algorithm in OpenMP, with a similar algorithm to the GPU algorithm. Nevertheless, Deco's GPU-based searches achieves 12X, 10X and 20X speed-up over CPU-based searches on six cores for the Montage-1, Montage-4 and Montage-8 degree workflows respectively. This demonstrates the efficiency of GPU accelerations.

Figure 11 shows the monetary cost and average execution time of Montage-8 workflow under different deadline settings. Deco obtains smaller monetary cost than Autoscaling under all settings. As the deadline gets loose, the monetary cost decreases and the

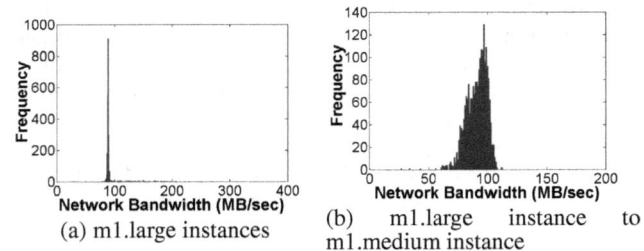

(a) m1.large instances

(b) m1.large instance to m1.medium instance

Figure 7: Network performance histograms of different instance types of Amazon EC2.

average execution time increases. This is because more cheap instances are selected for tasks when the deadline gets loose.

6.3.2 Workflow Ensemble

Overall, for all ensemble settings, Deco obtains better than or the same scores as SPSS [24]. Figure 9 shows the scores with different ensembles of Ligo, with the deadline D3 and budget Bgt1 to Bgt5. Under budget Bgt1 and Bgt5, SPSS and Deco always obtain the same scores because they can only make the same decision, that is, to execute one smallest workflow and all the workflows in the ensemble, respectively. Under budget Bgt2, Bgt3 and Bgt4, Deco obtains better scores than SPSS. This is because the workflow transformation operations in Deco can highly reduce the monetary cost of a workflow, and allow more workflows to be executed within the budget and deadline constraints. The average monetary cost of a workflow optimized by the SPSS algorithm is 1.4 times as high as that optimized by Deco.

When the probabilistic deadline requirement increases from 90% to 99.9%, Deco always obtains higher score than SPSS. The number of completed workflows in Deco is up to 60% higher than that in SPSS.

To evaluate the influence of memory access, we compared the performance of GPU-based search engine with different sizes of workflows. The average speedup of Deco over the CPU-based counterpart on the six cores is 36X, 22X, and 18X for 20-task, 100-task and 1000-task workflow ensembles respectively. As a result, the optimization overhead of Deco takes 4.3-63.17 ms per task for a workflow with 20-1000 tasks.

6.3.3 Follow-the-Cost

Figure 10a shows the normalized monetary cost obtained by Deco under different workflow sizes. Deco obtains the lowest monetary cost under all workflow sizes. As the workflow size increases, the cost reduced by Deco compared to the heuristic increases. The cost reduction by Deco mainly comes from two aspects. First, Deco dynamically changes the selected data center for the workflows to exploit the price difference between the two Amazon EC2 regions. The workflows deployed in the Singapore region are eventually migrated to the US East region due to the relatively low price in this region. Second, the cloud performance is dynamic and re-optimization at runtime generates more accurate configuration and migration solutions than offline optimizations. For example, when a task finishes earlier than its scheduled time, Deco chooses more cost effective and usually cheaper instance types for its child tasks after the re-optimization. Another case is, when the network performance between two clouds degrades at runtime, Deco changes the migration decision after the re-optimization. This is because the migration may increase the execution time of tasks and also increase the overall monetary cost.

Figure 10b shows the monetary cost results with different threshold settings. Deco obtains a smaller total cost under all threshold values. As the threshold decreases, the cost optimization result of the heuristic algorithm decreases. This is because the heuristic method performs more re-optimization operations under a smaller threshold. However, the optimization takes a long time, which cannot catch up with the workflow executions. In contrast, with the GPU power, Deco is still able to reduce the cost when the threshold is smaller than 10%.

7. RELATED WORK

There are a lot of works related to our study, and we focus on the most relevant ones on workflow optimizations on IaaS clouds, generalized optimization engines and GPU-based search strategies.

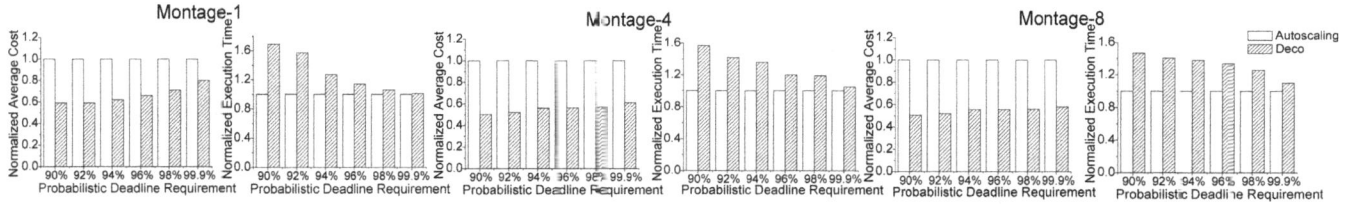

Figure 8: The average monetary cost and execution time of compared algorithms on Montage workflows.

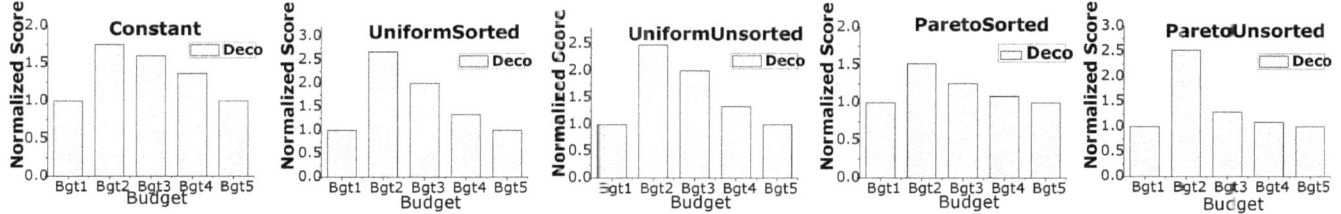

Figure 9: Scores of SPSS and Deco with different ensemble types under budget Bgt1 to Bgt5. Workflow type is Ligo and the deadline constraint is D3.

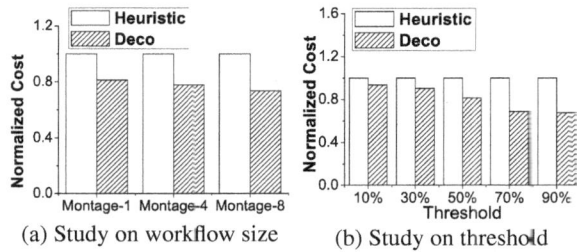

(a) Study on workflow size   (b) Study on threshold

Figure 10: Monetary cost of Deco and Heuristic of follow-the-cost: (a) workflow sizes; (b) performance change threshold.

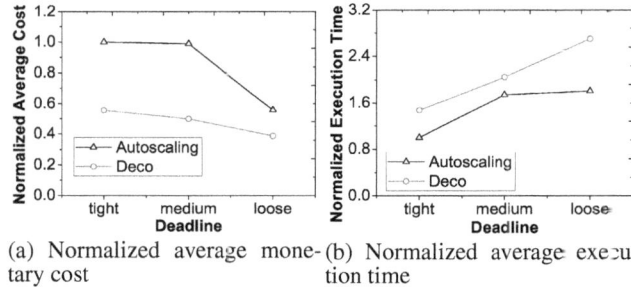

(a) Normalized average mone-tary cost   (b) Normalized average execution time

Figure 11: Sensitivity study on the deadline parameter using Montage-8 workflow.

Workflow optimizations. Workflow management systems (WM-Ses) are a fruitful research area in the cluster and grid environments [13, 23, 42, 9, 2]. Compared with grid and cluster environments, IaaS clouds have their own unique features in many system and economic aspects [15]. Many WMSes (such as Pegasus [13] and Kepler [23]), originally designed for grid and local clusters, are redesigned to cloud environments [18, 38].

There have been a lot of studies working on various optimization problems for scientific workflows in the cloud (e.g., [25, 26, 24, 14, 6, 45]). However, most of them target at specific goals or constraints for performance and monetary cost optimizations for workflow. In contrast, we propose a declarative and flexible workflow optimization engine which can be applied to a wider range of workflow optimization problems. Also, we demonstrate that GPU accelerations are viable for workflow optimizations, whereas none of above-mentioned related work has attempted GPU accelerations.

Previous works have demonstrated significant variances on the cloud performance [33, 16]. Machine learning techniques are used to adapt various applications in the changing execution environment [10]. In this paper, our declarative engine exposes the probabilistic performance distributions to users and abstracts the dynamic performance details from users with a declarative interface.

Generalized optimization engines. There have been some general optimization frameworks proposed to solve domain-specific optimization problems in the cloud. Alvaro et al. [3] propose to use a declarative language called Overlog to reduce the complexity of distributed programming in the cloud. Cologne [21] is another declarative system to solve a wide range of constrained optimization problems in distributed systems. They model the optimization problems in the form of Datalog with extensions for constraints and goals. Inspired by their design, this paper has the similar spirit in extending ProLog to hide the internal system details from users. Differently, this paper further makes a series of extensions that go beyond the previous studies [3, 21]. The significant ones include 1) formulate probabilistic extensions of cloud dynamics to ProbLog, 2) workflow specific constructs for reducing the complexity of developing workflow applications, and 3) a GPU-accelerated parallel solver for workflow optimizations.

There are some other studies on resource provisioning. Zhang et al. [44] proposed to formulate the mapping of users resource requirement to cloud resources with SQL queries. ClouDiA provides instance deployment solutions for users [49]. Rai et al. [32] proposed a novel bin-ball abstraction for the resource allocation problems. Different from bin-ball abstractions, workflows have more complicated structures. Moreover, bin-ball abstractions are static, which cannot capture cloud performance dynamics.

GPU-based search strategies. There have been a number of previous studies [5, 37, 32] that use the GPU to accelerate the performance of local search algorithms by means of exploring multiple neighbors in parallel. Different from those studies, our GPU-based implementation are specially designed for general workflow transformation-based optimizations.

8. CONCLUSION

In this paper, we have developed a declarative optimization engine *Deco* for WMSes to address the resource provisioning problem of scientific workflows in IaaS clouds. Deco works as an effective alternative to the existing schedulers of WMSes. With Deco, users can implement their workflow optimizations in a declarative manner, without involving the tedious and complicated details on dynamic cloud features and workflow processing. The declarative engine provides a series of practical constructs as building blocks to facilitate users to develop resource provisioning mechanisms for workflows. Moreover, a novel approach of probabilistic optimizations on goals and constraints is developed to address cloud dynamics. Deco also takes advantage of the available GPU power to accelerate the probabilistic evaluations. We integrate Deco into Pegasus (a popular workflow management system) and evaluate Deco with real scientific workflows on both Amazon EC2 and simulator, in comparison with the state-of-the-art heuristics based approaches. Our experiments show that 1) Deco can achieve more effective performance/cost optimizations than the state-of-the-art approaches, with the monetary cost reduction by 30-50%. 2) The optimization overhead of Deco takes 4.3-63.17 ms per task for a workflow with 20-1000 tasks. We have made Deco open-sourced at http://goo.gl/jZatcF.

9. ACKNOWLEDGEMENT

The authors would like to thank anonymous reviewers for their valuable comments. We acknowledge the support from the Singapore National Research Foundation under its Environmental & Water Technologies Strategic Research Programme and administered by the Environment & Water Industry Programme Office (EWI) of the PUB, under project 1002-IRIS-09. This work is partly supported by a MoE AcRF Tier 1 grant (MOE 2014-T1-001-145) in Singapore. Amelie Chi Zhou is also with Nanyang Environment and Water Research Institute (NEWRI).

10. REFERENCES

[1] L. Abeni and G. Buttazzo. Qos guarantee using probabilistic deadlines. In *ECRTS 1999*, pages 242 – 249.

[2] S. Abrishami, M. Naghibzadeh, and D. H. J. Epema. Deadline-constrained workflow scheduling algorithms for infrastructure as a service clouds. *FGCS*, pages 158–169, 2013.

[3] P. Alvaro, T. Condie, N. Conway, K. Elmeleegy, J. M. Hellerstein, and R. Sears. Boom Analytics: Exploring Data-centric, Declarative Programming for the Cloud. In *EuroSys '10*, pages 223–236.

[4] Amazon Case Studies. *http://aws.amazon.com/solutions/case-studies/.* accessed on July 2014.

[5] A. Arbelaez and P. Codognet. A GPU Implementation of Parallel Constraint-based Local Search. In *PDP '14*, pages 648 – 655.

[6] E.-K. Byun, Y.-S. Kee, J.-S. Kim, and S. Maeng. Cost Optimized Provisioning of Elastic Resources for Application Workflows . *FGCS*, pages 158–169, 2011.

[7] R. N. Calheiros and R. Buyya. Meeting Deadlines of Scientific Workflows in Public Clouds with Tasks Replication. *IEEE TPDS*, pages 1787 – 1796, 2013.

[8] R. N. Calheiros, R. Ranjan, A. Beloglazov, C. A. De Rose, and R. Buyya. CloudSim: A Toolkit for Modeling and Simulation of Cloud Computing Environments and Evaluation of Resource Provisioning Algorithms. *Softw. Pract. Exper.*, pages 23–50, 2011.

[9] J. Cao, S. Jarvis, S. Saini, and G. R. Nudd. GridFlow: Workflow Management for Grid Computing. In *CCGrid '03*, pages 198 – 205.

[10] Z. Chen, S. W. Son, W. Hendrix, A. Agrawal, W. keng Liao, and A. Choudhary. Numarck: Machine learning algorithm for resiliency and checkpointing. In *SC '14*, pages 733–744.

[11] DAGMan. *http://research.cs.wisc.edu/htcondor/dagman/dagman.html.* accessed on May 2014.

[12] L. De Raedt, A. Kimmig, and H. Toivonen. ProbLog: a Probabilistic Prolog and its Application in Link Discovery. In *IJCAI '07*, pages 2468–2473.

[13] E. Deelman, G. Singh, M.-H. Su, J. Blythe, Y. Gil, C. Kesselman, G. Mehta, K. Vahi, G. B. Berriman, J. Good, et al. Pegasus: A Framework for Mapping Complex Scientific Workflows Onto Distributed Systems. *Sci. Program.*, pages 219–237, 2005.

[14] K. Deng, J. Song, K. Ren, and A. Iosup. Exploring Portfolio Scheduling for Long-term Execution of Scientific Workloads in IaaS Clouds. In *SC '13*, pages 55:1–55:12.

[15] I. Foster, Y. Zhao, I. Raicu, and S. Lu. Cloud Computing and Grid Computing 360-Degree Compared. In *GCE '08*, pages 1 – 10.

[16] A. Iosup, S. Ostermann, M. N. Yigitbasi, R. Prodan, T. Fahringer, and D. H. Epema. Performance Analysis of Cloud Computing Services for Many-Tasks Scientific Computing. *IEEE TPDS*, pages 931 – 945, 2011.

[17] Iperf. *http://iperf.sourceforge.net.* accessed on July 2014.

[18] G. Juve, A. Chervenak, E. Deelman, S. Bharathi, G. Mehta, and K. Vahi. Characterizing and Profiling Scientific Workflows. *FGCS*, pages 1–10, 2013.

[19] K. Keahey, R. Figueiredo, J. Fortes, T. Freeman, and M. Tsugawa. Science Clouds: Early Experiences in Cloud Computing for Scientific Applications. In *CCA '08*.

[20] A. Kimmig, B. Demoen, L. De Raedt, V. S. Costa, and R. Rocha. On the Implementation of the Probabilistic Logic Programming Language Problog. *Theory Pract. Log. Program.*, pages 235–262, 2011.

[21] C. Liu, B. T. Loo, and Y. Mao. Declarative Automated Cloud Resource Orchestration. In *SoCC '11*, pages 26:1–26:8.

[22] J. W. Lloyd. *Foundations of Logic Programming*. 1984.

[23] B. Ludäscher, I. Altintas, C. Berkley, D. Higgins, E. Jaeger, M. Jones, E. A. Lee, J. Tao, and Y. Zhao. Scientific Workflow Management and the Kepler System: Research Articles. *Concurr. Comput. : Pract. Exper.*, pages 1039–1065, 2006.

[24] M. Malawski, G. Juve, E. Deelman, and J. Nabrzyski. Cost- and Deadline-constrained Provisioning for Scientific Workflow Ensembles in IaaS Clouds. In *SC '12*, pages 22:1–22:11.

[25] M. Mao and M. Humphrey. Auto-scaling to Minimize Cost and Meet Application Deadlines in Cloud Workflows. In *SC '11*, pages 49:1–49:12.

[26] M. Mao and M. Humphrey. Scaling and Scheduling to Maximize Application Performance within Budget Constraints in Cloud Workflows. In *IPDPS '13*, pages 67 – 78.

[27] Montage Archive. *http://hachi.ipac.caltech.edu:8080/montage/.* accessed on July 2014.

[28] Montage Workflow. *http://montage.ipac.caltech.edu/docs/download2.html.* accessed on July 2014.

[29] D. Nurmi, R. Wolski, C. Grzegorczyk, G. Obertelli, S. Soman, L. Youseff, and D. Zagorodnov. The Eucalyptus Open-Source Cloud-Computing System. In *CCGRID '09*, pages 124–131.

[30] R. A. O'Keefe. *The Craft of Prolog*. 1990.

[31] I. Pietri, G. Juve, E. Deelman, and R. Sakellariou. A Performance Model to Estimate Execution Time of Scientific Workflows on the Cloud. In *WORKS '14*, pages 11–19.

[32] A. Rai, R. Bhagwan, and S. Guha. Generalized Resource Allocation for the Cloud. In *SoCC '12*, pages 15:1–15:12.

[33] J. Schad, J. Dittrich, and J.-A. Quiané-Ruiz. Runtime Measurements in the Cloud: Observing, Analyzing, and Reducing Variance. *Proc. VLDB Endow.*, pages 460–471, 2010.

[34] P. Sevon, L. Eronen, P. Hintsanen, K. Kulovesi, and H. Toivonen. Link Discovery in Graphs Derived from Biological Databases. In *DILS '06*, pages 35–49.

[35] W. Tang, J. Wilkening, N. Desai, W. Gerlach, A. Wilke, and F. Meyer. A Scalable Data Analysis Platform for Metagenomics. In *BigData '13*, pages 21–26.

[36] J. Van der Merwe, K. Ramakrishnan, M. Fairchild, A. Flavel, J. Houle, H. A. Lagar-Cavilla, and J. Mulligan. Towards a Ubiquitous Cloud Computing Infrastructure. In *LANMAN '10*, pages 1–6.

[37] T. Van Luong, N. Melab, and E.-G. Talbi. GPU Computing for Parallel Local Search Metaheuristic Algorithms. *IEEE TC*, pages 173 – 185, 2013.

[38] J. Wang and I. Altintas. Early Cloud Experiences with the Kepler Scientific Workflow System. In *ICCS '12*, pages 1630–1634.

[39] L. Wang, J. Tao, M. Kunze, D. Rattu, and A. C. Castellanos. The Cumulus Project: Build a Scientific Cloud for a Data Center. In *CCA '08*, 2008.

[40] Windows Azure Case Studies. *http://azure.microsoft.com/en-us/case-studies/.* acessed on July 2014.

[41] Workflow Generator. *https://confluence.pegasus.isi.edu/display/pegasus/WorkflowGenerator.* accessed on July 2014.

[42] J. Yu and R. Buyya. A Taxonomy of Scientific Workflow Systems for Grid Computing. *SIGMOD Rec.*, pages 44–49, 2005.

[43] J. Yu, R. Buyya, and C. K. Tham. Cost-based Scheduling of Scientific Workflow Applications on Utility Grids. In *e-Science '05*, pages 140–147.

[44] M. Zhang, R. Ranjan, S. Nepal, M. Menzel, and A. Haller. A Declarative Recommender System for Cloud Infrastructure Services Selection. In *GECON'12*, pages 102–113.

[45] A. Zhou and B. He. Simplified resource provisioning for workflows in iaas clouds. In *CloudCom'14*, pages 650–655, 2014.

[46] A. C. Zhou and B. He. Transformation-based Monetary Cost Optimizations for Workflows in the Cloud. *IEEE TCC*, pages 85–98, 2013.

[47] A. C. Zhou and B. He. A Declarative Optimization Engine for Resource Provisioning of Scientific Workflows in IaaS Clouds. Technical Report 2015-TR-Deco, http://pdcc.ntu.edu.sg/xtra/tr/2015-TR-Deco.pdf, 2015.

[48] A. C. Zhou, B. He, and C. Liu. Monetary Cost Optimizations for Hosting Workflow-as-a-Service in IaaS Clouds. *IEEE TCC*, page PrePrints, 2015.

[49] T. Zou, R. Le Bras, M. V. Salles, A. Demers, and J. Gehrke. ClouDiA: a Deployment Advisor for Public Clouds. In *PVLDB'13*, pages 121–132.

HeteroDoop : A MapReduce Programming System for Accelerator Clusters

Amit Sabne
Purdue University
asabne@purdue.edu

Putt Sakdhnagool
Purdue University
psakdhna@purdue.edu

Rudolf Eigenmann
Purdue University
eigenman@purdue.edu

ABSTRACT

The deluge of data has inspired big-data processing frameworks that span across large clusters. Frameworks for MapReduce, a state-of-the-art programming model, have primarily made use of the CPUs in distributed systems, leaving out computationally powerful accelerators such as GPUs. This paper presents HeteroDoop, a MapReduce framework that employs both CPUs and GPUs in a cluster. HeteroDoop offers the following novel features: (i) a small set of directives can be placed on an existing sequential, CPU-only program, expressing MapReduce semantics; (ii) an optimizing compiler translates the directive-augmented program into a GPU code; (iii) a runtime system assists the compiler in handling MapReduce semantics on the GPU; and (iv) a tail scheduling scheme minimizes job execution time in light of disparate processing capabilities of CPUs and GPUs. This paper addresses several challenges that need to be overcome in order to support these features. HeteroDoop is built on top of the state-of-the-art, CPU-only Hadoop MapReduce framework, inheriting its functionality. Evaluation results of HeteroDoop on recent hardware indicate that usage of even a single GPU per node can improve performance by up to 2.78x, with a geometric mean of 1.6x across our benchmarks, compared to a CPU-only Hadoop, running on a cluster with 20-core CPUs.

Categories and Subject Descriptors

D.1.3 [**Software**]: PROGRAMMING TECHNIQUES—*Concurrent Programming, Distributed programming*; D.3.3 [**Software**]: PROGRAMMING LANGUAGES—*Frameworks*; D.3.4 [**Programming Languages**]: Compilers

Keywords

Distributed Frameworks; MapReduce; Accelerators; Source-to-source Translation; Scheduling

1. INTRODUCTION

A growing number of commercial and science applications in both classical and new fields process very large data vol-umes. Dealing with such volumes requires processing in parallel, often on systems that offer high compute power.

For this type of parallel processing, the MapReduce paradigm has found popularity. The key insight of MapReduce is that many processing problems can be structured into one or a sequence of phases, where a first step (Map) operates in fully parallel mode on the input data; a second step (Reduce) combines the resulting data in some manner, often by applying a form of reduction operation. MapReduce programming models allow the user to specify these map and reduce steps as distinct functions; the system then provides the workflow infrastructure, feeding input data to the map, reorganizing the map results, and then feeding them to the appropriate reduce functions, finally generating the output.

The large data volumes involved may not fit on a single node. Thus, distributed architectures with many nodes may be needed. Among the systems that support MapReduce on distributed architectures, Hadoop [1] has gained wide use. Hadoop provides a framework that executes MapReduce problems in a distributed and replicated storage organization (the Hadoop Distributed File System – HDFS). In doing so, it also deals with node failures.

Big-data problems pose high demands on processing and IO speeds, often with emphasis on one of the two. For general compute-intensive problems, accelerators, such as NVIDIA GPUs and Intel Phis, have proven their value for an increasing range of applications. To obtain high performance, their architectures make different chip real-estate tradeoffs between processing cores and memory than in CPUs. A larger number of simpler cores provide higher aggregate processing power and reduce energy consumption, offering better performance/watt ratios than CPUs. In GPUs, intra-chip memory bandwidth is high and multi-threading reduces the effective memory access latency. These optimizations come at the cost of an intricate memory hierarchy, reduced memory size, data accesses that are highly optimized for inter-thread contiguous (a.k.a. coalesced) reference patterns and explicitly parallel programming models. Using these architectures therefore requires high programmer expertise.

While accelerators tend to perform well on compute-intensive applications, IO-intensive MapReduce problems may not always benefit. Previous research efforts on MapReduce-like systems employ either GPUs [2, 3, 4] alone, disregarding IO-intensive applications, or CPUs [1, 5, 6, 7] alone, losing out on GPU acceleration. In this paper we present our

HPDC'15, June 15–20, 2015, Portland, Oregon, USA.
Copyright © 2015 ACM 978-1-4503-3550-8/15/06 ...$15.00.
http://dx.doi.org/10.1145/2749246.2749261.

HeteroDoop[1] system, which exploits *both* CPUs and GPUs in a cluster, as needed by the application.

The first challenge in developing such a heterogeneous MapReduce system is the programming method. In a naive scheme, the programmer would have to write two program versions, one for CPUs and the second for GPUs. This need arises as accelerators rely on explicitly parallel programs, be it either low-level programming models such as CUDA [8] and OpenCL [9], or high-level ones, such as OpenACC [10] and OpenMP 4.0 [11]. Although available high-level programming models relieve the user from having to learn model-specific APIs, such as in CUDA or OpenCL, they still require explicit parallel programming. On the other hand, in CPU-oriented MapReduce systems, programmers write only sequential code; the underlying framework automatically employs all cores in the cluster by concurrently processing the input data, which is split into separate files. Previous research on GPU uses for MapReduce has either relied on explicitly parallel codes with accelerator-specific optimizations [3, 4, 12, 13], and/or on specific MapReduce APIs [2, 3, 13, 14]. Programmability in both approaches is poor; the former requires learning low-level APIs and the latter necessitates application rewriting. To overcome these limitations, our contribution enables programmers to port already available sequential MapReduce programs to heterogeneous systems by annotating the code with *HeteroDoop directives*. Inserting such directives is straightforward, requires no additional accelerator optimizations, and leads to a single input source code for both CPUs and GPUs. Furthermore, the resulting code is portable; it can still execute on CPU-only clusters.

The second key challenge in exploiting accelerators is their limited, non-virtual memory space. The default parallelization scheme used in MapReduce/Hadoop engages multiple cores by processing separate input files in parallel – typically one per core, as an individual task. Data input is appropriately partitioned into separate *fileSplits*, which are fed to the different compute nodes and their threads. Simultaneous accesses by many threads to their fileSplits require a large memory. This size requirement is not a problem in today's typical CPUs with 4 to 48 cores and virtual memory support; however, in GPUs with several hundred cores and possibly thousands of threads, the available, non-virtual memory is insufficient. Our second contribution addresses this challenge by processing the data records *within* a fileSplit in parallel on the accelerator, while retaining the default processing scheme on the CPU.

The third challenge is to translate the annotated, sequential source code in a way that maximizes performance. Our contribution includes an optimizing source-to-source translator, assisted by a runtime system, that generates CUDA code and splits the work across CPUs and GPUs. In doing so, several issues arise. The first one is load imbalance across GPU threads, as the records processed in parallel may be of different size. A global work-stealing approach would incur high overheads, due to excessive atomic accesses by the GPU threads. HeteroDoop overcomes this issue by using a novel record-stealing approach that partitions the records statically across threadblocks but dynamically within threadblocks. Another issue is that GPU memory is statically allocated but the size of the map phase output, the key-value pairs, is not known a priori. Over-allocation would lead to

inefficient sorting of the key-value pairs, which follows the map phase. To resolve this issue, HeteroDoop includes a fast runtime compaction scheme, resulting in efficient sort. Furthermore, the runtime system executes the sort operation on the GPU rather than on the slower CPU. Other optimizations include efficient data placement in the complex GPU memory hierarchy and automatic generation of vector load/store operations.

A final challenge in developing such a heterogeneous MapReduce scheme is to account for the different processing speeds of CPUs and GPUs for work partitioning. While prior work [15, 16] has dealt with load balancing across nodes, intra-node heterogeneity has remained an issue. HeteroDoop's *tail scheduling* scheme addresses this issue. Our contribution is based on a key observation: the load imbalance only arises in the execution of the final tasks in a job; careful GPU-speedup-based scheduling of the tailing tasks can avoid the imbalance.

We have evaluated the HeteroDoop framework on eight applications, comprising well-known MapReduce programs as well as scientific applications. We demonstrate the utility of HeteroDoop on a 48-node, single GPU cluster with large datasets, and on a 64-node, 3-GPU cluster with in-memory datasets. Our main results indicate that the use of even a single GPU per node can speed up the end-to-end job execution by up to 2.78x, with a geometric mean of 1.6x, as compared to CPU-only Hadoop, running on a cluster with 20-core CPUs. Furthermore, the execution time scales with the number of GPUs used per node.

The remainder of the paper is organized as follows: Section 2 provides background on GPUs, MapReduce, and Hadoop. Section 3 describes the HeteroDoop constructs, followed by the compiler design in Section 4. Section 5 describes the overall execution flow of the HeteroDoop framework and details the runtime system. The tail scheduling scheme is explained in Section 6. Section 7 presents the experimental evaluation. Section 8 discusses related work, and Section 9 concludes the paper.

2. PRELIMINARIES

We introduce the basic terminology used in this paper for the GPU/CUDA architecture and programming model as well as the MapReduce and Hadoop concepts. We keep the discussion of GPUs and CUDA brief, assuming reader familiarity, but we do refer to introductory material [17].

2.1 CUDA Basics

In the CUDA [8] GPGPU architecture, the many GPU cores are structured into multiple Streaming Multiprocessors (SM). CUDA threads execute in SIMD fashion, where a *warp* consisting of 32 threads executes a single instruction and multiple warps time-share an SM in multi-threading mode. Storage is separate from the CPU address space; it is structured into the global (or device) memory, the per-SM shared memory (user managed cache), and specialized memories. The latter include the read-only constant and texture memories as well as the registers.

CUDA programming is explicitly parallel with user-driven *offloading*; i.e, the user identifies compute-intensive code sections, *kernels*, which are to be run on the GPU (the device) and inserts data transfers between CPU and GPU. The threads are organized into threadblocks. All threads within a threadblock execute on the same SM. The programmer manages most of the storage hierarchy explicitly, including fitting the data into the limited-size memories. There is no virtual memory support.

2.2 MapReduce and Hadoop

In the MapReduce model, programmers write a *map* and a *reduce* function, with the system organizing the overall execution workflow. The input data is placed on a distributed file system, such as the HDFS [18] (Hadoop Distributed File System). HDFS stores the input in blocks, or *fileSplits*. A job consists of a set of map and reduce tasks. In Hadoop, one node usually acts as master and the others as slaves. The master node runs a *JobTracker*, while each slave runs a *TaskTracker* – together they orchestrate the necessary map and reduce tasks in a way that exploits data locality, engages all available nodes and cores, and provides fault tolerance. The total number of concurrent tasks in a Hadoop cluster is typically the same as the number of available cores.

In Hadoop, each map task processes one fileSplit. The map function applies a map operation to each data record in this fileSplit. The map task emits a set of <key, value> pairs (or *KV pairs*). The framework puts these KV pairs into different partitions, each partition targeted at a particular reduce task. To form these partitions, the KV pairs are sorted by their keys and split by a default or user-provided partitioning function.

Each partition is then sent to its target reduce task. This task typically resides on a different node, making this a costly step. To reduce the cost, a task-local, user-provided reduction operation, known as the *combiner*, is applied first on each partition, minimizing the size of the communicated data. This communication is also known as the *shuffle* phase.

In the next phase, the *sort phase*, each reduce task merges the incoming partitions into a sorted list. Then the *reduce phase* applies the reduce function to these data. The output is written back to the HDFS. As the data volumes involved are typically very large, the intermediate results between map and reduce are typically written to the local disk.

Hadoop uses a *heartbeat* mechanism for communication between the JobTracker and TaskTracker. TaskTrackers send heartbeats to the JobTracker at regular intervals. These heartbeats include items such as status of tasks and free cores or *slots*. If the JobTracker finds that a TaskTracker has free slots, it schedules new tasks on the particular TaskTracker in the heartbeat response.

Hadoop is written in Java, and hence the baseline system supports input functions written in Java. Hadoop Streaming [19] is an extension that supports other languages for writing MapReduce programs. It is implemented so that the map, combine, and reduce functions obtain their input from standard input and write the output onto standard output; map, combine, and reduce can be written as unix-style "filter" functions, using a language of choice.

3. HETERODOOP DIRECTIVES

Recall that the HeteroDoop directives are designed to exploit both CPUs and GPUs in a cluster with a single source program. They identify the *map* and *combine* functions and their attributes in a serial, CPU-only MapReduce program. From this information, our translator generates code that exploits both the CPUs and GPUs available in the nodes of a distributed architecture. While the concept of HeteroDoop directives is language-independent, our HeteroDoop proto-

Listing 1: Wordcount Map Code with HeteroDoop Directives

```
1  int main() {
2    char word[30], *line;
3    size_t nbytes = 10000;
4    int read, linePtr, offset, one;
5    line = (char*) malloc(nbytes*sizeof(char));
6    #pragma mapreduce mapper key(word) value(one) \\
7    keylength(30) kvpairs(20)
8    while( (read = getline(&line, &nbytes, stdin)) != -1) {
9      linePtr = 0;
10     offset = 0;
11     one = 1;
12     while( (linePtr = getWord(line, offset, word,
13       read, 30)) != -1) {
14       printf("%s\t%d\n", word, one);
15       offset += linePtr;
16     }
17   }
18   free(line);
19   return 0;
20 }
```

type supports programs written in C. Our implementation makes use of the Hadoop Streaming framework, which we extend to enable efficient execution on both CPUs and GPUs.

3.1 HeteroDoop Directives with an Example

A key insight used in the design of HeteroDoop constructs is the observation that both map and combine functions iterate over a non-predetermined number of records. The bulk of the computation of the map and combine functions is performed inside a *while* loop. HeteroDoop directives identify these loops and express attributes that allow the translator to generate efficient parallel code for the GPUs.

Listing 1 shows an example *map* code, written in C, for *Wordcount*. This application counts the occurrences of each word in a set of input files. The code reads each input line and applies to it an elementary map operation. For each word in the line, this map operation emits a KV pair < word, 1>. Notice that the input is read from STDIN using the *getline* function, while the output is written to STDOUT via *printf*.

In general, the elementary map operation is applied to every record. By default a record is a line of input. The bulk of the map computation lies within the loop iterating over these records – lines 8–17 in the example. The *mapreduce* directive on line 6 with the *mapper* clause tells the compiler that this loop applies the map operation. The *key* and *value* clauses identify the variables used for emitting KV pairs. The *keylength* and *vallength* clauses indicate the lengths of the respective variables; the clauses are needed if these variables do not have a compiler-derivable type. Table 1 lists all HeteroDoop directives and clauses. Some of these clauses are optional; users need to provide them only for further optimizations and tuning of the generated GPU code.

Listing 2 shows an example *combine* code for the same *Wordcount* application. Recall that, before the combiner is run, the underlying HeteroDoop system sorts the KV pairs emitted by the map according to their keys and places them into different partitions. The combiner function operates on each partition and sums up the occurrences of each word. Note that the *while* loop in the map function can execute in parallel, but the one in the combine function cannot, except for reduction-style parallelism. The only readily available parallelism in the combine and reduce executions exists across partitions. Typically, the number of partitions is not high enough to exploit the GPU completely. For this rea-

Listing 2: Wordcount Combine Code with HeteroDoop Directives

```
1  int main() {
2    char word[30], prevWord[30]; prevWord[0] = '\0';
3    int count, val, read; count = 0;
4    #pragma mapreduce combiner key(prevWord) value(count)
5    keyin(word) valuein(val) keylength(30) vallength(1)
6    firstprivate(prevWord, count) {
7      while( (read = scanf("%s %d", word, &val)) == 2 ) {
8        if(strcmp(word, prevWord) == 0 ) {
9          count += val;
10       } else {
11         if(prevWord[0] != '\0')
12           printf("%s\t%d\n", prevWord, count);
13         strcpy(prevWord, word);
14         count = val;
15       }
16     }
17     if(prevWord[0] != '\0')
18       printf("%s\t%d\n", prevWord, count);
19   }
20   return 0;
21 }
```

son, HeteroDoop provides no directives for reduce functions and executes them on the CPUs only. For combine functions, however, as the data is already present in the GPU memory, HeteroDoop employs an economical way for GPU execution (Section 4.2).

Two extra clauses are necessary on the combiner function : *keyin* specifies the variable that receives the map-generated key and *valuein* does the same for the map-generated value.

3.2 Clauses for Memory and Thread Attributes

HeteroDoop directives also allow for clauses that improve performance by specifying the attributes of the data and threads. The following constructs exist:

Read-only variables: The *sharedRO* clause lists read-only variables. The compiler places such variables in faster GPU memories, such as the constant memory and the texture memory. By default, our compiler places read-only scalars in the constant memory. Arrays whose sizes are known at compile time are placed in the texture memory, otherwise in the global memory. The *texture* clause forces placement in the texture memory. Placing data in the texture memory is especially useful for random array accesses, as this memory comes with a separate on-chip cache.

Firstprivate: This clause specifies variables that can be privatized during the map or combine operation but are initialized beforehand. In the absence of this clause, the compiler tries to identify such variables automatically. It issues a warning if the analysis is inaccurate, e.g., due to aliasing.

Notice that in the MapReduce programming model, all written variables are privatizable during the map and combine operations. There is no shared written data. The translator performs the privatization without the need for user directives.

Space Allocation for KV Pairs: The space needed for the KV pairs output by map is not known at translation time. The translator allocates all free GPU memory for storing these KV pairs. In practice, this leads to an over-allocation. To reduce the memory required for storing these KV pairs, the users can indicate the maximum number of KV pairs emitted by each record using the *kvpairs* clause. This reduction in the storage space required for the KV pairs improves the aggregation efficiency for this storage, as will be described in Section 4.3.

Thread Attributes: The *blocks* and *threads* clauses allow programmers to choose the number of threadblocks and number of threads in a threadblock on the GPU, resp. These clauses help tune the map and combine kernel performance.

Table 1: HeteroDoop Directives

Clause	Arguments	Description	Optional
mapper		Specifies that the attached region performs map operation	No
combiner		Specifies that the attached region performs combine operation	No
key	Variable name	Specifies the variable that contains the key	No
value	Variable name	Specifies the variable that contains the value	No
keyin	Variable name	Specifies the variable that contains the incoming key. Valid only on the combiner	No
valuein	Variable name	Specifies the variable that contains the incoming value. Valid only on the combiner	No
keylength	Integer variable	Specifies the length of the key being emitted	No
vallength	Integer variable	Specifies the length of the value being emitted	No
firstprivate	A set of variable names	These variables are initialized before being used in the attached region	No
sharedRO	A set of variable names	These are read-only inside the map or combine regions	Yes
texture	A set of variable names	These variables are read-only and hence can be placed in GPU texture memory	Yes
kvpairs	Integer variable	This is an optional clause on map region specifying the maximum KV pairs that can be emitted from a single record	Yes
blocks	Integer variable	Specifies the number of threadblocks to use	Yes
threads	Integer variable	Specifies the number of threads in a threadblock	Yes

4. COMPILER

This section describes the HeteroDoop source-to-source translator, which converts an input MapReduce code annotated with HeteroDoop directives into a CUDA program. It is built using the Cetus [20] compiler infrastructure. Translating directly into CUDA, rather than a higher-level model such as OpenACC or OpenMP 4.0, provides direct access to GPU-specific features which are exploited by the compiler optimizations. For the code running on the CPUs, the same Hadoop Streaming code is compiled using the *gcc* backend compiler. In this manner, a single MapReduce source is sufficient for the execution on both CPUs and GPUs. The next two subsections describe the key translation steps of generating GPU kernel code for the map and the combine functions, respectively. Section 4.3 describes the code generation for the host CPU, which offloads the kernels.

4.1 Map Kernel Generation

Each thread in the map kernel fetches a record, performs the elementary map operation, and stores the generated KV pairs into its portion of a central GPU storage, called the *global KV store*. The process repeats until all records are done.

The compiler begins by locating the annotation with the *mapper* clause. The annotated *while* loop is the target region for kernel generation. The compiler extracts this region into a new function, *newGPUKernel*, which contains the kernel code. A key step in doing this is the transformation of the

Algorithm 1 Handling Variables in Generated Kernels

Input: *region* - Region attached to the annotation
Input: *newGPUKernel* - Extracted region copy (kernel)
Input: *sharedROSet* - Set of shared read-only variables inside *newGPUKernel*
Input: *textureSet* - Set of shared read-only variables to be placed on texture memory
Input: *firstPrivateSet* - Set of firstprivate variables
Output: Correct placement of variables in *newGPUKernel*, along with necessary GPU memory allocation and data transfer generation

---

```
1:  function HANDLEVARIABLES(region, newGPUKernel,
       sharedROSet, textureSet, firstPrivateSet)
2:    usedVars = newGPUKernel.getUsedVars()
3:    For each var ∈ usedVars do
4:      if (sharedROSet contains var) then
5:        if (var is scalar) then
6:          newVar = addParameter(var, newGPUKernel)
           //gets placed on constant memory
7:        else   //a shared read-only array
8:          newVar = addParameter(var, newGPUKernel)
9:          insertMallocAndCpyIn(region, newVar, var)
10:       end if
11:     else if (textureSet contains var) then
12:       tex = createNewTexture(var)
13:       newVar = addParameter(var, newGPUKernel)
14:       bindTexture(tex, newVar, region)   //cudaBindTexture
15:       insertMallocAndCpyIn(region, newVar, var)
         //inserts cudaMalloc and cudaMemCpy
16:     else   //a private variable
17:       newVar = addPrivateVar(newGPUKernel, var)
18:       if (firstPrivateSet contains var) then
19:         newFPCopy = addParameter(var, newGPUKernel)
20:         if (var is array) then
21:           insertMallocAndCpyIn(region, newFPCopy, var)
22:         end if
23:         insertInKernelCopyCode(newFPCopy, newVar);
24:       end if
25:     end if
26:   end for
27:  end function
```

---

different variable types. Algo. 1 shows the procedure. From the user annotations, the compiler generates *sharedROSet*, which lists the shared read-only variables. *TextureSet* consists of read-only array variables that are to be placed in the texture memory. *FirstPrivateSet* contains all variables that are firstprivate, either specified by the programmer or identified by the compiler. The scalar *sharedRO* variables are passed as arguments to the kernel; the underlying CUDA compiler places these arguments in *constant* memory (lines 5–6). A pointer to each array *sharedRO* variable is passed through a kernel parameter (lines 8–9); storage is allocated on the GPU and the array data is copied from the CPU into this space. The transformation for using the texture memory is essentially the same as for *sharedRO* arrays (lines 11–15). The functions *addParameter* and *addPrivateVar* create new variables and automatically rename the previous variable names in the *newGPUKernel* respectively.

The remaining variables inside the *newGPUKernel* are private (lines 17–24). For each private variable, a new variable is created inside the kernel body using the *addPrivate-Var* function. For firstprivate variables, there is an extra step. For scalars, the initial value is passed through a kernel parameter. For arrays, storage is allocated and a reference is passed via kernel parameter. The initial values of the array elements are copied into the corresponding memory locations before the kernel. Inside the kernel body, each thread copies these values into the private spaces using the *insertInKernelCopyCode* function.

Listing 3 shows the translated CUDA map kernel for *Wordcount* (Listing 1). The kernel generation procedure

---

Listing 3: Translated Wordcount Mapper Code

```
1   __global__ void gpu_mapper(char *ip, int ipSize,
2   int *recordLocator, char * devKey, int * devVal,
3   int storesPerThread, int * devKvCount,  int keyLength,
4   int valLength, int * indexArray, int numReducers) {
5     char gpu_word[30];
6     int gpu_read, gpu_one, gpu_offset, gpu_linePtr;
7     int index, tid, start;
8     __shared__ unsigned int recordIndex;
9     mapSetup(&start, &tid, &index, ipSize, storesPerThread,
10        ip, devKvCount, numReducers, &recordIndex);
11    while( ( gpu_read = getRecord(ip, &recordIndex, &start,
12        recordLocator) )!= - 1) {
13      gpu_linePtr = 0;
14      gpu_offset = 0;
15      gpu_one = 1;
16      while( (gpu_linePtr = getWord(ip + start, gpu_offset,
17          gpu_word, gpu_read, 30)) != -1) {
18        emitKV(gpu_word, &gpu_one, devKey, devVal, &index,
19        devKvCount, keyLength, valLength, numReducers,
20        storesPerThread, indexArray);
21        gpu_offset += gpu_linePtr;
22      }
23    }
24    mapFinish(index, storesPerThread, devKey, keyLength,
25    indexArray, numReducers, devKvCount);
26  }
```

adds internal parameters for bookkeeping. *Ip* represents the input file buffer; *ipSize* is the input file size. *RecordLocator* is a data structure that keeps a list of starting addresses of all input records. *DevKey* and *devVal* are the GPU variables for keys and values of the global KV store, respectively. *StoresPerThread* holds the storage size allocated to each thread in the global KV store. *DevKvCount* array keeps a count of the KV pairs emitted by each thread.

The first GPU-specific translation step is the insertion of a *mapSetup* function call (line 9) for the map execution. This function sets up internal variables for GPU execution e.g. *tid*, which stores the thread ID. Next, the algorithm replaces the CPU record input function, such as *getline*, with a GPU equivalent *getRecord* function (line 11). Similarly, the KV-emitting function, which is *printf* in the CPU code, is replaced with a GPU equivalent *emitKV* function (line 18). The *emitKV* function puts the generated KV pairs into the global KV store. The translation scheme replaces the calls to all C standard library functions with GPU counterparts. Since the current GPUs do not support all C standard library calls, their equivalent implementations are provided by the runtime system. The runtime system also includes other functions used in the translated code, such as *mapSetup*, *getRecord*, and *emitKV*. At the end of the map kernel execution, the *indexArray* holds the locations of individual KV pairs in the global KV store. This array is useful in indirectly accessing the global KV store.

The *mapFinish* function (line 25) performs bookkeeping after a thread is done with the map execution. Most importantly, it keeps a count of the total number of KV pairs emitted by each thread.

Record Stealing: The execution time taken by the map operation for each record can vary greatly among different records in certain MapReduce applications due to the differences in the amount of data in each record. For example, in the *kmeans* application, where each record contains a list of movie ratings, some records have fewer reviews than others. This leads to load imbalance among threads if the records are statically partitioned. A better strategy is therefore to perform dynamic record distribution, or *record stealing*. However, a global record distribution scheme would require global atomic functions on the GPU, which are expensive. We therefore devise a scheme where the records are statically and equally split among the threadblocks used in the map kernel, and threads of a given threadblock steal a new record from the threadblock's pool. As it is common for larger records to get distributed across threadblocks, record stealing implemented at the threadblock level is effective. The variable *recordIndex* (Listing 3, Line 9) acts as a counter for the records used by the threads of a threadblock. This variable is placed in the GPU shared memory for fast atomic increment operations. The maximum record stealing that a thread can perform is limited by the *storesPerThread* it has in the global KV store.

Using Vector Data Types: For array keys/values, the generated code uses an optimization of internally using CUDA-specific vector data types, such as *char4*, which increase the memory accessing performance. The functions that exploit such a vectorization include *emitKV*, and string functions called within the map code, e.g. *strcpy*.

4.2 Combine Kernel Generation

As the combine function operates on one partition at a time, there is no explicit parallelism. However, different partitions can be processed in parallel. Unfortunately, we have found that the number of partitions i.e., the number of reducers can be low in certain MapReduce applications. Therefore, the degree of exploitable parallelism can be low, leading to underutilization of the GPU. Our scheme therefore exploits in-partition, reduction-style parallelism, while sacrificing full functional equivalence with respect to the CPU code. The idea for this approach is simple: e.g. for the *Wordcount* code, a particular partition received the following KV pairs <a,1>, <a,1>,<a, 1>, <b,1>. The output from a CPU combiner would be <a,3>, <b,1>. However, if two different threads were to operate on the partition, with the first operating on the first two KV pairs, and the second on the last two, the intermediate output would be <a,2>, <a,1>, <b,1>. In this manner, the functional equivalence of the combiner is traded off for parallelism. Due to the presence of the global reducers, however, this trade-off is legal; the global reducer will eventually produce the same output. In practice, as the number of KV pairs in each partition is typically high, this small dissimilarity has a negligible impact on the communication volume.

A second design choice in the combine kernel generation deals with the fact that the degree of exploitable in-partition parallelism is still usually much less than the number of GPU threads. The compiler-generated code forces all threads in a warp to execute the same combine function redundantly. This way, intra-warp thread divergence is eliminated. Listing 4 shows the generated kernel for the *Wordcount* combine code of Listing 2. The compiler inserted a number of parameters: *Keys* and *values* hold the KV pairs emitted by the map for the particular reducer. *OpKey* and *opVal* store the combine-emitted KV pairs. The lengths of keys and values for both map and combine functions are passed as parameters. The *handleVariables* pass (Algo. 1) adds two parameters *prevWordFP* and *countFP* for firstprivate variables.

Similar to the map setup function, the *combineSetup* function (line 11) initializes the internal variables of the combiner operation. The compiler performs an optimization of placing the private array variables in the faster shared memory for each warp. In this example, *gpu_prevWord* and *gpu_word* are placed in the shared memory. The scalars are placed

Listing 4: Translated Wordcount Combiner Code

```
1  __global__ void gpu_combiner(char *keys, int *values,
2  char *opKey, int *opVal, int *indexArray, int *finalCount,
3  int size, int mapKeyLength, int mapValLength,
4  int combKeyLength, int combValLength,
5  char *prevWordFP, char *countFP) {
6    int laneID, kvsPerThread, warpID, ptr, gpu_val;
7    int high, kvCount, index, gpu_read, gpu_count;
8    //WARPS_IN_TB = number of warps in a threadblock
9    __shared__ char gpu_prevWord[WARPS_IN_TB][30];
10   __shared__ char gpu_word[WARPS_IN_TB][30];
11   combineSetup(kvsPerThread, &laneID, &warpID, &ptr,
12     &high, &kvCount, &index, size);
13   for(int i=0; i < 30; i++) { //init firstprivate data
14     gpu_prevWord[warpID][i] = prevWordFP[i];
15   }
16   gpu_count = countFP;
17   while(getKV(gpu_word, keys, &gpu_val, values, ptr,
18     high, index, mapKeyLength, mapValLength)!= -1) {
19     if(strcmpGPU(gpu_word, gpu_prevWord[warpID],
20        mapKeyLength)==0){
21       gpu_count += gpu_val;
22     } else {
23       if(gpu_prevWord[0] != '\0') {
24         storeKV(gpu_prevWord[warpID], &gpu_count, &index,
25         combKeyLength, combValLength, opKey, opVal,
26         &kvCount);
27       }
28       strcpyGPU(gpu_prevWord[warpID], gpu_word,
29         mapKeyLength);
30       gpu_count=gpu_val;
31     }
32   }
33   if (gpu_prevWord[0] != '\0') {
34     storeKV(gpu_prevWord[warpID], &gpu_count, &index,
35     combKeyLength, combValLength, opKey, opVal, &kvCount);
36   }
37   finalCount[warpID]=kvCount;
38 }
```

in the thread registers. The compiler replaces calls to *scanf* that read in the KV pairs with a GPU-specific *getKV* call (line 18). The *keyin* and *valuein* clauses are necessary for this function. The original *printf* function for outputting the KV pairs is replaced by the *storeKV* function (lines 24, 34). *FinalCount* keeps track of the KV pairs emitted by each thread so that the final output can be combined and written back to the CPU.

While each thread in the warp executes the combiner function redundantly, for *getKV* and *storeKV* the threads perform vectorized loading and storing of KV pairs, respectively. This method loads/stores one element in an array key/value from one thread. It improves performance as it enables coalesced memory accesses. This same optimization is also performed on string functions, such as *strcpy* in the combiner kernels. Note that in order to dynamically switch between the vector and non-vector modes, all threads in the warp must be active for the entire code execution, making redundant execution in non-vectorizable code sections necessary. This redundant execution comes without any side-effects, owing to the warp-level SIMD model. If neither the key nor the value is an array, the compiler would generate a code where only a single thread per warp is active.

4.3 Host Code for Offloading

Since the GPU code execution is orchestrated by the host, the compiler must generate the necessary host code. Fig. 1 displays a flowchart for the structure of the generated code. First, the code copies the input fileSplit from HDFS into the GPU memory. A GPU kernel is then launched to collect and count the records in the input. Next, necessary storage is allocated on the GPU for map and combine kernels. To allocate the global KV store, all available GPU memory is used in the absence of the *kvpairs* clause. Otherwise, the global KV store memory allocation can be reduced, because the to-

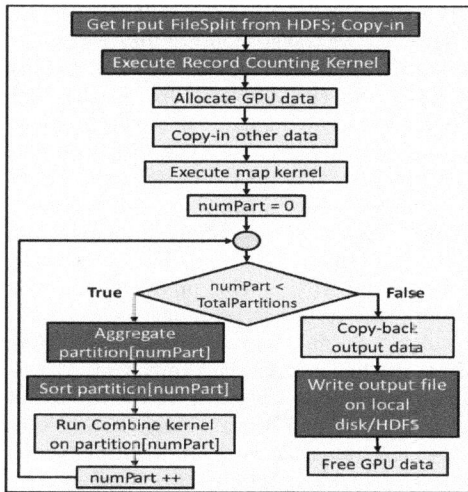

Figure 1: Flowchart for the driver code on the host CPU : Dark boxes indicate functions provided by the runtime system

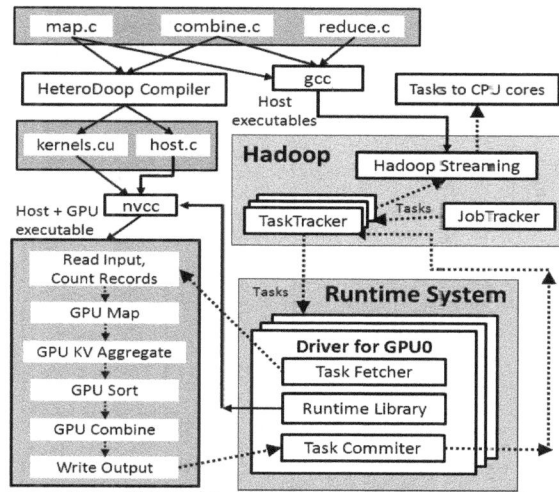

Figure 2: Execution Scheme of HeteroDoop : Dashed arrows represent the execution flow; solid arrows represent the compilation flow

tal number of records is already known. Each GPU thread in the map kernel generates KV pairs in its own portion of the global KV store. Note that each thread may not completely use its own portion of the global KV store, leading to *whitespaces*, which are the empty slots in the global KV store. This leads to a scattering of the KV pairs belonging to each partition. These KV pairs must be aggregated by removing the whitespaces before they are sorted in the next phase, reducing the sort size. The indirection array (*indexArray*) is useful for performing this aggregation as the KV pairs do not need to be shuffled directly. Note that smaller global KV store size results in better aggregation efficiency. Next, sort, followed by the combine kernel, are run on each partition. The generated output is written back to a local disk. For map-only jobs, the output is written directly to the HDFS. Finally, the allocated memories are freed.

5. OVERALL EXECUTION AND RUNTIME SYSTEM

This section describes the overall flow of the HeteroDoop framework and the runtime system. The runtime system assists the compiler-optimized code to run on a GPU by providing a number of library functions (Section 5.2), and helps implement the MapReduce semantics (Section 5.3).

5.1 Overall Execution

Fig. 2 shows the overall workflow in HeteroDoop and the roles of the runtime system. First, the user-written map and combine functions are translated by the HeteroDoop source-to-source compiler. Next, the generated CUDA code is compiled by the *nvcc* compiler for the GPU executable. The original source is compiled by *gcc* for the CPU executable. The executables are inserted into the Hadoop Streaming mechanism. When the execution starts, the Job-Tracker sends tasks to TaskTrackers, which schedule them either on the CPU cores, using native Hadoop Streaming, or on a GPU. The latter is coordinated by the *GPU driver* of the runtime system. The GPU driver fetches new tasks and invokes the GPU executables to perform map, combine and other MapReduce semantic-specific operations. Upon completion of a task, the GPU driver informs the TaskTracker

about the task completion details, which comprise execution time, task log, etc.

Hadoop Integration and Fault Tolerance: Fault tolerance of HeteroDoop for GPU tasks manifests itself in two ways: i) a task failure is communicated to the Hadoop scheduler so that it can reschedule the task; ii) the failed GPU is revived so that future tasks can still be issued to it. To obtain this fault tolerance and to achieve issuing of tasks to GPUs, we have modified Hadoop's *MapTask* class implementation to signal a new task to be run on the GPU to the GPU driver. TaskTrackers on each slave keep one slot reserved per GPU. Note that these slots simply offload the tasks on GPUs; no CPU time is consumed. Scheduling decisions on the GPU are described in the next section. Internally, the driver runs one thread for each GPU on the node. The driver assures that only a single task runs on the GPU at a time. If a thread's execution fails, the error is communicated to Hadoop TaskTracker, and the driver restarts the thread. In this manner, the GPU driver is made fault tolerant.

5.2 Assisting GPU Execution

The following runtime library functions help facilitate the GPU kernel execution.

File Handling: HDFS is not POSIX API compliant for file handling; directly reading the input fileSplit from a C-code is not supported. The runtime system uses lib-HDFS [21], which provides a C/C++ function for fetching the input fileSplits from HDFS. The output of the map + combine execution is written to the local disk in a Hadoop-compatible binary format (*SequenceFileFormat*). For map-only jobs, the output is written directly to the HDFS.

Record Handling: The records in an input file must be pre-determined to support record stealing. The runtime system implements a GPU kernel that pre-determines and counts the records in the input file. This kernel is executed before the map kernel. The runtime system provides a thread-safe function, *getRecord*, which can be called by each thread of the map kernel to fetch a new record.

5.3 Implementing MapReduce Semantics

Performing Partition Aggregation: After the map execution, KV pairs in each partition of the global KV store

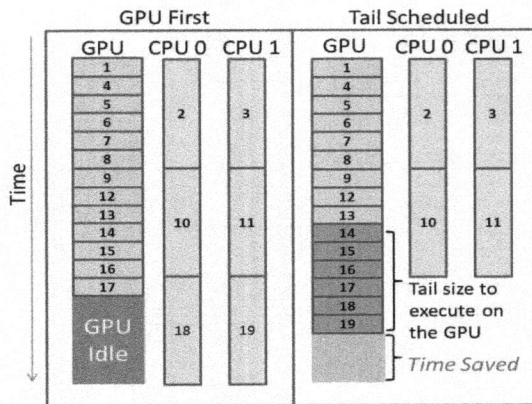

Figure 3: Key Idea of Tail Scheduling

must be compacted to get rid of the whitespaces, resulting in improved sorting efficiency. The runtime system provides an aggregation function that operates in parallel. It utilizes the count of the KV pairs emitted by each thread of the map kernel and an indirection array to locate KV pairs in the global KV store. A fast, parallel scan method for GPUs [22] is used to compute the prefix sum of the emitted KV pairs for each thread. From this information and the count of KV pairs emitted by each thread, a GPU kernel converts the old indirection array into a new one, wherein the generated KV pairs are aggregated.

Intermediate Sort: Recall that the MapReduce model sorts the KV pairs after the map operation. HeteroDoop uses a modified version of the efficient GPU merge sort implementation [23]. The original implementation operates on fixed, short-length integer keys and values, making efficient use of the GPU shared memory. For long keys and values, this method would make inefficient use of the shared memory and thus restrict the partial merge size. Our implementation therefore forgoes direct key-based sorting. We instead modify the original method [23] to employ indirection for accessing the KV pairs. The use of indirection avoids expensive movements of the KV pairs in the device memory. We chose this implementation over an alternative merge sort approach [24] for variable-length keys. This alternative approach hashes the first few characters of the variable-length keys, breaking ties by comparing the next characters. We chose not to use this method, since hashing requires additional memory on the GPU.

6. TAIL SCHEDULING

Hadoop's default scheduler does not take into account the disparity in the computational capabilities of the processors. When employing both CPUs and GPUs, task execution times vary substantially, requiring more advanced scheduling decisions. This section describes the HeteroDoop scheduler, aiming at optimal execution on accelerator clusters where each node has a CPU and one or more GPUs.

6.1 GPU-First Execution vs Tail Scheduling

A simplistic scheduler for CPUs and GPUs would act as follows. Whenever a new task is issued on a node, the task is scheduled on a GPU if such a device is free; otherwise, the CPU is chosen. We refer to this method as *"GPU-first."*

GPU-first scheduling keeps all CPU and GPU cores busy until the final tasks show up. Consider the example scenario in Fig. 3, which uses 1 GPU and a 2-core CPU for scheduling

a total of 19 tasks. The GPU slot is 6x faster than the CPU slot. The figure shows the sequence number of each task. In GPU-first scheduling, shown on the left, the 1st task would go on the GPU and the 2nd and 3rd on the CPU. Since the GPU finishes early, the 4th task would go again on the GPU. Continuing in this manner, the 17th task goes on the GPU, while the 18th and 19th stay on the CPU. Since the CPU tasks are much slower, the faster GPU remains idle at the end stage, which is sub-optimal. A smarter scheme, as shown on the right side of Fig. 3, would force tasks 18 and 19 to execute on the GPU, saving on overall execution time. This is the key idea of tail scheduling.

A key challenge in realizing tail scheduling in HeteroDoop is for the slaves to know when their tails begin. As this information is not available to the slaves in the baseline Hadoop, in our algorithm, the JobTracker will estimate the number of remaining tasks for each node and communicate this information to the TaskTrackers, as described next.

Algorithm 2 Tail Scheduling on JobTracker and Task-Tracker

1: **function** TAILSCHEDULEONJT(*numGPUs*, *maxSpeedup*, *numSlaves*) //this function executes on the JobTracker before sending heartbeat response
2:    *jobTail* = *numGPUs* × *maxSpeedup* × *numSlaves*
3:    **if** (*jobTail* < getNumRemainingMaps()) **then** //identifying tail
4:       *taskSet* = scheduleNumGPUTasksAtMax() //assures fairness
5:    **else**
6:       *taskSet* = useHadoopDefaultScheduling();
7:    **end if**
8:    *numMapsRemainingPerNode* = getNumRemainingMaps()/*numSlaves*
9:    heartBeatResponse.add(*numMapsRemainingPerNode*, *taskSet*)
10: **end function**
    //TaskTracker calculates GPU speedup over CPU for each task
11: **function** TAILSCHEDULEONTT(*task*, *numGPUs*, *aveSpeedup*, *numMapsRemainingPerNode*)
12:    *taskTail* = *numGPUs* × *aveSpeedup*
13:    **if** (*taskTail* <= *numMapsRemainingPerNode*) **then**
14:       forceGPUexecution(*task*) //tail is forced on GPU
15:    **else**
16:       useGPUFirst(*task*);
17:    **end if**
18: **end function**

6.2 Tail Scheduling Algorithm

We implement tail scheduling in HeteroDoop at two levels: on the JobTracker and on the TaskTracker. Algorithm 2 describes the mechanism. The TaskTracker continually calculates the average GPU slot speedup over the CPU slot and informs the JobTracker. The Hadoop heartbeat mechanism has been modified to carry this information. The JobTracker remembers the maximum speedup from the TaskTrackers. For the TaskTracker, the tail size (*taskTail*) is the number of GPU tasks that execute in the same amount of time as one CPU task. It is computed as the number of GPUs on the current node (*numGPUs*) multiplied by the average GPU speedup (*aveSpeedup*) seen on that TaskTracker.

The JobTracker notifies each TaskTracker about the remaining number of map tasks to be scheduled (*numMapsRemainingPerNode*). As task scheduling on the JobTracker is on a first-come-first-serve basis, it does not exactly know how many tasks would go on a given TaskTracker. The Job-Tracker estimates *numMapsRemainingPerNode* as the total number of remaining tasks divided by the number of

Table 2: Description of the Benchmarks Used

Benchmark	%Exec. Time Map + Combine are Active	Nature (Intensiveness)	Combiner	Total Reduce Tasks		Total Map tasks		Input Size (GB)	
				Cluster1	Cluster2	Cluster1	Cluster2	Cluster1	Cluster2
Grep (GR)	69	IO	Yes	16	16	7632	2880	902	340
Histmovies (HS)	91	IO	Yes	8	8	4800	640	1190	159
Wordcount (WC)	91	IO	Yes	48	32	5760	1024	844	151
Histratings (HR)	92	Compute	Yes	5	5	4800	2560	591	160
Linear Regression (LR)	86	Compute	Yes	16	16	2560	3840	714	356
Kmeans (KM)	89	Compute	No	16	16	4800	NA	923	NA
Classification (CL)	92	Compute	No	16	16	4800	3200	923	72
BlackScholes (BS)	100	Compute	No	0	0	3600	5120	890	210

slaves (line 8). Whenever *taskTail* is greater than *numMapsRemainingPerNode*, GPU-first scheduling is used (lines 13–17). Otherwise, all the next tasks - across all slots of the TaskTracker - are forced for GPU execution. As all slots on a TaskTracker force their tasks on the GPU(s) once the *taskTail* begins, queuing might occur on the GPU(s). To counter this effect, the JobTracker only schedules at most *numGPUs* tasks on a TaskTracker per heartbeat once the *jobTail* begins. *JobTail* is the total number of tasks all GPUs in the cluster can finish in the same amount of time as a single CPU core. It is estimated as $numGPUs \times maxSpeedup \times numSlaves$, where *numSlaves* is the total number of slave nodes in the cluster and *maxSpeedup* is the maximum GPU speedup seen across the cluster. *ScheduleNumGPUTasksAtMax* replaces the original Hadoop scheduling scheme, which schedules tasks up to the number of empty GPU and CPU slots per heartbeat (lines 3–7).

7. EVALUATION

This section evaluates the HeteroDoop system. We present the overall performance achieved on our heterogeneous CPU-plus-GPU system versus a CPU-only scheme, i.e. baseline Hadoop. To analyze the performance in further detail, we show individual task speedups of GPU over CPU execution. We also present the performance benefits of HeteroDoop compiler optimizations on individual kernels.

Table 3: Cluster Setups Used

	Cluster1	Cluster2
#nodes	48 (+1 master)	32 (+1 master)
CPU	Intel Xeon E5-2680	Intel Xeon X5560
#CPU cores	20	12
GPU(s)	Tesla K40 (Kepler)	3×Tesla M2090 (Fermi)
RAM	256GB	24GB
Disk	500GB	none
Communication	FDR InfiniBand	QDR InfiniBand
Hadoop Version	Hadoop 1.2.1	Hadoop 1.2.1
CUDA Version	CUDA 6.0	CUDA 5.5
HDFS Block Size	256MB	256MB
HDFS Replication Factor	3	1
Max. Map Slots Per Node	20 (+1 for GPU runs)	4 (+1/GPU for GPU runs)
Max. Reduce Slots Per Node	2	2
Speculative Execution	Off	Off
% map tasks to finish before reduce starts	20	20

7.1 Benchmarks

We used eight benchmarks for our experiments. *Grep*, *wordcount*, *kmeans*, *classification*, *histmovies* and *histratings* are taken from the PUMA benchmark suite [25]. They represent typical MapReduce applications, including both IO-intensive and compute-intensive ones. Apart from these we

evaluate two scientific computation applications, *blackScholes* and *linear regression*, that have been shown to be amenable to MapReduce [12, 3]. *Grep* and *wordCount* are well-known MapReduce applications, and both are IO intensive. *Kmeans* is an iterative clustering application. While *kmeans* is a centroid-based clustering algorithm, other variants such as distribution-based or density-based clustering are popular as well. All these clustering algorithms are known to be compute intensive. *Classification* benchmark is derived from statistical classification algorithms. It is similar to *kmeans*; however, there is no clustering involved. The application ends after classifying the input dataset to respective centroids in a single iteration. Histograms are common in big-data applications. *Histmovies* and *histratings* are two such applications. *Histmovies* averages the review ratings for each movie in a given dataset and puts these averages into bins. *Histratings* directly bins each review rating for all movies in the dataset. Since the combiner receives larger data to operate on, *histratings* becomes more compute intensive than *histmovies*. *BlackScholes* is a financial pricing model, with explicit parallelism. Other financial applications with similar workloads include *binomial options* and *SOBOL quasi random number generator*. *Linear regression* is commonly used in curve-fitting applications. For *blackScholes*, we ran 128 iterations per option. For *linear regression*, each input file contained data for 12 regressors, with 32 rows each. The details of the benchmarks, data sizes and tasks are presented in table 2.

7.2 Cluster Setups

Table 3 shows the configurations of the two XSEDE [26] clusters used in this evaluation. Cluster1 is our primary platform. Each node has one GPU, which is a newer generation device. To evaluate the scalability of HeteroDoop on a multi-GPU system, we use Cluster2, which includes three older-type GPUs per node. Cluster2 is an in-memory system, i.e., there are no disks. Input, output, and temporary storage exist in the main memory of the Cluster2 nodes.

7.3 Overall Improvements

Fig. 4 shows the overall performance of HeteroDoop over the CPU-only Hadoop baseline. We ran each experiment three times, and report the best run. The variation across runs was low (<5%). The benchmarks are arranged by increasing speedup. As expected, HeteroDoop greatly outperforms CPU-only Hadoop on compute-intensive benchmarks owing to the GPU acceleration. Compute-intensive applications are therefore ideal candidates for HeteroDoop. For IO-intensive benchmarks, the use of CPUs brings about most of the achievable performance, indicating that execution on CPUs is essential in IO-intensive applications. In these benchmarks, HeteroDoop speedups are higher for Cluster2

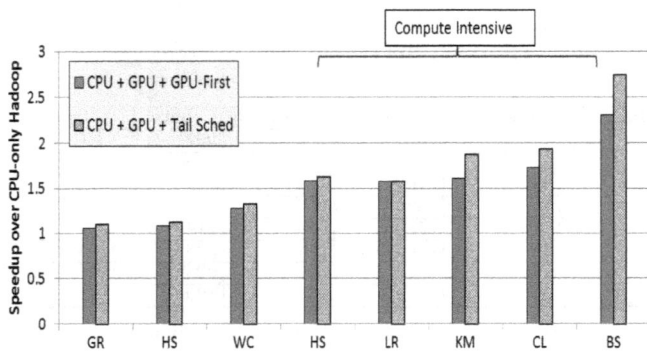

(a) Performance gains of HeteroDoop normalized to CPU-only Hadoop on Cluster1

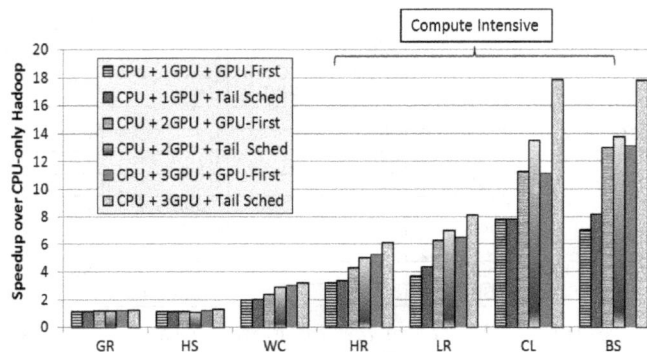

(b) Performance gains of HeteroDoop normalized to CPU-only Hadoop on Cluster2

Figure 4: Performance evaluation of HeteroDoop

than for Cluster1 because i) Cluster1 uses more CPU cores than Cluster2, and ii) Cluster2 is an in-memory system, reducing the IO-intensiveness of the applications. Fig. 4b shows multi-GPU scalability results of HeteroDoop. *KM* is not shown, as the memory requirement exceeds the capacity of Cluster2. The figures also show the effectiveness of *tail scheduling* over *GPU-first* scheduling. Note that tail scheduling improves performance only if the GPU(s) go idle at the end of the execution. For *LR* on Cluster1, this imbalance does not arise. For the IO-intensive benchmarks, the GPU speedup over a CPU core is low, resulting in only marginal benefits of HeteroDoop and tail scheduling.

7.4 Detailed Analysis

We present detailed analyses of the performance obtained on our primary cluster, Cluster1. Cluster2 showed similar trends. Fig. 5 shows the speedups obtained by a GPU task over a CPU task run by a single core, with the compiler-translated baseline code and with the optimizations. The optimizations include vectorization of map and combine kernels, using texture memory, record stealing and performing KV pair aggregation prior to sort. The GPU task comprises input copy, record counting, map, aggregate, sort, combine, and output write operations. The benchmarks are sorted by increasing speedups of their tasks. We attribute the increasing speedup to higher compute intensiveness. Each bar in the figure shows the speedup achieved by the baseline-translated code and the additional benefit of the optimizations. In *GR*, *KM*, *CL*, and *LR*, the optimizations gain substantial additional performance. Note that even for IO-intensive applications, such as *GR* and *HS*, the GPU achieves speedups over a single CPU core, and therefore, executing MapReduce tasks on GPUs along with CPU cores is still beneficial in these applications.

Fig. 6 breaks down the execution time for a single GPU task on each benchmark. Input reading time is the time for reading the HDFS file. Output writing time measures the time required for formatting the generated GPU output in Hadoop binary format, calculating the checksum, and writing the data on the HDFS/local disk, depending on whether or not the application is map-only. Fig. 6 shows that different stages of the MapReduce scheme can form a bottleneck on the GPU for different benchmarks. Note that the partition aggregation times are negligible in all benchmarks. Both these experiments (fig. 5, Fig. 6) made use of input data-local map + combine tasks. These figures indicate that a single-task speedup can be as high as 47x for

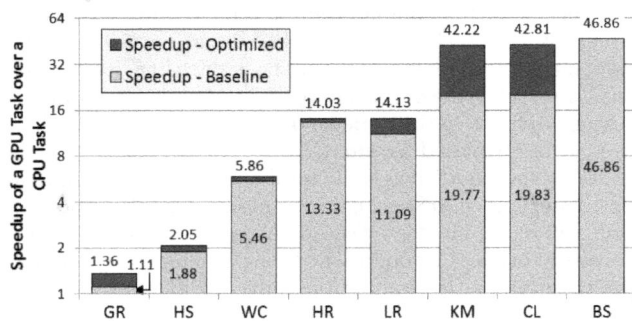

Figure 5: Speedup of a single GPU task over a CPU task : Optimizations have high impact on four benchmarks

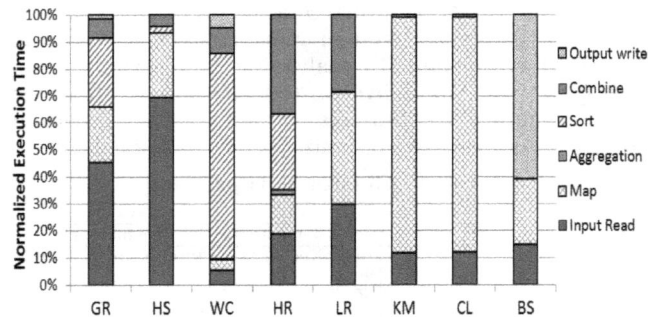

Figure 6: Execution time breakdown of a GPU task

BS, which is our most compute-intensive application. The GPU task of *BS* spends 62% of its execution time writing the output, which is up from 1% in a CPU task. Evidently, the high computational power of GPUs moves the bottleneck from computation to disk write. *CL* and *KM* are both map-heavy operations. *Wordcount* shows an interesting case where most of the execution time is spent in sorting since it emits many long-length keys. *HR* and *LR* spend substantial execution time in the combine operation.

Fig. 7 shows the effects of individual optimizations. The first is the usage of texture memory, which can speed up the map kernel in *KM* and *CL* benchmarks by 2x (Fig. 7a). Vectorized read and write of the KV pairs in the combine kernel can improve this operation by 2.7x, as shown in Fig. 7b. Vectorized read and write in the map kernel can yield gains of up to 1.7x (Fig. 7c). A speedup of up to 1.36x is gained by the record stealing scheme on map kernels as shown in Fig. 7d. Aggregating KV pairs in each partition prior to

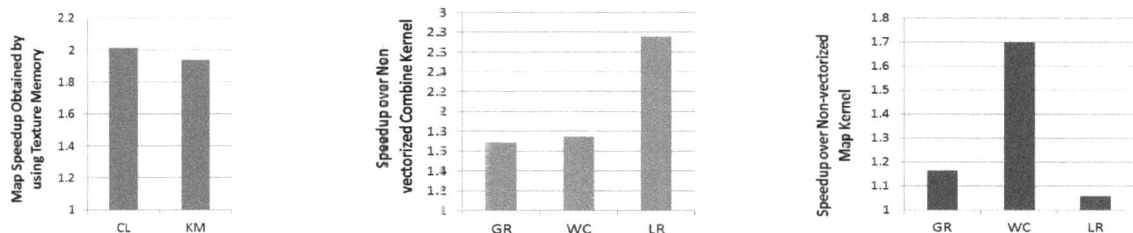

(a) Effects of using Texture Memory

(b) Effects of Vectorized Read-Write on combine kernels

(c) Effects of Vectorized Read-Write on map kernels

(d) Effects of Record Stealing on map kernels

(e) Effects of KV Pair Aggregation on sort kernels

Figure 7: Effects of Optimizations : Only the benchmarks affected by the optimizations are shown

sorting can improve the sort kernel's performance by up to 7.6x (Fig. 7e).

8. RELATED WORK

We classify related work into the following five categories:

Single Node Systems: MapReduce has been studied as a programming model for several architectures. Two approaches [27, 28] target multi-cores. Catanzero et al. [4] proposed a MapReduce system for GPUs. Mars [2] uses MapReduce as a programming model for a single GPU node. MapCG [14] offers a MapReduce API that is portable across CPUs and GPUs. But all these systems lack a distributed framework, and do not scale across a cluster.

Distributed Systems: GPMR [3] uses CUDA + MPI as a platform for writing applications, but does not employ CPUs in a cluster. As both CUDA and MPI require significant programmer expertise to organize the parallelism and manage communication, programmability of GPMR is low. MITHRA [12] is a system that shows the effectiveness of using Hadoop and GPUs together in two scientific applications. Unlike HeteroDoop, MITHRA relies on the programmer to write CUDA code for the application. It uses Hadoop Streaming as well, and utilizes only the GPUs in a cluster. Glasswing [13] uses either CPUs or GPUs for MapReduce. It requires the input map and reduce kernels to be written with OpenCL and offers a unified API to feed these kernels to the framework.

Employing both CPUs and GPUs: HadoopCL [29] presents a Java-based approach, where the programmer writes map and reduce functions in GPU-friendly classes. Java bytecode is translated into an OpenCL program. A key difference between HadoopCL and HeteroDoop is the parallelism exploitation: for a given fileSplit of a task running either on the CPU or GPU, HadoopCL launches many small, asynchronous OpenCL kernels. This leads to IO overheads, as the input data chunk of the fileSplit for each kernel must be copied separately into its buffer, and output must be written into a buffer which is shared across kernels, requiring serialization. Further, for multi-core CPUs, this strategy results in one task occupying all the CPU cores, and

would require significant changes in the Hadoop scheduler when jobs have to share a cluster. Architecture-specific optimizations and CPU-GPU work partitioning decisions are not considered.

Scheduling Hadoop Tasks on a CPU-GPU Cluster: Shirahata et. al. [30] present a strategy where map tasks can be run on both CPUs and GPUs. The programmer is expected to provide the corresponding CPU/CUDA codes. This work employs a mathematical performance model for a heterogeneous scheduling strategy that minimizes the overall execution time for the given constraints. However, such minimization requires evaluation of the performance model throughout the job execution. By contrast, tail scheduling affects only the final tasks, reducing the scheduling overhead.

GPU-Specific MapReduce Optimizations: Chen et. al. present a system [31] for running MapReduce on CPU-GPU coupled architectures, where the CPU and GPU share the system memory. Another approach [32] presents a system that makes better use of the on-chip shared memory of the GPU for running reduction-intensive applications. Both these systems present important optimizations for MapReduce as a programming model on a single node. However, they are not directly applicable to distributed MapReduce since the map and reduce stages may run on different nodes. Also, GPU-shared-memory based optimizations for storing intermediate KV pairs would be precluded.

9. CONCLUSION

This paper has presented HeteroDoop, a MapReduce framework and system that employs both CPUs and GPUs in a cluster. It has introduced HeteroDoop directives, that can be placed on an existing sequential, CPU-only, MapReduce program for efficient execution on both the CPU and one or more GPUs on each node. The optimizing HeteroDoop compiler translates the directive-augmented programs into efficient GPU codes. HeteroDoop's runtime system assists in carrying out the compiler optimizations and handling MapReduce semantics on the GPUs. HeteroDoop is built on top of Hadoop, the state-of-the-art MapReduce framework for CPUs. The HeteroDoop runtime system plays a vital role in this integration. A novel scheduling scheme optimizes the execution times of jobs on CPU-GPU heterogeneous clusters. Our experiments with HeteroDoop in eight benchmarks demonstrate that using a single GPU per node can achieve speedups of up to 2.78x, with a geometric mean of 1.6x, compared to a cluster running CPU-only Hadoop on 20-core CPUs. The proposed tail scheduling scheme works well for intra-node heterogeneity. We leave handling of extreme inter-node heterogeneity to future work, where the trade-off between data locality and execution speed will be an important additional consideration.

Acknowledgements

We thank T. N. Vijaykumar and anonymous reviewers for their valuable feedback that helped improve this paper. This work was supported, in part, by the National Science Foundation under grants no. 0916817-CCF and 1449258-ACI. This work used the Extreme Science and Engineering Discovery Environment (XSEDE), which is supported by National Science Foundation grant no. ACI-1053575. We also thank NVIDIA corporation for the equipment grant.

10. REFERENCES

[1] Apache, "Hadoop." [Online]. Available: http://hadoop.apache.org/. (accessed December 30, 2014).

[2] B. He, W. Fang, Q. Luo, N. K. Govindaraju, and T. Wang, ""Mars: a MapReduce framework on graphics processors"," in *Proceedings of the 17th international conference on Parallel architectures and compilation techniques*, PACT '08, pp. 260–269, ACM, 2008.

[3] J. Stuart and J. Owens, ""Multi-GPU MapReduce on GPU Clusters"," in *Parallel Distributed Processing Symposium (IPDPS), 2011 IEEE International*, pp. 1068–1079, may 2011.

[4] B. Catanzaro, N. Sundaram, and K. Keutzer, "A map reduce framework for programming graphics processors," in *In Workshop on Software Tools for MultiCore Systems*, 2008.

[5] M. Zaharia, M. Chowdhury, M. J. Franklin, S. Shenker, and I. Stoica, "Spark: Cluster computing with working sets," in *Proceedings of the 2Nd USENIX Conference on Hot Topics in Cloud Computing*, HotCloud'10, (Berkeley, CA, USA), pp. 10–10, USENIX Association, 2010.

[6] M. Isard, M. Budiu, Y. Yu, A. Birrell, and D. Fetterly, "Dryad: Distributed data-parallel programs from sequential building blocks," in *Proceedings of the 2Nd ACM SIGOPS/EuroSys European Conference on Computer Systems 2007*, EuroSys '07, (New York, NY, USA), pp. 59–72, ACM, 2007.

[7] Y. Yu, M. Isard, D. Fetterly, M. Budiu, U. Erlingsson, P. K. Gunda, and J. Currey, "Dryadlinq: A system for general-purpose distributed data-parallel computing using a high-level language," in *Proceedings of the 8th USENIX Conference on Operating Systems Design and Implementation*, OSDI'08, (Berkeley, CA, USA), pp. 1–14, USENIX Association, 2008.

[8] NVIDIA, "CUDA." [Online]. Available: http://bit.ly/1xnvPXr, 2015. (accessed January 5, 2015).

[9] OpenCL, "OpenCL." [Online]. Available: http://www.khronos.org/opencl/. (accessed Jan. 4, 2015).

[10] OpenACC, "OpenACC: Directives for Accelerators." [Online]. Available: http://bit.ly/1Bx3pWk. (accessed June. 11, 2014).

[11] OpenMP, "OpenMP: Version 4.0." [Online]. Available: http://bit.ly/1Bx3IjT, 2013. (accessed July 31, 2014).

[12] R. Farivar, A. Verma, E. Chan, and R. H. Campbell, "Mithra: Multiple data independent tasks on a heterogeneous resource architecture.," in *CLUSTER*, pp. 1–10, IEEE, 2009.

[13] I. El-Helw, R. Hofman, and H. E. Bal, "Scaling mapreduce vertically and horizontally," in *Proceedings of the International Conference for High Performance Computing, Networking, Storage and Analysis*, SC '14, (Piscataway, NJ, USA), pp. 525–535, IEEE Press, 2014.

[14] C. Hong, D. Chen, W. Chen, W. Zheng, and H. Lin, "Mapcg: Writing parallel program portable between cpu and gpu," in *Proceedings of the 19th International Conference on Parallel Architectures and Compilation Techniques*, PACT '10, (New York, NY, USA), pp. 217–226, ACM, 2010.

[15] M. Zaharia, A. Konwinski, A. D. Joseph, R. Katz, and I. Stoica, "Improving mapreduce performance in heterogeneous environments," in *Proceedings of the 8th USENIX Conference on Operating Systems Design and Implementation*, OSDI'08, (Berkeley, CA, USA), pp. 29–42, USENIX Association, 2008.

[16] F. Ahmad, S. T. Chakradhar, A. Raghunathan, and T. N. Vijaykumar, "Tarazu: Optimizing mapreduce on heterogeneous clusters," *SIGARCH Comput. Archit. News*, vol. 40, pp. 61–74, Mar. 2012.

[17] J. Sanders and E. Kandrot, *CUDA by Example: An Introduction to General-Purpose GPU Programming*. Addison-Wesley Professional, 1st ed., 2010.

[18] K. Shvachko, H. Kuang, S. Radia, and R. Chansler, "The hadoop distributed file system," in *Proceedings of the 2010 IEEE 26th Symposium on Mass Storage Systems and Technologies (MSST)*, MSST '10, (Washington, DC, USA), pp. 1–10, IEEE Computer Society, 2010.

[19] "Hadoop streaming." [Online]. Available: http://bit.ly/1Hc17Rg. (accessed January 02, 2015).

[20] C. Dave, H. Bae, S.-J. Min, S. Lee, R. Eigenmann, and S. Midkiff, "Cetus: A source-to-source compiler infrastructure for multicores," *IEEE Computer*, vol. 42, no. 12, pp. 36–42, 2009.

[21] libHDFS, "API http://wiki.apache.org/hadoop/LibHDFS."

[22] S. Sengupta, M. Harris, Y. Zhang, and J. D. Owens, "Scan primitives for gpu computing," in *Proceedings of the 22Nd ACM SIGGRAPH/EUROGRAPHICS Symposium on Graphics Hardware*, GH '07, (Aire-la-Ville, Switzerland, Switzerland), pp. 97–106, Eurographics Association, 2007.

[23] N. Satish, M. Harris, and M. Garland, "Designing efficient sorting algorithms for manycore gpus," in *Parallel Distributed Processing, 2009. IPDPS 2009. IEEE International Symposium on*, pp. 1–10, May 2009.

[24] A. Davidson, D. Tarjan, M. Garland, and J. Owens, "Efficient parallel merge sort for fixed and variable length keys," in *Innovative Parallel Computing (InPar)*, pp. 1–9, May 2012.

[25] F. Ahmad, S. Lee, M. Thottethodi, and T. N. Vijaykumar, "Puma: Purdue mapreduce benchmarks suite," Tech. Rep. Paper 437, School of Electrical and Computer Engineering, Purdue University, West Lafayette, Indiana, October 2012.

[26] J. Towns, T. Cockerill, M. Dahan, I. Foster, K. Gaither, A. Grimshaw, V. Hazlewood, S. Lathrop, D. Lifka, G. D. Peterson, R. Roskies, J. R. Scott, and N. Wilkens-Diehr, "Xsede: Accelerating scientific discovery," *Computing in Science and Engineering*, vol. 16, no. 5, pp. 62–74, 2014.

[27] W. Jiang, V. T. Ravi, and G. Agrawal, "A map-reduce system with an alternate api for multi-core environments," in *Proceedings of the 10th IEEE/ACM International Conference on Cluster, Cloud and Grid Computing*, CCGRID, (Washington, DC, USA), pp. 84–93, IEEE Computer Society, 2010.

[28] C. Ranger, R. Raghuraman, A. Penmetsa, G. Bradski, and C. Kozyrakis, "Evaluating mapreduce for multi-core and multiprocessor systems," in *Proceedings of the 2007 IEEE 13th International Symposium on High Performance Computer Architecture*, HPCA '07, (Washington, DC, USA), pp. 13–24, IEEE Computer Society, 2007.

[29] M. Grossman, M. Breternitz, and V. Sarkar, "HadoopCL: Mapreduce on distributed heterogeneous platforms through seamless integration of hadoop and opencl," in *Proceedings of the 2013 IEEE 27th International Symposium on Parallel and Distributed Processing Workshops and PhD Forum*, IPDPSW '13, (Washington, DC, USA), pp. 1918–1927, IEEE Computer Society, 2013.

[30] K. Shirahata, H. Sato, and S. Matsuoka, "Hybrid map task scheduling for gpu-based heterogeneous clusters," *2013 IEEE 5th International Conference on Cloud Computing Technology and Science*, vol. 0, pp. 733–740, 2010.

[31] L. Chen, X. Huo, and G. Agrawal, "Accelerating mapreduce on a coupled cpu-gpu architecture," in *Proceedings of the International Conference on High Performance Computing, Networking, Storage and Analysis*, SC '12, (Los Alamitos, CA, USA), pp. 25:1–25:11, IEEE Computer Society Press, 2012.

[32] L. Chen and G. Agrawal, "Optimizing mapreduce for gpus with effective shared memory usage," in *Proceedings of the 21st International Symposium on High-Performance Parallel and Distributed Computing*, HPDC '12, (New York, NY, USA), pp. 199–210, ACM, 2012.

Monte Carlo Based Ray Tracing in CPU-GPU Heterogeneous Systems and Applications in Radiation Therapy

Kai Xiao, Danny Z. Chen, X. Sharon Hu
Dept. of Computer Science and Engineering
University of Notre Dame
South Bend, IN 46556
{kxiao, dchen, shu}@nd.edu

Bo Zhou
Altera Corp.
San Jose, CA 95134
allen.bo.zhou@gmail.com

ABSTRACT

Monte Carlo based ray tracing (MCBRT) is the foundation of simulating the transport of particles in an inhomogeneous medium, and arises in different applications such as global illumination in graphics rendering and dose calculation in radiation therapy. Due to the computation intensive nature of MCBRT, GPUs have been extensively adopted to accelerate it. However, memory bandwidth becomes a new bottleneck for GPU-based implementations due to the lack of data locality in the MCBRT random memory access patterns. To tackle this issue and consequently improve performance of MCBRT, we present a new locality enhancing method, called LE-MCBRT, on CPU-GPU heterogeneous systems. LE-MCBRT is based on task partitioning and scheduling, which enhances both the spatial and temporal data locality by organizing random rays into coherent groups. We also develop a CPU-GPU pipeline scheme to reduce the overhead in such ray organization process. To show the applicability of our LE-MCBRT method, we apply it to a dose calculation problem in radiation cancer treatment, achieving 6-8X speedup over the best-known GPU solutions on various clinical cases of radiation therapy.CCL11

Categories and Subject Descriptors

C.1.4 [**Computer Systems Organization**]: Processor Architectures—*Parallel Architectures*; I.3 [**Computing Methodologies**]: Computer Graphics

Keywords

Data locality; cache; heterogeneous systems; ray tracing

1. INTRODUCTION

Monte Carlo based ray tracing (MCBRT) appears in various applications such as graphics rendering [11], radiation dose calculation [34], and neutron transport simulation [12].

HPDC'15, June 15–20, 2015, Portland, Oregon, USA.
Copyright © 2015 ACM 978-1-4503-3550-8/15/06 ...$15.00.
http://dx.doi.org/10.1145/2749246.2749271.

The goal of ray tracing in these applications is to compute the intersection points between the particles and geometric objects, or to calculate the interactive impacts (e.g., energy diffusion) of the particles to the surrounding medium areas based on their transport lengths. In MCBRT, massive numbers of stochastically generated rays are traversed along their trajectories in a 3D scene.

MCBRT mimics the physical behaviors to obtain highly accurate results for particle transport simulations. In contrast to deterministic methods, which commonly use discrete models to approximate the physical transport of particles, MCBRT methods model particle transport in a virtually continuous space by stochastically sampling and tracing massive numbers of particles. Hence, MCBRT is often considered to be able to faithfully capture the real physical interaction processes [16]. For example, in radiation treatment planning, Monte Carlo (MC) dose calculation methods using MCBRT are viewed as the most accurate approach and used to evaluate the quality of deterministic dose calculation methods [14]. But, achieving high accuracy using MCBRT often requires to process a huge number of randomly generated rays. For instance, in MC dose calculation, millions of particles (i.e., primary rays) are typically sampled from the radiation source, while each primary ray also generates hundreds to thousands of secondary rays at each interaction point to simulate the transport of radiation energy in the patient body. Thus, MCBRT is extremely computationally intensive, and is usually too slow to be used for real-time applications. In daily clinic planning of radiation therapy, the performance of dose calculation plays a central role and dictates the entire radiation treatment process, ranging from pre-treatment planning to post-treatment verification. Despite vast efforts on accelerating MC dose calculation, the current full dose engines using MCBRT can still take several hours for processing, which prevents such a "gold standard" method from being applied to routine clinical scenarios [19].

Recent advances in GPU architecture present new opportunities to speed up MCBRT methods. Since the rays are independent of each other, it is a conventional wisdom that MCBRT is extremely parallelization-friendly by using different computation units to handle different rays concurrently. Also, since GPUs typically work with CPUs asynchronously in CPU-GPU heterogeneous systems, it is intuitive to utilize both CPU and GPU cores to process as many rays as possible in parallel. Due to the difference in computation power (i.e., GFLOPS) of CPU and GPU, it is common to find an MCBRT application running hundreds of times faster on

GPU than on CPU. By Amdahl's law, straightforward partition of MCBRT on a CPU-GPU heterogeneous platform would only slightly improve the performance than on GPU alone (e.g., within 10% [19]).

It is well known that the performance of MCBRT implementations on GPUs is bounded by the memory bandwidth, since the inherent randomness in MCBRT presents a unique challenge to achieving high efficiency. Because many GPU cores compete with one another for accesses to the external memory, memory efficiency on GPUs is much more important to performance than on CPUs. For example, in NVIDIA's Kepler GPU architecture, since the latency of an off-chip memory transaction is 400-600 times longer than the average time of computation instructions, the GPU computation power will be wasted if each memory access needs to go through the external memory interface. The main cause of the memory bandwidth bottleneck in MCBRT is the lack of spatial and temporal data locality in its random memory access patterns, which leads to several memory efficiency issues such as un-coalesced transactions and cache thrashing.

Lots of work attempted to improve data locality for irregular memory access applications on CPU-GPU heterogeneous systems, e.g., packet ray sorting [31], coherency grouping [35], data reorganization [28], and thread remapping [32]. But, none of them was specifically designed for MCBRT in particle transport simulations. There is also no previous work on enhancing temporal locality for random memory requests generated at different times.

In this paper, we propose a new locality enhancing MCBRT method, called LE-MCBRT, to exploit both the spatial and temporal data locality for efficient memory accesses on CPU-GPU heterogeneous systems. We improve data locality with LE-MCBRT by using several task partitioning and scheduling mechanisms during the parallel processing of massive stochastic ray tracing. With this objective, we develop and adopt a set of schemes, including spatial partitioning, coherent ray grouping, grouped ray tracing scheduling, writing-efficient data transformation, and a CPU-GPU pipeline. Compared with existing techniques, we offer the following unique contributions:

(1) A systematic approach to reduce the penalty of random and irregular patterns for an important application. We show data locality could be effectively improved without losing computational accuracy;

(2) A novel way of exploring CPU-GPU systems. Instead of using CPU and GPU as same resource of data parallelism, we decouple the computational tasks so that different processors can work with their most efficient operations (e.g., scatter writing for CPU and coalesced writing for GPU);

(3) An analysis of extending our methods to other applications having similar issues of randomness and irregularity.

To demonstrate the effectiveness of our new approach, we apply LE-MCBRT to the Monte Carlo Convolution Superposition (MCCS) dose calculation approach [29] for radiation cancer treatment on a CPU-GPU heterogeneous system. Experiments are conducted using radiation therapy cases, including water phantoms and clinical CT image sets for various cancer cases. The results show that LE-MCBRT can accelerate the MCCS computation by 6-8X on CPU-GPU comparing with the best known implementation on the same system [19, 38]. Besides the MCCS application, LE-

MCBRT can also be extended to other applications, such as neutron transport simulations and graphics rendering.

2. RELATED WORK

In graphics rendering, MCBRT is used to synthesize photo-realistic images of sophisticated scenes. Wald *et al.* [31] first proposed to use packet ray tracing to take advantage of SIMD architecture of CPUs. Garanzha *et al.* [5] then extended the ray sorting and packeting techniques to GPUs. However, incoherent rays in Monte Carlo based global illumination give rise to extremely low SIMD utilization. Some work [2, 20, 22] adopted ray reordering schemes to improve SIMD efficiency for incoherent ray tracing. Yang *et al.* [35] developed a CPU-GPU based data management scheme to exploit ray coherency by bucket sorting and dynamic traversal scheduling, in order to enhance the spatial locality. The Optix framework [24] adopts many acceleration techniques, including efficient implementations of BVH and kd-tree. However, the spatial and temporal data locality, as an important issue for MCBRT, is not explicitly addressed. Note that the memory access patterns of graphics ray tracing do not contain random writing, which is commonly found to be a big performance hurdle (e.g., writing conflicts) for other MCBRT applications such as radiation dose calculation.

GPU based MCBRT dose calculation is an active research topic. Many approaches [13, 15, 18, 39] were proposed to reduce execution divergence and improve memory access efficiency. For memory efficiency, Jia *et al.* [17] developed a data duplication method to eliminate writing conflicts. However, the data locality problem was not studied. All known GPU-based MC radiation dose calculation implementations suffer from memory efficiency issues, such as un-coalesced transactions and cache thrashing.

Particle-in-cell (PIC) is a widely used algorithm in plasma physics simulation, where the dynamic of the plasma constituents is computed using particle tracking and collision detection [4]. Due to the large scale of plasma simulation, the PIC algorithm is often executed in a cluster of GPUs. Several acceleration strategies [3, 4] were developed to overcome the problems of high latency to scale PIC to match such a cluster of GPUs, including domain decomposition (partitioning the space into tiles and sorting the particles by positions and directions) and simplification of depositing steps (computing the mean field of particle values). But, the efficiency issue of parallel memory transactions in individual GPU is not addressed, which can be a limiting factor for the performance of PIC running on GPU clusters.

Data locality enhancement is crucial for all memory intensive applications running on GPU. Several studies [27, 36] aimed to regularize data locality of dynamic irregular memory accesses, using run time or compile time data transformations. Zhang *et al.* [37] first used a CPU-GPU pipeline scheme to reorganize data and threads for efficient memory accesses and hide the reorganization overhead. Wu *et al.* [32] then proposed several heuristic methods to enhance the spatial locality by asynchronous operations and software-level scheduling. However, temporal data locality has received much less attention in these studies. The applications (e.g., molecular dynamics simulations and sparse matrix multiplication) in these studies have less irregularity and randomness in their memory accesses compared with MCBRT.

Several of our proposed techniques bear similarity to some existing methods in other applications, but we also provide

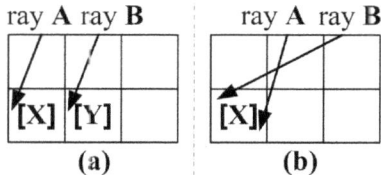

(a)   **(b)**

Figure 1: Illustration of data locality in memory accesses during tracing rays A and B: (a) A and B exploit spatial locality for $K = 1$ in accessing X and Y concurrently; (b) A and B exploit temporal locality in accessing X contiguously in time.

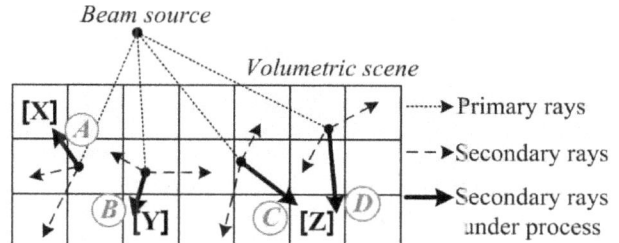

Figure 2: Illustration of the data locality issues in the common GPU-based MCBRT model, in which each thread is assigned to handle one primary ray r and all secondary rays generated from r. Due to the randomness of the rays, a group of threads may concurrently process incoherent rays (e.g., the solid secondary rays labeled with circles), which lead to random memory accesses.

unique improvement and extension for the MCBRT problem and CPU-GPU heterogeneous systems. Specifically, our spatial partitioning in Section 4.2, different from the gridding idea [21], coherently groups the massive number of random rays. Our conflict-free writing in Section 4.5, different from the two-phrase writing scheme in histogram calculation [7], decouples the writing and uses CPU-GPU pipeline to further reduce the overhead. Our scheduling model presented in Section 4.4 is improved with fine-grained scheduling to address the limitation of parallelism at the start/end of each scheduling phase (see Section 6.1), which is a common issue for other "wavefront" models on GPU [23, 25]. Another related approach is tiling and overlapping [30], which divides the scene into regions and extends each region's working space to partially overlap with the neighbors. However, this approach cannot handle long rays traversing through many regions, which need to be regrouped as discussed in Section 4.3 (otherwise, they are terminated incorrectly). One may extend the overlapping to further delay the regrouping, but that leads to considerable overhead in memory usage.

3. DATA LOCALITY ISSUES IN MCBRT

In this section, we describe the spatial and temporal locality using the quantitative model in [10], and highlight the memory access patterns and data locality issues in MCBRT.

Spatial locality.

If at one point in time, a memory address X is being accessed, then it is likely that a nearby address Y, whose *spatial locality distance* K from X in the memory space (i.e., $|X - Y| = K$), is also being accessed concurrently. In the GPU architecture, multiple memory accesses can benefit from spatial locality by one transaction (i.e., *coalesced transaction*) if $K \leq Q$, where Q is the size of consecutive memory addresses to be transferred in a single transaction. In NVIDIA Kepler, Q can be up to 128 bytes.

Temporal locality.

Suppose a memory address X is accessed by two memory requests X_A and X_B issued in different times t_A and t_B, respectively. We define the *temporal locality distance* T as the number of different memory addresses accessed between times t_A and t_B such that X is not accessed in this time duration. Given that X_A has loaded X at time t_A, temporal locality can be exploited if X is retained in the on-chip memory when X_B is issued at time t_B. In NVIDIA Kepler, a shared cache with a total number C of address entries is provided, and memory requests may benefit from temporal locality when $T \leq C$.

In the above model, K and T are key measurements for evaluating the spatial and temporal data locality, respectively. Maintaining good data locality means to minimize the values of K and T for large numbers of memory requests [9]. Fig. 1 illustrates two ray tracing examples whose memory access patterns efficiently exploit the spatial or temporal locality. However, such regular patterns are difficult to attain in MCBRT due to the high randomness in the generated rays. In practical MCBRT applications, K and T are often very big, leading to several memory efficiency issues such as un-coalesced transactions (e.g., if $K > 128$ bytes) and cache thrashing (e.g., $T > 3.84 \times 10^5$, which is the maximum number of address entries in the L2 cache of NVIDIA's Kepler architecture based GPU).

We now consider the specific locality challenges in MCBRT. In a general scenario of particle transport simulation, beams of particles are traced within a volumetric scene to calculate their energy distributions. With MCBRT methods, a large number of rays are randomly sampled at the beam source (e.g., primary rays, the dotted lines in Fig. 2) or at the particle-medium interaction points (e.g., secondary rays, the dashed or solid lines in Fig. 2). In all known MCBRT implementations on GPU [2, 20, 13, 15, 18, 35], a thread is assigned to process each primary ray r and all secondary rays generated at the interaction points of r. For each voxel traversed by r, the thread needs to *read* the local medium information (e.g., density) and *accumulate* the energy result by accessing (i.e., reading and writing) the corresponding memory address. As a result, the randomly distributed rays lead to incoherent execution and random memory access patterns for the concurrent GPU threads. Thus, performance benefits of spatial and temporal data locality are difficult to exploit.

We use the example in Fig. 2 to demonstrate the data locality problems in MCBRT. For the spatial locality measurement K, consider two threads processing rays A and B (labeled with circles in Fig. 2) simultaneously. The concurrent memory requests for addresses X and Y have a spatial distance $K = |X - Y|$, which can be too big to be coalesced into one transaction. Thus, the threads for A and B generate two memory transactions separately, to access X and Y. For the NVIDIA Kepler architecture, the threshold is 128 bytes. If $K > 128$ bytes, multiple memory transactions are needed. For temporal locality, we assume that two threads for rays C and D in Fig. 2 generate separate requests Z_C and Z_D to access the data in Z, respectively. Due to the round-robin thread scheduling mechanism in GPU architecture, T

different memory addresses could be accessed between Z_C and Z_D and none of them accesses Z. If T is larger than the size of the L2 cache on the GPU chip (e.g., 1536 KB in Kepler architecture), the data in Z loaded onto the cache by Z_C will be replaced before the execution of Z_D. Hence, Z_D results in a cache miss and an off-chip memory transaction for Z, giving rise to the cache thrashing issue for GPU.

In general, for MCBRT in a 3D scene with N voxels along each dimension, the average values of both the spatial locality distance K and temporal locality distance T are within N^3. In many applications, N is usually too big (e.g., $N = 200$) for memory accesses in MCBRT to attain good coalesced transactions and cache hits.

4. THE LE-MCBRT METHOD

We propose a new locality enhancing MCBRT method, called LE-MCBRT, to improve both spatial and temporal data locality on CPU-GPU heterogeneous systems. Our idea is to reduce the amount of data being accessed by concurrent threads, in order to decrease the average values of the *spatial locality distance K* and *temporal locality distance T* for the memory accesses involved. A set of schemes are employed in LE-MCBRT, including spatial partitioning, coherent ray grouping, grouped ray tracing scheduling, data transformation, and a CPU-GPU pipeline.

4.1 Approach Overview

A key observation on the MCBRT memory access patterns is that the spatial and temporal locality distances (i.e., K and T) are closely related to the scene size S. Since the ray trajectories of MCBRT applications are randomly distributed in the entire 3D scene space, the average values of K and T during processing a group of incoherent threads[1] are mainly determined by S. In practice, S is generally much bigger than the coalesced transaction size Q or cache size C on GPU. For temporal locality, we would like to somehow reduce S to be smaller than C, so that all data can be retained in cache during the MCBRT processing. To reduce the locality distances, we partition the whole space of ray tracing into a set of regions, each of which can be entirely retained in GPU caches. We then organize the randomly generated rays into coherent groups such that each group of rays can be scheduled to traverse within one partitioned region. With such partitioning and scheduling methods, GPU threads processing the rays in each coherent group access only the data of one region that is retained in caches, thus substantially reducing the locality distances K and T for their memory accesses.

Specifically, given a 3D scene (e.g., a space volume of inhomogeneous density media represented by a uniform grid structure) stored in memory of size S, we partition the scene into a set of rectangular regions, each containing an amount S' of data, with $S' \leq C$. Then all rays whose origins are spatially located inside a region R are put into a coherent group G (by a bucket sort method). When a ray r in G exits R, the traversal of r needs to be stopped to avoid accessing data outsides R (i.e, the set of size S'). This maintains the effective amount of data accessed by G and avoids the cache thrashing problem. The un-traversed trajectories of

[1]Rays are incoherent if their trajectories are not close in space. The threads for processing incoherent rays are referred to as *incoherent threads*.

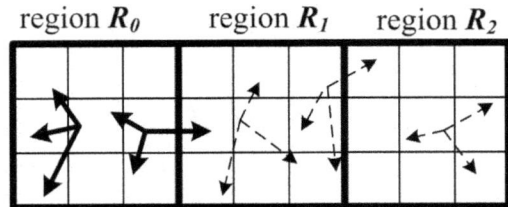

Figure 3: A scene is partitioned into three regions and the rays traversing in each region are grouped into one coherent group (e.g., the solid rays in region R_0) to be processed concurrently.

rays r are regrouped with another group G' corresponding to the next region R' that r enters, in which data locality can be exploited together with other coherent rays of G' in R'. Fig. 3 gives an example of the spatial partitioning and ray grouping schemes in LE-MCBRT, where the scene space is partitioned into three regions with the corresponding coherent groups of rays.

There are two key factors to the efficiency of LE-MCBRT: maximizing the parallelism by packing more rays into each coherent group and minimizing the overhead in the ray grouping process, especially for the rays traversing multiple regions. Subject to the data size constraint of $S' \leq C$, both factors can be enhanced by reducing the number of partitioned regions (i.e., enlarging the spatial space of each region), which also reduces the average number of regions visited by a ray. Furthermore, if a ray r traverses from a region R_0 to another region R_1, ray regrouping is needed after processing the ray group G_0 in R_0, in order to add r to the group G_1 for R_1. Thus, there is an *execution dependency* between ray groups G_0 and G_1. We use a graph model to analyze this group dependency problem and develop a scheduling scheme to reduce the ray regrouping overhead.

Although our partitioning and scheduling schemes enhance temporal locality for memory reads, they introduce additional issues for concurrent memory writes, such as writing conflicts. In order to address such issues, we use a CPU-GPU pipeline based data transformation scheme, which enhances spatial locality and eliminates writing conflicts.

LE-MCBRT can considerably improve memory access efficiency. Given a uniform grid based 3D scene U with N voxels in each dimension, for a ray r traversing $O(N)$ voxels in U, $O(N)$ memory transactions could be generated without exploiting data locality. In LE-MCBRT, U is decomposed into a set of rectangular regions with M voxels in each dimension. Since the data in each region R visited by r is already retained in cache (e.g., by other rays in group G for R), all $O(N)$ memory requests of r could be fulfilled by cache hits without memory transactions. Every time r visits a new region R', two transactions are needed to regroup r into the corresponding ray group G', which leads to $O(N/M)$ transactions for r to traverse through U. Hence, LE-MCBRT can reduce the transactions by a factor of M.

4.2 Spatial Partitioning Scheme

Our spatial partitioning scheme subdivides a 3D scene space U into a set of disjoint rectangular regions, each containing an amount S' of data. The data layout of the scene is then modified according to this partition such that the data of each region is stored consecutively in memory, which enhances the spatial locality for $K \leq S'$. By ensuring $S' \leq C$ (C is the cache size of GPU), we can retain all data of a region R in GPU cache during the tracing of a ray group G in R. With $T \leq S'$, all memory accesses for processing rays in G can be fulfilled by cache hits (e.g. in L2 cache), instead of the expensive off-chip memory transactions.

In determining the specific partitioning parameters, we aim to maximize the spatial space of each region R so long as the memory size S' of R is no bigger than the cache size C of the target GPU platform. This partition strategy is based on two facts: (1) the number of (random) coherent rays to be put into a group G is related to the spatial size of region R for G; (2) larger regions lead to a smaller number of regions in the partition, which reduces the number of rays to be regrouped upon their intersections with the region boundaries. In a uniform grid based 3D scene, the decomposed regions are typically of the same spatial size and shape, which is common for many MCBRT applications such as radiation dose calculation. Such regularity of the regions helps to attain the efficiency of our partitioning scheme.

As shown in Fig. 2, the MCBRT ray tracing in general exhibits poor data locality due to the incoherency in concurrently tracing random rays (e.g., the solid secondary rays in Fig. 2). When the scene is subdivided into a set of small regions (e.g., in Fig. 3), the coherent rays traversing within each region could exploit temporal and spatial data locality. The next challenge then is to efficiently identify and group such coherent rays for each region, e.g., grouping together the solid rays for region R_0 in Fig. 3.

4.3 Coherent Ray Grouping

Given a region R whose data has been retained in GPU cache, it is essential to find and schedule as many coherent rays as possible to traverse in R to benefit from cache hits during accessing the memory addresses for R. To achieve this, for a set of stochastically distributed rays, we group them into coherent groups and associate each group with the region where the origins of the rays reside. There are two scenarios in which the coherent ray grouping scheme is needed: (1) when a ray r is newly generated, we need to store it into a coherent group G; (2) when r exits from region R and enters a neighboring region R', we need to regroup r from G to another group G' for R'.

Coherent ray grouping for newly generated rays is not difficult. It is common that all new rays are originated at the interaction points randomly generated along the trajectories of some existing rays (e.g., all secondary rays are generated at the interaction points on the primary rays, as shown in Fig. 2). Hence, for a new ray r whose originating point p is located in a region R, we insert r into the coherent group G for R. For a large number of rays randomly generated in MCBRT, a location based bucket sort (in which the space of each region is a bucket) is conducted to build the coherent ray groups. For example, in Fig. 4, all solid rays in region R_0 are put into the same group G_0 for R_0 to be scheduled to run concurrently on GPU. Due to the homogeneousness of the partitioned regions in a volumetric scene (i.e., the regions form a uniform grid structure in the scene), such bucket sort based ray grouping is efficient to execute.

For a group G of rays traversing within a region R, the locality distances of their memory accesses are guaranteed such that $K \leq S'$ and $T \leq S'$. The computation for the coherent rays in group G should not process their traversal to space outsides the region R. Otherwise, the working domain size (i.e., the number of memory locations) for G would

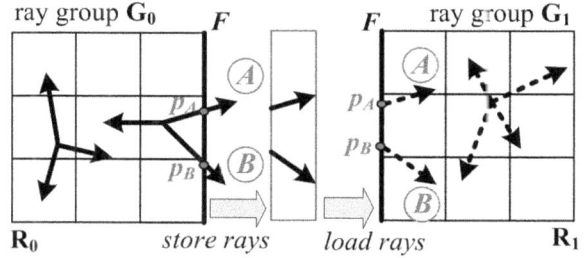

Figure 4: Upon crossing the boundary face F between regions R_0 and R_1, rays A and B need to be regrouped from group G_0 to group G_1. Specifically, when A and B cross the common boundary of R_0 and R_1, they are removed from G_0 and stored into G_1 to maintain the data locality of both ray groups.

increase, resulting in memory efficiency issues such as cache thrashing. To avoid this problem, we need to regroup the rays when they exit a region. As illustrated in Fig. 4, when rays A and B traverse from a region R_0 to a neighboring region R_1 by crossing a shared boundary face F at points p_A and p_B, to avoid loading data outsides R_0, we stop the processing of A and B in group G_0 and add them to the coherent group G_1 for R_1. The ray tracing task for the remaining trajectories of A and B from p_A and p_B is then migrated to G_1, and will exploit data locality with the other coherent rays (the dashed rays) in region R_1.

This regrouping mechanism introduces the main overhead to LE-MCBRT. Each time when ray r traverses from region R to region R', we need to write r to the group G' for R' and read it again when G' is scheduled to be processed (see the *store* and *load* operations in Fig. 4). In a 3D scene with N voxels in each dimension, suppose every region R contains M voxels in each dimension. Then a ray r may cross $O(N/M)$ region boundaries, which could induce significant overhead if N/M is big. To alleviate such overhead, we have developed several techniques, which are discussed in the following subsections.

4.4 Scheduling of Grouped Ray Tracing

With the above ray regrouping mechanism, execution dependency exists between any two coherent ray groups G and G' if a ray in G traverses from a region R to a neighboring region R' and thus is regrouped to the ray group G' of R'. We design a scheduling scheme to process all ray groups while minimizing the number of regrouping operations. If a ray r is to be regrouped from G to G', the processing of G' should not start until the ray tracing for G is finished. Given a set of partitioned regions and their associated ray groups, we introduce a graph model to capture the group dependency relations, and design a scheduling scheme based on this model to efficiently process all rays.

Our graph model for capturing the dependency in processing coherent ray groups is illustrated in Fig. 5. Let a directed graph H model the partition of a 3D scene U; each node in H represents a group of rays to be traversed in a region, and each directed edge (either solid or dashed, whose difference will be explained later) stands for the rays to be regrouped from one group to a neighboring group in the partition. (Note that H is directed but in general is not acyclic.) Scheduling the execution of the ray groups (including both ray tracing within each region R and ray regrouping at the boundary of R) hence corresponds to finding a sequence for

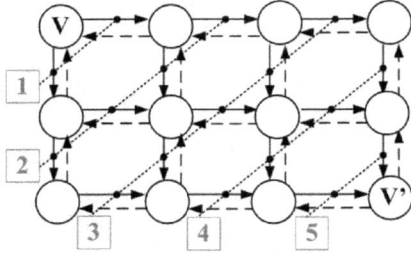

Figure 5: A graph model capturing the inter-group dependency relations in the partition of a scene with 12 regions. Each node represents a coherent ray group and a directed edge stands for the rays regrouped from one group to another. Each dotted line segment indicates the solid edges that can be simultaneously processed in our scheduling of the forward phase from V to V'.

visiting every node and every edge, while making as few visits to each node and edge as possible.

Suppose along each dimension of the 3D scene U, the voxels are labeled as $1, 2, \ldots, N$. We partition the x-axis of U into N/M region intervals Lx_i, $i = 1, 2, \ldots, N/M$, such that each region interval Lx_i covers the voxel positions along the x-axis consecutively between $(i-1)*M+1$ and $i*M$. Region interval Ly_i on the y-axis of U and Lz_i on the z-axis are defined similarly. Then each region in our partition can be viewed as defined by three intervals Lx_i, Ly_j, and Lz_k on the three axes of U and labeled as $R(i, j, k)$. Correspondingly, the ray group for the region $R(i, j, k)$ is denoted by $G(i, j, k)$ and the node of H for this group is $v(i, j, k)$. Note that each directed edge in H must have one of the following forms: $(v(i, j, k), v(i+1, j, k))$, $(v(i, j, k), v(i, j+1, k))$, $(v(i, j, k), v(i, j, k+1))$, $(v(i, j, k), v(i-1, j, k))$, $(v(i, j, k), v(i, j-1, k))$, and $(v(i, j, k), v(i, j, k-1))$. We call all edges of the form $(v(i, j, k), v(i+1, j, k))$, $(v(i, j, k), v(i, j+1, k))$, or $(v(i, j, k), v(i, j, k+1))$ the *forward edges* (e.g., the solid edges in Fig. 5), and all other edges of H the *backward edges* (e.g., the dashed edges in Fig. 5)[2].

We first assume that all rays to be traced have already been grouped (into the nodes of H). Our schedule for tracing these rays consists of eight phases, two phases for each of the four diagonals of U. We show only the two phases for the main diagonal $D(V, V')$ of U defined by the two nodes $V = v(1, 1, 1)$ and $V' = v(N/M, N/M, N/M)$ (those for the other three diagonals of U are similar). The two phases for the diagonal $D(V, V')$ are called the *forward phase* and *backward phase*. In the forward phase, we start the processing at the node V, and proceed iteratively following only the forward edges in H, until reaching node V'. Intuitively, the order in which the nodes are visited (i.e., the coherent ray groups are processed) is guided by sweeping a plane P through the 3D scene U such that P is always orthogonal to the diagonal $D(V, V')$. The forward phase has $1 + 3(N/M - 1)$ iterations. In iteration i, $i = 1, 2, \ldots, 1 + 3(N/M - 1)$, the sweeping plane P intersects all nodes of H whose shortest distances from V (i.e., the minimum numbers of directed edges from V) are exactly $i - 1$. All such nodes for iteration i can be processed in any order, one node (i.e., its ray group) per

---

[2] Theoretically, diagonal edges in Fig. 5 are also valid, which represent the rays directly traverse into diagonal regions. However, such a ray must exit from a region's vertex or edge, which is rarely happened in practice. We omit modeling the diagonal edges and handle such rays by traversing through two/three orthogonal regions in implementation.

GPU at a time, while the nodes for iteration j are processed after those for iteration i if $j > i$.

Though it may seem that all nodes have been visited after the forward phase of one diagonal direction, there can still be rays in the reverse diagonal direction which have not been processed for ray tracing. We handle these rays in the backward phase. That is, we reverse the direction of the sweeping, going from V' to V following only the backward edges, and perform $1 + 3(N/M - 1)$ iterations in a similar fashion. With these two phases, each node of H is processed exactly twice and each edge is visited once. There are three other diagonal directions which are processed similarly in six additional phases.

In our eight-phase schedule above, it was assumed that all rays to be traced are already given. But, new rays can be randomly generated during the ray tracing process, in order to account for the cases of backscattered rays (e.g., the reflection rays in light transport). Thus, in general, our schedule proceeds in *rounds*, each round consisting of eight phases as above. When new rays are generated during processing a node v of H in one round (by ray group G_v), we put the new rays into a new group G'_v for v, to be processed in the next round. In the MCBRT scenario, if new rays are generated in one round (e.g., secondary rays are generated by tracing primary rays), then new ray groups are created and another round is scheduled for such new rays.

Note that all nodes involved in each iteration are independent of one another (i.e., no edge in H connecting any two). Thus, we can process these nodes (i.e., their ray groups) simultaneously or in any order among them; we then process in parallel all their out-going edges (i.e., their ray regrouping to neighboring nodes, such as those forward edges crossed by a dotted line segment in Fig. 5). At the end of each iteration, all nodes for the next iteration are ready for processing. The above scheduling scheme presents more parallel opportunities for using multiple GPUs, making LE-MCBRT a scalable method on heterogeneous systems with multiple GPUs. Because the number of independent nodes is quite small at the start and end of each phase, a multi-GPU system could suffer from the limited parallelism at such steps. To alleviate this issue, we exploit the fine-grained parallelism opportunity within a single node. Our method partitions a node into a set of smaller independent blocks and processes them simultaneously on different GPUs. The details of this fine-grained method are discussed in Section 6.1.

4.5 CPU-GPU Pipeline Design for Resolving Writing Conflicts

For the ray tracing of a coherent group in a partitioned region, memory read operations can benefit considerably from the enhanced temporal locality in LE-MCBRT due to the improvement in the cache hit ratio. But, concurrent memory write operations during coherent ray tracing may cause writing conflicts when two threads attempt to write to the same memory location simultaneously, which is common in radiation dose calculation.

A writing operation in the MCBRT memory accesses can be expressed as: $result[address]+=\{\text{"value"}\}$, where a *value* is accumulated (i.e., added) to the entry at *address* (i.e., $result[address]$). Conflicts occur when multiple *values* are added to the same *address* concurrently. In LE-MCBRT, there are two scenarios when such writing conflicts may occur: (i) in the process of ray grouping or regrouping, multiple rays can be stored into the same coherent group concurrently; (ii) in depositing the ray tracing results (e.g., dose values in dose calculation) for the ray-traced voxels, two or more rays may simultaneously write to the same voxel. Current GPU architecture can correctly resolve writing conflicts by atomic operations. However, atomic writing operations result in serial execution of parallel threads, which can significantly lower the performance.

To reduce the impact of writing conflicts on the performance, we divide the writing operations of MCBRT into two separate steps: (1) *parallel-write* running on GPU, and (2) *sequential-write* running on CPU. We then operate the CPU and GPU in a pipelined fashion to overlap these two steps. The details are discussed below.

We allocate a buffer space on GPU, referred to as *G_buffer*, and also allocate a similar buffer space on CPU, referred to as *C_buffer*. On GPU, the step of *parallel-write* carries out the operation shown below, which leads to fully-coalesced and conflict-free transactions.

parallel-write:

   G_buffer[thread_id]={ "address", "value"};

After executing *parallel-write* on GPU, the data in *G_buffer* is transferred to *C_buffer* on CPU. Then, the step of *sequential-write* is performed on CPU to accumulate the buffered data (i.e., *values*) to the *result* volume. Specifically we store the *value* of each buffer entry x into the *result* volume according to the *address* of x, as shown below:

sequential-write:

   result[C_buffer[x].address]+= C_buffer[x].value;

By letting GPU carry out the *parallel-write* steps and CPU carry out the *sequential-write* steps, we can effectively exploit the capability of each processor. However, this introduces an additional memory transfer between GPU and CPU. Furthermore, since the amount of information (i.e., *addresses* and *values*) generated in MCBRT can be huge, it is difficult to allocate a large enough *G_buffer* to store all such information.

To tackle the challenges induced by our two-step writing approach, we adopt a dual-buffer mechanism, which is a common technique in the rasterization frameworks [1]. The dual-buffer mechanism in LE-MCBRT creates multiple small buffers in the GPU and CPU memory, and alternately uses different buffers to store and accumulate data (i.e., performing *parallel-write* and *sequential-write*). Specifically we create two copies of *G_buffer* and *C_buffer*, referred to as G_b_1 and G_b_2 for *G_buffer* and C_b_1 and C_b_2 for *C_buffer*. The buffer sizes are fixed such that each GPU thread has a limited number of entries in each *G_buffer* (e.g., 100). During execution, *parallel-write* and *sequential-write* are simultaneously operating on different copies of the buffers. For example, suppose a group of ray tracing threads W is performing *parallel-write* in G_b_1. When G_b_1 is full, W continues to execute *parallel-write* in G_b_2, while the data in G_b_1 is transferred to C_b_1 so CPU can perform *sequential-write* with C_b_1. When G_b_2 is full, G_b_1 should have finished the data transfer and be ready for accesses from W.

Fig. 6 illustrates the CPU-GPU pipeline scheme. The following three steps are executed in a pipelined fashion: (a) coalesced and conflict-free writing on GPU; (b) GPU-CPU data transfer using the direct memory access (DMA) mode of the PCI-E bus; (c) random sequential writing on

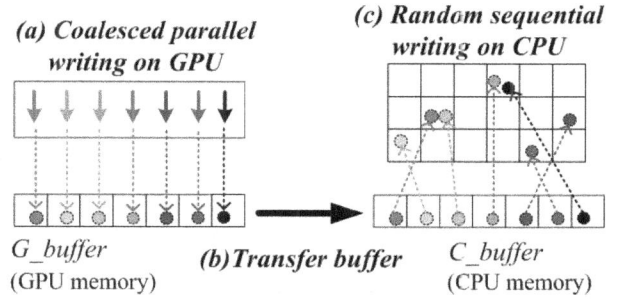

Figure 6: Our data transformation scheme using CPU-GPU pipeline. The random memory writing patterns are moved to CPU, leaving GPU with efficient regular writing operations.

CPU. With the CPU-GPU pipeline, the random memory writing patterns are migrated from the high-latency GPU memory to the low-latency CPU memory. To ensure the efficiency of our pipeline scheme, steps (b) and (c) need to be executed in a speed no slower than step (a), which increases the performance demands for PCI-E bus and CPU processors. The dual-buffer scheme described above allows smaller buffers (G_b_1 and G_b_2) to be used, and thus the memory bandwidth demand for PCI-E bus is modest [1]. In our experimental evaluation of LE-MCBRT, the PCI-E bandwidth (up to 16GB/s [6]) is proved to be sufficient for the required data transferring speed between CPU and GPU (4.3GB/s on average), while the CPU processing is also fast enough by using multi-threading techniques. In our implementation, we detect potential conflicts pre-compilation: for any write needed to be implemented as "atomic" operation, we rewrite the code and apply our dual-buffer technique.

5. EVALUATION

To evaluate LE-MCBRT on CPU-GPU heterogeneous systems, we apply this method to the Monte Carlo Convolution Superposition (MCCS) dose calculation approach [29, 38] for radiation therapy. In this section, we first briefly introduce the MCCS dose calculation method and our CPU-GPU platform. We then show the performance evaluation of using LE-MCBRT in a GPU-based MCCS implementation [38], obtaining a speedup of 6-8X. Key parameters and schemes in LE-MCBRT are also quantitatively analyzed to examine their impacts on the overall speedup results.

5.1 MCCS Background

MCCS dose calculation is a hybrid approach combining the strengths of the stochastic and deterministic dose calculation methods. First, a stochastic MC method [18] is used to transport a large number (on the order of millions) of randomly generated particles from a radiation beam source (e.g., a linear accelerator) through the patient volume. The locations of particle-medium interactions (and the amount of transferred energy) are randomly sampled. Second, the deterministic convolution superposition (CS) method [14] is used to spread energy around the interaction points. The speed advantage of MCCS over the MC methods and its accuracy advantage over the CS methods make it a good candidate for constructing a routine dose calculation tool for clinical radiation treatment planning.

Computationally, the MCCS method consists of three steps: (1) randomly sample and transport a particle P (called a *pri-*

mary ray) from the beam source to the patient body surface through a radiation beam-shaping device called *multileaf collimator* (MLC); (2) from the patient body surface, transport P until an interaction point L is randomly generated on the trajectory of P, and determine the energy deposited at L; (3) spread the energy of L to its surrounding area using multiple rays randomly generated from L (called *secondary rays*). Energy is deposited to each voxel along these rays based on a pre-calculated dose-spreading array. P continues along its trajectory and the processing of P also continues as above. Processing a particle by these three steps is called a *history*, where steps (1)-(2) correspond to the primary ray tracing and step (3) corresponds to the secondary ray tracing, as shown in Fig. 2. The cross-section of the MLC determines the shape of a radiation beam.

5.2 Evaluation Setup

In our evaluation, we use two sets of water phantoms (Ph1 and Ph2) and six sets of clinical CT images for various cancer cases (media), including lung (L1 and L2), head-and-neck (H1 and H2), and breast (B1 and B2). To show the effectiveness of LE-MCBRT in accelerating the MCCS dose calculation for each case, we configure the geometric structures of these phantoms and CT images such that each of them uses two different spatial settings (i.e., different uniform grids) to represent its scene. The configuration details of our evaluation cases are shown in Table 1.

The MCCS program that we use for comparison is based on the GPU implementation in [38], which is the best known GPU implementation of the MCCS approach. We further add to this implementation several techniques for accelerating GPU-based MC dose calculation, including particle separating [15], divergence control [18], and data duplication for eliminating writing conflicts [17]. To ensure a fair comparison, we extend this GPU-based MCCS implementation to the CPU-GPU system by concurrently executing ray tracing threads on both the CPU and GPU processors. We take this CPU-GPU implementation as the "base version" and refer to it as base-MCCS.

Our experiments are conducted on a CPU-GPU heterogeneous system consisting of an NVIDIA Titan GPU processor (Kepler architecture, 2688 cores, 0.8GHz core frequency, L2 cache of 1536KB) and an AMD Phenom II quad-core CPU processor (2.8GHz frequency). All experiments are developed using CUDA v5.5 under Windows 7 and the Visual Studio 2012 environment. Performance metrics such as the L2 cache hit ratios and transactions per request are obtained by the NVIDIA Visual Profile tool in CUDA toolkit.

5.3 Overall Speedup

Fig. 7 summarizes the performance results of applying LE-MCBRT to the MCCS implementation (labeled as LE-MCCS) over the base-MCCS. The results in Fig. 7 show that the processing time of a single beam is reduced from 1.5-3 seconds to 0.2-0.4 seconds, which yields speedup factors between 6-8X for LE-MCCS over base-MCCS. Note that a typical treatment planning procedure can involve hundreds of planning iterations, each commonly computes for thousands of beams. The 6-8X speedup factors obtained in our approach can accelerate such procedure by several hours, which is significant to the modern clinical radiotherapy.

We further evaluate the accuracy of the dose calculation results computed by both implementations. The results

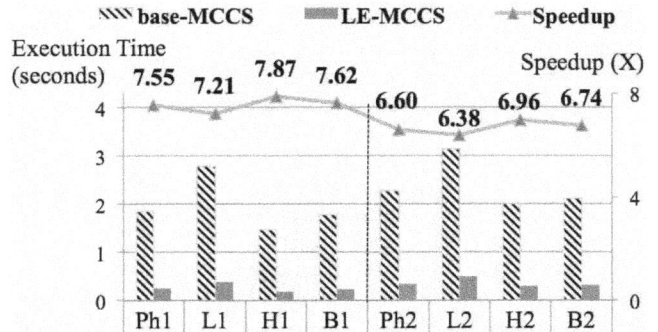

Figure 7: Overall performance comparison of LE-MCBRT on MCCS: 6-8X speedup is obtained by LE-MCCS over base-MCCS.

indicate that our modifications to the MCBRT method have no impact on the accuracy of the MCCS dose calculation. This is expected since our changes do not affect the distributions of the random rays but merely modify the method for processing the rays.

It is interesting to note that both the L1 and L2 cases have the lowest speedup in their respective groups, even though the configuration parameters for each group are the same. This behavior can be attributed to the fact that the media in the lung cases have lower average density than other cases. A ray with certain energy propagates far in low density areas, resulting in a longer ray trajectory and more traversed regions than in high density areas. Hence, in low density areas, more ray regrouping operations are needed, which reduce the speedup factors. Another pattern in Fig. 7 is that the speedup for the cases with smaller scene sizes is bigger than that for the cases with larger sizes (e.g., 7.55X for Ph1 but 6.6X for Ph2, in Fig. 7). This pattern is due to the less ray regrouping overhead incurred by the cases with smaller scene sizes, since they have less partitioned regions.

5.4 Performance Analysis of Key Parameters and Schemes

There are three key parameters to the performance of LE-MCBRT: the partitioned region size M, coalesced transaction size Q, and L2 cache size C. Since Q and C are fixed in a GPU (e.g., $Q = 128B$ and $C = 1536KB$ in NVIDIA Titan), the region size M is the most important parameter. Subject to the constraint of $M^3 \leq C$, the value of M determines the execution efficiency of the schemes in LE-MCBRT, such as ray grouping, coherent ray tracing, and data transformation. For a given case and a CPU-GPU platform, a good choice of M can yield significant speedup, while an inappropriate configuration of M often leads to performance issues. For example, if M is too large, GPU may suffer from workload imbalance across different regions, where the numbers of rays in each region could be significantly different.

To evaluate the performance impact of the region sizes, we select two cases (B1 and B2) and test them on various partition settings. Fig. 8 shows the impacts of different region sizes on the speedup factors. Starting at a small-size partition (e.g., $M = 2$), with the increase of the region size, the speedup becomes higher (due to the reduction of the ray regrouping overhead), until the regions are too large to allow any temporal data locality benefit (e.g., when $M > 50$, as shown in Fig. 8). Nevertheless, even without the help of temporal locality, LE-MCBRT can still gain speedup

Table 1: Configurations of the evaluation cases.

Case	Scene Volume (# of voxels)	Voxel Size (mm)	# of Beams[a]	MLC Width[b]	# of Histories
Phantom1 (Ph1), Lung1 (L1), Head-and-neck1 (H1), Breast1 (B1)	$200 \times 200 \times 200$	$2.5 \times 2.5 \times 2.5$	6	100	5.76×10^7
Phantom2 (Ph2), Lung2 (L2), Head-and-neck2 (H2), Breast2 (B2)	$256 \times 256 \times 256$	$2 \times 2 \times 2$		128	

[a] Each beam is from the radiation source and has a different orientation.
[b] The maximum width (# of voxels) of the MLC cross-section.

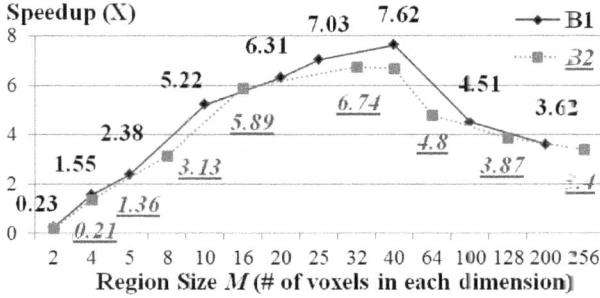

Figure 8: Speedup factors vs. sizes of partitioned regions. The x-axis is for the number of voxels along each dimension of a region.

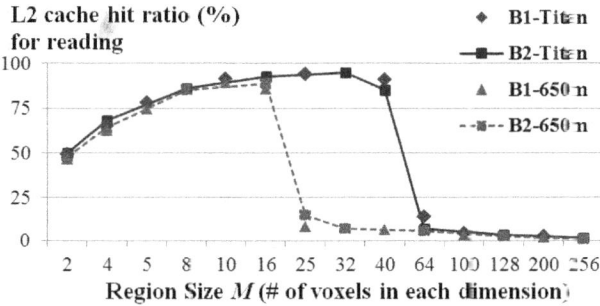

Figure 9: L2 cache hit ratios for different region sizes on Titan GPU (with a bigger L2 cache) and 650m GPU.

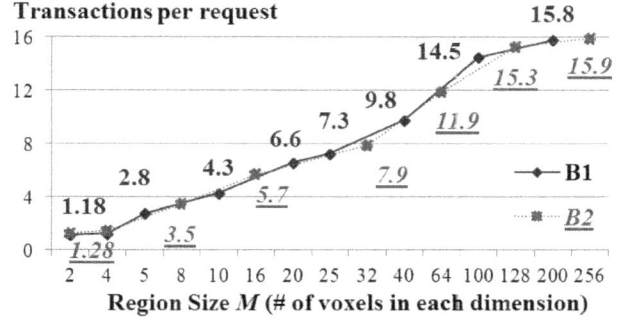

Figure 10: Comparison of memory transaction efficiency for different region sizes. A larger number of transactions per request is the effect of more un-coalesced transactions.

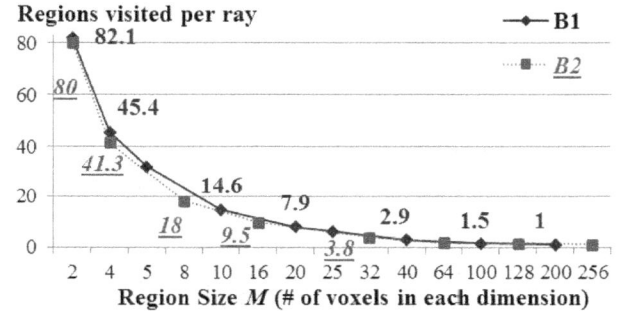

Figure 11: Evaluation of ray regrouping overhead: Comparing the average numbers of traversed regions of the rays for different region sizes. Smaller regions generally lead to larger ray regrouping overhead, and hence smaller speedup factors.

of 3-4X because of the improvement in spatial locality for efficient writing using the CPU-GPU pipeline based data transformation scheme (e.g., the results for the range of the M values between 64 and 256 in Fig. 8).

We further examine two performance metrics, transactions per request and cache hit ratios, to analyze the spatial and temporal locality, respectively. Note that when the region size is equal to the scene dimension (e.g., $M = 200$ in B1 and $M = 256$ in B2), there is only one region for the entire scene, yielding the same data locality in LE-MCBRT as in the base-MCCS implementation. The cache hit ratios (reflecting temporal locality) for different region sizes are presented in Fig. 9. Two GPU processors with different L2 cache sizes are compared (i.e., 256KB in NVIDIA 650m and 1536KB in NVIDIA Titan). For both platforms, the L2 cache hit ratios drop drastically when the region sizes become larger than the L2 cache size. For the 650m GPU (with a small L2 cache), the drastic drop of its L2 cache hit ratio occurs at a smaller region size (e.g., $M = 20$), which indicates the loss of temporal locality and the effect of cache thrashing problem. On the Titan GPU (with a larger L2 cache), temporal locality can be better maintained (e.g., until $M > 50$, as shown in Fig. 9). Fig. 10 plots transactions per request (reflecting spatial locality) for different region sizes. Clearly, spatial locality holds well for small regions

(see the left portions of the curves in Fig. 10), yielding more coalesced transactions (i.e., less transactions per request).

Smaller region sizes, however, lead to more ray regrouping operations, and hence limit the performance of LE-MCBRT. Fig. 11 compares the ray regrouping overhead on different region sizes, measured by the average numbers of traversed regions of the rays. For each region traversed by a ray, we need to perform a number of memory accesses for regrouping the rays. Since each ray is regrouped only once for each traversed region, the ray regrouping operations cannot benefit from temporal locality. Thus, with small region sizes such as $M < 10$, the large amounts of ray regrouping operations lead to reduction in both the cache hit ratios and speedup factors, though with more coalesced transactions (see the left portions of the curves in Fig. 8 to Fig. 11).

5.5 Comparison of Performance on CPU-GPU and GPU-only Systems

The CPU-GPU pipeline scheme is important to the performance of LE-MCBRT. It accelerates the data transformation scheme used in the result depositing, ray grouping, and

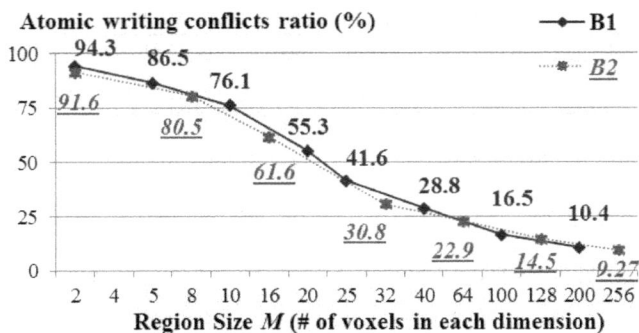

Figure 12: Writing conflict overhead (ratios of atomic writing conflicts in all write operations) of using LE-MCBRT only on GPU (i.e., without the CPU-GPU pipeline based data transformation).

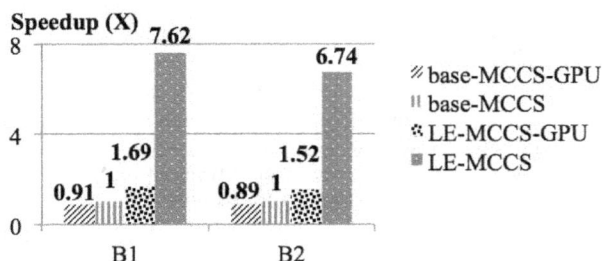

Figure 13: Comparison of speedups for LE-MCBRT using only GPU or using both CPU and GPU processors. The CPU-GPU version (i.e., LE-MCCS) is about 4-5X faster than the GPU-only version (i.e., LE-MCCS-GPU).

ray regrouping processes. Without the CPU-GPU pipeline based data transformation scheme, LE-MCBRT would suffer significantly from writing conflict issues. Fig. 12 illustrates the percentage of atomic writing conflicts over the total write operations as a function of the partitioned region sizes, for using GPU alone. One can see that atomic writing conflicts are a significant portion of all write operations for the more desirable partitioned region sizes (e.g., $M \in [16, 64]$).

Fig. 13 compares the speedups over base-MCCS when using LE-MCBRT on a CPU-GPU based system and on a GPU-only system. For the GPU-only scenario, without the CPU-GPU pipeline to support efficient memory writing and execution time overlapping, LE-MCCS-GPU only achieves around 1.5X speedup, which is 4-5X lower than what LE-MCCS can achieve. The readers might be surprised to find that base-MCCS-GPU is only slightly slower (around 10%) than base-MCCS which uses both CPU and GPU to execute MCCS. Note that base-MCCS simply executes the ray tracing task of MCCS on CPU in parallel with GPU. Since the CPU processor is not that powerful in terms of GFLOPS (e.g., over 20X less than GPU [19]), base-MCCS only achieves 1.1X speedup over base-MCCS-GPU.

In summary, the results and analyses in this section show that LE-MCBRT gains larger speedup on GPUs with bigger L2 caches. For a given CPU-GPU system, we should try to maximize the region size M, as long as it satisfies the $M^3 \leq C$ constraint by the L2 cache size C, in order to gain more temporal locality and reduce the ray regrouping overhead. To further enhance the memory writing efficiency, we should use the CPU-GPU pipeline scheme to eliminate atomic operations and overlap the execution of data transformation on different hardware components.

6. DISCUSSION

This section discusses the extension of LE-MCBRT to multi-GPU systems and other particle transport applications, including radiation dose calculation, neutron transport simulation, and graphics rendering.

6.1 Parallel Execution on Multi-GPU Systems

Our scheduling scheme demonstrated in Section 4.4 provides opportunities to scale LE-MCBRT to match the heterogeneous systems with multiple GPUs. Such a system generally consists of a CPU as host and multiple GPUs as devices. As shown in Figure 5, in each iteration of a scheduling phase, we have a number of independent nodes to be processed simultaneously on different GPUs. However, this parallelism is limited by the number of such nodes, especially at the start and end steps of a phase. Specifically, for an iteration with X independent nodes running in a system with Y GPUs, parallelism is limited if $X < Y$. In the example shown in Figure 5, there is only one node ($X = 1$) to be processed in the first (node V) and last (node V') iteration of the forward scheduling phase.

We further exploit the fine-grained parallelism opportunities within a single node such that the processing task of a node can be split and simultaneously executed in multiple GPUs. We can use two approaches for different scenarios, as shown in the following.

(1) Splitting the ray group:

Assume that each GPU has a capability of simultaneously processing z rays, given a node containing a total of Z rays such that $Z > z \times Y$. We can simply split those Z rays into Y subgroups and use each GPU to process one subgroup. Since each GPU could keep a copy of the node's data, this ray splitting approach is quite straightforward and efficient to execute in the multi-GPU systems.

(2) Partitioning the domain space:

In the case of $Z < z \times Y$, however, the ray splitting method cannot create enough rays for each GPU to process, which wastes the resources of the multi-GPU system. To solve this problem, we can partition the space of a single node into a set of rectangular blocks, and use each GPU to process the ray tracing operations inside one block.

In order for this method to work, we need to remove the dependence relationships when processing different blocks. For a node A whose domain space is partitioned into a set of blocks B_is, we assign each block B_i to GPU Y_i, respectively. Each GPU Y_i will compute the trajectories of all rays in A, but only perform the actual ray tracing operations for the portion of ray paths inside its assigned block B_i, respectively. For example, in radiation dose calculation, Y_i only computes and deposits the dose results for the rays traversing in block B_i. Therefore, the processing of each block is independent from the others, and can be simultaneously executed on multiple GPUs.

By these fine-grained partitioning methods, the processing task of a single node can be divided and assigned to different GPUs, which alleviates the parallelism limitation at the start and end iterations of a scheduling phase.

6.2 Extension for Other Applications

Besides the MCCS approach considered in Section 5, there are many other MC based dose calculation approaches in radiation therapy. Since the patient treatment space is commonly represented as a uniform grid in dose calculation applications, LE-MCBRT can be directly applied to known MC based dose calculation implementations, such as GPUMCD [13], gDPM [15], and GMC [18]. Other than stochastic MC dose calculation methods, some deterministic approaches (e.g., collapsed cone convolution superposition [14] and pencil-beam [8]) also use ray tracing algorithms to calculate the energy propagation for massive numbers of particles. LE-MCBRT can also help accelerate these approaches. On the other hand, the deterministic methods deal with less randomness in the ray distributions, and certain degrees of ray coherency could be utilized without applying LE-MCBRT. Thus, LE-MCBRT techniques may be less beneficial to deterministic dose calculation methods.

In MCBRT neutron transport simulation, the memory access patterns are similar to those in MC dose calculation, i.e., information of a scene such as density is read and the neutron energy is stored along the trajectories of random rays in the scene. But, the spatial scene structure differs significantly between neutron transport simulation and MC dose calculation. To accurately represent the geometric scenes (e.g., reactor shields), the spatial structures used in neutron transport simulation are typically a set of inhomogeneous triangles (i.e., triangle mesh) instead of uniform grids [12]. Each triangle contains some material information, and the energy results are accumulated to the triangles along the neutron trajectories. Due to the non-uniform distributions of the triangles, partitioning the scene space into regions containing the same amount of data can lead to different region sizes and shapes. The regular pattern of neighboring regions (i.e., the uniform grid graph structure for all nodes and edges in our graph model such as that in Fig. 5) may not be common in neutron transport scenarios. Hence, more sophisticated scheduling schemes are needed to process coherent ray tracing and reduce the ray regrouping operations, say, based on a more general graph model to capture the neighboring relations among non-uniform regions. This can allow efficient implementations of LE-MCBRT for neutron transport simulation.

Some memory access patterns of graphic rendering are different from MC dose calculation and neutron transport simulation in that no result needs to be stored along the ray trajectories. Thus, our spatial locality enhancement techniques, such as the data transformation scheme for efficient memory writing, need not be applied to graphics rendering. Still, LE-MCBRT can accelerate graphics ray tracing by enhancing temporal locality with coherent ray tracing. Since the geometric scenes in graphics rendering are typically decomposed into regions with hierarchical structures (e.g., kd-tree [25]), we can adopt such regions in LE-MCBRT. However, it is not easy to attain efficiency in exploiting the neighboring region relations of a hierarchical structure on GPU. To solve this problem, a new structure, called Shell [33], was recently developed to efficiently capture and organize the neighboring region relations in hierarchically partitioned scenes. We believe the Shell structure could be utilized by LE-MCBRT to accelerate graphics ray tracing in static scenarios. But, for dynamic scenes where objects are constantly moving or deforming, we need to develop real-time methods to update the region shapes and neighboring relations based on object movement and deformation. Several data structures (e.g., BVH [23]) are often used to support efficient structural adjustment in dynamic scenes. Yet, how to combine these structures with LE-MCBRT is an interesting open problem.

7. CONCLUSIONS

We proposed a new approach, called LE-MCBRT, for efficiently implementing MCBRT on CPU-GPU heterogeneous systems. LE-MCBRT enhances both spatial and temporal data locality by organizing random rays into coherent groups using a set of task partitioning and scheduling schemes. We evaluated LE-MCBRT by applying it to the MCCS dose calculation approach in radiation therapy, obtaining considerable performance improvement over the best-known GPU solutions for MCCS. LE-MCBRT can be applied to other applications involving particle transport simulations.

Acknowledgments

This research was supported in part by NSF under Grant CCF-1217906 and by a research contract from the Sandia National Laboratories.

8. REFERENCES

[1] M. Bailey. Combining GPU data-parallel computing with OpenGL. In *ACM SIGGRAPH Courses*, pages 14–26, 2013.

[2] S. Boulos, D. Edwards, J. D. Lacewell, J. Kniss, J. Kautz, P. Shirley, and I. Wald. Packet-based Whitted and distribution ray tracing. In *Proceedings of Graphics Interface*, pages 177–184, 2007.

[3] H. Burau, R. Widera, W. Honig, G. Juckeland, A. Debus, T. Kluge, U. Schramm, T. E. Cowan, R. Sauerbrey, and M. Bussmann. PIConGPU: A fully relativistic particle-in-cell code for a GPU cluster. *IEEE Transactions on Plasma Science*, 38(10):2831–2839, 2010.

[4] V. K. Decyk and T. V. Singh. Adaptable particle-in-cell algorithms for graphical processing units. *Computer Physics Communications*, 182(3):641–648, 2011.

[5] K. Garanzha and C. Loop. Fast ray sorting and breadth-first packet traversal for GPU ray tracing. *Computer Graphics Forum*, 29(2):289–298, 2010.

[6] A. Gharaibeh, E. Santos-Neto, L. B. Costa, and M. Ripeanu. The energy case for graph processing on hybrid CPU and GPU systems. In *Proceedings of the 3rd Workshop on Irregular Applications: Architectures and Algorithms*, pages 2–13, 2013.

[7] J. Gomez-Luna, J. M. Gonzalez-Linares, J. I. Benavides Benitez, and N. Guil Mata. Performance modeling of atomic additions on GPU scratchpad memory. *IEEE Transactions on Parallel and Distributed Systems*, 24(11):2273–2282, 2013

[8] X. Gu, D. Choi, C. Men, H. Pan, A. Majumdar, and S. B. Jiang. GPU-based ultra-fast dose calculation using a finite size pencil beam model. *Physics in Medicine and Biology*, 54(20):6287–6299, 2009.

[9] S. Gupta, P. Xiang, Y. Yang, and H. Zhou. Locality principle revisited: A probability-based quantitative approach. *Journal of Parallel and Distributed Computing*, 73(7):1011–1027, 2013.

[10] S. Gupta, P. Xiang, and H. Zhou. Analyzing locality of memory references in GPU architectures. In *Proceedings of the ACM SIGPLAN Workshop on Memory Systems Performance and Correctness*, pages 12–13, 2013.

[11] M. Hapala and V. Havran. Review: Kd-tree traversal algorithms for ray tracing. *Computer Graphics Forum*, 30(1):199–213, 2011.

[12] A. Heimlich, A. Mol, and C. Pereira. GPU-based Monte Carlo simulation in neutron transport and finite differences heat equation evaluation. *Progress in Nuclear Energy*, 53(2):229–239, 2011.

[13] S. Hissoiny, B. Ozell, H. Bouchard, and P. Després. GPUMCD: A new GPU-oriented Monte Carlo dose calculation platform. *Medical Physics*, 38(2):754–764, 2011.

[14] S. Hissoiny, B. Ozell, and P. Després. A convolution-superposition dose calculation engine for GPUs. *Medical Physics*, 37(3):1029–1037, 2010.

[15] L. Jahnke, J. Fleckenstein, F. Wenz, and J. Hesser. GMC: A GPU implementation of a Monte Carlo dose calculation based on Geant4. *Physics in Medicine and Biology*, 57(5):1217–1227, 2012.

[16] X. Jia, X. Gu, Y. J. Graves, M. Folkerts, and S. B. Jiang. GPU-based fast Monte Carlo simulation for radiotherapy dose calculation. *Physics in Medicine and Biology*, 56(22):7017–7028, 2011.

[17] X. Jia, J. Schuemann, H. Paganetti, and S. Jiang. Development of GPMC V2.0, a GPU-based Monte Carlo dose calculation package for proton radiotherapy. *Medical Physics*, 40(6):498–498, 2013.

[18] X. Jia, J. Schümann, H. Paganetti, and S. B. Jiang. GPU-based fast Monte Carlo dose calculation for proton therapy. *Physics in Medicine and Biology*, 57(23):7783–7795, 2012.

[19] X. Jia, P. Ziegenhein, and S. B. Jiang. GPU-based high-performance computing for radiation therapy. *Physics in Medicine and Biology*, 59(4):151–174, 2014.

[20] E. Mansson, J. Munkberg, and T. Akenine-Moller. Deep coherent ray tracing. In *IEEE Symposium on Interactive Ray Tracing*, pages 79–85, 2007.

[21] M. Murphy, M. Alley, J. Demmel, K. Keutzer, S. Vasanawala, and M. Lustig. Fast-SPIRiT compressed sensing parallel imaging MRI: Scalable parallel implementation and clinically feasible runtime. *IEEE Transactions on Medical Imaging*, 31(6):1250–1262, 2012.

[22] R. Overbeck, R. Ramamoorthi, and W. R. Mark. Large ray packets for real-time Whitted ray tracing. In *IEEE Symposium on Interactive Ray Tracing*, pages 41–48, 2008.

[23] J. Pantaleoni and D. Luebke. HLBVH: Hierarchical LBVH construction for real-time ray tracing of dynamic geometry. In *Proceedings of the Conference on High Performance Graphics*, pages 87–95, 2010.

[24] S. G. Parker, J. Bigler, A. Dietrich, H. Friedrich, J. Hoberock, D. Luebke, D. McAllister, M. McGuire, K. Morley, A. Robison, and M. Stich. Optix: A general purpose ray tracing engine. *ACM Transactions on Graphics*, 29(4):66–77, 2010.

[25] T. G. Rogers, M. O'Connor, and T. M. Aamodt. Cache-conscious wavefront scheduling. In *Proceedings of the 45th Annual IEEE/ACM International Symposium on Microarchitecture*, pages 72–83, 2012.

[26] A. Santos, J. M. Teixeira, T. Farias, V. Teichrieb, and J. Kelner. Understanding the efficiency of kd-tree ray traversal techniques over a GPGPU architecture.

[27] I. Sung, G. D. Liu, and W. Hwu. DL: A data layout transformation system for heterogeneous computing. In *Innovative Parallel Computing*, pages 1–11, 2012.

[28] I. Sung, J. A. Stratton, and W. Hwu. Data layout transformation exploiting memory-level parallelism in structured grid many-core applications. In *Proceedings of the 19th International Conference on Parallel Architectures and Compilation Techniques*, pages 513–522, 2010.

[29] W. Ulmer, J. Pyyry, and W. Kaissl. A 3D photon superposition/convolution algorithm and its foundation on results of Monte Carlo calculations. *Physics in Medicine and Biology*, 50(8):1767–1790, 2005.

[30] B. Van Werkhoven, J. Maassen, H. E. Bal, and F. J. Seinstra. Optimizing convolution operations on GPUs using adaptive tiling. *Future Generation Computer Systems*, 30:14–26, 2014.

[31] I. Wald, P. Slusallek, C. Benthin, and M. Wagner. Interactive rendering with coherent ray tracing. *Computer Graphics Forum*, 20(3):153–165, 2001.

[32] B. Wu, E. Z. Zhang, and X. Shen. Enhancing data locality for dynamic simulations through asynchronous data transformations and adaptive control. In *International Conference on Parallel Architectures and Compilation Techniques*, pages 243–252, 2011.

[33] K. Xiao, D. Z. Chen, X. S. Hu, and B. Zhou. Shell: A spatial decomposition data structure for 3D curve traversal on many-core architectures. In *21st Annual European Symposium on Algorithms*, pages 815–826, 2013.

[34] K. Xiao, B. Zhou, D. Z. Chen, and X. S. Hu. Efficient implementation of the 3D-DDA ray traversal algorithm on GPU and its application in radiation dose calculation. *Medical Physics*, 39(12):7619–7626, 2012.

[35] X. Yang, D. Xu, and L. Zhao. Efficient data management for incoherent ray tracing. *Applied Soft Computing*, 13(1):1–8, 2013.

[36] E. Z. Zhang, Y. Jiang, Z. Guo, and X. Shen. Streamlining GPU applications on the fly: Thread divergence elimination through runtime thread-data remapping. In *Proceedings of the 24th ACM International Conference on Supercomputing*, pages 115–126, 2010.

[37] E. Z. Zhang, Y. Jiang, Z. Guo, K. Tian, and X. Shen. On-the-fly elimination of dynamic irregularities for GPU computing. *ACM SIGARCH Computer Architecture News*, 39(1):369–380, 2011.

[38] B. Zhou, X. Y. Cedric, D. Z. Chen, and X. S. Hu. GPU-accelerated Monte Carlo convolution/superposition implementation for dose calculation. *Medical Physics*, 37(11):5593–5603, 2010.

[39] B. Zhou, K. Xiao, D. Z. Chen, and X. S. Hu. GPU-optimized volume ray tracing for massive numbers of rays in radiotherapy. *ACM Transactions on Embedded Computing Systems*, 13(3):42–53, 2013.

International Journal of Parallel Programming, 40(3):331–352, 2012.

Automated GPU Kernel Transformations in Large-Scale Production Stencil Applications

Mohamed Wahib
RIKEN Advanced Institute for Computational
Science
Kobe, Japan 650–0047
mohamed.attia@riken.jp

Naoya Maruyama
RIKEN Advanced Institute for Computational
Science
Kobe, Japan 650–0047
nmaruyama@riken.jp

ABSTRACT

This paper proposes an end-to-end framework for automatically transforming stencil-based CUDA programs to exploit inter-kernel data locality. The CUDA-to-CUDA transformation collectively replaces the user-written kernels by auto-generated kernels optimized for data reuse. The transformation is based on two basic operations, kernel fusion and fission, and relies on a series of automated steps: gathering metadata, generating graphs expressing dependencies and precedency constraints, searching for optimal kernel fissions/fusions, and generation of optimized code. The framework is modeled to provide the flexibility required for accommodating different applications, allowing the programmer to monitor and amend the intermediate results of different phases of the transformation. We demonstrate the practicality and effectiveness of automatic transformations in exploiting exposed data localities using a variety of real-world applications with large codebases that contain dozens of kernels and data arrays. Experimental results show that the proposed end-to-end automated approach, with minimum intervention from the user, improved performance of six applications with speedups ranging between 1.12x to 1.76x.

Categories and Subject Descriptors

D.3.3 [**Language Constructs and Features**]: Frameworks; D.3.4 [**Programming Languages**]: Processor—*Code generation, Optimization*

Keywords

GPU; stencil computations; source-to-source translation; CUDA

1. INTRODUCTION

To achieve performance improvement beyond the memory wall, memory-bound applications are in an increasing need for advanced optimizations such as kernel fusion. Kernel fusion is an advanced optimization at which codes of different memory-bound kernels are aggregated to expose inter-kernel data localities. Performance can then potentially improve if opportunities of data reuse in the transformed code are exploited effectively. Applying kernel fusion to

real-world large-scale applications, however, is difficult. A main challenge is the need for a scalable method to search for the optimal choice of which kernels to fuse among the enumeration of feasible fusions. Real-world large applications can have over a hundred kernels using dozens of data arrays, as will be shown in the results section (Table 1). For example, SCALE-LES [29] weather model is estimated to have ~2.6e45 feasible combinations of kernels to fuse together. Another main challenge is to design an architecture-aware method for collectively applying fusion as a transformation: exposing locality does not guarantee actual performance improvement unless the architecture-related features were taken into consideration when optimizing for data reuse. Finally, a transformation method for applying kernel fusion that is automated and applicable to a diversity of applications is a non-trivial challenge.

This paper addresses GPU kernel fusion for a class of memory-bound applications[1]. In particular, Partial Differential Equation (PDE) solvers comprise a significant fraction of scientific applications in a variety of areas. Those applications are often implemented using memory-bound finite-difference techniques: iteratively sweeping over a spatial grid to perform nearest neighbor computations called stencils. Stencil codes such as the Jacobi and Gauss-Seidel kernels are used in many scientific and engineering applications. Optimized stencil codes in GPU typically depend on the on-chip memory to enhance performance [19]. Kernel fusion further optimizes the use of on-chip memory in stencils and can be increasingly important in the future of performance optimization driven by the increased dependence on on-chip memory. Note that the effective on-chip memory capacity in Nvidia GPUs, for instance, has increased from one generation to another with the trend expected to continue.

The ideal realization of improving the performance of real-world GPU applications via kernel fusion is based on scalable and architecture-aware end-to-end automated transformation. Moreover, this automated transformation should be usable by stencil applications from different domains in science and engineering. The main requirements of the ideal realization are: a) expressing the complicated dependencies of kernels and data arrays in the large codebases of real-world applications, b) a scalable and robust method for identifying the prospective fusions that would give best locality, c) a method for generating code that would apply fusion such that the exposed localities lead to actual performance improvement, d) implementing the prospective fusions collectively for the entire application, and e) most importantly, using a transformation method that is automated and flexible in order to be generic (i.e. beneficial for applications from different areas).

HPDC'15, June 15–19, 2015, Portland, Oregon, USA
© 2015 ACM 978-1-4503-3550-8/15/06 ... $15.00
DOI: http://dx.doi.org/10.1145/2749246.2749255

---

[1] Kernel fusion is a general concept, however, GPU is the target architecture in this paper

The work in this paper targets this ideal realization: make the process of applying kernel fusion to improve performance a practical choice for real-world applications. The paper's main proposal is an end-to-end automated kernel transformation framework. The end-to-end solution includes the following steps. First, gathering of metadata via instrumentation and static analysis to understand the dependencies among kernels. Second, searching for the optimal fusion of kernels using a customized optimization algorithm. Third, auto-generating new optimized kernels to replace the original kernels. A positive consequence of the automated approach is an opportunity for improving the optimization algorithm. More specifically, this paper proposes the use of kernel fission to improve the search space exploration by increasing the number of feasible solutions through relaxation of the on-chip memory capacity constraint. This in turn increases the chances of finding kernel fusions that could expose higher locality.

Attending to applications from different domains having different levels of complexity is a challenge. Hence we provide the programmer with the option to guide the transformation. The programmer-guided optimization of the transformation works as follows. Initially, The programmer is provided with a report on the output of each phase including hints of possible inefficiencies. Next, the programmer can intervene by changing the output of any given stage before passing it to the next stage. It is worth mentioning that the programmer can guide the framework to execute until/from any given stage of the transformation. To clarify, in this paper, *automated transformation* is analogous to compilation and *programmer-guided transformation* is analogous to how the programmer can manually intervene at any of the compilation steps, e.g., using pragma directives in the source code to guide the compiler or changing the source code so that the compiler can automatically vectorize the code.

We build on previous work [28], which took the following steps. First, we formulated the kernel fusion problem as a combinatorial optimization problem. Second, we modeled the projected performance bound of prospective fusions. Third, it was demonstrated that manually applying kernel fusion is effective in enhancing performance for both a test suite and two real-world weather models. However, the steps taken in the previous work had limitations that hindered the ideal realization. First, massive effort is required in applying the transformation by manually rewriting the kernels, which includes non-trivial on-chip memory optimizations. Second, as an inherent nature of code transformation, modifications and expansion in the original codebase means redoing the whole process from the beginning. Third, the manual transformation inhibits the possibilities for improving the transformation when the manual efforts for those transformation improvements grow exponentially with the number of kernels and arrays in the application (kernel fission is an example). Therefore, manually applying kernel fusion is prohibitive vertically, for continuously growing applications, and horizontally, in limiting generality with respect to diversity in applications' features and areas. To summarize, the transformation method is not complete if not automated and not amenable for use by a variety of applications having different features. The main contributions in this paper are:

- A framework for automatically exploiting data locality exposed via a transformation based on kernel fission/fusion. The framework is modeled such that the programmer has the option to guide the transformation; the programmer can intervene at any of the transformation phases and change the intermediate results (Section 3).

The transformation framework contains: a) a metadata gathering tool based on instrumentation and static analysis, b) a tool for creating and optimizing the data dependency and order-of-execution graphs, c) an optimization algorithm for identifying optimal fissions/fusions, and d) a code generator that creates the new kernels (Section 5).

- Capitalizing on the utility of automation, this paper proposes the use of kernel fission to relax the constraints on the search space explored for kernel fusion, which in turn increases the number of feasible kernel fusions and solutions with better localities. In the same context, tuning thread block size at the final transformation phase is also introduced (Section 4).

- We evaluate the proposed end-to-end solution by applying automated kernel transformations to enhance the performance of six real-world scientific applications in such diverse areas as weather modeling, seismic simulations, oceanic circulation modeling, electromagnetics, and fluid dynamics. The transformation resulted in speedups ranging between 1.12x to 1.76x compared to the original CUDA codebases.

To assess the effectiveness of the automated approach, we compare the achieved speedup of two of the applications against the speedup of the manual approach used in the previous work. The automated framework is shown to achieve more than 85% of the performance of the previous manual approach. Applying a programmer-guided transformation by changing the transformation intermediate results drove the performance up to 92%. Investigation revealed the loss in performance was a result of suboptimal code generation when fusing: a) kernels having deep nested loops, and b) kernels having highly varied loop sizes.

In a separate experimentation, using kernel fission and tuning block size overly improved the effectiveness of kernel fusion and resulted in speedups higher than the manual approach which relied on kernel fusion only (Section 6).

2. BACKGROUND

The following is an overview of terms that will be frequently used. *kernel fusion* is the aggregation of the codes of several kernels into a single new kernel. Next, shared memory[2] is used to exploit exposed localities and hence improve performance through data reuse. In an application with dozens of kernels, those *original kernels* that use *data arrays* residing on the device memory are fused to generate *new kernels*. Data Dependency Graph (*DDG*) is a DAG composed of vertices that can be either kernels or data arrays to reveal the data inter-dependencies between kernels. Order-of-Execution Graph (*OEG*) is a DAG composed of vertices that represent the kernels and edges that correspond to the inter-kernel precedence that should not be violated.

This paragraph briefly overviews the scalable method for GPU kernel fusion introduced in previous work [28]. Initially, the search for the best prospective combination of kernels to be fused together was formulated as an optimization problem and a customized Grouped Genetic Algorithm (GGA) was used to solve the optimization problem. Next, a performance projection model for stencil kernels was derived to evaluate if any given fusion would potentially improve the performance or not. The performance model is codeless to be lightweight, i.e., relies on performance data and no form of code abstraction. Operating the optimization algorithm requires the following: a) *problem-related constraints* extracted from DDG and OEG, b) *architecture-related constraints* extracted from metadata

_____

[2]Nvidia's term for on-chip scratchpad memory

260

related to the device and stencil operations in the kernels, and c) *objective function* derived from the performance projection model.

Finally, the output of the optimization algorithm, i.e., best promising fusions, was used as a basis for manually transforming the code such that the original kernels are replaced by new kernels.

3. AUTOMATED END-TO-END TRANSFORMATION

This section discusses the design and functions of different stages of the transformation. Figure 1 illustrates the end-to-end approach for multi-kernel transformation. Note that all of the steps of the transformation were done manually in the previous work with the exception of the genetic algorithm (enclosed in a red dotted rectangle in the figure in comparison to the entire end-to-end transformation that we automate in this paper).

First, metadata about the individual kernels, inter-kernel dependencies, and the target device is extracted using different methods. Next, the source code and metadata are used to construct and optimize the DDG and OEG. The metadata and graphs are then used to provide the input and constraints to the optimization algorithm. The optimization algorithm, a customized grouped genetic algorithm, identifies optimum kernel fusions that can enhance the performance. Next, new DDG and OEG are generated to reflect the dependencies and precedencies of the new kernels. Finally, a new set of kernels is created to replace the original kernels and the host side code is changed to invoke the new kernels. Note that kernel fission is embedded in the optimization algorithm. A detailed discussion of the motivation of kernel fission and how it works is discussed later in Section 4.1. Note also that tuning the thread block size, introduced later in Section 4.2, is embedded in the last step (i.e. when generating the code for the new kernels).

3.1 Design Considerations

3.1.1 Programmer's Intervention and Interaction

Real-world applications have different forms and levels of complexity regarding data localities (complexities are defined primarily by the algorithm and implementation). Pure automated approaches, i.e., compilation and transformation frameworks, can generally work well on most of the applications but do not give optimal performance as finding an optimal strategy for a given application is NP-hard [2]. From that perspective, we designed the framework to be fully automated, in the sense of automating every single stage of the transformation. Yet the programmer has the option to intervene at any of the steps to cater for specific features of his application without being obscured by the otherwise transparent framework.

3.1.2 Amenability for Use in Compilation Frameworks

The proposed framework is intended to be used as a standalone source-to-source transformer. However, it is of worth to use a set of constructs that can extend an existing compilation framework. Several programming standards support GPU, i.e., OpenACC, OpenMP, and OpenCL. Other high-level frameworks support specific types of computations, such as stencil, implicitly [15, 14]. For the proposed kernel fission/fusion to be an extended functionality in OpenACC for example, clauses can be added to the OpenACC's *parallel* construct to mark the kernels and data arrays that are target for fusion. Such a concept is aligned with how the framework is implemented as will be seen in Section 5. Granted that using a compilation framework will limit the programmer's intervention as explained in the previous section, yet automated transformation can still be beneficial to a large extent as will be shown in Section 6.2.2.

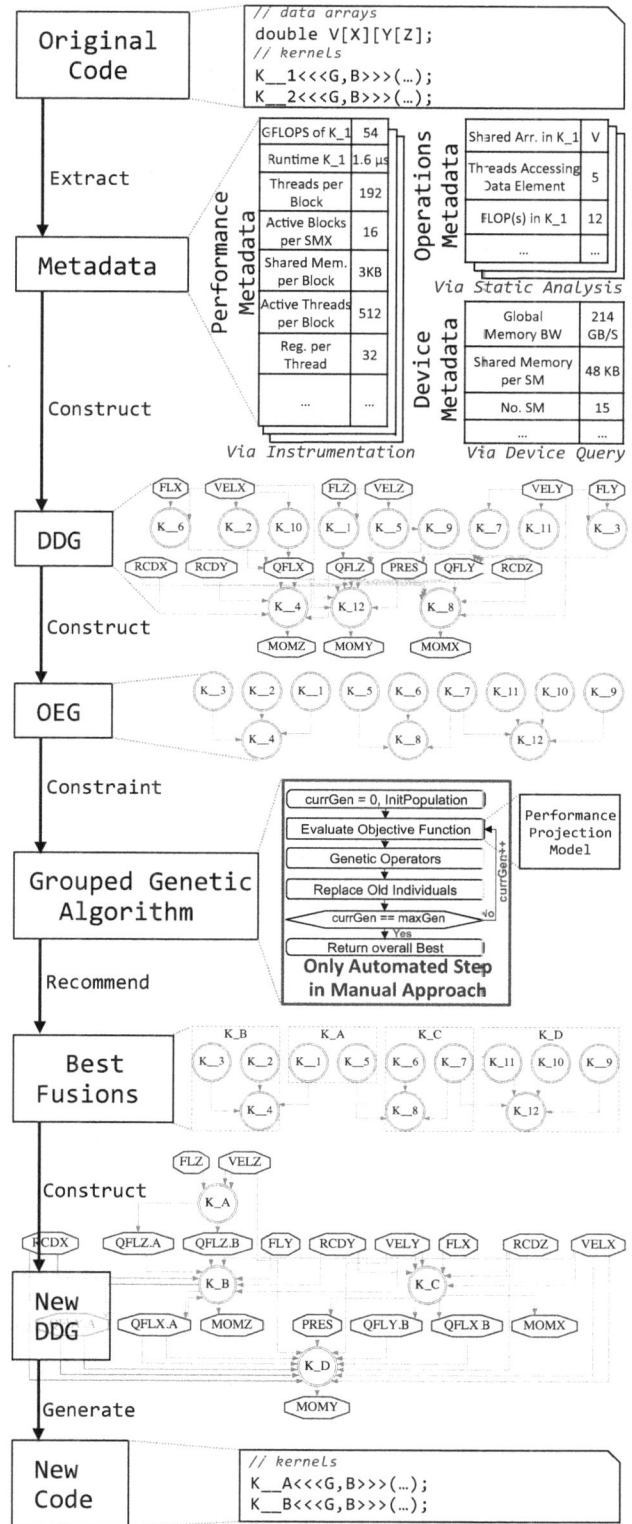

Figure 1: Workflow of end-to-end transformation including an example extracted from SCALE-LES [29] (workflow steps are on the left-hand side with an example for each step on the right-hand side). Metadata is extracted from source code using different methods. Source code and metadata are used to generate DDG and OEG. An optimization algorithm finds the optimal fission/fusions, which act as a guide for generating new kernels

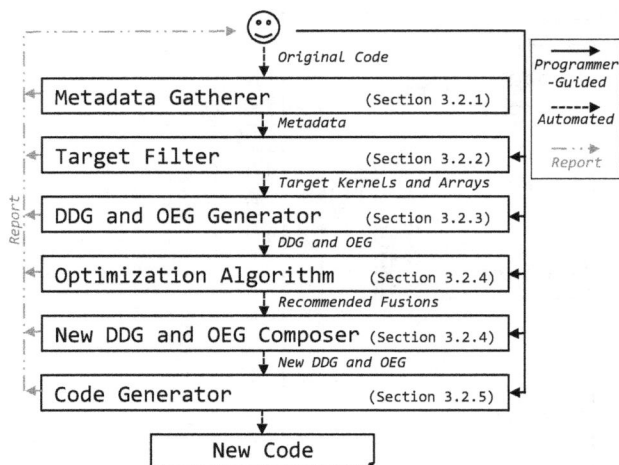

Figure 2: The Programmer can guide the transformation by amending the output of any transformation stage before using it as input to following stage. The programmer can favor an automated transformation, if intervention deemed unnecessary

3.2 Transformation Workflow

The programmer can choose to use the framework to apply the entire transformation without interfering with any of the stages (we call it *automated transformation*). Otherwise, in a *programmer-guided transformation*, the programmer can administer the workflow of stages and at each step he can choose to intervene or skip intervention. The programmer can execute up to a certain stage or starting from a certain stage by passing command-line arguments when executing the framework.

Figure 2 shows how the programmer can apply the transformation with the option of intervening at any step. The workflow is designed to allow the programmer to intervene at the pivotal points of the transformation: after data is collected about the program, after the kernels and data arrays are filtered to choose the targets of fusion, after the DDG and OEG are generated from the code, before/after the search, and after the new graphs are created.

3.2.1 Metadata

In its first stage, the framework will output the metadata in three text files. These are the files that the programmer can amend and pass to the next stage if he wishes to intervene. First, a file containing performance metadata that quantify performance metrics and device utilization for each original kernel, including: FLOPS, runtime, effective memory throughput, shared memory per thread block, registers per thread, the number of active threads, and active blocks per Streaming Multiprocessor (SM). Second, a file containing operations metadata that describe the features of the stencil operation(s) in each original kernel, such as: the stencil shape, access stride, loop size, arrays that are shared with other kernels, and FLOP(s) related to each data array. Finally, a file containing device metadata that include information about the target device required for use by the objective function, such as the number of SMs and available shared memory.

3.2.2 Identifying Targets

In an ideal scenario, all kernels in the application, by default, would be set as targets for optimization. However, passing all kernels as targets to the optimization algorithm would exponentially increase the size of the solution space, which can cause the optimization algorithm to converge significantly slower. Therefore,

filtering out irrelevant kernels before passing the input to the optimization algorithm is necessary.

In this stage of transformation, the code is analyzed to decide on the kernels to target for fission/fusion. The framework automatically excludes two types of kernels. First are the compute-bound kernels. Compute-bound kernels do not benefit from kernel fusion. Thus, they have no effect on the optimal fusions recommended by the optimization algorithm yet they increase the search space size. Compute-bound kernels are identified by mapping the operational intensity (FLOPS to bytes ratio) to the Roofline model [32]. Note that the information required for calculating the operational intensity exists in the operational metadata.

The second type of kernels that the framework excludes are memory-bound kernels that operate on a small subset of the data arrays target of locality, e.g., kernels applying boundary conditions on a few 2D planes of a 3D grid. Those kernels that apply boundary conditions do not have much benefit from fusion: the spatial locality is limited to a few 2D planes only. Moreover, the objective function evaluation time would significantly increase due to the complex analysis required. Finally and more importantly, leaving those kernels in the search space can lead to missed positives, i.e., they mask alternative fusions that could have exposed better locality.

The boundary kernels in stencil applications vary from doing the same operation as in non-boundary kernels up to kernels applying complex boundary conditions. Using the metadata, the boundary kernels are identified by the framework as kernels operating on a small number of iterations on a subset(s) of the data array(s).

3.2.3 DDG and OEG

As shown in Algorithm 1, the DDG is constructed by adding a node for every kernel invocation and every data array target of locality. Edges are added to express the intention of data arrays; an edge connects an input data array to the kernel using it and an edge connects a kernel to the output data array. The DDG is generated when doing the static analysis required for metadata gathering. The OEG is generated from the DDG by adding nodes to the OEG equivalent to all kernel nodes in DDG and then adding edges to express the precedency as dictated by the control flow or host side operations, i.e., copying data between device and host.

In addition to creating the graphs from the original code, the framework applies optimizations on the graphs that could require changing the original code. The following is an example for a case in which the graphs are optimized. Assume a kernel A touches arrays X and Y for reading and writing, respectively. Another kernel B touches X and Y but for writing and reading, respectively. This case, which actually occurs in one of the applications evaluated, creates a cycle in the DDG, causing incorrect constraints being passed to the optimization algorithm. The problem is resolved by the OEG generating heuristic that adds precedency for the kernel invoked first by the host. Another optimization is to add redundant instances for arrays having several kernels writing into them to relax dependencies (elaboration on this optimization in previous work [28]). After this stage in the transformation a report is given to the programmer regarding changes that were done to the original code to optimize the two graphs. The programmer can intervene and change the DDG if he finds it improperly representing the actual dependencies in his program.

3.2.4 Identifying the Best Kernel Fissions/Fusions

At this step of the workflow, the input is the metadata, DDG, and OEG. In addition to that, a parameter input file for the optimization algorithm is required. The parameter file configures the population, genetic operators, generations, and constraints [27]. There is a default parameter file provided for the programmer. The default values were chosen based on empirical tests. One more important input to the optimization algorithm is the objective function. The previous work derived an objective function based on the projected performance bound. However, other objective functions, i.e., performance models, can be used as an objective function. The programmer can add his own objective function, written in standard C language, and recompile the framework. Next, the programmer can change an entry in the parameter file to use his objective function. Note that the objective function is a black box, i.e., it receives individual solutions as an input and returns the float value of a projected performance bound in GFLOPS.

Running the optimization algorithm results in a new DDG and OEG representing the new program with the recommended fusions and fissions. Note that the new OEG is different from the original OEG in that the fissions and fusions can be visualized in the DOT file (see red dotted lines in new OEG in Figure 1). The programmer, if not satisfied by the output of the optimization algorithm, can amend the OEG DOT file and have another run to automatically amend the new DDG. Once the programmer is satisfied, the new DDG and OEG can now be used as an input to the final transformation stage as shown in the following section

3.2.5 Applying Kernel Fission/Fusion

The programmer can pass the command-line argument to run only the code generator using as input the original code, the new DDG and OEG, and the metadata. The code generator generates new CUDA code that the programmer can compile using CUDA's *nvcc* compiler without any external dependencies. The programmer can also amend the new CUDA code with relative ease considering that the generated CUDA kernels are highly readable, with the exception of CUDA kernels that require a complex fusion as will be explained in Section 5.5. High readability is an outcome of the tool used for source code manipulation.

4. IMPROVED TRANSFORMATION AS ENABLED BY AUTOMATION

The automated approach for transformation gives an added opportunity for improving the transformation itself by introducing

---

Algorithm 2 Heuristic for Fission of a Kernel

INPUT:
Original kernel K to be fissed
$D \leftarrow$ set of N arrays residing in shared memory and used in K
$G \leftarrow$ empty graph representing dependencies among arrays in D
OUTPUT:
$F \leftarrow$ set of kernels resulting from fissing K
1: **BEGIN**
2: **for** every array $D_i, i = 1, \ldots, N$ **do**
3:     arrayNode = G.addNode(D_i, Tag = i)
4: **end for**
5: **for** every array $D_i, i = 1, \ldots, N$ **do**
6:     **for** each data array $D_j, i = 1, \ldots, N$ and $i \neq j$ **do**
7:         **if** dependencyExists(D_i, D_j) **then**
8:             G.addEdge(i, j)
9:         **end if**
10:     **end for**
11: **end for**
12: **while** G is Not Empty **do**
13:     $Root \leftarrow$ random node $Root$ from G
14:     $SubG \leftarrow$ subgraph returned by breadth first_search($Root$)
15:     $F_i \leftarrow$ kernel fissed from K by extracting all instructions related to arrays in $SubG_k$
16:     **for** every node in $SubG_i, i = 1, \ldots, |SubG|$ **do**
17:         delNode($SubG_i$)
18:     **end for**
19: **end while**

---

transformation components that would have been a prohibitive burden on the programmer's end in the manual approach. This section discusses two components in the transformation that are enabled by the automation.

4.1 Kernel Fission

Kernel fission in this paper refers to splitting a kernel into several kernels such that each data array and the operations acting on it for all iterations are kept together and not split among kernels. So for a set D of n arrays residing in shared memory and used in original kernel K, find m kernel subsets $K_1, \ldots, K_m \subseteq K$ such that a) the subsets are pairwise disjoint and complete (i.e., their union via code aggregation is exactly K), b) if $x_{ij} = 1$ when array D_i appears in kernel subset K_j, $x_{ij} = 0$ otherwise, $\sum_{j=1}^{m} x_{ij} = 1, \forall i \in \{1, \ldots, n\}$, and c) all operations related to array D_i only exist in kernel K_j at which D_i appears. D_i is in this case called a *separable data array*. Figure 3 shows a simple example of kernel fission.

Algorithm 2 shows the heuristic for splitting a kernel into many kernels by fission. Initially, a graph representing the dependencies among the data arrays using shared memory is constructed. An array A is not dependent on array B if all instructions touching elements in B have no effect on the value of any element in A and vice versa, i.e., altering values of one array has no side effect on the values of the other arrays. The dependency between two arrays is determined based on a scalable method for polyhedral analysis at the granularity of individual statements [16]. Further details of the analysis of the dependency are not included due to space limitation. If separable data arrays exist, the graph will be a disconnected graph, i.e., there exists pairs of nodes having no path between them. Next, a random node is picked and a breadth first search is conducted to find all nodes connected to it. The nodes are then removed from the graph and the process repeats with a new random node until there are no more nodes left in the graph. The enumerated disconnected subgraphs guide the auto generation of the new kernels fissed from the original kernel by confining the instructions reading/writing to the arrays in each disconnected subgraph. Note that if no separable arrays exist, a single subgraph identical to the original graph will be returned by the breadth first search.

While kernel fission intuitively seems to reduce the chances for data locality, we argue that fission can be a useful tool in searching for optimal data locality. This is based on two observations: a) many applications have large sized CPU kernels and when ported to GPU the device kernels are consequently of large size (i.e., include many data arrays), and b) the main constraint affecting fusion is the capacity of shared memory. Therefore, in the evolving search for solutions in the genetic algorithm, candidate solutions, i.e., proposed kernel fusions, can often be stuck on the boundary of the feasible area of the search space. This means attempting to fuse any more kernels to a candidate fusion on the boundary of the search space will make the solution infeasible and be penalized by the penalty function. We relax the boundaries of the search space by applying fission to the kernels that hit the shared memory capacity constraint such that breaking up the kernel can provide shared memory space to explore new fusions. Kernel fission can also have significant impact of performance for applications that already have fused-like kernels. In such applications kernel fission is not only a strategy for relaxing the search space but can be the main force driving performance improvement in comparison to kernel fusion. The results section shows two applications of this type.

There are two prospective methods for including kernel fission in the transformation. The first prospective method is to apply an initial round of iterative fission before running the optimization algorithm such that all the kernels provided as input to the optimization algorithm can not be fissed any more, i.e., none of the kernels have any separable data arrays. This method is impractical, as it will cause an explosive expansion in the search space size, i.e., search space size is exponentially proportional to the number of kernels. The other prospective method for fission is to start with the original kernels without a fission pre-step, and apply fission on-demand for candidate solutions if required. This method is not possible because the performance projection method used as an objective function depends on empirically measured metadata, i.e., kernels fissed on-demand have no such metadata.

We introduce a compromising solution, *lazy fission*, at which fission is applied in a pre-step in which the metadata of the fissed kernels is gathered. Next, the optimization algorithm starts with the original kernels and not with the fissed ones. When the genetic algorithm is evolving, and upon investigating solutions on the search space boundary, fission is applied to relax the boundary. Therefore, the metadata gathered in the pre-step enables the use of the performance projection while avoiding the increase in search space size had the fissed kernels been used at the start of the search process. The decision to apply fission, when needed, is embedded in a dynamic penalty function. Hence the kernels that would benefit from fission would be less penalized, i.e., relaxed:

$$f_p(x) = f(x) + \sum_{i=1}^{m} C_i \delta_i - C_{SM} \delta_{SM}$$

Where
$$\begin{cases} \delta_i &= 1, \text{constrain } i \text{ is violated} \\ \delta_i &= 0, \text{constrain } i \text{ is satisfied} \\ \delta_{SM} &= 1, \text{shared memory capacity constrain is violated} \\ \delta_{SM} &= 0, \text{shared memory capacity constrain is satisfied} \end{cases}$$

$f_p(x)$ is the penalized objective function, $f(x)$ is the unpenalized objective function, C_i is a constant imposed for the violation of constrain i, and C_{SM} is a positive variable corresponding to the anticipated relaxation in shared memory constraint if fission for any of the cached data arrays is possible. Otherwise C_{SM} is a negative number to penalize solutions on the boundary of the search space that cannot be fissed.

Before Fission

```
Kern_A<<<G, B>>>(R, S, T, Q, P, V, U, W, nz, c);

__global__Kern_A(R, S, T, Q, P, V, U, W, nz, c){
int i = blockIdx.x*blockDim.x + threadIdx.x;
int j = blockIdx.y*blockDim.y + threadIdx.y;
for(int k=0; k<nz;k++)  {
  R[i,j,k]= S[i,j,k] * (V[i-1,j,k]/V[i,j,k]);
  W[i,j,k]= V[i-1,j,k] - V[i,j,k];
  P[i,j,k]= c*(Q[i-1,j,k]+Q[i,j,k]+Q[i+1,j,k]+Q[i,j+1,k]);
  U[i,j,k]= T[i,j,k]-Q[i,j,k]*(Q[i-1,j,k]-Q[i,j-1,k]);
 }
}
```

After Fission

```
Kern_X<<<G, B>>>(R,S,V,W,nz);           __global__  Kern_Y(P,Q,U,T,nz,c){
Kern_Y<<<G, B>>>(P,Q,U,T,nz,c);         int i= //absolute index in X-Dir
                                        int j= //absolute index in y-Dir
__global__ Kern_X(R,S,V,W,nz){          for(int k=0; k<nz;k++) {
int i= //absolute index in X-Dir          P[i,j,k]= c*(Q[i-1,j,k]+Q[i,j-1,k]
int j= //absolute index in y-Dir          +Q[i,j,k]+Q[i+1,j,k]+Q[i,j+1,k]);
for(int k=0; k<nz;k++) {                   U[i,j,k]= T[i,j,k] - Q[i,j,k]
  R[i,j,k]= S[i,j,k]                            * (Q[i-1,j,k]- Q[i,j-1,k]);
    * (V[i-1,j,k]/V[i,j,k]);              }
  W[i,j,k]= V[i-1,j,k]-V[i,j,k]);        }
 } }
```

Figure 3: Example of CUDA Kernel fission. Kernel A is fissed to kernels X and Y

4.2 Tuning Thread Block Size

A main opportunity for a simple yet effective optimization not addressed in the previous work is the tuning of thread block size to maintain high occupancy. Occupancy is the ratio of sustained active warps to maximum possible active warps. The factors affecting the occupancy are the thread block size, shared memory used by each thread block, and the registers used by each thread. Tuning thread block size can have a significant effect on performance [24]. Therefore, we operate towards the target of keeping the occupancy of the new kernel as high as possible by tuning the thread block size. We leverage the analysis done by the performance model to estimate the shared memory used per block and registers used per thread. We then enumerate all possible sizes of thread block and substitute in a series of equations using the same method as in the CUDA occupancy calculator tool. A block size giving the highest occupancy is chosen to be the new block size used in kernel invocation.

It is important to note that tuning is done in the final step of generating the new code and not included in the optimization algorithm as an additional degree of freedom. This is because occupancy is a measure of utilization and is not equivalent to performance. If occupancy becomes part of the optimization algorithm, the performance projection model would have an added inaccuracy not related to the performance.

5. IMPLEMENTATION

ROSE compiler infrastructure [21] is used for source-to-source transformation. ROSE supports manipulating the AST (Abstract Syntax Tree), and automatically transforming CUDA code to AST, and vice-versa. Initially, the AST of the CUDA program is constructed. To gather metadata, new statements are injected in the AST to instrument the code. Next, a shell script runs the instrumented program in profiling mode and the metadata is later extracted from the output. To construct the DDG and OEG, we locate the statements in the AST that would be statically analyzed. Examples of the static analysis are identifying the kernels order of invocation and identifying the shared arrays. Next, the GA is executed independently to identify the best fissions/fusions. Based on the output of the GA, the AST is modified to remove the original kernels and create the new kernels. The new kernels include statements from the original kernels plus new statements that are injected, e.g. loading/storing to shared memory. Finally, the AST is unparsed to generate the new source code.

The following sections briefly present the implementation of the metadata gatherer, target kernel identifier, DDG and OEG constructor, the optimization algorithm, and the code generator.

5.1 Metadata Gathering

First, performance metadata is gathered using code instrumentation. The code is instrumented, using ROSE, by injecting CUDA APIs dedicated for creating, destroying, recording, and measuring elapsed time of events such as kernel invocations. A shell script runs CUDA command-line profiler, *nvprof*, with the appropriate parameters to generate the metadata of the program. The required values are then automatically extracted from the profiler's output file. Note that only a single run of the instrumented code, on the target device, is required to gather the metadata.

Second, operations metadata is gathered using static analysis. The metadata is gathered by a static analysis of the program. To be more specific, the subset AST corresponding to each kernel is examined to identify the stencil operations, intra-kernel dependencies, and the data access pattern, i.e., shape of stencil, loop(s) size, and access stride. There are restrictions on the stencil operations in kernels. The limitations section will later discuss those restrictions.

Third, device metadata is gathered using a device query program. A small program queries the device for the required information; the program is named *deviceQuery* and is readily available with CUDA SDK samples. Note that device query can be done using the instrumentation being done for gathering operations metadata. However, since the device query is required only once per target device, we choose to leave it as a separate step.

5.2 Identifying Targets

To identify compute-bound kernels, operational intensity for all kernels in the program is calculated using the metadata. A precedency constraint can occur between two memory-bound kernels due to an intermediate invocation of a compute-bound kernel, hence the compute-bound kernels are added to the DDG and OEG. However, they are tagged as ineligible for fusion and are not used when randomly making an initial population in the optimization algorithm. Similar to the compute-bound kernels, boundary kernels are added to the DDG and OEG but not used when searching for fusions. Boundary kernels are identified as kernels having a small number of iterations applying stencil operations.

5.3 Constructing DDG and OEG

The following are functions related to the DDG and OEG: generation from parsed code, parsing them to guide generation of new code, and programmers amending them. The AST is used to generate and parse the graphs. An output file is generated in DOT format where the programmer can visualize the graphs using various tools such as GraphViz [1] (DDG and OEG in Figure 1 are generated with GraphViz). If the programmer changes the DDG, another run with an appropriate command-line argument is required just to generate a new OEG from the DDG the programmer amended.

5.4 Optimization Algorithm: GGA

Kernel fusion is defined as a combinatorial optimization problem. A customized grouped genetic algorithm is used to search the space of possible fissions/fusions while catering for the multivariate nature of the problem. The algorithm is implemented to be flexible; the programmer can tune the parameters of the optimization algorithm, write his own objective function, and add constraints.

Details about the implementation of the optimization algorithm are not covered by this paper and can be found elsewhere [27].

5.5 Code Generation

As mentioned earlier, ROSE parses CUDA code into an AST at which transformations can be applied before unparsing the AST to generate the new code. Fission is applied iteratively as long as there is at least one separable data array in the target kernel(s). The following sections introduce the code generation process when fusing kernels, i.e., different cases for generating a new kernel.

5.5.1 No Fusion

This is the case when the framework decides that a kernel is not to be fused, i.e., fusing of the kernel is not expected to improve performance. The new kernel is a copy of the original kernel.

5.5.2 Simple Fusion

This is the case when the framework reaches a decision that two or more original kernels are to be fused together into one new kernel. Note that in simple fusion, unlike complex fusion, all of the original kernels to be fused together have no precedency constraints between them appearing in the OEG. This means that no operation in any kernel relies on data generated from operations in the other kernel(s). First, the codes of the original kernels are aggregated in a new kernel. Next, the code is changed such that the arrays that are target of locality are stored into shared memory before the relevant stencil operation(s). The statements operating on the arrays are adjusted accordingly to read from shared memory. Next, the code segments are aligned to the same loop boundaries by offsetting the indices of every element accessed. Finally, for code segments of fused kernels requiring iterations less than the largest of loop boundaries, conditional statements are added.

5.5.3 Complex Fusion

This is the case when the original kernels have at least one precedence constraint appearing among them in the OEG. This causes the fusion process to be complex because the operations appearing the new kernel must follow some order. First, the steps of the previous simple fusion steps are applied. On top of that, appropriate barrier(s) are used to prevent data races. In addition to the barrier(s), this type of fusion introduces a type of problem related to the architecture of GPUs: the scope of shared memory in GPU is a thread block, and shared memory is not coherent with off-chip cache and device memory. Therefore, the boundary threads of a thread block become unaware of the change of intermediate values held in the shared memory of other thread blocks. We resolve this problem using the common approach of temporal blocking in GPU stencil applications [8]. An extra layer(s) of values is initially loaded to the shared memory of each block. The number of layers depends on the radius of the stencil neighborhood. Hence the stencil operations before the barrier are applied to an extra layer(s) of stencil sites at each thread block. After the barrier, the stencil operations are only applied to the number of stencil sites originally intended per thread block.

5.5.4 Host Code

For the host code, the code generator replaces the invocations of the original kernels with those of the new kernels. The size of thread blocks for each invocation is determined according to the tuning method mentioned earlier. The order of invocation is extracted from the new OEG.

Table 1: Applications Attributes and the Effect of Automated Transformation

Application	No. Original Kernels	No. New Kernels	No. Fused Kernels	No. Kernels Output of Fusion	Avg. Fissions/-Generation	No. Arrays Targeted	No. Array Sharing sets
SCALE-LES	142	63	117	38	0.07	64	103
HOMME	43	30	22	9	0.163	27	51
Fluam	169	144	42	17	0.01	84	201
MITgcm	37	29	14	6	0.010	35	61
AWP-ODC-GPU	12	24	6	3	1.062	21	48
B-CALM	23	24	8	3	0.783	44	58

6. EVALUATION

This section does not demonstrate the effectiveness and limitations of the GPU kernel fusion introduced in the previous work (demonstrated in [28]). The aim of this section is to: a) demonstrate the effectiveness of the automated end-to-end approach in speeding up real-world applications and evaluating the effect of kernel fission and tuning thread block size (Section 6.2.1), and b) quantify the efficiency of the automated transformation, by comparison to manual kernel fusion, and highlighting the experience when using a programmer-guided transformation (Section 6.2.2).

6.1 Methodology

6.1.1 Applications

SCALE-LES [29]: a next generation weather model having over a hundred kernels and tens of data arrays. Most of the kernels, in the dynamical core, are memory-bound kernels applying iterative stencils. SCALE-LES is liberally estimated to have 41% of reducible off-chip traffic from which 26% was achieved [28] (1.35x speedup). The problem size used is 1280x32x32.

HOMME [4]: the dynamical core within the Community Atmospheric Model (CAM). Similar to SCALE-LES, most kernels are memory-bound yet not all modules of HOMME are ported to GPU so we report the speedup of the kernels and not the entire application. The problem size used is 4x26x101.

Fluam [25]: a fluctuating particle hydrodynamics application based on an hybrid Eulerian-Lagrangian approach. Fluam relies on finite volume stencils with explicit time stepping formulated as 3rd order Runge-Kutta scheme. Fluam includes a large number of kernels, 207, of which 169 are stencil-based. The problem size used is 1000x8000x8000x384000.

MITgcm [12]: is an oceanic general circulation model relying on a finite volume numerical method with partial cells. The setting used for experimentation [20] is for a non-hydrostatic flow mode, which makes the simulation's hotspot a set of kernels with simple stencil operations: a 3D conjugate gradient solver for surface pressure. The problem size used is 804x2064x(24.9x10^6)x25m.

AWP-ODC-GPU [9]: an earthquake wave propagation simulator. 3D velocity-stress wave equations are solved by explicit staggered-grid 4th order finite difference. AWP-ODC-GPU includes vector and stress computation kernels using 3D arrays each having the same size as the 3D simulation domain. It is worth mentioning that AWP-ODC-GPU is highly optimized for GPU architecture features; overlapping computation with communication highly influenced the design of the kernels and ghost cell regions. The problem size used is 3500x2500x1500.

B-CALM [30]: a 3D-FDTD simulator which models the permittivity of dispersive material, i.e., propagation of electromagnetic waves in metallic nanostructures. B-CALM breaks down the update equations for both the electric and magnetic fields into separate kernels to optimize for minimizing thread divergence in simulating materials with high number of poles. The approach of breaking the kernels in such way adds extra memory traffic to hold intermediate results in global memory in-between kernel invocations. Hence a

setting of high resolution, i.e., large problem size, is used in this evaluation to amplify the effect of the extra memory traffic. The problem size is 208x208x400 cells with $0.1nm$ resolution.

6.1.2 Platform and Tools

The results were collected using CUDA 6.0 for Nvidia's Kepler K20X and K40 GPUs. Two of the applications, SCALE-LES and CAM-HOMME, were written originally in CUDA Fortran. For experimentation purposes, the kernels were manually translated to CUDA C while the host related computation remains in Fortran 90. The non-hydrostatic flow mode setting used for MITgcm in experimentation was also translated to CUDA C. Performance results are averaged for 10 runs compiled at the highest possible compiler optimization. Output of the automated method was verified against the output of the original code base for every single run. All the results reported are for double precision in a single node execution. Stencil-based scientific applications widely favor weak scaling to be the major evaluation criterion, e.g., adding new nodes to a weather application means expanding the 3D grid atmospheric space in the horizontal direction. Hence the speedup achieved on a single node is expected to carry over to multi-node execution for applications having almost linear weak scaling. Initialization and output writing parts are excluded from this calculation. The I/O time is negligible when time iterations of tens to hundreds of thousands of time steps are involved.

The framework is implemented in C++, parallelized by OpenMP, and executed using an Intel Xeon E5-2670 2.60GHz machine (8 cores). The optimization algorithm runs for 500 generations, the population size is 100 individuals. Evaluation of the objective function constituted more than 90% of the total runtime of the optimization algorithm for all applications (total runtime for an automated transformation averages around 11 minutes).

6.2 Results

We start this section by summarizing the important results. The transformations applied on the six applications resulted in speedups ranging between 1.12x to 1.76x compared to the original CUDA codebases. Kernel fission appeared to have the primary influence on performance improvement for applications that have original kernels that are already fused to some extent. Tuning thread block size proved to be effective for most applications. The automated transformation of framework is shown to enhance performance within high proximity to performance enhancement due to manual fusions. Programmer-guided transformation proved to be of value in identifying sub-optimal transformations that were the reason of difference in performance improvement between the manual and automated methods.

Section 6.2.1 quantifies the effect of automated transformation on performance and investigates the impact of applying kernel fission and thread block tuning. Section 6.2.2 analyzes the efficiency of the automated transformation in comparison to the manual transformation and discusses the effectiveness of programmer-guided transformation.

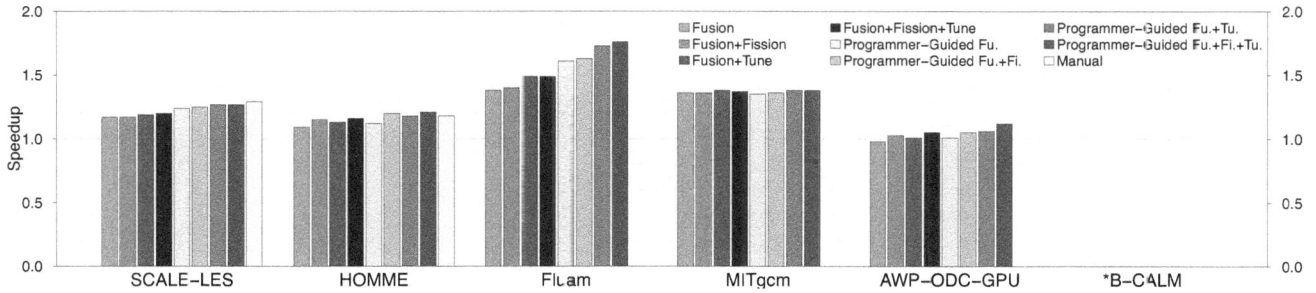

Figure 4: K20X speedup compared to baseline CUDA version with no kernel fission/fusion (*B-CALM run not possible due to limited device memory capacity)

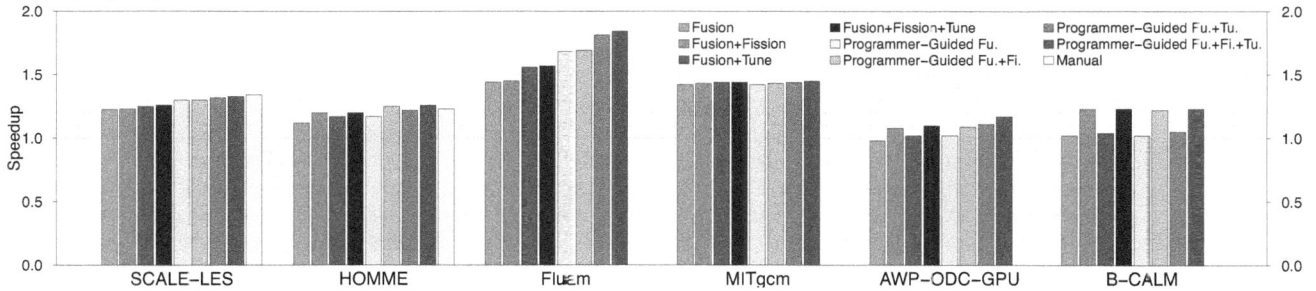

Figure 5: K40 speedup compared to baseline CUDA version with no kernel fission/fusion

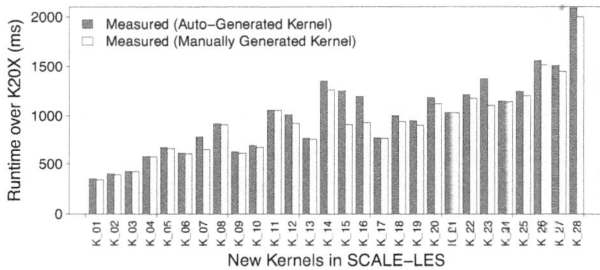

Figure 6: Runtime on K20X for new kernels of SCALE-LES. Manually generated vs. auto-generated kernels

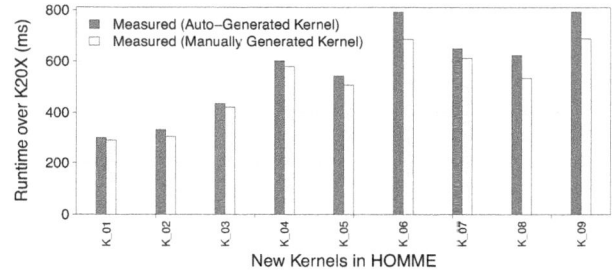

Figure 7: Runtime on K20X for new kernels of HOMME. Manually generated vs. auto-generated kernels

6.2.1 Performance and Speedup

Table 1 summarizes the collective effect of transformation on kernels. The two factors affecting the size of the optimization problem are the number of original kernels and the number of array sharing sets (array sharing sets is an enumeration of possible reuse combinations). Note that the number of original kernels can potentially increase during the optimization process if fissions are feasible. As a consequence, for two applications, AWP-ODC-GPU and B-CALM, the number of new kernels is more than the number of original kernels. This means that the actual number of kernels available for fusion, after applying fission, was higher than the number of original kernels (27 rather than 12 for AWP-ODC-GPU and 29 rather than 23 for B-CALM). Analyzing the reason for this effect on those two applications revealed that the original kernels of the two applications were large in code size compared to the other applications. This implies the kernels of both applications are already in an almost-fused state. It also indicates a higher possibility of finding separable data arrays that can be fissed. The other applications, however, have tight kernels, which decreases the opportunity for fission. The difference is demonstrated in Table 1 where the average number of fissions per generation of the optimization algorithm is orders of magnitude higher in the two applications. It is worth mentioning that the higher tendency towards fission rather

than fusion in these two applications was made possible by the performance model and optimization algorithm. Had a naive fission been applied, best fissions, which are the fissions that would relax the penalty for desired fusions, would have not been guaranteed.

Figures 4 and 5 show the speedups achieved when using the framework in both automated and programmer-guided modes. Note that speedup for the "Manual" kernel fusion is included for only SCALE-LES and HOMME, while the other four applications were transformed only automatically with no reference implementation for manual fusion existing. Several points are important to note from the figures. First, kernel fusion showed no speedups for AWP-ODC-GPU and B-CALM. Surprisingly, kernel fission+fusion results in significant improvement in performance for those applications. Second, thread block tuning shows worthwhile improvement in performance. Finally, programmer-guided transformation shows significant improvement over the automated transformation for SCALE-LES, HOMME, and Fluam. The following section discusses the role of programmer-guided transformation.

Table 2 shows the effect of thread block tuning on the occupancy of the new kernels (1.0 is top occupancy). The occupancy reported in the table is the occupancy measured after kernel fusion and not the estimated occupancy that guided the tuning.

Table 2: Tuning Thread Block Size for New Kernels

Application	No. Kernels Output of Fusion	No. Tuned Kernels	Avg. Occupancy Before Tuning	Avg. Occupancy After Tuning
SCALE-LES	38	14	0.65	0.80
HOMME	9	4	0.55	0.85
Fluam	17	11	0.81	0.90
MITgcm	6	3	0.95	0.96
AWP-ODC-GPU	3	2	0.75	0.77
B-CALM	3	0	0.72	0.72

6.2.2 Efficiency of Automated Transformation

This section discusses two issues. The first issue is the source of inefficiencies in automated transformation, i.e., the reason for the difference in performance between the automated vs. manual transformation. This was done by analyzing the reports of each transformation stage to understand the behavior of the framework components, which in turn helped in identifying the reason in performance gap between the manual and automated kernel fusion.

The second issue discussed is how the programmer-guided transformation was used in this context to close the performance gap; after identifying the inefficiencies of the automated transformation, manual intervention was minimally introduced to improve the performance. As will be shown, in the case of SCALE-LES and HOMME, the manual changes were to address problems in the auto-generation of code. In the case of Fluam, the manual changes were to address a problem in filtering target kernels.

There are four possible reasons why the automated transformation can result in lower performance than the manual transformation are: a) inaccuracy in gathering metadata, b) inaccuracy in generation of the DDG and OEG, c) failing to generate new kernels that reuse data optimally, and d) failing to filter the target kernels automatically. We used the programmer-guided transformation to identify which of the four reasons was the source of performance difference for each application:

SCALE-LES: When compared against the speedup of the previously reported manual method [28], baseline automated transformation for SCALE-LES achieves 85% of manual method compared to 92% for the programmer-guided transformation (Figures 4 and 5). Thread block tuning showed improvement in performance for both automated and programmer-guided transformation, while fission did not show a significant difference.

We identified the performance gap to be caused by the auto-generated kernels, i.e., auto-generated kernels have lower aggregate performance compared to the manually generated kernels. Accordingly, we analyzed the auto-generated kernels that show the highest difference in runtime from the manually generated kernels. Figure 6 shows the runtime for the new kernels of SCALE-LES executed on K20X. Note that few kernels are contributing the highest in the total performance difference: kernels K_07, K_15, K_16, and K_23. The problem in the generated code of the mentioned kernels was the inefficiency in fusing kernels that had deep nested loops inside them. Normally, kernels would have a single loop that iterates on the vertical 3D space. However, some kernels can have nested loops where stencil operations would be applied to arrays with more than three dimensions. The programmer that manually fused the kernels aggregated the two codes such that they share the most inner loop if codes of both kernels do not share the external loops. The auto-generated code on the other hand did not aggregate the codes in same manner. Therefore iterations for the code of the first kernel were entirely finished before the iterations of the second kernel started and shared data was never reused. Automatically resolving this problem by running a polyhedral model is a main point in the future work.

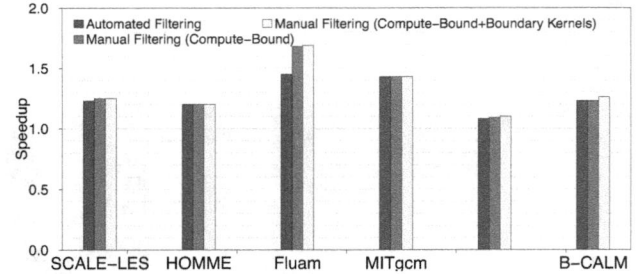

Figure 8: K40 speedup for automated vs. manual kernel filtering compared to baseline CUDA version with no kernel fission/fusion

HOMME: Like SCALE-LES, HOMME's performance gap was caused by the auto-generated kernels. However, the exact cause of the difference in performance in HOMME was found to be of different nature. The runtime comparison in Figure 7 shows a more even distribution of difference in performance with two kernels slightly higher than the others. Analysis showed that the reason of performance degradation was auto-generating code that incurs intra-warp divergent branches, which does not appear in manually fused kernels. In the proposed method for fusion, the code segments originating from different kernels are dimension-aligned by offsetting the indices of every element accessed. Conditional statements are added to account for the difference in dimension lengths. When loops bounds are different on both ends of the warp dimension, i.e., tx, the manual code accumulated the diverging threads in the last thread block on the warp dimension. The automated version, however, adds branches for the first and last thread blocks, which increases the intra-warp divergence. Optimizing the generation of branching statements to close the performance gap is part of the future work. Finally, it is worth mentioning that due to the significant effect of fission on performance for HOMME, the programmer-guided transformation with fission exceeds the manual approach in speedup.

Fluam: In Fluam, we observed that the optimization algorithm converged poorly in comparison to the other applications. This implies the excessive size of the solution space, i.e., original kernels that unnecessarily appear as targets. To understand this behavior, we evaluated the effectiveness of filtering the kernels by comparing the automated kernel filtration of the framework with a version that was filtered manually. Similar to the automated method, the manual filtration filters out the compute-bound kernels and boundary memory-bound kernels. Figure 8 shows a comparison in speedups generated by both the automated and manual filtering. All applications, excluding Fluam, give the same speedup when comparing the automated with manual versions. This implies the effectiveness of the framework in automatically filtering out kernels that are not worthy of being targets. The transformation of Fluam was further investigated and the anomaly is likely to be a number of kernels that have latency problems (i.e., poor computation and memory overlapping). Those kernels falsely appeared to the framework as memory-bound kernels and populated the search space. Which in turn caused less convergence in the optimization algorithm running to a pre-defined number of steps. Finally, it is worth mentioning that when no filtering out at all was applied, automated or manual, the optimization algorithm converged 2.5x slower on average.

7. LIMITATIONS

Despite demonstrating promising results for real-world applications, the proposed framework is certainly not complete. Limitations and restrictions that the programmer must be aware of are summarized in the following points:

Table 3: Related Work Summary

Domain	Technique	Relationship/*What is lacking*
GPU Kernel Fission and Fusion	GROPHECY [17]	Analytical model based on code skeletons. *Writing code skeletons is a significant effort and requires the kernel code to already exist.*
	Fuse kernels applying basic operations [11, 10]	Using building blocks, e.g. map-reduce operations, simplifies the search process at the expense of bounding the kernels to a fixed set of problem-specific elementary functions.
	Fuse kernels to optimize for power [31]	The problem is represented as a dynamic programming problem of fusing a small number of kernels. Reported fusion of two kernels was shown effective for power optimization. *Effective for demand balancing of hardware resources and not locality.*
CUDA Code Generation	PPCG [26], PLUTO [3]	Tiling strategy and a code generation scheme for the parallelization and locality optimization of imperfectly nested loops. *Targets fine-grain locality i.e., nested loops and polyhedral iterations. Not for coarse-grain locality spanning entire programs.*
	Stencil DSL generating CUDA [14, 15]	Generate CUDA code implicitly, via directives or leveraging C++ templates. Optimizations, such as computation-communication overlapping, are applied. *No optimization available for exploiting inter-kernel locality.*
Coarse-grained Data Locality	Pipeline parallelism of stream programs [23]	Changing the boundaries of the pipeline stages by fission/fusion to optimize for load balance on multicores. *Assumes load balance to be the objective of optimization with locality implicitly optimized. Works for cache systems having coherency*
	Task clustering in data-intensive scientific workflows [22, 6]	Task clustering is aggregating multiple workflow tasks into a single job to reduce the job execution overhead. Locality in workflows is focused on assigning tasks to where the data resides and not merging tasks using the same data. *Runtime and dependency imbalances [7], if not considered in task clustering, could degrade the performance.*

Pointer aliasing: Pointer aliasing is extremely complicated in static analysis. Hence we limit the programmer to restrict the pointers for data arrays that are targets for locality. The following improvement is under consideration for the future work. For the majority of stencil applications, the data operated-on across the kernels is stable throughout the lifetime of the program. By stable we mean that the memory dependences between different kernels is predictable. A pre-run of the program for a few iteration to detect the data usage pattern can provide a more practical method to address the pointer aliasing problem (this approach was originally proposed in pipelined parallelism for stream programs [23]).

Supported stencils: Our framework specifically targets stencils for dense multidimensional Cartesian grids, e.g., 3D atmospheric grid. For example, stencils for unstructured grids are not possible. One approach is to extend the framework to introduce support for different stencil operations. Another radical approach is to have the proposed framework sit on top of a framework that can support different stencils via intrinsic data models, e.g., Chapel programming language [5]. The proposed framework would then extend the runtime and compiler to leverage the data models.

Data access: As mentioned earlier, the static analysis can detect the access stride. However, the code generator will assume that the stencil is following the common horizontal mapping to CUDA grid and iterating in the vertical direction [19] and will not be effective in translating stencils with irregular access. Furthermore, stencils with large neighborhood size can limit the performance in some cases, i.e., when thread block halo layers are exceedingly large in size.

Sensitivity to input: The analysis done by the framework is dependent on the properties of the original kernels. More specifically, the performance model projects the performance of the kernels based on empirically measured properties of stencil operations. Using a different problem size with the transformed code could negatively impact the effectiveness of kernel fusion. However, we argue that this is unlikely to happen considering that, in practice, stencil applications favor design for weak scaling. Hence as the problem size grows with the number of nodes, the input size per node remains the same. Another point of concern is the change in program behavior if specific values are used as input. The supported stencils in this work, however, are unlikely to have such

problem. Nonetheless, a proper analysis of the sensitivity of the performance of transformed code to change in input is important.

8. RELATED WORK

Table 3 contrasts with related work on GPU kernel fusion, CUDA code generation, and coarse-grained data locality in literature. We elaborate on a few other related works below.

Auto-tuning CUDA by traversing the space of possible implementations can be used to generate optimal code variants [13]. The work is reported to be based on a compiler framework, which makes it extendable, in concept, to more advanced optimizations such as kernel fusion. Meng at al. [18] proposed an automated optimization for selection of the optimal ghost zone size depending on the characteristics of both the architecture and the application. The optimization addresses single kernels, unlike kernel fusion, yet it demonstrated the effectiveness of complex automated memory optimizations for GPU kernels.

9. CONCLUSION

This paper introduces an automated end-to-end method for exposing and exploiting hidden localities in a class of GPU applications with stencil-based CUDA kernels. The proposed work builds on previous work, which successfully formulated the GPU kernel fusion problem and demonstrated effectiveness, yet lacked a practical automated approach. The main contribution introduced in this paper is an end-to-end framework for applying kernel fission/fusion transformations. The framework includes a set of automated components starting from analysis of the original code and ending with generation of new code. The programmer can compile the new code using the native CUDA compiler without runtime dependencies. In addition, the paper introduced optimizations for the transformation mainly enabled by the automation. One improvement is a scheme for lazy fission that enables on-demand use of fission in the search process. Another optimization is tuning of thread block size for kernels generated from fusion to achieve high occupancy.

The effectiveness of the proposed framework is demonstrated by achieving speedups ranging between 1.12x and 1.75x for six real-world applications and with speedups comparable to a previous manual kernel fusion of two of the applications. Using the programmer-guided transformation for investigation, potential areas of improvement in code generation were identified: a polyhedral model for guiding fusion in kernels having deep nested loops, and a more efficient loop alignment scheme.

Acknowledgments

This project was partially supported by JST, CREST through its research program: "Highly Productive, High Performance Application Frameworks for Post Petascale Computing."

10. REFERENCES

[1] http://www.graphviz.org.

[2] L. Almagor, K. D. Cooper, A. Grosul, T. J. Harvey, S. W. Reeves, D. Subramanian, L. Torczon, and T. Waterman. Finding Effective Compilation Sequences. LCTES '04, pages 231–239, 2004.

[3] U. Bondhugula, M. Baskaran, S. Krishnamoorthy, J. Ramanujam, A. Rountev, and P. Sadayappan. Automatic Transformations for Communication-Minimized Parallelization and Locality Optimization in the Polyhedral Model. ETAPS CC '08, 2008.

[4] I. Carpenter, R. Archibald, K. Evans, J. Larkin, P. Micikevicius, M. Norman, J. Rosinski, J. Schwarzmeier, and M. Taylor. Progress Towards Accelerating HOMME on Hybrid Multi-core Systems. *Int. J. High Perform. Comput. Appl.*, 27:335–347, 2013.

[5] B. Chamberlain, D. Callahan, and H. Zima. Parallel Programmability and the Chapel Language. *Int. J. High Perform. Comput. Appl.*, 21:291–312.

[6] W. Chen and E. Deelman. Integration of Workflow Partitioning and Resource Provisioning. CCGRID'12, pages 764–768, 2012.

[7] W. Chen, R. F. D. Silva, E. Deelman, and R. Sakellariou. Balanced Task Clustering in Scientific Workflows. e-SCIENCE '13, pages 188–195, 2013.

[8] M. Christen, O. Schenk, P. Messmer, E. Neufeld, and H. Burkhart. Accelerating Stencil-Based Computations by Increased Temporal Locality on Modern Multi- and Many-Core Architectures. HipHaC '08, pages 47–54, 2008.

[9] Y. Cui, E. Poyraz, K. B. Olsen, J. Zhou, K. Withers, S. Callaghan, J. Larkin, C. Guest, D. Choi, A. Chourasia, Z. Shi, S. M. Day, P. J. Maechling, and T. H. Jordan. Physics-based Seismic Hazard Analysis on Petascale Heterogeneous Supercomputers. SC '13, pages 1–12, 2013.

[10] J. Filipovic, M. Madzin, J. Fousek, and L. Matyska. Optimizing CUDA Code By Kernel Fusion: Application on BLAS. *CoRR*, 1305, 2013.

[11] J. Fousek, J. Filipovič, and M. Madzin. Automatic Fusions of CUDA-GPU Kernels for Parallel Map. *SIGARCH Comput. Archit. News*, 39(4):98–99, 2011.

[12] C. Hill, C. DeLuca, V. Balaji, M. Suarez, and A. d. Silva. The Architecture of the Earth System Modeling Framework. *Computing in Science and Eng.*, 6:18–28, 2004.

[13] M. Khan, P. Basu, G. Rudy, M. Hall, C. Chen, and J. Chame. A Script-based Autotuning Compiler System to Generate High-performance CUDA code. *ACM Trans. Archit. Code Optim.*, 9:1–25, 2013.

[14] X. Lapillonne and O. Fuhrer. Using Compiler Directives to Port Large Scientific Applications to GPUs: An Example from Atmospheric Science. *Parallel Processing Letters*, 24(1), 2014.

[15] N. Maruyama, T. Nomura, K. Sato, and S. Matsuoka. Physis: An Implicitly Parallel Programming Model for Stencil

[16] Computations on Large-scale GPU-accelerated Supercomputers. SC '11, pages 1–12, 2011.

[16] S. Mehta, P.-H. Lin, and P.-C. Yew. Revisiting Loop Fusion in the Polyhedral Framework. PPoPP '14, pages 233–246.

[17] J. Meng, V. A. Morozov, K. Kumaran, V. Vishwanath, and T. D. Uram. GROPHECY: GPU Performance Projection from CPU Code Skeletons. SC '11, pages 1–11, 2011.

[18] J. Meng and K. Skadron. Performance Modeling and Automatic Ghost Zone Optimization for Iterative Stencil Loops on GPUs. ICS'09, pages 256–265, 2009.

[19] P. Micikevicius. 3D Finite Difference Computation on GPUs Using CUDA. In *Proceedings of 2ND Workshop on General Purpose Processing on Graphics Processing Units*, GPGPU-2, pages 79–84, 2009.

[20] O. Padon. Using graphics processing unit computing to improve the performance of an oceanic general circulation model the mitgcm and implementation to dead sea circulation. Master's thesis, Ben-Gurion University, 2014.

[21] M. Schordan and D. Quinlan. A Source-To-Source Architecture for User-Defined Optimizations. In *Modular Programming Languages*, volume 2789 of *Lecture Notes in Computer Science*, pages 214–223. 2003.

[22] G. Singh, M.-H. Su, K. Vahi, E. Deelman, B. Berriman, J. Good, D. S. Katz, and G. Mehta. Workflow Task Clustering for Best Effort Systems with Pegasus. In *Proceedings of the 15th ACM Mardi Gras Conference*, MG '08, pages 1–8, 2008.

[23] W. Thies, V. Chandrasekhar, and S. Amarasinghe. A practical approach to exploiting coarse-grained pipeline parallelism in c programs. MICRO'07, pages 356–369, 2007.

[24] Y. Torres, A. Gonzalez-Escribano, and D. Llanos. Understanding the Impact of CUDA Tuning Techniques for Fermi. HPCS'11, pages 631–639, 2011.

[25] F. B. Usabiaga, I. Pagonabarraga, and R. Delgado-Buscalioni. Inertial Coupling for Point Particle Fluctuating Hydrodynamics. *J. Comput. Phys.*, 235:701–722.

[26] S. Verdoolaege, J. Carlos Juega, A. Cohen, J. Ignacio Gómez, C. Tenllado, and F. Catthoor. Polyhedral Parallel Code Generation for CUDA. *ACM Trans. Archit. Code Optim.*, 9(4), 2013.

[27] M. Wahib and N. Maruyama. A Hybrid Grouped Genetic Algorithm for Optimizing GPU Kernel Fusion. http://mt.aics.riken.jp/publications/GGA.pdf. 2014.

[28] M. Wahib and N. Maruyama. Scalable Kernel Fusion for Memory-Bound GPU Applications. SC'14, pages 191–202.

[29] M. Wahib and N. Maruyama. Highly Optimized Full GPU-Acceleration of Non-hydrostatic Weather Model SCALE-LES. CLUSTER'13, pages 77–85, 2013.

[30] P. Wahl, D.-S. Ly-Gagnon, C. Debaes, J. Van Erps, N. Vermeulen, D. Miller, and H. Thienpont. B-CALM: An Open-Source GPU-based 3D-FDTD with Multi-Pole Pispersion for Plasmonics. *Progress In Electromagnetics Research*, 138:467–478, 2013.

[31] G. Wang, Y. Lin, and W. Yi. Kernel Fusion: An Effective Method for Better Power Efficiency on Multithreaded GPU. In *GreenCom'10*, pages 344–350, 2010.

[32] S. Williams, A. Waterman, and D. Patterson. Roofline: An Insightful Visual Performance Model for Multicore Architectures. *Commun. ACM*, pages 65–76, 2009.

A Numerical Soft Fault Model for Iterative Linear Solvers

James Elliott[1,2]
jjellio3@ncsu.edu

Mark Hoemmen[2]
mhoemme@sandia.gov

Frank Mueller[1]
mueller@cs.ncsu.edu

[1] Department of Computer Science, North Carolina State University, Raleigh, NC
[2] Center for Computing Research, Sandia National Laboratories, Albuquerque, NM

ABSTRACT

We present a fault model designed to bring out the "worst" in iterative solvers based on mathematical properties. Our model introduces substantially higher overhead, but smaller variance, than a fault model based on random bit flips. We also relate the statistics from our experiments back to the solvers' configuration, and briefly address the computational effort that each model requires. Our approach requires significantly fewer resources, while punishing our solvers with undetectable errors that require notable overhead for recovery. This work also illustrates the robustness of our resilient algorithms: Not only do we make forward progress in the presence of pathological faults, we always obtain the correct answer.

Categories and Subject Descriptors

G.4 [**MATHEMATICAL SOFTWARE**]: Reliability and robustness; G.1.3 [**NUMERICAL ANALYSIS**]: Numerical Linear Algebra—*Linear systems (direct and iterative methods)*

Keywords

Algorithm-Based Fault Tolerance; Sparse Iterative Methods; Pessimistic Fault Modeling

1. INTRODUCTION

Recent studies indicate that large parallel computers will continue to become less reliable as energy constraints tighten, component counts increase, and manufacturing sizes decrease [8, 5]. This unreliability may manifest in two different ways: either as "hard" faults, which cause the loss of one or more parallel processes, or as "soft" faults, which cause incorrect arithmetic or storage, but do not kill the running application.

This paper focuses on soft faults. Specifically, we consider those that corrupt data or computations, without the hardware or system detecting them and notifying the application

Publication rights licensed to ACM. ACM acknowledges that this contribution was authored or co-authored by an employee, contractor or affiliate of the United States government. As such, the United States Government retains a nonexclusive, royalty-free right to publish or reproduce this article, or to allow others to do so, for Government purposes only.
HPDC'15, June 15–20, 2015, Portland, Oregon, USA.
Copyright is held by the owner/author(s). Publication rights licensed to ACM.
ACM 978-1-4503-3550-8/15/06 ...$15.00.
http://dx.doi.org/10.1145/2749246.2749254

that a fault occurred. We call this type of soft fault Silent Data Corruption (SDC). SDC is much less frequent than process failures, but much more threatening since the application may silently return an incorrect answer. In physical simulations, the wrong answer could have costly and even life-threatening consequences. Users' trust in the results of numerical simulations can lead to disaster if those results are wrong, as for example in the 1991 collapse of the Sleipner A oil platform [11]. Unlike with hard faults, applications currently have few recovery strategies. Hardware *detection* without correction may cost nearly as much as full hardware correction. Hardware vendors can harden chips against soft faults, but doing so will increase chip complexity and likely either increase energy usage or decrease performance. An open field of research and the focus of this paper is designing algorithms that can tolerate SDC.

2. PRECONDITIONED LINEAR SOLVERS

Our fault model assesses iterative, possibly preconditioned, linear solvers under faults that are not detectable in standard implementations, and that can remain undetectable using low overhead detectors. The model introduces a *pessimistic* fault. This accounts for our lack of knowledge of exactly which physical events can lead to the worst case for a particular problem and solver combination. We argue that if a numerical approach can tolerate these types of perturbations, then it should be able to tolerate transient arithmetic errors. This minimizes fruitless speculation about how faults manifest in real hardware, and instead asks whether an algorithm can handle challenging numerical faults. The latter presents a fault model that we show produces a much worse case than random bit flips. If it is true that future hardware will allow some transient soft errors, we should assess fault tolerance in algorithms based on a worst-case scenario, rather than the extremely biased case of random bit flips.

2.1 Soft Faults and Iterative Methods

Given a direct solver, if a soft fault corrupts arithmetic, the method will reach a (possibly unacceptable) solution in a bounded, known number of steps. Iterative methods behave differently. They may 1) "converge through" the error, taking no more iterations than in the error-free case; 2) converge but take more iterations; 3) *stagnate* — reach the maximum iteration count without improving the initial approximation; or 4) become divergent — oscillate wildly or have rapid error growth such that the solver "explodes" toward infinity. In the latter two cases, the solver fails to produce an acceptable solution. Stagnation relates to the *maximal attainable ac-*

curacy, which bounds below the accuracy an iterative solver can reach in finite-precision arithmetic. If a soft error introduces error sufficient to damage the maximal attainable accuracy, then the solver may stagnate.

Pessimistic faults have mathematical interpretations. For example, they may introduce a fictitious, abnormally large eigenvalue to the matrix A. Iterative solvers approximate the solution as a linear combination of basis vectors that are weighted by the largest eigenvalues in the system. The fault will thus make the solver converge to a bogus solution dominated by the fictitious eigenvalue. Also, iterative solvers are often used for solving discretized versions of elliptic partial differential equations (PDEs). Their solutions must satisfy the *maximum principle*: their maximum must be found on the boundary. One may view a soft fault as a (transient) violation of this principle. Alternatively, a "bad" soft error may make the problem appear to have a nonmathematical discontinuity.

Our fault model evolves from these mathematical interpretations. We model faults as a specific MPI process returning a bad vector from its preconditioner application. We generate faults in two ways: a fault may 1) scale its contribution to the global vector, or 2) permute its local portion of the global vector. Permutations preserve the vector's norm, while making its contents incorrect. This models discontinuity. Scaling increases or decreases the norm of the vector predictably. This, or directly corrupting inner product or norm results, perturbs the eigenvalue approximations. Corrupting the basis vectors also makes the algorithm search for a solution in the wrong direction. Our numerical fault model suffices to cause stagnation or divergence in non-restarted solvers.

2.2 Selective Reliability

Our fault-tolerance strategy rests on relating numerical methods that naturally correct errors to system-level fault tolerance. In particular, we assume a *selective reliability* or "sandboxing" programming model [6] that lets algorithm developers isolate faults to certain parts of the algorithm in a coarse-grained way. In our scheme, we enforce that the outer solver be reliable, while letting the inner solver run in an unreliable mode. We aim to spend most of our computation time in cheap "unreliable" computations, while minimizing the time we spend in the presumably expensive outer solve.

Analytically, any faults that occur in the inner solver manifest as a "different preconditioner" to the outer solver. We choose Flexible GMRES [9] as the outer solver, since it can tolerate a preconditioner that changes between iterations. As an inner solver, we use the Generalized Minimal Residual Method (GMRES) from Saad and Schultz [10]. We show results for the resulting system, called FT-GMRES, that uses a multigrid preconditioner (MueLu) and solves a Poisson problem. Multigrid is the preferred preconditioner for Poisson problems.

2.3 Implementation

We implemented our solvers using the Tpetra [1] sparse linear algebra package in the Trilinos framework [7] and validated them against both MATLAB and the solvers in Trilinos' Belos package [2]. Implementing our solvers using Trilinos lets us benefit from the scalability and performance of its sparse matrices and dense vectors.

3. RESULTS

3.1 Methodology

We previously described how we corrupt the preconditioner's output. To evaluate the impact of our preconditioned solvers in the presence of SDC, we perform the following steps:

1. Solve the problem injecting no SDC, and compute the number of times, K, the preconditioner was applied.

2. For all j in $[1, K]$, reattempt the solve, introducing SDC at the j-th preconditioner application. This results in K total solves.

3. For all K solves with SDC, compute the relative percent of *additional* preconditioner applies over the SDC-free solve[1], e.g., $\frac{Applies_{observed} - Applies_{FailureFree}}{Applies_{FailureFree}} \times 100$

4. Repeat Steps 2 and 3, letting various numbers of MPI processes participate in the SDC injection.

5. Repeat Steps 2-4, varying the scaling factor applied to the SDC.

6. For each combination of scaling factor and number of faulty processes, plot the *average* number of additional preconditioner applies as a percentage. 0% means no additional applies; 100% means twice as many.

3.2 Model Comparisons

Fig. 1 shows a side-by-side comparison of the overhead introduced from random bit flips and our numerical fault model. Here, we use no detection mechanism and force our solver to roll through all errors.

Each plot represents a different fault model, so the results cannot be compared geometrically. The intent of the figure is to illustrate the overhead we observe given faults from each model. Recognize the overheads have roughly the same range, yet the variance in Fig. 1a is considerably higher than our model (Fig. 1b). We address this in greater detail in § 3.4.

Note, Fig. 1a shows the highest overhead when all 32 subdomains inject the 58th or 59th exponent bit flips. This is not a weakness in our model. Those specific faults introduce very large magnifications into the vector, but not large enough to create an infinite or not-a-number value. Elliott et al. [3] explored exactly this scenario of faults and proposed a low overhead detector that efficiently filters such errors with $O(1)$ cost. For this exact reason our results analyze scaling factors that would slip through such a filter. Only the largest scaling factor, 1×10^5, would be detected by a projection bound.

Next, we enable both explicit residual ($\|Ax - b\|$) and projection bound tests per each inner iteration in Fig. 2. The resulting colorbar bounds are similar for both the numerical model and the bit flip model. That is, both models require a maximum overhead in the range of $100\% - 120\%$. This also exposes the trouble with bit flip injection: bit position does not affect the introduced overhead consistently. For example, exponent bits sometimes introduce high overhead, while mantissa bits can introduce overhead proportional to exponent bits. Notice that the right-most column of the numerical fault model is not the highest overhead — this is

---

[1]If $Applies_{observed} - Applies_{FailureFree} < 0$, i.e., SDC accelerated convergence, we record zero overhead.

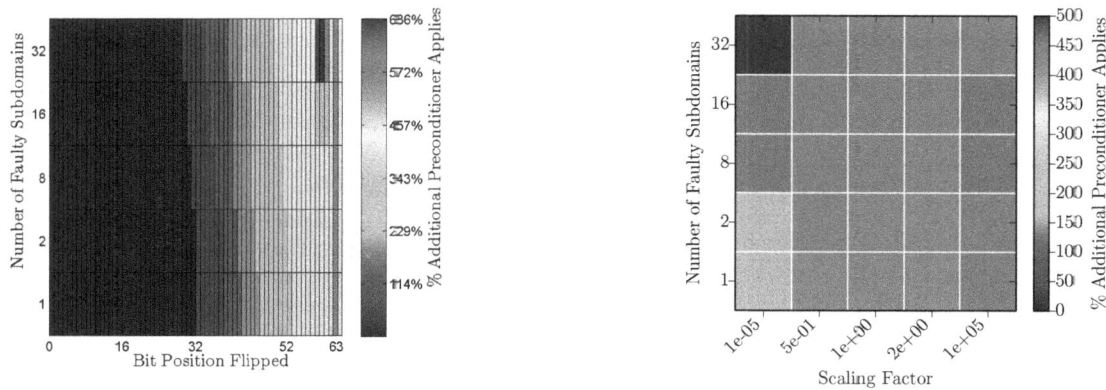

(a) Overhead given no attempt to detect and respond to faults with a random bit flip model.

(b) Overhead given no attempt to detect and respond to faults with a numerical fault model.

Figure 1: Overhead comparison with no fault detection, for a numerical fault model (right) and random bit flip injection (left)

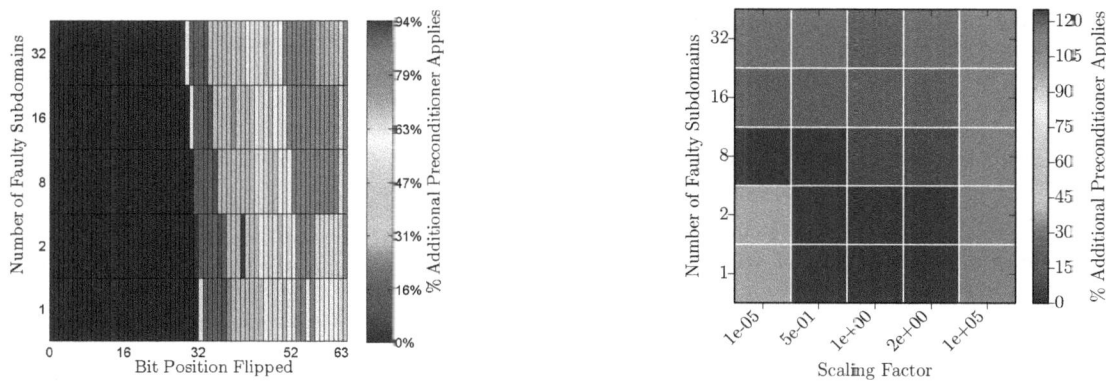

(a) Overhead when utilizing detection with a random bit flip model.

(b) Overhead when utilizing detection with a numerical fault model.

Figure 2: Overhead comparison with fault detection on, for a numerical fault model (right) and random bit flip injection (left)

due to a very low overhead detector, whereas checking the explicit residual requires a preconditioner apply.

3.3 Computational Effort

Our fault model captures hard to detect, yet numerically challenging faults. The largest overhead is easily characterized by our model and requires substantially less experimentation. For example, each shaded region constitutes one trial (of which we compute a mean). Clearly evaluating 25 unique experiments is much cheaper than evaluating 64×5 experiments. Moreover, if the experiment is not designed to account for the bias introduced by random bit flips, the mean will approximate optimistic overheads.

3.4 Expected Overhead Comparison

We compute the expected overhead across all experiments, i.e., compute the expected value for each row of these graphs. It becomes clear by inspection that our approach captures a worst-case scenario well beyond that of random bit flipping. That is, we are ensuring our algorithms can tolerate "bad" undetectable errors — error cases that random bit flips fail to expose — since we lack knowledge of exactly which val-

ues are the most sensitive. If an algorithm can handle our fault model, it can certainly handle the errors introduced by random bit flips.

We now compute the expected overhead given all samples for a given number of faulty subdomains. This computes the expected value for a "row" of the prior figures. For our numerical model, this entails grouping all scaling factors together, while for the bit flip model this considers an equally likely chance of flipping any of the 64 bits in the IEEE-754 representation.

Table 1 summarizes the expectation across all experiments for a given number of faulty subdomains when no reactive fault tolerance is used. This corresponds to Figures 1a and 1b. Clearly, our numerical faults are much worse than bit flips. Our model tends to create roughly **25** additional preconditioner applies, because our inner solver iterates 25 iterations (max) per inner solve. Our faults are sufficient to require an entire inner solve. We then obtain our solution in the next inner iteration, requiring roughly the failure free number of iterations (6). This gives a total iteration (and preconditioner apply) count of approximately 25+6. Our model has significantly smaller variance than what random bit flips would have introduced. This indicates that our model *consistently* introduces poor behavior, which is our intent.

Table 1: Additional preconditioner applies given no fault detection; percent additional applies in parentheses.

| Faulty Subdomains | Additional Preconditioner Applies | | | |
| | Bit Flips | | Numerical | |
	mean	StdDev	mean	StdDev
1	7.28 (121%)	10.94	24.73 (412%)	5.05
2	7.56 (126%)	11.08	24.93 (416%)	5.07
8	8.11 (135%)	11.35	26.40 (440%)	1.90
16	8.56 (143%)	12.08	26.43 (441%)	1.89
32	9.51 (158%)	13.38	26.93 (449%)	2.85

Table 2 analyzes the overhead if we check explicit residuals and projection lengths [3] inside the inner solver (Fig. 2a). Again, we show that random bit flips present very optimistic overheads. The reason for this was rigorously addressed by Elliott et al. [4]. Even with fault detection enabled, our fault model is still sufficient to show high overhead. This is desired. The faults we introduce are not necessarily detectable immediately. This forces our solvers to iterate 2-3 iterations before finally reaching a divergent state that is detectable. These are precisely the events we wish to study — faults that are undetectable, yet cause the solvers to eventually reach an invalid state. This motivates the study of low-overhead detection mechanisms.

Table 2: Additional preconditioner applies **with reactive fault tolerance**; percent additional applies in parentheses.

| Faulty Subdomains | Additional Preconditioner Applies | | | |
| | Bit Flips | | Numerical | |
	mean	StdDev	mean	StdDev
1	1.49 (25%)	2.54	7.00 (117%)	2.12
2	1.56 (26%)	2.48	7.00 (117%)	2.12
8	1.69 (28%)	2.35	7.27 (121%)	1.72
16	1.81 (30%)	2.74	7.07 (118%)	1.74
32	1.83 (30%)	2.54	6.97 (116%)	1.83

4. CONCLUSION

We have presented results based on a fault model that allows us to characterize the numerical errors introduced by faults, and have shown that this model encompasses the range of overhead that the random bit flip model can introduce. Our fault model does not aim to predict the actual behavior of SDC. Rather, it shows a case sufficiently "bad" for us to assess how our fault-tolerance strategies behave when presented with very damaging SDC.

Our approach is a very different way of assessing preconditioned iterative linear solvers given an uncertain fault model. Rather than focus on what specifically constitutes a fault, we force our solvers to work through numerically challenging events. We specifically tune our fault model to inject errors that are not necessarily detectable. Our errors live inside the solvers' valid norm bounds, and empirically we observe our errors may cause divergence in latter iterations rather than immediately.

We compare our model to that of random bit flips, showing that random bit flip injection is *not* likely to show worst-case overhead. We support this through a methodical injection of bit flips, and by computing statistics over all experiments, as well as per bit position. Furthermore, we show our approach produces very predictable variance, irrespective of the number of processes that are faulty.

Acknowledgment

This work was supported in part by grants from NSF (awards 1058779 and 0958311) and the U.S. Department of Energy Office of Science, Advanced Scientific Computing Research, under Program Manager Dr. Karen Pao. Sandia National Laboratories is a multiprogram laboratory managed and operated by Sandia Corporation, a wholly owned subsidiary of Lockheed Martin Corporation, for the U.S. Department of Energy's National Nuclear Security Administration under contract DE-AC04-94AL85000.

5. REFERENCES

[1] C. G. Baker and M. A. Heroux. Tpetra, and the use of generic programming in scientific computing. *Scientific Programming*, 20(2):115–128, 2012.

[2] E. Bavier, M. Hoemmen, S. Rajamanickam, and H. Thornquist. Amesos2 and Belos: Direct and iterative solvers for large sparse linear systems. *Scientific Programming*, 20(3):241–255, 2012.

[3] J. Elliott, M. Hoemmen, and F. Mueller. Evaluating the impact of SDC on the GMRES iterative solver. In *28th IEEE International Parallel & Distributed Processing Symposium (IEEE IPDPS 2014)*, Phoenix, USA, May 2014.

[4] J. Elliott, M. Hoemmen, and F. Mueller. Exploiting data representation for fault tolerance. In *Proceedings of the 5th Workshop on Latest Advances in Scalable Algorithms for Large-Scale Systems*, ScalA '14, pages 9–16, 2014.

[5] A. Geist. What is the monster in the closet? Invited Talk at Workshop on Architectures I: Exascale and Beyond: Gaps in Research, Gaps in our Thinking, Aug. 2011.

[6] M. Heroux. Scalable Computing Challenges: An Overview. Minisymposium talk at SIAM Annual Meeting: Supercomputing Challenges: Petascale and Beyond, July 2009.

[7] M. A. Heroux et al. An overview of the Trilinos project. *ACM Trans. Math. Softw.*, 31(3):397–423, 2005.

[8] P. Kogge et al. ExaScale computing study: Technology challenges in achieving exascale systems. Technical report, Defense Advanced Research Project Agency, Information Processing Techniques Office, 2008.

[9] Y. Saad. *Iterative Methods for Sparse Linear Systems*. Society for Industrial and Applied Mathematics, Philadelphia, PA, USA, 2nd edition, 2003.

[10] Y. Saad and M. H. Schultz. GMRES: A generalized minimal residual algorithm for solving nonsymmetric linear systems. *SIAM J. Sci. Stat. Comput.*, 7(3):856–869, July 1986.

[11] J. Schlaich and K.-H. Raineck. Die Ursache für den Totalverlust der Betonplattform Sleipner A. *Beton- und Stahlbetonbau*, 88:1–4, 1993.

Lightweight Silent Data Corruption Detection Based on Runtime Data Analysis for HPC Applications

Eduardo Berrocal
Illinois Institute of Technology
Chicago, IL
USA
eberroca@iit.edu

Leonardo
Bautista-Gomez
Argonne National Laboratory
Argonne, IL
USA
leobago@anl.gov

Sheng Di
Argonne National Laboratory
Argonne, IL
USA
sdi1@anl.gov

Zhiling Lan
Illinois Institute of Technology
Chicago, IL
USA
lan@iit.edu

Franck Cappello
Argonne National Laboratory
Argonne, IL
USA
cappello@anl.gov

ABSTRACT

Next-generation supercomputers are expected to have more components and, at the same time, consume several times less energy per operation. Consequently, the number of soft errors is expected to increase dramatically in the coming years. In this respect, techniques that leverage certain properties of iterative HPC applications (such as the *smoothness* of the evolution of a particular dataset) can be used to detect silent errors at the application level. In this paper, we present a pointwise detection model with two phases: one involving the prediction of the next expected value in the time series for each data point, and another determining a range (i.e., normal value interval) surrounding the predicted next-step value. We show that dataset correlation can be used to detect corruptions indirectly and limit the size of the data set to monitor, taking advantage of the underlying physics of the simulation. Our results show that, using our techniques we can detect a large number of corruptions (i.e., above 90% in some cases) with 84% memory overhead, and 13.75% extra computation time.

Index Terms—Fault Tolerance; Resilience; High-Performance Computing; Silent Data Corruption; Soft Errors; Time Series

1. INTRODUCTION

High-performance computing (HPC) is changing the way scientists make discoveries. Science applications require ever-larger machines to solve problems with higher accuracy. While future systems promise to provide the power needed to tackle those science problems, they are also raising new challenges. For example, transistor size and energy consumption of future systems must be significantly reduced.

Such steps might dramatically impact the soft error rate (SER) according to recent studies [4].

Random memory access (RAM) devices have been intensively protected against silent data corruption (SDC) through error-correcting codes (ECCs) because they have the largest share of the susceptible surface on high-end computers. Recent studies, however, indicate that ECCs alone cannot correct an important number of DRAM errors [10]. In addition, not all parts of the system are ECC-protected: in particular, logic units and registers inside the processing units are usually not protected by ECC but by other methods because of the space, time, and energy cost that ECC requires in order to work at low level. Historically, the SER of central processing units was minimized through a technique called *radiation hardening*, which consists of increasing the capacitance of circuit nodes in order to increase the critical charge needed to change the logic level. Unfortunately, this technique involves increasing either the size or the energy consumption of the components, which is prohibitively expensive at extreme scale.

Runtime data analysis can be used to leverage the fact that some datasets produced by iterative HPC applications (i.e., the applications' state at a particular point in time) evolve *smoothly* from one time step to the next. This characteristic can be used effectively to design a general SDC detection scheme with relatively low overhead. In particular, we will show that an interval of *normal* values for the evolution of the datasets can be predicted, such that any corruption will *push* the corrupted data point outside the expected interval of *normal* values, and it will, therefore, become an *outlier*.

Previous work in this area have tried to solve the SDC problem using different strategies. Namely: by hardware-level detection [11], process replication [7], algorithm-based fault tolerance (ABFT) [9], and approximate computing [3]. These techniques, however, are either too expensive resource-wise, such as hardware-level detection (energy intensive) or process replication (2x or 3x in extra resources), or not general enough, such as ABFT or approximate computing (algorithms need to be adapted manually and only a subset of the kernels can be protected).

In our previous work [5, 2, 6], we showed the feasibility of using data analysis with simple and lightweight linear

HPDC'15, June 15-19, 2015, Portland, OR, USA
©2015 ACM 978-1-4503-3550-8/15/06 $15.00
DOI: http://dx.doi.org/10.1145/2749246.2749253.

predictors to detect SDC efficiently. In [6] we used *error-feedback control* to improve prediction recall (See Equation (2) for a definition of recall), and a technique called *even sampling* to reduce memory overhead.

In this paper, we introduce a new detection model based on the user-expected accuracy and past prediction errors. In addition, we perform a comprehensive evaluation during live executions with two popular DoE applications: Nek5000 and HACC. We also observe that it is viable to detect, using the underlying physics of the simulation, corruptions in one dataset by just using another, thus opening the door for memory saving strategies.

The rest of the paper is organized as follows. In Section 2 we present our proposed detector. In Section 3 we present our evaluation and results. Finally, in Section 4 we summarize our key findings and future work.

2. ANOMALY DETECTION

Our pointwise SDC detection model has two phases: the first phase involves the prediction of the next expected value in the time series for each data point, while the second determines a range (i.e., normal value interval) surrounding the predicted next-step value. Soft errors can be detected by observing whether a particular value falls outside this computed range. The range size, or normal value interval, will play an important role in obtaining high precision and recall, defined in Equations (1) and (2), respectively. Here TP, FP, and FN refer to *true positives*, *false positives*, and *false negatives*, respectively.

$$precision = \frac{TP}{TP + FP} \quad (1)$$

$$recall = \frac{TP}{TP + FN} \quad (2)$$

The magnitude of the range size depends on the relative location of the predicted value and the user-expected accuracy. The key notations used to formulate the pointwise detection

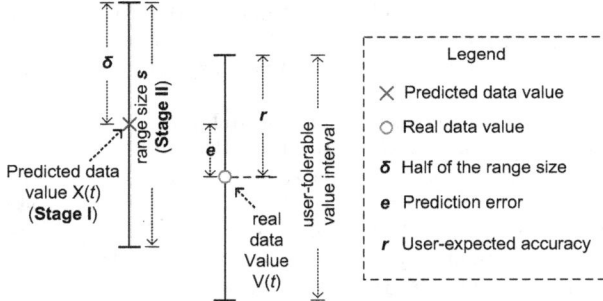

Figure 1: Illustration of our one-step prediction model (at time step t).

model are presented in Figure 1. $X(t)$ is the predicted value at time step t. The prediction error (denoted by e) is equal to the difference between the predicted value $X(t)$ and the real data value (denoted by $V(t)$) computed at the current time step. In practice, we find that $\delta = r + e$ works well (zero false positives) when predictions are very good (i.e., $e < r$). Here r represents the user-expected accuracy. The real error e, however, is unknown at runtime, so we approximate it by using the last-step prediction error (see Equation (3)), since we have observed that prediction errors at adjacent time steps exhibit a high degree of autocorrelation.

$$\hat{e}(t) = |V(t-1) - X(t-1)| \quad (3)$$

The first predictor, called linear curve fitting (LCF), uses the two most recent previous time steps to fit a linear curve, which is then projected to the next time step in order to predict the next value in the time series. Equation (4) shows how this prediction is calculated. $\Delta(t-1)$ is the slope of the curve (velocity) at time $t-1$.

$$\begin{aligned} X(t) &= \Delta(t-1) + V(t-1) \\ &= (V(t-1) - V(t-2)) + V(t-1) \quad (4) \\ &= 2V(t-1) - V(t-2) \end{aligned}$$

The acceleration-based predictor (ABP)[1] uses the two and three most recent previous time steps to extract the velocity ($\Delta(t-1)$) and acceleration ($\Delta^2(t-1)$) of the data, respectively, and then combines them to compute the prediction for the next value in the time series.

$$\begin{aligned} X(t) &= \Delta^2(t-1) + \Delta(t-1) + V(t-1) \\ &= 3V(t-1) - 3V(t-2) + V(t-3). \end{aligned} \quad (5)$$

The autoregressive (AR) and the autoregressive moving average ($ARMA$) models assume that every value in the time series depends linearly on its previous values. Equation (6) describes AR, where c is a constant, φ_i are the coefficients of the model, p is the number of coefficients, and $\varepsilon(t) \sim \mathcal{N}(0, \sigma^2)$ is the noise at time t. Similarly, Equation (7) describes ARMA, which adds the moving average part to AR. The errors $\varepsilon(t - i)$ are computed by using the past prediction errors:

$$\varepsilon(t-i) = V(t-i) - X(t-i)$$

The coefficients φ_i and θ_i (we set $p = q = 4$) are computed by using the first 10 time steps of the simulation by least squares with the Yule-Walker equations. We assume that no errors occur during this period; otherwise the coefficients would not reflect the reality of the application's data behavior.

$$X(t) = c + \sum_{i=1}^{p} \varphi_i V(t-i) + \varepsilon(t) \quad (6)$$

$$X(t) = c + \sum_{i=1}^{p} \varphi_i V(t-i) + \varepsilon(t) + \sum_{i=1}^{q} \theta_i \varepsilon(t-i) \quad (7)$$

3. EVALUATION

In this section, we present a set of experimental results to verify the efficacy of our SDC detector in production-level iterative HPC applications. All our predictors, as well as our bit-flip fault injector, are already implemented transparently in the fault tolerance interface (FTI) toolkit [1] to protect the execution against silent data corruptions.

We evaluate two well-known and widely used DoE HPC applications: Nek5000 [12] (a CFD kernel), and HACC [8] (an N-body cosmology application). Nek5000 is a CFD solver based on the spectral element method. It is also being used for a large number of applications in diverse fields such as reactor thermal-hydraulics and biofluids. HACC (for Hybrid/Hardware Accelerated Cosmology Code) is a cosmology code aimed at understanding the nature of dark matter and dark energy in the universe.

3.1 Prediction Errors

We characterize the distribution of the prediction errors under different predictors with the two mentioned iterative

---

[1]It can also be called quadratic curve fitting (QCF).

HPC application traces regarding different variables. The variables inlcude the position's coordinates (x) cf the particles in HACC, and the vertical flow and pressure (in a large eddy simulation) for Nek5000. We performed the prediction at each time step for each data point, measuring the error by taking the absolute difference between the real value and the predicted one: $e(t) = |V(t) - X(t)|$. Each trace involves millions of prediction results, which allow us to build a cumulative distribution function (CDF) of the prediction error e, as shown in Figure 2.

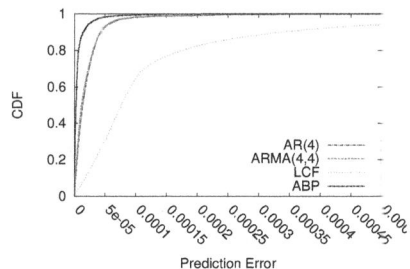

(a) HACC (particles' position)

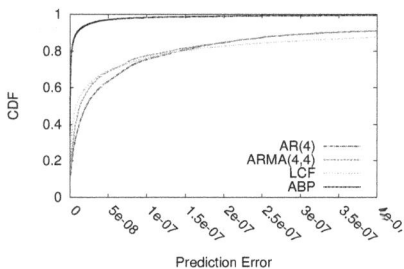

(b) Nek5000 (vortex)

Figure 2: Cumulative distribution function of prediction errors for different predictors and HPC datasets.

The most interesting result from these experiments is that a relatively simple predictor such as ABP is able to achieve smaller prediction errors than more complex linear models such as the well-known AR and $ARMA$ models for the selected HPC applications. In absolute terms, for the HACC application, up to 90% of the predictions have an error less than or equal to 10^{-5} under ABP, whereas only 8% to 56% of other predictors can reach such low errors. In the case of Nek5000, the prediction errors (90% of predictions) for vorticity and pressure are less than or equal to 8×10^{-9} and 2.8×10^{-10}, respectively. By comparison, other predictors are not able to achieve errors below 10^{-7}. In addition, the AR and $ARMA$ models require more memory sizes per data point (since they need to store the coefficients), and a coefficient learning phase for a number of time steps (in our case 10) in the training period.

3.2 Detection Results

In the second set of experiments, we test our detector using traces and real application runs. We choose the ABP predictor because it has the smallest prediction error, as seen in Section 3.1. In the case of real application runs, we run HACC with 512 MPI ranks and around 16 million particles, protecting the position and velocity variables. Nek5000 is run with 64 MPI ranks and a grid of 573,440 data points

per rank. Seven variables are protected: position(x,y,z), velocity(vx,vy,vz), and pressure.

In Figure 3 we inject bit-flips at random particles and/or data points on particular bit positions on different datasets. In the case of HACC (single-precision datasets), we set $r = 10^{-6}$; and for Nek5000 (double-precision datasets), we set $r = 10^{-8}$. In the figure, *vel* refers to injection and detection on the particles' velocity dataset, and *pos+vel* refers to injection on velocity while *detecting on position*. In the latter case (Figure 3(b)), we want to explore the idea of leveraging datasets' correlation for detection (i.e., having a corruption in one dataset visible by the other). In the case of HACC, *velocity* is used to move a particle to a new *position*.

Three conclusions can be extracted from these results. First, if we consider only the corruptions outside the range of the user-expected accuracy, our method can cover over 90% of all possible corruptions for HACC (Figure 3(a)). Similarly, our method can cover 66% of corruptions for Nek5000 (Figure 3(c)).

Second, the performance of our detector depends heavily on the underlying dataset (Figure 3(b)). We have observed that position changes are smoother than velocity changes, thus making the next values for velocity more difficult to predict. The good news is that leveraging datasets correlations works. Apart from the savings in memory overhead, these results indicate that we can achieve a similar recall by monitoring only position, rather than monitoring both.

Third, we see that our predictors have different results depending on whether we work with traces or real application runs. The reason for such disparities is that traces do not represent the totality of the application's data state and are used only to construct distributions to help us understand different predictors and parameters. In any case, the results are indeed similar enough to make us confident in our experiments using traces.

3.3 Performance Overhead

Our SDC detector (using ABP as predictor) is always below 90% memory overhead, 15% runtime overhead, and has a 0% extra network communication for both applications. By comparison, 2x-replication will produce an overhead of 100% in all three dimensions. The overheads for HACC are 84% extra memory consumption and 13.75% extra computation time. For Nek5000, the memory overhead is only 9.5%, while the extra computation time never goes above 1%.

4. CONCLUSION AND FUTURE WORK

We have developed a new model to tackle the problem of SDC detection using user-expected accuracy and past prediction errors. We compared a large number of linear predictors that take advantage of the characteristics of iterative HPC application datasets, and also implemented and evaluated our detector model with production-level scientific applications using both traces and real experiments on supercomputers. The detection results are promising. Considering only the corruptions outside the range of the user-expected accuracy, our method can cover 90% of all possible corruptions for HACC (single-precision), and over 66% for Nek5000 (double-precision).

We have shown that it is viable to detect corruptions in one variable (such as velocity) by using another (such as position) in one of our applications (HACC), taking advantage of the fact that these variables are interconnected by the underlying

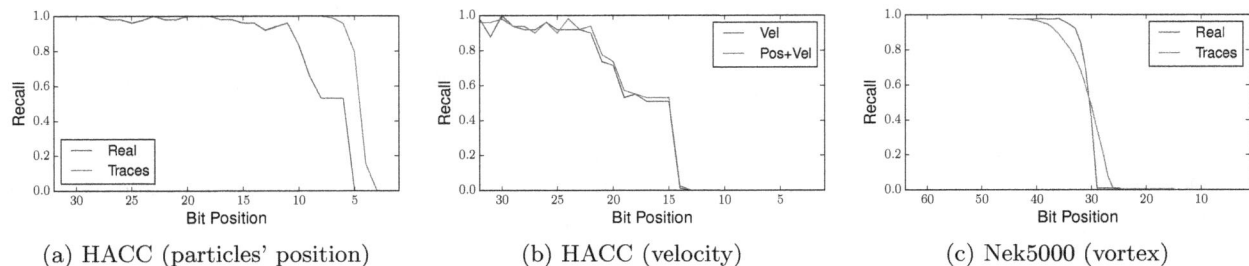

(a) HACC (particles' position)   (b) HACC (velocity)   (c) Nek5000 (vortex)

Figure 3: Comparing recall for bit-flips injected at random particles and/or data points.

physics of the application. Based on this initial observation, we plan to explore further the use of variable correlation to reduce the memory requirement of detection while keeping the detection recall high for all variables.

One limitation of our approach is the number of false positive (FP) detections. Although the FP rate is always below 10^{-4} for HACC, and always below 10^{-3} for Nek5000, this is still too high for a production level SDC detection tool. Consider that the large number of detections involved (one per data point, with millions of potential points per application) would produce a *positive* in every iteration. There are two ways in which this problem can be solved: (1) making our predictors more accurate, and (2) by optimizing the detection range parameter δ to find the optimum value that would maximaze *recall* by producing almost zero FP. We plan to follow these two paths in our future research.

Another limitation is performance overheads (see Section 3.3), especially for applications such as HACC that are memory bound. For such cases, we plan to investigate compression methods to group close points together in order to reduce the memory footprint significantly without incurring in a big reduction in detection recall.

We note that these techniques would only work for iterative HPC applications. Although such applications are the majority today, especially in the scientific area of computational physics, other types of applications are becoming important in the HPC community in areas such as computational biology and statistics. Also, simulations with abrupt variable changes, like applications involving collisions, may need different types of detectors. For those, much work remains to be done.

Acknowledgments

This material was based upon work supported by the U.S. Department of Energy, Office of Science, Advanced Scientific Computing Research Program, under Contract DE-AC02-06CH11357, and also in part by the ANR RESCUE, and INRIA-Illinois Joint Laboratory for Petascale Computing. The work at Illinois Institute of Technology was supported in part by US National Science Foundation grant CNS-1320125 and CCF-1422009. The software used in this work was developed in part by the DOE NNSA ASC- and DOE Office of Science ASCR-supported Flash Center for Computational Science at the University of Chicago

5. REFERENCES

[1] L. Bautista-Gomez, S. Tsuboi, D. Komatitsch, F. Cappello, N. Maruyama, and S. Matsuoka. Fti: High performance fault tolerance interface for hybrid systems. In *SC'11*, pages 32:1–32:32, 2011.

[2] L. A. Bautista-Gomez and F. Cappello. Detecting silent data corruption through data dynamic monitoring for scientific applications. In *PPoPP'14*, pages 381–382, 2014.

[3] A. R. Benson, S. Schmit, and R. Schreiber. Silent error detection in numerical time-stepping schemes. *International Journal of High Performance Computing Applications*, pages 1–20, 2014.

[4] S. Borkar. Designing reliable systems from unreliable components: The challenges of transistor variability and degradation. *IEEE Micro*, 25:10–16, Nov. 2005.

[5] S. Di, E. Berrocal, L. Bautista-Gomez, K. Heisey, R. Guptal, and F. Cappello. Toward effective detection of silent data corruptions for hpc applications. SC '14 - poster, 2014.

[6] S. Di, E. Berrocal, and F. Cappello. An efficient silent data corruption detection method with error-feedback control and even sampling for hpc applications. CCGRID, 2015.

[7] D. Fiala, F. Mueller, C. Engelmann, R. Riesen, K. Ferreira, and R. Brightwell. Detection and correction of silent data corruption for large-scale high-performance computing. In *SC'12*, pages 78:1–78:12, 2012.

[8] S. Habib, V. A. Morozov, H. Finkel, A. Pope, K. Heitmann, K. Kumaran, T. Peterka, J. A. Insley, D. Daniel, P. K. Fasel, N. Frontiere, and Z. Lukic. The universe at extreme scale: Multi-petaflop sky simulation on the bg/q. In *SC'12*, pages 1–11, 2012.

[9] K.-H. Huang and J. A. Abraham. Algorithm-based fault tolerance for matrix operations. *IEEE Transactions on Computers*, 100(6):518–528, 1984.

[10] A. A. Hwang, I. A. Stefanovici, and B. Schroeder. Cosmic rays don't strike twice: Understanding the nature of dram errors and the implications for system design. In *ASPLOS'XVII*, pages 111–122, 2012.

[11] S. S. Mukherjee, J. Emer, and S. K. Reinhardt. The soft error problem: An architectural perspective. In *HPCA'05*, pages 243–247. IEEE, 2005.

[12] J. Shin, M. W. Hall, J. Chame, C. Chen, P. F. Fischer, and P. D. Hovland. Speeding up nek5000 with autotuning and specialization. In *ICS'10*, pages 253–262, 2010.

Exploring Failure Recovery for Stencil-based Applications at Extreme Scales

Marc Gamell[†], Keita Teranishi[‡], Michael A. Heroux[‡], Jackson Mayo[‡], Hemanth Kolla[‡], Jacqueline Chen[‡] and Manish Parashar[†]

[†]Rutgers Discovery Informatics Institute, Rutgers University, Piscataway, NJ, USA
{mgamell, parashar}@cac.rutgers.edu

[‡]Sandia National Laboratories, Livermore, CA, Albuquerque, NM, USA,
{knteran, maherou, jmayo, hnkolla, jhchen}@sandia.gov

ABSTRACT

Application resilience is a key challenge that must be addressed in order to realize the exascale vision. Previous work has shown that online recovery, even when done in a global manner (i.e., involving all processes), can dramatically reduce the overhead of failures when compared to the more traditional approach of terminating the job and restarting it from the last stored checkpoint. In this paper we suggest going one step further, and explore how local recovery can be used for certain classes of applications to reduce the overheads due to failures. Specifically we study the feasibility of local recovery for stencil-based parallel applications and we show how multiple independent failures can be masked to effectively reduce the impact on the total time to solution.

1. INTRODUCTION

The mean time between failures (MTBF) for current petascale systems is measured in days (e.g., production runs on ORNL's Titan Cray showed 9 node failures/day, as shown in [4]), but it is estimated that the MTBF for an exascale system would be measured in minutes [2]. An important class of failures that must be addressed is process and node failures, including correlation effects. These failures are often recovered by terminating the job and restarting it from the last checkpoint found in stable storage. While coordinated, stable-storage-based global checkpoint/restart (C/R) is currently the most widely accepted technique for addressing processor failures, it is unclear whether this approach will scale to exascale since the time to checkpoint will often be longer than the expected MTBF, and researchers continue to actively address this issue. For example, runtimes that aim to offer an abstraction of a fault-free system to the application have been developed (e.g. redMPI [3]). However, as suggested by recent studies [6], the abstraction of a failure-free machine will not be sustainable at extreme scales, which will require application-aware resilience.

While programing models such as task-DAG can include resilience features, SPMD and message passing are not designed to handle process failures by default. In previous studies, [4] we have shown how online (i.e., without disrupting the job) global recovery (i.e., involving all the cores in the system in the recovery process) can be used in conjunction with application-guided checkpointing to support high failure rates (i.e., every 47 seconds) for message passing applications using the Fenix framework. In that approach, every failure triggered a global recovery, which required all survivor processes to recover the MPI environment. Then, all surviving processes, along with the newly spawned ones, had to rollback to the last commonly available checkpoint. The advantage of global recovery is that it can be done in a semi-transparent way: the application does not necessarily have to be aware of the failure. However, due to the intrinsic global nature of the recovery algorithms, global recovery present scalability challenges.

In this paper we explore the local recovery for stencil-based parallel applications, which represent a significant set of physical simulations. In addition to its inherent scalability, local recovery provides several benefits. For example, the environment does not need to be recovered globally after a failure, and only the newly spawned processes have to rollback to the last checkpoint.

The key idea underlying the local recovery approach is as follows. Stencil-based parallel applications, such as simulations that solve partial differential equations (PDEs) using finite-difference methods, typically consist of a number of iterations (timesteps) with each iteration consisting of two key steps, computation on local data to advance the simulation, and communication with the immediate neighbors. This communication pattern implies that, upon failure, by allowing the rest of the domain to continue the simulation, only the immediate neighbors will be immediately affected by that failure. When a failure occurs, we can substitute the failed process with a spare one, rollback to the last saved state for the failed process (i.e., the last checkpoint), and resume computation for that process. In this paper we show how the effect of the failure will slowly propagate through the machine. If subsequent failures occurs at a distant node *before* the original failure delay has spread to that node, we demonstrate that the delay of the second failure will be masked with the delay of the first one. In general, we show that the overhead due to several separate failures on the total execution time can appear to be the same as the overhead due to a single failure. This effect is what we call **failure masking**.

One of the key contributions for this work is a study of the applicability of local recovery approaches to stencil-based parallel applications in order to understand the propagation of failure recovery delay.

2. BACKGROUND AND RELATED WORK

Global recovery. Process and node failures and their characteristics have been well documented in [12].Checkpoint and restart (C/R) [7] is the most widely used technique for implementing resilience for HPC systems. In this model, the application state is periodically saved (e.g., using BLCR [5]) so that, upon failure, global rollback can be used to restart the application from the last globally committed checkpoint. This process is independent of the number of nodes affected by the failure, i.e., if a node or process failure occurs, all processes are typically forced to rollback to the previous strongly consistent checkpoint. In contrast, by recovering locally, only failed processes need to rollback to the previous checkpoint.

Checkpointing. Typically, checkpoints are saved to a centralized parallel file system [7] but may also be stored in local memory [11], in both local and peer-memory [14], in non-volatile memory [8], in node-local storage (such as SSD) [1, 10], or at different storage layers [9]. In order to enable local recovery, our technique suggests to store checkpoints at a peer node. Other strategies, such as storing checkpoints in the parallel file system or compressing them would add performance overheads that makes them prohibitive, despite their advantages.

Combining optimized checkpointing with global recovery. Systems such as Fenix [4] and LFLR [13] show how advanced in-memory diskless checkpointing can be used in conjunction with global recovery to enable execution in a failure-prone scenario.

3. LOCAL RECOVERY FOR STENCIL-BASED SCIENTIFIC APPLICATIONS

This section presents the local recovery approach and our underlying reasoning for exploring this approach for stencil-based applications. Recovering from failures in a local manner implies that (1) only the re-spawned processes have to rollback to the last checkpoint and (2) only the processes that communicate with the failed ones will notice the failure and might be involved in the recovery process. These requirements are in contrast with global recovery, in which all the processes are involved in the recovery and rollback to the last consistent checkpoint. Global recovery can be costly and presents scalability challenges, and, in many situations, may be unnecessary. Note also that local recovery is by definition an online recovery approach, i.e. the job does not have to be disrupted.

In this section we first describe the key relevant characteristics of the targeted stencil-based applications. We then explore the local recovery approach for this class of applications, its benefits in case of single and multiple failures, as well as associated challenges.

3.1 Stencil-based Scientific Applications

In this work, we target iterative applications with stencil-based domain partitioning and communication properties,

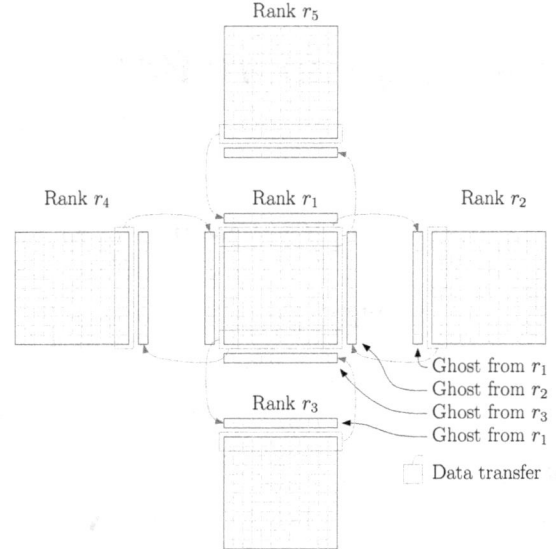

Figure 1: Partitioning of a 2D domain across five processes. This figure shows the ghost region buffer exchange between neighboring processes in a typical implementation of a stencil-based parallel application.

such as for example, typical parallel implementations for PDE solvers using finite-difference methods. In these applications, the application domain is typically partitioned using a block decomposition across the processes, and each process perform two key tasks at every timestep: (1) computation on its local data to advance the simulation, and (2) communication with its immediate neighbors that based on the specific stencil used. A typical block decomposition for a 2-D stencil-based application is illustrated in Figure 1. The figure also illustrates the communication pattern between blocks on neighboring processes. In a typical implementation, each process maintains a "ghost region" corresponding to the width of the stencil used around its blocks, and populates this region from its neighbors in a "ghost region exchange" communication step. The exchange shown in Figure 1 is for a 5-point stencil.

Not all scientific applications offer the described iterative behavior from the beginning of the execution until the end. Sometimes, collective operations are performed every certain number of timesteps, for example, for analysis, error checking, etc. In this paper we focus the execution between two consequent such synchronizations, and assume that this interval is long enough so that, at extreme scales, several failures can occur within it. For example, in case of the S3D application, this interval is typically every 16 minutes [4]. Our focus is to enable the application to continue the execution between these such synchronizations despite the number of failures occurring and the system size. If this assumption is unrealistic, we can assume, instead, without loss of generality, that the collective operations can be done in an asynchronous manner. Asynchronous collectives are promising, because they can naturally support imbalance between the processes without imposing barrier-like constraints. We leave understanding how local recovery can be beneficial even with periodic blocking collective operations as future work.

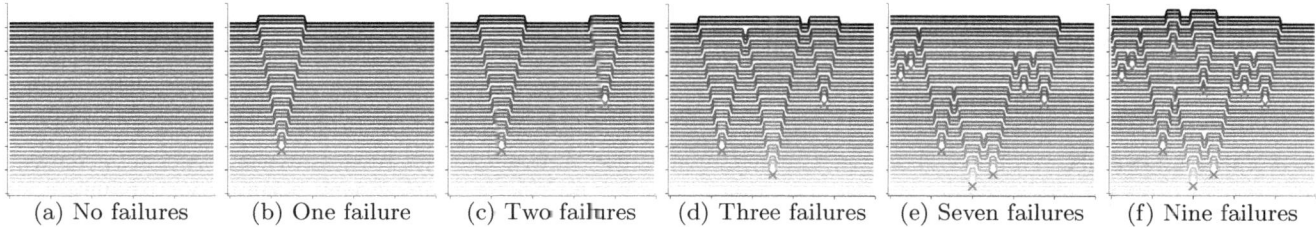

|(a) No failures|(b) One failure|(c) Two failures|(d) Three failures|(e) Seven failures|(f) Nine failures|

Figure 2: Behavior of local recovery for a stencil-based 1-D partial differential equation (PDE) solvers. X axis represents process number (or rank) and Y axis indicates wallclock time. Each line in a figure represents a timestep, and the color of the line represents how advanced the simulation is (i.e., it advances from yellow to dark purple). Each red 'X' represents a failure. A straight line means all processes compute the timestep at the same physical time. When a failure occurs, the recovery delay does not get propagated immediately to the entire domain. Instead, the immediately adjacent neighbor processes are the first to be delayed, which in turn propagate the delay to their immediate neighbors, resulting in the delay eventually spanning across the entire domain. Note how Figures 2(b), 2(c), 2(d) and 2(e) have the same recovery overhead, i.e., as if only one failure occurred, even though they have different numbers of failures. In case of Figure 2(f), however, the total recovery time is equal to sequentially recovering from two failures.

3.2 Local Recovery, challenges and benefits

Realizing local recovery for target stencil-based parallel applications, implemented using message passing (MPI), presents several challenges and benefits.

Consistency. As neighbor processes must communicate, guaranteeing consistency in a message passing environment can be challenging. In the approach suggested in this paper, we log messages that have been transferred since the last checkpoint, and store them in local memory. Specifically, for the 1D case, only two messages are stored every timestep: the message sent to the node in the right, and the message sent to the node in the left. In the 3D case, 6 messages need to be logged at each timestep. However, note that the overhead of logging the messages is negligible compared to the cost of checkpoint because the checkpoint is several orders of magnitude larger.

Delay propagation. Assume that a node failure occurs while the processes mapped to the node are between iterations C_{i-1} and C_i. Once the failure is detected, the last checkpoint can be fetched from the checkpoint store used to restart the execution of the failed node on either a node from a spare pool or a re-spawned node. While this is happening, the rest of the processes can continue working as usual. The fact that the failed process advanced beyond C_{i-1} guarantees that all their immediate neighbors were also already past this point. Note that, in order for a process to advance beyond a certain communication point, it has to exchange information with their immediate neighbors. This is also true even when the ghost exchange is non-blocking, because sender-based message logging guarantees the availability of the data even when the failure occurs between the data transfer. The iterative and stencil-like nature of the targeted applications will eventually require immediate neighbor processes (i.e., L_1 neighbors) that communicate directly with the failed node to wait. Even though these processes can continue executing the next iteration, it is likely that when they reach the next communication phase (i.e., C_i), the restarted neighbors will not have reached that point yet. Therefore, the immediate neighbors will have to wait. In turn, second-level (L_2) neighbors (i.e., the immediate neighbors of L_1) will be able to continue its execution up to iteration C_{i+1}, and will then be blocked. This is possible

because the L_1 processes are waiting at C_i, which means they are not able to exchange data with the L_2 processes at iteration C_{i+1}. In general, kth-layer neighbors would be able to continue until iteration C_{i+k-1} without blocking. This wave-like delay propagation behavior can be seen in Figure 2(b) for a 1-D stencil. While we use 1-D to illustrate the process, this behavior also applies to higher dimensions.

Failure masking. When using a large number of processes, it is possible that another failure occurs on distant processes where the delay from the first failure has not yet reached. In this case, the recovery delay of the second failure will begin propagating from the second location, as see in Figure 2(c). At some point in space and time, the delay of both failures will *merge*. At this point, the total delay will be the maximum of both delays. We call this effect *failure masking*, and an example can be seen in Figure 2(d). This situation is beneficial at large scales, because the impact of several failures on end-to-end execution time will be comparable to that of a single failure. Note that this effect can also happen with multiple failures, as seen in Figures 2(d) and 2(e). Comparing these four figures, we see that the total overhead is the same. Note that the larger the machine is, the more plausible this effect becomes, which is an ideal property for good scalability.

There may be cases, however, where failures occur after the delay of previous failures have already reached the failed node. An example can be seen in Figure 2(f), in which the total execution time is comparable to that of recovering from two failures sequentially. The likelihood of this situation is dependent on the communication pattern of the application and the checkpointing approach used. Specifically, it depends (1) on the dimension of the application domain (i.e. 1D, 2D, 3D), (2) on the size of the domain assigned to each process (which will determine the checkpoint latency), (3) the communication frequency, and, (4) the amount of computation per iteration (which will determine the latency between iterations, and is a factor of the size of the domain per node).

Low power and energy footprint. Local recovery has better power and energy behavior as compared to global recovery as the entire system does not have to roll back and redo computations. Furthermore, in case of local recovery, while the neighboring processes wait for the re-spawned ones to catch up their CPU will be idle, and their power consumption can be reduced by using techniques such as Dynamic Voltage and Frequency Scaling (DVFS).

4. CONCLUSION

In this paper we have explored online, local recovery from high-frequency node failures for stencil-based parallel applications, using application guided checkpointing as a means for failure masking and data resilience. The approach is based on understanding the propagation of delays associated with local recovery for stencil-based computation/communication pattern, and the observation that the impact of the delay associated with multiple failures is often not additive, allowing this approach to be feasible and scalable. Based on this observation, we demonstrated that local recovery enables failure masking, i.e., the overheads on the total execution time due to recovery from multiple failures is comparable to that due to only one failure.

Our ongoing and future work include implementing and experimentally evaluating the techniques described in this paper using real applications.

Acknowledgments

The authors would like to thank Josep Gamell, Robert Clay and George Bosilca for interesting discussions related to this work. The research presented in this work is supported in part by National Science Foundation (NSF) via grants numbers ACI 1339036, ACI 1310283, CNS 1305375, and DMS 1228203, by the Director, Office of Advanced Scientific Computing Research, Office of Science, of the US Department of Energy Scientific Discovery through Advanced Computing (SciDAC) Institute of Scalable Data Management, Analysis and Visualization (SDAV) under ward number DE-SC0007455, the Advanced Scientific Computing Research and Fusion Energy Sciences Partnership for Edge Physics Simulations (EPSI) under award number DE-FG02-06ER54857, the ExaCT Combustion Co-Design Center via subcontract number 4000110839 from UT Battelle, and by an IBM Faculty Award. The research at Rutgers was conducted as part of the Rutgers Discovery Informatics Institute (RDI2). Sandia National Laboratories is a multi-program laboratory managed and operated by Sandia Corporation, a wholly owned subsidiary of Lockheed Martin Corporation, for the U.S. Department of Energy's National Nuclear Security Administration under contract DE-AC04-94AL85000.

5. REFERENCES

[1] L. Bautista-Gomez, S. Tsuboi, D. Komatitsch, F. Cappello, N. Maruyama, and S. Matsuoka. FTI: High Performance Fault Tolerance Interface for Hybrid Systems. In *Proceedings of International Conference for High Performance Computing, Networking, Storage and Analysis*, SC 2011, 2011.

[2] J. Dongarra and et al. The International Exascale Software Project Roadmap. *International Journal of High Performance Computing Applications*, 25(1):3–60, 2011.

[3] D. Fiala, F. Mueller, C. Engelmann, R. Riesen, K. Ferreira, and R. Brightwell. Detection and correction of silent data corruption for large-scale high-performance computing. In *Proceedings of the International Conference on High Performance Computing, Networking, Storage and Analysis*, SC 2012, pages 78:1–78:12, 2012.

[4] M. Gamell, D. S. Katz, H. Kolla, J. Chen, S. Klasky, and M. Parashar. Exploring Automatic, Online Failure Recovery for Scientific Applications at Extreme Scales. In *Proceedings of the International Conference on High Performance Computing, Networking, Storage and Analysis*, SC '14, 2014.

[5] P. H. Hargrove and J. C. Duell. Berkeley Lab Checkpoint/Restart (BLCR) for Linux clusters. In *Journal of Physics: Conference Series*, volume 46, page 494. IOP Publishing, 2006.

[6] M. A. Heroux. Toward Resilient Algorithms and Applications. In *Proceedings of the 3rd Workshop on Fault-tolerance for HPC at Extreme Scale*, FTXS 2013, pages 1–2, New York, NY, USA, 2013. ACM.

[7] J. Hursey. *Coordinated checkpoint/restart process fault tolerance for MPI applications on HPC systems*. PhD thesis, Indiana University, Indianapolis, IN, USA, 2010. AAI3423687.

[8] S. Kannan, A. Gavrilovska, K. Schwan, and D. Milojicic. Optimizing Checkpoints Using NVM as Virtual Memory. In *IEEE 27th International Symposium on Parallel Distributed Processing*, pages 29–40, May 2013.

[9] A. Moody, G. Bronevetsky, K. Mohror, and B. R. d. Supinski. Design, Modeling, and Evaluation of a Scalable Multi-level Checkpointing System. In *Proceedings of the ACM/IEEE International Conference for High Performance Computing, Networking, Storage and Analysis*, SC 2010, pages 1–11, Washington, DC, USA, 2010. IEEE Computer Society.

[10] X. Ouyang, S. Marcarelli, and D. K. Panda. Enhancing Checkpoint Performance with Staging IO and SSD. In *Proceedings of the International Workshop on Storage Network Architecture and Parallel I/Os*, SNAPI 2010, pages 13–20, Washington, DC, USA, 2010. IEEE Computer Society.

[11] R. Rajachandrasekar, A. Moody, K. Mohror, and D. K. D. Panda. A 1 PB/s file system to checkpoint three million MPI tasks. In *Proceedings of the 22nd international symposium on High-performance parallel and distributed computing*, HPDC 2013, pages 143–154, New York, NY, USA, 2013. ACM.

[12] M. Snir, R. W. Wisniewski, J. A. Abraham, S. V. Adve, S. Bagchi, P. Balaji, J. Belak, P. Bose, F. Cappello, B. Carlson, and et al. *Addressing Failures in Exascale Computing*. U.S. DoE, 2013.

[13] K. Teranishi and M. A. Heroux. Toward Local Failure Local Recovery Resilience Model Using MPI-ULFM. In *Proceedings of the 21st European MPI Users' Group Meeting*, EuroMPI/ASIA '14, pages 51:51–51:56, New York, NY, USA, 2014. ACM.

[14] G. Zheng, X. Ni, and L. V. Kalé. A scalable double in-memory checkpoint and restart scheme towards exascale. In *IEEE/IFIP 42nd International Conference on Dependable Systems and Networks Workshops (DSN-W)*, pages 1–6, 2012.

Author Index